Fighting With FEMA

In this book, disaster finance and cost recovery expert Michael Martinet provides unparalleled coverage of the practical, real-world key principles necessary to successfully navigate the nuances of federal regulations surrounding FEMA's Public Assistance program. Accessibly written, Martinet demystifies the many policies, procedures, and administrative processes a local government agency should adopt before a disaster to prepare themselves for a greater financial recovery after the disaster. The intent is to awaken local authorities to the realities of the process and assist them in preparing for a day which they all hope they will never see.

Designed for financial officers, purchasing officials, Public Works officials, Building & Safety officials, public construction project managers, and emergency management professionals at all levels of government, *Fighting With FEMA* will also earn a place in the libraries of consulting disaster recovery specialists and students interested in the financial aspects of disasters.

Michael Martinet is Principal with The Martinet Group, LLC, specializing in teaching Disaster Finance and Cost Recovery programs. For over 25 years, Martinet has trained local government officials on how to maximize their disaster cost recovery under FEMA's Public Assistance program. Attendees have come from cities, counties, states, special districts, and private non-profit agencies across the nation. He has a master's degree from California State University at Long Beach and is a Certified Emergency Manager through the International Association of Emergency Managers (IAEM). Martinet is the founder and chair of the IAEM Disaster Cost Recovery Caucus and former Principal of the National Fire Protection Association's Standard 1600, the Standard on Disaster/Emergency Management and Business Continuity Programs. Martinet has also worked as a local government emergency manager since 1989 and retired in 2013 from the City of San Francisco, where he worked as the Emergency Planning Manager in the Controller's Office. Since 2013, he has focused exclusively on disaster cost recovery training for local government agencies and eligible private non-profit agencies.

Fighting With FEMA

A Practical Regulations Handbook

Michael Martinet, MS, CEM

Routledge
Taylor & Francis Group

NEW YORK AND LONDON

Cover image: © Getty Images

First published 2025
by Routledge
605 Third Avenue, New York, NY 10158

and by Routledge
4 Park Square, Milton Park, Abingdon, Oxon, OX14 4RN

Routledge is an imprint of the Taylor & Francis Group, an informa business

Library of Congress Cataloging-in-Publication Data
Names: Martinet, Michael, author.
Title: Fighting with FEMA : winning strategies to avoid the disaster after the disaster / Michael Martinet.
Description: New York, NY : Routledge, 2024. | Includes bibliographical references and index.
Identifiers: LCCN 2024007150 (print) | LCCN 2024007151 (ebook) | ISBN 9781032770338 (hardback) | ISBN 9781003487869 (ebook)
Subjects: LCSH: Disaster relief—United States—Finance. | Emergency management—United States—Finance. | Public Assistance Grant Program (U.S.) | United States. Federal Emergency Management Agency.
Classification: LCC HV555.U6 M363 2024 (print) | LCC HV555.U6 (ebook) | DDC 363.34/820973—dc23/eng/20240409
LC record available at https://lccn.loc.gov/2024007150
LC ebook record available at https://lccn.loc.gov/2024007151

ISBN: 978-1-032-77033-8 (hbk)
ISBN: 978-1-003-48786-9 (ebk)

DOI: 10.4324/9781003487869

Typeset in Times New Roman
by Apex CoVantage, LLC

Access the Support Material at: www.routledge.com/9781032770338

This book is dedicated to my loving wife, Karen, who has stood by me through thick and thin, and especially for encouraging me to write this book. P.S. She is a great copy and content editor too!

Contents

Introduction

The FEMA Fallacy

Somewhere in the collective subconscious mind of America, this thought rests like a sleeping giant: the Federal government is waiting to help me, the average citizen, at my moment of greatest need, and it will lift me up from the ashes to make me whole again. This is the ultimate act of hope, the ultimate fantasy, and the ultimate setup for great disappointment.

But this wishful thinking isn't limited to individuals. It's a 3D, technicolor, holographic fantasy actively practiced by cities, counties, school districts, and other local government agencies from Bangor to Barstow and from Key West to Klamath Falls.

These local government agencies labor under the very misguided belief that the Federal government, and FEMA specifically, will arrange for Brinks Armored trucks to arrive within days of a disaster with pallets of cash to help the local governments rebuild and recover.

In fact, a FEMA "Public Assistance" grant may be the most dangerous grant a local government may receive. Not because there are some inherently malevolent forces at work within FEMA, but because the local government agencies have not bothered to understand the fundamental premise which guides FEMA in its grant-making process.

I envision the process of FEMA's Public Assistance program as a chain. A chain composed of serial interconnected links, both strong and at the same time flexible and able to accomplish great things. However, when even one link is broken, the entire chain fails.

FEMA Grants versus Other Federal Grant Programs

Disasters are very costly events in terms of human life, and in the United States, they are even more costly in terms of financial loss to the public at large and individuals as both homeowners and business owners. The single focus of this book is about how local governments and certain eligible private non-profit organizations may be able to recover some of those disaster-related losses from the Federal government through the Federal Emergency Management Agency's (FEMA) Public Assistance program.

In the process of describing how the program works, many facets of emergency and disaster management will be touched on and explained. However, the focus will always return to the process of obtaining Federal grants for disaster cost recovery.

A Federal Emergency Management Agency (FEMA) Public Assistance grant may be the most difficult Federal grant to obtain, and the most challenging to keep. From the Federal perspective, there are some very good reasons why this is the case.

Most Federal agencies that provide grants to local government agencies receive an annual allotment in the current Federal fiscal year's budget for grant-making purposes. These Federal agencies

DOI: 10.4324/9781003487869-1

generally provide a competitive process for grant applications. Once those grants are awarded and the grant cycle is completed, there is no further funding available in that fiscal year. There is a finite limitation on the grant funds available for most Federal agencies within a given Federal Fiscal Year.

FEMA, on the other hand, has no budget allocation in the federal fiscal year for the Disaster Relief Fund, or DRF. When the President declares a disaster, Congress then appropriates funding for the DRF, and that specific Disaster. But there is no limit to the amount of money for which the local jurisdiction may apply, unlike the usually limited funds available through other Federal grant programs. However, not all disaster-related damages and costs are eligible for FEMA reimbursement.

To provide funding for the Disaster Relief Fund and a specific Presidential disaster declaration, Congress must allocate funding which often comes from budget allocations taken from other federal agencies. Hence, although its purpose and intent is to provide Public Assistance grant funding to local jurisdictions for response and recovery from disasters, FEMA is under continuous and intense pressure to minimize the amount of funds provided for disaster relief. Simply put, the cost of disasters is steadily increasing over time and placing strains on all levels of government agencies, particularly the Federal government.

Federal spending for disaster relief is continuing to grow at an almost-unrestrained rate.

"To get a sense of the significance of these figures in relation to other, more familiar obligations of the Federal Government, we take the expected annual expense over the next seventy-five years and compute a net present value (NPV) of this 'unfunded liability.' Doing so yields a figure between $1.2 and $7.1 trillion, depending on assumptions of growth and discount rates. For comparison, the trustees of Social Security project a shortfall with an NPV of $4.9 trillion over this same horizon."[1]

The Fundamental Flaw: Fiscal Responsibility without Planning Control

There is one overriding and underpinning flaw in relation to the Public Assistance program. It is this: Local governments have control over their planning and zoning and building construction. The local agency may choose to allow building of homes, businesses, and all other manner of facilities in disaster-prone areas. The author has seen firsthand where dozens of new and expensive homes were built at the mouth of a normally-dry riverbed – a riverbed that on occasion turns into a torrent of deadly floodwaters. This happens everywhere, and it happens all the time. Developers buy the least expensive land they can find, and then build the most expensive structures they can in order to maximize their profits. FEMA has virtually no control over this helter-skelter way of running a local agency. Yes, FEMA does now have mandatory consensus-based building codes, but a well-built structure built on a flood plain will still flood. Furthermore, decades of structures built in harm's way still remain in place, and in some parts of the country are repeatedly damaged over the course of years from the very same hazards which existed even before they were built.

Thus, FEMA and the nation face an ever-worsening problem, and FEMA's only real play is to attempt, as is best possible under the current regulations, to limit the amount of Federal tax dollars paid out. This is in part why FEMA is so terribly demanding of substantial proof that damage was caused by the disaster, and only by the disaster, without contributions from deferred maintenance or pre-existing conditions.

Fraud, Waste, and Abuse

Although the post-disaster environment brings out the very best in many people and the organizations that they serve, it also brings out the very worst in some other individuals and organizations, both public and private. These bad actors will attempt to scam the disaster grant process.[2] As a matter of routine, both individuals and organizations will attempt to defraud either the local governments affected by a disaster, or the federal government, because so much money is in play following a disaster. In this regard, the Feds simply have no sense of humor, nor should they, given that these are Federal tax dollars in play.

As a result, FEMA must be constantly on guard to prevent waste, fraud, and abuse in the disaster assistance grant programs. This real-world aspect of fraud and abuse has created a situation where many stringent FEMA and other Federal regulations are required to protect the Federal Treasury as well as the treasuries of state, local, tribal, and territorial governments. These stringent rules and regulations have the unintended consequence of creating a much more burdensome administrative process for the local governments, the respective state governments, and the Federal government.

Local Administrative Capabilities

Additionally, state and local jurisdictions are often overwhelmed with the different demands of clean-up, repair, reconstruction, and replacement of damaged infrastructure and facilities. As a result of being administratively overloaded in the immediate aftermath of a disaster, many juris-dictions have difficulty in rapidly moving ahead with their recovery work. As a result, FEMA will sometimes seek to "clawback" grant funds that it perceives are not being used in a timely manner.

Another aspect of the disaster grant process is this: Many local government agencies do not normally collect and maintain records which fully address the requirements of FEMA's Public Assistance program in sufficient detail to ensure that they will be able to: a) qualify for a Public Assistance grant; b) permanently retain the grant funds; and c) survive a Federal audit of those grant funds.

Program Challenges

In part, I liken FEMA's Public Assistance program to the process of filing and paying Federal income taxes. Both the Internal Revenue Service and FEMA's Public Assistance program were created by Congress and Federal bureaucrats. Both make honest efforts to fulfill the needs of society, but inevitably bad actors from many sectors and conflicting goals in the programs create serious administrative, financial, and public relations problems at the local level.

Ideally, FEMA would provide Public Assistance grants quickly in a manner which promotes efficiency, and eliminates waste, fraud, and abuse. But this is the age-old problem of conflicting goals, i.e., Fast, Cheap, and Good. A program may deliver two of these three goals, but never all three. If something is fast and cheap, it will not likely be very good. If it's good and cheap, it prob-ably won't be fast. And, if it's good and fast, it probably won't be cheap. However, from a political perspective, all three must be stated goals which FEMA seeks to achieve.

Regulations and Their Interpretations

Unlike many other single-purpose grants from other federal agencies, there is also the fact that FEMA Public Assistance grant regulations are also subject to differing interpretation by the 10 different FEMA regions and the thousands of individual FEMA employees.

FEMA's job in relation to the Public Assistance program is not a simple one to do. When FEMA staff arrives at a disaster, local people are physically suffering; they are certainly suffering financially; and their lives are generally and severely disrupted. Working in an environment where people are greatly upset places harsh demands on the employees of any organization involved in disaster response and recovery. One result is that FEMA has had trouble maintaining a highly qualified and well-trained cadre of workers – workers who not only must deal with unhappy clients, but workers who often have sub-optimal living conditions in terms of lodging, food, and ordinary creature comforts.

This said, in many disasters, the FEMA staff on-scene may not be as knowledgeable and experienced as they could be. In trying to do the best job possible, these employees may often either approve or disapprove of projects without all of the requisite knowledge and skills needed. In some cases, the local jurisdiction may have to go through a lengthy appeals process to rectify errors made by nominally qualified FEMA staff. These same nominally qualified staffers may also approve work which will later be determined to be ineligible, to the financial detriment of the local agency.

In a case from the FEMA Appeals Database, in the aftermath of Hurricane Katrina, the Village of Key Biscayne, FL, received $208,522 for a contract for debris removal.[3] As a result of inconsistencies in the documentation, FEMA deobligated $37,817 of the total funding. Key Biscayne appealed against the deobligation. In a subsequent review of the appeal, FEMA further determined that none of the original $208,522 was eligible. In this case, a more experienced FEMA employee determined that the Project Worksheet was not eligible. Key Biscayne would have been better off forgoing the first appeal in this case.

Guide for Maximizing Recovery

The focus of this book will be on how local public agencies can maximize their cost recovery under FEMA's Public Assistance program and minimize their Project Worksheet denials, deobligations, and adverse audit findings.

Since 1998, I have been teaching local government agencies across the country how to be better prepared to work their way through FEMA's Public Assistance program.

For years I intentionally avoided writing a book on this topic because of the continuously changing FEMA policies and regulations. Maintenance of such a book would be more than a full-time job.

However, my thinking has recently undergone a sea change. While there is every reason to expect that the policies and regulations will continue to evolve, there are certain bedrock principles which for FEMA's 40+ years have not changed, and indeed in many cases may never change.

I do not intend this book to be a re-working of the Public Assistance Program and Policy Guide (PAPPG). Rather, I see it as a hands-on working guide with very specific information and useful perspectives, including working forms to ensure the proper documentation which FEMA requires.

As I do in my training programs, the book will make use of extensive real-world information, i.e., Department of Homeland Security, Office of the Inspector General (DHS-OIG) audits, and FEMA appeals from the online searchable Appeals Database. My library includes over 400 DHS-OIG audits and 500 appeals cases which illustrate the hard reality of noncompliance with FEMA's Public Assistance grant requirements.

The Public Assistance program is not a perfect program, nor will it ever be. This is simply the reality of any bureaucracy. Regulations, no matter how perfectly drawn, cannot cover every possible permutation of fact. However, local agencies are often their own worst enemies because of their failure to understand, adopt, and follow the policies and regulations required.

My ultimate intent is to assist local agencies to be better able to navigate the Public Assistance program for their cost recovery efforts. An additional benefit should apply to both FEMA and its state partners in that better-prepared local agencies will also reduce the administrative burden for both the Feds and the states.

Keeping Up to Date on Changes

Any time a disaster affects an agency or organization, it is imperative that the latest rules, regulations, and forms are located and used correctly. Failure to do so imperils the disaster cost recovery process.

Note: Both on the internet in general and on FEMA and other government websites more specifically, out-of-date rules, regulations, and forms may be found. Always double check that you have the most up-to-date information available. That said, it is my observation that in some instances FEMA forms may be used past their respective nominal expiration dates.

What Is Not Covered in This Book

While this book will attempt to cover the major issues relative to FEMA's Public Assistance program, there are many topics that, while important, are not critical to what I call Disaster Cost Recovery.

The broad concept of Disaster Cost Recovery naturally includes FEMA's Public Assistance program, but it also includes cost recovery from insurance policies, the receipt of donations for disaster assistance and recovery, and any other form of monetary or monetary equivalent resources available to local jurisdictions or eligible private non-profit organizations. All play a part in total Disaster Cost Recovery.

This book will not cover the Incident Command System (ICS), the National Incident Management System (NIMS), the National Response Framework (NRF), or the National Disaster Recovery Framework (NDRF). There are ample resources available from www.fema.gov or other websites for information on these programs.

This book will not cover Fire Management Assistance grants (FMAG) or FEMA's Individual Assistance program (IA). Similarly, the Small Business Administration's disaster loans for individuals and small businesses are generally not covered. An exception will be made in regard to Small Business Administration loans for eligible private non-profit organizations.

Neither will the book address FEMA's Emergency Declarations. "The President can declare an emergency for any occasion or instance when the President determines federal assistance is needed. Emergency declarations supplement State and local or Indian tribal government efforts in providing emergency services, such as the protection of lives, property, public health, and safety, or to lessen or avert the threat of a catastrophe in any part of the United States. The total amount of assistance provided for in a single emergency may not exceed $5 million. The President shall report to Congress if this amount is exceeded."[4]

However, the administrative and documentation procedures for Emergency Declarations are largely consistent with the Public Assistance program.

Other significant components of comprehensive Disaster Cost Recovery are the disaster assistance programs from more than a dozen other Federal agencies. Among others, these agencies include the Federal Highway Administration (FHWA), the Federal Transit Administration (FTA), the U.S. Army Corps of Engineers (USACE), the U.S. Department of Agriculture (USDA), and many others. To review all of the Federal disaster assistance programs available would be far beyond the scope of this book.

What This Book Is Not

This book is absolutely not a substitute for a good working familiarity with FEMA's Public Assistance Program and Policy Guide (the PAPPG), and many other FEMA books, policy statements, and Fact Sheets. This book should be used as a supplement to the FEMA literature.

Using this book will not be a substitute for experienced subject matter expertise, which may often be called for depending on the depth and breadth of the disaster-caused damage.

Reading this book will be of little help in the disaster cost recovery process if specific actions are not also taken to develop local policies and procedures, where necessary, to improve the capabilities of the local agency and its staff to properly document costs and otherwise comply with FEMA's sometimes-bewildering array of regulations and policies.

There are tens of thousands of pages of FEMA publications and documents; this book is an attempt to synthesize the most important policies and practices necessary to navigate the Public Assistance program. The book will introduce the reader to the vast complexities of the regulations, but it cannot and does not include every possible permutation of the facts which vary with each disaster, each agency, and each individual project.

FEMA's Web-Based Grants Portal

This book will generally not discuss FEMA's web-based Grants Portal. The Grants Portal is the method by which local agencies submit documentation for the disaster and each individual Project Worksheet. The Grants Portal is a relatively new approach to gathering documentation and submitting it to FEMA. As such, it is still evolving, and new programmatic elements continue to be introduced and improved upon. Because the Grants Portal is somewhat in a state of flux, information on how to use it continues to evolve, and that information could become quickly outdated. This book's aim is to discuss those fundamental principles of the Public Assistance program, which change slowly and rarely, if at all.

FEMA Publications Available Online

FEMA has a staggering amount of information available on its website, FEMA.gov. First and foremost for local governments is the Public Assistance Program and Policy Guide (PAPPG), Version 4.0, issued on June 1, 2020. A new revision is already in the works.

However, therein lies a problem. There is so much information available that it may be difficult to keep up with the latest revisions. Some FEMA materials are readily available for download. Other FEMA documents may be mentioned, but are only available to FEMA employees and contractors.

The Department of Homeland Security's auditors and the Government Accounting Office (GAO) also periodically issue reports dealing with FEMA and the Public Assistance program. Some, but not necessarily all, of this information will apply in certain circumstances, but not in other situations.

This book will not substitute for reading and understanding the Public Assistance Program and Policy Guide (PAPPG). However, it should serve as an enhancement and guide to many of the principles contained in the PAPPG. This book will contain numerous case studies based upon both DHS-OIG audits and published second appeals from FEMA's Appeals Database.

Disaster Cost Recovery Lifecycles

There are differing disaster cost recovery lifecycles. The cost recovery lifecycle for local governments, i.e., city, county, special district, tribal nation, or U.S. Territory,[5] as well as non-profit hospitals and medical centers and certain eligible non-profit organizations, including colleges and universities, may vary from the disaster cost recovery cycle experienced by the states or the Federal government itself. The nature of the disaster and the damages caused will also partially determine the complexity and timelines of the disaster cost recovery process.

In disaster cost recovery, it is important to recognize that for the locally affected organizations, the disaster lifecycle appears to move at a crawling pace. People are suffering, and their needs are often most immediate. But larger governments, i.e., the states and Federal government, by necessity move at a much more measured cadence. The pace of state and Federal governments can rarely move fast enough to satisfy the local government and its suffering citizens. At no level does any government move like Amazon. Except for fire, emergency medical services, and law enforcement, there is no same-day or next-day delivery, and disaster cost recovery is no exception.

Disaster Recovery Perspectives

For each level of government – local, state, and Federal – there are differing disaster perspectives. The local perspective is one of great urgency, intense drama, and often staggering loss. The state perspective is still urgent, but slightly less so if only because the disaster will typically affect only a relatively small portion of the state. The Federal perspective is about providing various forms of disaster assistance, but FEMA's actions are always measured in full compliance with applicable laws and regulations. For Federal employees, the current disaster is another day in the life. They were assisting at an equally bad disaster last week, and next week there will be yet another disaster.

Consider the perspective of someone who has just called 911 because of a heart attack. This is a traumatic and often life-changing event; however, for the firefighter/paramedic, this is just one of many 911 calls they will respond to this week. So too do we at the local level appear to have a greater sense of urgency than those outside of the disaster area who have come to assist us.

A colleague of mine, the elected Auditor-Controller of a Northern California county, suffered through eight Presidentially declared disasters in the 2010s. She reported that in each case, the Public Assistance program was administered with differences, as policies changed and state and Federal personnel rotated in and out.

And although they are different, from each government's point of view, these perspectives are all valid, meaning that each level of government has a different job to do relative to both overall disaster recovery and disaster cost recovery. These differing perspectives often make for confusion, complexity, and conflict among the parties, especially the locals who seldom if ever deal with disaster cost recovery. Understanding the validity of the various perspectives may help smooth out some of the issues. If a local government understands the Federal requirements for proper documentation and fully complies with those requirements, the local government will find the path to grant funding much less strewn with administrative rubble.

Acknowledgments

Over the decades since I was first exposed to FEMA's Public Assistance program in training, scores of my colleagues have played a role in guiding me along the way to writing this book. Because they are so many and have contributed so much in both major and minor ways, I shall list them alphabetically and with their significant affiliations as best I can.

- Ria Aiken, formerly with the City of Atlanta, GA
- Ernie Abbott, former Chief Counsel at FEMA, now an attorney at Baker, Donelson
- Fan Able, Retired Disaster Management Area Coordinator, Los Angeles County
- Doug Ahlers, Harvard Kennedy School of Government
- Karl Bruchhaus, Calcasieu Parish School Board, LA
- Mike Byrne, formerly with FEMA, now at Deloitte
- Tim Campbell, The Campbell Group

- Arrietta Chacos, Policy Advisor on Urban Resilience
- Christy Crosser, formerly with Lyons and Estes Park, CO
- Chris Donegon, formerly with the City of Fort Colllins
- Caroline Egan, Assistant Emergency Management Coordinator for Sugarland, TX
- Don Florence, Retired, Mariposa County Emergency Management
- Mark Fratkin, Adjusters International
- Carolyn Harshman, President of Emergency Planning Consultants
- Gary (J.R.) Hatfield, Imperial Irrigation District
- Michael Herman, Former FEMA Chief Regulatory and Legislative Counsel
- Steve Hynes of Deloitte
- Brenda Hundemiller, Retired Disaster Management Area Coordinator, Los Angeles County
- Matt Jadacki, Former FEMA CFO, Deputy Inspector General, Ernst & Young
- Ed Johnson, Former FEMA CFO
- Paul Johnson, Director of Douglas County Emergency Management Agency, NE
- Dr. Bijan Karimi, formerly with the City of San Francisco, Department of Emergency Management
- Chief Stan Lake, Adjunct Instructor at the National Fire Academy
- Margaret Larsen, formerly with FEMA and now with AG Witt Global
- Herman B. (Dutch) Leonard. George F. Baker, Jr. Professor of Public Management, Harvard Kennedy School of Government
- Andrew Lockman, Tulare County, CA
- Edward Martinet, Lima Consultants
- Paul Migdal, Adjusters International
- Vanessa Paulson, City of Los Angeles
- Vernon Poe, Franklin County Emergency Management, Ohio
- Gerard Quinn, Gerard Quinn & Associates
- Dr. Karen Scott-Martinet, Retired Contingency Planner, Northrop Grumman Corp.
- Melissa Shirah, Florida Division of Emergency Management Recovery Bureau Chief.
- Jesse St. Amant, Retired, Plaquemines Parish, LA
- Dr. Ellis Stanley, Former Director of the Los Angeles City Emergency Preparedness Division
- Betsy Thomas, Grants Administrator, County of Galveston, Texas
- Brandalyn Tramel, Purchasing Agent, City of Santa Rosa, CA
- Darrell Wolfe, Battalion Chief, Cal-Fire
- Jeannie Wong, Director of Finance & Administration, San Francisco City Controller's Office
- Monique Zamuda, Retired, Deputy Controller, City of San Francisco

Policies, Procedures, and Programs

This book contains certain policies, procedures and programs that are highly recommended, and in some cases, absolutely necessary to effectively work within FEMA's Public Assistance program and gain the maximum possible level of Public Assistance grant funding and protect the agency/organization from "claw backs" and adverse audit findings.

FEMA Simplifications

Over the years, FEMA has made many efforts to improve, simplify and expand the Public Assistance program. However, sometimes these efforts have produced unintended consequences which have had the exactly opposite effect, or at least an effect with little or no financial benefit for all the administrative efforts put forth.

Some of FEMA's efforts to both simplify and enhance the flexibility of Public Assistance do create tangible benefits; however, for some smaller agencies which have very little knowledge of and experience with the Public Assistance program, these advantageous programs may be a confusing waste of time and may not produce the desired results.

Therefore, this book will focus on the underlying fundamentals and will limit the discussion of some of the financially beneficial but administratively challenging options available within the Public Assistance program.

This is not to say that some of the program options are not worthwhile; indeed, many are. But the local government's ability to navigate these waters, with often deep and swift undercurrents, may be best left to larger agencies with more adequate levels of staffing, or to those smaller agencies which choose to hire an experienced consultant to assist them with the intricacies of these "advanced" program options.

Pre-Emptive Strategies

Pre-emptive strategies for Disaster Cost Recovery under FEMA's Public Assistance program are critical to obtaining the maximum funding available, and to reduce the likelihood of a FEMA deobligation or adverse audit findings. We will discuss several pre-emptive strategies throughout the book.

Strategies versus Tactics: The Long Perspective versus Down-in-the-Weeds

In my opinion, to successfully navigate FEMA's Public Assistance program and recover the maximum possible for disaster damages, the local agency must have a Financial Recovery Strategy to cover the long haul of disaster cost recovery.

Some damages may occur in a jurisdiction where it makes good business sense to simply walk away from making a claim. There are reasons for this:

1) There is limited staff to pursue the recovery of damages. Their time should be focused on those projects of the greatest value and where the need for immediate restoration is the greatest.
2) The lifecycle costs of a project may simply not be worth the time and effort. One way this can occur is when there is a very high-cost and relatively new facility (let's say a $50,000,000 city hall), with a very low damage cost ($250,000). At a 75% reimbursement, this would yield $187,500 in Federal funding. However, FEMA requires the agency to 'obtain and maintain' an insurance policy for $187,500, but local agencies, except for states, cannot be self-insured. Therefore, over the life of the facility, the local agency may make insurance payments many times over the value of the $187,500 FEMA reimbursement. More about this in Chapter 10: Insurance and Risk Management.

Another key strategy is the prioritizing of damages and restoration of facilities and infrastructure. Some agencies initially would like to fix it all and fix it right now. If a disaster is large enough to warrant a Presidential declaration, there is usually so much damage that this is not possible. Neither the state nor FEMA will know what the local priorities are or should be. This is the job of the local agency to determine what the priorities should be and then convey that information to both the state and FEMA.

Another very effective strategy for the local agency is to have enacted, before the disaster, certain policies which will enable the agency to obtain reimbursement for costs which are not otherwise eligible absent such a policy. These and various other strategies and recommended pre-emptive policies will be discussed in greater detail later in the book.

However, without good tactics, the best strategies in the world will come to naught.

Good tactics include having proper procedures and policies in place and then carefully adhering to these procedures and policies.

For over 25 years, as I have trained scores of agencies in the disaster cost recovery process, most agencies were initially focused on tracking their labor, equipment, and materials. This is only one of the in-the-weeds pieces of cost recovery. In fact, these costs are a very small part of the total disaster cost recovery. Far more important are the agency's purchasing policies and issues related to its insurance or self-insurance coverages.

Another important tactic is to be aware of and closely follow the requirements for Special Considerations.[6]

Complete denials of FEMA funding, or partial deobligations from procurement, insurance, and special considerations far outweigh the losses for improper documentation of labor, equipment, and materials. Yet most public agencies are blissfully unaware of the implications of their failure to know and adhere to these requirements – until funding is reduced or lost altogether.

Disaster Cost Recovery Challenges: The Almond Brain

The human brain contains two almond-shaped elements called the amygdala, which are understood to form the core of a neural system for processing fearful or threatening situations and events. This includes the detection of threats and the activation of appropriate behaviors in responding to threats or perceived dangerous situations. When humans become stressed, they often revert to these previously learned behaviors to successfully cope with a threatening situation, even though those previously learned behaviors may not be appropriate to the current situation.

Disasters are stressful events, whether we are a victim, a first responder, or a staff member of an organization which must respond in some way. When we are stressed, it is easy to fail to take the appropriate action, or even to recognize which actions are most appropriate.

Public safety employees, those in emergency medical services, law enforcement, or the fire service, often receive extensive training to help them automatically and appropriately respond in emergencies and disasters.

However, local government agency employees working in non-public safety functions may not receive appropriate training for disaster response activities, the administrative aftermath, or working with FEMA's Public Assistance program.

This book will help these governmental and non-profit employees to know which disaster-related activities are appropriate and supportive of their efforts in Disaster Cost Recovery.

Some of the most valuable tools for appropriately following the regulatory requirements associated with FEMA's Public Assistance program are checklists and the proper use of the forms documenting the process for receiving FEMA grants. Such check lists and forms are an integral part of this book and are listed in the Appendix, with a link to the support material at www.routledge.com/9781032770338.

A standard statement in many check lists for Emergency Operations Center positions states: "Keep the required documentation," or "Keep the appropriate documentation," without ever specifying in any detail what might constitute "proper" documentation. This book will provide many specific forms and MS Excel spreadsheets for tracking disaster-related costs and generally managing the necessary disaster documentation. No one agency will need to use every form offered in a single disaster, but various forms are provided to meet differing needs.

The approach to Disaster Cost Recovery will vary from agency to agency because every agency has slightly, and sometimes significantly, different ways of accomplishing the same or similar tasks. However, all agencies, regardless of size or purpose, will have to meet certain and very specific documentation requirements to obtain and retain FEMA's disaster assistance.

Disaster Cost Recovery Challenges: Garnering Support for the Cost Recovery Job

In his book "The 8th Habit,"[7] Stephen R. Covey describes a remarkable Harris Poll study conducted with 23,000 participants. He reports the findings in a comparison with an eleven-player soccer team: "If, say, a soccer team had these same scores, only four of the eleven players on the field would know which goal is theirs. Only two of the eleven would care. Only two of the eleven would know what position they play and know exactly what they are supposed to do. And all but two players would, in some way, be competing against their own team members rather than the opponent."

These research findings, while staggering, are an everyday occurrence in the world of disaster cost recovery. In my work with client cities and counties, I observed that many employees of these disaster-affected agencies were either apathetic to FEMA's requirements for proper record-keeping and documentation, or worse, actively refused to follow the appropriate processes necessary to ensure the maximum cost recovery by the agency. In the least offensive situations, employees were merely ignorant of the proper procedures and uninterested in learning what they should do.

Alternatively, many very experienced and capable public sector managers "freeze up" when confronted with a disaster situation, because they have no prior experience in the disaster arena.

This is then another challenge for the team assigned to the disaster cost recovery. In addition to all the administrative challenges, disaster cost recovery done well involves a large component of change management within the organization.

Disaster Cost Recovery Challenges: The Zombie Apocalypse – *(The Disaster Doesn't Matter; The Rules Are the Rules)*

Some years ago, I was delivering a cost recovery training program for a county in Texas and garnered some criticism because I was not including more information about the region's most recent disaster, Hurricane Ike. My reply was that the specific disaster does not matter; the FEMA rules are printed in black and white and are the same for any and all disasters.

In some cases, this may be a plus if your disaster was a flood, hurricane, or tornado, for which the Stafford Act (Robert T. Stafford Disaster Relief and Emergency Assistance Act, Public Law 93–288, as amended, 42 U.S.C. 5121 et seq., and Related Authorities) was written. However, if your disaster is an earthquake, tsunami, or drought, then there may be more squeaky issues at hand. Indeed, those same rules would theoretically apply in a zombie apocalypse or an extraterrestrial alien invasion. We certainly saw a mishmash of rules and regulations evolving from the recent Covid-19 pandemic, in addition to massive funding streams which were far beyond the purview of FEMA.

The Language of Public Assistance

One of the fundamental but often nearly invisible concepts of FEMA's Public Assistance program is the language used throughout the process. For example, the term "standby," meaning the "waiting in the wings" status of some disaster workers, may attract unwanted scrutiny regarding eligibility for that time. If, on the other hand, the employees are assigned to a "staging area" there is less chance of denial for that time if the workers were in fact in an on-duty status awaiting dispatch to some disaster incident. Putting lipstick on a pig results in a pretty pig, but nonetheless a pig.

Similarly, requesting a "reimbursement" for volunteer time or donations, will be ineligible even though they are likely to be eligible for a local cost share credit for the value of their time and/or donations. There is no single source of the proper vocabulary of words to use or not use, as the proper words to use may be highly dependent on the individual facts of a case. And for many, if not most, local government or non-profit organization employees, the next disaster may be their very first experience in "speaking" this strange language with its inscrutable nuances. Because this "language" is so different, do not hesitate to ask FEMA staff precisely what they mean if you do not understand what was said.

Self-Inflicted Gunshot Wounds

After reading literally thousands of published cases from FEMA's searchable online Appeals Database and audits from the Department of Homeland Security, Office of the Inspector General, certain trends and errors become readily apparent. One of those issues is that many – indeed most – of the denied first and second appeals are the result of what I term a "self-inflicted gunshot" wound, sometimes disabling and sometimes quite fatal, but almost never a "just a scratch." These self-inflicted gunshot wounds can come at any step in the disaster cost recovery process and are made by local agency employees in virtually every department of the agency. Throughout the book, I will endeavor to point out many of the most common failings or outright intentional missteps made by local officials which result in the partial or total deobligation of FEMA funding. And by "self-inflicted gunshot wound," I'm not talking about outright fraudulent or criminal behavior of local officials. Fraud and Criminal behavior will be addressed in Chapter 39. There will be more on this in Chapter 35 (Catch-22s, Conflicting Regulations) and Chapter 36 (Self-Inflicted Gunshot Wounds)

In the book, some paragraphs or topics will be marked by either a ⬚ (a bandage) or a ✎ (bullet) which will indicate a cost recovery aid or a dangerous situation to be avoided.

Terminology

Throughout the text, I will endeavor to avoid the runaway use of acronyms. The Public Assistance process is arcane and convoluted enough without hiding the meaning of words behind a cloud of acronym fog.

The words "jurisdiction," "agency," and "organization," and "applicant" are generally used interchangeably to describe the many different types of local government; these include cities; counties; special districts, including school districts, water districts, and others; non-profit hospitals; other eligible non-profits; colleges and universities; tribal nations; and U.S. insular territories. The common Federal acronym for local governments is "SLTT," which stands for State, Local, Tribal, and Territorial governments and their respective agencies.

However, in some cases the use of these terms does not necessarily apply to private non-profit organizations, which are sometimes treated differently by FEMA. These exceptions will be noted in the text.

For Whom Is This Book Written?

It is my observation, gathered over 25 years of teaching, responding to disasters, and consulting work, that unless someone has had the misfortune to work on disaster cost recovery for a local government agency, they are probably very unfamiliar with the different aspects of Federal disaster assistance, both FEMA's Public Assistance program and the many other Federal disaster assistance programs which may be available. Even for many of those with prior experience, their experience is usually limited and not filled with happy memories.

This appears to be especially so among many of my colleagues in the world of emergency management. Often their attitude is, "This is a finance problem, not an emergency management one," whereas many financial staff, at all levels, believe that disaster cost recovery is an emergency management task. Neither view, in my experience, is correct. Disaster cost recovery is a TEAM sport, and successful disaster cost recovery depends on the knowledgeable input and efforts of most of the different departments within a local government agency. Not everyone needs to read all of this book. But there are some members of staff in every department that will benefit from doing so. As one who may read most or all of this book, to them falls the responsibility of parsing out the different chapters of the book as appropriate.

For instance, the building & safety officials may provide a perfect damage assessment; the purchasing agent may fully comply with the Federal procurement regulations; the project manager may direct the repairs and reconstruction by the book; and yet FEMA may deny some or all the funding because of HOW the invoices were paid out. Disaster cost recovery is an intricate symphony of many different musicians, and any one of them will ruin the performance if they hit a false note. Every local government agency is organized slightly differently, and so it depends on one individual to rise to the occasion and be the conductor of this complex orchestra.

Use of This Book

The intent of this book is to provide a window through which to understand FEMA's Public Assistance program, and the audits and cases which are reviewed herein are powerful examples of how not to navigate the Public Assistance program.

However, this book should not be used as a reference or point of argument when working with FEMA on Project Worksheets or filing an appeal. If only because FEMA did not write this book, they are likely to ignore its provenance as an authoritative resource. That said, all the appeals cases are from FEMA's own online database, and the audits referenced are from the Department of Homeland Security's, Office of the Inspector General's website, and many other FEMA documents, including the Public Assistance Program and Policy Guide (the PAPPG) and FEMA's Disaster Operations Legal Reference (the DOLR). All of these documents and resources can provide readers with a trail of breadcrumbs to follow as they work through the Public Assistance program.

Covid-19: The Outlier Event

For the most part, this book will not deal with the Covid-19 pandemic. This disaster clearly was an outlier event which had not occurred since the so-called Spanish Flu outbreak of 1918. Covid-19 resulted for the very first time in a national declaration of disaster and resulted in virtually every government agency in the country having the option to apply for FEMA funding to cover Covid-19-related costs. Covid-19 was also largely an outlier event insofar as eligible expenses were only for Emergency Protective Measures and did not provide any funding for repair or replacement of damaged facilities. The elimination of Covid-19 as a covered topic will in no way reduce the value of this book. Virtually all of FEMA's procedural and documentation requirements are consistent across all disasters, including a pandemic.

Disaster Information Transitions

Disaster cost information is our financial lifeblood, and if information doesn't support the cost recovery, we don't need it. This book is focused on the collection, organizing, and communication of information from those who generate it to those who need it, in the form which they need at the time when they need it.

The Disaster Information Paradox

The information we have now is not the information that we want.

The information we want is not the information we need.

The information we need is not yet available.

When the information does become available, it may no longer be as useful because the situation has changed.

Our cost recovery information needs will change as the event moves through time.

Initially, we need high-level summary information to develop strategies, to define tactical responses, and to further our financial recovery. As the situation begins to mature, the information must get more specific and more detailed. As the situation further matures, more people will need access to more of the information. As the situation continues to mature, we do not want to reprocess the same information over and over to meet our evolving needs for disaster cost recovery.

Our information needs, priorities, qualities, and details will change and evolve as the disaster matures and moves from emergency situation to a set of stable problems that need to be resolved, restored, repaired, or rebuilt through our bureaucratic processes.

This Book Is a Start

For many of the topics in this book, this is only a starting point. Some of these topics could easily sustain a full book all by themselves. In the 40+ years of FEMA's existence, to my knowledge, no one has ever attempted a book like this. I have over 100 hours of programmed classroom training, and the training only scratches the surface of the Public Assistance program. For those who may be interested, there are many good resources available online at FEMA.gov.

Repetitions, More Repetitions, and Then Some More

This book is massive, and many readers do not need to read the entire book. Procurement staff will not necessarily need to read about damage assessment, and most building inspectors don't need to know much about procurement, etc.

In several cases, some of the appeal case studies may appear to be repetitions from an earlier chapter. These so-called repeat cases typically examine additional issues from these same cases which were not examined in the previous chapter. Appeals cases frequently contain multiple issues, any one of which could be fatal to the Project Worksheet in question.

Finally, there are some aspects of the Public Assistance program that are so important, that they bear repeating multiple times, if only because of their singular importance in the process.

Looking Forward

Should the reader or their agency be fortunate enough not to experience a disaster for some time after reading this book, always check the for current edition of the Public Assistance Program and

Policy Guide, the Disaster Operations Legal Reference, a host of other FEMA publications, and other important regulations, especially Title 2 of the Code of Federal Regulations, Part 200. Each of these documents is periodically updated, and any changes will have the potential to change the Public Assistance program.

The Weasel Words

The Weasel Words, aka My Attorney Said This Had to Be in the Book.

Every effort has been made to make this a comprehensive and current how-to text on FEMA's Public Assistance program.

That said, the Public Assistance program is in a near-continual state of revision, upgrading, and introduction of new options and processes. Therefore, anything in this book may be out of date, or incorrect the day after I sent it to the publisher. This is the nature of all bureaucracies and their regulations. Things change.

However, by avoiding as much as possible the process-oriented specific details and focusing instead on the underlying principles of disaster cost recovery, this book should outlast some of the procedural changes which will routinely occur in any bureaucratic program.

The focus of this book is on those principles of the Public Assistance program which have seldom if ever changed since FEMA was established in 1979.

Caveat Emptor

(Note All pictures in this book were created using Chat GPT's Dall-E creative program.)

Notes

1 Cummins, J.D., Suher, M., Zanjani, G. February 2010. *Federal Financial Exposure to Natural Catastrophe Risk*. University of Chicago Press. ISBN: 0-226-49658-9, http://www.nber.org/books/luca07-1
2 Brown, R.B. February 21, 2019. *NYC Admits Defrauding FEMA Out of Millions after Superstorm Sandy*, http://www.governing.com/topics/transportation-infrastructure/tns-nyc-lies-to-fema-storm-sandy.html
3 https://www.fema.gov/appeal/debris-removal-70
4 https://www.fema.gov/disaster/how-declared
5 Usually abbreviated by FEMA as SLTT, for state, local, tribal, or territorial government.
6 The 'Special Considerations' FEMA form number is FF-104-FY-21–134 (formerly 009–0-120)
7 Covey, S.R. 2004. *The Eighth Habit: From Effectiveness to Greatness*. Free Press, New York.

Part 1

Before the Event

1 FEMA's Public Assistance Program Overview

"We can throw stones, complain about them, stumble on them, climb over them, or build with them."

William Arthur Ward

Disaster response and recovery is a multi-agency, multi-faceted, multi-timeline concept which often goes far beyond the capabilities of any one local, state, or Federal jurisdiction or organization.

There are 17 Federal agencies alone with some involvement in either disaster response or recovery planning and operations, including FEMA.

Within FEMA, there are dozens of disaster response and recovery programs grouped into several categories, such as: Public Assistance, Individuals and Households Program Assistance, Mass Care and Emergency Assistance, Crisis Counseling Assistance, Disaster Case Management, Disaster Legal Services, and Voluntary Agency Coordination, among others.

This book, however, has a narrow focus on the Public Assistance program. Unlike most state-run "public assistance" programs, which is a euphemism for what might be otherwise called "welfare" programs, FEMA's "Public Assistance" program provides financial assistance for government agencies and in some cases for private non-profit agencies for their costs in responding to or recovering from disasters.

Since the early 1800s, the Federal government has been involved in assisting local jurisdictions following disasters.[1] For decades, Federal disaster assistance was done on a disaster-by-disaster basis, as the needs arose. As time went on, the Federal government got more involved and began enacting more disaster legislation in the 1950s. In the 1960s and 1970s, there was a series of significant disasters requiring major federal support for the response and recovery efforts, and the Federal government focused attention on natural disasters. These disasters included Hurricane Carla, 1961; the Alaska Earthquake, 1964; and Hurricane Betsy, 1965.

After these events, Congress passed the Disaster Relief Act of 1966, authorizing a 50% federal cost share to support the repairs, restoration, and reconstruction of public facilities damaged and destroyed following a major disaster. In the years following, the disasters kept on coming: Hurricane Camille, 1969; the San Fernando Earthquake, 1971; Hurricane Agnes, 1972; Love Canal, 1978; and the nuclear accident at Three Mile Island in March of 1979.

By this time, more than 100 federal agencies were somehow involved in some aspect of disasters. As a result, in April 1979, President Jimmy Carter created the Federal Emergency Management Agency, or FEMA, by executive order. This executive action placed the primary responsibility for all things related to disasters on one single Federal agency. However, many other Federal agencies still retained ownership of disasters and disaster-related damages to those areas over which they had their respective authorities, such as the Federal Highway Administration for the interstate highway network and other Federally supported roads.

DOI: 10.4324/9781003487869-3

FEMA has many other responsibilities related to disaster prevention, preparedness, response, and recovery. Since this book's primary focus is on the Public Assistance (PA) program, and more specifically about how local jurisdictions can take advantage of Federal financial support to restore their communities as much as possible to their pre-disaster conditions, very little will be said regarding these other programs.

Nonetheless, knowledge of these other non-FEMA programs is important insofar as these other Federal agencies and their respective programs may often be the source of problems because the disaster-affected local government agency mistakenly applies to FEMA for grant funding when they should have applied to another Federal agency – for instance, the U.S. Army Corps of Engineers or the Federal Highway Administration as the appropriate grant-funding source.

Throughout the book, instances of the sometimes-confusing array of Federal disaster grant funding streams will be mentioned, particularly when discussing "Eligibility" issues.

FEMA receives Federal funds through the Disaster Relief Fund (DRF), as appropriated by Congress. The challenge at all levels of government is that disasters are continuing to grow in numbers and severity. The following chart[2] clearly demonstrates this trend. The Public Assistance program itself accounts for 55% of all Disaster Relief Funds expended.[3]

As cities, counties, and special districts grow both in population and in physical footprint, the likelihood of a catastrophic disaster increases while the jurisdiction's public and private infrastructures continue to deteriorate with age.

Risks which formerly did not exist or existed as a pale shadow of themselves have grown very significantly over the decades because of the increasing urbanization of society. Furthermore, the widespread failure to maintain and replace aging infrastructure sometimes gives FEMA an out on certain projects, because projects which have deferred maintenance may be denied. There will be more about this concept in Chapter 26: Eligibility.

For example, take the County of Los Angeles at the time of the 1857 Fort Tejon Earthquake. The County at that time had less than 9,000 residents, zero miles of roads other than dirt tracks, zero

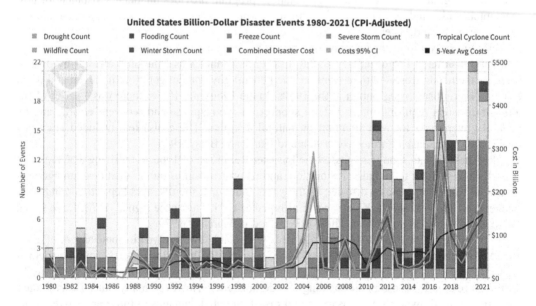

Figure 1.1 United States Billion Dollar Disaster Events 1980–2021.

Source: climate.gov/media/13979

utilities other than water wells, and the total assessed value of the real estate was approximately $750,000 in 1857 dollars.

Today this same region, all of L.A. County, has nearly 10 million residents; 22,000 miles of paved roads of all types, approximately 15,000 miles of electrical lines, tens of thousands of miles of water, wastewater, and storm drain piping, to say nothing of 2,000 miles of petroleum pipelines. The assessed value of real property in the county is approaching 1.9 trillion dollars in current value.

A similar earthquake to the 1857 Fort Tejon temblor will have massive humanitarian and financial implications for almost every aspect of life in this entire country, and global economic implications will reverberate as commerce and communications are affected in ways most people cannot yet fathom.

"According to the National Centers for Environmental Information of the National Oceanic and Atmospheric Administration, from 1980 through 2021, the United States has averaged more than seven weather-related disaster events that each cost $1 billion or more each year. The frequency of these events is increasing. From 1980 through 2007, more than seven billion-dollar events occurred in only one year (1998). Since 2007, these events have become more frequent: only one year since 2007 has seen *fewer* than seven such events. Ten or more such events have occurred each year since 2015. The United States was struck by 22 such events in 2020, an annual record."[4]

This sustained trend in the increased number of disasters and in their average cost continues to put pressure on the U.S. economy, and FEMA in particular, as the source of the most significant portion of all disaster related spending. I believe that as a result of this growing economic pressure, Congress, and by extension FEMA, will have to make adjustments in how disasters are paid for at the Federal level.

This anticipated trend will thus put greater pressure on local government agencies to be much better prepared to understand and follow FEMA's Public Assistance grant requirements or lose massive amounts of otherwise eligible Federal grant funds.

Meanwhile, small and rural local agencies continue to struggle mightily with the complex challenges of running a local government on a day-to-day basis. Following a disaster, these same communities are often overwhelmed by the onslaught of Federal regulations which have a tsunami-like tendency to flatten everything in their path.

The responsibility for knowing, understanding, and following the often-complex rules for obtaining FEMA Public Assistance falls completely on the shoulders of local government. This is a serious challenge, as many units of local government live from paycheck to paycheck as it were. Very few units of local government have the economic resources, the foresight, and the discipline to have a well-trained cadre of disaster cost recovery personnel. Training is often difficult to come by; there is normally a continuous turnover of trained staff; and Congress and FEMA are continually tweaking the process.

These challenges notwithstanding, the Federal regulations must be strictly followed equally by all agencies, large and small. The Stafford Act provides no equitable relief for those agencies with few resources and fewer trained employees.

This book aims to provide an easily accessible working guide to the Public Assistance program and shine a light on some of the program's sometimes frustrating and costly idiosyncrasies.

There are occasionally important differences between the way the program is supposed to work and the way it works in reality. These differences can arise when the unit of local government doesn't understand how the process is supposed to work, and sometimes the differences arise when the local government doesn't follow the rules even when they know the rules.

The respective states also may play a contributory role in the process. Most states do not have sufficiently trained and qualified staff to assist the local jurisdictions in the process. Several years ago, I examined all the Department of Homeland Security audits of local agencies in a single

Federal Fiscal Year and found that in exactly one-half of those same audits, the Office of the Inspector General also criticized the states for their failure to properly support the local government agencies in their quest for Public Assistance grants.

There is no other government agency nor anyone who will better look after the financial affairs of a single local government agency than its own employees. The ultimate burden for a successful Disaster Cost Recovery program rests with the officers and staff of each local agency.

Is It Worth It?

Is it worth it to go through FEMA's Public Assistance program? This is sometimes literally the million-dollar question. The Public Assistance program is clearly a challenge for local government agencies, be they large, medium, or small. This question is a valid one which deserves serious thought.

Some smaller disasters may be large enough to warrant a Presidential disaster declaration, but the individual city, county, or special district may not have enough serious damage to absolutely need the Federal disaster assistance, given the amount of staff time involved for the cost recovery. Over time, if a local agency could have an energetic disaster cost recovery program, be able to keep up with the frequent FEMA policy changes and maintain the proper level of training to ensure a successful cost recovery, they might spend more money than a single disaster will generate in Federal assistance.

But working with the Public Assistance program is an important practice for all staff, because when a truly catastrophic disaster happens, the local agency may be completely lost in the process and have to struggle mightily because they have had no recent experiences with the Public Assistance program.

Perspective on 'Is It Worth It?'

It is important to note that 25% of all U.S. disasters account for 93% of all disaster relief funding. For 75% of all Federally declared disasters, the local agency might not 'need' to apply to FEMA or any other Federal agency for disaster relief, certainly not in the same way as for a '25% worst-case' disaster.

However, when the local agency experiences one of those one-in-four worst-case-scenario disasters, there are no viable options for recovery except for Federal assistance. If the local agency is not familiar with FEMA regulations and experienced in providing proper documentation, it will be extremely difficult to obtain and retain a satisfactory level of financial assistance from the Federal government. As the old oil filter commercial said: "You can pay me now, or you can pay me later."

Real-Life Experience

In 1989, I traveled with three colleagues to observe the response of local agencies to the Loma Prieta earthquake in California. We visited four small cities to see how they handled the earthquake response. Of the four cities we visited, one of them appeared to have the situation well in hand because in the previous decade they had had three flooding events, which gave them important practice in resolving issues. One of the other cities we visited seemed like a bug on its back, with all six legs wiggling hopelessly in the air. They were clearly behind the 8-ball in so many ways. This community had previously been lucky and had not had a serious disaster in its recent past and was thus very much out of practice. I continued to follow these agencies over the next year, and those first impressions were pretty much unchanged. Experience counts and it counts a lot, especially in high-stress situations such as a disaster.

Chapter Questions

1) Do we have some of the basic FEMA documents in-house, such as the Public Assistance Program and Policy Guide?
2) Do we have FEMA's Publication 325 on Debris Management?
3) Do we have FEMA's Publication 327 on Debris Monitoring?
4) Has anyone on our staff attended the state-run Applicant's Briefing to see what happens there, even if we ourselves did not have damage from a disaster?

The FEMA PA program is a simple process with very complicated and non-linear moving parts.

Sources and Resources

This book makes extensive use of the FEMA website and the many FEMA publications, policies, and Fact Sheets contained therein, especially the Public Assistance Program and Policy Guide, or PAPPG. FEMA's 'Disaster Operations Legal Reference,' or the DOLR, is another often-used source.

The FEMA Appeals Database (https://www.fema.gov/assistance/public/appeals) and the Department of Homeland Security Office of the Inspector General's webpage (https://www.oig.dhs.gov/reports/audits-inspections-and-evaluations) are both treasure troves of real-life instances of both failure and success in how local jurisdictions fare with the Public Assistance program.

In the more than 25 years I have been providing training programs and consulting services, I have developed a national network of colleagues who have shared the stories of their successes and problems with the Public Assistance process.

On many occasions, I have also been privileged to assist in Emergency Operations Centers, where I have observed firsthand many of the issues discussed in this book.

Lastly, in my years of providing training for thousands of students from local government agencies, I have run across many real-life stories, far too many of them without a happy ending. I believe that I learn more from them than they do from me.

Notes

1 "An Act for the Relief of the sufferers by fire, in the town of Portsmouth", Ch. 6, 2 Stat. 201 (1803).
2 Painter, W.L. January 2022. *Congressional Research Service: The Disaster Relief Fund: Overview and Issues*, p. 22, https://crsreports.congress.gov, R45484
3 Ibid, p. 5.
4 Ibid, pp. 23–24.

2 General Pre-Emptive Strategies

"Every battle is won before it is ever fought."

Sun-Tsu, Chinese General circa 2500 BC

General Pre-Emptive Disaster Cost Recovery Strategies

Case Study: Feeding Force Account Labor – City of Atlanta, GA

"From February 10 to 15, 2014, a severe winter storm resulted in sleet, ice, and snow accumulation in the City of Atlanta, Georgia (Applicant). FEMA prepared Project Worksheet (PW) 322 to address the Applicant's request for costs associated with its force account labor (FAL) compensatory time and overtime, materials (food costs for FAL), and equipment used to establish an Emergency Operations Center (EOC) and perform emergency protective measures for a portion of the Hartsfield-Jackson Atlanta International Airport (Airport) located in Fulton County. In addition, the PW documented costs associated with salting nearby bridges and roads. FEMA subsequently determined the work captured in PW 322 was ineligible and notified the Georgia Emergency Management Agency (Grantee) of its decision by email on September 22, 2014. PW 322 stated that the FAL was not eligible per FEMA Recovery Policy RP9525.7, Labor Costs – Emergency Work, and the Applicant's employee overtime policy did not allow for reimbursement of overtime for exempt employees. PW 322 further stated that snow assistance costs, equipment and materials to salt roads and bridges were also ineligible per FEMA Disaster Assistance Policy DAP9523.1, Snow Assistance and Winter Storm Policy. Additionally, FEMA noted that the Applicant did not have a food and lodging provision in its predisaster employee policy, which would require it to pay such expenses, and consequently, costs to feed employees working regular shifts were ineligible for Public Assistance (PA) funding."[1]

In this case, the lack of pre-disaster policies resulted in the denial of compensatory time off for exempt employees and overtime pay for hourly employees.

Two years later, I was invited to present my disaster cost recovery training program in Atlanta. Ria Aiken was at that time the Director of Atlanta's Office of Emergency Preparedness. Ria opened the training on the first morning with this question directed at the audience: "What would you do if you won the lottery?"

Ria chose several people to respond to the question. One person said they would buy a house, another said they would pay off their student loans, yet another said they would buy their mother a home, etc.

Ria then asked: "What would you do if you lost the lottery ticket?"

A very audible groan spontaneously rose up within the room. "Oh, no, we lost the ticket."

DOI: 10.4324/9781003487869-4

Ria then stated: "This is what happened to the City of Atlanta. We lost the ticket; that is to say, we didn't have the documentation necessary to recover the eleven million dollars of damage and response costs from the 2015 storm." At that point in time, according to Ria, the city had only recovered $200,000 dollars of the total of $11,000,000 spent for the disaster response.

Effective disaster cost recovery depends on knowing what to do, doing those things in the proper order, and doing the important things in a timely manner.

In this chapter and the next, we will look at a series of strategies and policies which can make a significant difference in the local agency's disaster cost recovery process.

There are many disaster-related costs which FEMA will reimburse IF AND ONLY IF certain actions are taken before the disaster occurs. There is no set time frame to take some of these actions, with the exception that those we will discuss in this chapter and the next must be taken BEFORE the onset of the disaster – preferably long before the onset of the disaster, not the week before.

These policies, which we will discuss one at a time in the next chapter, cover expenses related to the agency's own employees; the survivors of the disaster; the use, care, and feeding of volunteers; and the proper handling of donations of all types and sizes.

We will look at more than two dozen different policies an agency may want to have. The need for, and importance of, these policies will vary from disaster to disaster; indeed, they may vary from one agency to another. Some of the policies may result in relatively small financial recovery, while others may be worth millions of dollars, lost or gained, because the relative policy was or was not in place, properly adopted, and consistently followed.

This chapter will be a brief discussion of the underlying elements which must be present in all of these policies. These key elements do apply to all these policies, but rather than repeat them time after time, we will do this once in this chapter.

All this said, having the proper policies in place will not substitute for the work, goods, and or services being otherwise eligible. All the terms of the policy may be met; however, if the underlying work to which the policy is applied is ineligible, then the policy will not make a difference.

One policy which will not be in this chapter is the policy, and the supporting documentation, for Private Property Debris Removal (PPDR). This may be one of the most important pre-disaster policies for any local agency, particularly for cities and counties. Private Property Debris Removal will be dealt with in Chapter 15, Debris Monitoring and Debris Management. However, the underlying principles for adopting a PPDR policy are the same as for all other policies explained in this chapter.

Six Important Factors for Every Policy

There are six factors which must be present for any pre-emptive policy to be honored by FEMA. These factors are:

1) The policy, the MOU (Memorandum of Understanding), or contract must be in writing. Hereinafter "policy."
2) The policy must have been adopted before the disaster occurred. Adopting a policy on the day of the disaster or the day after the disaster will not work. The policy must be a standing policy of the agency.
3) The policy must be adopted by a formal action of the elected officials of the agency at a public meeting. So-called "Administrative Policies", i.e., those approved by the city manager, chief executive officer, county judge, or other senior official will not be sufficient to warrant FEMA's acceptance of the policy.

4) The policy must be consistently enforced. For example, if the agency has a feeding policy for Emergency Operations Center staff, FEMA may require that the agency provide receipts for those meals provided during prior EOC training sessions and EOC exercises. Failure to continually adhere to the feeding policy will result in deobligation of funding.

Many agencies have a general policy which prohibits feeding during training sessions or meetings. This policy notwithstanding, FEMA will not honor a disaster feeding policy if the agency does not have a consistent practice of feeding during EOC training, exercises, or locally/gubernatorially proclaimed disasters.

5) The policy must not be discretionary, i.e., invoked at the discretion of the city manager, or the discretion of the mayor, etc. As far as FEMA is concerned, a discretionary policy is no policy at all. If the local agency has the discretion to activate and enforce the policy, then FEMA will choose not to allow the policy.
6) The policy and the resulting costs may not be dependent on FEMA funding. If the language of the policy in any way hints that the cost will be paid only if FEMA reimburses them, or only when FEMA reimburses them, then the policy is void and not worth the paper on which it is printed.

Without compliance with these six conditions, any disaster-related policy is a waste of time, and even worse, may give the agency a sense of well-being when in fact the agency may be treading water in the Mariana Trench. Under the terms of an improperly created pre-disaster policy, the local agency may have obligated itself to cover certain disaster related costs, i.e., feeding, but by faulty adoption or lack of consistent application made the policy ineligible for FEMA reimbursement.

In drafting any of these policies, it is important to understand that some of the normal rules affecting non-FEMA policies may not be appropriate for use. I have seen policies drawn up by staff, then reviewed by agency legal counsel, which after all was said and done were useless.

There are relatively few attorneys who are fully conversant with the Stafford Act and with FEMA regulations. Great care must be taken to ensure that language which might otherwise be appropriate and necessary in legal documents, contracts, and policies may not be embedded explosives in pre-disaster policies.

In 2014, I assisted a local agency with its initial efforts for disaster cost recovery following the Napa Earthquake. The local agency had requested Mutual Aid assistance from a neighboring agency. The "invoice" which we received contained the following language: "Payment shall be due to the sending party within sixty (60) days of receipt of funds from FEMA by the requesting party." This single sentence in the agreement made it a contingent agreement, depending on FEMA reimbursement, and therefore an ineligible expense. It is difficult for me to imagine that anyone familiar with FEMA regulations would have allowed such a statement to be inserted into the agreement.

It is highly recommended that when an agency intends to create certain policies, the staff conduct extensive research in FEMA's Appeals Database to understand and comply with the nuances needed for these policies.

Notes on Conducting Research in FEMA's Appeals Database

• Spelling and typography count. For example, searching for terms like "nonprofit" and "nonprofit" will yield substantially different search results.

- Typing in certain search terms may bring up hundreds of cases to review. The use of quotation marks around a search term will usually bring more limited and specific results.
- Many appeals cases in the database will have multiple issues included in a single appeal. Cases will have to be read carefully to filter out the cases and the issues which do not apply.
- Do not stop researching after finding only one or two cases. Some of the cases may be on point but still not be the most definitive answer. Other cases will be an apparent answer but in fact do not apply at all. The research will take time to ensure that the researcher has obtained a full comprehension of the pertinent issues of the case.
- In the Appeals Database, there are apparent instances of a single agency with two or more appeals with the same title. They may or may not be the same case or the same set of issues.
- In the Appeals Database, there are sometimes three different 'versions' of the appeals case. They are:

  - The Appeal Brief, which is a brief, often one-page summation of the key facts of the appeal.
  - The Appeal Letter, which is a copy of the actual letter sent to the state director of emergency services, requesting that the state notify the local agency of FEMA's determination of the appeal. The letters are generally more detailed than the 'Brief.'
  - The Appeal Analysis, which is my personal favorite. When it is included, it provides the greatest detail and usually abundant footnotes which provide references to other appeals cases, the relevant sections of the Stafford Act, or the relevant regulations, usually in Title 44 of the Code of Federal Regulations, Section 206 et seq.

However, some cases, particularly older ones, will not include the Appeal Analysis. The Appeal Analysis may sometimes run to a dozen pages or more and be written in such a style that it appears it was written by an attorney.

Having some familiarity with FEMA's Appeals Database will also provide a leg up if and when the local agency is considering filing an appeal of an adverse ruling by FEMA.

Reading either or both appeals cases and Department of Homeland Security, Office of the Inspector General audits of local agencies will open the door to understanding how FEMA administers the Public Assistance program, and what is expected of us as applicants.

Further Thoughts on Policy Development

When formulating a new disaster policy, base the policy implementation on the most likely worst-case scenario, knowing that actual implementation will probably be at a lower level in most cases. However, a policy developed with a worst case in mind should cover most, if not all, possible eventualities.

Make the policy as specific and well-defined as possible without making it too restrictive to activate. While flooding may be the most likely threat for one community, that community should not exclude the possibility of other threats arising which would potentially create a misapplication of the policy.

And always know that FEMA will likely read a policy differently than how you expect. Both the letter of the law and the intent of the law are important, but if the intent does not match the letter, then there is room for interpretation.

The following is an example of a policy poorly drafted for the desired outcome.

"The SEMA*/FEMA rates shall only be used or implemented when there is a declaration of disaster for an incident directly involving primary mutual aid and the mutual aid departments listed in this Agreement."

In this paragraph, the problem areas are underlined.

"The SEMA*/FEMA rates[1] shall only be used or implemented[2] when there is a declaration[3] of disaster for an incident[4] directly[5] involving primary[6] mutual aid and the mutual aid departments listed in this Agreement."

Here are the issues I see:

1. Which rates are they talking about? Labor rates, equipment rates, or some other rates? We must be specific or provide inclusive language as necessary.
2. What is the difference between "used" and "implemented"? Implemented is extraneous verbiage, which adds nothing, but gives a reader the opportunity to question what the word means in this context.
3. This is the fatal word, because only the President may 'declare' a disaster. This single word would make this a contingent agreement.
4. More extraneous verbiage which adds little or nothing to the statement.
5. How is Mutual Aid directly or indirectly involved? Yet more added but useless wording. "Direct mutual aid" is defined as Mutual Aid directly coordinated between agencies. However, FEMA only reimburses Mutual Aid coordinated by the respective state, and only when the Mutual Aid resources obtain a "resource request number" or "mission assignment number" per state Mutual Aid policy.
6. What is "primary" Mutual Aid, and how would it differ from secondary or tertiary Mutual Aid, whatever they may be? In this case, primary and secondary Mutual Aid are firefighting-related terms for Mutual Aid. But what if the Mutual Aid is for police or public works or any other function? This again places artificial limits on the policy.
7. Why would access to Mutual Aid be limited to only signatory departments? In a worst-case scenario, a desperate agency would likely take help from any qualified source. This sentence would give FEMA a great rationale for denying payment for Mutual Aid provided by non-signatory agencies.

It is apparent that this agreement was drafted by someone within the fire service, which is perfectly acceptable. However, to use this as a broad-based policy for other than the fire service could cause problems. The team drafting a policy should have representation from all those functions which may use or be affected by the policy.

Note

1   https://www.fema.gov/appeal/force-account-labor-emergency

3 Pre-Disaster Strategies and Policies

"Some people don't like change, but you need to embrace change if the alternative is disaster."

Elon Musk

In the previous chapter, we looked at the general conditions for all pre-disaster policies, Memoranda of Understandings, and non-commercial contracts. Following in this chapter are the individual documents which a well-prepared local agency would have to enable recovery of the maximum amount of eligible costs from FEMA. They are broken down into three major groups: 1) Employee pay and benefits; 2) Survivor's services for the disaster victims; 3) Volunteers and donations.

As previously mentioned, Private Property Debris Removal (PPDR), which is often a major expense in any disaster, will be dealt with in Chapter 15, Debris Monitoring and Debris Management.

As explained in the previous chapter, these policies and agreements have some common elements of information and some common prohibitions which would otherwise invalidate them.

The relative importance of these policies and agreements will vary with each disaster and with each different local agency.

Caveat: Having a perfectly drawn up and properly approved and implemented policy will not guarantee FEMA reimbursement if the work performed and/or goods and services provided do not meet the underlying requirements for emergency work.

In the case of the city of Atlanta,[1] where we previously addressed the issue of employee feeding, the city also requested overtime pay for its employees. The city's overtime pay policies were properly drafted and implemented. However, the work done by the city's employees was ineligible work as defined in the Stafford Act §403 (a)(3), meaning that the emergency work performed must be necessary to deal with imminent threats to life safety, to protect the public health, or to protect improved property.

Employee Related Pre-Disaster Policies

- Employee Overtime Pay (For both hourly & exempt employees)
- Employee Feeding

    a. Specify who is fed, & under what conditions, i.e., activation levels, etc.

- Employee Lodging
- NO FEMA-funded employee Childcare

DOI: 10.4324/9781003487869-5

Survivor's Services for the Public

- Shelters
  - Congregate
  - Transitional

- Feeding
- Medical Care
- Pet Rescue & Care
- Emergency Transportation
- Evacuation/Repatriation
- Local Transportation and Direct Federal Assistance (DFA)
- Family Re-unification
- Childcare for Survivors
- Points of Dispensing (PODS)
- Points of Distribution (PODS)
- Mental Health Care
- Restoration of disaster-use facilities
- Miscellaneous Post-Disaster Services (Generally Non-Eligible)

Volunteers and Donations

- Individual Volunteer Hours & Equipment
- Volunteer Registration
- Volunteer Assignments
- Volunteer Time Tracking
- Volunteer Organizations (VOADs: Volunteer Organizations Active in Disasters)
- Informal or ad-hoc volunteer groups
- Pre-Disaster Service Agreements
- In-Kind Donations of Goods & Services
- Small Donations & Crowdfunding Donations
- Legacy Donations

Employee Disaster Pay Policy for Hourly Employees

A pre-disaster policy for employee overtime may be one policy with two parts or two separate policies: one for hourly employees and a second policy for FSLA (Fair Labor Standards Act) or exempt employees. Here we will deal with these two separate classes of employees in two different policies. In this way, should the disaster overtime pay for one group be found ineligible, all may not be lost vis-a-vis the other group of employees.

In the following case, there are multiple issues; however, FEMA has chosen to deny eligibility on only one of those issues. This overtime request for 32,200 hours is also defective insofar as these were actually regular hours worked, which makes them ineligible, even though they may have been worked in support of the disaster response.

Case Study: East Carolina University (ECU) – Overtime, Force Account Labor

"In this case study, the university requested $537,310 for employee 'overtime' following Hurricane Floyd in September of 1999. Critical employees were asked to work during this period and were compensated with premium pay and overtime, in addition to their regular salaries. The premium pay rate was 100 percent of the employee's regular hourly wage. ECU claimed 'overtime labor costs' for 35,111 hours (32,200 regular hours and 2,911 overtime hours). FEMA denied these costs as ineligible."[2]

"On June 19, 2000, ECU submitted its first appeal requesting $537,310 in 'overtime costs associated with the premium pay for 32,200 regular hours' and fringe benefits. It claimed that the premium pay was warranted due to the emergency circumstances and was approved in accordance with the State's in-range salary adjustment policy. FEMA denied the appeal on October 6, 2000, stating that ECU had not demonstrated it had a uniformly applied overtime policy in place at the time of the disaster."[3]

"ECU submitted its second appeal on December 4, 2000. It included the State's policy on in-range salary adjustments, which was implemented prior to the disaster. ECU explained that while the university was closed, essential employees who performed emergency work were provided with premium pay. It was provided in addition to their regular salary but applied to regular hours worked. ECU states that it uniformly applied the premium pay scheme to all such employees. It claims that the fact that other state agencies did not use the premium pay scheme during Hurricane Floyd is of no consequence because agencies were impacted differently. Finally, ECU asks that these premium pay expenses be recognized as eligible overtime costs."[4]

"The State's in-range salary adjustment policy allows salary adjustments for permanent employees to 'recognize permanent and significant job change, resolve bona fide inequitable salary relationships, and/or respond to unique labor market conditions.'" The policy only allows for a salary increase of up to 10 percent, and requires administrative documentation, such as a new position description. ECU acknowledged in the PW and in its first appeal that a special exception to the in-range salary adjustment policy was made in this case. It stated, 'University policy and North Carolina Office of State Personnel guidelines did not specifically address compensation for the specific circumstances.' A memorandum dated September 30, 1999 *(two weeks after the storm)*, and sent via email to university employees, documents ECU's rate of premium pay in this situation. The in-range salary adjustment policy does not address labor costs in emergency situations, as is clear from the language of the policy and the fact that the Office of State Personnel made a special exception in order to apply it in these circumstances."[5]

"FEMA may pay extraordinary costs for critical employees who are asked to perform disaster-related emergency work when otherwise on administrative leave. However, applicants must provide for such labor costs in a written policy prior to the disaster. In accordance with the Office of Management and Budget, Circular A-87, Attachment A, Section C (1)(e), costs must be consistent with policies, regulations and procedures that apply uniformly to federal awards and other activities. ECU had no relevant written policy in place at the time of the disaster. As such, FEMA cannot reimburse ECU for these costs. For this reason, I am denying this appeal."[6]

This case also points out how university administrators chose to read the state's in-range salary adjustment policy from a "permissive" angle, i.e., "We can interpret the policy to allow this." However, FEMA will in most cases read the same language from a "restrictive" perspective, i.e., "The policy does not address this situation."

Dealing with overtime for employees is not a simple matter in many cases. A search of the Appeals Database for the term "overtime" will yield nearly 200 cases, or almost 10% of all the cases in the Appeals Database.

Furthermore, having a properly drawn and approved overtime pay policy does not necessarily mean that all costs will be eligible for reimbursement.

In a case from a South Carolina city,[7] the city's "Emergency/Extraordinary Pay Policy" is defective from the very first line of the policy which states in part: "the Office of the Mayor *may* (emphasis added) declare" This single phrase makes the policy a discretionary policy, and therefore not FEMA-eligible.

Even absent this single damning line, there are further provisions in the policy which would be ineligible. i.e., provisions for "sleep time pay" which does not apply since FEMA regulations state that only hours actually worked on bona fide emergency response work are eligible.

Many local public agencies already have a written overtime policy in place for their hourly employees as a regular part of the agency's pay and benefits policy or labor bargaining unit agreements. For many local agencies, the standard overtime pay language may be sufficient; however, a careful review is probably warranted since overtime pay is often a substantial portion of the costs for disaster response and recovery. Of course, the number of overtime hours worked will mean nothing without detailed documentation regarding the disaster-related problem and what was done to reduce or eliminate the threat posed.

Another interesting twist on the implementation of a policy which had the specter of ineligibility looming large comes from a Texas county.[8] In this case, the county's policy authorized overtime pay when employees were sent home on "administrative leave" and then required to return to work for emergency purposes. However, in this particular case, the employees were already at work and were required to remain at work. Because employees had not been officially placed on administrative leave, the county was not eligible for the overtime reimbursement of $34,000.

In this case, an apparently minor mistake in policy application turned out to be a fatal error for the disaster cost recovery process.

Further complicating this case is that the employees were paid a 100% premium over their normal wages while working straight-time hours. Because the premium was paid on straight-time, none of the cost was eligible.

There are no doubt many more apparently minor flaws possible in policy creation, adoption, interpretation, and implementation for overtime pay.

The following text from this same appeals case spells out in agonizing detail the responsibility of the local agency regarding receiving FEMA funding not only for disaster overtime, but for ALL disaster-related costs for which reimbursement is sought. "It is the applicant's responsibility to substantiate its claim as eligible. If the Applicant does not provide sufficient documentation to support its claim as eligible, FEMA cannot provide PA (Public Assistance) funding for the work. Documentation should provide the 'who, what, when, where, why, and how much' (emphasis added) for each item claimed. The burden to fully substantiate an appeal with documented justification falls exclusively on the applicant and hinges on the applicant's ability not only to produce its own records, but to clearly explain how those records support the appeal."

The discussion continues: "Here, the Applicant has not provided documentation to substantiate that the FAL *(Force Account Labor)* costs claimed on second appeal are tied to the performance of eligible work. While the Applicant has provided documentation, via the Incident Action Plan, that identifies a group of planned emergency response activities conducted through the incident period, including but not limited to flood fighting, EOC operations, sandbagging, etc., this does not identify the who, what, when, where, why, and how much for each claimed activity. Similarly, although the Applicant provided validation summary spreadsheets and timesheets which show the hours claimed by each employee as O.T. *(overtime)* during the incident period, the documentation does not provide detail or specificity regarding what the employees were doing during those hours. *It simply contains general descriptions, such as pre-storm prep and storm response.* Additionally, the Applicant has not provided activity logs or other documentation which tie O.T. hours claimed to eligible emergency protective measures. Therefore, the claimed costs on appeal cannot be tied to the performance of eligible work."[9] (Emphasis added)

And an overtime pay policy for hourly employees is the simpler of the two possible overtime pay policies, if only because employers normally pay their employees overtime when they work extra hours, in a disaster or not.

The payment of overtime wages for FLSA (Fair Labor Standards Act) exempt employees working disaster overtime are subject to greater scrutiny, if only because this is not a normal course of events for either the employers or the employees.

Perhaps the most definitive case regarding the payment of overtime for otherwise FLSA exempt employees comes to us from a county in North Carolina[10] which properly adopted a policy to pay exempt employees overtime during a disaster. The policy was adopted in November of 2002, and the disaster in question occurred in September of 2003. Therefore, the adoption of the policy was clearly done prior to the disaster. There were no disasters in the county between the adoption of the policy in 2002 and the disaster in 2003, so there was no opportunity for the county to follow its own policy in a locally proclaimed disaster. The amount of money in question in this case was approximately $26,000.

There are two problems with the policy that resulted in deobligation of funds. First is a technicality to be sure, but the wording of the policy states in part: "The decision paper recommended the following policy change: 'In the case of a *__declared__* (emphasis added) state of emergency/disaster employees generally exempt under the Fair Labor Standards Act (FLSA), *__will be considered__* (emphasis added) for overtime pay.'"[11]

Local officials and governors of states may "proclaim" disasters, but only the President may "declare" a disaster. The use of the single term "declare" is an indication that the policy would only be used when Federal assistance is available, and therefore an ineligible cost.

The second fault of this policy is the phrase "will be considered," which makes this a discretionary policy and therefore ineligible for FEMA funding.

All this is bad, but the county seemed to make an extra effort to make things even worse. One of the back-up documents which it submitted during the appeals process by the county included the explanation that: "the Personnel Policy Committee recommends amending the policy in order to be eligible for FEMA reimbursement,"[12] specific language which makes this a contingent policy and therefore ineligible.

In a continuing denial of the reality of the supremacy of Federal regulations, this same county in its 2020 version of its "Pay Plan" contains the following language: "This additional compensation does not apply when specific extraordinary working conditions warrant such as extreme weather conditions, acts of terrorism, pandemic conditions or declaration of state of emergency, *__unless otherwise approved by the County Manager__*. This is a privilege granted by Northampton County Local Government and is subject to change."[13] Once again, this language makes the policy discretionary by the County Manager.

If the policy has even a whiff of the scent of being a contingent or discretionary policy, it will be dead on arrival.

In a final case on ineligible employee overtime, also from North Carolina, the city requested reimbursement of $28,000 for overtime paid to its employees who worked in support of a shelter for the survivors of Hurricane Katrina. The overtime was authorized under a very broad brush reading of a fire department bulletin dated a year prior to Hurricane Katrina. The bulletin was specific to the deployment of a hazardous materials response team and not to sheltering activities; therefore, FEMA denied funding.

Comp Time Issues

Comp Time, or more properly Compensatory Time Off, occurs when an hourly employee works overtime and chooses in lieu of paid overtime to put time on the books, usually an hour of comp time for each hour of overtime worked.

Comp time also often also applies to FSLA (Fair Labor Standards Act) exempt employees who are not eligible to be paid overtime. The same situation applies: one hour of comp time accrued for each hour of extra time worked past their normal 40-hour workweek. FEMA does not reimburse an agency for those hours of comp time accrued because the agency did not "pay" cash for the work done. The exception to this rule is that if the hourly employee has the right to elect either paid overtime or comp time, or convert comp time to paid overtime, then reimbursement may be possible. However, there must be a written policy giving the employee the discretion to take either paid overtime or comp time. The local agency's pay policy must be precise and specific as to how comp time is earned and used or paid out and which groups of employees are covered by the policy.

Employee Feeding During a Disaster Response

Text from the Public Assistance Program and Policy guide:

"M. Meals

Applicants often provide meals for emergency workers. Provision of meals, including beverages and meal supplies, for employees and volunteers engaged in eligible Emergency Work, including those at EOCs, is eligible provided the individuals are not receiving per diem and one of the following circumstances apply:

- Meals are required based on a labor policy or written agreement that meets the requirements of Chapter 6 (of the PAPPG), *Cost Eligibility*;
- Conditions constitute a level of severity that requires employees to work abnormal, extended work hours without a reasonable amount of time to provide for their own meals; or
- Food or water is not reasonably available for employees to purchase.

FEMA only reimburses the cost of meals that are brought to the work location and purchased in a cost-effective and reasonable manner, such as bulk meals. FEMA does not reimburse costs related to group outings at restaurants or individual meals."[14]

What is not said in this quotation is that for such meals to be eligible for reimbursement, the local agency must document and account for every meal served under the qualifying conditions. For this purpose, in Form 21 (see Appendix), there is a sample form, the Disaster Operations Meal Sign-In Sheet. This is not a FEMA form, but it is a form which will meet the need to document every meal served. A fresh set of forms should be set out with each meal that is served, and the employees are reminded to sign-in for each separate meal. The fact that an employee is signed in and working in the Emergency Operations Center or other qualified disaster site is not sufficient documentation that they also received a meal. This form, or one similar to it, should be in constant use during disaster operations.

Upon receiving a request for reimbursement for meals, FEMA will probably require a copy of the agency's written and properly adopted disaster meals feeding policy. They may also ask for copies of the receipts for meals served during Emergency Operations Center training and exercises, perhaps going back two or three years, as proof that this is a regularly and consistently enforced agency policy. Failure to provide this documentation will likely result in deobligation of these costs.

In a case from the State of Iowa, the State's Emergency Operations Center was activated for the response to a series of tornadoes which struck the State in August of 2008. The State Emergency Operations Center (SEOC) provided meals for the SEOC staff and personnel from "a variety of other federal and state agencies (such as FEMA and the Iowa State Police), National Guard members, and a handful of private entities such as the American Red Cross."[15] Meal costs were approximately $60,000.

The appeal discussion also noted that: "On most days, there were more meals ordered than signatures collected, and on a few days, there were more signatures than meals.[16]

In the first appeal, the State "explained that providing meals to individuals charged with emergency work at the SEOC was necessary due to the 24-hour operation of the SEOC, *was part of the state's established practice,* and was already determined to be eligible in the obligated PW Version 1.

FEMA denied the first appeal, ruling that: '. . . all of the requested costs were ineligible. Its rationale was that:

- meals that were purchased but not signed for were unreasonable and could not be tied to an emergency function,
- providing refreshments was unnecessary, and
- the Grantee had not established that meals were only provided to personnel performing emergency work because the roles of the individuals on the sign-in sheets were unclear.'"[17]

So, in creating a disaster worker feeding policy, the policy should not only address the needs of the agency's own employees, but also other personnel from all other agencies who may be involved with the disaster response operations. The policy should also spell out in detail that each meal must be signed for and provide a template sign-in sheet. The policy would also appropriately provide parameters for the purchasing of meals.

An appropriate if time-consuming task would be to circulate a meal sign-up sheet BEFORE ordering each meal. This would avoid the problem of leftover meals and obtain the necessary signatures before the meals are served. Depending on the in-and-out transitory staffing of an emergency operations center, it could be reasonable to order a limited number of meals for those who arrive after the sign-up sheet has been circulated.

When writing a disaster feeding policy for employees, the language should include specific groups that might need to be fed, including Emergency Operations Center staff, field personnel responding to incidents, all paid and volunteer shelter workers, Amateur Radio Operators (Hams), disaster call center staff, Mutual Aid forces, workers at Points of Distribution, and any other eligible groups of workers. If the list is specific and limited, for instance, to Emergency Operations Center staff, then FEMA may choose to limit reimbursement to that specific group. The meals policy should also describe the specific documentation requirements to document the meals served and eaten and include sufficient documentation to substantiate that each of the workers receiving meals was in fact actively involved in eligible disaster response activities, i.e., saving lives, protecting the public health, and/or protecting improved property.

Workers who may be staffing a Local Assistance Center, which is not a FEMA-eligible activity, could not be fed with the expectation of reimbursement. However, as a practical matter, the local agency would probably choose to provide those workers with meals as well, at its own expense. In many cases, the cost of pursuing an appeal for a relatively small number of meals could easily exceed the cost of the meals themselves.

Note for Non-Profit Hospitals and Other Non-Profit Agencies

Because private non-profit organizations do not have the same disaster response legal responsibilities as do cities and counties, the provision of meals for staff, even though they are doing disaster-related work, will likely be determined by FEMA to be increased operating costs and therefore ineligible expenses. This includes facilities which may be in a 'lockdown' status.

However, all may not be lost, and this is the confusing and frustrating part of disaster cost recovery: the eligibility or ineligibility of certain expenses sometimes depends on the specific facts of the case, and most importantly, how the arguments for eligibility are framed during the initial application process, and during any subsequent appeals, as shown in the following Appeals Database case.

Note: Any case arising out of Hurricane Katrina should be taken with a grain of salt, insofar as that hurricane was a truly catastrophic national disaster; exceptions may have been made and regulations interpreted in a way that might only again occur in a similarly massive disaster. FEMA makes every effort to be consistent in the application of the regulations, as much as is possible with ten different Regions and more than 10,000 employees.

"Hurricane Katrina severely damaged the Applicant's kitchen facilities, thereby preventing the Applicant from preparing meals on site. <u>Because the Applicant's hospital was the only one of its type and capability in Hancock County, the Applicant had to find alternative means of preparing meals until repair of the facility was completed</u>. While the Applicant routinely provides meals to the hospital's patients, the lack of available food services in the surrounding storm-damaged community following Hurricane Katrina compelled the Applicant to provide meals to critical staff that worked extended hours. In order to meet the need, the Applicant arranged for its dietary staff to use the kitchen facilities at a nearby public high school to prepare meals for patients and hospital staff. The Applicant transported the meals prepared at the school to the hospital for distribution."[18] (Emphasis Added)

In this case, while the emergency feeding of employees was an eligible expense, the feeding of the patients was not an eligible expense because "For the costs of patients' meals, the Applicant has other mechanisms for recoupment of those costs, such as billing and/or patients' medical insurance."[19]

The FEMA Appeals reviewer further continues: "Conversely, the Applicant has demonstrated that the circumstances which compelled the Applicant to prepare and supply meals to staff, emergency responders, and non-admitted 'patients', justifies the argument that the work was necessary to save lives and preserve public health in accordance with the intent of Section 403 of the Stafford Act. As this work was not normally performed by the Applicant prior to the event, the eligibility of the work cannot be disqualified as an increased operating expense for the hospital under R&RP 9525.4."[20]

There is a very old appeals case wherein the applicant, upon noticing that not all meals had been signed for, had a staff member sign in on all the blank lines to account for all meals served. However, the FEMA reviewer noticed that many of the signatures were in the same handwriting, and therefore denied eligibility.

Employee and Prisoner Meals – Audit Findings

With feeding, as with all other expenses for which the applicant seeks reimbursement, compliance with Federal procurement regulations is critical. Following is an excerpt from a Department of Homeland Security, Office of the Inspector General (DHS-OIG) audit report DD-l0–08.

"Finding C: Employee Meal Costs

The Orleans Parish Criminal Sheriff's Office (OPCSO) employee meal costs were excessive because OPCSO did not solicit proposals through full and open competition or conduct a price analysis. OPCSO generally paid from $40 to $46 per day for employee meals over a 9-month period, while it reduced its inmate meal cost from $46 to $7.50 per day after only 3 months. OPCSO should have solicited proposals from contractors to reduce its employee costs along with its inmate costs."

If meals are provided to the EOC or other operations at no cost by local restaurants, it would be appropriate to request a donations receipt, since the value of the donation may be used as a part of the local agency's 25% cost share. More on this later in the chapter about donations.

Employee Lodging During a Disaster Response

The instances of employee emergency lodging are not to be found in the FEMA Appeals Database. However, the same fundamental principles apply to employee lodging, albeit with more restrictive parameters than for employee feeding.

In creating an Employee Disaster Lodging policy, great care must be taken to limit the reasons for and use of such a policy.

In any disaster, not all employees would be or could be provided lodging. The policy should carefully lay out to which persons, and under which conditions, lodging could be provided.

First of all, only certain key employees should be eligible, depending on:

1) The criticality of their experience and position within the emergency response organization. A fire or police chief versus a rank-and-file firefighter or police patrol officer;
2) The number of continuous hours for which they will have to work either in the emergency operations center or at a disaster incident;
3) The individual employee's total round-trip commute time;
4) The impact on the personal safety of an employee working extended hours, day after day, and then having to make a long-distance commute and getting enough sleep to then safely make the return commute to the emergency operations center or disaster incident;
5) The number of consecutive days this grueling work/commute schedule is anticipated to last;
6) The safety conditions on the roads over which the employee must commute (including washed-out roads and damaged bridges which would lengthen the total commute time);
7) The wildcard factor of weather conditions existing during the period of the disaster response;
8) The general stress levels under which the employee must safely operate;
9) The livable condition of their personal residence and its effect on the employee's ability to get proper rest while off-duty;
10) Other factors which may vary depending on the nature of the disaster and how it has affected the community.

Therefore, a public safety chief who lives within the affected community and whose home is undamaged would not be eligible for lodging reimbursement. However, the same employee who has a 50-mile commute over unsafe roads in poor weather conditions and is working 16 or more hours per day could qualify for lodging reimbursement while dangerously adverse conditions exist.

A proper employee lodging policy might name, by job title, those positions which could be eligible for lodging assistance, and other parameters of the policy.

If an employee does qualify for lodging, then the lodging should be appropriate to the situation, i.e., nearby, safe, and secure, and if at all possible within the allowable Federal, state, or local per diem rates for lodging.

For instance, if the hotel or motel provides breakfast, then the employee should not also sign up for a breakfast meal at the emergency operations center, unless the breakfast provided by the hotel is not served until after the employee had to leave to return to their respective disaster post. Also, use of a hotel mini-bar or room service would not be acceptable charges for reimbursement.

In addition to documenting the night's stay at the hotel with a printed receipt, the employee should sign-in on a lodging sign-up sheet at the emergency operations center. The lodging must always be approved by the City or County manager or the Emergency Operations Center Director or equivalent.

Employee Disaster Childcare Policy

The local agency SHOULD NOT have a policy to provide childcare for its employees AND expect to be reimbursed by FEMA. Childcare for disaster victims who are in congregate shelters is an eligible expense when properly documented, which will be addressed in the next section on Public Survivor's Services. The local agency may see fit to provide childcare for its employees, but the associated costs will not be FEMA-eligible under current FEMA policy.

The policies we have just discussed for overtime pay, meals, and lodging absolutely must be in place prior to a disaster to be eligible for reimbursement. With many of the suggested policies we will now discuss, that one requirement of "adopted before the event" has not been rigidly enforced by FEMA, or the auditors for that matter. To date, FEMA has allowed Memoranda of Agreements or Memoranda of Understanding to be post-dated, i.e., signed after the disaster has occurred, thus enabling local agencies to be reimbursed for goods and services provided frequently by volunteer non-profit organizations.

Employee Disaster Policies in Summary

Of these employee-related policies for overtime, lodging, and meals, employee overtime policies would clearly be the most important, because that is likely to be the greatest cost to the agency. For hourly employees, most agencies already have a legal obligation to pay overtime for all reasons, not just disasters. Based upon the Texas case previously cited, the current hourly employee policy might need some attention so that when the agency wishes to recoup straight time, they would have language in the policy about recalling employees from an official furlough. However, as we saw, it is crucial to actually place the employees on furlough, send them home, and then selectively recall those employees needed for the disaster response. Of course, the employee's documentation must absolutely indicate that is the case. Naturally, for those employees who are on duty and must remain on duty, i.e., law enforcement and firefighters, their regular, non-overtime wages will not be eligible in any case, and the agency must have a method of properly accounting for these two different classes of employees when preparing the application for a Project Worksheet. Such a recoupment of costs may be possible for noticed events, such as hurricanes, winter storms, and flooding. However, application of such a policy would not be eligible for sudden-onset events such as tornadoes, earthquakes, and hazardous materials incidents, all of which happen with little advance notice and therefore no time to send employees home on furlough. Naturally, the furlough would have to be in writing and approved by the appropriate authority, strictly following the requirements of the policy itself.

Note that calling employees back from vacation time, scheduled holidays, or weekend time off is not the same as a disaster-related furlough.

The payment of a premium over regular wages for straight time will generally be ineligible in any case.

For FSLA-exempt employees, an overtime policy, unless a proper one already exists, must be written and approved by the elected officials and properly applied in a non-discretionary and non-contingent manner.

Depending on the disaster, the agency, and other factors, it may be a toss-up whether meals or lodging would be the next most important policy to have on the books legally obligating the agency to cover those costs for employees who are doing qualifying disaster work.

As for meals, it is entirely probable that while some employees' meals would be eligible, there will be other employees doing other important work which may be necessary, but is non-qualifying work. An example of non-qualifying work would be employees working in a Local Assistance Center, which is an ineligible expense. As a practical matter, all employees should be provided with meals even though some of the meals will not be eligible. Again, the internal cost tracking for all the meals must discriminate between eligible and ineligible meals served. A failure to properly account for the eligible/ineligible provision and distribution of meals can result in the denial of funding for all the meals.

Public Survivor's Services

Shifting gears, we will now look at several situations for providing disaster-related services to the survivors of the event.

Under the aegis of written agreements, private non-profit organizations can provide many different forms of disaster assistance sorely needed by the survivors of the disaster. These agreements may be covered by memoranda of agreement, memoranda of understanding, contracts, and or policies.

Many of these private non-profit organizations are faith-based; in fact, nearly every faith-based group in the country has a disaster operations element. Certain of these organizations specialize in the services they can provide. For instance, the Southern Baptist Convention is known and greatly respected for its capabilities to provide mass feeding. The American Red Cross is the go-to first agency for congregate or mass sheltering. I know of one instance where the Seventh-Day Adventists provided donation management services for a disaster-affected community.

Most of these faith-based organizations are organized under the umbrella organization, the National Volunteer Organizations Active in Disaster (NVOAD, or VOAD for short).

These "official" volunteer organizations are distinguished from spontaneous or ad hoc groups of volunteers which can often spring up, literally overnight, to provide assistance to the survivors. However, FEMA sees and treats these spontaneous or ad hoc groups differently than the formally organized and continuously established private non-profit groups.

Our discussion will only deal with the formally organized groups which are both legally incorporated and certified as non-profit via an IRS letter which recognizes them as a non-profit organization.

Key Understandings

Certain private non-profit organizations may be directly eligible for FEMA funding if their facilities are damaged or destroyed in a disaster.

These same organizations, however, cannot apply directly to FEMA to recover the costs of the disaster-related work which they perform.

But these same organizations can, under the terms of a formal written agreement with a city or county, provide services and then be reimbursed by the city or county, which in turn may apply to FEMA to be reimbursed for the costs incurred in the delivery of disaster-related goods and services, such as mass feeding, operation of a shelter, pet rescue and care, etc.

Alternatively, using the same or similar agreements, the private non-profit may donate the value of the goods and services, and the city or county may then claim the fair market value of the goods and services as a part of the local agency's 25% cost share.

In either case, the residents of the city or county receive much-needed assistance, and the city or county either gets FEMA reimbursement or the credit to use against its local cost share.

As an example, if a local Southern Baptist Church with a large campus allows the Southern Baptist Convention to set up their mobile kitchens and a tent on the campus and begin feeding operations on its own initiative, the value of the meals served is not an eligible or creditable expense. Only when the work is done at the behest of and at the general direction of the host city or county is work an eligible cost or credit against the local cost share.

As mentioned previously, FEMA currently allows these agreements to be post-dated. This is a practice which could change, and therefore the best defense in this case is to have the signed written agreement in place prior to the private non-profit beginning disaster operations.

This key understanding applies to all disaster services provided by private non-profit organizations, faith-based or otherwise.

Shelter Operations

There are two types of sheltering: congregate or mass care sheltering and transitional sheltering.

We will first dispense with transitional sheltering.

ONLY FEMA can provide "transitional" sheltering.

Transitional sheltering differs from congregate or mass care sheltering insofar as the shelterees are provided individual living accommodations, such as hotel or motel rooms. If a local agency provides transitional sheltering, it is not an eligible expense. Simple and done. Transitional sheltering is not eligible. In reading hundreds of audits and appeals cases, I have only seen one case where a local agency was reimbursed for transitional sheltering, and that was due to an extraordinary set of circumstances, where an entire class of people was refused sheltering in a congregate shelter based upon their race.

Note of Exception for Transitional Housing

During the Covid-19 pandemic, FEMA delegated the authority to the states to provide on a case-by-case basis transitional sheltering due to the extreme risk of infection which would have resulted from a conventional congregate shelter situation.

In this chapter, I will frequently refer to cities and counties because these are the agencies most frequently involved in providing these survivor's services. However, there may also be tribal nations, territorial governments, and possibly a limited number of special districts that will be involved in the provision of these survivor's services.

Congregate or Mass Care Sheltering

Congregate or mass care sheltering is a common activity following major disasters. People's homes are damaged and destroyed, and these people are in desperate need of sheltering from the elements and a safe place to sleep on a short-term basis.

The American Red Cross is every local agency's go-to Plan A to provide congregate shelters. However, in catastrophic disasters, even the Red Cross gets tapped out and may be unable to provide shelter operations, at least in the short term.

In sudden-onset events, such as a tornado or hazardous materials incident, it takes time to notify and mobilize the staff and supplies necessary to operate a shelter. Therefore, the local agency should have at least a Plan B, if not also a Plan C, to provide shelters.

Many local agencies, particularly cities and counties, will have their staff trained in shelter management and operations by the good folks at the Red Cross. These same forward-looking agencies may also have a cache of cots, blankets, pillows, and personal "comfort" kits stored in a city or county facility nearby.

There is also a sound financial logic in this advanced planning and training by the Red Cross; even if the Red Cross cannot fully set up and staff the shelter, they will have a trained cadre of city or county staff (typically from the Parks and Recreation Department) to initially set up and open the shelter. But with close coordination with the Red Cross, the Red Cross can then assume the costs of sheltering from the moment the doors open because they know they have Red Cross-trained city or county staff on hand. The arrangement reduces the out-of-pocket costs to the host city or county agency for mass sheltering.

Although the city or county may have some ancillary costs to open a shelter in a public building, for electricity, heating, and other utilities, the greatest burden of the cost of staff time and supplies over the life of the shelter operations will be substantially less with the Red Cross underwriting the costs.

Because the Red Cross does sheltering on a frequent basis, they have excellent experience and will take a heavy load off of an overburdened city or county staff.

The Red Cross also knows from years of experience how to track costs and generate and maintain proper documentation. That is not often the case with cities and counties. In my years of working for and with local governments and in reading many different kinds of emergency and disaster plans, I have NEVER seen a shelter cost recovery plan. Some local government officials have the good presence of mind to know they need a shelter plan, a mass feeding plan, a pet rescue and care plan, etc., But I have never seen where they went to the next step and created a cost recovery plan for any of these activities.

Such a plan would follow the guidance in the FEMA publications, particularly the Public Assistance Program and Policy Guide, and it would comply with the requirements of Title 2 of the Code of Federal Regulations, Part 200 for procurements.

In this chapter, I will introduce a series of forms which I created to provide some basic documentation for tracking the costs associated with these disaster relief operations. See Form 22 in the Appendix for a sample Memorandum of Understanding between a local agency and a private non-profit agency for Cost Recovery.

Form 59 (see Appendix) is the Special Disaster Operations Report, which may be used for such operations as mass feeding, Points of Distribution, etc.

Although the city or county may be fortunate enough to have all the shelters operated by the Red Cross, the local agency may still have out-of-pocket expenses for the shelter operations. In the case where the Red Cross or other private non-profit operates a shelter and underwrites the costs for personnel, equipment, and supplies, the local agency may provide the facility for the shelter, such as a community center or gymnasium. It is likely that the local agency will have a paid staff person on-site to manage the building and take care of minor maintenance issues which may arise. The local agency will also have increased costs for utilities, possibly including a portable electrical generator. If these added costs are properly documented, they should be eligible expenses.

However, if the facility includes a kitchen for the preparation of meals for mass feeding, the use of the kitchen equipment is not an eligible expense.

Use of the Daily Shelter Report for Cost Recovery

First, if the shelter is operated by the Red Cross, the Red Cross has a long-established system for managing its costs, including tracking the time for its volunteers and paid staff. That said, they probably will not be able to track the added operating expenses for utilities and the local agency paid staff who may support the shelter operation.

It is not the intent of this cost tracking form to supplant the normal operating procedures of the Red Cross or any other private non-profit shelter operator. The purpose of this form is to track any expenses incurred by the local agency which may be eligible.

Some of the information requested on this form may be obtained from the data collected by the Red Cross or other shelter operator. The local agency should collect this information daily, as much of the data may simply not be available after the shelter closes.

This is Form 60 in the Appendix. At the bottom of the form are the daily counts for ancillary services. This data is collected to clearly show that this was a full-on shelter operation, and may have provided much more than just basic overnight sheltering for the disaster survivors.

This form, along with a number of the other sample forms provided, should be printed on 8½-inch by 11-inch label stock, and the label attached to a 9-inch by 12-inch envelope, with all the supporting documents enclosed in the envelope. Each day of shelter operations, a new form should be filled out, and the forms from all the shelters, if there is more than one, maintained in a plastic filing tub labeled "Shelter Daily Reports." In this way, all the daily shelter reports will be tracked in one single file.

If the form is created in Excel, then the daily totals for all shelter operations can be beautifully tracked using the Excel Cross-Tab report function. One single form will contain the totals for all shelter activities, updated each day of shelter operations.

Shelter Appeals Cases

The first case comes out of Tulsa, Oklahoma, where "from February 8–20, 2021, a severe winter storm affected the State of Oklahoma. The Center for Housing Solutions, Inc. (Applicant), a Private Nonprofit (PNP) that administers low-income housing, requested $2,878,429.90 in Public Assistance (PA) funding for the reimbursement of force account labor, materials, and contract costs associated with operating congregate and non-congregate sheltering (NCS). The Applicant claimed it provided sheltering in local hotel rooms to homeless individuals from February to July 2021, and coordinated associated services such as transportation for the homeless individuals to the shelters, cleaning of the shelters, and minor repairs to habilitate one of the hotels. Also, the Applicant stated that the sheltering services were provided at the request of the City of Tulsa and that it entered into an agreement to that end with the State of Oklahoma."[21]

"FEMA denied PA funding for all project costs and stated that the Applicant did not have legal responsibility to provide the services claimed. Specifically, FEMA stated that FEMA policy states that emergency services are the responsibility of State, Local, Territorial, or Tribal (SLTT) governments, and if a PNP *(private non-profit)* provides emergency services at the request of, and certified by, the legally responsible government entity, FEMA provides PA funding through that government entity as the eligible Applicant."[22]

What is not said in this appeal case is that while the city would be the appropriate and eligible agency to request reimbursement for these nearly three million dollars of sheltering expenses, the city must have listed these expenses on its list of damages (the damage inventory) and done so within 60 days of the Recovery Scoping Meeting.

We have not yet come to the Recovery Scoping Meeting but will do so in Chapter 28, Beginning the Paperwork Process. This may have been a rather staggering loss to a well-intentioned private non-profit.

The next case[23] is a complex one that comes to us from the Hurricane Katrina era. Hundreds of thousands of people were evacuated before, during, and after the storm, resulting in the largest evacuation in U.S. history. One shelter was set up at the Louisiana CajunDome arena and convention center in Lafayette. The CajunDome is owned by the State of Louisiana through the University of Louisiana and is operated by a five-member commission. Under the terms of an Intergovernmental Contract, the University may use the CajunDome free for 22 days per year, but the Lafayette Parish government and all others must pay for use. Lafayette Parish was the applicant, and the shelter was set up under its auspices.

Normally when a local government sets up a shelter in a facility that it owns, the cost for the facility is not eligible; however, the increased cost of utilities and maintenance would be eligible when properly documented. In this instance, however, because Lafayette Parish did not own the facility, the daily rental costs were eligible.

Another part of this appeal dealt with a "lost revenue" claim while the CajunDome was repaired and refurbished following the closure of the shelter on October 28, 2005. The refurbishment process lasted from October 29, 2005, until January 26, 2006. FEMA denied this portion of the claim, arguing that the facility was no longer being used as a shelter and was therefore ineligible for funding during the refurbishment period. This two-month period represented "lost revenue," which is an ineligible cost.

However, there is a caution in this appeals case. The appeal documents reference a "Disaster Specific Guidance," which indicates that the decision in this case may not set a precedent for future disasters.

The third appeals case also involves the same "Disaster Specific Guidance," so care is advised in relying on this case, although the general principles probably remain intact. This appeal,[24] filed by the State of Utah, again involved Hurricane Katrina evacuees who were sheltered in Utah. Five of the shelterees were removed from the shelter and hospitalized. The costs of their medical care were a total of $70,975. However, while the evacuees were in the hospital the shelter was closed and at that time, the cost eligibility ceased, causing a loss of $20,744. FEMA only covered the cost of the evacuees' medical care as long as the shelter where they initially resided was open.

For Colleges and Universities Only

There are appeals cases for post-disaster sheltering from colleges and universities for transportation and sheltering for "student-athletes." These appeals were determined to be ineligible expenses. Some colleges and universities, when disaster was imminent or had just occurred, elected to have their student-athletes maintain their intercollegiate athletic competitions, including travel and lodging.

These same institutions then requested FEMA reimbursement for these activities. Athletic endeavors of any sort are not eligible for reimbursement. These athletic activities do nothing to save lives, protect the public health, or protect improved property. In fact, from FEMA's published perspective, these athletic endeavors are not a part of the educational mission for these institutions. These initial applications and the subsequent appeals simply waste the time of both college and university personnel and the good people at FEMA.

Post-Shelter Use Refurbishment

Disaster shelters are hard-use facilities. Most facilities used as shelters were not designed or constructed with 24-hour a day, seven-day a week occupancy, and generally for many less people than will be in temporary residence. Every day, shelters need to be cleaned and maintained to provide a safe and healthy environment for the shelterees. Over the term of use of the facility, the interior surfaces will be dirtied and possibly damaged and plumbing will receive hard use, far beyond that for which it was designed. Inevitably, walls may be marred and written upon. Gymnasium floors, usually designed only for sneaker footwear, will be damaged. During the shelter operation, maintenance will be ongoing and costly. The ongoing maintenance when properly documented and supported as necessary, with photographs for notable damage, should be eligible expenses.

However, once the shelter is closed, there will usually be quite a mess to clean up, if only from the wear and tear of such heavy around-the-clock occupancy. The good news is that these costs to restore the facility to its pre-disaster condition are eligible costs when properly documented. It is critical to have a pre-opening written assessment of the facility prepared, including thorough and extensive photo documentation of the pre-existing conditions. Following the closure of the shelter, before ANY clean-up or repairs are begun, the facility must be reinspected in a similar manner to the comprehensive pre-use inspection. All cost items must be listed, line by line, in a similar manner to costing out a new construction project. All individual damages must be listed and supported with photographs. Only once the full damage and clean-up report is complete can clean-up, painting, repairs, and other necessary work begin. The intent of the work is to restore the facility to its condition just prior to use as a shelter.

DO NOT attempt to make any improvements to the facility beyond its pre-use condition. This will gum up the entire process and position the agency for a partial or full denial of funding. See the sample Form 67 in the Appendix for a guide to documenting the pre- and post-use condition of the facility.

The costs for restoring the facility are properly made by the public agency which owns the facility. If the facility is owned by an entity other than the local government that has the legal responsibility for sheltering, then the costs for facility restoration must be assigned within the written agreement between the legal owner of the facility, the local government agency, and possibly the shelter operator. In all cases, the simplest and cleanest arrangement is to assign restoration costs to the local city or county that has the legal responsibility for sheltering.

If the local agency which owns the shelter wishes to recoup the increased costs for utilities during the shelter period, it should be prepared to gather the utility bills for the period of shelter operations, as well as the corresponding utility bills for possibly the previous two to three years, to irrefutably demonstrate to FEMA the incremental increase for each of the utilities. FEMA will not pay for the baseline utility use, only the incremental increase during the period of shelter use.

It is the complete responsibility of the local agency to clearly demonstrate to FEMA the prior condition of the shelter site and all damage which occurred as a result of the shelter operation. FEMA will assume nothing in this regard.

Mass Feeding

Most mass feeding operations for the public in disasters are often provided by private non-profit agencies with little cost to the communities for which they provide the meals. In the FEMA Appeals Database, there are no appeals cases regarding mass feeding operations other than providing meals for employees working in a disaster.

We have already dealt with the question of providing meals for public agency employees while performing eligible disaster work. There are, however, several appeals cases from private non-profit convalescent care facilities, hospitals, and residential care facilities.

These cases for the most part are quite similar. For the convalescent care and residential care facilities, the applicants argue that as a result of mandatory evacuation orders, they had to relocate their patients/residents because of the mandatory evacuation order and they request, in addition to the actual evacuation expenses, that they be reimbursed for providing meals for their clients. In some cases, they also request reimbursement for meals which they provided to their on-duty staff. Uniformly, FEMA denies these applications for providing meals to both patients and staff as increased operating expenses. For hospitals, the denials of funding are for meals provided to on-duty staff, even when in a "lockdown" situation.

In one case, the applicant private non-profit argued that "it was unreasonable for FEMA to expect it to have a written policy in place requiring it to provide complimentary meals to employees, given the unprecedented nature of the disaster."[25] In the case of hospitals and residential care facilities, having an employee feeding policy would make no difference to FEMA since it sees these meals as "increased operating costs."

Pet Rescue and Pet Shelter Care

The Pets Evacuation and Transportation Standards (PETS) Act was passed by Congress and signed into law in October of 2006, the very first post-Katrina disaster legislation.

The PETS Act requires local emergency planners to prepare for the needs of individuals with household pets and service animals when developing their emergency plans.

This law was passed in response to the difficulties that were encountered during Hurricane Katrina, when many pet owners were forced to leave their pets behind during evacuations, resulting in many animal deaths and injuries.

This of course entails costs, not only for planning a preparedness, but for the actual response of rescuing and caring for the household pets.

The law is very specific on the household pets covered, and only costs associated with the specified animals are eligible for reimbursement. The Public Assistance Program and Policy Guide lists the following species of animals as eligible for reimbursement for their rescue and care:

"Household pets are domesticated animals that:

- Are traditionally kept in the home for pleasure rather than for commercial purposes
- Can travel in commercial carriers
- Can be housed in temporary facilities.

Examples are dogs, cats, birds, rabbits, rodents, and turtles.

Household pets do not include reptiles (except turtles), amphibians, fish, insects, arachnids, farm animals (including horses), or animals kept for racing purposes.

Service animals are dogs that are individually trained to do work or perform tasks for people with disabilities or access and functional needs.

Assistance animals are animals that work, provide assistance, or perform tasks for the benefit of a person with a disability, or provide emotional support that alleviates identified symptoms or effects of a person's disability.

Although dogs are the most common type of assistance animal, other animals can also be assistance animals."[26]

At present, there are no appeals cases dealing with the PETS Act. However, there are some important financial considerations when dealing with the rescue and care of domestic pets as specified in the Public Assistance Program and Policy Guide.

Many cities and counties have their own animal control departments, and the employees and related expenses for animal rescue and care will require the same high level of documentation as any other eligible disaster response activities.

If a city or county is a member of the local or regional animal care agency, such as the American Society for the Prevention of Cruelty to Animals (ASPCA) or the Humane Society, then the local agency has effectively transferred its legal authority for animal rescue and care to that agency and is not otherwise eligible for FEMA reimbursement.

However, if the local agency has retained the legal authority for animal control, then it can seek reimbursement for those services provided during the disaster.

Perhaps more importantly, volunteer animal lovers and volunteer veterinary professionals may come out of the woodwork to assist the local agency in rescuing and caring for animals during the disaster. Similarly, providers of pet care food, supplies, and equipment may make substantial donations for the rescued animals.

Reimbursement of actual expenses all depends on proper and complete documentation of the out-of-pocket expenses.

Donations received for pet care will be discussed later in the Donations section.

As a beginning point, see the sample Special Disaster Operations Report (SP-1) on page 59 (see Appendix). This form may need to be modified for the particular needs of veterinary care, including veterinary medical care that may be needed. "This includes the use of animal microchips for the purpose of tracking evacuated animals."[27]

Given that many of the rescued animals may not be tagged or microchipped, it is a good idea to attach a photograph of each animal to their shelter census card. The shelter census card should also have sufficient space to itemize any veterinary medical treatment required.

As for the volunteers, who will be discussed in greater detail later in this chapter, the volunteer roster must include any licenses or certificates of training which individual volunteers may hold.

The reason for this is that the value of the volunteer's time when caring for the animals is eligible for a credit against the local agency's 25% cost share. A licensed veterinary medical doctor's time will have a higher value than that of a licensed veterinary technician, whose hourly rate will be higher than an off-the-street volunteer "kitty hugger."

The documentation of all volunteers' hours and any licenses or certificates they may hold should be part of the documentation package, along with the days, hours, and locations where they worked.

The value of any donations made for animal rescue and care must be well documented.

As we will discuss later, these veterinary volunteers must be registered with the local agency or their respective private non-profit agency.

Another way a city or county may benefit is to establish a memorandum of understanding or contract with an established animal care group, under whose auspices and at the direction of the city or county provides donated services for animal care. In this instance, as with the mass feeding previously discussed, the city or county may reimburse the private non-profit agency and then request reimbursement from FEMA, or it may use the value of the donated labor, equipment, and materials against the local city or county local cost share.

In reference to the previous discussion on meals, the memorandum of agreement or the volunteer agency's own internal policies should provide for the cost of meals.

Therefore, in addition to the planning efforts and actual rescue and care efforts required under the PETS Act, the local agency needs to have procedures in place for proper documentation and cost tracking. In developing such policies and procedures, licensed veterinary professionals and organized animal rescue groups should be involved to get the best perspective, with the caveat that many of these individuals and organizations may not have previous experience with the FEMA Public Assistance reimbursement process and its strict recordkeeping requirements.

Evacuation and Emergency Transportation

It is important to identify the separate transportation issues present in a disaster. Evacuation is the first and most common transportation activity associated with disasters.

Not all residents of a disaster-threatened or disaster-affected area will evacuate, even under mandatory evacuation orders. Not all residents are able to or have the means to evacuate. Each of these scenarios presents real-time problems for emergency managers and first responders in addition to the disaster cost recovery issues.

We will take these different scenarios in order and discuss issues related to each.

First, some of those residents who will heed the warnings and evacuate themselves and their families may have occasion to use toll roads. In a case from the State of Florida, the governor ordered that the state's toll roads not collect tolls to help speed the flow of traffic. The state requested reimbursement for more than $51,000,000 in uncollected tolls for eight different hurricane evacuations.[28] Uncollected tolls are a form of lost revenue which are not FEMA-eligible expenses, and the appeal was denied. We will further discuss the issue of lost revenue in Chapter 26: Eligibility.

There are multiple appeals cases from colleges and universities for evacuation of student-athletes which have been denied by FEMA for two different reasons. In the case of a South Carolina University,[29] FEMA found that 1) the university did not have the legal responsibility for evacuating its students, as it was not a city or county; and 2) the university only provided evacuation for its student-athletes, then sheltered them in a non-congregate care setting, i.e., the student-athletes were housed in hotel rooms, rather than a mass shelter as would ordinarily be required for sheltering. The appeals case goes on to list seven different athletic teams, some of whom traveled out-of-state, far beyond the distance normally required for a disaster-related evacuation.

For purposes of clarity, the following language is taken directly from the Public Assistance Program and Policy Guide, which quite clearly spells out the eligible evacuation tasks:

"Transportation to evacuate (and subsequently return) survivors, household pets, service animals, assistance animals, luggage, and durable medical equipment is eligible. This includes emergency medical transportation. The mode of transportation should be customary and appropriate for the work required.

Eligible activities include, but are not limited to:

- Transferring patients from inoperable, compromised, or overwhelmed eligible medical or custodial care facilities to another medical facility or to a shelter;
- Transferring patients back to original medical or custodial care facility, when appropriate;
  - Transporting survivors, including shelterees, who require emergency medical care to and from the nearest existing or temporary medical care facility equipped to adequately treat the medical emergency. Transport may include emergency air, sea, or ground ambulance services if necessary;
  - Use of equipment such as buses, trucks, or other vehicles (including accessible vehicles) to provide one-time transportation to evacuate survivors and their household pets and service and assistance animals to emergency shelters from pre-established pick-up locations. This includes standby time for drivers and contracted equipment while waiting to transport survivors;
  - Paratransit transportation services, such as vans, minibuses, and buses, (including accessible vehicles) to transport senior citizens, individuals with disabilities (including mobility disabilities) or access and functional needs, individuals in nursing homes and assisted-living facilities, and homebound individuals impacted by the incident;
- Tracking of evacuees, household pets, service animals, luggage, and durable medical equipment. This includes the use of animal microchips for the purpose of tracking evacuated animals;
  - Food and water provided during transport;
  - Emergency medical care provided during transport, including emergency medical personnel and supply costs;
  - Stabilization of individuals injured during evacuation; and
  - Costs incurred in advance of an incident necessary to prepare for evacuations in threatened areas. Costs may include mobilization of ambulances and other transport equipment.

Contracts for staging ambulance services must be part of the State, Territorial, Tribal, or regional evacuation plan. Costs of staging ambulances are eligible even if the incident does not impact the area normally served by those ambulances. PA funding for activating, staging, and using ambulance services ends when any of the following occurs:

- FEMA, and the State, Territorial, or Tribal government, determines that the incident did not impact the area where it staged ambulances;
- Evacuation and return of medical patients and individuals with disabilities or access and functional needs is complete; or
- The immediate threat caused by the incident has been eliminated and the demand for services has returned to normal operation levels.

FEMA does not provide PA funding for ambulance services that are covered by private insurance, Medicare, Medicaid, or a pre-existing private payment agreement."[30]

Where agencies can get into trouble with evacuation costs is in the failure to properly document the names of the evacuees along with the pickup points and drop-off locations when the local agency is providing the transportation.

The staging of vehicles, in some cases including ambulances, may become questionable if the circumstances are not properly documented, particularly in those instances when the ambulances and their crews are in a "standby" status, and not actively engaged in rescue and/or transport work.

If it is truly the case, the work orders and time sheets should reflect that the ambulances are located in a "staging area." A staging area differs from standby in that the crews and equipment are physically located in the staging area and are able to respond within 3 to 5 minutes of dispatch.

While FEMA does allow and reimburse "standby" time in some cases, the use of "standby" as a generic term will usually result in much closer scrutiny of the time and activities described as standby if and only if the crews and their equipment were actually located in a staging area and immediately able to respond.

A staging area is a temporary location, usually separate and distinct from a fire station, police facility, or other public safety venue, although it may be adjacent to the public safety location. The staging area should be staffed by a "Staging Manager" and other support staff.

Medical Evacuations

There are several appeals cases regarding the evacuation of individuals in hospitals, convalescent care, and residential care facilities.

Typically in these appeals, the agency involved, whether it's a government agency or a private non-profit, will initially request the actual evacuation of patients/residents, the cost of meals for the patients/residents and in some cases the cost of meals for the care staff. As discussed, the cost of staff meals is seldom an eligible expense.

For post-evacuation transportation, there are two significant cases in the Appeals Database. The first one comes from San Mateo, California where the disaster caused the failure and subsequent closure of a stretch of highway between Montara, CA and Pacifica, CA. "The Applicant provided supplementary bus service to ensure continuation of public transportation for the affected communities while Highway 1 was closed. FEMA denied the Applicant's request for $155,044 and additional costs related to the supplemental transportation stating that the cost was an increased operating expense."[31] The applicant appealed the denial of funding.

"FEMA denied the appeal stating that the work may meet eligibility criteria established under 44 CFR §206.225(d), but FEMA is authorized to provide emergency transportation only in the form of Direct Federal Assistance under Section 419 of the Stafford Act."[32]

"Section 419 of the Stafford Act is separate from, and administered differently from, authorities which allow reimbursement to applicants for disaster costs. Section 419 of the law states that the President is authorized to provide temporary public transportation service. FEMA implemented this authority through the Direct Federal Assistance mechanism described in 44 CFR §206.208. Emergency transportation is not otherwise eligible for PA Program Assistance."[33]

The second notable and seemingly contradictory case comes from the City of Lubbock, TX, where Hurricane Katrina survivors were provided temporary shelter. Some of the shelterees were provided with bus passes "for a period of one month, to allow mobility throughout the city to access grocery stores, medical facilities, drug stores, schools, etc. The cost was $35.00 per bus pass for 175 evacuees for a total cost of $6,125."[34] FEMA denied the request, and the City appealed the decision.

In the appeal: "The City stated that Lubbock is a very spread-out city, and the evacuees apartments were not within walking distance of grocery stores, medical facilities or schools. The city asserts that it acted according to the guidance dated September 10, 2005, from the Federal Coordinating Officer and the Texas State Coordinator. This memorandum states that, 'Cost for bus passes and taxis services incurred by local jurisdictions are eligible as long as it is limited to a "reasonable amount." ' The City also cited Disaster Specific Guidance #2, which states in part, Eligible Category B sheltering costs may include, but are not limited to, the reasonable costs for: 'limited essential transportation to shuttle evacuees to and from aero medical transport sites, post offices, banks, shopping, and other essential trips while in congregate shelters.' FEMA denied the appeal in April 2006, stating that in order for the decision to be reconsidered, the Applicant would need to supply detailed documentation such as who received the passes and for what purpose. The City of Lubbock submitted a second appeal on June 8, 2006, and provided a list of 175 evacuees who had received bus passes."[35] On the second appeal, FEMA approve the full funding.

Note here that once again, Hurricane Disaster Specific Guidance #2 was in play. This might not hold true in disasters of a lesser magnitude. However, the clear explanation of the situation provided, along with the detailed accounting of every person who received a bus pass, no doubt played a role in this appeal victory.

Evacuation Documentation Afterthought

In terms of documenting the force account labor involved in planning and executing a disaster evacuation, it is critical that the public safety personnel involved clearly spell out their individual roles in both the planning and execution,

This should include the direct planning activities, the role of the local Roads and Highways agency staff on setting up signs and barricades, the efforts of the Public Information staff in the messaging efforts, time for law enforcement traffic direction, and other time and activities directly involved in the evacuation. For those staff working in the field, specific locations should be included, along with the hours involved.

Public Information Officer (PIO) Functions

In any disaster, the dissemination of information to the public is an important part of the planning and response efforts. However, not all work done to disseminate this important information is FEMA-eligible. We have a case out of Florida,[36] following Hurricane Opal in the 1990s. In this case, the Florida Department of Business and Professional Regulation formed task forces to assist homeowners in avoiding contractor and consumer fraud following the hurricane. State employees held public seminars and meetings with local building officials; they appeared in interviews with the local media; distributed pamphlets; posted warnings about contractor fraud; and conducted investigations. For all these activities, FEMA found that: "the activities were ineligible for funding on the basis that the work performed was not eliminating immediate threats to life and property as provided for under Section 403 of the Stafford Act."[37] "The threat of fraudulent activities is not recognized by FEMA as an immediate emergency issue."[38]

In 2004, in a similar case also out of Florida, Hurricanes Charley and Frances struck. "The Applicant was concerned that the public would be vulnerable to unscrupulous merchants and opportunists. As such, the Applicant warned both the public and merchants about price gouging through public service announcements aired on television. The Applicant also investigated and enforced State price gouging laws. The Applicant claimed a total of $34,548.92, of which $23,568.75 related to public service announcements and $10,980.17 related to travel expenses incurred while investigating public assertions of price gouging. FEMA deemed airing public service announcements and investigating public assertions of price gouging ineligible because they do not qualify as emergency protective measures."[39]

The appeals case goes on to state: "In accordance with 44 CFR §206.63, the assistance authorized by an emergency declaration is limited to that essential to save lives, to protect property and public health and safety. Educating the public on price gouging is not essential to save lives, protect property and public health and safety. Similarly, emergency work is defined in 44 CFR §206.201(b) as work which must be done immediately to save lives and to protect improved property and public health and safety, or to avert or lessen the threat of a major disaster. An example of this would be a public service announcement instructing residents where to seek emergency assistance and shelter before and immediately after the disaster. The public service announcements warning of price gouging were not necessary to immediately save lives or to protect improved property and public health and safety."[40]

Apparently, if the state had limited the information in the brochures to specific information about evacuation, sheltering, food availability, etc. the mailing would have been eligible. The reality, of course, is that mailing residents about evacuation and emergency services available may not be possible in a timely manner before or following a major disaster, although information disseminated via the broadcast and electronic media could be timely.

Disaster Assistance Centers and Local Assistance Centers

In the past, following major disasters, some local agencies opened "Local Assistance Centers." These centers provided a place where disaster survivors could go to obtain information regarding disaster recovery. Many non-profit agencies, the local building and safety department, and some insurance companies, among others, would have booths where both paid staff and volunteers provided important information to the survivors to assist them in rebuilding their lives. These Local Assistance Centers were not FEMA-eligible for reimbursement.

In some cases, FEMA would support "Disaster Recovery Centers" for a limited time. However, now neither of these centers are mentioned in the Public Assistance Program and Policy Guide (PAPPG), nor are any cases to be found regarding these centers in FEMA's Appeals Database.

Therefore, a local jurisdiction should be prepared to shoulder these costs entirely on its own, absent a future change in FEMA policy.

Childcare for Congregate Shelters

"FEMA reimburses State, Local, Tribal and Territorial governments for the cost of providing licensed childcare services to support sheltered populations. This includes the cost of the labor, facility, supplies, and commodities. Additionally, FEMA may provide PA funding for the cost of childcare services that the eligible Applicant provides to other survivors, and beyond the period of emergency sheltering, with certification that temporary childcare is necessary to meet immediate threats to life, public health and safety, or property.

- Childcare includes services such as:
- Day care for children; and
- Before- and after-school care.

The Applicant may provide these services within a shelter facility or in a separate facility, as appropriate. FEMA Public Assistance and Individual Assistance staff coordinate to ensure no duplication with IHP (Individuals and Households Program) assistance."[41]

The critical issue here is that this must be licensed and stateapproved childcare as opposed to unlicensed childcare, even when provided by a legitimate private non-profit.

Points of Distribution Center (PODS)

Following a major disaster, the local agency may establish points of distribution. These PODs may provide the distribution of emergency food, water, ice, and possibly tarps for roof coverings. Other emergency supplies may be available in some instances. However, as with all else, proper documentation of these expenses, and detailed records of the workers and equipment used, must be provided along with the invoices for the emergency supplies distributed.

Points of Dispensing (Also Called PODS)

Following the outbreak of the Covid-19 virus and the subsequent Presidential disaster declaration, which simultaneously covered the entire country, many cities, counties, and other local public health agencies set up vaccination centers to dispense Covid-19 shots. Once again, full and complete recordkeeping is required, as many agencies saw during the Covid-19 response. Also, many agencies saw their applications for Project Worksheets denied by FEMA as increased operating costs, even though these were frequently extraordinary and never-before-experienced costs.

Volunteers, Donations, and Survivor's Services

In this section, we will deal with these three important topics in the listed order.

Disaster Volunteers

Disasters are extreme events in many ways. Disasters bring out the very best in some people, and the very worst in others. We will address the worst aspects of humanity in Chapter 39, "Fraud."

However, the greater good that comes out of disasters is often manifest in the volunteers who will always show up to aid the survivors and help to restore the affected communities. The good work that disaster volunteers perform in and of itself is a blessing to the community in direct relief. But the value of the work done by disaster volunteers also can have a direct monetary benefit to the community as well.

FEMA allows that for bona fide disaster response work, the value of the volunteers' time may be taken as a credit against the city's or county's local cost share. In a hypothetical $1,000,000 disaster, if all costs are eligible, FEMA will **_reimburse_** the city or county for not less than 75%, or in this case, $750,000. This leaves a 25% balance, or $250,000, as the local cost share.

Some, but not all, states may also contribute to this local cost share. The amount varies from state to state. Some states pay nothing, while others may pay 10% to 18.75% (California). So, the value of the volunteers' time may be much more important in some states than others.

To get this valuable benefit, the work done by the disaster volunteers must meet the same documentation criteria as for the local agency's own employees. The work performed must address an immediate threat to life safety, public health, or a threat of damage to improved property.

Furthermore, the written documentation must provide the "Five Ws": the "who" (did the work); "what" (disaster work did they perform); "when" (was the work done); "where" (was the work done); "why" (was the work done); and "how" (long did it take to do the work).

With complete documentation of the workers' time and the work done, the local agency then requests a Project Worksheet for that value. This dollar amount then becomes a credit against the (nominal) 25% local cost share.

However, as with all things FEMA, there are some unique rules to know and heed.

1) The work done by the volunteers must be the actual saving of lives, protecting public health, and/or preventing damage to improved property.
2) A volunteer's time must be tracked and documented the same as for regular employees.
3) The volunteers must be working directly or indirectly for the local government agency and properly registered as volunteers. If a local church's volunteers set up a shelter or a mass feeding program, and do this independently of the local government agency, then their time is not eligible. However, if the church sets up the shelter or mass feeding program at the direction of and with the approval of the local government agency, then their time is eligible for counting toward the credit when properly documented.
4) "High dollar value" volunteers, such as a licensed veterinary medical doctor, may have their time credited at a higher rate than a licensed veterinary medical technician, who in turn would be accounted for at a higher hourly "pay" rate than someone who walks in and has no special training or expertise. Therefore, for these "high dollar value" volunteers it will be necessary at some point to get a copy of their license or credentials to document that this volunteer is credited at a higher dollar value than another volunteer with no special credentials.
5) If the volunteers perform work which is important but not necessarily bona fide disaster work, such as saving lives, protecting public health, and/or preventing damage to improved property, then their time may not be counted for the cost share match. An example of this would be when volunteers distribute grocery store gift cards to disaster survivors. Because the distribution of food cards falls under the aegis of the U.S. Department of Agriculture, under the theory of "duplication of benefits" FEMA would not count the time of volunteers doing this work even, though it may be important to the community.
6) Furthermore, if the volunteers are doing work for an agency which does not have the legal authority to do that work, then their time is not countable. Thus, if a school district sets up a mass feeding program, which is something for which they generally do not have the legal responsibility, then that would not be countable, unless the operation was somehow authorized on behalf of the local city or county government.

In a case from Missouri: "From April 29 to July 6, 2019, Missouri experienced severe storms, tornadoes, and flooding. Following damage to its levee, the Applicant enlisted volunteers to construct a temporary levee and inspect it to ensure it continued to function. The Applicant requested Public Assistance funding and FEMA wrote Project Worksheet 814 to document the request for donated resources. FEMA denied PA funding for the project following several attempts to request documentation to support the Applicant's claimed costs. FEMA found that the Applicant did not provide information documenting its donated resources claim."[42]

"The Applicant submitted a first appeal, stating that due to the time sensitive nature of the emergency situation, it did not provide volunteer sign-in sheets at various points on the levee."[43]

"The Missouri State Emergency Management Agency recommended FEMA deny the appeal because proper documentation is required in order to validate volunteer labor and equipment and the Applicant did not provide it. The FEMA Region VII Acting Regional Administrator denied the appeal on September 20, 2021, finding that the Applicant did not provide documentation with enough detail to support the claimed donated resource amount. The Applicant submitted a second appeal, reiterating previous arguments. FEMA finds that the Applicant did not provide documentation to support the claimed costs for donated labor and equipment. Therefore, the appeal is denied."[44]

In a second appeal case on "Volunteers," this time from Tennessee: the appeal brief states: "From May 1 through May 2, 2010, Tennessee experienced high winds and flooding which resulted in widespread loss of power. The disaster forced residents to vacate their homes and to require food and basic housing. The Applicant opened a disaster recovery center and staffed it with volunteers. The Applicant requested credit toward the calculation of the non-Federal cost share for volunteer labor, donated equipment, and donated materials. FEMA initially granted Applicant's request for a $65,416 credit but later de-obligated $57,714 because volunteer hours were not properly documented. FEMA also indicated that a church organization, not the Applicant, organized the emergency work. In its first appeal, the Applicant asserted that it was entitled to de-obligated funds and that, although volunteers came from several churches, volunteers from other places also participated. The FEMA Region IV Regional Administrator partially approved the first appeal, noting that FEMA policy does not preclude faith-based organizations from volunteering their resources. The Regional Administrator validated 3,534 volunteer hours and approved a credit of $45,435. In its second appeal, the Applicant argues that it should receive an additional credit of $12,279, the amount that was not awarded on first appeal."[45] (Emphasis Added)

One of my favorite cases comes out of Kentucky: "During early February 1998, McCreary County, Kentucky experienced a record snowfall event causing damage to utilities and widespread debris. As a result, FEMA-1207-DR-KY was declared. The severity of the snow stranded even the county's emergency personnel and snow removal equipment. In response to this, the County Judge requested that citizens assist with the removal of downed trees and snow to facilitate bringing the county emergency resources back online. Damage Survey Report (DSR) 53499 was written on March 25, 1998, in the amount of $380,407 to cover costs associated with the debris removal effort. However, the DSR was determined ineligible because the work performed was volunteer labor and there was insufficient documentation to support those costs. The first appeal was denied because the documentation submitted did not allow the tracing of funds to specific tasks such that a determination could be made as to the eligibility of the work. To support the second appeal, additional documentation and clarification of the details surrounding the events during the snowstorm have been submitted. The request is that credit for the donated resources be approved."[46] This appeal was approved for the amount of $318,000.00 once the proper documentation was provided.

"To support eligibility of Force Account Labor (FAL) costs claimed, the Applicant should submit, for each individual, their name, job title (if any) and function, type of volunteer, days and hours worked, pay rate and fringe benefit rate, description of work performed with a representative sample of daily logs/activity reports, representative sample of Time sheets, fringe benefit calculations, and pay policy."[47]

"The burden to fully substantiate an appeal with documented justification falls exclusively on the applicant and hinges on the applicant's ability not only to produce its own records, but to clearly explain how those records support the appeal."[48]

The registration of disaster volunteers is important for several reasons. First, the local agency needs some baseline information regarding the volunteers, like their name, address, and other contact information. Second, some states provide a worker's compensation umbrella for registered disaster volunteers. In these states, if a volunteer is injured during the course and scope of their disaster volunteer activities, they are covered by worker's compensation insurance at no cost to the local agency. Third, at some point following the disaster, it will be important to thank these wonderful people for their good work. Fourth, the registration process is a great time to impress upon each volunteer the importance of how they track their volunteer time, so it is eligible for counting in the local cost share credit. This is also an opportunity to share with the disaster volunteers a "Volunteer's Code of Ethics," which may help protect the local agency in the event of volunteer malfeasance.

Voluntary Organizations Active in Disaster (VOADs)

Now we move from individual volunteers to formally organized groups of disaster volunteers.

VOADs, or Voluntary Organizations Active in Disaster, are collaborative networks of non-profit organizations, faith-based groups, and other voluntary organizations that work together to provide assistance and support during times of disaster or emergency. VOADs coordinate resources, services, and expertise to effectively respond to and recover from disasters.

VOAD Characteristics

- Collaboration: VOADs bring together various voluntary organizations to collaborate and coordinate their efforts in disaster response and recovery.
- Preparedness and Response: VOADs focus on disaster preparedness and response activities.
- Resource Sharing: VOADs facilitate and share resources among member organizations. This can include supplies, equipment, personnel, and expertise.
- Long-Term Recovery: VOADs play a crucial role in long-term recovery efforts following a disaster. They collaborate with community stakeholders, government agencies, and other organizations to help communities rebuild.
- National and Local Networks: VOADs exist at both the national and local levels. National VOADs, such as the National Voluntary Organizations Active in Disaster (NVOAD) in the United States, provide coordination, support, and guidance to local VOAD chapters across the country.
- Local VOADs operate within specific regions or communities, tailoring their efforts to the unique needs and challenges of their respective areas.

VOADs play a vital role in disaster management by providing timely assistance to disaster affected communities.

Every major faith in the U.S. has a disaster volunteer cadre, as do other private non-profit agencies with increasing frequency, notably Team Rubicon, the "Cajun Navy," Habitats for Humanity, and of course, the American Red Cross, which has been active in disaster relief since the late 19th century.

Any and all of these disaster volunteer organizations can play a significant role following a disaster. First, obviously, are the services they will provide, including the provision of congregate shelters, mass feeding, donations management, and numerous other community needs.

However, our focus here is the financial recovery which must follow a disaster, large or small. When any one of these voluntary disaster relief organizations provides assistance, the value of the services they provide may be claimed by a city or county as a part of their local cost share, thereby reducing its out-of-pocket expenses.

Generally, however, this does not apply to school districts, colleges and universities, and other special districts, because these organizations generally do not have the legal responsibility for mass feeding, congregate sheltering, or donations management.

One notable exception might be a local independent animal control authority, which would have the legal responsibility for pet care. In this case, a volunteer pet rescue organization could provide valuable support to the animal control authority.

The most important key to success in obtaining the value of donated services is to have a written agreement with EACH volunteer organization providing services to the city or county. Absent such a written agreement, the chances of getting the credit diminish considerably.

Currently, FEMA has allowed such agreements to be post-dated. However, I can see a future where this may no longer be so. Therefore, a best practice would be to have agreements, be they Memoranda of Agreement or other similar documents, already in place before a disaster strikes.

In the support material, Form 22 (see Appendix) is a comprehensive pre-disaster agreement which was carefully structured to avoid the most common pitfalls in these types of agreements and provide the full range of documentation which FEMA may require, depending on the nature and extent of the understanding between the parties to the agreement. Not all pages will apply to every agreement. Rather than delete these pages when signing the agreement, I recommend typing in large, bold-face characters "Does Not Apply for This Agreement" or something to that effect.

Not all work done by disaster volunteers may be eligible for inclusion in the local cost share credit requested. There is a case out of Texas that is on point in this regard. The county in question distributed food cards to disaster survivors and was denied funding for its employees' time for this task, because the distribution of food cards comes under the auspices of the U.S. Department of Agriculture, and therefore would represent a duplication of benefits under FEMA regulations. In theory, had the county used volunteers instead of employees to perform this function, the volunteer hours would have also been considered ineligible for the same reason, i.e., a "duplication of benefits."

Disaster Donations, Monetary and In-Kind

Beyond the very valuable donations of volunteer time, whether as individual volunteers or as members of a Volunteer Organization Active in Disasters, there are both monetary and in-kind donations. We will deal with each type of monetary and in-kind donations in turn. We will discuss very large monetary donations, which I refer to as "legacy" donations. We will also discuss small monetary donations, like GoFundMe donations.

Then we will turn to in-kind donations which can cover a great deal of territory, including consumable supplies, permanent donations of equipment, and temporary donations of equipment; think of tractor or excavator equipment time donated for a specific purpose, such as constructing a flood levee.

Finally, we will look at donations which have been and should be refused because they often cost the local agency money for no tangible or intangible benefit to anyone.

Legacy, or Very Large Monetary Donations

Disasters are events which can stir human compassion in complex manifestations. Some people give of their time, and some of those who have been financially successful may give serious money to deal with the disaster aftermath.

However, there is a huge caveat in play here. FEMA is prohibited from providing a duplication of benefits by the Stafford Act.[49] Therefore, if a person or organization provides monetary or in-kind aid to the local agency or eligible private non-profit, then FEMA must deduct that amount from what it would otherwise grant to the applicant.

Here is a quotation from a Department of Homeland Security-Office of the Inspector General's report, in part: Finding B: Duplicate Funding:

"Jesuit received $4,693,265 of duplicate funding for damages resulting from the disaster. After the disaster, Jesuit received $4,693,265 in donations designated for a 'Katrina Fund.' Jesuit's 2009–2010 President's Report states that the fund was set up to help pay for the extensive repairs and renovation to Jesuit's facilities. Jesuit officials said these funds were not used for the repair and renovation purposes stated in the President's Report but were used to offset revenue decreases after the disaster. Jesuit later provided previous versions of the President's Report, which state that the 'Katrina Fund' donations were to be used for facility repair costs not covered by insurance and FEMA grant funding. However, Jesuit has not provided documentation to prove these funds were not used for the same purpose as the FEMA grant funds."[50]

"Section 312(a) of the Stafford Act states that no entity will receive assistance for any loss for which financial assistance has already been received from any other program, from insurance, or from any other source."[51]

"Further, Public Assistance Policy Digest (FEMA 321, p. 34) states that grants and cash donations from nonfederal sources designated for the same purpose as public assistance funds are considered a duplication of benefits. Therefore, because Jesuit designated its 'Katrina Fund' for the same purpose as its FEMA grant, we question $4,693,265 of ineligible duplicate costs claimed."[52]

Arguably, had the money been donated for the repairs to chapel or the campus landscaping, which would have been FEMA-ineligible at that time, the school might have been able to keep the $4.7 million dollars and receive full eligible funding from FEMA as well.

Consequently, when an agency receives an offer of a legacy donation, it needs to go into "tax planning" mode or risk losing a great deal of money. If a check is presented, it should not be deposited directly into an agency account, but rather locked in a fireproof safe until it is best determined how to appropriately (and legally) respond to the donor's generosity.

"GoFundMe" Types of Donations

This isn't an endorsement of a particular way of raising funds, but a reference to what might otherwise be called "crowdfunding," where many people or organizations offer to donate relatively small individual donations, which sometimes amount to a great deal of money. Here the same prohibition of a duplication of benefits still applies.

General Note on Accepting Disaster Relief Cash Donations

Any time there is money involved, some people will attempt to take advantage of the cash surplus, and other people will have arguments as to why they should have gotten some or more of the money. Even wise Solomon might have difficulty navigating these swirling rocky shoals. Take for example the millions of dollars raised to aid the victims of the September 11 terrorist attacks. These were some of the problems which otherwise distracted the fund managers:

- Lack of coordination;
- Inadequate disbursement speed;

- Eligibility criteria and documentation;
- Long-term financial planning; and
- Emotional and psychological support.

Many of these problems may be alleviated by proper pre-planning, before the event occurs because once the event occurs local or agency officials will have more trouble than they can handle.

One option is (ideally, pre-disaster) to enter into a well-structured financial agreement with an existing and highly reputable local charity organization to receive and distribute these donations when the donations are provided for community relief, as opposed to support the repair and reconstruction of agency facilities.

If, on the other hand, the funds were donated with the express purpose of repairing and rebuilding public facilities and infrastructure, then the local agency would again need to go into "tax planning" mode to minimize the hit taken to prevent the duplication of benefits.

In either case, this goes to the issue of properly "inventorying" donations as they are received. Who is the donor? Are they donating for a specific purpose or is the donation's purpose unspecified? How does the agency properly thank each donor, whether large or small? Does the donor expect a tax deduction? Can the agency provide a proper tax deduction?

There was an interesting case I am personally aware of from a disaster several years ago. Good people in the community would stop by the government offices or the Emergency Operations Center and simply drop off one or more grocery store gift cards because "they felt they had to do something to help the community." Over the course of the weeks, the total of all these unrestricted, spontaneous, and deeply personal donations totaled up to nearly $75,000.

The question was put to me: "What do we do with these gift cards? They're not redeemable for cash, they were from several different businesses, and the donors specified no particular purpose." I suggested that first of all the gift cards be inventoried and locked up in a safe; then later donated to community feeding programs on an equitably distributed basis; and slowly distributed to appropriate feeding programs or food banks. To donate all of them at once would surely create public and media interest which would immeasurably complicate matters, and no constructive purpose would be served.

Perhaps the best donation of all is money, regardless of whether the recipient is a local government agency or a private non-profit organization providing some form of disaster relief. Money may also be the most difficult to deal with in terms of proper financial reporting and public accountability. Disasters are always "stressor" events, and donated money is one of those very high-visibility stressors.

One Possible Donations Option

My last "paycheck" job was with the City of San Francisco. San Francisco is a unique city in so many ways, and one of those unique facets is that people in the City donate to all kinds of causes. On the City's web page there is a donations portal, where one may choose to donate to feeding people, or the opera or symphony, or various other worthy causes. When I started work, one of my first projects was to be a part of the disaster donations project. The plan is that if a major disaster were to strike, the City's web page would shut off all links for these worthy donations and redirect those potential donors to the 'Disaster Donations' page, thereby funneling all internet-based donations to disaster purposes.

In-Kind Donations – Consumable Supplies

Donations are wonderful assistance, and they may be a massive headache for whomever is designated the "Donations Manager."

First, in-kind donations must be fully documented and tracked from receipt to distribution, like financial donations. But unlike money, in-kind donations need to be temporarily stored, sorted, and finally distributed in some fashion. Typically, this requires physical space like a storeroom or warehouse space. The logistics challenges are substantial. Going, in some cases overnight, from no operations to full-blown warehousing and distribution functions requires experienced staff, supplies, equipment, and of course money to pay for utilities, fuel, communications, etc.

The good news is that some Volunteer Organizations Active in Disasters have experienced people on their volunteer call-up lists. They can provide volunteer disaster-experienced personnel to manage and operate a full-blown, large-scale donations management program. Some possible resources for donation management are Goodwill, the Salvation Army, Habitats for Humanity ReStore, food banks, American Red Cross, Seventh-Day Adventists, and other crisis relief organizations.

The organization best suited to the needs of any particular disaster may depend on the types of donations being made.

Caroline Egan of Sugarland, Texas, has a truly innovative story about disaster donations. After Hurricane Harvey in 2017, her agency was able to connect with a Las Vegas hotel that was undergoing a major renovation, and the hotel donated the surplus furniture for the use of the hurricane survivors. This particular donation does not apply to the Public Assistance program, but it would be a boon for the general disaster recovery.

Form 22 (see Appendix), previously mentioned in this chapter, contains an in-depth sample of the logistical needs for setting up a large-scale donations management program.

For all in-kind donations, each donation must be documented with a donations acceptance form. A sample form is given in the support material (Form 23, see Appendix). It is important to document the cost of the donation. If an individual purchases a case of disposable diapers at a big-box store for use in a shelter, the cost may be $X, i.e., the retail cost. However, if the big-box store itself donates the same case of disposable diapers, the cost may be only $X/2 or the wholesale cost. Determining the actual cost is most easily done if the donor can provide a register receipt for purchased goods.

This leads to the next point regarding unsolicited donations, often made by good-hearted souls, who in some cases take the opportunity to get rid of old clothing and household goods which may or may not work. These donations drives are often spontaneously put together with no thought to the logistical nightmares which they may create.

I have photos taken by a good friend after Hurricane Katrina, where unannounced trailer loads of clothing and household goods are literally dropped off in a supermarket parking lot, unsorted, unwashed, and largely unusable, except perhaps as rags. The last photo in the series is of a U.S. Army Corps of Engineers heavy-duty front loader literally plowing up these now-dirtier and mildewing items of clothing to haul them to the dump.

My good colleague Brenda Hunemiller tells of a well-intended donation in post-hurricane Puerto Rico of 10,000 microwave meals, delivered to an island where there was no electricity and possibly few working microwave ovens, even if there were electricity.

In another donations fiasco following one of the massive fires which have rocked Northern California in the past many years, local officials turned away a donated truckload of hay from another state because the hay contained noxious weeds not found in California.

As a side note, it's entirely possible that this donation of hay could easily be denied as a part of the local cost share even if accepted, because the hay would not meet FEMA's requirement that the use of the hay address an immediate threat to life safety, the public health, or protect improved property.

In-kind donations have been for decades and will probably continue for decades to be an ongoing, costly, and distracting problem for local officials. The best that can be done is to issue and enforce, as best as possible, strict guidelines on how and if these donations would be accepted.

In a major disaster, donations management is one of those wildcard issues that will create many distracting problems if an experienced donations manager is not immediately assigned, and in the long run, it will cost the city or county a great deal of money that's desperately needed for recovery. Furthermore, the hauling-away of this donated rubble will likely not be eligible for FEMA reimbursement because the donated rubble was not a direct result of the disaster.

In-Kind Donations – Equipment

Donations of equipment fall into two categories: donations of equipment time and permanent donations of equipment itself.

For equipment donated for a limited time, such as someone donating a truck or tractor to be used to help a sandbagging operation during a flood flight, the time must be fully documented as to the hours used or miles driven during the flood flight. The time the equipment was used and the name(s) of the operator(s) must be tracked in the same manner as the local agency's own equipment. Obviously, if the donor operates their own equipment, then the donor/operator's time could also be counted as a donation. The dollar value of the equipment will be charged based on the FEMA Equipment Rate Sheet for similar equipment. Fuel, if provided by the donor, could also be included when properly tracked and documented. Routine wear and tear and normal maintenance are included in the FEMA Equipment Rate. However, if the equipment is damaged while in use and the fault is not operator error, then the damage might be eligible. However, if the equipment is destroyed and FEMA determines that the damage is eligible, FEMA would only reimburse at the Blue Book value, which is often far below the cost of replacing the equipment.

The second, and frankly quite rare, situation is one that occurred in a Southern California county some years ago. The county had rented a large water pump from a local vendor. The county used the pump for several months during the rainy season to pump out a low-lying area that repeatedly flooded. At the end of the term, the county called the vendor and advised them they no longer needed the pump. The vendor told the county, "Since you first rented the pump from us, you have more than paid for it. Why don't you just keep it?" So, the county picked it up and kept it. The use of the pump was eligible for FEMA reimbursement, until that point when the county took legal possession of it. Then the pump was no longer a rental but a purchase, and was no longer eligible as a purchase. The county also had violated its own procurement policy because it hadn't obtained the necessary number of quotations or bids for the equipment.

General Note on Donated Labor, Goods and Services, and Equipment

For more specific information on Donated Resources, see FEMA's current Recovery Policy, dated February 9, 2022. To receive a credit for the value of donated labor, materials and supplies, and equipment, the donations must be used for otherwise eligible disaster response activities within the Period of Performance (POP) for the related activities. For Debris Clearance and Emergency Protective Measures the period of performance is nominally for a six-month period; however, in some cases, FEMA may approve an extension of time.

Notes

1 https://www.fema.gov/appeal/force-account-labor-emergency
2 https://www.fema.gov/appeal/force-account-labor
3 Ibid.
4 Ibid.

5 Ibid.
6 Ibid.
7 https://www.charleston-sc.gov/DocumentCenter/View/14733/employee_handbook?bidId=
8 https://www.fema.gov/appeal/force-account-labor-equipment-costs-7
9 https://www.fema.gov/appeal/force-account-labor-equipment-costs-5
10 https://www.fema.gov/appeal/overtime-labor-policy
11 Ibid.
12 Ibid.
13 http://cms1files.revize.com/northampton/3_Article_III_The_Pay_Plan_NHC%20updated%20sec-tion%2015–20%20(10.2020).pdf
14 Public Assistance Program and Policy Guide, Version 4, Effective June 1, 2020, FP 104–009–2, p. 117.
15 https://www.fema.gov/appeal/legal-responsibility-705c
16 Ibid.
17 Ibid.
18 https://www.fema.gov/appeal/hospital-food-services
19 Ibid.
20 Ibid.
21 https://www.fema.gov/appeal/legal-responsibility-34
22 Ibid.
23 https://www.fema.gov/appeal/cajundome-shelter
24 https://www.fema.gov/appeal/medical-cost-evacuees
25 https://www.fema.gov/appeal/increased-operating-expenses-2
26 Public Assistance Program and Policy Guide, Version 4, Effective June 1, 2020, FP 104–009–2
27 Ibid.
28 https://www.fema.gov/appeal/uncollected-toll-road-revenue
29 https://www.fema.gov/appeal/legal-responsibility-evacuation-medical-care-and-sheltering
30 Public Assistance Program and Policy Guide, Version 4, Effective June 1, 2020, FP 104–009–2, pp. 119–120.
31 https://www.fema.gov/appeal/transportation-service
32 Ibid.
33 Ibid.
34 https://www.fema.gov/appeal/eligible-costs
35 Ibid.
36 https://www.fema.gov/appeal/emergency-response
37 Ibid.
38 Ibid.
39 https://www.fema.gov/appeal/emergency-protective-measures-7
40 Ibid.
41 Public Assistance Program and Policy Guide, Version 4, Effective June 1, 2020, FP 104–009–2, p. 124.
42 https://www.fema.gov/appeal/donated-resources-0
43 Ibid.
44 Ibid.
45 https://www.fema.gov/appeal/donated-resources
46 https://www.fema.gov/appeal/volunteer-labor
47 https://www.fema.gov/appeal/force-account-labor-and-equipment-costs-6
48 Ibid.
49 Title 42/Chapter 68/Subchapter III/§ 5155, **(c) "Recovery of duplicative benefits**
    A person receiving Federal assistance for a major disaster or emergency shall be liable to the United States to the extent that such assistance duplicates benefits available to the person for the same purpose from another source."
50 FEMA Public Assistance Grant Funds Awarded to Jesuit High School, New Orleans, Louisiana; FEMA Disaster Number 1603-DR-LA; Audit Report Number DD-11–21
51 Ibid, p. 5.
52 Ibid.

4 The Local Government Cost Recovery Planning Process

"Success in any endeavor requires single-minded attention to detail and total concentration."
Willie Sutton, American Bank Robber, Circa 1930

The lack of a disaster cost recovery program and planning process may be the single most glaring defect for any local government organization or eligible private non-profit agency at the time they experience a disaster. This is my observation from working with and training scores of local government agencies across the U.S. for the past 25 years.

No local government agency's chief financial officer would consider operating without a budget. No agency risk manager would want their agency to operate without the appropriate levels of affordable insurance. No agency employing law enforcement officers would want to be absent a Police Policy and Procedures manual with an appropriate training regimen.

Yet it is more often the rule rather than the exception that most local agencies have absolutely no plans, policies, or procedures in place to describe and facilitate the disaster cost recovery process.

In fact, in my experience most agencies do not even have a single employee designated to manage the disaster cost recovery process. It is often the case that the emergency manager will imagine that the responsibility lies with the Finance department, while the Finance department will correspondingly imagine that disaster cost recovery will be the exclusive purview of the Emergency Manager. Neither could be more wrong.

As a result, no one pays any attention to this critical gap in agency knowledge and experience. I have taught classes for agencies that I expected, because of their frequent experience with catastrophic disasters, would have sophisticated policies, plans, and procedures in place for disaster cost recovery.

I wondered, "What can I possibly tell these people that they don't already know?" It turns out quite a lot. Although one agency in particular had frequent and severe disasters, they had no formal plan for training their employees. Much of the experience they garnered from their disasters was eroded by normal staff turnover and a lack of post-event lessons learned.

In my study of the Department of Homeland Security, Office of the Inspector General's audits, it is a frequent complaint of local agencies that either the state or FEMA's employees provided the local agency personnel with incomplete or inaccurate information.[1] This often-repeated complaint is simply a non-starter. The responsibility for knowing, understanding, and following the requisite Federal regulations falls exclusively on the local government agency or private non-profit agency.

It is a fact of life, more so now than ever before, that local government does not have the resources to do all that is asked of it. This is understandable and acceptable until such a time as a disaster occurs, and the local government needs access to those sometimes difficult-to-obtain Federal disaster grants.

DOI: 10.4324/9781003487869-6

The cost of having such expertise on staff is an economic burden on a community. But in the same way that the agency spends money on the budget process, buys the needed insurance, or has the expense of police department policies and procedures, it is necessary to be prepared to recover the cost of disaster response, repairs, and reconstruction efforts.

I have seen many so-called disaster cost recovery plans over the years. Most of them consist of the FEMA forms for tracking Force Account Labor, Force Account Equipment, Rented Equipment, Materials, Small Contracts, and perhaps 10 to 20 pages of other explanatory materials with instructions on how to fill out the FEMA forms. Valuable information, no doubt, but wholly insufficient for the task at hand when a disaster has struck. I recall one significant exception to this list of pithy plans. I reviewed a 200+-page disaster cost recovery document. However, it was mostly useless insofar as it was nearly 20 years old and had never been updated to include all the changes implemented by FEMA over the years.

Who Is on the Disaster Cost Recovery Team . . . Whether They Like It or Not

The disaster cost recovery process is a TEAM sport for all but the smallest of local government agencies.

In a catastrophic disaster, virtually every department and/or division can and should have a role in the disaster cost recovery process. If the disaster is significant enough to warrant a major Presidential disaster declaration, there is a substantial chance that any of the declared jurisdictions will have disaster-related losses in the hundreds of thousands if not the millions of dollars.

Here is a sample list of departments/divisions, allowing that every local government and private non-profit agency works with a different organizational structure. Some or many of these functions may not be provided by the local jurisdiction, and/or may be combined within smaller jurisdictions. Some of these functions may also be provided by a local "Joint Powers" authority or council of governments.

- Airport: A key location for logistics support; also, outlying areas may be used for a Temporary Debris Reduction Site (TDRS)
- Animal Control: A primary disaster response department may also provide coordination and support for disaster-related pet rescue and care. May require a great deal of Mutual Aid in the early phases of the disaster.
- Building & Safety Department: Conducts post-disaster health and structural safety inspections and posts occupancy restrictions; managing all aspects of Building & Safety Inspector's Mutual Aid.
- Business Licenses: Post-disaster rebuilding will bring in a plethora of building contractors and allied trades.
- City Attorney/Prosecutor, County Counsel: The attorney's office will be involved in preparing the local proclamations and reviewing FEMA's legal requirements.[2]
- City Auditor: The auditor's office should be reviewing Project Worksheets prior to uploading the documents to FEMA's online portal.
- City Manager: Overall responsibility for disaster recovery and disaster cost recovery.
- City/County Clerk: May co-prepare the local proclamations with others; provides local agency documents to support the Project Worksheet files.
- Code Enforcement: Responsible for coordination with either Public Works or the Environmental Department for the removal of disaster-damaged and abandoned vehicles and vessels.
- Economic Development: Will have a significant role in planning and executing jurisdiction-wide physical recovery and financial recovery.

- Emergency Management: Co-responsible but subordinate to the Finance Department for disaster cost recovery operations.
- Environmental Issues, Refuse removal: Co-responsible with Public Works and/or Engineering for the Debris removal program. Also, may lead to post-disaster household hazardous waste collections.
- Facilities: Responsible for surveying all agency facilities for damage; once projects are approved and funded, then responsible for construction and repair projects.
- Finance Department: Overall management and coordination of the disaster cost recovery process. Responsible for collection and analysis of disaster damage.
- Fire/EMS: A primary disaster response department; may also be an advisor for the debris management program; may also be responsible for repairs and reconstruction of departmental facilities.
- Harbor, Port, or Marina: May be a key location for logistics support; if a marina, it may have significant debris clean-up issues and partially submerged watercraft.
- Health & Human Services: A primary provider of survivor's services, including providing food, shelter, pet care, emergency medical care, etc.
- Historic Preservation: Many communities have important historic structures. Such structures require special handling in terms of their repair and reconstruction. Historic Preservation staff may need to assist those managers of Project Worksheets who are involved with a historic structure.
- Human Resources: Must provide the written bargaining unit labor agreements as a part of the documentation for any Project Worksheet involving the agency's own employees, aka Force Account Labor, if not done by payroll.
- Library: Always my first choice for support staff in an EOC because librarians are great record-keepers and organizers of information.
- Mayor & City Council: Provide overall community leadership throughout the disaster and recovery. The time for these officials may be used as a part of the local cost share when their time is properly tracked and tied to bona fide disaster-related activities.
- Municipal Health Services: A primary disaster response function for the treatment of injuries and illnesses caused by the disaster.
- Parks & Recreation: Usually the primary department for providing care and shelter for disaster survivors. It may also provide childcare services for shelter residents and provide for other disaster survivor needs.
- Payroll: Responsible for providing the written bargaining unit labor agreements as a part of the documentation for any Project Worksheet involving the agency's own employees, aka Force Account Labor, if not done by Human Resources.
- Planning/Community Development: May need to be involved in the community notifications program if FEMA has approved "private property debris removal" (PPDR). Will have substantial involvement in the post-disaster rebuilding of the community.
- Police: A primary disaster response department; may also be responsible for repairs and reconstruction of departmental facilities.
- Public Transit: Will be responsible for repairs to public transit equipment, facilities, and infrastructure. Will <u>not be eligible</u> for FEMA funding for providing disaster transportation along regular or special routes.
- Public Utilities, water, sewer, etc.: A first response agency, particularly when there is damage to the utility system(s); may also be responsible for repairs and reconstruction of departmental facilities/systems. May also be charged with bottled drinking water distribution when water quality issues arise.

- Public Works: A primary disaster response department; may also be a co-manager or advisor for the debris management program; may also be responsible for repairs and re-construction of departmental facilities.
- Purchasing/Procurement: Complies with Title 2 of the Code of Federal Regulations, Part 200, and state and local purchasing regulations, whichever is most restrictive when the local agency is spending Federal grant dollars. This applies to both FEMA disaster grants and non-disaster grants from FEMA and from other Federal agencies.
- Risk Management: Providing all required insurance information to FEMA; pursuing timely and complete insurance recovery; purchasing new insurance policies for repairs to facilities that are FEMA-funded.
- Roads and Bridges: Another primary disaster response department; may also be responsible for repairs and reconstruction of departmental facilities and roads and bridges.
- Street Lighting: May be a first-responder department when damage occurs to municipal lighting; responsible for lighting system repairs and restoration.
- Technology & Communications: In many local jurisdictions, very little is done which does not involve information technology and communications, as well as GIS Mapping. Maps are required as a part of every Project Worksheet written. Technology and communications will essentially play a first-responder role to get systems back in operation to support all other responders and departments.
- Towing & Lien Sales: Flood-, tornado-, and hurricane-ravaged communities usually have large numbers of damaged/destroyed and abandoned vehicles and vessels; this function will likely have to integrate with the debris management programs set up by the local agency.
- Utility Billing: When properties are damaged to the point that they are not livable, property owners will request reductions or elimination of certain utility fees. While this is caused by the disaster, the administrative efforts to address these issues, such as rate reductions or rebates, are not generally FEMA-reimbursable.
- Voter Registration: Civic life goes on, even after a disaster. However, the costs to set up alternate polling places are generally not FEMA-reimbursable.
- Other: Any department that has employees working as a part of the disaster response or reconstruction, and any department which has actual physical damage.[3]

So, virtually every department and/or function of local government may be called upon to play an active role in both the disaster response and/or recovery. In my experience, there is virtually no function of local government which categorically could not have one or more disaster-related functions, and most importantly, those tasks related to the disaster cost recovery process.

Obviously, in small agencies where most staff wear multiple hats, all this is even more challenging. I have a colleague in Colorado who, because she worked part-time for two different towns, was the entire team for each town. She coordinated with other officials, but she had the primary responsibility for disaster cost recovery for these two different jurisdictions.

Documentation on Steroids

In his book *The Devil in the White City*,[4] author Erik Larson reports the following interaction between a group of Chicago businesspeople and the Federal government about the World's Columbian Exposition of 1890s:

"The conflict between Burnham and Davis again flared to life. The directors of the Exposition Company did decide to seek a direct appropriation from Congress, but their request triggered a congressional investigation of the fair's expenditures. Burnham and *(Exposition)* President Baker expected a general review but instead found themselves grilled about the most mundane expenses. For example, when Baker listed the total spent on carriage rental, the subcommittee demanded the names of the people who rode in the carriages."

This is a picture of the Federal government doing what it often does: protecting the Federal treasury, albeit sometimes in ways of questionable cost efficiency.

The Federal requirements for detailed information of the sort which may never be tracked by the local jurisdiction is not personal; it's not just for one agency; it is simply the way the Federal government does business every day.

This is one of those aspects of receiving Federal funding which will likely never change: the near-obsessive attention to details of which the local government is often unaware.

However, to measure up to these unrelenting Federal requirements, local government agencies, as well as non-profit agencies, must have prior knowledge of the requirements, have plans and procedures in place to gather and process the information, and be prepared to ensure that its employees, volunteers, and contractors provide reams of data that the local agency itself does not normally require for its own purposes.

There is a benefit for a local agency that tracks its expenses, particularly those expenses for force account labor, force account equipment, rented equipment, and materials. Using the more detailed, Federally-required tracking of job data provides the local agency with real-time data on expenses, and work performance throughout its normal budget cycle. More importantly, the practice of daily detailed work and time reporting means that employees, on the day of a disaster, do not have to suddenly switch to a new, unfamiliar, and untested method for tracking disaster response and repair costs.

One of the challenges which local government agencies often fail to execute well is the need for an instantaneous transition from routine day-in-and-day-out recordkeeping to the much more stringent Federal documentation requirements. In this book, we will specifically detail many of these differing standards for local versus Federal recordkeeping.

While the ongoing cost of such a program is not inconsequential, to not have a program when disaster strikes may be more than the local community can financially sustain. The net result is that the local agency may not have the funds, nor ready access to the funds necessary to rebuild and recover after the disaster.

In March 2008, I visited New Orleans with a Louisiana colleague. We visited a small fire station which had been flooded and damaged in Hurricane Katrina. Adjacent to the fire station was a Starbucks shop where the high-water mark of nine feet still remained on the outside storefront. The captain at the firehouse said that the community was almost through renovating the fire house. But all the work done was through community support and donations. The fire captain said that the City of New Orleans was unable to provide any funding for the project. This is not a one-off situation; most communities have to prioritize their projects, and for some, there is simply no source of funding without access to FEMA's Public Assistance program.

The bottom line is that failure to properly document response and recovery costs often results in Project Worksheet denials or partial deobligation of the requested funds.

One potential alternative would be to, upon the onset of a disaster, reach out and hire someone who has the requisite knowledge and experience. But in the midst of the disaster, hunting for someone with such a specialized skill set is a daunting task at best. The middle of a battle is not a good time to go hunting for a better general.

Another possible option is to send one or two staff members on a "Mutual Aid" assignment to assist a disaster-affected agency with its cost recovery work early in the process. This is highly recommended as a "live" learning tool. On numerous occasions, I have volunteered my time to assist agencies during their disasters. Virtually every time I have done so, I have learned important lessons which I have incorporated into my working knowledge of the Public Assistance program and my training programs.

Furthermore, if the local agency could find such a unicorn, that person would still not be able to meet all of FEMA's possible requirements, because FEMA requires that certain policies must be adopted, and certain actions may only be taken prior to the onset of the disaster.

We will look at many of these issues in depth as we start to move into the next chapters.

Absent spending the necessary funds on planning, preparation, and training for a comprehensive disaster cost recovery program, the local agency must be willing to consider the option of hiring an experienced disaster cost recovery consulting firm. Much more about this in "Hired Guns and Consultants" in Chapter 13.

The Disaster Cost Recovery process probably isn't what most people think it is. In the scores of classes that I have taught across the country, the initial focal point of the attendees is that Disaster Cost Recovery is primarily a process of capturing the costs for the first responders' labor, equipment, and materials, with something left over for the costs of evacuation, sheltering, feeding, and other survivor's services. This picture is not only incomplete, but dangerously false. As we move through the book, we will see that disaster cost recovery is much more, in most cases, than a recapturing of the response costs. Disaster cost recovery is also the recovery of all possible insurance available, the proper acceptance of volunteer time and donations, and the repair and reconstruction of damaged facilities, equipment, and infrastructure.

Chapter Questions

1) For our agency, who is the designated disaster cost recovery team leader?
2) Who else is designated as a team member?

   a. What departments do they represent?
   b. Do they know they're on the team?

3) What, if any, disaster cost recovery plans do we have?
4) When were those plans last reviewed and revised?
5) Do we have an organizational chart or process map of how we will work through the Public Assistance program?
6) If we had a disaster next week or next month, are there colleagues in other nearby jurisdictions we could call on to provide us with some Mutual Aid?

   a. Can we arrange that in advance with other nearby financial officials?

Notes

1 DHS-OIG Audit, OIG-14-46-D, FEMA's Dissemination of Procurement Advice Early in Disaster Response Periods, February 2014, "During our deployment to the Oklahoma City Joint Field Office, we observed instances where FEMA personnel provided incomplete and, at times, inaccurate information to Public Assistance applicants regarding Federal procurement standards. Based on our audit reports and personal observations, similar instances have been occurring for several years." Author's Note: In the years since this audit was released, FEMA has made great strides in providing proper procurement information to applicants. FEMA is now very intent on ensuring that applicants assiduously adhere to the requirements of 2 CFR, Part 200.
2 FEMA – Disaster Operations Legal Reference, Version 4.0, September 25, 2020
3 This does not generally apply to a department whose workload has increased due to the disaster. For instance, a Tax Assessor's office that is overwhelmed by requests for property tax reductions due to disaster damage is not eligible for FEMA funding to cover its increased operating costs for preparing those tax reductions.
4 Larson, E. 2003. *The Devil in the White City*. Vintage Books, New York.

5   Disaster Cost Accounting Systems and Details

Audit Case Study: The High Cost of Dirt

"Jackson County is located in northwestern Florida. It is the third oldest county in Florida, established by an act of the Territorial Legislature in 1822. The County, named after Andrew Jackson, originally extended from the Choctawhatchee River on the west to the Suwannee River on the east. Jackson County is the only county in Florida to border two states, Alabama and Georgia."[1]

"On April 28, 2014, heavy rains and excessive water flow resulted in extensive flooding in the County. As a result, County roads were damaged by heavy water flow, standing water saturation of surface and base materials, and heavy runoff washouts of roads and ditches . . . On May 6, 2014, the President declared a major disaster (DR-4177-FL) to assist Florida and local government with recovery efforts for damages incurred during the disaster period of April 28 to May 6, 2014."[2]

Lack of Documentation to Support Costs

"Jackson County did not comply with the Federal cost principles requiring grant recipients to adequately document costs under a Federal award. Under the CFR (Code of Federal Regulations, Part 200), grant recipients must maintain records that adequately identify the source and application of Federal funds and maintain source documentation to support those records."[3]

"The County claimed $402,409 in force account materials for Projects 900, 980, and 981, without adequately documenting the costs. Force account materials are those purchased or taken from an applicant's inventory and used for eligible work. During road repairs following the April and May 2014 disaster, the County used daily activities sheets to document the use of dirt, a force account material. Specifically, County truck drivers and truck loaders documented the dirt they took every day from the County's dirt pits on daily activities sheets, which include the location, site details, date of use, employee's name and hours worked, equipment unit and hours used, task performed, quantity, and materials. County officials explained that truck drivers normally recorded the number of loads hauled, which pits the loads came from, and where the loads were hauled on a daily activities sheet. However, the truck loaders' daily activities sheets the County provided were incomplete; they did not include the quantity of dirt loaded or identify which truck had been loaded."[4]

"We determined the County's normal practice involving the daily activities sheet did not meet the requirements for documenting costs incurred using Federal grant funds. Even though, in keeping with the County's normal practice, truck drivers documented the quantity of dirt loaded, we could not trace this quantity to the daily activities sheet of the employees who loaded the trucks. Therefore, the County could not provide documentation verifying the materials were delivered and used at project sites damaged in April and May 2014. County officials also said that supervisors typically told employees how many loads to haul to a location, but that has not been documented

DOI: 10.4324/9781003487869-7

in the activities sheets either. If properly documented, the sheets would have enabled us to trace the dirt quantity recorded in drivers' activities sheets to the dirt quantity recorded in the loaders' activities sheets."[5]

"The inadequate documentation occurred because the County does not have an operating procedure for its employees working at the dirt pit with respect to loading the trucks. Also, according to County officials, they do not have an individual designated to monitor the loading of trucks at the dirt pits."[6]

"Because the County did not adequately document $402,409 of project costs used for these force account materials, FEMA has no assurance that those costs are valid and eligible, which puts Federal funds and taxpayers' money at risk of fraud, waste, and abuse. Therefore, all costs associated with the force account materials are ineligible."[7]

The Cost Recovery Conundrum

Cost accounting for disasters and the disaster cost recovery process have some requirements which may not be a part of the local agency's normal accounting and work tracking processes. No matter how much the local agency may need Federal financial assistance to recover from a disaster, if the contemporaneous records of the work done do not support the costs, they are ineligible.

The requirements of GAAP, the Generally Accepted Accounting Principles; the GAAS, Generally Accepted Auditing Standards; and the GAGAS, Generally Accepted Government Auditing Standards remain relevant and in force following a disaster.

However, FEMA requires very detailed information on how response, repair, clean-up, and reconstruction work is tracked, far more detailed than most agencies normally provide for their own internal purposes.

Many government agencies have a unique accounting code for emergencies and disasters. Let's use the six-digit number 999–999 as an example.

While this is a useful code for internal use, it is not sufficiently robust in detail for FEMA. In the first instance, if a jurisdiction has a disaster in one fiscal year and a second or even a third disaster, either within the same fiscal year or in subsequent fiscal years, the use of a single account code will be the cause of immediate confusion, because each disaster must be accounted for separately, and should have different tracking codes, hence 999–998, 999–997, etc.

FEMA needs to see a unique disaster cost accounting code for each separate disaster. When the first disaster hits, there is no way to anticipate whether or not there will be another disaster. One of the fastest ways to create a problem with FEMA is to code disaster damages incorrectly. This can result in a deobligation or an adverse audit finding.

Second, the use of a single disaster cost accounting code, in this case 999–999, will not allow tracking of the incurred costs for multiple incidents which may occur in a disaster.

For instance, a hurricane event may create the need for search and rescue for persons who refused to evacuate. The same disaster may involve human shelter operations; it may also require evacuation area perimeter control and operation of a pet rescue and care facility. Each of these separate incidents under the disaster code must be uniquely identifiable. Let's now add another data field to the 999–999 code, making the code now 999–999-1, 999–999-2, 999-999-3, etc.

FEMA separates the various kinds of disaster response, repair, and recovery into seven groups or categories, A through G.

- Category A: Debris removal
- Category B: Emergency Protective Measures, which includes all emergency work other than debris clean-up, i.e., evacuations, flood fight, congregate sheltering, mass feeding, emergency repair work, etc.

- Category C: Repair of roads and bridges
- Category D: Water control facilities
- Category E: Repair and reconstruction of facilities
- Category F: Public Utilities
- Category G: Recreation facilities and miscellaneous

FEMA requires the *local* jurisdictions to code the disaster work under one, and only one of these categories. The failure to properly code the work done by the appropriate category often may result in an outright denial or a partial deobligations of grants funds.

So, we have to add yet another field to the cost accounting code. Our 999–999–1 becomes 999–999–1-A (for debris removal) or 999–999–1-B for other emergency protective measures, etc.

Imagine that a water main has burst in the street. First, the rushing water creates a sinkhole. The sinkhole grows in size, the root system of a large tree is exposed, and high winds topple the tree into the sinkhole. A number of different FEMA damage categories are now in play.

The sinkhole needs traffic control barricades *(Cat B)* to prevent anyone from driving into the deep hole. Once the water is shut off, the hole will need to be pumped *(also Cat B)*. The tree must be removed *(Cat A)* before the pipe can be excavated, replaced *(Cat F)*, and the street repaired *(Cat C)*.

Therefore, we need to track the placing of barricades as a Category B activity. Tree removal is nominally a Category A activity. The excavation and repair of the pipe would be a Category F, and the repair and repaving of the street are Category C. Failure to properly isolate and identify each different and separate problem/activity could result in a denial of FEMA funding for this incident.

Here's the confusing and frustrating thing: FEMA staff may later choose to combine all these different activities into a single Project Worksheet. They may say that the debris removal (of the tree, in this case) is incidental to the repair of the pipe and the street. The dry pumping of the sinkhole could also be work incidental to the pipe and street repair. However, there is no way for us to know in advance if FEMA personnel will choose to handle the incident as several different categories of work, or as work incidental to the primary problem of the broken water main.

Let's carry this discussion a bit further. Let's say that on a given street, Main Street, there are five geographically separate breaks on the same 24" water supply main line. The total distance separating the first to the last of the five pipe breaks is 7 miles, and none of the water main breaks is closer than ¾ of a mile to the next break. These then are essentially 5 separate water main breaks, albeit on the same water main line and within the same jurisdiction.

As the Water Department crews arrive at location #3, right in the middle of the series of breaks, they see archeological artifacts from a tribal nation that originally lived in and around the community. The discovery of historical artifacts, or the presence of hazardous materials in the hole, will bring this specific site to a screeching halt. FEMA will require an in-depth investigation of such an occurrence.

Because the Water Department tracked all five water main breaks as a single event, FEMA funding will be considerably delayed until the historical or environmental investigation is completed. However, if the Water Department tracked each break as a separate incident, the remaining four sites can be repaired, and only the one problem site will be delayed pending the historical or environmental review.

Therefore, the disaster cost tracking process must be detailed, flexible, and robust enough to track all the various components of the incident in great detail, without overlap. The challenge for many local agencies is that this detailed process of tracking each element of the response separately is not the normal way the field departments do cost tracking.

Under some of FEMA's newer "simplified" procedures all this data may not need to be initially submitted to FEMA, but if questions arise, they may request the project be broken into an agonizing level of appropriate detail.

Counterintuitive Recordkeeping

In a hypothetical situation, a water department crew arrives at the site of a broken pipe which has resulted in a large sinkhole forming in the street. The curb and gutter have collapsed into the hole, and a large tree has also fallen into it.

The water department crew spends half a day at the site working to stabilize the problem and set up traffic barricades.

Theoretically, the crew must document the time to pump out the hole separately from the time they spent removing the tree. They must also separately document the time spent placing the traffic control measures.

Another water department crew may later return to make a temporary or permanent repair to the pipe, also documenting their time separately. Another crew, or the same crew, may also backfill the sinkhole and lay down a temporary asphalt patch, which is again more separate documentation.

This detailed documentation probably flies in the face of the department's normal method of documentation, which would be to group all work under the same project documentation.

There is no doubt that getting the field forces to detail this work in compliance with FEMA requirements will be a hard sell to the agency's employees, but this is the cost of receiving Federal disaster assistance.

Deobligation Case History

I worked with a client who suffered through a devastating wildfire that destroyed a facility located in the Sierra Nevada foothills. The entire campus burned to the ground, and not a single building survived. As part of the initial response once the fire was under control, the agency hired a firm to a) clean up the debris, and b) perform erosion control measures required since the campus was in a foothill environment where winter weather could result in flooding and erosion.

Upon receipt of the invoice from the contractor, the agency paid the bill, and in turn requested that FEMA reimburse the eligible expenses for debris removal and erosion control. FEMA rejected the invoice because the contractor had combined both the debris clearance and erosion control work into a single invoice.

The contractor alleged that they had done previous work for agencies receiving funding from FEMA. However, they did not separately track the labor, the equipment used, and the materials used as required by FEMA under separate categories, in this case Category A and Category B.

FEMA requires specific information for each incident or event. For those locations with a street address this will generally suffice. However, where there is not a street address, FEMA uses geographic positioning system (GPS) coordinates. This generally should not be a problem insofar as GPS positioning is available on most smart phones, and separate GPS location devices can be purchased. There will be more regarding GPS coordinates in subsequent chapters.

The Five Ws

Anyone who takes a beginning journalism class learns about the 5 Ws: Who, what, where, when, why, and how long. The 5 Ws are also the basic building blocks of information tracking for the Public Assistance program.

1) "Who" did the work? Track by first and last name and employee I.D. number. If the workers are part of a crew, then the names and I.D. numbers for each employee are required. It is inappropriate to use group names, such as Engine Company 22 or police patrol unit 33, etc.

2) "What" refers to the specific work or activities performed by an individual or a crew and really has two parts. The first part is what happened, what was the root cause of the problem or damage. The "What" also needs to include why or how the problem arose or how the damage was done. To specify that the problem was a hurricane is short sheeting. A proper description might be that this event was a Category 3 hurricane with winds gusting to xxx mile per hour, with a tidal storm surge that rose to xx feet above normal tide.

   The second part of the "What" is what was the specific damage done by the hurricane? XX square feet of roofing materials were torn from a roof, or so many square feet of glazing were broken, accounting for xx individual broken windows.

3) The "Where" naturally refers to the physical location, either by street address or GPS coordinates. The "Where" might also include a reference that the third floor of the city hall at the specific address was where most of the damage occurred.

4) The "When" is important, as each day's activities must be accounted for separately. The "When" also provides FEMA information that the work was accomplished within the defined disaster timeline, or what FEMA refers to as the "POP" or period of performance.

5) The "Why" must explain why it was necessary to do the work. In general, during the response phase of the disaster, the work done must involve: 1) the saving of lives, 2) the protection of public health, or 3) preventing further damage to improved property or the environment.

   FEMA requires that the work done must address an immediate threat to either life safety, the public health or prevention of damage to improved property. In fact, any work done by the local agency that does not address one of these three reasons is quite likely to be ineligible.

6) The "How Long" obviously tracks the total number of hours that the disaster response activity took, for each separate day that the specific work was done.

I was teaching a class in Douglas County, Colorado, several years ago, and heard this story from one of the attendees. The agency had an employee I call Jimmy Bob Baker. Actually, Mr. Baker's parents named him James Robert Baker. However, since he was a small child, he was known as Jimmy Bob. Most people can follow the logic that "James" became "Jimmy" and "Robert" became "Bob," hence the moniker "Jimmy Bob" Baker. However, his timecard was printed with James Robert Baker. The FEMA employee reviewing and comparing the timesheets with the work records said that James Robert Baker was not the same person as "Jimmy Bob" Baker and disallowed all of the time for "Jimmy Bob," which amounted to a $12,000 loss to the agency.

FEMA may not always be this picky on issues, but they have a legitimate right and reason to ensure that proper documentation is provided.

Adding to the paperwork burden, and this burden is the price of Federal assistance, is the fact that every day that single employees or crews of employees work at various sites and incidents, they must submit complete documentation for each day, AND for every location where they work. This level of documentation typically goes well beyond the *de minimis* paperwork that many government employees must normally submit as part of their jobs.

The 5 Ws not only apply to every individual employee and crew for their work hours; they also apply to all equipment (typically rolling stock and not hand tools) used, and all the materials and supplies needed for the work.

The tracking of equipment also requires that for each piece of equipment used, an operator is assigned and identified in the paperwork. Thus, if John Doe drives a dump truck and/or operates an excavator, he must be listed on the field paperwork as the operator of each piece of equipment, or the agency risks a deobligation for that equipment which is reportedly used without identifying the operator(s).

Some equipment, such as temporary electrical power generators, stationary water pumps, and similar equipment which can run unattended for extended periods of time, need not identify an operator for every hour of operation, but they should note who set up the equipment and who fuels it daily.

The 5 Ws for materials and supplies used require similar detailed reporting. Following a high-wind event, if a public works or facilities crew spends two days boarding up broken windows on government buildings and has used 100 sheets of plywood and 50 each of 2" x 4" x 8" wood studs for the work, then they must specify how many sheets of plywood and how many studs were used on each building. They cannot simply report 100 sheets of plywood and 50 studs used. Materials and supplies must be accounted for on a site-by-site basis.

Both materials purchased specifically for the disaster work and any materials taken from existing inventories are normally eligible for reimbursement, However, materials charge tickets must account for any material taken from inventory. Furthermore, the materials taken from inventory must be cost accounted for on the same basis as that which the agency normally uses for cost accounting purposes, i.e., FIFO, (first-in-first-out); LIFO (last in, first out) or five-year running average, etc.

A colleague, the former emergency manager for his county in the Sierra Nevada mountains told me of an incident following the Rim Fire in 2013. A section of road in the county was damaged by the fire, and the county's own crews did the repair work on the highway. However, at close-out, the FEMA official noted a discrepancy between the amount of material used, and the amount of material which would be necessary for the complete repair job. The amount requested for reimbursement was far less than the total amount of materials needed. Because of this discrepancy, the materials were disallowed. Because the materials were disallowed, the equipment used to place the materials was also disallowed, as was all the labor for the project. The only thing that made any sense was that the crew used materials from inventory, and when that ran out, the crew ordered enough additional materials to finish the work. But there was no charge ticket to indicate how much material was taken from inventory.

There is additional information that must be included on various forms. One of these is the FEMA 'DR' number. This is a unique number FEMA assigns to every major disaster. It is an essential piece of documentation required once the number has been assigned by FEMA.

Once individual Project Worksheets are authorized, the Project Worksheet number becomes part of the essential information chain. This is an important number because, when the project is first approved, FEMA issues a Version 0 Project Worksheet. However, on large projects where there are cost increases for any reason, FEMA may issue a subsequent version of the Project Worksheet, now called Version 1 or Version 2, as may be the case when there are continuing changes.

And lastly, but perhaps most importantly, no form which requires a signature is complete until the form has been signed, with the **full** required number of signatures.

I have a copy of a Project Worksheet originally written to pay for damages to a Colorado fire engine when the fire agency was on Mutual Aid in California. A tree fell and damaged the engine, and damage cost slightly less than $19,000. California agreed to cover the damages under the Mutual Aid agreement. However, when the vehicle operator filled out the damage form, he only signed in one of the three signature boxes. As a result, FEMA disallowed those costs because of faulty documentation. Once documentation is submitted, it stands on its own, for better or worse.

My recommendation for filling out both state and Federal paperwork is: **"Never Leave a Box Blank."** As needed, enter "n/a" for "not applicable," or "unk" for "unknown," etc.

The FEMA Summary Forms for Labor, Equipment, Materials, and Contracts

There are six FEMA forms for tracking the costs associated with the disaster response which require close attention to the 5 Ws. They are the:

1) Force Account Labor Summary (FEMA Form FF-104-FY21–137; Formerly 90–0-123)[8]
2) Force Account Equipment Summary Record (FEMA Form FF-104-FY21–141; formerly FEMA Form 90–0-127)[9]
3) Materials Summary Record Summary (FEMA Form FF-104-FY21–138; formerly FEMA Form 90–0-124)[10]
4) Rented Equipment Summary Record Summary (FEMA Form FF-104-FY21–139; formerly FEMA Form 90–0-125)[11]
5) Contract Work Summary Record Summary (FEMA Form FF-104-FY21–140; formerly FEMA Form 90–0-123)[12]
6) Applicant's Benefits Calculation Worksheet (FEMA Form FF-104-FY21–135; FEMA Form 90–0-128)[13]

When a disaster hits a local jurisdiction, it is a best practice to go to the internet and download the most recent versions of these FEMA forms. In fact, it is a best practice to ensure that all the forms used for the disaster cost recovery process be the current FEMA and related state forms.

These six forms are used to document the disaster-related work and the costs related to the disaster response activities in great detail.

The Disaster Field Unit Incident Work Report, AKA "The Scary Form"

Following the discussion of these six FEMA forms, we will discuss the Disaster Field Unit Incident Work Report, aka the "Scary Form." This form consists of data fields extracted from the FEMA forms for tracking labor, equipment, both owned and rented, and the materials used for a project. The "Scary Form" is found in the Appendix, Form 10.

Many frontline employees do not like paperwork. In fact, some may simply detest it; however, without proper documentation, our disaster response and reconstruction costs will not be eligible for FEMA reimbursement. The challenge for the disaster cost recovery process is to get sufficiently detailed information to support our requests for grant funding. The theory is that we are more likely to get the documentation we need if we simplify and reduce the total amount of paperwork required from our frontline employees. The "Scary Form" combines four different FEMA forms into one single form for frontline employee use. A properly completed "Scary Form" will provide all the information we need to later complete four of the six FEMA forms listed previously.

Later in the book, we will discuss how to further simplify and reduce the documentation workload when using the "Scary Form."

The Applicant's Benefits Calculation Worksheet

This is a required form. However, the local agency need only fill out examples of this form rather than filling out the form for each employee. A best practice would be to fill out one of these forms for each of the different bargaining units within the agency's labor units or unions.

This form is important because in addition to the overtime and, in some cases, straight time wages paid to each employee, the benefits paid to the employee are also generally FEMA-eligible for reimbursement. These forms, once filled out, will be uploaded to FEMA's web-based Portal as part of the documentation for EVERY Project Worksheet where wages are paid to agency employees.

The purpose of this form is to demonstrate to FEMA that the local agency knows how to properly calculate their employee benefits, and that those benefits were also paid out to each employee.

This form has limitations, however, insofar as not all the benefits paid to employees are listed on this form. Therefore, the local agency will have to add in those other paid benefits, such as shoot pay for police officers, boot pay for public works and other field employees, bilingual pay for certain qualified employees, etc.

Most public agencies have benefit packages that are much more generous than many private employers, and in the public sector, straight time benefit rates will sometimes approach, and may even exceed, the base hourly pay rate itself.

However, FEMA pays close attention to how the local agency applies the benefit rates. Typically, almost all benefits are fully accrued in the first 40 hours of straight time. These are vacation, sick leave, holiday pay, medical and dental insurance, pension, and other miscellaneous benefits, such as shoot pay, boot pay, cafeteria plans, etc.

The overtime benefits usually consist almost entirely of taxes, i.e., Social Security, disability, unemployment, Medicare, etc. However, some agencies may pay certain benefits other than taxes. An example of this might be multilingual pay. Multilingual pay may only be paid for the first 40 hours, or it might also be paid for each hour of overtime, in which case this would be eligible for when properly documented. Perhaps an agency has a very liberal policy that multilingual during overtime hours is paid on the basis of multilingual pay and a half. If properly documented and the normal practice of the agency, this overtime benefit should be eligible when the practice is consistently applied for any disaster, Federally declared or not.

Because the overtime benefit rates are mostly taxes, the typical overtime benefit rates are usually near or below 10% of the hourly base pay rate versus the straight time benefit rates. Local government benefit rates typically range from 50% to 90% or more of the base pay, depending on the individual agency's benefit packages. FEMA closely checks how the local agency has applied the benefit rates and this form, the Applicant's Benefit Calculation Worksheet, is part of that checking process.

FEMA uses a standard 2080-hour workweek (52 weeks at 40 hours per week) as the annual hours basis for determining the benefit percentages. If the local agency uses a "productive hourly rate" based on a denominator of anything less than 2080 hours, FEMA will either adjust the benefit rates based on 2080 hours, or simply deobligate funding to reflect the 2080-hour basis for calculating the benefit rate.

Additionally, each Project Worksheet that contains costs for labor must include as back-up material the labor bargaining unit agreement for the respective employees who worked on a specific project.

Force Account Labor Summary

The Force Account Labor Summary is used to document the time local agency employees spend on qualified disaster response and recovery work. The form will be explained, moving from left to right and top to bottom. Following is the breakout for how to properly use this form.

The Force Account Labor Summary is only used to report actual disaster-related work. However, when filling out the form all worked hours must be reported, even though only actual disaster-related work is eligible for reimbursement. This is to show FEMA that the employee(s) have

Table 5.1 Force Account Labor Summary Notes

Box Name	Notes & instructions
Applicant	Insert the full, legal name of the applicant agency.
PA ID #	Enter the Public Assistance Identification Number. (This is the 'DR' number assigned by FEMA)
Project #	Enter the unique number for an approved Project Worksheet. This may be entered once the Project Worksheet has been approved.
Disaster	Enter the name of the disaster based upon the name given in the Presidential disaster declaration.
Location/Site	Detail here is critical. Use a street address or the GPS coordinates.
	The building name, e.g., "City Hall" may be used, but does not substitute for the street address or GPS coordinates.
Category	Enter the appropriate FEMA Category using the correct category, A through G.
Period Covering	Enter the date(s) the work was done. For each different date worked at an individual location or incident, prepare a separate form.
Description of Work Performed	Detail here is critical. Enter a complete description of what the disaster was, i.e., fire, flood, tornado, etc. Enter how the disaster caused the specific problem and what specific work was necessary to mitigate the problem. If the work done was Category B, "Emergency Protective Measures," the explanation of the work done should clearly indicate that any repair work was an emergency or temporary repair measure.[14]
Date	Enter the date worked.
Total Hours	Enter the total hours worked for BOTH straight time AND overtime as two separate numbers, total regular time hours, AND total overtime hours worked.
Hourly Rate	Enter the straight time hourly pay rate and the overtime hourly rate, both in dollars and cents. Do not use a benefit rate as a percentage of the hourly pay rate.
Benefit Rate/Hour	Enter the benefit rate per hour in dollars and cents, NOT as a percentage.
Total Hourly Rate	Add the straight time wages to the straight time benefit rate for the hourly total cost. Add the overtime wages cost to the overtime benefit rate for the total overtime wages cost.
Total Costs	If appropriate, add the total straight time costs and the overtime costs for each employee.
Name	Enter the employee's full name as reflected in the payroll/timecard system. Do not use nicknames or abbreviations unless identical to the payroll/timecard data.
Job Title	Enter the job title for each employee as reflected in their personnel file.
Total Costs for Force Account Labor Regular Time[15]	Add up all employee straight time, if any, and enter.
Total Cost for Force Account Labor Overtime	Add up all employee overtime and enter the total here.
Certified	Each form must be signed by the person preparing the form.
Title	Enter the preparer's job title.
Date	Enter the date the form was completed.

worked a full shift of straight time, AND additional hours of overtime. The straight time may be for normal duties and the overtime for disaster-related work, or any combination thereof, but only disaster-related work is eligible for reimbursement.

In filling out the Force Account Labor Summary, it is critical to properly demonstrate that the work done was directly related to the disaster and not otherwise ineligible emergency work. For example, the time for which firefighter/paramedics treat a heart attack victim will be ineligible unless a nexus is clearly shown between the disaster and the heart attack.

While it's not normally an eligible expense, if paramedics treat a heart attack patient who has been sitting on the roof of their house for 2 or 3 days in the heat and humidity and without their normal medications, this could qualify as a "flood-induced" heart attack.

Similarly, a police officer who reports 4 hours of overtime for "routine patrol" will not be eligible. However, if their time was actually for traffic control for a mandatory evacuation, then the overtime will be eligible. All work must have this disaster nexus clearly documented to be eligible for reimbursement. This is one area where many local agencies' time recording systems often fail to meet FEMA's stringent tracking requirements.

Force Account Equipment Summary Record

The header parts of this form are identical to the Force Account Labor Summary. The following table provides instructions on the use of this form.

Force Account equipment is FEMA-reimbursable based upon standard nationwide rates published by FEMA in its Equipment Rate Sheet. This list of rates is periodically revised, so ensure that the staff is using the current rate. In some cases where the agency has had disasters in two

Table 5.2 Force Account Equipment Summary Notes

Box Name	Notes & instructions
Applicant	Insert the name of the applicant agency.
PA ID #	Enter the Public Assistance Identification Number. (This is the 'DR' number assigned by FEMA)
Project #	Enter the unique number for an approved Project Worksheet. This may be entered once the Project Worksheet has been approved.
Disaster	Enter the name of the disaster based upon the name given in the Presidential disaster declaration.
Location/Site	Detail here is critical. Use a street address or the GPS coordinates. The building name, e.g., "City Hall" may be used but does not substitute for the street address or GPS coordinates.
Category	Enter the appropriate FEMA Category using the correct category, A through G.
Period Covering	Enter the date(s) the work was done. For each different date worked at an individual location or incident, prepare a separate form.

(Continued)

Table 5.2 (Continued)

Box Name	Notes & instructions
Description of Work Performed	Detail here is critical. Enter a complete description of what the disaster was, i.e., fire, flood, tornado, etc. Enter how the disaster caused the specific problem and what specific work was necessary to mitigate the problem.
Type of Equipment	Use the equipment descriptions from the current FEMA Schedule of Equipment Rates.[16]
Equipment Code Number	Use the four-digit code from the FEMA Schedule of Equipment Rates.
Operator's Name	For each piece of equipment, an operator's name must be attached. Failure to identify the operator will result in disallowance of those costs.
Date	Enter the date the equipment was used.
Hours	Enter the total hours the equipment was used at the site. If the equipment is used intermittently throughout the day, the full day may be charged. However, if the equipment is only used part-time, then only the run time hours are eligible. This form does not have a space for "Miles Driven," so the person preparing the form will have to annotate the form to indicate that the vehicle was used to transport people and not used on an hourly basis.
Total Hours	Enter the total hours for the day in question.
Equipment Rate	Pull the equipment rate from the FEMA Schedule of Equipment Rates. If FEMA does not list the piece of equipment, the usual practice is to use the state's department of transportation's equipment rates. If the state's DOT rates are used, indicate this on the form.
Total Cost	Enter the total cost for all equipment used at the site.
Certified	Sign the form.
Title	Enter the employee's job title.
Date	Date the form was prepared.

different years, it may be necessary to cost out the equipment used at two different rates if FEMA revised the Equipment Rate Sheet between the two disasters.

If the equipment in question is a piece of stationary equipment such as an emergency electrical generator, a water pump, air compressor, or similar item, the operator may not be attending the equipment all day, but there should be an operator of record, the person who starts up the equipment or refuels it. The total run hours must be documented each day.

For each hour that a piece of equipment is used, there must be an operator identified for each hour, with the exception of the types of equipment mentioned in the previous paragraph.

Therefore, there is a maximum of 24 hours in a single day for which equipment charges may be incurred. However, this has not stopped some agencies in the past from attempting to claim more than 24 hours in a single day for a piece of equipment. Remember, this is Federal money, and FEMA does not have a sense of humor in this regard.

Regarding equipment maintenance or repairs, NEVER enter the time for a mechanic's time, parts, or supplies used to maintain or repair the equipment used for disaster-related activities. The costs for maintenance and repairs are included when using the FEMA Equipment Rate Sheet.

The Materials Summary Record

Table 5.3 Materials Summary Record Notes

Box Name	Notes & instructions
Applicant	Insert the name of the applicant agency.
PA ID #	Enter the Public Assistance Identification Number. (This is the 'DR' number assigned by FEMA)
Project #	Enter the unique number for an approved Project Worksheet. This may be entered once the Project Worksheet has been approved.
Disaster	Enter the name of the disaster based upon the name given in the Presidential disaster declaration.
Location/Site	Detail here is critical. Use a street address or the GPS coordinates. The building name, e.g., "City Hall" may be used but does not substitute for the street address or GPS coordinates.
Category	Enter a FEMA Category, using the correct category A through G.
Period Covering	Enter the date(s) the work was done. For each different date worked at an individual location or incident, prepare a separate form.
Description of Work Performed	Detail here is critical. Enter a complete description of what the disaster was, i.e., fire, flood, tornado, etc. Enter how the disaster caused the specific problem and what specific work was necessary to mitigate the problem. If the work done was Category B, "Emergency Protective Measures," the explanation of the work done should clearly indicate that any repair work was an emergency or temporary repair measure.[17]
Vendor	Enter the vendor's name.
Description	Enter the standard description for the materials or supplies used. It's a good idea to copy word-for-word the description from the invoice, if the invoice provides a sufficient description.
Quantity	Enter the quantity of materials or supplies used at each individual job site. Include the case or pack, i.e., one gallon, case of 24 55-gallon drum, 6 cubic yards, etc.
Unit Price	Include the billing unit as per the invoice so there are no differences between this form and the invoice. A copy of the invoice will also need to be provided as a back-up document.
Total Price	Enter the total price based upon the earlier-cited unit costs for the total cost.
Date Purchased	Enter the date(s) purchased.
Date Used	Enter the date(s) the equipment was used.
Info from Invoice	If the materials are supplied by a vendor, the invoice should be sufficient documentation.
Info from Stock	If the materials are taken from stock on hand, then all materials must have a "chit" or an "inventory used" tag to document their use. Cost of the materials must be charged on the same basis as the local agency normally uses for costing its inventory, FIFO, LIFO, five-year running average cost, etc.
Grand Total	Enter the grand total in the box at the bottom of the "Total Price" column. If this is a multi-page list of materials and supplies and there is a sub-total, indicate on each page what the page sub-total is, separate from any grand total.
Certified	Each form must be signed by the person preparing the form.
Title	Enter the preparer's job title.
Date	Enter the date the form was completed.

Eleven Ways to Ensure a Deobligation on a Single Form[18]

In this example from a large transit agency, it is easy to see how these forms in general, and the Materials Summary Record specifically, can be misused and potentially result in a partial or total denial of FEMA funding. Please see form 66 in the Appendix.

1) Note first the "Description of Work Performed" box. The first line "Disinfection of public facilities/disinfection and cleaning of train cars" is correct, since these costs were for the Coronavirus response efforts and within the approved Category B, Emergency Protective Measures. However, the remaining text, i.e., "repair and maintenance of train cars and other district facilities, etc." describes work which is permanent work, and not eligible under the Presidential disaster declaration. This error alone could torpedo this entire document and result in a total de-obligation.

2) At the bottom of the first page, KN95 masks are listed at a cost of $4.09 each with a quantity of 20,000 units. This purchase and a second one (See Star # 4) effectively set the price range that FEMA will most likely pay for all KN95 masks.[19] In this case, these two purchases of 48,000 KN95 masks set the price floor. These are reasonable costs against which FEMA can measure all other purchases for KN95 masks, some of which were purchased for more than $100 for each mask.

3) On the second page, there is a purchase listed for alcohol. Is this Budweiser, Berringer, or Jim Beam? There are no specifics as to the type of alcohol or the package size. These alcohol purchases could have been in pints, quarts, or gallons, etc. Based upon the information, there is no way to determine the cost reasonableness of this purchase.

4) Star #4 is the second purchase, at a reasonable cost, for KN95 masks.

5) Star #5 is again for alcohol, with no further information provided as to package size or quantity, or if these were master cases of a gross of small pocket dispensers of sanitizer.

6) Star #6 could be a beautiful refrigerated wine cabinet. It doesn't specify anything about this storage container. And why, if you're buying alcohol in some sort of container, is an alcohol storage cabinet needed?

7) Star #7 is for hand sanitizer, purchased from the same company only two days apart, at different prices. Again, there are no specifics as to quantity or case pack to determine cost reasonableness.

8) Star #8 is yet again for more alcohol, with absolutely no specifics that would provide for a determination of cost reasonableness.

9) Star #9 references four different purchases of KN95 masks at over 100 dollars per mask. This is clearly not a reasonable cost when compared to the 48,000 masks purchased for an average price of $3.76.

10) Star 10 is probably a page subtotal, but this is anyone's guess. The number should be labeled as a subtotal. This is a fact which FEMA may choose not to assume.

11) Star #11 is the coup de grace. The actual total for all these pages is $0.00, because that is what is entered in the "Grand Total' box at the bottom of the page. FEMA might accept this document, but there's more than a slight chance that it will not be honored as written, with a net obligation of zero dollars.

Rented Equipment Summary Record

When the local agency does not have sufficient equipment for the disaster response and repair tasks, it may rent or lease the needed equipment, and FEMA will reimburse those eligible costs

Table 5.4 Rented Equipment Summary Record Notes

Box Name	Notes & instructions
Applicant	Insert the name of the applicant agency.
PA ID #	Enter the Public Assistance Identification Number. (This is the 'DR' number assigned by FEMA)
Project #	Enter the unique number for an approved Project Worksheet. This may be entered once the Project Worksheet has been approved.
Disaster	Enter the name of the disaster based upon the name given in the Presidential disaster declaration.
Location/Site	Detail here is critical. Use a street address or the GPS coordinates. The building name, e.g., "City Hall" may be used but does not substitute for the street address or GPS coordinates.
Category	Enter the appropriate FEMA Category using the correct category, A through G.
Period Covering	Enter the date(s) the work was done. For each different date worked at an individual location or incident, prepare a separate form.
Description of Work Performed	Detail here is critical. Enter a complete description of what the disaster was, i.e., fire, flood, tornado, etc. Enter how the disaster caused the specific problem and what specific work was necessary to mitigate the problem. If the work done was Category B, "Emergency Protective Measures," the explanation of the work done should clearly indicate that any repair work was an emergency or temporary repair measure.[20]
Date & Amount Paid	Enter (later in the process) the date and amount of the payment. A copy of the cancelled check (both sides) will need to be attached as a back-up document.
Check Number	Enter the Check number, even though the invoice copy will show the check number. If this box is left blank, it may be cause for denial of the document.
Grand Total	Enter the grand total for all rented equipment used at a single incident or work site.
Certified	Each form must be signed by the person preparing the form.
Title	Enter the preparer's job title.
Date	Enter the date the form was completed.

based upon the reasonable rental rates of local vendors. When ordering rental equipment, the local agency should specify that it requires a separate invoice for each separate piece of equipment rented, and if possible, where it was delivered, i.e., the job site.

Furthermore, the local agency should also require that the vendor use the FEMA 4-digit equipment code when preparing the invoices. The contract should stipulate that invoices which do not contain the required information shall not be paid until the invoice is properly submitted.

Having separate and properly formatted invoices will make the task of cost accounting much easier when dealing with FEMA regulations.

Contract Work Summary Record

This form should not be used for large or complex projects. This form cannot account for change orders, percentage of completion payments, and other factors which regularly affect large and complex projects.

Table 5.5 Contract Work Summary Record Notes

Box Name	Notes & instructions
Applicant	Insert the name of the applicant agency.
PA ID #	Enter the Public Assistance Identification Number. (This is the 'DR' number assigned by FEMA)
Project #	Enter the unique number for an approved Project Worksheet. This may be entered once the Project Worksheet has been approved.
Disaster	Enter the name of the disaster based upon the name given in the Presidential disaster declaration.
Location/Site	Detail here is critical. Use a street address or the GPS coordinates. The building name, e.g., "City Hall" may be used but does not substitute for the street address or GPS coordinates.
Category	Enter the appropriate FEMA Category using the correct category, A through G.
Period Covering	Enter the date(s) the work was done. For each different date worked at an individual location or incident, prepare a separate form.
Description of Work Performed	Detail here is critical. Enter a complete description of what the disaster was, i.e., fire, flood, tornado, etc. Enter how the disaster caused the specific problem and what specific work was necessary to mitigate the problem. If the work done was Category B, "Emergency Protective Measures," the explanation of the work done should clearly indicate that any repair work was an emergency or temporary repair measure
Dates Worked	Enter the date(s) worked from and to as appropriate.
Contractor	Enter the contractor's name.
Billing/Invoice Number	Enter the invoice number. A copy of the invoice with back-up material will also be required.
Amount	Enter the total amount for the work done at each individual site, or per the contract specifications if a multi-site job.
Comments/Scope	As necessary
Grand Total	Enter the grand total per individual job site or per the contract specifications.
Certified	Each form must be signed by the person preparing the form.
Title	Enter the preparer's job title.
Date	Enter the date the form was completed.

The best use of this form is for limited-scope emergency and temporary work, such as boarding up buildings with broken windows and/or damaged doors, or surrounding a facility with safety barricades as a temporary protective measure, or the provision of security guards.

Ideally, each different incident or work site will have a separate form to account for the small contracts at that location. Work or services provided should be separately invoiced by each site.

General Note for These FEMA Forms

When filing out these FEMA forms, there are two reasons for describing the work done as a temporary measure, if in fact the work is of a temporary nature. 1) If the work is done as a temporary or emergency repair, then the work is eligible, and later the permanent work to properly redo the work, including any applicable codes and standards upgrades, will also be eligible. 2) If the work is done by another agency's Mutual Aid forces, then by definition the work must be of a temporary nature, as Mutual Aid forces are prohibited from performing any Category C through G permanent work.

The "Scary" Form Alternative for Documentation

For each different incident or work site and on each and every day worked, field crews must document their labor, their equipment use, the materials used, and any rented equipment used at the specific site on a given day. This is a lot of paperwork for field crews who normally do not like paperwork.

Years ago, I synthesized all the critical information from these four forms into a single document, the Disaster Field Unit – Incident Work Report in order to simplify and minimize the documentation requirements while retaining all of the key information required by FEMA to document the costs associated with disaster response and repair activities.

Note: THIS IS NOT A FEMA FORM. However, by properly using this form, the local agency will be able to fully document its costs for FEMA reimbursement.

When this form is properly filled out, it provides all the necessary information to later fill out the four forms: the Force Account Labor Summary; the Force Account Equipment Summary; the Materials Summary; and the Rented Equipment Summary. When the "Scary" form is properly filled out, office staff can weeks or even months later complete these FEMA forms fully.

Using the FEMA forms is not exactly intuitive, and I have seen these four forms very badly filled out due to a lack of understanding how FEMA expects these forms to be used. The incidence of errors will be quite high when front line staff are required to complete these forms. There will be illegible entries, miscalculations, data transpositions, and general imprecision in the forms' completion. Once the forms are submitted, it is often not possible to make corrections.

Error-Free and Automation, Too

In 1995 I experienced my first disaster, albeit a disaster of minor flooding which affected several homes in the city for which I worked. I had to fill out the FEMA forms for labor, equipment, and materials, which at that time were strictly paper-and-pen documents. Being familiar with Excel, I thought it ridiculous to fill out the forms by hand and perform all the necessary calculations. I did not know it then, but this became the beginning of my decades-long journey into disaster cost recovery.

I created my first simple imitations of FEMA's form for tracking our costs and programmed the spreadsheet to perform all the calculations. That first spreadsheet was modified and improved many times in the years since.

This master form can be located in the Appendix, Form 25. While this is not a FEMA form per se, it is a perfect imitation of the FEMA forms with a great deal more added in to speed up the process of filling them out, to completely eliminate miscalculation errors, and insure across-the-board consistency between the local agency's payroll data and the information provided on the forms.

The spreadsheet form consists of 11 different tabs. They are, in order:

1) The Recap Sheet, which summarizes the data from the other remaining pages.
2) The Force Account Labor Summary sheet, which tracks the employee data identically to FEMA's form FF-104-FY-21–137 (formerly 009–0-123).
3) The Donated Labor sheet, which tracks donated labor in the same way as for employees but must be tracked separately for reasons which we will later discuss. Other than the fact that it is used only for volunteers, it is the same form.
4) The Force Account Equipment sheet, used to track the equipment utilized for disaster response activities and later for permanent work. This is FEMA Form FF-104-FY-21–141 (formerly 009–0-127).
5) The Rented Equipment Summary Record, which is used to track any rented equipment used for response or recovery activities. This is FEMA Form FF-104-FY-21–139 (formerly 009–0-125).
6) The Donated Equipment tab is for any equipment that may have been donated for emergency response activities.
7) Tab 7 is the Materials Summary Record, identical to FEMA Form FF-104-FY-21–138 (formerly 009–0-124), and tracks all materials used, including both purchased materials and any materials taken from inventory. Materials taken from the local agency inventory will also need a Materials Charge Ticket or other form to document that they were taken from inventory.
8) Tab 8 is used for any materials that might be donated for emergency response activities. Please see form 68 in the Appendix.
9) Tab 9 is used for tracking and accounting for small contract work done on a project. This form is insufficient for large projects because it does not allow for progress payments, change orders, or retention, etc.
10) Tab 10 is where the data is stored for the employees' information, i.e., name, job title, regular hourly pay rate (or annual salary calculated on an hourly basis), the employee I.D. number, the overtime ratio (typically 1.5 for time and one-half), the employee's regular time benefit, and their overtime benefit rate.
11) Tab 11 is the FEMA Schedule of Equipment Rates form, which lists hundreds of line items of the equipment most often used by local government agencies.

These 11 tabs in one spreadsheet work together to fully document the labor, equipment, and materials, both agency-owned and rented or purchased used for disaster response and recovery operations. The spreadsheet also provides for any donated labor, equipment, and/or materials that may be used.

Included with the spreadsheet are cell-by-cell instructions on how to use the form, including the downloading of the payroll data and the FEMA Schedule of Equipment Rates.

The Force Account Equipment Summary Record (Tab 4) provides the capability to compile a list of the local agency's owned equipment which identically matches up using FEMA own 4-digit codes to ensure proper tracking. The correct use of FEMA's 4-digit equipment codes sends the message to FEMA that the agency is on the ball and more than likely keeping the necessary documentation.

When using this spreadsheet, do not delete any of the individual tabs as that may cause a corruption of the calculations within the spreadsheet.

City of – Disaster Field Unit – Incident Work Report (LEM – 1)

Use one form per crew, per location, each day

Table 5.6 City of – Disaster Field Unit – Incident Work Report (LEM – 1)

Incident Address		Incident #
Description of Problem		FEMA Work Category: A B C D E F G
Description of Work Done		
Date	Start Time	Is this a Mutual Aid Crew? Y □ N □ Mixed □
My Supervisor	Stop Time	Mutual Aid Agency Department
Are Damage Photos Attached? Y □ N □		Mission # Radio/Phone #

Mutual Aid

Materials

Personnel

Unit Opr.	Employee's Name	Employee's I.D. #	Job Title & Department or Agency			**Hours**		
				Reg.	O.T.	C.O.		

A Equipment

Unit #	Eq. License #	Equipment Description	City Eq.	Rented	Donated	Vendor Name 1	P.O. #	Hours	Miles

Personnel

Materials

Materials Description 1	Units	Stock	Unit Cost	Total Cost	Vendor Name 2	P.O. #	Purpose

Fees

Receipt #
Cost

Name of employee completing form, please print

3DC Use Only Dept   3DC Use Only Log Number   Phone #

3DC Name   3DC Phone #   Prepares Signature

3DC Signature

Originator: All Field Personnel or Supervisors   Routing: Send forms to the Finance Section of the EOC daily; attach any receipts or invoices.
A separate form should be filled out for each different work location. All personnel, equipment, supplies, materials, and fees should be accounted for.

"Scary" Form Add-on Information

Included in the "Scary" form are some data fields which are not required by FEMA but may be extremely important to the local agency. See the following table for the instructions on properly using the "Scary" form.

Table 5.7 "Scary" Form Add-on Information

City of - Disaster Field Unit - Incident Work Report (LEM - 1)	Title
Use one form per crew, per location, each day	Instructions
Incident Address	Enter the location of the incident or project.
Incident #	Enter the incident name or number if available.
Description of Problem	Enter the nature of the disaster, i.e., fire, flood tornado, etc.
FEMA Work Category: A B C D E F G	Enter the FEMA damage category.
Description of Work Done	Enter the description of the work done and explain how the work was necessary to protect life, protect the public health, or protect improved property. *(This information may be later amplified when filling out the four FEMA forms for tracking labor, equipment, and materials.)*
Date	Enter the date of the activity.
Start Time	Enter the start time.
Mutual Aid	*This data field is not on the FEMA forms, but may be important if the work is performed by Mutual Aid.*
Is this a Mutual Aid Crew? Y□ N□ Mixed□	Check the appropriate box. If "Yes" or "Mixed," enter the name of the agency providing the Mutual Aid.
My Supervisor	Enter the crew's supervisor's name.
Stop Time	Enter the time the work was completed on that day.
Mutual Aid Agency	Enter the Mutual Aid agency's name.
Department	Enter the Mutual Aid agency's department, if any.
Are Damage Photos Attached? Y□ N□	Check the appropriate box. Upload the photographs to the event or project file.
Mission #	Enter the state-issued mission number or resource request number. To be FEMA-eligible, all Mutual Aid must be authorized by the state. The mission number or resource request number documents that authorization.
Radio/Phone #	Enter the contact number(s) for the Mutual Aid staff.
Unit Opr. *(Operator)*	If any employee uses or operates equipment, the employee must be tied to the specific piece(s) of equipment used. Failure to assign an operator will result in denial of funding for that piece of equipment.
Employee's Name	Enter the employee's name using the same name format as appears in the payroll system. Do Not Use nicknames.
Employee's I.D. #	Enter the employee's identification number as per the payroll system.
Job Title & Department or Agency	Enter the employee's department or division.
Reg. *(Regular time worked on disaster events)*	Enter each employee's regular hours worked, if any.
O.T. *(Overtime worked on disaster events)*	Enter each employee's overtime hours, if any.
C.O. *(Call-Out Time)*	If the employee is called out while in an off-duty status and that employee is entitled to 'call-out' pay, enter those hours here. Note: this would apply only on the first day of the disaster.

(Continued)

Table 5.7 (Continued)

City of - Disaster Field Unit - Incident Work Report (LEM - 1)	Title
Unit #	Enter the unique identification number for each piece of equipment used.
Eq. License #	Enter the Equipment license number or other unique identifier.
Equipment Description	Enter the 4-digit FEMA equipment number from the current FEMA Equipment Rate Sheet.
City Eq.	Check this box if this is Force Account (i.e., local agency owned) equipment.
Rented	Check this box if the equipment is rented or leased specifically for the disaster response.
Donated	Check this box if the equipment was loaned to the local agency for disaster response activities.
Vendor Name	If the equipment was rented or donated, provide the vendor or donor's name and contact information.
P.O. #	If the equipment was rented, leased, or purchased, enter the P.O. number.
Hours	Enter the number of hours the equipment was used.
Miles	If the equipment is a passenger vehicle or light pickup truck used as a passenger vehicle, enter the miles driven.
Materials Description	Enter the description(s) of the materials used for this activity.
Units	Enter the number of individual units of material used. For materials used from inventory, ensure that a chit or charge tag is issued for the materials.
Stock	Check this box if the materials used were taken from on-hand inventory.
Unit Cost	This data field may be filled out later by staff, rather than by field crews, who may not have access to this information.
Total Cost	This data field may be filled out later by staff rather than by field crews, who may not have access to this information.
Vendor Name	Enter the vendor's name
P.O. #	This data field may be filled out later by staff rather than by field crews, who may not have access to this information.
Purpose	This box refers to Special Fees, such as dump charges or road tolls.
Receipt #	Enter the receipt number and take a photo of the receipt in case the original is lost. An excellent app for this is Turbo Scan. With a smart phone and the Turbo Scan app, the employee can take a photo of the receipt or other document and email it to themselves or to a "central receipts" electronic library.
Cost	Enter the charges pertaining to the receipt(s).
Name of employee completing form; please print	Enter the name of the employee completing the form.
Phone #	Enter that employee's phone number, email, or both.
3DC[21] Use Only Dept	The 3DC will enter the name of the department which will be performing the Quality Control audit of the daily work reports.
3DC Use Only Log Number	The 3DC employee will enter the log number, if any.
Preparer's Signature	This is where the person who completes the form will sign their name. Each and every form must be signed.

(*Continued*)

Table 5.7 (Continued)

City of - Disaster Field Unit - Incident Work Report (LEM - 1)	Title
3DC Name	The 3DC person will enter their name when checking the for accuracy and completeness.
3DC Phone #	The 3DC person will enter their phone number.
3DC Signature	The 3DC person will sign the form upon completion of the Quality Control audit.
Originator: All Field Personnel or Supervisors	Note on form distribution.
Routing: Send forms to the Finance Section of the EOC or the Departmental Emergency Operations Center (DOC) each day. Attach any receipts or invoices.	
A separate form should be filled out for each different work location. All personnel, equipment, supplies, materials, and fees should be accounted for.	Note on form use.

"Scary Form" Shortcuts

The local agency field crews should create a new set of documents for each specific site where they perform disaster-related work and for different categories of work performed at the same site. They should not attempt to cram an entire day's work of responding to disaster incidents on a single form. Each work site should have new paperwork. This may be very important later when trying to summarize the costs on a project-by-project basis.

FEMA requires that we specify minutes and hours worked at each individual incident or work site. FEMA does not allow an allocation of time or other costs based on percentages or other estimates.

One way to reduce the amount of time spent filling out time reporting, whether using the "Scary Form" or other type of documentation, is to enter the day's "standard" data, such as the employee's names, their job titles, and the equipment they use, and then make multiple photocopies of these semi-filled out forms. Then at each new site, the employee or crew leader takes a fresh photocopy of the form and enters the site-specific information regarding type of problem, length of time, materials used, etc.

For local agencies with multiple field departments or divisions, we recommend color-coding the forms so that all light orange forms are from Public Works, light green forms are from Parks and Recreation, and so on. Use caution and avoid certain shades of colored papers which may not photocopy very well.

Affirmative Paperwork Quality Control

The City of Torrance, CA, developed a concept called the "3DC" or "Department Disaster Document Coordinator." With this concept, at the end of each shift or end of each day, an employee from the department doing the work will quality check the paperwork turned in. If there are any errors or omissions, then the 3DC' will return the incorrect forms to the employee or crew leader who prepared the form to make the necessary changes before the form is accepted and approved.

Using the 3DC concept and properly completing the "Scary Form" or other work tracking document(s), the FEMA forms for tracking labor, equipment, and materials can be filled out weeks or even months later, because all the critical data has already been captured, properly documented, and approved by the 3DC. The City of Torrance had at least two 3DCs in each department, and periodically provided them with training.

There will be much more about what constitutes proper documentation in the following chapters.

Notes

1 DHS-OIG Audit 19–12, FEMA Should Recover $3,061,819 in Grant Funds Awarded to Jackson County, Florida, December 4, 2019, p. 2.
2 Ibid.
3 Ibid, p. 6.
4 Ibid.
5 Ibid.
6 Ibid.
7 Ibid, p. 7.
8 See Form 4 in the Appendix.
9 See Form 5 in the Appendix.
10 See Form 6 in the Appendix.
11 See Form 7 in the Appendix.
12 See Form 8 in the Appendix.
13 See Form 9 in the Appendix.
14 There are two reasons for describing the work done as a temporary measure. 1) If the work is done as a temporary or emergency repair, then the work is eligible, and later the permanent work to properly redo the work, including any applicable codes and standards upgrades, will also be eligible. 2) If the work is done by another agency's mutual aid forces, then by definition the work must be of a temporary nature, as mutual aid forces are prohibited from performing any Category C through G permanent work.
15 If an employee is working on a temporary or "acting" capacity and is receiving a higher rate of pay and benefits, this pay "bump" must be explained and supported with the proper documentation.
16 Search FEMA.gov for "Schedule of Equipment Rates. Be sure to get the most current version of this list."
17 There are two reasons for describing the work done as a temporary measure. 1) If the work is done as a temporary or emergency repair, then the work is eligible, and later the permanent work to properly redo the work, including any applicable codes and standards upgrades, will also be eligible. 2) If the work is done by another agency's mutual aid forces, then by definition the work must be of a temporary nature, as mutual aid forces are prohibited from performing any Category C through G permanent work.
18 See Example 66 in the Appendix.
19 Both FEMA and the Department of Homeland Security auditors frequently "comparison shop" to determine if costs are reasonable.
20 There are two reasons for describing the work done as a temporary measure. 1) If the work is done as a temporary or emergency repair, then the work is eligible, and later the permanent work to properly

Type of Equipment	First, enter the 4-digit code from the FEMA Equipment Rate Sheet, followed by the description provided on the Rate Sheet.
Dates & Hours Used	Enter the date the rented equipment is used and the total hours for each date.
Rate Per Hour, w Opr (Operator)	Typically, use the equipment daily rental rate, unless the equipment is rented for three or more days, in which case the weekly rate will apply. If a piece of equipment is used for three weeks or more, continuously, then the monthly equipment rental rate should be used. These are the typical rental rates applied in the rental industry. The rental rate may also include a charge for fuel. In this case, the equipment is rented "wet." If the vendor does not provide the fuel, the equipment is rented "dry." Annotate the form to indicate whether the equipment is rented "wet," since this will increase the rental rate.

Rate Per Hour, w/o Opr (Operator)	Typically, use the equipment daily rental rate, unless the equipment is rented for three or more days, in which case the weekly rate will apply. If a piece of equipment is used for three weeks or more, continuously, then the monthly equipment rental rate should be used. These are the typical rental rates applied in the rental industry. The rental rate may also include a charge for fuel. In this case, the equipment is rented "wet." If the vendor does not provide the fuel, the equipment is rented "dry." Annotate the form to indicate whether the equipment is rented "wet," since this will increase the rental rate.
Total Cost	Enter the total cost from the invoice for each separate piece of equipment.
Vendor	Enter the vendor's name.
Invoice Number	Enter the invoice number.

redo the work, including any applicable codes and standards upgrades, will also be eligible. 2) If the work is done by another agency's mutual aid forces, then by definition the work must be of a temporary nature, as mutual aid forces are prohibited from performing any Category C through G permanent work.

21 3DC stands for Department Disaster Document Coordinator.

6 Work Activity Documentation and Work Process Flow

Disaster Realities, Actual and Augmented

When a disaster strikes, there are different and distinct realities in play, although in the heat of the moment they may not be recognized as such.

One reality is those tasks like public safety, where the agency staff rescue people and save lives and protect property much as they do any other day of the year, except that during the disaster the public safety staff is working harder, faster, and much longer hours than they normally do, and under a great deal of stress. Fortunately, most public safety employees have some experience in documenting their time during disasters.

A second reality is that the local agency finds itself having to do things that it has never before or seldom done, i.e., providing congregate sheltering, mass feeding, pet care and rescue, debris management, etc., with staff that has little experience performing those tasks, and are working under a great deal of stress throughout the long hours of the emergency. Unfortunately many, if not most, local government employees do not have experience in how to properly track their time and other costs during a disaster.

Yet one more reality is that the local agency staff must document all their disaster response activities, whether those activities are familiar or not, to a degree which they seldom if ever had to do before the disaster struck.

The staff must create documentation proving that the work was done as a direct result of the disaster, the costs were reasonable, and all was done in compliance with Federal regulations, which they often don't know exist. This is especially true for Federal procurement requirements. The attention to detail for all this recordkeeping is usually quite beyond their previous experiences in local government.

A common perception of disaster is that it is an emergency response activity, with intense media, covering a very short time frame. The true reality of a disaster is that most of the post-response-phase disaster work is a stifling bureaucratic process with virtually no media coverage, except when there are negative audit findings.

This chapter is broken up into sections, to deal with the different types of information needed to initiate and fulfill the needs of the disaster cost recovery process. For each of these different information categories and needs, the local agency Financial Officer, and by extension the disaster cost recovery team, will be involved with collection, processing, and sharing of the different types of information.

The first category of information, which is needed immediately, is the damage assessments. The damage assessments themselves will be carried out by different departments.

DOI: 10.4324/9781003487869-8

Variable Solutions

This book cannot prescribe a single one-size-fits-all approach or form for tracking much of the information FEMA requires for the submission and completion of Project Worksheets. Every government agency is unique in some regard, particularly how they are organized, the services which they do or don't provide, and those state laws affecting jurisdictions differently in every state. The same is also true for tribal nations, U.S. territories, and private non-profit agencies. Some small agencies may have only a few employees and a very informal work culture; larger agencies have hundreds or even thousands of employees and highly structured and formalized operations.

Unfortunately, the regulations governing the provision of FEMA's Public Assistance program do not provide any accommodation for these sometimes-great differences between agencies. Throughout this book, I will provide suggested policies, forms, and best practices to help increase the likelihood of a successful disaster cost recovery process. However, each agency will have to determine its own best approach after familiarizing themselves with the Federal requirements and suggested forms and practices.

Safety Assessments versus Damage Assessments

There is a very important distinction between "Safety Assessments" and "Damage Assessments." Safety Assessments, those inspections made to determine if a facility, road, or utility is safe to occupy or use, are FEMA-eligible for reimbursement.

Damage Assessments, those inspections made to determine what will be the cost to clean up, repair, or reconstruct a facility, road, or utility, are NOT FEMA-eligible for reimbursement.

Therefore, the local inspectors must be educated in how to properly document their time when making these inspections.

If an inspector logs all their time as "Damage Assessment," their time may be determined to be ineligible, even if some or all of their work was actually Safety Assessments.

Conversely, if the inspector logs all their time as "Safety Assessment" but in fact they were performing Damage Assessments some or all of the time, then their time may be ineligible.

If the inspector performs a Safety Assessment, then their time should be so logged. If, on the other hand, they were doing Damage Assessment, then their logs should reflect that as well.

The inspector's time for Damage Assessments and Safety Assessments must be logged using hours and minutes. FEMA will not allow us to use a percentage estimate, i.e., 33% of the time was for safety assessment and 67% was for damage assessment.

In this book, we may use the term "Damage Assessment" although some of the time, the work being done will actually be a "Safety Assessment."

The first category of damage assessment is to determine the damages to agency-owned facilities. This damage assessment may be carried out by the Facilities Department, or the Building and Safety Department. This is a high priority insofar as the local agency needs its facilities in order to carry out its disaster response missions.

Secondary to these inspections are the inspections of other public agency facilities, such as water districts, schools, and other facilities which may also serve the various disaster needs.

Following the government facilities inspections, the Building and Safety inspectors will move on to private property, both residential and commercial.

For both government facilities and private property, some thought must be given to how these inspections will be prioritized.

Building Occupancy Resumption Planning (BORP)

When I worked in San Francisco, the Building & Safety Department had worked out a system for prioritizing which facilities, both public and private, would be inspected first.

In the rating system for public buildings, the Building & Safety Department evaluated each City-owned building to determine how many disaster response-related activities were housed in each building. The eight-story office building at One South Van Ness was the highest-rated building, higher rated than City Hall itself, because it had more disaster-related functions than City Hall. Therefore, One South Van Ness is first in line to be inspected.

On the private property side, those residential buildings with the lowest amount of damage, which could be returned to full residential occupancy at the earliest possible date, received the highest priority for inspections.

Depending on the nature and extent of the damages caused by disaster, the BORP priorities may change. In San Francisco, their number one threat is a catastrophic earthquake, and so that was their primary threat criteria.

Slow and Inaccurate Damage Assessments Will Delay Federal Assistance

I performed an analysis of all the disasters which were Presidentially declared in 2020 and 2021. During those 104 weeks, the President declared a disaster 105 times. The average time between the onset of the respective disaster and the issuance of the Presidential disaster declaration was 62 days. The lowest time delay was one day, and the greatest time delay in this period was 185 days.

I attribute this average delay, in part, to ineffective and delayed damage assessments. If the local agencies cannot demonstrate that there is enough damage to meet the Federal thresholds for a Presidential disaster declaration, then one will not be issued.

Therefore, it is incumbent upon the local agencies to rapidly ramp up their damage assessment processes to initiate the disaster cost recovery process. For this to happen, there needs to be a plan and process in place before the disaster hits.

Damage Assessment Is an Iterative Process

Often, the damage assessment process cannot be completed in a single inspection. Early in the disaster, non-registered engineers or non-licensed Building and Safety personnel may visit sites and report that the facility was damaged.

However, to get a more detailed picture of the full nature and extent of the damage done, registered civil engineers, licensed architects, and/or licensed building and safety inspectors will have to visit the site to make a detailed report, including photographs, of the nature and extent of the damages. In some cases, it may take weeks or months to perform a complete inspection to determine the full extent of the damage, including often-hidden damages that won't become evident until repair or reconstruction begins.

Update Damage Assessment Information on a Regular Basis

Once the process of conducting safety and damage assessments has begun, it is important to regularly update any changes in the status of properties that were already inspected.

Years ago, a city with which I worked had a major explosion in a residential neighborhood. An empty home had been tented for termite fumigation and filled with gas. However, during the tenting process the natural gas line was broken, and the tent filled up with the explosive natural gas. Something triggered an explosion, and the home was completely destroyed. Other adjacent homes had damage ranging from serious structural damage to merely cosmetic damage and broken windows.

I visited the scene and witnessed firsthand the complete destruction of what had been a good-sized private home. However, when I later visited the EOC, which had been activated as though this were a disaster of much greater magnitude, I noticed that the posted report of the home in question listed the home as "damaged." It went far beyond damage; it no longer existed, except as rubble. Obviously, the initial damage report, although in error, had not been corrected. In a major disaster, this oversight could lead to a gross undercounting of the total dollar value of the damage.

Disaster Damage – Missing in Action

Some years later, during the response to the Napa Earthquake of 2014, the water department of the city where I was working as a disaster cost recovery volunteer had a water main break posted at an address of 1800 Oak Street.

However, the actual water main break was located 1½ blocks away. This error started because the convalescent home at 1800 Oak Street had reported the lack of water pressure at 4:30 on the morning of the earthquake.

The people in the EOC and the water department did not catch this error until we went to look for the damage site and could not locate it.

We started out the day with a list of over 50 reported water main breaks, but after we failed to find even one of the first seven pipe breaks, we returned to City Hall for a meeting with the Public Works Director to see what was going on. He insisted that the pipe breaks really did exist, and had us revisit the list, this time with the supervisor who was at many of the sites.

Every one of the first seven breaks we tried to find had been mislocated or misreported, which would have caused the City a serious problem if the breaks could not be easily located during the Preliminary Damage Assessment or PDA.

If FEMA and the state cannot find the reported damage, this goes very badly for the local agency, and FEMA could easily delete unlocated sites from the list of reported damages. FEMA will not waste time looking for damage if our recordkeeping is inaccurate or erroneous.

So, the damage assessment process is an iterative process which also requires continual updating as events unfold and the damage data is enhanced and clarified.

Furthermore, for facilities where the utilities have failed, it may not be possible to determine whether there was damage to the electrical system, the plumbing system, elevators, and other building components until the utilities have been restored, possibly days or weeks later.

Additionally, some specialized facilities such as hospitals or schools may need to be checked by special inspectors authorized by the respective level of government which has jurisdiction.

So, we have damage assessments of improved property (property which has been built upon) as one important element of a comprehensive damage assessment.

A second and distinct element of damage assessment is the roads, highways, and bridges/tunnels network.

Damage inspections of the transportation infrastructure, roads, bridges, tunnels, etc., will be performed by road maintenance personnel and/or registered civil engineers.

In some cases, Federal, state, or county roads will have to be inspected by employees of the agency that "owns" a road or bridge. Although the local agency is aware of the damage, it does not have the authorization to make the definitive damage assessment for the record. FEMA plays very close attention to who has the legal responsibility for road repair. In this audit case,[1] the county had an informal decades-long agreement with its townships to repair the township roads, because the small townships did not have the capacity to do so for themselves. However, there was no documentation to substantiate this arrangement and make it an official policy which FEMA could otherwise honor.

Tallying All the Damage

Another element of the comprehensive damage assessment process is all the facilities and property of all special districts and eligible private non-profit agencies within a city or county. Under the U.S. system, cities are responsible for collecting and reporting ALL disaster damage, even though the city itself may not be responsible for repairing the damage. Similarly, counties are responsible for tracking and reporting all disaster damage within the county borders, even without the legal responsibility for making the repairs.

Although a particular facility or component of the local infrastructure may be the responsibility of some higher or different level of government, it is the responsibility of the city or county to track the costs related to the damage of non-owned facilities and infrastructure. A Presidential disaster declaration requires states to meet a per-capita threshold of damage from a disaster. Each county that is covered by a Presidential disaster declaration must also meet a higher per-capita threshold of disaster damage. These per-capita indicators typically are adjusted upward based on the consumer price index (CPI) on an annual basis.[2]

Thus, even if a state meets its per-capita threshold, each county covered by the Presidential disaster declaration must also meet its respective per-capita threshold. To ensure that the county is covered by the declaration, it must collect ALL disaster damage from the private sector, special districts, and eligible private non-profits.

Tracking All Sub-Agencies' Damage

A highly recommended practice for cities and counties is to maintain a list of all the special districts and eligible private non-profits within its jurisdiction.

For example, various special districts and private non-profits may report their damages to their headquarters, which may be in another city or county, or to the county or state Board of Education. However, that higher authority may not (and probably won't) report the damages back to the city or county where the damaged facility is located.

Disaster Tunnel Vision

It is a near-universal phenomena that government officials and staff experiencing a disaster will often focus on relatively few critical problems and will often fail to see the much larger composite picture. People will hunker down to solve their most pressing problems, even when there are more significant, longer-term problems waiting just around the proverbial corner. In these cases, the personnel at special districts or private non-profits will often fail to report damage estimates to a higher level of government, i.e., the city or county in which they are located. A school district with individual schools in multiple cities or towns will usually not think to report their damages to each respective city or county where their campuses are located.

This is also a complicating factor for some larger cities. For instance, Denver, Colorado and Houston, Texas both reside in multiple counties. Therefore, these cities must each report their respective disaster damage to the county in which the damaged facility lies. Unless they are a city and county combination, cities do not receive disaster declarations; only the county in which they are located does.

So in a hypothetical disaster, damages to City of Houston facilities located in Harris County, TX could be eligible, while City of Houston facilities located in Fort Bend County might not be eligible because Harris County met its per-capita threshold while Fort Bend County did not meet its threshold, or vice versa.

The best practice is to have the hub city or county affirmatively contact all special districts and eligible private non-profits to determine if they had any disaster damage. It would be at least unusual for one of these "child" districts or non-profits to have the presence of mind to contact their respective city or county to advise them of their damages.

Debris Management

A third element of damage assessment is debris management. Disasters typically leave in their wake thousands or even millions of cubic yards of debris. Debris removal is a major component of disaster recovery. There likely will be debris on public lands and on private property. These are dealt with separately and given more attention in Chapter 15: Debris Monitoring and Debris Management.

Financial Damage Assessment

The fourth element of damage assessment is the financial impact on the local agency's revenue streams. Disasters disrupt the normal flow of community life. The day-to-day revenue streams are often affected by the disaster, and it may be weeks, months, or in severe cases years before the revenue streams return to something approaching "normal."

In some cases, there are marked shifts in revenue. In a disaster-affected community where tourism was a significant income stream, tourism will wither for a time. But the loss of tourism dollars may be partially supplanted by a marked increase in sales taxes as people spend money to repair and replace their disaster losses.

All of this may factor into the financial distress or well-being of a disaster-affected community, and in some cases it may be a significant factor in determining whether the jurisdiction will receive a Presidential disaster declaration.

No Reimbursement for Lost Revenue

FEMA never reimburses for lost revenue, regardless of the source. Similarly, FEMA does not reimburse for increased operational expenses. If a local agency has an enterprise function, such as a water utility, port, or airport, lost revenue is simply gone and not an eligible cost.

Private Utility Damage

A fifth element consists of damage to the private utilities infrastructure, which may affect electrical power, water, natural gas, wastewater, storm drains, and communications and internet services. If these utilities are investor-owned (privately held), the local agency has no responsibility for repairing or maintaining them and cannot request FEMA funding to repair the damages. However, these losses still need to be counted as a part of the totality of disaster damage, even though the utility and its rate payers will have to pay for the necessary repairs.

So far, we have not discussed "Work Documentation and Work Process Flow." But as you can see, the work process flow for each of these various disaster damage elements, i.e., buildings versus roads, etc., could vary within a single agency, to say nothing of differences between two or more differing but similar agencies.

Moving Forward

It is seldom if ever the responsibility of the financial officials within local government to develop a disaster damage assessment program for any of the elements previously discussed. However, the financial chickens will absolutely come home to roost outside the finance director's office when such plans are not in place.

A Presidential disaster declaration, as well as FEMA funding, may be delayed because of the lack of complete damage information from both the agency itself, and possibly any "child" agencies within the "parent" agency's jurisdiction. Or worse, the county and all agencies within the county may fail to qualify for the Presidential disaster declaration because of "insufficient" damages being reported below the county's per-capita damage threshold.

Damage Assessment Planning Challenges

First of all, building inspections will have different requirements than those of the transportation infrastructure. And even within the rubric of the transportation infrastructure, where we have roads and highways, free-standing buses, and light and heavy rail systems, etc., there will be mixed approaches for each system which contain some similarities in their data, with notable differences also present.

Therefore, each different department and/or division within the local agency must develop its own damage assessment protocols to provide sufficient damage data in the most expeditious manner possible. However, it is important for the local agency to have a consolidated plan and process to tabulate all the damage assessments from the various departments.

According to James Featherstone, former head of the Los Angeles City Emergency Preparedness Division, following the Northridge Earthquake in 1994 the City received 40 damage reports in 40 different formats, each from a different department.

This no-format damage reporting raises several questions:

1) Did we ensure that we got damage reports from every department?
2) How can we rapidly collate similar damages from the different departments?
3) When a department updates its damage estimate, how can we roll the added information easily into the existing list of damages without incurring duplicate information?

Later in the book, in Chapter 20, we will look at damage assessment reporting in greater detail. In that chapter, I will provide an Excel-based program for tracking and consolidating damage reports from both city/county departments, special districts, and private non-profit organizations.

For the post-disaster safety inspections to be considered FEMA-eligible, the inspectors must be either registered architects or civil engineers, or licensed building inspectors. FEMA can deny the cost of safety assessments performed by non-licensed or non-registered workers, whether they're agency employees or Mutual Aid forces.

Inspection Plans and Inspection Reports

With increasing frequency, FEMA is demanding the submission of both written inspection plans and written inspection reports for facilities, including buildings, transportation, and public utility infrastructures, before awarding eligibility for damaged facilities.

Local government-owned facilities and infrastructure elements are generally FEMA-eligible for Public Assistance, but when there is evidence of deferred maintenance and/or pre-existing damage, FEMA may deny eligibility for the repair work.

For instance, "alligatored" pavement is typically ineligible for FEMA funding because the cracked pavement has had maintenance deferred, even if the road is otherwise eligible, meaning that it is not a Federal Aid road. Federal Aid roads are those roads and highways which were built or are maintained in whole or in part with Federal Highway Administration funds. FEMA does not provide funding for Federal Aid roads, even if and when, the Federal Highway Administration has no Emergency Relief Funds. Therefore, it is very important for the local Roads and Highways Department to have a current list with the status of its roads and streets.

In the same manner, the roof of a building should be inspected at least annually, typically before the "threat season," i.e., in the spring if the agency is subject to hurricanes, or the fall if the agency typically has heavy winter rains or snow, etc.

Inspection Plans

Each local agency and the departments within the agency must have a program of regular inspection to be able to prove to FEMA that prior to the disaster, the facilities were in good working order and properly maintained.

This does not mean that all defects or deterioration must be fixed immediately in order for the facility to be eligible. However, the local agency must be able to show that it has a maintenance budget, and repairs are made according to a budgeted plan on a regular basis.

There are some excellent inspection plan forms available on the internet.[3] There is also a sample Annual Building Inspection Checklist in the Appendix, Form 11. For smaller jurisdictions, good inspection forms for a variety of local agency assets, including buildings, roads, and utilities, may be available from either the local county or the respective state. The advantage of using these forms from nearby local agencies is that much of the work has already been done to put the form together, and most likely these same forms will reflect the hazards most likely to affect the local agency.

The important thing is to have an inspection form and an inspection plan and to use it regularly on at least an annual basis or a pre-disaster seasonal basis.

Ineligible Flood Damage

Following the winter storms in California in 2017/2018, I worked with a large wholesale water agency. They believed that due to the very heavy rains, three of their water storage dams had large amounts of sediment deposited in them, which reduced their overall capacity. They wanted to request Federal assistance to dredge the dams. However, the last time the agency had done a bathymetric survey to determine the level of pre-storm sedimentation was over a dozen years prior to the current storm. This made it doubtful that FEMA would approve any dredging work, since there was no recent documentation to prove any amount of sedimentation was deposited by those winter storms.

Pre-Disaster Photo Documentation

Photographs will also play a key role in the regular inspection process. It's difficult to argue with an in-focus photograph which clearly shows the damaged facility before the disaster struck. To paraphrase the proverb, "A picture is worth $10,000" . . . or more.

Some Good News

When a property owner files a claim for storm damage to a roof, the insurance companies will pro-rate the life of the roof, which results in a reduced payout of the claim. If a structure has a roof built and guaranteed for a life of 20 years and the roof is damaged in year 10 of the projected 20-year life, the insurer will typically pay for one half of the roof replacement cost.

With FEMA, however, the full cost of the roof will be otherwise eligible if the local agency can prove that the roof was in good repair and condition prior to the storm.

However, the roof will only be eligible if the local agency can prove, with documentation including photographs, that the cause of the roof failure was directly due to the storm.

The Dark Side of a Leaky Roof

Be careful of having more than one roof inspection following a damaging event, if the first inspection does not meet the needs of the local agency. In one second appeals case,[4] the eligible entity had three inspections of the same roof. FEMA then had the opportunity to pick and choose among the three inspections, resulting in a denial of funding of $1,315,455.00.

This topic, relating to damage assessments and eligibility, will be covered in greater detail in coming chapters.

Introducing the Role of the Emergency Operations Center for Disaster Cost Recovery

Typically, agencies of various sizes and shapes will have an Emergency Operations Center (or EOC) to manage the sometimes-vast array of incidents and response activities. But care should be taken not to overload the EOC and assign recordkeeping functions that are better taken care of at the departmental level. The flow chart "Sample Cost Recovery Process Flow Chart for Field Operations" shows that there are numerous cost centers for eligible activities and expenses to track properly to ensure their reimbursement. And these tracking requirements will be somewhat different for the various facets of the disaster response and recovery work, with some common elements among all activities that need to be tracked.

It is important to recognize that this flow chart may be different for different departments, and possibly within activities within a single department. Visualizing both these differences and similarities will help clarify the documentation process

Some agencies try to track all field response activities in the EOC. However, this is ill-advised because: 1) The EOC isn't familiar with all the nuances of tracking field activities like the department would be; 2) The EOC will most likely shut down within a few days or a couple of weeks, which will require the transfer of all the records of field activities back to their respective departments; 3) If the departments have a paperwork quality control function,[5] it will make the job of the quality control staff more difficult if the physical records are in the EOC instead of the respective departments.

The EOC should focus on the big-picture agenda and trust the detailed recordkeeping to each department. In this chart, the solid lines represent direct tracking of information, while the broken lines represent the related procurements for the field activities.

If the local agency is a larger city/county/special district, it may be advisable to establish a Department Operations Center (or DOC) for some of the more involved departments that have numerous field activities. In these instances, tracking would be appropriately done at the department level and reported in a daily summary of activities, hours worked, and costs incurred to the EOC.

We're on Our Own Much of the Time

FEMA has very detailed regulations with documentation requirements that often are far beyond the normal administrative procedures of many local governments and non-profit agencies.

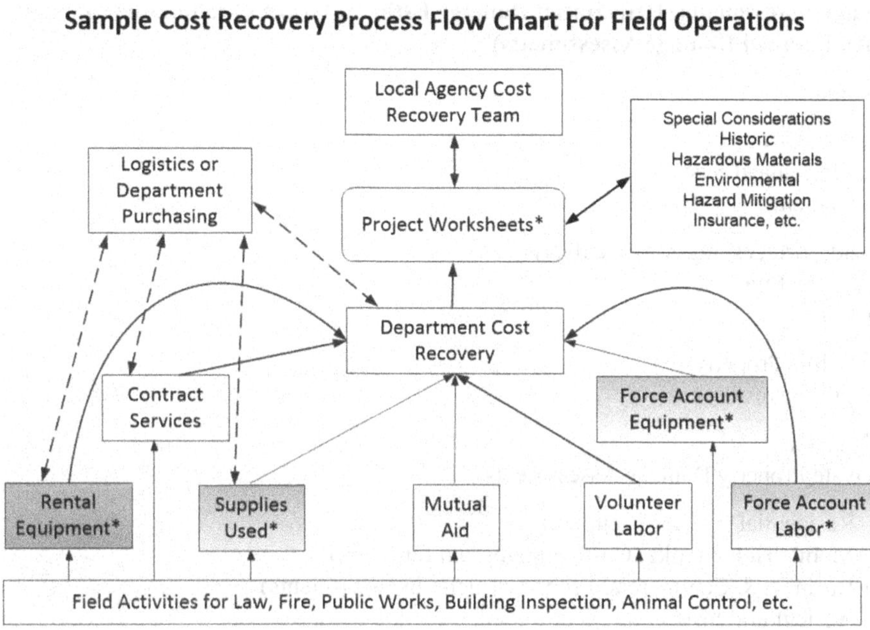

Sample Cost Recovery Process Flow Chart For Field Operations

Figure 6.1 Sample Relationship Chart For Field Response Cost Tracking.

The good news is that FEMA does not specify how we comply with these requirements, only that we *do* comply with them. The bad news is that FEMA does not specify how we comply with these requirements, only that we *do* comply with them. In many cases, we are truly left to our own devices.

The FEMA forms are not necessarily difficult to use if you are familiar with them. But most people are not.

That said, I have seen many forms filled out so badly that the net value of costs requested to be reimbursed is zero dollars. We will get into the nitty-gritty details of all this in the following chapters.

Types of Disaster Information Which Need to Be Collected, Organized, and Managed

Depending on the type and scope of the disaster, this list may not be all-inclusive:

1) **Administrative Information**

    a. Disaster proclamations and declaration

    b. Agency budget and current monthly budget report

    c. Insurance policies, including the loss adjuster's reports

    d. Pre-emptive disaster policies (See Chapters 2 and 3)

    e. Labor bargaining unit agreements

    f. Purchasing policy (compliant with Title 2 of the Code of Federal Regulations, Part 200)

    g. Mutual Aid agreements (if any)

    h. Articles of agency incorporation

    i. Tax ruling letter if a non-profit agency

2) **Damage Assessments (IDE (Initial Damage Estimate), PDA (Preliminary Damage Assessment), Detailed Damage Assessments)**

   a. Buildings

      i. Structures
      ii. Mechanical Systems
      iii. Contents

   b. Roads, bridges, highways, culverts
   c. Infrastructure
   d. Debris

      i. Public Property
      ii. Private residences

   e. Financial
   f. Private Property Damage Assessments

      i. Residential (Owner-occupied)
      ii. Mobile Home Parks (Co-operatives and for-profit)
      iii. Business & Commercial Property (including apartments)
      iv. Agricultural losses

3) **Response Costs**

   a. Labor, Equipment, & Materials
   b. Small contracts
   c. Survivor's Services

      i. Evacuation/re-entry
      ii. Sheltering
      iii. Mass Feeding
      iv. Animal Control/Pet rescue & sheltering

4) **List of Projects/Damage Inventory** sorted by FEMA Categories:

   a. FEMA-eligible work
   b. Other Federal Agency-covered work:

      i. Federal Highway Administration (FHWA)
      ii. Federal Transit Administration (FTA)
      iii. U.S. Army Corps of Engineers (USACE)
      iv. U.S. Department of Agriculture (NRCS)
      v. Housing and Urban Development (HUD – CDBG)
      vi. Others

5) **Project Worksheets**

   a. Small Projects
   b. Large Projects
   c. Improved Projects
   d. Alternate Projects
   e. Mitigation
   f. Special Considerations

Following is a brief description of the information needed and, when available, the form(s) which may be used to document the information. Some of the forms will be official FEMA forms; there may be other forms which are required by your respective state. Also included in some cases are forms I have developed over the years, which may be helpful in tracking and managing the required information. Much more detail will follow in the ensuing chapters.

Currently, FEMA has an online computer portal where all the documents related to the disaster and each individual Project Worksheet are uploaded.

Administrative Information

- Disaster Proclamations & Declaration (Each of the proclamations and the declaration should be maintained in the main disaster information file AND in each individual Project Worksheet file when the Project Worksheets are written)
- Agency Budget and Current Monthly Budget Report (FEMA expects to see the local agency budgets and financial statements as part of the eligibility determination process)
- Insurance Policies (FEMA requires the agency to submit its insurance policies (if any) to determine what amount of insurance is available for all projects)

Flood insurance is required in certain parts of the country, and the applicability of having flood insurance may be determined by reviewing the Special Flood Hazard Maps published by FEMA. More on this in the chapter on insurance.

- Pre-Emptive Disaster Policies (See Chapters 2 and 3): There are a number of best practice policies which should be in place to maximize the disaster cost recovery; among others, these include policies for overtime labor, disaster feeding for employees, receiving donations, etc. More on this in Chapters 2 and 3.
- Labor Bargaining Unit Agreements (FEMA will reimburse both hourly wages and fringe benefits. Therefore, we must document the pay scales and authorized fringe benefits on every Project Worksheet where local agency staff work. This may include some of those projects which are done entirely by contract, insofar as the agency may want to claim and qualify for Direct Administrative Costs or DAC)
- Purchasing Policy (Far and away the single greatest reason for denial of funding or partial deobligation of funding is failure at the local level to strictly follow the Federal procurement requirements as specified in Title 2 of the Code of Federal Regulations, Part 200 (2 CFR, Part 200). Local agencies must follow their own purchasing regulations AND those of 2 CFR, Part 200, whichever are more restrictive. This also includes following those state purchasing requirements where they exist at the local level.)
- Mutual Aid Agreements (if any) (If during the disaster response the local agency makes use of Mutual Aid agreements for debris clearance or "emergency protective measures," those costs must be for appropriate activities and properly documented. Generally, both fire and law enforcement agencies do a good job of documentation. However, non-public safety staff (animal control, public works, etc.) who seldom if ever go on Mutual Aid probably will not be familiar with these requirements.)
- Articles of Agency Incorporation (FEMA regulations require that each agency document that it is in fact a government agency by providing its articles of incorporation in its respective state. If the agency is a private non-profit agency, it must also provide an Internal Revenue Service letter ruling establishing it as a tax-exempt, non-profit agency.)

6) **Damage Assessments** (IDE, PDA, Detailed)

Damage Assessment is a multi-stage process which will likely evolve over days and weeks. In some cases, damage may not be apparent for months, which can be a serious problem and will be discussed in Chapters 19 and 20.

The first phase of the damage assessment process will begin almost immediately, depending on the type and severity of the disaster. For purposes of this discussion, disasters are generally one of two types: 1) rapid-onset, no-notice events, such as a tornado, an earthquake, a transportation accident, or explosion; 2) the slow-onset, advance-notice event, such as a hurricane, severe winter storm, or downriver flooding. Neither is welcome in the community, but the slow-onset events at least give the local jurisdiction some time to prepare.

In either case, the first level of damage assessment is sometimes referred to as the Initial Damage Estimate (IDE), which also may be referred to as the "Windshield Survey." In this activity, local law enforcement and firefighters will drive pre-described routes to check the most critical facilities within the local agency.

Fire and law will check city/county facilities, particularly hospitals, fire stations, police stations, critical infrastructure, i.e., major roads and bridges, major utility facilities, and any major industrial facilities which could pose a serious threat to life safety and public health if the facility is damaged.

During this first critical phase of the damage assessment, typically both fire and law enforcement will not respond to individual incidents regardless of the severity, until the initial survey is complete and local officials have a handle on the scope and severity of the disaster. Both the Preliminary Damage Assessment (PDA) and the detailed damage assessments will follow, often by at least several days, until local officials believe they have full knowledge of the situation, which incidents are the most pressing of the problems, and which present the greatest threats to life safety, public health, and improved property, generally in that order of importance.

Typically, inspectors with different areas of expertise will make the inspections based upon the nature of the facilities or infrastructure. Some facilities will require multiple inspections, depending on the disaster and kinds of damage done.

Building inspections should be prioritized based on the needs of the community and how those buildings will support the disaster response and recovery.

*   Structures may be public buildings, owner-occupied homes, multi-family housing, and commercial and industrial buildings. Initially, buildings are inspected to determine if they are safe to enter and be safely occupied.
*   Mechanical systems in buildings may be evaluated during the safety inspection if the utilities are fully functional. However, if one or more of the utilities is off-line, then another inspection will have to be made to determine if the building systems are fully functional or not.
*   Contents of a building may also need to be inspected for potential threats. A high school or college may have laboratories with hazardous materials. Hospitals have a great deal of expensive medical testing and treatment equipment, which:

    1) may be damaged and dangerous or ineffective to use; 2) are very costly and in need of replacement. In these specialized instances, engineers or technical specialists may be the only persons qualified to determine the safety of the equipment in the facility. Building inspectors can determine if the structure is safe to use, but other serious hazards may be present which require other special expertise.

    *   Roads, bridges, and highways will have to be inspected by registered civil engineers when damage is observed or suspected.

In California and other earthquake-prone regions, it should be a standard practice immediately following a major earthquake, when damage is suspected, for all bridges to be closed pending a safety inspection.

When there is ground movement, a landslide or subsidence, the inspections will only be the first step, as a geo-technical evaluation will have to be done to determine how extensively the under-pinning ground may be damaged. FEMA may pay for damage done to structures or infrastructure, but generally it will not pay to restore the land to its prior condition.

- Infrastructure consisting of roads, bridges, etc., and publicly owned utilities are generally eligible, unless the roads or bridges are part of the Federal highway system or fall under the purview of another Federal agency.

  - Debris of all types is typically eligible for Federal funding, so long as it is on public property.

    - Public Property includes publicly owned land and roadways; however, unimproved or raw land is not generally eligible. Exceptions have been made for those instances where there is biological contamination, i.e., animal carcasses.
    - Private Residences with debris are only eligible for cleanup and debris removal when FEMA specifically authorizes the cleanup in writing. Property owners are responsible for moving the debris on their property to the public right-of-way for pickup and hauling.

  - A financial damage assessment at the local level is important to provide local officials with a comprehensive financial analysis of the total damages done to the community and each of its segments, i.e., public facilities, private residences, multi-family dwellings, businesses, and industries. Without integrating a financial damage assessment with the local agency's projected post-disaster revenue streams, it will be difficult to plan and prioritize the disaster recovery effectively.
  - Private Property Damage Assessments are an initial part of the local agency's responsibility for disaster response. No other agency is responsible for preparing the damage estimate for privately owned homes, multi-family housing, business, and industry. Without this information, the Presidential disaster declaration will likely not include any provisions for Individual Assistance (IA), FEMA's aid for private citizens, whether homeowner or renter. Without damage information tallying the losses for business and industry, there will probably not be access to Federal Small Business Administration loans. For both Individual Assistance and Small Business Administration loans, the property owner is responsible for filing their claim for damages directly with FEMA, without assistance from the local government agency.

    - Residential (Owner-occupied) homeowner's financial assistance is covered under the Individual Assistance programs. The homeowner must file their claim directly with FEMA.
    - Mobile Home Parks themselves are a bit more complicated insofar as they may be publicly owned, owned by a non-profit association, or owned by a private business. The individual mobile homes may be owned by the occupant or owned by a private company as a rental unit. In some states, mobile home inspections may fall under the Department of Motor Vehicles (California) or another state agency, which may complicate the timing and logistics of mobile home inspections.
    - Business & Commercial Property (including apartments) are the responsibility of the owners, who should have insurance to cover their losses. Private businesses are not

eligible for Federal disaster assistance beyond Small Business Administration loans when these loans are made available.

- Agricultural Losses are not covered by FEMA but may be covered under the programs of other Federal agencies, particularly the U.S. Department of Agriculture.

7) **Response Costs** are generally eligible, provided that the costs for labor, equipment, and materials used are properly documented, properly procured, and used for the disaster response.

   a. Labor, Equipment, & Materials are tracked officially with four FEMA forms which are addressed in Chapter 5. However, the local agency may want to use an intermediate form to track these costs and later transfer the information to the FEMA forms.

   b. Small contracts may be an expeditious way to obtain urgently needed disaster-related services. Such small contracts may include boarding up buildings which have sustained damage and emergency repairs to facilities so they may be restored to use for the disaster response.

      a. Survivor's Services, which FEMA describes as part of Category B, "Emergency Protective Measures," should be eligible expenses when properly documented.

         i. Evacuation and Re-entry costs may be eligible for FEMA reimbursement. However, not all expenses may be eligible. One notable exception is the suspension of highway toll fees. If a jurisdiction, including the state, normally charges for the use of certain roads, and those tolls are waived for purposes of the evacuation, the losses of those fees are not reimbursable costs.

         ii. Sheltering costs incurred for "congregate" or mass care shelters are normally eligible cost items when they are properly documented, necessary, and procured.

           "Transitional" housing, where disaster survivors are placed in individual living units such as motels or FEMA trailers, are not eligible for reimbursement. More on this in Chapter 3.

         iii. Mass Feeding for disaster victims is usually an eligible expense so long as the costs are reasonable and properly documented. Mass feeding for the agency's own employees may or may not be an eligible expense. This is further addressed in Chapter 3: Pre-Disaster Strategies and Policies.

         iv. Animal Control/Pet rescue & sheltering costs are eligible when done in compliance with FEMA's policies. This is also addressed in Chapter 3.

8) **List of Projects/Damage Inventory** sorted by FEMA Categories as described in Chapter 24.

- FEMA-eligible work for the seven categories, A through G, is generally eligible for reimbursement, with the caveat that categories of work may not be mixed, i.e., debris clearance cannot be combined with any other category of work without FEMA's specific approval, which is usually only given on a Project Worksheet by Project Worksheet basis.
- Other Federal Agency-Covered Work:
- It is very important to understand that the FEMA Public Assistance program is only one of many Federal programs available for disaster relief.
- Each Federal agency will have regulations and guidelines which cover the types of assistance they may provide when authorized to do so by the Presidential disaster declaration. These rules are somewhat different for each agency, as are the amounts for which they may provide funding. The timelines for applying for and completing the projects may also be different.
- There are more than a dozen different Federal agencies which may provide both financial and non-financial forms of assistance. When these **O**ther **F**ederal **A**gencies (OFA) have jurisdiction, e.g., the Federal Highway Administration (FHWA) has authority over

Federal aid roads, then FEMA will not provide assistance under the Public Assistance program, even if these other Federal agencies do not have money budgeted for disaster relief.

This greatly complicates the disaster cost recovery process. If the local jurisdiction misapplies to FEMA for work covered by another Federal agency, FEMA will deny the application. But by the time the application is denied, the application period for the other Federal agency may have already passed by. It is very important to consult with both your respective state and the FEMA Program Delivery Manager (PDMG) to determine as soon as possible which may be the appropriate Federal agency to apply to.

- The Federal Highway Administration has authority over all "on-system" roads and highways in the U.S. When a road is thus designated, it will not be FEMA-eligible.
- Similarly, the Federal Transit Administration has authority over public transportation and rail systems. If your community has Federally funded transit projects, they may not be FEMA-eligible.
- The U.S. Army Corps of Engineers (USACE) has a large portfolio of public works projects across the country, including many flood control projects. These projects are typically FEMA-ineligible.

In some disasters and for some communities, the U.S. Army Corps of Engineers may also conduct debris management operations. However, this is not a given, and the ultimate responsibility for debris clearance remains with the local agency unless delegated, under an agreement, to the Corps of Engineers.

b. The U.S. Department of Agriculture (USDA) plays a significant role in disaster response and relief work by providing various forms of assistance to farmers, ranchers, and rural communities affected by natural disasters. The Department can provide emergency assistance to farmers and ranchers; it may distribute food and supplies; it can help to rebuild rural infrastructure; and can provide technical assistance and support through the Department's Natural Resources Conservation Service (NRCS).

c. Housing and Urban Development (HUD – CDBG) may provide disaster relief in a variety of ways. It can provide Community Development Block Grants – Disaster Recovery (CDBG-DR). This is flexible funding that can provide communities with resources to address a wide range of disaster recovery needs, including housing, infrastructure, and economic revitalization. This is one of the few Federal funding streams which can be integrated with FEMA funding.

The Department may also provide temporary rental assistance and case management services to individuals and families who are displaced from their homes due to a disaster.

Through the Federal Housing Administration (FHA), it may provide mortgage insurance to help homeowners rebuild or purchase new homes following a disaster. These are just a few of the programs available through Housing and Urban Development.

There are many other Federal agencies which may be authorized under a specific Presidential disaster declaration to provide disaster financial relief to both local agencies, individual homeowners, renters, and businesses.

This cornucopia of Federal disaster assistance is in addition to FEMA's Public Assistance program, which is the focus of this book. Depending on the nature, scope, and severity of a single disaster, the Presidential disaster declaration may or may not include authorization for many of these additional programs. Depending on the disaster, it may be advisable for the local jurisdiction to seek the help of experienced disaster cost recovery consultants to assist the agency in maximizing its disaster cost recovery under all available Federal programs.

9) **The Project Worksheet** is nominally about 10 pages long, although multiple copies of certain of the pages may be required to fully document the damages and the costs incurred to repair them. That said, the total count of pages provided in support of the Project Worksheet may run into the thousands of pages, or much more, for some projects.

    a. Small Projects are those projects in any FEMA damage category which may be completed for less than $1,037,000. Small projects are funded based on estimated costs and are fully funded, typically at 75%,[6] upon project approval. Cost overruns, if any, may only be addressed through a process called the Net Small Project Overrun or NSPO, which may only be applied for when ALL of the small projects have been completed. More on NSPO in Chapter 42: Close-outs and Net Small Project Overruns.

    b. Large Projects are those projects estimated to cost over $1,037,000. These projects are obligated and paid for on a reimbursement basis as the work is completed. When cost overruns occur, the local agency should immediately request a revision of the Project Worksheet. A new version of the Project Worksheet will replace the original Project Worksheet.

    c. Improved Projects are projects where the local agency wishes to make some improvements to the existing facility while repairing the disaster damage. Improved projects require the written approval of the state (in FEMA parlance, the Grantee, or Recipient). An example of an improved project might be the addition of another bay to a local fire station which was damaged by the disaster. Certain "improved" projects will trigger additional requirements, such as compliance with the National Environmental Protection Act (NEPA). Compliance with these additional requirements will probably delay the start of work on such projects.

    d. Alternate Projects are projects where the local agency wishes to repair or build a facility to a different purpose or location than that for which it was originally built. Such "alternate" projects require FEMA's written approval. An example of an alternate project might be the conversion of a building formerly used as a warehouse to serve as additional office space for agency staff.

    e. Mitigation funding is typically provided by FEMA to make a facility more damage-resistant to a future event. Mitigation may take many forms, including beefing up the structure to make it more wind-, flood-, fire-, etc., resistant. In some cases, mitigation may include the elevation or relocation of at-risk structures. Mitigation has a 75%-25% Federal-Local cost share, although some states may also contribute funding for mitigation.

    f. Special Considerations apply to all projects. The special considerations include historic structures, insurance, hazardous materials, and other environmental issues. These special consideration issues must be addressed for every Project Worksheet. The special consideration issues may or may not apply in some cases, but the form must always be part of the application package.

10) **Alternative Procedures Projects:** FEMA's Alternative Procedures projects provide a different approach to the traditional cost-share requirements for federal disaster recovery funding.

Alternative Procedures projects allow the state and local governments to submit proposals for fixed amounts of federal funding and help to ensure that critical recovery projects can be undertaken, even in jurisdictions with limited resources.

FEMA's Alternative Procedures program may be used for a variety of disaster recovery projects, including the construction of levees, the repairing of roads and bridges, and the implementation of hazard mitigation measures.

However, the program is only available for certain types of disasters and is subject to specific eligibility criteria.

If your agency is considering using the Alternative Procedures program, I highly recommend that serious consideration be given to working closely with a disaster cost recovery specialist firm, as these projects have both serious advantages and serious disadvantages, some of which may not be apparent to an agency without prior experience in the Alterative Procedures approach to disaster cost recovery.

Notes

1 FEMA Should Disallow $1.1 Million in Grant Funds Awarded to Richland County, North Dakota, OIG-19–63, September 25, 2019.
2 The per capita indicators for the Federal Fiscal Year 23–24 are $1.84 for the state, and $4.60 for the county.
3 One of the best sample forms available online is from the Government of the Northwest Territories in Canada, https://www.inf.gov.nt.ca/sites/inf/files/roof_inspection_checklist.pdf
4 *Baptist Hospitals of Southeast Texas – Result of Declared Incident*, https://www.fema.gov/appeal/result-declared-incident-18
5 Described in Chapter 5 as the 3DC concept for quality control.
6 Although in most disasters FEMA funds 75% of the eligible costs, the President may order a 90% of higher rate of reimbursement. This special added funding, however, is usually reserved for the most damaging of disasters.

7 Criticality of Effective/Comprehensive Documentation

At this point, the book will be getting deeper into the weeds to explain the challenges of obtaining FEMA's Public Assistance Grants.

Acronyms

FEMA, like all Federal agencies and most other units of state and local government, makes liberal use of acronyms. There is a logic to this, because governments and other large organizations must track vast volumes of information; and in this process, some form of shorthand is a valuable time-saving tool. Acronyms make it possible to have some compression of terms which are in frequent and constant use for those who are familiar with the subject matter.

But the very dark side of these acronyms is that those who do not frequently use this shorthand are sometimes unaware of both the meaning and nuances of an acronym. This makes it very diffi-cult to read, understand, and carefully follow the regulations to which we must adhere in the Public Assistance process. For this reason, in this book there are limited acronyms.

With this in mind, while FEMA and other government agencies all use acronyms of various stripes on an all-too-frequent basis, local government agencies should strive to eliminate and, as much as is possible, NEVER use acronyms when filling out Public Assistance forms. At the local level, our energies should be completely focused on making information and data as transparent and as easy to understand as possible. We should strive to convey information with great clarity and simplicity, not to obscure it in a fog of administrative jargon.

Furthermore, the use of acronyms by local government agencies can only damage the likeli-hood of full disaster cost recovery. When I worked for the City and County of San Francisco, the internal and generally accepted abbreviation for the City and County of San Francisco was CCSF. However, this same acronym also stands for City College of San Francisco. The misinterpretation of local government acronyms by the state or Federal agencies may result in delays or denial of Project Worksheets.

I worked for years in Los Angeles County, CA, which also has Los Angeles City wholly con-tained within the County's boundaries. Again, the use of the acronym LAC can mean different things depending on who is talking and who is listening. The very safest recommendation is NEVER to use local acronyms that might confuse others, especially when we're trying to get money from those others.

Avoid Administrative Jargon

Government agencies at local, state, and Federal levels also use certain phrases specific to the work they do and how they're organized. Because the levels of local government are asking for help

DOI: 10.4324/9781003487869-9

for disaster response and recovery, it is incumbent upon those same agencies to be sure that they ask specifically for what they need to avoid confusing other government agencies. All during the process, the local agencies should ask themselves: "Are our messages clear and unambiguous, and have we provided sufficient information to present our case?"

Rigorous Tracking of Labor, Equipment, and Materials

This single tenet of disaster cost recovery is absolutely critical to getting and keeping Federal disaster assistance from any agency, particularly FEMA.

The failure to properly document damages and costs incurred may be one of the most serious risks attached to the Public Assistance process. Front-line employees, those who work in the field, whether it is in the Public Safety, Public Works, Facilities or Maintenance, or other functions of local governments, generally do not like paperwork. Pushing paper is a scourge on the best of days, and when these same front-line employees are tasked with saving lives, protecting the public health, or preventing further damage to improved property, they do not first think about how they must properly document their activities, the use of equipment, and the supplies consumed in the process.

From the perspective of many front-line workers, these detailed regulations about how to dot an 'i' and how to cross a 't' are nothing short of ridiculous. They do not understand that these are not the rules of the department head or the Finance Director. These rules are the strings that are attached to government money. This is not something unique to American governments; it is to some degree common practice within any and all levels of government anywhere in the world.

Over the years, when I was called upon to train front-line workers in the importance of the documentation process, I liked to change the entire presentation to make it relevant to the field employees. I would tell them that perhaps they were told by a supervisor that the training was about disaster preparedness or emergency response procedures. Continuing, I said: "Nothing could be further from the truth; we are here today to talk about your [the employees'] pay and benefits." I explained that in some cases, pay and benefits could be frozen, and in the worst cases, pay and benefits may be reduced because of the economic aftermath of the disaster. This reframing of the need for detailed record-keeping for engaged employees is much better than simply making a demand for proper documentation, which might not be heeded in any case.

Taco Tuesdays

- While teaching disaster cost recovery for a group of cities in the Tidewater area of Virginia a few years ago, I came across an excellent practice. One of the local agencies had a practice which they called "Taco Tuesdays." On the first Tuesday of each month, all employees would fill out the forms which they would use to track labor, equipment, and materials during a disaster response. In this way, all employees would be readily familiar with the agencies' forms for tracking costs on a regular monthly basis.

Dual Use – Daily Use

I ran across a similarly related practice while teaching in Anne Arundel County, Maryland. There, they espoused the concept of "Dual Use, Daily Use." Jurisdictions there had adopted the practice of using forms every day that would provide the information required by FEMA. The ideal situation is to track the costs associated with disaster response exactly the same way normal or "blue sky" everyday work is done.

Dual Use – Daily Use – On Steroids

The lady who was then the Chief Financial Officer for the City of San Francisco's Public Works Department took my disaster cost recovery training and recognized, through a class exercise, that their normal cost tracking procedures failed to meet FEMA's requirements.

After the training, she pulled together her Information Technology and Accounting staff and they created a software application for smartphones and tablets which every day collects work and cost information in a way that meets FEMA's requirements.

Now, every day, San Francisco City Public Works Employees are properly tracking their activities and costs. Their system will print out the FEMA forms with no intermediate steps.

Having automated data collection reduces the workload for proper documentation and eliminates typographical and miscalculation errors. When the state and FEMA see this high-quality documentation, they will check a few forms to prove to themselves that the records are properly completed, and then relax their scrutiny of that part of the process.

The Five 'Ws' of Cost Tracking (Reprise)

For tracking and accounting for the costs of the emergency response, debris clearance, and temporary emergency repairs to government-owned facilities and infrastructure, the 5 Ws mentioned in Chapter 5 are essential.

I worked with a client agency that had two large sinkholes develop in one of their major roads. The invoices from contractors involved in the repair work stated the invoice was for "storm work." Such a description is entirely insufficient for FEMA to consider reimbursement.

The words "storm work" could apply to dozens of different response tasks occurring after a disaster. In this case, the work description should have been enhanced to fully describe the work done. The invoice might have specified: "Pumped out two sinkholes in the roadway, measuring approximately 20 long feet by 14 feet wide by 5 feet deep. Pump time total for both sinkholes was 6 hours. Pump used was a 4-inch capacity, 55-horsepower trailer-mounted trash pump."

The documentation should specify what event (tornado, hurricane, fire, flood, etc.) caused the damages and the precise damage done by the specific event. "Flooding washed out 40 lineal feet of the roadway, centered at Mile Marker 21," followed by the GPS coordinates for both latitude and longitude, with GPS readings at the beginning and end of the damaged area. Furthermore, the complete documentation will also state what specific threat the damage presented. "The washed-out roadway was a threat to the safety of emergency vehicle traffic."

According to FEMA: "It is critical that the applicant establish and maintain accurate records of events and expenditures related to disaster recovery work, and the documentation must describe the 'who, what, when, where, (why), and how much' for each item of disaster recovery."[1]

In the same appeal case, FEMA further states: "Applicants must maintain their financial and programmatic records for three years following submission of the recipient's final expenditure report. The burden to fully substantiate an appeal with documented justification falls exclusively on the applicant and hinges on the applicant's ability not only to produce its own records, but to clearly explain how those records support the appeal."[2] (Emphasis Added)

Incident Command System (ICS) Forms – Use Extreme Caution

Many agencies use the Incident Command System forms. This can be dangerous unless your agency is a fire department. ICS forms were designed by and for the fire service, and they work beautifully *for the fire service*. However, non-fire service documentation needs are different and require data which may be hard to extract, or impossible to extract in non-fire uses. This is particularly the case with the ICS-214, which is probably the most misused of the ICS forms. For starters, there is no place to track both straight time and overtime separately, as FEMA requires. For firefighters, who are on continuous overtime when responding to a major brush or forest fire, they do not need to track straight time. City and county crews need to track both straight and overtime separately. There is no place in the standard ICS-214 form for equipment and materials. There are other ICS forms for those purposes. However, if staff is unfamiliar with how to properly use the ICS forms, critical data may be forever lost.

Electronic Document Management Systems

The larger the disaster, the more valuable an electronic document management system will be to the local agency.

Large disasters will generate thousands, even tens of thousands, of pages of documentation. Managing this documentation will require a great deal of staff time and will result in enormous costs for document storage and retrieval over the years.

The FEMA Project Worksheet document is nominally fewer than 10 sheets of paper, although for some projects there will be additional copies of some of the pages.

The vast bulk of the documentation will be the supporting documents, i.e., timecards, fieldwork reports, contracts, change orders, invoices, copies of paid checks, etc.

Federal regulations require that documentation for Project Worksheets be maintained for no less than three years. However, this minimum of 3 years of document retention can be misleading because for small projects (those less than $1,037,000), all the documentation must be retained for three years AFTER the close of the last small project. Most Presidentially declared disasters will remain open administratively for several years, and some will remain open for a decade or more.

Hurricane Katrina (2005) remains open. The Loma Prieta Earthquake (1989) for one agency did not close for 22 years. In the case of the Loma Prieta disaster, the local agency would have had to maintain their documentation for no less than 25 years. That is a long and costly time to store those records.

If the local agency already has an electronic document management system, care needs to be taken that the system has some user-defined fields for the disaster name, the 'DR' number, the Project Worksheet number, and other data that will be needed throughout the cost recovery process.

The Parallel Document Filing System

In some cases, the local jurisdiction may need what I call the "Parallel Filing System." This deals with FEMA's requirement for original invoices.

Inevitably, some back-up documents, including some invoices, will work their way into the paperwork. Let's imagine that the local agency has 6 similar projects (sinkholes) for which they had to rent equipment (water pumps) for each separate location. In spite of the purchasing officer's request for separate invoices, the vendor put all 6 water pumps on the same invoice. We want to have an original invoice in each file; in this case, that is not possible. Therefore, we create a 'parallel filing system.'

First, we create a unique master location where the original invoice is located, e.g., File Drawer #2, Pendaflex Folder #23. The one-of-kind original document is placed in the parallel filing system, which is a fireproof and lockable file cabinet. Before filing this document, it is annotated with the exact location where it will be stored, and then a copy is made for each of the different Project Worksheet files. The photocopies are then placed in their respective files. If the state, FEMA, or the auditors then request the original document, it can be easily found by referencing the location which was annotated before the document was copied.

Not every document needs to be in the parallel filing system, but there will be certain one-of-a-kind documents that will need this special treatment as a hedge against a FEMA deobligation or adverse audit finding.

Time and Date Stamping of Correspondence

Throughout the Public Assistance process, the local agency will receive correspondence from either the state or FEMA, and many of these documents will require a response within a limited time frame. A typical example is an 'RFI' or Request for Information. The normal response time for such a request is 15 calendar days. FEMA begins the response time period from the date on the correspondence. If the letter was mailed, this may result in a loss of 2 to 4-5 days' time. As a defense against this, a recommended practice is, upon receipt of the correspondence, to timestamp both the envelope and the document itself, and staple both together. This resets the time to the date of receipt, not the date of writing.

While the time and date stamping of physical documents may be important, the local agency must also constantly check the FEMA Portal and email for any documents transmitted electronically. Once FEMA or the state sends an electronic communication, that agency considers the communication to be received timely by the local agency. The local agency is responsible for checking these files every day.

This will not apply when documents require a signature upon delivery. This practice should be consistent for all documents received from either the state or FEMA. Furthermore, the staff in the mailroom must be advised that any correspondence from the state or FEMA must be delivered on the same date on which it was received. This requirement should be rigidly enforced for the protection of the disaster cost recovery process.

The Public Assistance Grant Program Hierarchy

The disaster cost recovery team should be knowledgeable regarding the hierarchy of law and regulations regarding the Public Assistance process.

At the top of the pile is the Stafford Act, Public Law 93–288 et seq. This is the law which enables FEMA to provide financial assistance to local government agencies and certain private non-profit organizations.

Next in line is the Code of Federal Regulations, Title 44 – Emergency Management and Assistance, Part 206. Herein lie the specific regulations which expand on the Stafford Act.

Then follow the public policy requirements, such as environmental and historic preservation regulations.

Next in this hierarchy are the Administrative Regulations, including those in Title 2 of the Code of Federal Regulations, Part 200, (2 CFR, Part 200) which deals primarily with procurement and audits.

The next level is the 'Grant Agreement Letter,' a document unique to every Presidentially declared disaster. This is an agreement between FEMA and the respective state which specifies which Federal programs, including non-FEMA Federal Assistance, such as funding from the Federal Highway Administration, the Federal Transit Administration, Housing and Urban Development, etc., will be made available for this disaster.

The Federal government has many agencies and many different varieties of both monetary and non-monetary disaster assistance. However, a Presidential disaster declaration does not automatically open the door for every possible avenue of Federal disaster assistance. Different programs are authorized from one disaster to another. It's a lot like looking at a menu in a restaurant, except that the waiter (FEMA) tells us what we're having for dinner. It's not our choice which Federal disaster programs will be in play, although a complete damage assessment will help define our need for assistance.

In the Napa Earthquake of 2014, Public Assistance was initially authorized and Small Business Administration loans were approved, but only for non-profits. It was some time later, when the damage assessments were more fully developed, that the Presidential disaster declaration was amended to include 'Individual Assistance' for homeowners.

Finally, we come to the approved Project Worksheet itself. This is the document which authorizes a specific dollar amount, or an estimated dollar amount, for response activities or repair and/ or reconstruction work.

However, just because someone from FEMA has signed off on a Project Worksheet does not mean that there's smooth sailing ahead. If anything in the Project Worksheet violates any of the aforementioned laws, regulations, or agreements, then that part of the Project Worksheet may be void in whole or in part. The order of legal and regulatory precedence is important.

Color Coding of Forms for Use and Filing Purposes

- One simple way to make some sense of all the paperwork and better organize the documentation is to color-code the documents by department or purpose. In this way, a misfiled document can stick out like a sore thumb.

A Case of Proper Documentation

In text from the Second Appeal of Lowe County, KS, we find a good example of effective documentation of road maintenance: "On first appeal, FEMA determined the Subrecipient did not demonstrate pre-disaster maintenance of the culvert sites. The determination was based in part on an examination of the annual budgets, finding they did not contain enough detail to determine the specific type or location of maintenance work completed in a given FY (*Fiscal Year*). However, close scrutiny of the budget data shows the Subrecipient apportioned all expenses into one of two categories: 'general' or 'roads.' This indicates the priority the Subrecipient places on public road maintenance; indeed, maintenance of road networks is one of the primary historical reasons a township exists as a subdivision of local government in Kansas. For each year represented, the Subrecipient never allocated less than 40 percent of its total budget to its roads."[3]

"In other words, in the years prior to the disaster, it is clear the Subrecipient earmarked and then spent funds to perform the work described in its annual budgets. Finally, because it covers multiple successive years, the budget execution data demonstrate the Subrecipient performed work to maintain its roads routinely. The Subrecipient's annual budgets therefore document an annual program of prioritized, routine pre-disaster road maintenance."[4]

Notes

1 https://www.fema.gov/appeal/force-account-labor-equipment-costsfinancial-accounting-reconciliation-section-705
2 Ibid.
3 https://www.fema.gov/appeal/roads-direct-result-disaster
4 Ibid.

8 Pre- and Post-Disaster Photo Documentation

"Badges? We ain't got no badges. We don't need no badges. I don't have to show you any stinkin' badges!"
Alphonso Bedoya, aka Gold Hat, from the movie
"Treasure of the Sierra Madre," 1948

Photographs: We Don't Need No Stinkin' Photographs . . . or Do We?

"On October 14, 2016, the Applicant filed a supplement to its September 9, 2016 letter. In this letter, the Applicant reiterated its previous arguments and, further, argued that there was no requirement to show photographs of the damage and that there were other ways to prove the damage."[1] (Emphasis Added)

"The Applicant argued there was no law or policy in effect at the time of the disaster that required applicants to submit pre- and post-disaster photographs of each and every damaged site."[2] (Emphasis Added)

This is absolutely true. There is no law or regulation which requires the use of pre- and/or post-disaster photographs of damage.

However, the use of pre- and post-disaster photographs is the easiest way to effectively and comprehensively document what existed before the disaster, and how that same facility was damaged by the disaster. Without these photographs, the task of fully proving the damage becomes substantially more difficult and will take a great deal more staff time. The only party hurt by the lack of pre- and post-disaster photographs is the applicant, i.e., the local agency.

The Best Deal in Town

Not only is proper "before and after" photo documentation of damages the simplest and most effective way to prove that the disaster caused certain damages, but the process may also be done at very low cost, i.e., the cost of digital cameras and digital storage are remarkably inexpensive; and the labor to take the photos may be free or at very low cost.

In many cases, when FEMA cannot determine what damage was caused, how it was caused, or if there was any pre-existing damage; etc., FEMA will send out a Request for Information (RFI). The request may include a request for either or both pre- and post-disaster photographs showing the claimed damage.

Pre- and post-disaster photos are critical. We must remember that the Grants Portal process has many moving parts, which may not perfectly always support the transfer of damage information. First, we have the Site Inspector (SI) who visits the damage site. This person takes some photos and writes up their report. Next, this information goes to one of four different regional

DOI: 10.4324/9781003487869-10

Consolidated Resource Centers (CRC), where another individual, who has no firsthand knowledge of the damages, will write up the Project Worksheet, including the Scope of Work, without benefit of a site visit or any other firsthand knowledge.

If damages exist but the Site Inspector doesn't see them, they won't be in the Site Inspection Report (SIR). This means that any hidden damages won't be included in the Scope of Work, which means that FEMA won't pay for those costs.

Free and Low-Cost Labor

The process of taking pre- and post-disaster photographs will vary from jurisdiction to jurisdiction. In San Francisco, when I worked there, the City owned or leased nearly 1,200 buildings of all sizes and shapes. In the small city where I began my career in government, we had only four buildings. Therefore, how long the process will take and how many people will be needed will vary. And inevitably, some prioritization may be needed.

In San Francisco, we hired four summer interns for the job. When the team got to the Justice Center, aka the Police Department and Jail, a light duty officer escorted the team into the sensitive areas.

There are many potential labor resources for this project. Many cities and counties have active volunteer groups which might be tapped for the project. There are community and four-year colleges with photography classes and knowledgeable students. These same schools also may have GIS (Graphic Information Services), geography, or urban planning students, many of whom have to turn in projects as part of their classwork. Eagle Scout candidates need a project, or there may be a local photography club with interested members. It will take some staff time to get things rolling, but once the protocols are in place, the project should move along nicely.

A Pre-Disaster Photo Documentation Guide

Overview

The objective is to have sufficient photographic documentation of government agency-owned facilities, including roads, bridges, and culverts to establish the baseline condition of these facilities before a disaster causes damage to them. In the event of a natural disaster where buildings or equipment are damaged, we will then have photographs as proof that the building or equipment existed and what their condition was prior to the disaster. These photos become an important part of proper documentation to receive FEMA Public Assistance funding or other Federal disaster assistance.

Photographic documentation of a sampling of infrastructure is also important. For instance, storm water channels should be photographed at key locations before each major storm to show the level of soil and debris that may be in the channels before the storm adds additional debris and fill to the system. FEMA will only pay for the increment of damage caused by a disaster, and we must prove the prior levels to insure eligibility for Federal reimbursement.

A colleague of mine, Anjila Lebsock, was the emergency manager for the City of Palm Springs. Although Palm Springs is a desert community, it does periodically experience flash flooding. When the city received a storm warning, Anjila would run a route and take pictures of the known low spots where flood debris would normally accumulate. By using the foot markers painted on the side of culverts, she got perfect pre-storm documentation of any existing debris and sediment in the channel. After the flooding subsided, Anjila would then revisit each site and take another photo, if warranted, to prove exactly how much debris and sediment the storm deposited at a given location. Anjila knows how cost recovery works.

A Simple Process and Easily Executed

The beauty of this process is that when properly done, very little writing or note-taking is required. When you use a consistent and systematic approach, it will be easy to locate photographs of specific buildings, areas, or offices even years later.

Getting Started: Contact and Notify

Try to make a contact who has the authority to send out an email to the entire department or building that you intend to document. This email is a very important part of the project. For people to allow you to do your job smoothly, you must make sure that there is an email or some sort of advance notice given to workers that will clearly describe what the project is about, why it needs to be done, and that access has been granted to their workspace. This allows less time-wasting and more productivity for all parties involved.

Dealing with People

Make sure that your agency identification badge is always showing or is at least easily accessible. This ensures your legitimacy to the people you are meeting.

Be clear about what it is exactly that you are doing. Go into a little detail and have a concise activity description prepared for people who have questions.

If concern arises, let it be known that all pictures taken are confidential and will only be used for disaster cost recovery purposes. Most people do not want to be photographed, so be sure to give the option of stepping out of the workspace for a quick moment, and if necessary, to flip over or cover any confidential documents in the area.

Sample Dialogue

"Hello, we are doing photo documentation of the building for our disaster cost recovery planning. I believe an email was sent out that we would be coming. Could I take a few pictures of your office? It will only take a minute."

If they ask what it is for, then you might say: "In a way, it is like insurance. The photos are taken in case a natural disaster such as a hurricane, a flood, or an earthquake damages the building or equipment. If anything is damaged, the photos will be submitted to FEMA to prove our losses for disaster cost recovery."

When working through many individual offices, an employee will frequently be on the phone or in a meeting. In these cases, just write down the room number and move on to the next office, and come back after the rest of the rooms are complete to check back with that employee to see if they are available.

Never get angry or frustrated with people who are objecting to having their area documented. First, tell them who you have clearance from and reference the email that was sent out as a notice. If that does not work, note the problem room or area, and bring it up to your contact after the rest of the work has been completed. At that point you will either be escorted by the contact to the problem area, or you will be told that the area will not be documented for a given reason.

Covering All the Bases

Ask your contact or someone who is helping you about locked rooms or cabinets that contain expensive equipment such as electronics. These are important to document because they can be very expensive.

Most tenants in an office do not have access to electrical and mechanical rooms, and some of these can be the most expensive rooms in the building. Make sure that a building engineer is contacted to find out if these rooms exist and if they can be documented.

Ask a building engineer about boiler rooms, fan rooms, or other mechanical equipment necessary to run a large building.

Each floor or tenant usually has a server room also. If you do not find it or you think it is behind a locked door, try to gain access to it by asking someone or finding Information Technology (IT) in the building.

In addition to the photographs on the inside of the building, make sure the exterior of the building is photographed, as well as the roof and any belowground areas like basements or underground parking.

Photography

The main objective of the project is to capture the value of a building and its current condition. When taking photographs, be sure that the photos represent the fair value of the building.

Good lighting is crucial. Turn on lights in dark rooms if possible. Be careful when photographing a room with a window, because sometimes the only thing you will be able to see is a glare from the outside.

Try to keep a steady hand, and wait for the camera to complete the photo before moving on to the next to avoid blurry pictures.

What to Photograph

Photograph everything that is valuable.

Examples: Walls, ceilings, floor coverings, desks, chairs, computers, printers, lights, fire sprinklers, alarms, vents, combination locks, security cameras, windows, blinds, good building architecture, appliances, and especially any fancy architectural touches, etc.

Art, plants, and personal items are all things that do not need to be photographed; they won't be replaced by FEMA because they are either not government-owned or are ineligible for FEMA funding (artworks).

If possible, obtain a building plan or map. This can be very helpful when organizing photos. Frequently, maps or plans can be found on the walls in the form of an emergency exit route. These are good to photograph and provide a floor plan of each floor.

Try to take a lot of photos. You cannot have too many, but you can have too few.

A good rule of thumb is "If it's different or expensive, photograph it."

Methodology

No Written Documentation

This is important. There is no writing involved. If the process is set up properly, create file folders for each building and each floor of a building, and always take pictures in a clockwise direction from the point of entry, then there is no need to write anything down.

No Video, No Drones

I generally recommend not taking video footage. First, videos are usually of a lower resolution than a good digital camera picture. Second, sometimes the videographer may make gratuitous statements which may cause a problem later, such as, "We were going to tear that building down later this year." Third, it takes time to scan videos for the exact location from which you need photos. In some cases videos or drone videos may be called for, but not as a general rule unless you are documenting roads or utility lines. Usually, video won't show as much detail as still photographs.

The Establishing Shot

For each building you will photograph, use what Hollywood calls an "establishing shot." The establishing shot in a movie or TV show clearly identifies the location shown as New York City, London, Hong Kong, or Paris. We do the same by going to the street corner and taking a photograph of the street sign. The very next photo is of the building number. If the building has a name, this should be the very next shot after the street number. This identifies the building without any writing necessary. Always keep these shots in order for each new building photographed.

When you have finished photographing a facility, close the series of photos with another photograph of the main entrance of the building. Then take one more photograph of the street sign that you photographed before starting the facility. These sets of "bookend" photographs will identify all the photos between the "bookends" as belonging to one single facility.

Exteriors

Always photograph the exterior next, after the establishing shots, and use the same systematic approach. From the street side of the building, shoot the front first. Again, begin with a full frontal shot and then move to any important details, working from left to right, clockwise around the exterior of the building. Photograph the doors and windows and any decorative elements that give the building its unique character and would be more expensive to repair or replace if damaged in a disaster.

Once the front of the building is completely photographed, then move to the left side and repeat the process similar to the front of the building. Next, go to the rear of the building and repeat the process. Finally, go to the right side of the building (as seen from the street) and repeat the process once more. Then, if you consistently use this method, anyone can find the photographs by mentally repeating the process to figure out where a photo should be found. If the building has more than four sides, simply take each face in order, beginning from the street side and working your way around the building in a clockwise fashion.

Interiors

Use the same process when you enter the building. First, photograph the lobby or entry area. Then move through the building in a clockwise direction from where you enter the building. Begin with the first floor and work up through each successive floor of the building and end up on the roof, if accessible. The last area to be photographed will be the basement(s), if any.

Rooftops and Basements

If the roof is flat and safely accessible, photograph it using the same approach, from general overview to important details, in a clockwise manner from your point of entry. Often, there is expensive mechanical equipment on the roof, such as elevator machinery, heating, ventilating, and air conditioning equipment (HVAC), and duct work. Also photograph details of the roof system and materials themselves. Good, clear photographs of the condition of a roof can be critical in qualifying for FEMA Public Assistance.

Basements also often have expensive equipment for elevators, electrical, plumbing, HVAC, and fire sprinkler systems. It is also common practice to install expensive computer equipment in basements. All of these items should be extensively photographed using the same general overview-to-specific details approach, in a clockwise manner from your point of entry.

Office Overviews

When taking photographs, it is important to start with a shot that will allow you to know where the photo was taken and when that room or area was completed, such as a room number or occupant's name. An example would be if the mayor's office had to be documented, the first picture of that office should be their room number or if that is not available, the title of the room ("Office of the Mayor"). The last shot (the "bookend") should be the same as the first. This makes it easy to differentiate offices when they are uploaded onto the computer and separated into different files.

When taking pictures of a room, have some sort of sequence that you can continue in every room. For example, you should always take pictures from left to right if possible. You should start with general overview photos to get a basic view of the room, and then take more detailed photos of smaller points in the room. If you keep doing the same sequence of steps every time you photograph a room, there will be less of a chance of anything being missed in the pictures.

Expensive equipment deserves a photo dedicated to it. For example, most offices have multiple large all-in-one printers, which can be very costly to repair or replace.

In rooms with repetitive features, such as cubicles, a few shots of a standard cubicle and its contents is sufficient to represent the room full of cubicles, as long as an overview photograph is taken of the room showing the size and number of cubicles.

Group Dynamic

When photographing with more than one person, you need to be careful. It is just as easy to photograph a room twice as it is to miss it entirely. Before starting a large room or floor, decide which parts each team member will photograph.

Care needs to be taken when dividing up work. The most effective and efficient way to divide up work is to completely split up, either by floor or by room. Sometimes, this is not possible in high-security areas where an escort is required.

When working in the same room, a good way to divide the work is to have one person take the common areas (hallways and cubicle space), while the others do everything that is separated from the common areas by a door (rooms and offices). In most cases it takes longer to complete the rooms and offices than the common areas, so the person who was working on the common areas then joins in working on the rooms and offices.

When working through rooms and offices with more than one person, it goes faster if you leapfrog through them. For example: in a line of offices, one person takes the first room and another takes the second room. When one finishes a room, they continue down the line of offices. This method works as long as all rooms are taken or noted why they were not taken. It works with more than two people as well, but close coordination is very important to ensure all significant building features are photographed.

The leapfrog method becomes more complicated when offices are not all lined up or when offices are on either side of a hallway. Completing these takes a little more communication, adaptation, and awareness, but it is still doable.

An important thing when working with others is being aware of where they are and what they have and have not photographed. This helps check each other to make sure a room or area is not missed and that time is not wasted photographing a room twice.

Uploading Pictures

This is a typical copying procedure; your exact process may vary.

Connect the camera to the computer using the USB to camera cord.

If an autorun option appears, select "Open folder" to view files. If the autorun does not appear go to Start -> My Computer, and then under "Devices with Removable Storage" select "Removable Disk." This should open the camera's picture folder.

Next, go to My Computer again and open up the common drive assigned for the photo documentation project, then locate the folder called "FEMA PICS."

To upload the pictures, copy and paste them from the camera to the appropriate folder in FEMA PICS.

Folder Structure

Use the following folder structure as an example.

Create a new folder for each building documented.

Create a folder within the building for each floor or separate area such as the garage, external pictures, or roof.

On each floor, create a folder for rooms, offices, cubicle space, common areas, and other obvious areas.

Within the rooms and offices folders, create a new folder for each room if needed.

Example Folder Structure:

100 South Grand Avenue

Exterior
Interior

   1st Floor

      Water Department
      Building & Safety Division
      Council Chambers

   2nd Floor

      Offices
      Room 201
      Room 202
      Room 203

   Common Areas
   Lobby
   Restrooms

Roof
Garage/Basement (if any)

Distributed File Storage

A highly recommended practice is to buy 3 or 4 portable hard drives for all the photos. When I worked in San Francisco, the main photo storage was on a hard drive in the Real Estate Division. However, I had a duplicate copy in my desk, our I.T. person had another at her home across the Bay, and I have another duplicate file at my home on the East Coast. It's hard to imagine a disaster that could destroy all four copies of the files.

Photo Documentation Cycle

I am often asked, "How often do we need to take the pictures?" One set of photos should last for years. But any time that the buildings are remodeled or redecorated would be an appropriate time to take a new set of photos. The most important set of photos is the first one. 1) It gets the practice started; 2) Subsequent re-shoots will only happen occasionally. Even if the photos are several years old, they will present a baseline for the condition of the facilities.

One exception to this would be building roofs, which continuously deteriorate due to the weather and daily exposure to solar radiation. For rooftops, I would recommend a maximum of 2 to 3 years between photo shoots. However, re-shooting a rooftop could easily be established as part of the annual roof inspection process.

Post-Disaster Photo Documentation

For post-disaster photo documentation, to the extent that it is safely possible, follow the same protocol described for pre-disaster photo documentation in those locations where damage has occurred.

A very important part of organizing post-disaster photographs is the naming convention when the photographs are stored on a hard drive. Unlike the pre-disaster photographs, post-disaster photographs will be grouped randomly by site. And the photographs from each site need to be filed separately according to the filing system set up by the disaster cost recovery team.

Each unique damage or activity site should have its own folder named with the street address or GPS coordinates. At a later date, a FEMA Project Worksheet number may be added to the end of the folder name.

Each photo should also have the street and number; in the event that a photo is misfiled, it can then be found by the street and number name data.

This is a sample photograph file naming convention. Every person taking photographs must use the same naming convention so the photographs can be properly filed and retrieved when necessary.

All photos should be filed using exactly the same naming convention so that any photo can be easily identified and located based on the location, date, and photographer.

This is considerable amount of work for each photo, but without a consistent file naming protocol, the agency may have thousands of useless damage photographs.

Useful Photography Apps: Solocator

There are many apps that enhance the photography process, and two of them may be very useful for damage documentation purposes. The first one is called "Solocator," and the second one is "Photo Trap."

Table 8.1 Sample photograph file naming convention

Street name or GPS coordinates	Street Number	Photographer, last name first	Date the photo was taken (Year-Month-Day). Use the zero in the month & day	Photo series # 001	Notes (Optional)
Main Street	729	Jones, John	2016-09-05	001	notes
Example: Main St-729#Jones, John#2016-03-09#001#notes					
33–49–44 (118–19–34)		Jones, John	2016-09-05	001	on Old Country Road
Example: 33-49-44 (118-19-34)#Jones, John#2016-09-05#001#on old country road					

Use a "#" without spaces between the data fields. Enter latitude and longitude as degrees, minutes, and seconds separated by a "-" with no spaces. Put the longitude in parentheses. The use of the "#" will enable someone to parse the data using the Excel program and create an index of all the photographs.

Figure 8.1 Sample photograph taken using the "Solocator" app.

When using Solocator on a digital phone, the app shows the longitude and latitude, the date and time, and the compass heading. The app also allows on-screen annotating, so you can make notes right on the photo. This information is very useful on pre-disaster photos because it allows the post-disaster photographer to duplicate the same picture, knowing the location where the original photo was taken.

This same important data, i.e., latitude and longitude, compass heading, and date and time is typically captured in every digital photograph, but software is needed to see this metadata embedded within the photo. A program such as Adobe's Bridge can extract the same information; however, with Solocator, it's right there and easy to use.

I shot this photograph in Goleta (Santa Barbara), California. Note that in the lower left corner is my name, and in the lower right corner is the name of the facility, along with the date and time. This information was entered directly into the app. The program itself entered the data across the top of the photo, the compass heading, the GPS coordinates, and the elevation.

Photo Trap Apps: Photo Trap

Another photo app that some may prefer is Photo Trap. This app allows you to take a photo and then at some later time take a second photo, then compare the two photos side by side. However, Photo Trap doesn't display the wealth of information Solocator does.

Tag-Along Volunteer Photo Documentarians

Particularly in those regions of the country where disasters may annually reoccur, it would be a great asset for a local agency to have a cadre of trained volunteers to tag along with field crews for the sole purpose of photo documenting the damages and the work done to reduce or eliminate the problems. Most certainly, not every volunteer would be able to do this, and some volunteers, those often referred to as high-maintenance volunteers (i.e., those who are more trouble than they are worth), should not be welcome for this sometimes-sensitive task.

To deal with issues of post-disaster access, perhaps the volunteers could ride with the crews where possible, to avoid being held up at security perimeter checkpoints. Each volunteer should have some form of official identification card and a reflective vest, hard hat, etc.

A maximum best practice would be to have an annual "Public Works Photo Day," where volunteers would meet with city/county crews to get to know each other and practice how to take photographs without: 1) endangering themselves, 2) endangering the work crews, 3) missing the "heart" of the damage or work to be done, 4) taking photos of people's faces, or imposing on people's privacy at a most stressful time.

A recommended best practice is to use agency-owned cameras, which should help with any potential future issues regarding any copyright infringement issues.

If such a program were set up, the volunteers would also have to sign a code of ethics regarding their personal behavior and assigning ownership of the photographs exclusively to the city/county.

Age Matters

If the local agency's facilities are older structures and/or historic structures, then pre-event photo documentation is even more important. Correctly or not, FEMA may make a presumption that an older facility has deferred maintenance and/or pre-existing problems, and the burden of proof lies completely with the local agency to prove otherwise.

This matter of age is particularly important with older roof systems. Roofs absolutely degrade with age, and in case after appeals case, FEMA's position has been that there were pre-existing issues.

Proactive Photo Defense

Following a disaster which generates a large amount of debris, it may be very important to photograph a sampling of the streets in the neighborhoods where the heavy equipment required for debris removal will operate. It is a frequent claim of local agencies that debris removal operations caused damage to local streets which were previously in good condition. However, in almost all appeals cases, the local agency loses out when it cannot demonstrate that the streets were in fact in good condition. This is important to do before the first piece of heavy equipment begins operation. This will be somewhat challenging if debris is covering the streets.

Another possible solution would be to drive those low-lying roads and streets which might typically flood using a dash camera immediately before a noticed storm. Not all streets need to be surveyed: only those which have a chance of flooding, and obviously only if those roads are in good condition, i.e., without alligator cracking of other obvious signs of deterioration or deferred maintenance. If the noticed storm is a hurricane and heavy debris is expected, then drive a sampling of streets and roads to establish that these facilities were in good condition before the disaster.

Photo Documentation Done Right

"Between March 12 and April 28, 2019, Minnesota experienced severe winter storms, straight-line winds, and flooding that impacted several counties, including Freeborn County. Freeborn County Highway (Applicant) requested Public Assistance (PA) to repair twelve roads (Facilities) damaged by the declared disaster. FEMA did not conduct site inspections because the Applicant indicated that the work was 100 percent completed at the time of the Recovery Scoping Meeting. The Applicant submitted invoices, maintenance records, and photographs of the damage to the Facilities, but FEMA was unable to determine whether the Facilities sustained damage directly due to the disaster or whether the damage was due to a lack of maintenance."[3]

"On May 20, 2020, FEMA issued a Request for Information (RFI) to the Applicant requesting documentation to demonstrate that the damage to the Facilities was disaster-related and the costs were necessary and reasonable. The Applicant responded to the RFI asking FEMA to reconsider the documentation it previously submitted, but did not provide additional information. However, the Applicant followed up in October 2020 with an email containing the 'Cost Ledger for 2018' showing the amount spent on the Facilities for 'spot graveling and culvert repair' as well as various other types of routine maintenance."[4]

"FEMA issued an RFI on May 10, 2021, requesting additional photographs or documentation demonstrating visible and quantifiable surface damages caused by the declared disaster after the flood waters receded, a spreadsheet listing the 12 claimed damaged locations, and corresponding invoices that indicate the amount of gravel and cost to repair each site to predisaster conditions."[5]

"As noted by the Applicant, the 'Damage Description and Dimensions' page of Grants Manager/Grants Portal breaks down the individual sites with starting and stopping GPS coordinates, and indicates how much gravel was used to repair the roads along those coordinates. The Applicant supported this information with its 'Contract Work Summary,' showing the materials and corresponding invoices, the labor summary, and the cost validation spreadsheet. Additionally, the Applicant provided photographs of the Facilities showing flooded sections which are labeled with site names and GPS coordinates. These photographs show standing water on and rutting of the roadway surface, as well as water overtopping the road and running off the opposite side. These photographs also show road closure and traffic guidance signs to prevent traffic and additional damage to the roads following the disaster. Finally, the Applicant submits its 'Road Cost Ledger,' showing the breakdown of work done to maintain the roads prior to the disaster. This document shows when the work was done and on which road, what materials were used, and the labor, equipment, material, and other costs."[6]

How Not to Do Photo Documentation

"Hurricane Harvey caused high winds, severe storms, and flooding in Texas from August 23 through September 15, 2017. The Ethician Foundation (Applicant), a Private Nonprofit (PNP) entity, sought FEMA assistance to repair damage caused by Harvey to the chimney at its Baird House, also known as the 1844 George Washington Rogers House (Facility)."[7]

"FEMA inspected the Facility on May 23 and June 6, 2018. The Facility is a two story, roughly 4,000 square foot wood-framed structure with wood floors, wood siding and a metal standing seam roof originally constructed in approximately 1845. The Facility has a 30-foot-tall brick chimney, constructed (or reconstructed) in the 1980s. According to FEMA's Site Inspection Reports (SIRs), the chimney was leaning away from the Facility at an angle of approximately 5 to 7 degrees. This lean began when the slope destabilized in 2005, following Hurricane Rita, and worsened following Hurricanes Ike (2008) and Harvey."[8]

"FEMA found the Facility to be ineligible for Public Assistance (PA) funding in an October 11, 2018 Determination Memorandum (DM). FEMA determined that both of its SIRs showed that the Facility was neither in active use nor undergoing temporary repairs during Hurricane Harvey. FEMA also noted that the Applicant had failed to establish that the Facility had been or would be in use within a reasonable time. Further, FEMA found, and the Applicant acknowledged, that the chimney began leaning away from the Facility before the disaster. FEMA therefore determined that the claimed damage was not the direct result of the disaster."[9]

"The RA (*Regional Administrator*) noted that photographs showed the Facility devoid of contents, exhibits, or documented collections, and the Applicant's first appeal acknowledged that the Facility suffered from chronic criminal trespass, criminal vandalism and theft. Ultimately, the RA found the lack of documented evidence regarding: a) the existence of guided tours of the Facility; b) exhibition of a documented museum collection with regular operating hours; c) any approved budget; or d) a schedule or end date for the ongoing remodeling/restoration work to be dispositive as to whether the Facility was in active use as a museum or not."

In this case the photographs submitted, rather than bringing salvation, were just one more nail in the coffin for this appeals case. Why someone would go to these lengths to prove they were wrong is a mystery and shows a substantial lack of understanding of how the Public Assistance process works.

Recap

Although there are no rules or regulations requiring photo documentation, it is one of the most important tools the local agency has in its arsenal to protect its claims of disaster-caused damage. The fact that photo documentation is a very low-cost effort is just frosting on the cake. I do not believe that it is an exaggeration to say that at least ½ of all denials of eligibility could be avoided with good pre-disaster and post-disaster photographs, if in fact the facilities were in good condition before the disaster.

If a facility clearly has pre-existing damage or deferred maintenance, then why bother? We won't need any help from FEMA to get denied eligibility.

Notes

1 https://www.fema.gov/appeal/direct-result-disaster-support-documentation
2 https://www.fema.gov/appeal/direct-result-disaster-support-documentation-1
3 https://www.fema.gov/appeal/result-declared-incident-33
4 Ibid.
5 Ibid.
6 Ibid.
7 https://www.fema.gov/appeal/inactive-or-alternative-use-facility
8 Ibid.
9 Ibid.

9 Disaster Procurement

Disaster Purchasing: An 800-Pound Public Assistance Gorilla

There are many different aspects of the Public Assistance process which are important, nay, critical, but few of these critical aspects are more important than proper procurement in full compliance with Title 2 of the Code of Federal Regulations, Part 200, (2 CFR, Part 200) specifically, sections 200.217 through 200.326, AND the local agencies' own procurement rules, whichever are more restrictive.

The short version is that a failure to comply with the provisions of 2 CFR, Part 200 will turn 24-karat solid gold eligibility into mud. Plain and simple, mud. And once a procurement is made, there is no undoing it.

Here's the Real Problem with Purchasing

Almost no one knows about the Federal procurement regulations in Title 2 of the Code of Federal Regulations, Part 200.

1) Emergency managers are generally unaware of these requirements. Emergency managers are usually tactical people, often retired police officers, firefighters, or former military. For the most part, they are doers, not management analysts or accountants.
2) Finance staff will seldom interface with FEMA and its procurement regulations, at least until it is too late. Most finance staff are not disaster procurement specialists.
3) Purchasing officials often have no knowledge of these Federal regulations. In the many training programs I have presented for purchasing officials, I was always amazed at the looks of total bewilderment that I would see in a room full of these otherwise very knowledgeable and experienced professionals.
4) Other than FEMA, there is almost no training available about proper disaster-related procurement.
5) Finally, FEMA is aggressively enforcing these regulations. At every turn in reviewing applications for Project Worksheets, FEMA now keeps one eye open for ANY procurement irregularities. In fact, FEMA has teams of attorneys dedicated to the enforcement of procurement regulations.

A Purchasing Worst-Case Scenario

In terms of Department of Homeland Security, Office of the Inspector General (DHS-OIG) audits, this audit is almost as bad as they get:

DOI: 10.4324/9781003487869-11

"On May 22, 2011, a slow moving, three-quarter-mile-wide EF-5 tornado struck Joplin, Missouri, with winds in excess of 200 miles per hour. Joplin Schools served 7,793 students in a 69.9 square mile area in Jasper County, Missouri, at the time of the disaster. The school district operated multiple facilities, including 13 elementary schools, three middle schools, and a high school. The tornado devastated the city and claimed 161 lives, including students and a school faculty member . . . the tornado destroyed multiple buildings, including Joplin High School, which had to be totally reconstructed. The tornado also extensively damaged several other school and district facilities."[1]

"Four days after the disaster, to allow immediate efforts to rebuild, the Missouri Governor waived the requirement for state and local agencies to adhere to normal state procurement regulations. Joplin School officials said they used the Governor's waiver and the school board's policy for waiving competition requirements to procure goods and services in emergencies. As a result, Joplin Schools hired a grant management contractor about 10 days after the tornado to assist with the disaster recovery process."[2]

"The community's need to reopen schools was an exigent circumstance. Accordingly, Joplin Schools' exigency period lasted from May 22, 2011, until August 17, 2011, the date Joplin Schools reopened schools. After the school year began, Joplin Schools' Chief Financial Officer (CFO) said normal competitive procurement procedures for disaster-related contracts had resumed."[3]

"We audited a FEMA Public Assistance (PA) Program grant of $152.7 million that the Missouri State Emergency Management Agency (Missouri), a FEMA grantee, awarded to Joplin Schools for damages sustained from the EF-5 tornado. Although granted $152.7 million, Joplin Schools claimed a gross amount of $218.5 million in reported disaster-related costs to replace and repair buildings and equipment. Of the $218.5 million that Joplin Schools claimed in costs, $187.3 million represented non-exigent contract work."[4]

"Key personnel, such as the CFO of Joplin Schools, with direct knowledge of the disaster work left the school district before our audit work was completed. In March 2018, Joplin School officials notified us about a district-wide reorganization of management personnel and staff turnover. The reorganization and turnover mean that many of the current Joplin School officials were not involved in the actions and decisions described in this report."[5]

Results of Audit

"Joplin Schools did not account for and expend $187.3 million of $218.5 million of the requested Federal share of grant funds according to Federal regulations and FEMA guidelines when it awarded 146 contracts for non-exigent work. Specifically, Joplin Schools:

- Did not comply with Federal procurement regulations for contract provisions and affirmative steps in awarding construction contracts;
- Did not comply with Federal procurement regulations in awarding its grant management contract; and
- Claimed ineligible direct administrative costs (DAC) related to its grant management contract."[6]

"This occurred because Joplin School officials were either unaware of or did not understand procurement regulations. Joplin School officials also disregarded Missouri's authority and relied heavily on the advice of their grant management contractor."[7] (Emphasis Added)

"Joplin Schools did not always follow Federal procurement regulations when it awarded $187.3 million in contracts for non-exigent disaster-related repairs and replacement. For its construction contracts, Joplin Schools did not include all required Federal contract provisions or take affirmative steps to ensure disadvantaged firms had opportunities to compete for the contracts. In awarding its grant management contract, Joplin Schools did not comply with all Federal procurement regulations. Specifically, in awarding the grant management contract, Joplin Schools did not comply with the requirement for full and open competition."[8]

The Federal Procurement Rules Are Different

When we as a local agency receive a Federal grant from FEMA or any other Federal agency, even one dollar, our entire pool of money becomes tainted and we are obligated to follow the Federal procurement rules, and any state and local purchasing regulations, whichever has the most stringent requirements. This requirement applies to <u>all</u> Federal grants, not just to FEMA Public Assistance grants.

In Federal procurement regulations, the "Simplified Acquisition Threshold" is $250,000. Any work contracted above $250,000 has certain requirements attached. However, if the local agency's sealed bid threshold is $50,000 or $100,000, then that lower dollar amount prevails because it is the more restrictive requirement. The "most stringent requirement" must be looked at for each individual section of 2 CFR, Part 200, not the regulations in their totality.

Why Is Proper Procurement So Important?

Figure 9.1 was taken from FEMA online data and shows the dollar amounts of Public Assistance distributed by damage Category A through G. The encircled bar, second from the left, is for all Category B

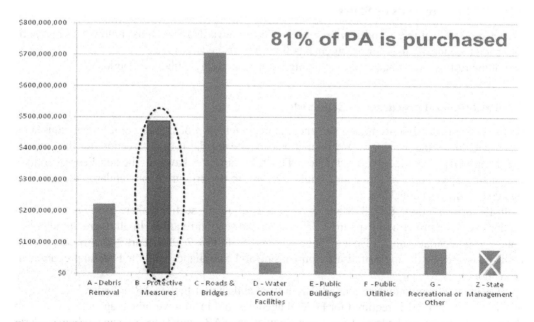

Figure 9.1 Chart derived from FEMA statistics showing allocations of Public Assistance grant funds distribution.

Emergency Protective Measures, which includes all disaster response and rescue activities, including evacuations, sheltering, and mass feeding, etc. In the two years of data sampled, all Category B costs were less than 20% of all Public Assistance funds. The remaining 81% of funding is most often used to pay for contracted work, since most agencies have neither the expertise, experience, nor equipment on hand to clean up the debris and make all the repairs necessary in a timely manner. Therefore, procurement is critical to the Public Assistance process. Most of our disaster costs are not police, fire, or other emergency responses; most of our costs are related to contracting activities.

Violations of Federal procurement violations may result in partial or complete deobligation of FEMA funding. And following the Federal procurement regulations is not a matter of substantial compliance; it is all or nothing. Consider Public Assistance funding as a boat. If there is a hole in the boat below the water line, it will sink. It doesn't matter where the hole is located, the boat will sink. Any violation of the regulations in 2 CFR, Part 200 is sufficient to lose money on a deobligation. That said, there are certain targeted 'go-to' regulations which are more often cited by both DHS auditors and FEMA staff. We will point these out in this chapter.

The Regulation Sections

The following are the leading sections within 2 CFR, Part 200. These introduce each of the sections; however, each of these sections contains additional details and requirements. Compliance with the following sections will not necessarily mean full compliance with 2 CFR, Part 200. For the full set of requirements, please see the full text version of 2 CFR, Part 200, available online. Be sure to download the most current version, as there may be out-of-date versions on the internet as well.

§ 200.317 Procurements by States

"When procuring property and services under a Federal award, a State must follow the same policies and procedures it uses for procurements from its non-Federal funds."[9]

For the rest of us non-states, the following regulations apply without exception.

§ 200.318 General Procurement Standards

"(a) The non-Federal entity must have and use documented procurement procedures, consistent with State, local, and tribal laws and regulations and the standards of this section, for the acquisition of property or services required under a Federal award or subaward. The non-Federal entity's documented procurement procedures must conform to the procurement standards identified in §§ 200.317 through 200.327."[10]

In the prior section, §200.318 and each of the following sections, there are numerous subsections which amplify and explain in detail what the section requires. In all, there are approximately 100 separate points of compliance required to follow 2 CFR, Part 200. An entire book could be written on the topic of disaster purchasing and compliance with the Federal procurement regulations.

These federal regulations are both different from and similar to the FAR or Federal Acquisition Regulations. The FAR is required for Federal agencies, not local government agencies. The main difference between the Federal Acquisition Regulation (FAR) and Title 2 of the Code of Federal Regulations (2 CFR, Part 200) is their scope and focus. The FAR governs federal procurement of goods and services, while Title 2 CFR, Part 200 deals with grants and agreements awarded to non-federal entities.

Case Study: Private Non-Profit, No Procurement Policy, Cost Plus a Percentage of Costs Contract

This case, like so many other appeals cases, has multiple issues; however, we will focus primarily on the procurement problems.

"From September 14–16, 2020, strong winds, rain, and flooding from Hurricane Sally caused damage throughout southern Alabama. St. Thomas by the Sea Parish (Applicant) used Belfor USA to remediate interior water damage and make temporary roof repairs at its church (Facility) in Orange Beach. Actual costs totaled $846,303.00. FEMA created Grants Manager Project (GMP) 180211 to document Category B (emergency protective measures) work for the remediation and temporary repairs Belfor completed."[11]

"On April 9, 2021, FEMA issued a Request for Information (RFI) to 24 subsidiary organizations under the Archdiocese of Mobile (Archdiocese), including the Applicant. FEMA requested documentation related to the claimed damages, insurance policies and settlements, and Small Business Administration (SBA) loan applications for each of the organizations. The Archdiocese responded to the RFI on May 7, 2021. It stated that each subsidiary organization had uploaded damage information and insurance documentation to Grants Portal. The Archdiocese also stated that it continued to pursue insurance claims and would provide updates as those claims were settled."[12]

"In a Determination Memorandum dated May 25, 2021, FEMA denied Public Assistance (PA) funding for GMP 180211. FEMA stated that the only documentation submitted to date was Belfor's invoice for the work at issue and a denied SBA loan application. Therefore, FEMA found that the Applicant had not submitted documentation that would enable it to develop the project and evaluate it for eligibility."[13]

"FEMA issued an RFI expressing concern that the available information did not support project eligibility. FEMA requested: (1) insurance documentation with information about the Facility and damage; (2) contract and procurement documentation; (3) a contractor's invoice with descriptions of the damage and the work performed; and GPS coordinates correlating to pre- and post-disaster photographs of the Facility and its roof and interior."[14] (Emphasis Added)

"Here, the available information does not fully clarify the contractual relationship between the Archdiocese, the Applicant, and Belfor. It appears that following Hurricane Sally, the Archdiocese used a predisaster contract with Belfor to engage their services on behalf of the Applicant. In order to receive PA funding for the work, the Applicant must demonstrate that both the pre- and post-disaster procurement actions were made in full compliance with federal requirements. On second appeal, FEMA examined the predisaster contract and the post-disaster contract, to determine compliance with federal procurement regulations."[15]

"The Applicant did not provide any written procurement policies or procedures with its appeal; it also stated affirmatively that the Archdiocese 'did not have a formal procurement process.' Thus, the Applicant has not demonstrated that the predisaster contract was procured using a documented contract procurement policy. It further indicated that no policy was in place for the procurement of the post-disaster contract. Therefore, FEMA determines that neither contract was procured in compliance with the federal procurement standard at 2 CFR § 200.318(a)."[16]

"Further, PNP (*private non-profit*) applicants are required to maintain records sufficient to document the procurement history. Without documented policies, FEMA is unable to identify how the procurement actions were conducted. For example, FEMA cannot determine whether the predisaster agreement was procured in a manner ensuring full and open competition, whether either contract was procured using one of the five procurement methods approved in regulation, whether the noncompetitive procurement of the post-disaster contract was warranted due to exigent or emergency circumstances, or whether a cost or price analysis was prepared for the post-disaster contract. The Applicant has not provided information documenting the procurement history for the contracted work, as required by the federal procurement standard at 2 CFR § 200.318(i)."[17]

"Finally, provisions in both the pre- and post-disaster contracts contained prohibited CPPC (*cost-plus-a-percentage-of-costs*) methods for determining costs. Both included a 21 percent markup on the total cost for unscheduled materials, unscheduled equipment, and subcontractors/vendors; a 15 percent markup on the total cost for reimbursables; and a 15 percent markup on the costs of airfare, hotels, rental car rates, and other travel expenses. Thus, for each markup: (1) the contracts used a predetermined percentage rate; (2) the contracts applied the percentage rate to actual performance costs; (3) the total amount of the markup was uncertain at the time of contracting; and (4) the amount of the markup increased commensurately with increased costs for each item. Therefore, FEMA determines that the contracts used prohibited CPPC costing methods in violation of the federal procurement standard at 2 CFR § 200.323(d)."[18]

At the end of the second appeal, the applicant was granted $262,930 of the $846,303 for which it filed the appeal, a net loss of $583,373.

§ 200.319 Competition

"(a) All procurement transactions for the acquisition of property or services required under a Federal award must be conducted in a manner providing full and open competition consistent with the standards of this section and § 200.320."[19]

Ernie Abbott, Former Chief Counsel at FEMA during the Clinton Presidency, states that a lack of competitive bidding is the most common cause for a FEMA deobligation. The language of 2 CFR, Part 200 §200.320 (b) (1) (i) (B) states, "Two or more responsible bidders are willing and able to compete effectively for the business." However, FEMA requires at least three sealed bids for those purchases over the Simplified Acquisition Threshold, or the lower limit as may be specified in the local agency's procurement regulations.

Audit Case Study: Minneapolis Park and Recreation Board Did Not Follow All Federal Procurement Standards for $5.1 Million in Contracts

"The Board owns and maintains parks, parkways, lakes, and waterways in and adjacent to the City of Minneapolis (City). The Board has control over the shores and waterways adjacent to any lake, waterway, or other body of water that it owns or governs. The Board is a semi-autonomous political subdivision of the City and may act on its behalf."[20]

"In June and July 2014, severe storms, straight-line winds, and flooding caused a mudslide and severe damage to two golf courses. The mudslide caused damage to the property of Fairview Hospital (Hospital), another FEMA applicant. The mudslide also caused slope failure that threatened additional damage to Hospital property requiring the Board to respond quickly. As a result, the Board and the Hospital entered into a memorandum of understanding to share costs related to the slope repair. The President declared the major disaster on July 21, 2014, and amended the declaration on August 21, 2014, to include Hennepin County, where the Board's damaged properties are located."[21]

Results of Audit

"Although the Board accounted for disaster-related costs on a project-by-project basis, it did not always comply with Federal procurement standards in awarding 15 contracts totaling $5.1 million. As a result, full and open competition did not always occur, and FEMA has no assurance that costs were reasonable or that small and minority firms, women's business enterprises, and labor surplus area firms received sufficient opportunities to bid on federally funded work. We generally do not question costs for work during exigent circumstances when lives and property are at risk. Therefore, we did not question $324,473 the Board expended for work performed to stabilize a slope failure during exigent conditions. However, we do question $4.8 million the Board claimed for non-exigent contract work."[22]

The following paragraph from the audit also points out a particularly pernicious fact which is a common finding in DHS-OIG audits. Per the auditors, the states fail to properly support the local agencies in their Public Assistance claims. I have seen this same finding in audits in more than a dozen different states. It's a fact of life that many states do not have the ready, knowledgeable, and experienced personnel resources to assist local agencies with Public Assistance. Therefore, the burden falls back upon the local agencies to take care of themselves or risk losing Public Assistance dollars.

"Minnesota, as the grantee, should have done more to ensure that the Board was aware of these standards. It is the grantee's responsibility to ensure that its subgrantees are aware of and comply with Federal requirements. Therefore, Minnesota should provide technical assistance and monitoring to the Board to ensure it complies with Federal procurement regulations, as well as reasonable assurance that the Board will spend the remaining $2,550,092 for eligible disaster work according to Federal procurement standards."[23]

In the follow-up, FEMA evaluated the facts in this case, and disallowed $1,239,567 dollars because of improper procurement.

"Federal regulation does not preclude the use of a pre-qualified list of firms, such as the one used by the Applicant. However, the Applicant may not merely select a candidate from such a list, it must still open the procurement so as not to preclude potential bidders from qualifying during the solicitation period. Not only did the Applicant not open the procurement, it also ruled out the only other firm from the pre-qualified list of contractors because of a prior contractual dispute. In doing so, it assumed that the other firm would not want to bid on the contract and in turn, did not allow that firm nor any others the opportunity to submit bids. By foregoing a solicitation for the specific work needed for this project, the Applicant precluded potential bidders that may have opted out of the City's solicitation for any number of reasons."[24]

Another aspect of compliance with § 200.319 Competition is a practice which is quite common among counties, but I have also seen the same practice at the city level. The practice is some form of a local vendor preference. These policies dictate that a bidder whose business location is within the jurisdiction is awarded a small percentage advantage when scoring the bids. This can be a good practice when only local funds are in play. However, when Federal funds are involved, this practice is prohibited because it creates a disadvantage for some bidders, contrary to Federal procurement policy. Geographical preferences of any kind are generally prohibited, as seen in this case from Kentucky.

"During the incident period of January 26 to February 13, 2009, freezing rain from winter storms caused the buildup of ice on woody vegetation, which resulted in hazardous limbs and the scattering of vegetative debris on roadways throughout the cities of Nicholasville and Wilmore and Jessamine County (Applicants) in Kentucky. The Applicants executed a Memorandum of Agreement (MOA) to share the contract costs incurred for debris removal and disposal. In order to address the immediate threat posed by the debris, the County initially hired a local contractor, CMC, Inc., for debris work on a time and materials (T&M) basis. Costs for the work to prepare two debris management sites in Nicholasville and Wilmore were charged against the T&M contract (debris management sites)."[25]

On February 6, 2009, Jessamine County initiated its Request for Proposal (RFP) process. The RFP requested unit pricing for six items of work to remove and dispose of debris from the event: (1) rights-of-way (ROW) vegetative collection (requesting separate prices for collection of debris based on zero to 15 miles and 16 to 30 miles); (2) private property vegetative collection (zero to 15 miles) and (16 to 30 miles); (3) removal of dangerous hanging limbs; (4) removal of hazardous stumps; (5) reduction through grinding of vegetative debris; and (6) haul-out of reduced vegetative debris. Additionally, the RFP directed respondents to submit completed price proposal forms and proof of insurance and bonding. The County required proposals to: (1) describe the contractor's knowledge and ability to provide expert guidance in accordance with guidelines and regulations relevant to disaster-generated debris; (2) include recently completed major debris removal projects, and information necessary to determine past performance; (3) provide references, a technical plan explaining how the work would be done, and a list of personnel with their qualifications; and (4) list all equipment available for the project. The RFP also explained that proposals would be evaluated and scored based on five criteria: knowledge of FEMA regulations and procedures (25 percent); operational plan (10 percent); proposed price (15 percent); past performance record (30 percent); and personnel qualifications and company experience (20 percent)."[26]

"Four Kentucky contractors, including CMC, and five contractors from other states submitted proposals by the County's deadline. The County Emergency Management Director reviewed the proposals and provided recommendations. In a memorandum dated February 9, 2009, the Emergency Management Director recommended selection of CMC for the following reasons: (1) the majority of debris was already collected and the remainder of work would not take long to complete; (2) the sites for collection were established and advertised and debris operations were stable; (3) the work was being handled by a local contractor and subcontractor; (4) CMC agreed to renegotiate pricing; and (5) a new contract would cause major delay and confusion. The County awarded the contract to CMC based on the renegotiated unit prices."[27]

"FEMA prepared separate Project Worksheets (PWs) to document each Applicant's share of claimed costs using the CMC debris work invoices billed through Jessamine County. As noted in the PWs, FEMA found that the Applicants did not follow Agency guidelines for debris documentation and federal procurement requirements. FEMA found that work performed was eligible, but that the County should have awarded the contract to Asplundh, the contractor with the lowest costs. FEMA determined that Asplundh submitted the lowest cradle to grave removal cost of $10.63 per cubic yard (CY) compared to CMC's $17.65 per CY rate. As a result, FEMA calculated eligible funding using Asplundh's unit costs for the quantities of debris as invoiced. As management costs for the debris management sites were not listed as a component in the RFP, FEMA applied an event-historical rate of $2.25 per CY, which was also the rate CMC charged on another project in a nearby county for the same event. While the County paid a total of $1,244,200.20 for CMC's work, FEMA determined only $753,126.22 was eligible."[28]

"On second appeal, the Applicants argue that CMC was selected as the lowest cost option out of the proposals submitted by **local** contractors, and further contend that Stafford Act § 307(a)(1) authorizes the use of local preference when making an award. However, FEMA has, within its discretion, declined to implement by regulation or policy alternative compliance requirements that would exempt PA applicants from local preference limitations established by 44 CFR § 13.36(c)(2). Failure to allow for full and open competition through the use of a local/state geographical preference does not comply with Federal procurement standards."[29] (Emphasis Added)

§ 200.320 Methods of Procurement to Be Followed

The non-Federal entity must have and use documented procurement procedures consistent with the standards of this section and §§ 200.317, 200.318, and 200.319 for any of the following methods of procurement used for the acquisition of property or services required under a Federal award or subaward.

This section spells out the various levels of procurement in 2 CFR, Part 200:

- Micro Purchases are those purchases made costing less than $10,000 per purchase, *
- Small purchases are those purchases made over $10,000 and less than $250,000 per purchase, *
- Formal procurements are those purchases over $250,000, and *
- Noncompetitive Procurements, which are used in very limited circumstances:

  1) The item is available only from a single source;
  2) The public exigency or emergency for the requirement will not permit a delay resulting from competitive solicitation;
  3) The Federal awarding agency or pass-through entity expressly authorizes noncompetitive proposals in response to a written request from the non-state entity; or
  4) After solicitation of an adequate number of sources, competition is determined inadequate.

* Or the lower limits which may be set in the state or local purchasing regulations.

This next case is from New York for a look at another fatal appeals case. "From September 7–11, 2011, Tropical Storm Lee caused flooding damage to the Susquehanna Apartments – North Shore Campus, a multi-family housing complex with five, two-story buildings owned and operated by the Binghamton Housing Authority (Applicant) in Binghamton, NY."[30]

"In response, the Applicant used its own Force Account Labor (FAL) and contracted with Homer C. Gow & Sons General Contractors (Homer Gow) and Keystone Associates, Architects, Engineers and Surveyors, LLC (Keystone) for campus repairs and associated project management. Repair work was initiated within a week of the disaster declaration and largely completed by January 6, 2012, although Keystone continued to coordinate with FEMA and contractors to review invoicing and design through July 2012. FAL *(force account labor)* work was documented in employee time-cards containing brief descriptions of tasks, such as 'flood,' 'security,' or 'snow removal.' For all other work, the Applicant's contractors issued purchase orders and invoices with descriptions of tasks, dates, employees, and costs based on the time and materials (T&M) involved."[31]

"There were 31 Homer Gow purchase orders totaling $589,955.10 and 6 Keystone invoices totaling $68,792.85. The Applicant claims that the Keystone invoices were based on a pre-existing, written, and competitively bid contract, dated February 2011. The Homer Gow purchase orders, however, were based solely on oral-agreements, including an agreement not to exceed $25,000.00 for any individual order."[32]

"As the Grantee *(New York State)* concedes, the Applicant did not competitively bid the services of Homer Gow or enter into a single contract for the overall restoration work. Instead, the Applicant accepted T&M Purchase Orders for individual items of work, ensuring through oral-agreement that no individual purchase order exceeded $25,000.00, but omitting total cost-ceilings or "do-not-exceed" provisions. The Applicant also did not submit any documentation demonstrating that it conducted a cost or price analysis prior to engaging Homer Gow. For these reasons, the RA found that the Applicant violated FEMA's procurement regulations requiring free and open competition and a cost or price analysis, and prohibiting T&M contracts that do not include a cost ceiling provision."[33]

In this case, for whatever reason the local agency decided to use a Time & Materials (T&M) contract when the work should have been solicited by sealed bid. Not only was an improper method of contracting used, but it also included the use of oral agreements, which simply never fly with the Feds. Furthermore, a proper Time and Materials contract would have included a not-to-exceed amount and would have been accompanied by a proper cost or price analysis, both of which were missing in this case. The local agency was lucky that FEMA did not completely deny all funding for this work and instead allowed $433,913 in reimbursements; however, this represented a loss of $203,992.

§ 200.321 Contracting with Small and Minority Businesses, Women's Business Enterprises, and Labor Surplus Area Firms

Affirmative Steps

"NFEs (*Non-Federal Entities*) must, at a minimum, take the following six 'affirmative steps' to assure that minority firms, small businesses, women's business enterprises, and LSA (*Labor Surplus Areas, i.e., areas of high unemployment)* firms are used when possible:

1) Solicitation Lists
   NFEs must include small and minority businesses and women's business enterprises on solicitation lists. NFEs must provide documentation of all prequalified lists or solicitation lists used in the procurement.
2) Soliciting
   NFEs must ensure that it solicits small and minority businesses and women's business enterprises whenever they are potential sources. An NFE must provide documentation to demonstrate compliance with this step (any communication, email, etc.).
3) Dividing Requirements
   NFEs must divide total requirements, when economically feasible, into smaller tasks or quantities to permit maximum participation by small and minority businesses and women's business enterprises. When applying this requirement, it is important to recognize that intentionally dividing up a large procurement into smaller parts in an effort to fall beneath the federal SAT or the micro-purchase threshold is prohibited. Additionally, bundling requirements so that small businesses, minority businesses, and women's business enterprises would be unable to compete is prohibited.
3) Delivery Schedules
   NFEs must establish delivery schedules, where the requirement permits, which encourage participation by small and minority businesses and women's business enterprises.
4) Obtaining Assistance
   NFEs must use the services and assistance, as appropriate, of such organizations as the Small Business Administration (SBA) and the Minority Business Development Agency (MBDA) of the Department of Commerce.
6) Prime Contractor Requirements
   NFEs must require the prime contractor, if subcontracts are anticipated or used, to take the five previous affirmative steps. FEMA recommends that the NFE include this requirement in the solicitation, as well as in the contract, to ensure contractor compliance.

NFEs must document its compliance with the six affirmative steps discussed above. Examples of documentation include prequalified, or solicitation lists used, communications, emails, online searches, etc." (Emphasis Added)

This section, §200.321, is a very high-risk part of the Federal procurement regulations, as it is frequently checked for compliance by both FEMA personnel and the DHS auditors.

It is highly recommended that local agencies begin doing this for all purchasing if they do not already do it regularly, since it will be very difficult to institute these practices flawlessly in the middle of a disaster. This is not a "set-aside" contracting requirement since the local agency must only notify these businesses of the potential opportunities to do business with the local agency. There is no requirement to award business to these firms if they are not the qualified low bidder.

Case Study: Rural Electric Cooperative

"From January 19 to 26, 2010, a severe ice storm with high winds damaged the Nishnabotna Valley Rural Electric Cooperative's (Applicant) electric distribution system. FEMA prepared 11 Project Worksheets (PWs) for conductor replacement. The Applicant hired a contractor to trim trees and vegetation in the right-of-way for the conductor replacement work. Between December 10, 2013 and March 14, 2014, FEMA issued eleven determination memoranda to notify the Applicant that tree trimming is maintenance and is therefore not eligible."[34]

Although this case initially centered around the question of tree trimming as a safety issue for electric utility workers, it quickly devolved into a treatise on procurement. Also, the references to Federal procurement regulations which follow are from 2010 and all the section citations have changed since the end of 2014.

"Subgrantees (*local agencies*) must comply with a variety of grant administrative requirements to be eligible and receive Public Assistance. When securing a contract for federally-funded work, an applicant is required to comply with the procurement requirements set forth in 2 CFR Part 215 (*now Part 200*). Among other requirements, applicants must (1) use the appropriate type of procuring instruments for the particular procurement; (2) consider small business, minority-owned firms, and women's business; (3) make pre-award and procurement documentation available to the awarding agency; (4) perform and document a cost or price analysis; and (5) include specific provisions in the contract."[35]

"The contract in this instance lists hourly rates for labor, equipment, and fuel, does not have a clear scope of work, and therefore meets FEMA's definition of a time and materials contract. The Applicant's contract was also signed on January 4, 2011, while the disaster occurred in January 2010 – a year earlier. The Applicant should have been able to develop a well-defined scope of work within twelve months of the disaster. The Applicant has not demonstrated that a time and materials contract was appropriate for the particular procurement or demonstrated that the contract was only used for a limited time for work that was necessary immediately after a disaster. Furthermore, the contract does not include a not to exceed provision."[36]

"An applicant must also demonstrate that it took positive efforts to utilize small businesses, minority-owned firms, and women's business enterprises whenever possible. While the Applicant states that 'every attempt was made to solicit bids from qualified small, minority-owned, and/or women-owned businesses' as required by 2 CFR § 215.44(b)(2), no explanation or documentation of those efforts was submitted. Furthermore, the Applicant has not provided documentation that it undertook the other positive efforts described at 2 CFR § 215.44(b)."[37] (Emphasis Added)

There were three more specific problems with the procurement, any one of which could have been fatal, and in this case, FEMA denied all funding, a loss to the agency of $191,629.00.

True-Life Tales

A Southern California county-wide water agency suffered from a damaging earthquake some years ago. To repair the system, the water agency hired many local firms to make the needed repairs. Virtually all the contractors were minority-owned construction firms, which would certainly comply with the spirit of §200.321 (Contracting with small and minority businesses, women's business enterprises, and labor surplus area firms). In fact, the agency hired only two non-minority owned firms, and that was for special technical expertise that could not be found within the county. However, the auditors cited the agency for its <u>failure to have a formal policy and include the policy requirements in its contracts</u>. We must not only do the right thing, but we must also have formal written policies and procedures that state we will do the right thing. In this case, although the auditors made the finding, FEMA waived any deobligation because the agency had substantially complied with the requirement. Although the local agency prevailed on this issue, the audit findings may have caused some heart palpitations, and then there were the largely unnecessary administrative costs to resolve the matter had a policy been in place.

§ 200.322 Domestic Preferences for Procurements

As appropriate, the non-Federal entity should, to the greatest extent practicable under a Federal award, provide a preference for the purchase, acquisition, or use of goods, products, or materials produced in the United States (including but not limited to iron, aluminum, steel, cement, and other manufactured products).

This is a relatively new addition to the list of procurement requirements, and there is little in the record currently. The requirements of this section must be included in all subawards, including all contracts and purchase orders for work or products under this award.

§ 200.323 Procurement of Recovered Materials

A non-Federal entity that is a state agency or agency of a political subdivision of a state and its contractors must comply with Section 6002 of the Solid Waste Disposal Act, as amended by the Resource Conservation and Recovery Act.

The requirements of Section 6002 include procuring only items designated in guidelines of the Environmental Protection Agency (EPA) at 40 CFR part 247, which contain the highest percentage of recovered materials practicable, consistent with maintaining a satisfactory level of competition, where the purchase price of the item exceeds $10,000 or the value of the quantity acquired during the preceding fiscal year exceeded $10,000; procuring solid waste management services in a manner that maximizes energy and resource recovery; and establishing an affirmative program for procurement of recovered materials identified in the EPA guidelines.

There is a technical nuance which must be mentioned here. It applies to many parts of the Public Assistance process, as per this example of § 200.323 Procurement of recovered materials requirement. Most public agencies have for years had a local and/or state requirement to purchase recycled materials when possible, and therefore may not include the Federal legal requirement in FEMA-funded contracts. However, when spending FEMA money, we are spending Federal funds, and therefore must comply with Federal requirements. Although the local agency might have a very similar, even identical, regulation, we must cite the Federal regulation in our contracts; in this case, specifically, the Resource Conservation and Recovery Act (RCRA) Section 6002.

Procurement Case Study: State Agency

This is another of those multi-fatality appeals cases which could have been lost for several reasons, including proper documentation of labor, equipment, and materials. We are focusing on the procurement aspects only.

"From February 1–23, 2017, severe winter storms, flooding, and mudslides caused damage throughout central and northern California. The University of California, Santa Cruz (Applicant) requested Public Assistance (PA) and reported erosion, mudslide, and slip damage to access roads and a wooden foot bridge in its Big Creek Ecological Reserve. FEMA conducted a site visit on September 22, 2017, and subsequently prepared Project Worksheet (PW) 1430 to document the Applicant's use of force account labor, force account equipment, materials, and contracted work to repair the roads and bridge. The scope of work (SOW) for PW 1430 describes completed work to restore a wooden foot bridge and roads at 12 separate sites."[38]

"In a June 3, 2019, email to the California Governor's Office of Emergency Services (Recipient), FEMA requested supporting documentation for the project, including: (1) timesheets, timecards, payroll information, or other documents supporting the force account labor claim; (2) invoices or receipts supporting the force account materials and contract claims; (3) information related to the materials the Applicant used; and (4) the Applicant's pay and procurement policies. The Recipient acknowledged receiving the request. It provided material purchase invoices and emails related to the project, and stated that it would send a request to the Applicant for the remaining documentation. In a follow-up email to the Recipient on June 6, 2019, FEMA again requested the supporting documentation."[39]

"In a Determination Memorandum (DM), FEMA denied $62,727.14 in PA funding for PW 1430. FEMA acknowledged that the work performed was necessary as a result of the disaster, however, it found that the Applicant had not submitted documentation supporting the costs claimed."[40]

On April 12, 2022, the FEMA Region IX Regional Administrator denied the appeal for costs of $63,558.

"FEMA provides PA funding for contract costs based on the terms of the contract if the applicant meets federal procurement and contracting requirements. State and territorial government applicants must follow the same policies and procedures they would use for procurements with non-federal funds; comply with 2 CFR § 200.322, 'Procurement of recovered materials'; and ensure that every purchase order or other contract includes any clauses required by 2 CFR § 200.326, Contract provisions."[41]

In some audits and appeals cases, the available records are sometimes vague and appear to be glossing over some important facts hiding in the administrative shadows. This is one of those cases. The appeals reviewer specifically mentions §200.326 but provides no details that would make the issue more relevant. So, we know there was a screw-up, but we do not have any clarity of the details.

"The Applicant claims $25,000.00 for contracted work performed to remove a rockslide and restore an access road at a site on its property. In support, it provides the contract it signed with Blaze Engineering, Inc., as well as a work proposal and price quote, an invoice for the completed work, and copies of two cancelled checks."

"Here, the SOW includes contracted work to remove and dispose of large rock debris at a site on the Applicant's property (Site 2). The SOW also includes a statement that the Applicant followed its own policy in procuring the contract with Blaze Engineering. However, the statement in the SOW is insufficient. In order to demonstrate compliance with federal procurement and contracting standards, the Applicant must provide supporting information establishing compliance with its own procurement policies and procedures. FEMA requested the Applicant's predisaster procurement policy in its emails to the Recipient in June 2019, prior to issuing the DM. However, the policy was not included in the administrative record. Therefore, FEMA determines that the Applicant has not demonstrated compliance with federal contract procurement standards. Consequently, the contract costs claimed are ineligible."

§ 200.324 Contract Cost and Price

1) The non-Federal entity must perform a cost or price analysis in connection with every procurement action in excess of the Simplified Acquisition Threshold (*currently $250,000*), including contract modifications.
2) The method and degree of analysis depends on the facts surrounding the procurement situation, but as a starting point, the non-Federal entity must make independent estimates before receiving bids or proposals.

The following case study is one of 15 similar appeals from the Port of Galveston, which lost a total of $1,257,118.82 in claimed Direct Administrative Costs (DAC) resulting from an improper procurement of a disaster cost recovery consultant following Hurricane Ike in 2008. In this case, there are multiple failures in compliance with the applicable Federal procurement regulations.

"From September 7 to October 2, 2008, Hurricane Ike impacted areas in East Texas. High winds and wind-driven rain damaged Pier 15 and a warehouse owned by the Port of Galveston (Applicant). FEMA developed Project Worksheet (PW) 13713 to document permanent work and costs for the repairs, including project-related Direct Administrative Costs (DAC). FEMA initially obligated Public Assistance (PA) funding based on estimated costs for the project but later deobligated all funding apart from DAC to account for actual insurance proceeds received by the Applicant. On September 19, 2020, the Texas Division of Emergency Management (Recipient) submitted a large project closeout request for PW 13713, validating costs for contracted work and DAC."[42]

"On February 7, 2022, FEMA Region 6 issued a closeout notice for PW 13713. FEMA stated that all PA funding related to repair costs for the project had been reduced due to actual insurance proceeds received by the Applicant. Therefore, FEMA stated that the only project funding at issue was associated with the Applicant's DAC claim. It then pointed to a previous first appeal decision for PW 15839, a separate project also associated with repairs the Applicant completed following the same disaster. FEMA explained that in the referenced first appeal decision, it found DAC the Applicant claimed for services performed by Beck Disaster Recovery (BDR) was ineligible due to improper contract procurement. FEMA found that the Applicant's DAC claim for BDR services under PW 13713, with costs totaling $19,981.10, was similarly ineligible."[43]

"The Applicant provided a lengthy analysis of the BDR contract procurement process under PW 15839, asserting that it complied with federal procurement requirements. The Applicant acknowledged that the BDR contract for that project was procured through an agreement in which an entity known as the Houston-Galveston Area Council Buy Board (HGAC-Buy) acted as its procurement agent. It asserted that HGAC-Buy procured the contract competitively, receiving 13 proposals in response to the bid solicitation, and that this was 'a direct indicator that adequate price competition was not lacking.' Thus, it asserted that BDR's costs were reasonable, and a cost analysis for the contract was not required. Finally, the Applicant asserted that the use of HGAC-Buy for procurement constituted 'an intergovernmental purchasing agreement' that fulfilled federal standards under Title 44 of the Code of Federal Regulations Part 13, which was in effect at the time of the disaster."[44]

"On October 12, 2022, the FEMA Region 6 Regional Administrator (RA) denied the appeal, finding that the BDR contract was not compliant with federal procurement regulations. FEMA explained that HGAC-Buy did not base the procurement of the contract on the Applicant's specific requirements. FEMA noted that the contract bid advertisement was completed before the Applicant requested HGAC-Buy's assistance and included 'an infinite quantity of services' that 'could be provided to users nationwide.' Thus, FEMA determined that the broad nature of the procurement action restricted competition for the specific requirements under PW 13713 and amounted to a prohibited sole-sourced contract. FEMA also determined that the Applicant failed to demonstrate compliance with other federal procurement standards, such as performing a cost analysis or taking steps to utilize socioeconomic procurement practices."[45] (Emphasis Added)

"On first appeal, FEMA determined that the Applicant's contract with BDR was not competitively procured. FEMA also found that the Applicant did not perform a cost analysis for the contract or take necessary steps to utilize small businesses, minority-owned firms, and/or women's business enterprises for the administrative services at issue. On second appeal, the Applicant does not contest the substance of these determinations. Rather, it states that FEMA applied authorities that were not in effect on the declaration date for the disaster (September 13, 2008) and 'retroactively [applied] policy to make determinations related to eligibility.'"[46]

"As a local government entity, the Applicant was required to comply with federal procurement standards found in 44 CFR § 13.36 at the time of the disaster declaration. In FEMA's first appeal decision, the Agency determined the BDR contract was noncompetitively procured, citing Title 2 of the Code of Federal Regulations (2 CFR) § 215.43. However, the applicable procurement standard in effect at the time was 44 CFR § 13.36(c)(1). Similarly, FEMA determined that the Applicant had not prepared a cost analysis for the BDR contract, citing 2 CFR § 215.46; in fact, the applicable procurement standard in effect at the time was 44 CFR § 13.36(f)(1)."[47]

Another issue in this case was the use of a contract through a "buy-group," a network of procurement officials which shares vendor and contract information among government agencies. We will address this complex issue later in this chapter.

§ 200.325 Federal Awarding Agency or Pass-through Entity Review

(a) "The non-Federal entity must make available, upon request of the Federal awarding agency or passthrough entity, technical specifications on proposed procurements where the Federal awarding agency or passthrough entity believes such review is needed to ensure that the item or service specified is the one being proposed for acquisition. This review generally will take place prior to the time the specification is incorporated into a solicitation document. However, if the non-Federal entity desires to have the review accomplished after a solicitation has been developed, the Federal awarding agency or pass-through entity may still review the specifications, with such review usually limited to the technical aspects of the proposed purchase."

This section of 2 CFR, Part 200, almost seems insignificant. However, it is clearly not, because this section gives both the state and the Federal government the right to review all documentation related to local agency procurements. The following appeals case is a perfect example of the failure, nay, the recalcitrant refusal to provide to FEMA the requested procurement information in a usable format. Once again, this is an appeal case with multiple problems, and we will focus exclusively on the Request for Information regarding the agency's procurements. In this case, FEMA made an initial deobligation of all 29 projects for a total loss of $2,018,593.

"In October 1999, Hurricane Irene (DR-1306) swept over the City of Sweetwater (Applicant), Florida, causing widespread flooding and damage. Afterwards, the Applicant initiated multiple repair projects and sought reimbursement from FEMA's Public Assistance (PA) Program. One year later, the Applicant was impacted by heavy rains and flooding, resulting in another major disaster declaration (DR-1345) with an incident period from October 3 to October 11, 2000. The subsequent disaster event adversely affected some of the ongoing repair work from the prior disaster. FEMA prepared multiple Project Worksheets (PWs) to document debris removal, emergency protective measures and permanent work related to the second disaster event (DR-1345). At the

May 2010 final inspection prior to project closeout, the Applicant was unable to provide complete documentation to substantiate the costs for each project. In May 2012, FEMA deobligated all funding from 29 PWs, 28 PWs related to DR-1345 and 1 PW related to DR-1306."[48]

First Appeal

"In a letter dated April 24, 2014, the Applicant appealed FEMA's deobligation of $2,018,593.29 in PA funding for the 29 PWs. The Applicant argued that, over the course of 14 years, it experienced substantial turnover among its employees including three different mayors, three different finance directors and four different grants administrators. As a result, the Applicant asserts it should not be expected to produce documentation attesting to the completion of the work associated with the various PWs. The Applicant emphasized the burden associated with trying to produce such documentation and stated that it did not have the financial capacity to pay back the deobligated funds. Through a July 16, 2014 letter, the State of Florida Division of Emergency Management (Grantee) forwarded the Applicant's appeal to FEMA and recommended approval."[49] (Emphasis Added)

This is no doubt a very sad story about a community that has difficulty retaining its key employees. However, they neglect to state that they had one city manager and one deputy city manager over that same time. Turnover is a fact of life in every sector, and all agencies experience staff turnover to some degree, all of which has nothing to do with compliance with Federal regulations.

"During the adjudication process, the Regional Administrator (RA) sent a Final Request for Information (RFI) to the Applicant. The Final RFI advised the Applicant that the Administrative Record did not validate reimbursement for incurred costs. The Final RFI made detailed requests for multiple, specific pieces of information, including but not limited to:

- Payroll information for all the Applicant's employees involved in the disaster work.
- Individual name, job title, and function to include the day the work was performed.
- Equipment logs and usage records, hourly pay rates and equipment rates, cost of materials purchased.
- Documentation of the City of Sweetwater's procurement process for this project.
- The request for proposal outlining the scope of work for each site.
- Any mutual aid agreements to which the Applicant may have been a party."[50]

"The Applicant responded to the Final RFI by sending FEMA a USB flash drive containing over 12,000 separate files."[51] (Emphasis Added)

"On January 13, 2016, the RA issued a decision denying the Applicant's appeal. The RA determined that the Applicant did not adequately document costs incurred for the projects. The Applicant's Final RFI response, provided on electronic media, did not contain a cover letter or any indication as to how the files document the eligible work performed or costs incurred for multiple projects. In upholding the deobligation, the RA found that the information provided did not assist FEMA in analyzing the 29 appealed PWs."[52] (Emphasis Added)

"Per FEMA regulation and policy, an appeal must contain documented justification supporting the applicant's position. The appeal must specify the monetary figure in dispute and the provisions in Federal law, regulation, or policy with which the appellant believes the initial action was inconsistent. When adjudicating appeals, FEMA relies on the Administrative Record, which includes documentation submitted by an applicant. An applicant is required to substantiate its appeal by not only producing records, but explaining how those records should be applied to support the appeal."[53] (Emphasis Added)

§ 200.326 Bonding Requirements

For construction or facility improvement contracts or subcontracts exceeding the Simplified Acquisition Threshold, the Federal awarding agency or passthrough entity may accept the bonding policy and requirements of the non-Federal entity, provided that the Federal awarding agency or passthrough entity has made a determination that the Federal interest is adequately protected.

If such a determination has not been made, the minimum requirements must be as follows:

1) A bid guarantee from each bidder equivalent to 5% of the bid price. The "bid guarantee" must consist of a firm commitment such as a bid bond, certified check, or other negotiable instrument accompanying a bid as assurance that the bidder will, upon acceptance of the bid, execute such contractual documents as may be required within the time specified.
2) A performance bond on the part of the contractor for 100% of the contract price. A "performance bond" is one executed in connection with a contract to secure fulfillment of all the contractor's requirements under such contract.
3) A payment bond on the part of the contractor for 100% of the contract price. A "payment bond" is one executed in connection with a contract to assure payment as required by law of all persons supplying labor and material in the execution of the work provided for in the contract.

There are virtually no appeals cases dealing with bonding requirements. However, bonding requirements might come into play if a local agency were to require bid, construction, and payments bonds higher than the Federal limits in an effort to screen out certain "undesirable" contractors and prevent them from bidding on work.

§ 200.327 Contract Provisions

The non-Federal entity's contracts must contain the applicable provisions described in appendix II to this part.

In addition to other provisions required by the Federal agency or non-Federal entity, all contracts made by the non-Federal entity under the Federal award must contain provisions covering the following, as applicable.

1) Contracts for more than the simplified acquisition threshold must address administrative, contractual, or legal remedies in instances where contractors violate or breach contract terms and provide for such sanctions and penalties as appropriate.
2) All contracts in excess of $10,000 must address termination for cause and for convenience by the non-Federal entity including the manner by which it will be effected and the basis for settlement.
3) Equal Employment Opportunity
4) Davis-Bacon Act
5) Contract Work Hours and Safety Standards Act
6) Rights to Inventions Made Under a Contract or Agreement
7) Clean Air Act and the Federal Water Pollution Control Act
8) Debarment and Suspension: A contract award must not be made to parties listed on the government-wide exclusions in the System for Award Management (SAM)
9) Byrd Anti-Lobbying Amendment
10) See § 200.323 (Procurement of recovered materials)

11) See § 200.216 (Prohibition of certain foreign manufactured telecommunications and video surveillance services or equipment)
12) See § 200.322 (Domestic preferences for procurements)

These required contract provisions must be included in every contract and should also be included in every request for bids. Even when one or more of these contract provisions does not apply, they must still be included in the contracts. A classic example of this is (4) The Davis-Bacon Act, which does apply to most Federal contracts, but very often does not apply to contracts with local agencies. Yet it must still be included in the contract as a requirement.

Each of these 12 contract provisions must be included in every contract as specified here, even when and if they do not apply to the project. A best practice is to have a separate add-in document when soliciting bids for Federally funded projects. One good practice is to have the bidders initial each of these contract provisions to ensure that each has been read and agreed to.

Stepping Back to Gain Perspective

These are the Federal procurement regulations which must be followed in conjunction with the local procurement regulations and any state procurement regulations which may also apply, whichever rule is more restrictive.

Over the past 25 years, I have trained thousands of public agency personnel on the Public Assistance program, and it is my observation that most public agencies, particularly those with no prior disaster cost recovery experience, believe that cost recovery is all about tracking the labor, equipment, and materials for disaster response. They have no inkling of the complexities involved in every step of the Public Assistance process, especially the procurement function.

Faulty procurement is a killer of eligibility, and most procurement officials, even those with decades of experience, have little or no experience in dealing with FEMA and its complex and demanding regulations, unless of course they learned the hard way.

One very important note of caution is taken from the FEMA Disaster Assistance Fact Sheet, 9580.4, Emergency Work Contracting: "Applicants should be advised that no contractor has the authority to make eligibility determinations, determinations of acceptable emergency contracting procedures, or definitions of emergency work. Eligibility determinations are made solely by FEMA."[54] (Emphasis Added)

Local agencies must recognize that vendors and contractors are in business to make a profit, and not necessarily to look out for the best interests of the local agency. Once awarded a contract, they might make efforts to "upsell" the agency on additional work. They may allege, and even absolutely state that the work which they are proposing is eligible, or that they did the same work in some other jurisdiction. Local officials should NEVER rely on any allegations of eligibility made by a vendor or contractor. This is purely a FEMA function.

In the past, FEMA itself has been the subject of more than one DHS-OIG audit on purchasing. This audit comes from Oklahoma City in 2014.

FEMA's Dissemination of Procurement Advice Early in Disaster Response Periods

Results of Audit

"During our deployment to the Oklahoma City Joint Field Office, we observed instances where FEMA personnel provided incomplete and, at times, inaccurate information to Public Assistance applicants regarding Federal procurement standards. Based on our audit reports and personal observations, similar instances have been occurring for several years. Thus, we were not surprised when we learned that FEMA officials did not emphasize contracting compliance training at the Joint Field Office. Contracting violations significantly increase the risk that contracts for disaster work will result in ineligible and excessive costs and that open and fair competition will not occur. Therefore, FEMA should take immediate steps to ensure that its Joint Field Office personnel provide complete and accurate information on Federal procurement standards."[55]

FEMA, to its great credit, has taken these and other audit findings to heart, and now vigorously enforces all aspects of Title 2 of the Code of Federal Regulations, Part 200. In fact, in terms of audits, there is no single audit finding which occurs more often than those related to procurement.

As a trainer, I have spoken about disaster procurement at state, regional, and national purchasing conferences, and one aspect of the presentations never fails to light up the room. It's as though I was throwing a five-gallon container of gasoline into an already-burning theater. The statement is this: As local agencies, we cannot "piggyback."

"Piggybacking," the practice of 'borrowing someone else's established contract for their own use, is almost always ineligible. There are a few cited exceptions, but they are as rare as a Gutenberg Bible. And "piggybacking" includes the use of cooperative purchasing agreements in almost every case.

"As a general matter, FEMA suggests that non-state applicants exercise caution when using cooperative purchasing programs because the Agency has observed problems with non-state applicants' ability to meet all of the requirements of the federal procurement standards found in 2 CFR §§ 200.317–200.326 when a non-state applicant uses these programs. Applicants are not permitted to use out-of-state cooperative purchasing programs."[56] (Emphasis Added)

In this case, the use of the word "suggests" is a felonious understatement. At a minimum, such a practice will invite intense scrutiny and may unnecessarily result in deobligation and the need to file an appeal in some cases. The document continues:

"FEMA will closely scrutinize the use of cooperative purchasing programs. If a non-state applicant decides to use a cooperative purchasing program, it will need to provide FEMA with documentation to show and explain how its use of a cooperative purchasing program complied with all federal procurement standards and applicable state, tribal and local procurement rules and policies."[57]

It should be noted, however, that FEMA distinguishes between "piggybacking" and true "joint procurements," where two or more agencies jointly seek out bids and jointly award contracts.

Cardinal Changes

Another important aspect of procurement is the matter of "cardinal changes." In some instances, the term "cardinal change" may substitute for a change in the "scope of work."

The best way to explain this is by example; this time it's a case from South Dakota, which is one of the longest appeals cases which I have studied and appears to have been written by someone with a legal background. The case is heavily edited because of its length.

"In the spring and summer of 2011, warm temperatures caused significant runoff and flooding in the state of South Dakota following a winter with above-normal snowfall. On May 13, 2011, the President declared a major disaster for the state (FEMA-1984-DR-SD), with an incident period of March 11 to July 22, 2011."[58]

"The flooding caused erosion and degradation of the sanitary sewer system operated by the City of Pierre (Applicant). The sewer system delivers sewage to the Applicant's wastewater treatment plant. A 72-foot long section of a 10-inch diameter clay sanitary sewer pipe on Missouri Avenue failed, creating a sinkhole that began developing during the disaster incident period. The sinkhole stretched due east along the sewer line (the 'East Line' to Pierre Street) from a manhole that serves as a connection point between additional sewer lines and a lift station. The Applicant used contract services, force account labor, and force account equipment to address resulting sewer backups, bypass pumping, and perform temporary repairs to the sinkhole."[59]

"The Applicant received two bids from contractors to perform permanent repairs to the sinkhole and remove and replace the sewer line, one bid for $86,000.00 and another for $160,400.00. On October 25, 2011, the Applicant awarded a contract to the lower bidder, Morris, Inc. (the 'Contractor'). The contract included work immediately adjacent to the manhole and included removal of a minimum of the top half of the impacted manhole. Under the contract, the Contractor was responsible for providing all materials, except for surface gravel, and the Applicant was responsible for replacing asphalt surface material, closing the water line valve, and bypass pumping."[60]

"On October 26, 2011, the Applicant issued a notice to proceed to the Contractor. During excavation and repair and after the pipe was exposed, additional damage was discovered on two additional sewer lines and the manhole. On November 29, 2011, a change order was issued for work to include: (1) removal of the manhole and placement of a concrete base under the replacement manhole, (2) excavation and removal of a damaged 12-inch line to the lift station to the north (the 'North Line' to lift station), (3) excavation and removal of a damaged 10-inch line flowing into the manhole from the west and installation of a new line (the 'West Line' to Fort Street), and (4) installation of sheet piling to protect structures and laborers. The change order amounted to $237,244.86."[61]

"On April 13, 2012, FEMA obligated $90,775.33 in Project Worksheet (PW) 2432, covering the contract and force account work and materials associated with the temporary repair of the sinkhole ($3,484.60), direct administrative costs (DAC) ($94.73), and the initial contract for the permanent repair of the sewer line ($86,000.00), plus a contract estimate for curb and gutter work ($1,196.00). PW 2432 did not include the costs of work performed under the $237,244.86 change order to the contract because, FEMA determined, there was a 'lack of specific documentation regarding costs and quantities' and 'proof that the damages were flood-related.'"[62]

"The Acting RA *(Regional Administrator)* also found that the Applicant improperly procured both the original contract and the change order. As to the original contract, the Acting RA stated that the Applicant failed to publicly advertise its solicitation for bids and, instead, merely solicited invitations to bid from local, capable contractors. The Acting RA also stated that the need for additional work was not discovered until after the contract completion date of November 21, 2011. As to the change order, the Acting RA stated that the Applicant failed to perform a necessary cost analysis and approved the change on a lump-sum basis, a change that increased the contract price by 276 percent. The Acting RA concluded that this increase could not be considered reasonable."[63]

Note: This case originated in 2011 when the old procurement regulations were in effect; hence the code citations are outdated but still relevant.

"The Applicant points out that the breaks in the three lines affected the main sewer line, which serves more than half of the city's population. The Applicant notes that above-normal precipitation continued during the repairs and that, given the extended length of the project, repair work – which involved exposed utilities and structures – would take place during below-freezing temperatures as winter set in. The freezing temperatures would affect not only the repairs but also bypass operations, the Applicant argues. In addition, the Applicant notes, the Contractor had already installed sheetpiling, which was actively protecting the site, and was the sole source of sheetpiling in the area. The Applicant also notes the numerous other sewer repairs were required following the disaster event and asserts that utility repairs and levee removals in progress in dozens of counties across South Dakota and in the surrounding state affected contractor availability. Thus, the Applicant argues, the Contractor, already in place, was the only practicable source to continue the repair work."[64]

"There are three procurement-related issues presented under the second appeal: (1) whether the method of procurement used by the applicant for the original procurement complied with 44 CFR § 13.36(d); (2) whether the procurement method followed by the applicant for the change order complied with 44 CFR § 13.36(d); and (3) whether the applicant conducted the proper cost or price analysis for the change order."[65]

"Once a contract is awarded, a local government may need to make changes to that contract to react to newly encountered circumstances, fix inaccurate or defective specifications, or modify the work to ensure the contract meets the local government's requirements. A contract 'change' is any addition, subtraction, or modification of work under a contract during contract performance. Notwithstanding the need to make appropriate contract changes, a local government may not make a 'cardinal change' to a contract so as to circumvent the requirements of 44 CFR § 13.36 for full and open competition . . . . A modification that comprises a cardinal change constitutes a sole source award, and FEMA evaluates such a modification to determine if the conditions precedent for a noncompetitive procurement at 44 CFR § 13.36(d)(4) have been met."[66]

"FEMA has determined that the Applicant was not required to use sealed bidding for the original procurement and that it was appropriate for the Applicant to have utilized the small purchase procedure method of procurement . . . . There is no indication that the Applicant improperly limited a known, larger requirement so as to avail itself of small purchase procedures."[67]

"The first step in analyzing a contract change is to determine whether the change is within the scope of the original procurement. If it is, then the change order is simply part of the original procurement, which means that such a change would be permissible if the Applicant had complied with all relevant procurement standards during the original procurement. FEMA treats a cardinal change, on the other hand, quite differently. A cardinal change is a significant change in contract work (property or services) that causes a major deviation from the original purpose of the work or the intended method of achievement, or causes a revision of contract work so extensive, significant, or cumulative that, in effect, the contractor is required to perform very different work from that described in the original contract. In effect a cardinal change creates a new procurement action that must meet all relevant procurement standards. Cardinal changes cannot be identified by assigning a specific percentage, dollar value, number of changes, or other objective measure that would apply in all cases."[68]

"FEMA has determined that the change order at issue comprised a cardinal change to the original contract based on the significant increase to the amount and type of repair work and total cost. The scope of work under the original contract included excavation and repair of the 10-inch line to the east of the manhole and removal and reset of a minimum of the top half of the manhole. The Applicant explained that the depth of the repair work was significantly increased from 16 to 20 feet in the change order and prompted a great deal of additional work, including the excavation and replacement of 12 feet of line west of the manhole, excavation and replacement of 16 feet of line to the north, and placement of a concrete pad beneath the new manhole. The cost of this work increased the costs of the contract by $237,244.86, which is an almost 300% increase to the original fixed-price contract for $86,000.

A contract change that comprises a cardinal change constitutes a sole source award, and FEMA evaluates such a modification to determine if the conditions precedent for a noncompetitive procurement at 44 CFR § 13.36(d)(4) have been met."[69]

FEMA determined that "The damage to the three sewer lines and manhole was caused by the disaster event, and the work as described in the change order was necessary to accomplish the needed repairs. The Applicant complied with the method of procurement requirements under 44 CFR § 13.36(d) for both the original procurement and the change order, but failed to comply with the cost analysis requirement for the change order required by 44 CFR § 13.36(f). Notwithstanding this noncompliance, FEMA will exercise its discretion to not take enforcement action by reducing otherwise eligible costs incurred by the Applicant for eligible work. FEMA will, therefore, increase the amount awarded under PW 2432 by an additional $213,570.86 for costs incurred under the change order, $3,397.10 for the manhole, $2,359.85 for curb and gutter repair and replacement, and $5,666.05 for DAC. However, FEMA is denying the requests for additional costs for the lift station and asphalt repairs."

This case represents a series of unique circumstances which allowed the city to largely prevail. The most significant fact is the freezing nature of winter life in South Dakota, and how the onset of winter would make the repairs virtually impossible, and therefore accelerated procurement was needed. Absent some similar level of threat, other jurisdictions in a similar but not identical situation might not fare as well.

Emergency Work versus Emergency Contracting

There is a huge difference between Emergency Work and Emergency Contracting. Imagine that in your community, the city hall, as a direct result of the disaster, i.e., hurricane, tornado, earthquake, fire, flood, etc. lies in a heap of rubble. Fortunately, the disaster struck at 2:00 A.M. on a Saturday morning; no one was in city hall; there is no lead or asbestos in the rubble; and the heap of rubble does not affect any other nearby facility. The rubble pile which was formerly the city hall is a mess; it is an embarrassment; but it is not an immediate threat to life, safety, public health, or other improved property. Therefore, that are no shortcuts which may be taken in letting the contract have the pile of rubble picked up and hauled away. If the contract for the debris clearance is greater than $250,000, The city will have to go with a full-on sealed bid process to select the contractor for the job if it is to qualify for FEMA funding.

Limited procurement shortcuts are only available on a very restricted basis, and certain requirements of 2 CFR, Part 200 are not waivable. If a disaster-caused problem poses an immediate threat to life, safety, the public health, or improved property, then under very restrictive conditions some of the 2 CFR, Part 200 requirements may be waived.

True-Life Tales

The devastating Santa Rosa Tubbs fire of 2017 burned over 5,000 structures to the ground. During the fire, purchasing agent Brandalyn Tramel called me with a question: "Mike, we have 5,000 sewer lines that need to be capped because of a threat to the public health. What do we do?" I asked her if she had a signed finding of a public health emergency from the County Health Officer. She did. Next, I asked her how many of these open sewer lines presented an "immediate threat" to public health. When she checked, she said needed about 100 locations to be capped immediately. I told her to write a Time and Materials contract to cap 100 homes, list them by their addresses, and attach the Public Health Officer's finding. The remaining 4,900 homes would have to go to a full bid contract.

So, even in one of the most damaging fires ever to hit California, there were limits and procedures to be followed. The following is a quotation from a now-archived FEMA Fact Sheet, 9580.4, which in principle still stands. Note in the quotation that reference is made to the old sections within 2 CFR, prior to the change in the regulations in late 2014. "Performing emergency work (Categories A and B) does not relieve the applicant from the requirements of competitive bidding. Not all emergency work is time sensitive to the point where competitive bidding is infeasible. In some situations, awarding a short-term non-competitive contract for site-specific work may be warranted; however, if the contract is for a long-term operation lasting weeks or months, the contract should be competitively bid as soon as possible. Contracts that are based on cost plus a percentage of the cost shall not be used for either competitive or non-competitive procurement. See 44 CFR §13.36 (1)(4)."[70] (Emphasis Added)

Have Pre-Disaster Purchasing Contracts in Place

The Federal government loves a deal, and they love to comparison shop. Consequently, it is not uncommon in audits or appeals cases to see comparison charts of what one local agency has paid for some service or commodity against what other local agencies have paid for the same or very similar goods or services. Usually, in an appeal, the presence of a price comparison chart does not bode well for the local agency in question. The following chart is taken from an appeal by a Louisiana parish following Hurricane Katrina.

In the second column of this table are the initial unit prices paid for work, with the cost comparison from other local agencies in the third column.

Why the Local Agency NEEDS Pre-Disaster Contracts

If a neighboring local agency has a pre-disaster contract in place for services or commodities it can reasonably assume will be needed in a disaster, the agency with a pre-disaster contract in place will set the bar for the other agencies needing the same service or commodity. For instance, the agency expects that it might need port-a-potties and sets up a pre-disaster contract at a rate of $75.00 per week, including regular pumping. Another nearby agency does not have such a contract and is forced to pay market rates of $150.00 for exactly the same service. FEMA will then use the $75.00 (pre-disaster) rate as the "reasonable" rate. The agency without the pre-disaster contract will be lucky if FEMA decides to pay them $75.00 and leave them short $75.00 per unit per week. Once a disaster strikes, many businesses will take full advantage of the seller's market conditions. Even if they don't engage in some form of price gouging, they generally will not fall all over themselves to provide discounts, even if the local agency is a regular customer. The general consensus is, "FEMA is paying the bills, so let's pile on the charges." Additionally, there are some firms that love

Table 9.1 Hurricane Katrina Price Comparison Chart

Contract line items	September 3, 2005 Contract Unit Cost	1st appeal reasonable unit price determination, based on cost matrix	December 9, 2005 Contract Unit Cost	1st appeal reasonable unit price determination, based on cost matrix
White Goods	$150.00 each	$49.00	$75.00	$49.00
Freon recovery	$250.00 each	$42.13	$35.00	$35.00
TDSRS Management	$6.00 per cubic yard	$2.94	$2.90	$2.90
Hanging Limbs		$215 per tree		$215 per tree
2" – 4"	$125.00 each	N/A	$125.00	N/A
5" – 12"	$200.00 each	N/A	$200.00	N/A
>12"	$250.00 each	N/A	$250.00	N/A
Car removal	$1,000.00 each	$36.05		
Boat Removal	$1,000.00 each	$36.05		

Source: https://www.fema.gov/appeal/debris-removal-reasonable-costs-1

disasters because they can charge what they want and get away with it because the need is great, and the available resources are so limited at the moment.

Disasters Are Open Season for Price Gouging

Here is a miniature copy of an unreasonable cost invoice for a board-up following the Napa Earthquake in 2014. At the agency where I was assisting, we immediately rejected the invoice and returned it to the Fire Department that had issued the purchase order. The invoice amount was for $4,153.50 for the installation of 2 each sheets of 4' by 8' plywood and 10 each of 2" by 4" by 8" wood studs.

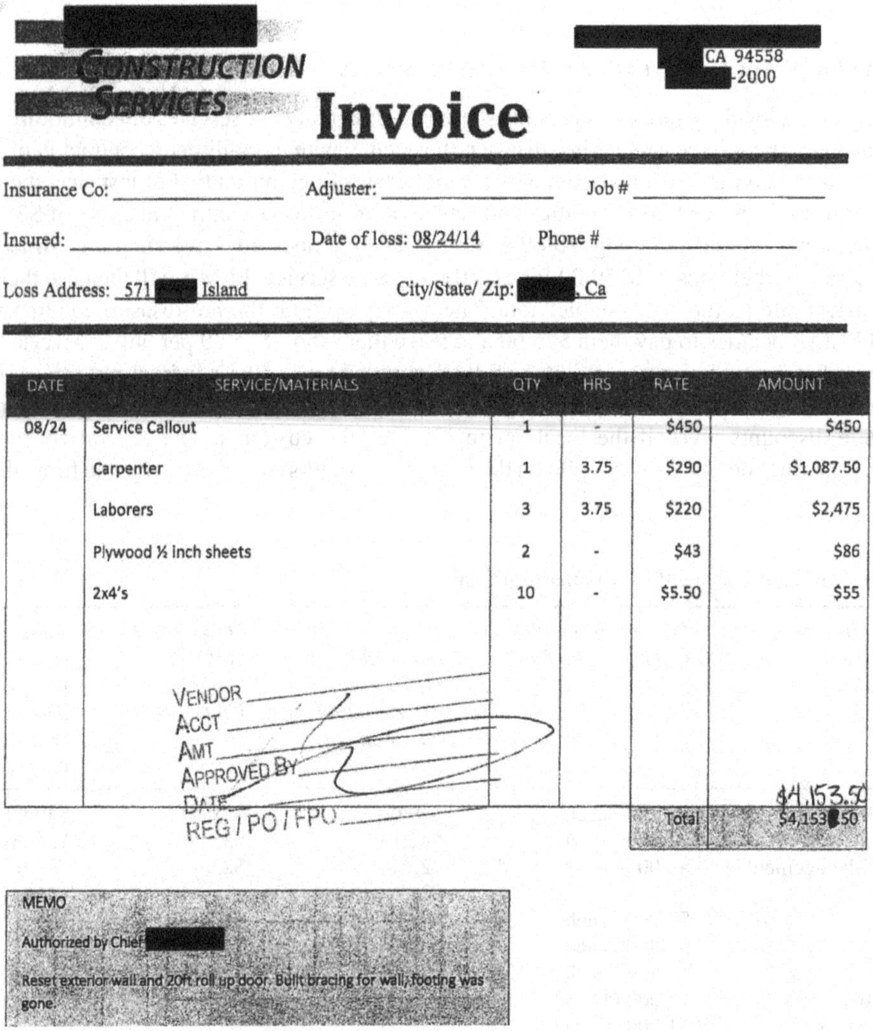

[redacted]
CONSTRUCTION
SERVICES

Invoice

[redacted]
[redacted] CA 94558
[redacted]-2000

Insurance Co: ________ Adjuster: ________ Job # ________

Insured: ________ Date of loss: 08/24/14 Phone # ________

Loss Address: 571 [redacted] Island City/State/ Zip: [redacted], Ca

DATE	SERVICE/MATERIALS	QTY	HRS	RATE	AMOUNT
08/24	Service Callout	1	-	$450	$450
	Carpenter	1	3.75	$290	$1,087.50
	Laborers	3	3.75	$220	$2,475
	Plywood ½ inch sheets	2	-	$43	$86
	2x4's	10	-	$5.50	$55
				Total	$4,153[redacted]50

VENDOR
ACCT
AMT
APPROVED BY
DATE
REG / PO / FPO

$4,153.50

MEMO

Authorized by Chief [redacted]

Reset exterior wall and 20ft roll up door. Built bracing for wall, footing was gone.

Figure 9.2 Redacted actual invoice from the 2014 Napa Earthquake.

I visited this site; in this case, as a former carpenter it appeared to me that there were too many laborers involved. This work could have easily been done with one carpenter and one laborer. This appeared to be a case of "packing it on."

The Local Agency Needs a <u>Disaster</u> Purchasing Policy

Each local agency is required to follow its own purchasing policy <u>AND</u> 2 CFR, Part 200, whichever is more restrictive. For instance, 2 CFR, Part 200 does not specify a proscribed length of time that a request for proposals must be advertised prior to the opening of sealed bids. The requirement is only that sufficient notice be given for the bid process. On the other hand, many local agencies have an established policy that the request for proposals be advertised in a newspaper of local circulation for not less than 21 days. These types of time restrictions are entirely a local condition, but when making disaster-related purchases which are over the Simplified Acquisition Threshold (currently $250,000), then that is the timeline which must be followed. Furthermore, if the day-to-day purchasing rules stipulate that any contract over $50,000 must be awarded through a sealed bid process. So, the local agency must advertise for 21 days for any contract over $50,000.

But this is a disaster; we don't have 21 days to advertise; and by the way, the local newspaper was damaged in the disaster, and there's no telling when they will be publishing again.

However, if the local agency has a specific disaster purchasing policy which specifies that in a properly proclaimed or declared disaster, the 21-day advertising period is foreshortened to 24 hours. Furthermore, the disaster purchasing policy continues, for bona fide disaster related purchases, <u>and only for bona fide disaster purchases</u>, the sealed bid limit is raised to the Federal Simplified Acquisition Threshold of $250,000. Language such as this which is consistently applied in a formal, written, board- or council-approved policy will give the local agency a great deal of flexibility in its disaster procurements.

Red Light Warning

A disaster purchasing policy must be carefully written by someone with extensive knowledge of both 2 CFR, Part 200, AND how FEMA interprets and enforces 2 CFR, Part 200. A poorly written policy could have catastrophic consequences for the adopting agency, with partial or total denial of FEMA funding. In the same way that one might not want their podiatrist to diagnose a heart condition and install a pacemaker or perform a quadruple bypass, not everyone who has some knowledge of the law or has even passed the bar may necessarily be qualified to draft a watertight disaster purchasing policy. In my career, I have seen too many legal documents written by otherwise competent professionals which grossly fail to appreciate the intricacies of dealing with FEMA and its legions of lawyers. Caveat Emptor.

Very Much Related to Pre-Disaster Contracts

Generally, the day-to-day contracts an agency may have with its vendors will be useless for disaster-related procurements. Let's take debris management as a horrible example of what might go wrong.

First off, I'm not making any of these up. I have read some of these contracts, and they are real. They are also useless, but they are real. A hypothetical local agency has a 10-year franchise agreement with its regular trash hauler, the company that goes around the neighborhoods every week and collects household trash and recycling. Somewhere, buried in the fine print of the contract language, someone thought about disaster debris removal and decided to make that a part of the franchise agreement with XYZ Environmental Services, Inc. Bad, Bad, Bad, and then Worse. This is a horrible idea for so many reasons:

1) The franchise trash hauler does not have the necessary equipment to collect, process, and properly dispose of disaster debris. Many trash trucks can only pick up specialized containers (50-to 80-gallon capacity), which are not suitable for bulk debris and large items.
2) The trash hauler would have to purchase or rent a substantial amount of specialized heavy equipment and do it immediately to meet the urgent need to clean up the community.
3) Its personnel have absolutely no experience in handling disaster debris and navigating all the environmental and other regulatory issues involved in disaster debris management.
4) The trash hauler is already at full staffing levels and would be hard pressed to double or triple their normal workforce literally overnight.
5) The debris cleanup, if they could perform it at all, would be at a much slower rate than would be acceptable to the community.
6) The debris cleanup, if they could perform it at all, would be at a much slower rate than would be acceptable to FEMA, and FEMA would see the costs as unreasonable because the cleanup would take so long.
7) While the franchise trash hauler is cleaning up the debris, who is now picking up the weekly trash and recycling?
8) FEMA would properly determine that the local agency paid too much to have the franchise trash hauler collect the debris, based upon an extension of the normal rates charge for weekly trash service.
9) Finally, as previously mentioned, expanding the contract to include disaster debris collection would trigger a "Cardinal Change" in the contract, which we previously discussed.

There are very few if any day-to-day contracts a local agency currently has with its vendors which could survive the issue of a cardinal change.

Pre-Disaster Contracts

That said, FEMA encourages local agencies to have properly drawn-up contracts in place for their disaster response needs. However, the pre-disaster contract must conform to 2 CFR, Part 200.

In this case from Florida, the local agency has a pre-disaster contract in place, but it fails to meet the required Federal standards. "Hurricane Irma made landfall in the Florida Keys on September 10, 2017 with strong winds, heavy rain, and storm surge that caused severe damage throughout Florida. In anticipation of the hurricane, the City of Key West (Applicant) declared a local emergency and used this authority to activate an existing sole source 5-year term contract (procured on April 21, 2016) for emergency management support services. FEMA prepared Project 10619 in the Grants Manager system to capture associated work and costs; however, in a memorandum dated February 26, 2019, FEMA determined that the Applicant failed to comply with federal procurement standards and denied funding."[71]

First Appeal

"The Applicant appealed on May 1, 2019 and stated: (1) its procurement complied with local procurement procedures and that federal procurement requirements (Title 2 of the Code of Federal Regulations (2 CFR) Part 200) did not apply because the procurement was not solicited in response to a disaster. . ."[72]

"FEMA issued a Request for Information (RFI) on August 6, 2019 requesting documentation demonstrating that the Applicant procured its contract in accordance with the procurement standards established by 2 CFR §§ 200.317–200.326. FEMA also requested documentation indicating that the consultant was the lowest responsive responsible bidder, and bid tabulations, analyses or other documents demonstrating the bid evaluation and selection."[73]

"The Region IV Regional Administrator denied the first appeal on March 16, 2020, *(for $185,193.00)* finding that the Applicant did not demonstrate compliance with its local procurement standards or that any of the four recognized circumstances for noncompetitive procurement existed at the time of its procurement per federal procurement standards under 2 CFR Part 200. Additionally, FEMA found that disallowance of funding was an appropriate enforcement action, as the Applicant did not provide documentation to determine reasonable costs for the consultant's work."[74]

"FEMA provides PA funding for reasonable contract costs based on the terms of the contract if the applicant meets Federal procurement and contracting standards set forth in the 2 CFR, Part 200. When choosing a contractor, local governments must follow their own procurement procedures, provided the procurement conforms to federal law and standards and is conducted in a full and open competition to ensure objective contractor performance and to eliminate unfair competitive advantage, organizational conflicts of interest, and arbitrary procurement processes. In addition, an applicant must document its procurement process through 'records sufficient to detail the significant history of procurement' and make available all procurement documents for FEMA or the pass though entity upon request."[75]

"FEMA permits pre-positioned or advance contracts procured before an incident occurs for the potential performance of work post-disaster as a basis for an award of funds but the contract must meet Federal procurement and contracting standards regarding the scope of work, term of work, reasonable price, and any changes made."[76]

Should a local agency wish to wrap disaster response services into a day-to-day contract, then the day-to-day contract must comply with 2 CFR, Part 200. Furthermore, it must deal with the issue of a "Cardinal Change" by including price de-escalation provisions based upon the total quantity of work, and these price de-escalation provisions should be stepped, so that as the total quantity of work increases, the unit prices decrease concurrently.

Also know that FEMA will look at mobilization costs and evaluate the reasonableness of the mobilization costs relative to the total amount of work performed. However, the cleanest method is to keep day-to-day contracts completely separate from pre-disaster contracts and contracts issued after the disaster occurs. The complications that can arise when attempting to marry a day-to-day contract with a disaster-related contracts increase geometrically and may contain hidden problems which will only surface after costs are incurred and reimbursement is sought.

Finding a Solution for a Difficult Situation

We all know that local government employees are asked to do more and more in the same amount of time. But in a disaster, they will be expected to do five or ten times the normal workload instantly, not next week. This is a serious challenge and a threat to effective time management. Would it not be better, at the beginning of the year (fiscal or calendar), to set a goal of creating one new disaster contract each month, or every two months as a way of gradually preparing for a disaster? Prior to implementing such a program, the local agency's Emergency Manager, and representatives from other involved departments, i.e., Finance, Police, Fire, Public Works, etc. would gather to determine the contracts most likely to be needed, and then to prioritize those necessary contracts so that the most important ones are contracted first. There may be cases where some of the more complex contracts, such as debris clearance may involve other departments, and might take six months or a year to complete because of their inherent complexities.

Returning to the Key West case: "The Applicant did not explain why sole sourcing was needed or in the best interests of the Applicant when the contract was procured, nor demonstrate it received approval from the City Commission pursuant to local ordinances prior to awarding the contract. In fact, the Applicant's resolution, which approved and ratified the contract, is dated nearly a year after the Applicant's procurement. Further, the Applicant failed to show solicitation of competitive bids at the time it activated the advance contract would have caused a delay or instability within recovery operations pertaining to this disaster."[77]

"The Applicant did not comply with its own procurement requirements or federal procurement requirements, nor did it demonstrate noncompetitive procurement was allowed due to its consultant being the sole source for emergency support circumstances or selected due to exigent or emergency circumstances."[78]

"While the Applicant provided documentation which identified utilized personnel by name and level of responsibility with a fee and total hours amount attributed to each, the Applicant did not provide descriptions of the type, category or complexity of work performed, supporting timesheets for all hours charged, or documentation that efficient methods and cost controls were utilized. In addition, the cost invoices provided by the Applicant for work performed by the same consultant for other local entities do not show that the rates were the market price for comparable service, e.g., were other consultants operating locally doing similar disaster related work, were the rates derived from the same incident time period as the disaster. Without such supporting information and documentation, FEMA is unable to verify the Applicant's cost analysis or determine the reasonableness of the claimed costs."[79]

Purchasing versus Renting or Leasing

"When the Applicant leases equipment, FEMA provides PA funding based on the terms of the lease. Leasing costs are eligible if:

- The Applicant performed an analysis of the cost of leasing versus purchasing the equipment; and
- The total leasing costs do not exceed the cost of purchasing and maintaining equipment during the life of the eligible project."[80]

"If the leasing costs exceed the cost of purchasing and maintaining the equipment, FEMA determines the amount of eligible costs based on an evaluation of the reasonableness of the costs claimed, including whether the Applicant acted with prudence under the circumstances at the time it leased the equipment."[81]

"If the Applicant has a lease-purchase agreement and obtains ownership during completion of eligible work, FEMA provides PA funding for the equipment use based on the hourly equipment rate."[82] For further information, see the FEMA Schedule of Equipment Rates at: https://www.fema.gov/sites/default/files/documents/fema_schedule-of-equipment-rates_2023.pdf

"If the Applicant has a lease-purchase agreement and completes the eligible work prior to obtaining ownership, FEMA provides PA funding based on the cost to lease the equipment."[83]

FEMA expects to see an analysis anytime that the local agency purchases equipment needed for a disaster response. The analysis must show that a purchase had a lower lifecycle cost than a rental or lease.

FEMA will not pay for equipment when that equipment can be rented or leased at a lower cost, and then they only pay for the actual hours that the equipment was used, unless the equipment had to be rented at a "day" or "weekly" rate in keeping with the rental industry's standard practices, so long as those practices do not conflict with Federal regulations.

Red Light Warning: Electrical Generators

One area where local agencies are repeatedly denied funding is for the use of permanently mounted electrical generators. These are not portable or trailer mounted generators, but rather those which are permanently mounted, i.e., bolted down, in service for a particular facility. There is an apparent error in the Public Assistance Program and Policy Guide (PAPPG), June 2020 Edition, which is quoted as follows:

"III. Applicant-Owned and Purchased Equipment

FEMA provides PA funding for the use of Applicant-owned (force account) equipment, *__including permanently mounted generators__*, based on hourly rates."[84] (Emphasis Added)

However, following this section of the PAPPG apparently is done at substantial risk to the local agency. In appeals cases, all that FEMA reimburses for permanently mounted generators is the added cost of the fuel for the generators. The following appeals case is from Ohio.

"During the incident period of June 29 through July 2, 2012, strong winds and severe storms produced extensive damage throughout Paulding County, causing downed utility lines and widespread power outages for multiple days. The Paulding County Emergency Management Agency (Applicant) utilized two permanently mounted generators during the event to support emergency protective measures at its Emergency Operations Center and communications tower. FEMA prepared Project Worksheet (PW) 510 for $3,803.32 to fund the fuel for the permanently mounted generators. Because both generators were permanently mounted, FEMA did not reimburse the use of those generators based on FEMA's equipment rates, but rather for fuel costs only."[85]

First Appeal

"The Applicant submitted a first appeal for $2,125.00 in a letter dated March 11, 2013, asserting that reimbursement for the permanently mounted generator usage should be based on FEMA's schedule of equipment rates because its permanently mounted generator was housed in a rented facility. The FEMA Region V Regional Administrator denied the first appeal in a letter dated May 7, 2013, explaining that the depreciation and ownership costs of permanently mounted generators are viewed as components of the cost of operating the facility."[86]

"FEMA policy specifically provides that the cost of obtaining power from alternate sources, with a few exceptions, is considered an increased operating expense and is generally not eligible for Public Assistance. FEMA's policy provides exceptions, however, for 'reasonable short-term additional costs to an applicant that are directly related to accomplishing specific emergency health and safety tasks as part of eligible emergency protective measures.' A specific example of such an exception is the 'increased utility costs of a permanently mounted generator at a hospital or police station.' The FEMA Public Assistance Guide also lists the use of 'temporary generators for facilities that provide health and safety activities' as an example of an emergency protective measure that can be undertaken by a community before, during, and following a disaster."[87]

"Recent appeals and appeal decisions have highlighted confusion with regard to distinguishing between the eligible costs associated with the use of permanently mounted generators compared to temporary generators and the underlying rationale for such distinctions. Use of the terms 'portable' and 'fixed' as interchangeable with 'temporary' and 'permanently mounted' has created additional ambiguity by primarily focusing on the physical placement of the generator rather than the duration, intent and purpose of the placement."[88]

"As such, it is important to reinforce the distinction between temporary and permanently mounted generators. FEMA reimburses the use of temporary generators based on FEMA equipment rates or similar set rates in large part because the purpose of the placement of those items at the facility is related to the disaster in question and temporary in nature. FEMA equipment rates include such costs as operation of equipment, depreciation, overhead, maintenance, field repairs, fuel, lubricants, tires, Occupational Safety and Health Administration equipment, and other costs incidental to operation. In contrast to temporary generators, permanently mounted generators, whether a fixture as described within OMB Circular A-87, mounted on a pad within a shed servicing a building, or affixed or otherwise bolted down to a slab adjacent to a building, typically have been placed in their locations for reasons that preceded the disaster and with an intent that they remain there afterward. Hence, the fundamental purpose, nature, and duration of the placement of a permanent generator differ from a temporary generator that is brought in to provide temporary emergency power during the time of the disaster in question. The purpose of permanently mounted generators is to provide backup power whenever necessary, and not only as a consequence of a disaster. Recognizing such a purpose, it is reasonable to assume the associated overhead costs for permanently mounted generators is covered by the applicant's operating budget and that the only out-of-pocket expense for operating them is the increased operating expense of fuel used. Accordingly, FEMA will reimburse fuel costs for permanently mounted generators if they are used to perform eligible emergency work because those are the only increased costs incurred by the applicant as a direct result of the event. This policy distinction applies to permanently mounted generators as a matter of principle, regardless of circumstances associated with an individual applicant's insurance coverage, the placement of a permanently mounted generator in a leased facility, or whether maintenance costs for a permanently mounted generator are included in an applicant's operating budget."[89]

"FEMA does not reimburse the use of permanently mounted generators based on equipment rates. However, if permanently mounted generators are used in the performance of eligible emergency work, FEMA will reimburse the fuel consumed during the performance of that work."[90]

Time and Materials Contracts (T&M)

"T&M contracts do not provide incentives to the contractor for cost control or labor efficiency. Therefore, use of T&M contracts are only allowed if all of the following apply:

- No other contract type was suitable;
- The contract has a ceiling price that the contractor exceeds at its own risk; and
- The Applicant maintains a high degree of oversight to obtain reasonable assurance that the contractor is using efficient methods and effective cost controls."[91]

"FEMA generally limits the use of T&M contracts to a reasonable timeframe based on the circumstances during which the Applicant could not define a clear SOW (Scope of Work)."[92]

"Therefore, the Applicant should define the SOW as soon as possible to enable procurement of a more acceptable type of contract."[93]

"Some entities, such as Rural Electrical Cooperatives, provide the materials necessary to restore the facilities and refer to such contracts as Time and Equipment (T&E) contracts. The limitations and requirements that apply to T&M contracts also apply to T&E contracts."[94]

In the past, FEMA limited T&M contracts to 70 hours. However, that specific limit no longer applies, which makes the call to use a T&M contract a higher-risk roll of the dice. The local agency may argue that it needed more time, while FEMA will allege that the work required less time under a T&M contract. In any case, T&M contracts are a dicey proposition in the best of circumstances. The following appeals case comes out of Florida.

"This letter is in response to your letter dated June 19, 2008, which transmitted the referenced second appeal on behalf of the City of Fort Meyers (Applicant). The Applicant is appealing the Department of Homeland Security's Federal Emergency Management Agency's (FEMA) de-obligation of $168,596 for work completed under a time-and-material (T&M) contract beyond the *(THEN)* allowable 70-hour work period."[95]

"FEMA prepared PW 6333 for $367,299 for debris removal from the Applicant's rights-of-way (ROWs) and other public property. The Applicant used a T&M contract to remove the debris for over one and one-half months. At final inspection, FEMA de-obligated $168,596 because the time period of the work performed under the T&M contract was in excess of the allowable 70-hour time limit. In addition, FEMA could not determine the reasonableness of the costs the Applicant incurred beyond the 70-hour limit."[96]

"The State submitted the Applicant's first appeal to FEMA eight months after regulatory deadline. The Regional Administrator denied the appeal because the State did not submit the appeal within the regulatory timeframe specified in 44 CFR §206.206(c). Therefore, the Regional Administrator did not evaluate the merits of the appeal."[97]

"Time-and-Material contracts should be limited to a maximum of 70 hours of actual emergency debris clearance work and should be used only after all available local, tribal and State government equipment has been committed. Time-and-Material contracts for debris clearing, hauling, and/or disposal should be terminated once the designated not-to-exceed number of hours is reached. On occasion, Time-and-Material contracts may be extended for a short period when absolutely necessary, for example, until appropriate Unit Price contracts have been prepared and executed."[98]

"T&M contracts may be appropriate beyond the initial 70-hour, provided that Applicant appropriately monitors the work. The Applicant did not provide any documentation to show that it appropriately monitored the contractor, or any other information that would allow FEMA to evaluate the reasonableness of the costs incurred after the initial 70-hour time period."[99]

"Based on these facts and the information submitted with the appeal, I have determined that the Applicant has not shown that the costs it incurred under the T&M contract were reasonable. Therefore, I am denying the second appeal."[100]

Debris management, which we shall deal with in Chapter 15, is the most frequently abused category of work regarding T&M contracts. Citizens of a local agency expect, nay, demand that the local agency immediately clean up following a disaster. Debris management becomes a bright spotlight on the inability and/or inefficiency of a local agency to respond to the disaster when debris management falters. As a result, local officials often feel that they must begin the cleanup process at all costs. It is not unusual to see debris management work begin on a handshake or verbal order.

The real dangers with T&M contracts, in no particular order, are as follows:

- Failure to provide proper and continuous monitoring of the T&M contractor by an independent third party or qualified local agency staff.
- Failure to have a contract with a not-to-exceed clause, which is strictly enforced.
- Failure to limit the T&M contract to truly emergency work, which presents an immediate threat to life safety, public health, or improved property.
- Failure to have a written contract in place which conforms to the requirements of 2 CFR, Part 200.

- Failure to quickly replace the T&M contract with a proper and compliant lump sum or unit price contract as appropriate.
- Failure to provide all the needed debris management documentation as described in chapter 15.

A Cautionary Note

The following case out of Missouri illustrates one of those "out-of-left-field" situations, which despite all the careful planning can sometimes occur and ruin the day.

"This letter is in response to a letter from your office dated July 23, 2010, which transmitted the referenced second appeal on behalf of the City of New Madrid (Applicant). The Applicant is appealing the Department of Homeland Security's Federal Emergency Management Agency's (FEMA) decision to limit Public Assistance funding for debris removal. The Applicant seeks reimbursement totaling $103,792."[101]

Background

"Between January 26 and January 28, 2009, a severe winter storm with high winds deposited ice throughout the City of New Madrid. The weight of the ice broke trees, tree limbs, damaged transmission lines and power poles that created city-wide power outages and widespread debris. The Applicant solicited bids by telephone from several contractors for debris removal along public rights-of way and awarded a unit price contract to M&M Tree Service (M&M) as it had submitted the lowest bid at $3.25 per cubic yard (CY). As the need for city-wide debris removal increased, the Applicant solicited additional bids over the telephone and awarded contracts to Scott's Lawn Service and Turf Max Lawn Care as these companies proffered bids of $3.00 per cubic yard."[102]

"At the kickoff meeting the Applicant reported that it was using force account labor for its debris removal operations. The Applicant completed 100 percent of its disaster-related debris removal work, including burning of all debris, before FEMA could inspect the debris burn sites to estimate debris amounts. FEMA prepared PW 440 [Category A – Debris Removal] for $365,517 using Applicant submitted invoices from Scott's Lawn Service for $99,630, Turf Max Lawn Care for $96,382, and M&M for $169,505. During project closeout, FEMA notified the Applicant that M&M's costs were not eligible as the services were billed on a time-and-material basis rather than per cubic yard as the contract specified. FEMA asked the Applicant to provide documentation that detailed the scope of work and quantities of eligible disaster debris removed by M&M."[103]

In this case, an otherwise properly procured contract went belly-up because of improper invoicing and payment. Had the city refused the invoices when first incorrectly presented and required the contractor to properly re-invoice the city prior to payment, then the costs would have arguably been eligible.

This points out a very common problem with contracts. Even if the contracts are properly written and executed in compliance with 2 CFR, Part 200 and the local purchasing rules, any inappropriate handling of the contract may create ineligibility after the fact.

Costs Plus a Percentage of Costs Contracts (CPPC)

2 CFR, Part 200 expressly forbids any cost plus a percentage of costs contracts. "§200.324 (d) The cost plus a percentage of cost (*CPPC*) and percentage of construction cost methods of contracting must not be used."[104]

A CPPC contract is where the contractor charges hourly unit rates for labor, equipment, and materials, and then applies an additional percentage charge on top of the unit rates for labor, equipment, and materials used on a project. In some cases, the contractors will charge a second mark-up on the already-marked-up unit costs. This is an example of CPPC mark-up taken from a contract from the state of Florida:

"Vendors, Unscheduled Materials & Unscheduled Equipment

1). Contractor's 10% overhead plus 10% profit (21%) will be added to the total of all documented costs for unscheduled materials, unscheduled equipment, and Subcontractors/Vendors . . ."[105]

This language was buried in the fine (6-point) print at the end of a seemingly otherwise well-prepared contract. This is a torpedo with no wake. No one ever reads all the fine print, except perhaps FEMA. However, FEMA has the advantage of dealing with this stuff every day and may know which contractors are likely to insert this poison language into a contract.

When a contract has CPPC language from the get-go, that's one thing. When the CPPC language is slipped into the contracts after all the compliance issues with 2 CFR, Part 200 are resolved, that's another matter entirely.

Even if a contract is not a CPPC contract, but contains any part of CPPC terminology, or CPPS billing practices, the entire contract is doomed.

One possible way to defend against a stealth CPPC contract, may be to insert a clause which states something to the effect that: ANY COST-PLUS-A-PERCENTAGE-OF-COSTS (CPPC) BILLING, OR ATTEMPT AT CPPC BILLING SHALL RESULT IN THE IMMEDIATE TERMINATION OF SAID CONTRACT, AND NON-PAYMENT OF ANY CHARGES BILLED, WHETHER BILLED AS CPPC, UNIT PRICE, OR LUMP SUM.

A slightly less draconian method would be to stipulate in the contract that any CPPC invoices, or invoices which contain any element of CPPC billing shall be returned unpaid to the vendor pending the proper re-invoicing as per the local agency's terms of payment, and not the contractor's terms of payment. No invoice containing any CPPC terms of payment or CPPC terminology shall be paid.

All of this goes back to the importance of having the time to properly solicit bids and evaluate them fully. This takes time, which is typically not available in the immediate aftermath of the disaster. That said, the following quotation is taken from a pre-disaster debris management contract, when arguably the purchasing officer should have had the time to thoroughly review the contractor's submission and should have rejected the bid as non-compliant. Worse still, this request for proposals was a collaborative effort for a group of public agencies, where more than 20 other public agencies trusted and relied upon someone else to take care of their interests in this solicitation. This alone is a good reason to avoid purchasing buy-groups.

"This Agreement results from a solicitation created in collaboration with the Florida College System Risk Management Consortium (FCSRMC) for the benefit of the 28 colleges in the Florida College System. The College of the Florida Keys, as one of the Florida College System colleges, may use these services when desired to comply with the solicitation and performance requirements of the Federal Emergency Management Administration (FEMA)."[106]

Billing Errors Can Be Deadly

To quote comedian Ron White, "But let me tell you something, folks: You can't fix stupid. There's not a pill you can take; there's not a class you can go to. Stupid is forever." And it may seem that stupid occasionally gravitates toward some disaster contractors.

After a very large fire destroyed a summer camp owned and operated by a client ten years ago, they hired a contractor who claimed that they were familiar with FEMA's regulations regarding debris clearance (FEMA Category A work) and erosion control work (FEMA Category B) work. The contractor completed the work and invoiced the local agency for $600,000. The local agency paid the contractor and sent the invoice in to FEMA for reimbursement. FEMA rejected the work as ineligible because the Cat A work was mixed in with the Cat B work, and FEMA could not make heads or tails of the mixed costs. The local agency believed that they had an ace up their sleeve because they still owed the contractor an additional $80,000 on the contract. They figured that the contractor would fix the invoices and submit all the proper paperwork to support eligibility. However, the contractor never kept the appropriate level of documentation. The contractor had arbitrarily moved workers from Cat A work to Cat B work, back and forth, with no records kept. In this case, the local agency was very fortunate that their insurance company did pay these incurred costs. It would have otherwise been a dreary rainy day in Camperville.

Debarment and Suspension

2 CFR,§ 200.327 Contract provisions (H) is a prohibition restricting contracts with Federally debarred or suspended businesses. For each procurement, the local agency must document that the contractors (prime contractors and subcontractors) are not debarred or suspended. This is done by checking the SAM.GOV website and searching for the proposed contractors to determine that they are not debarred or suspended. As documentation, the web page must be printed and entered in the procurement file. This is a good business practice which should be a consistent practice for all procurements, Federal money or not.

Some local agencies also check SAM.GOV for debarment or suspension status prior to making payments on invoices. For relatively small payments this may not be important; however, if the invoice is for five or six figures or more, it may be necessary to safeguard against deobligation.

Like for Like

The intent of the Stafford Act is to assist local agencies following a disaster and help those agencies to restore their facilities and infrastructure to their pre-disaster condition. The expression often used to describe this is: "Like for Like." If the local agency has a 5,000-square-foot facility used as a Senior Citizens' Center, then that is what FEMA will expect to replace. They will not expect to provide funding for a larger building, nor will they expect to fund the restoration as a Children's Center. These changes, however, may be funded through an improved project or an alternate project.

Like for like is also the rationale for FEMA only providing "Blue Book" values for replacement of vehicles and equipment which may have been damaged in the disaster.

The following text is from an audit of an Ohio hospital: "Columbus Regional Hospital is a branch of Bartholomew County and is a county nonprofit regional healthcare facility providing healthcare services to residents of multiple counties in southeastern Indiana. On June 7, 2008, flood waters inundated the entire basement of the Hospital, which contained much of the Hospital's medical and lab equipment. In addition, contaminated water and mud heavily damaged the first floor. Hospital officials closed the facility as a result of the flood and partially reopened it in October 2008. We determined that exigent circumstances existed until April 2009, when the hospital returned to full capacity."[107]

Results of Audit

"Of the 11 contracts we reviewed, totaling $74.7 million, the Hospital did not follow Federal procurement standards in awarding $64.8 million for 9 contracts. Two of the nine contracts were noncompetitive contracts for non-exigent work, another two were prohibited cost-plus-percentage-of-cost contracts for exigent work, and all nine contracts involved violations of other Federal procurement standards. As a result, open and free competition did not occur, and FEMA has no assurance that costs were reasonable. Therefore, we question $10.9 million, consisting of $8.7 million for the two noncompetitive contracts for non-exigent work and $2.2 million for prohibited markups on the two cost-plus contracts for exigent work. We did not question all the costs for the nine contracts because contractors performed the majority of the work under exigent circumstances to restore the Hospital to its full operating capability."[108]

This same hospital also had three appeals cases, dealing with the aforementioned audit, insurance, and equipment replacement, which text follows.

"Medical equipment at the Applicant's facility was damaged beyond repair as a result of the declared flooding event. The Applicant replaced several damaged items with new equipment and requested reimbursement of $3,700,171 for the cost of new equipment. FEMA prepared nine (9) Project Worksheets (PWs) to provide $2,484,081 for the eligible cost for replacement of the damaged items. The PWs reflected the value of destroyed equipment based on a fair market value for units of similar age and capacity."[109]

"The Applicant submitted its first appeal to the Indiana Department of Homeland Security (IDHS) on June 8, 2009. In its appeal, the Applicant claimed that the Stafford Act allows for replacement of equipment with new comparable items, not used or refurbished items."[110]

"The Applicant also claimed that it is entitled to full reimbursement because a FEMA representative stated that if it 'follow[ed] their own established procurement procedures in replacing equipment, there would be no issues of procurement to overcome at a later date.'"[111]

"The PA Guide (FEMA 322) *(now archived),* Chapter 2, states 'When equipment, including vehicles, is not repairable, FEMA will approve the cost of replacement with used items that are approximately the same age, capacity, and condition. FEMA may use 'blue book' values or similar price guides to determine the eligible cost for used equipment and vehicles. Replacement of an item with a new item may be approved only if a used item is not available within a reasonable time and distance.'"[112]

"In its second appeal, the Applicant claimed that PW MDF-073 does not provide full funding for refurbished equipment. The PW states that refurbished items for replacement of four (4) damaged ultrasound units were quoted from $33,000 to $38,000, each. PW funding was approved for $132,000 ($33,000 x 4) and the Applicant requested funding of $152,000 ($38,000 x 4). It is FEMA policy to provide funding for the most cost-effective alternative for completing the eligible scope. FEMA staff appropriately estimated the cost of the PW at the lowest quoted cost for replacement of the damaged equipment."[113]

"Refurbished medical equipment is readily available in the marketplace and can be effectively used in a health care facility. The Applicant is not required to use refurbished equipment to receive FEMA funding. The Applicant may apply the approved funding toward its cost to purchase new equipment through the use of improved projects."[114]

In the third paragraph on the previous page is another familiar theme: "someone allegedly relied on a verbal representation of a FEMA employee to their detriment."

1) We must never rely on any verbal representations from either the state or FEMA;
2) Improper written authorizations are subject to change at a later date;
3) The best defense for a local agency is to know the regulations well enough to know when something is squishy and should be investigated thoroughly.
4) If there's enough money at stake, it may be wise to hire a reputable and well-qualified cost recovery consultant to guide the agency through the mine field of public assistance.

Like for Like Reprised

This case, from Kansas, is another example of the "like for like" policy. "A violent storm system developed over the Midwest on May 4, 2007, spawning lethal tornadoes, one of which left a trail of debris 22 miles long and more than a mile wide, nearly destroying the entire City *(Greensburg, KS)*. The tornado turned brick and concrete buildings to rubble, rolled semitrailers, and left whole neighborhoods unrecognizable. The City, a small, rural farming community located in southwestern Kansas, had a population of 1,389 before the disaster."[115]

"The EF-5 (Enhanced Fujita scale) tornado touched down more than 75 times, killing 12. FEMA first responders noted that the City's facilities were destroyed, rendered unusable, or suffered major damage. In addition, the tornado damaged 90 percent of all street signs and signal lights and 90 percent of the City's vehicles."[116]

Finding C: Ineligible Costs

"The City claimed $33,988 for an extended warranty on a transformer purchased for the electrical distribution substation rebuilding project. However, extended warranty costs, essentially a form of insurance, are not eligible under the Public Assistance program. The purchase of the warranty was an improvement above the predisaster condition because the City did not have a warranty on the transformer that was replaced. FEMA Region VII officials agreed and said that the cost for improvements on a project is not a FEMA-eligible expense. FEMA's Policy Digest *(now archived)* states that the costs of restoring damaged facilities are eligible for Public Assistance funding, but only on the basis of the facility's predisaster condition. Also, the cost for the warranty was not necessary to complete the replacement of the transformer. Costs must be necessary to be allowable under a Federal award (2 CFR part 225, Appendix A, section C.1.a). Therefore, we question $33,988 as ineligible costs. City officials said that FEMA officials advised them to purchase the extended warranty, but could not provide physical evidence to support their statement. Because of the large number of FEMA officials who worked on this disaster, FEMA could not confirm the City's assertion."[117] (Emphasis Added)

Once again, we see the monster under the bed, where local officials allegedly accepted a verbal representation from someone at FEMA.

"Like for Like" Segues to Hidden Costs

From a financial perspective, disaster cost recovery is all about the money. Another money trap is any hidden costs associated with our response, repair, and reconstruction costs. Perhaps the most frequent "hidden" costs are those costs associated with debris removal. Certainly, if debris removal is being done under a Time & Materials contract, the contractor(s) must be diligently monitored to account for every haul trip and every load of debris claimed. These costs, properly procured, are FEMA-reimbursable, normally at 75%, which leaves the 25% balance due from the local agency, possibly in some cases with a state contribution.

However, all debris removal operations, whether unit price or lump sum contracts, must be monitored by an independent third party or by local agency staff. Either option results in disaster-related costs which do not contribute to directly to rebuilding the community, but which must be paid as a part of the debris clean-up process.

There are other "hidden" costs, particularly the administrative costs associated with the staff time to deal with the Public Assistance process. A very limited amount of these costs may be recoverable as Direct Administrative Costs, or DAC, which will be dealt with in Chapter 32. However, many of the administrative costs will simply be unrecoverable. This is the great cost of disasters for local agencies.

Contracts Must Provide the Required Information

The Public Assistance process is nothing if it is not about documentation. The contract documentation for goods and services must be a complete record that can stand up to the most intense scrutiny. The following text comes from an appeals case, which was the result of a DHS-OIG audit of a Texas County following Hurricane Ike in 2008. While this audit dealt with much more than procurement, the comments apply to all aspects of the case, including the procurement issues.

Lack of Supporting Documentation

"Pursuant to 44 C.F.R. § 206.206(a), an appeal must contain documented justification supporting an applicant's position. In considering the second appeal with respect to whether costs were reasonable and adequately documented, FEMA must rely exclusively on the documentation provided by the Applicant. On several previous occasions, including FEMA's response to the OIG *(Office of the Inspector General)* audit, first appeal decision, and at the oral meeting, the Agency reviewed the Applicant's supporting documentation and found it incomplete, unspecific or, otherwise deficient such that it did not substantiate eligibility. With the issuance of the RFI *(Request For Information)*, the RA *(Regional Administrator)* afforded the Applicant additional time to supplement its appeal with specifically requested documentation to support the Applicant's claim. The burden to substantiate appeals with 'documented justification' falls exclusively to the Applicant and hinges upon the Applicant's ability to produce not only its own records but to clearly explain how those records are relevant to the appeal. In response to the OIG audit, on first appeal and now on second appeal, FEMA has reviewed the Applicant's timesheets, sign-in sheets, invoices, descriptions of work, disposal tickets, training certificates, contracts and rates with Garner, Parker, and CERES, as well as the SO *(Sheriff's Office)* timesheets, corresponding submissions to FEMA, and employment policies."[118] (Emphasis Added)

"While the Applicant contends that it has provided documentation to demonstrate eligibility, the documentation reviewed by FEMA in response to the OIG audit, and on first and second appeal reveal the quality or substance of the documentation to be lacking, and not supportive of eligibility. As explained in the subsections below, the information submitted contains omissions, inconsistencies, and patterns of deviation that have not been explained to justify the eligibility of the work and the reasonableness of the costs claimed."[119] (Emphasis Added)

Documentation Requirements

The Applicant should submit the following to support contract costs claimed (not an all-inclusive list):

- Procurement policy (required when requested);
- Procurement documents (i.e., requests for proposals, bids, selection process, etc.) (required when requested);
- A cost or price analysis (required for contracts above the simplified acquisition threshold)
- Contracts, change orders, and summary of invoices (required);
- Dates worked (required when requested); and
- Documentation that substantiates a high degree of contractor oversight, such as daily or weekly logs, records of performance meetings (required for T&M contracts when requested).

$5,000 Residual Value

When the local agency receives funding from FEMA, and after completion of a project if there is residual value greater than $5,000, FEMA requires the local agency to refund the dollar value back to FEMA.

This requirement can take on many forms.

1) During debris removal operations, the salvage value of materials, when greater than $5,000, must be returned, unless the contract stipulates that this value is applied to the contractors benefit, i.e., as a part of their compensation under the contract.
2) The local agency purchases equipment for the disaster response, and then sells the used equipment, either with a remaining useful life or for scrap, and the sale price is greater than $5,000, the amount must be returned to FEMA.
3) The local agency has a facility which was so damaged that FEMA authorized the local agency to temporarily relocate the facility. The local agency then leases the temporary facility and uses it for six months, after which the original facility has been repaired and re-occupied. However, the best lease the local agency could negotiate was for a minimum term of one year. So, if the value of the lease for the remaining six months is greater than $5,000, then the local agency must make good faith efforts to sub-lease the facility to recoup the anticipated loss for non-use of the building. If the local agency cannot sub-lease the building, and if they have made a good faith effort to do so, then there is no payment due to FEMA. A good faith effort should at the least include the listing of the property with a licensed real estate broker and showing the property to prospective tenants, with all the relevant activities fully documented to prove the good faith effort.

Iowa Case Study: A Partial Winner

"This letter is in response to a letter from your office dated March 20, 2012, which transmitted the referenced second appeal on behalf of the Mahaska County Emergency Management Agency (Applicant). The Applicant is appealing the Department of Homeland Security's Federal Emergency Management Agency's (FEMA) deduction of $6,980 for the purchase of a boat and motor."[120]

"The Applicant purchased equipment and supplies in response to widespread flooding that threatened homes and the County water supply and sanitary systems as a result of severe storms occurring June 1, through August 31, 2010. Purchases included office supplies, safety vests and flares, generators, mobile telecommunication equipment, an outboard boat, and a gas-powered outboard motor. FEMA prepared PW 565 in the amount of $39,166 for force account labor ($4,212) and equipment and supplies ($34,954). FEMA determined, pursuant to Title 44 Code of Federal Regulations (44 CFR) §13.32(e)(2), Equipment, Disposition, and 44 CFR §13.33(b), Supplies, Disposition, that the Applicant was required to compensate FEMA for its portion of the fair market residual value of used and unused equipment and supplies with an aggregate value exceeding $5,000, when the materials are no longer needed for disaster work. A total of $24,695 was deducted from the eligible costs for equipment and supplies, and on January 26, 2011, PW 565 was obligated for $14,471."[121]

"In a letter dated December 7, 2011, the Regional Administrator responded to the first appeal and determined that only a portion of the equipment purchases required compensation to FEMA. The Regional Administrator explained that the boat ($3,695) and motor ($4,390) were purchased together and used together in function in the same way as an automobile. According to the Regional Administrator, the total purchase price of the boat and motor was greater than $5,000 and required a reduction to account for FEMA's share of that equipment. A reduction of $6,980 was calculated on the $8,085 purchase price of the boat and motor."[122]

"The Applicant purchased a Lowe R1760 Outboard boat ($3,695), a Mercury 25HP gasoline powered outboard motor ($4,390), a propeller ($174), a Karavan boat trailer ($899), and a battery ($103) from Malone Motorsports for its emergency response operations. The Applicant contends that the boat and motor were sold and purchased as separate units, not as a single piece of equipment. The Malone Motorsports invoice does not indicate that the boat comes equipped with an outboard motor as each piece of equipment is listed on the invoice with a separate serial number and corresponding purchase price. Likewise, the outboard motor does not indicate that it is equipped with a propeller, which FEMA previously reimbursed as an independent item. Each of the items purchased from Malone Motorsports has a fair market value of less than $5,000. Pursuant to 44 CFR §13.32(e)(1), Equipment, Disposition, items of equipment with a current per-unit fair market value of less than $5,000 may be retained, sold or otherwise disposed of with no further obligation to the awarding agency."[123]

Conclusion

"Based on the review of all information submitted with the appeal, I have determined that the boat and motor were separate purchases with a current fair market value of less than $5,000 each, and therefore, may be disposed of with no further obligation to FEMA. Therefore, I am approving this appeal to re-obligate $6,980 to PW 565."[124]

Following 2 CFR, Part 200, *AND* the Local Agency Purchasing Policy

This audit is from a California Wastewater Reclamation Authority, where the auditors questioned $33,000,000 in costs, due largely to improper procurement practices, including a failure to follow its own regulations.

"The Authority did not perform cost/price analyses, as required, in awarding and modifying its engineering contract (44 CFR 13.36(f)(1) and (3)). It did not develop independent estimates before receiving proposals or perform cost analyses for every procurement action, including contract modifications. For example, when the Authority approved Contractor C's change order requests, it accepted the contractor's own assessment of costs incurred and funds needed, without verification. In fact, the Authority was not able to verify Contractor C's costs billed because Contractor C did not itemize the costs by the agreed-upon tasks in its invoices. Without knowing actual costs incurred, the Authority was not able to determine the amount of additional funds needed for each task. A member of the Authority's Board publicly expressed his frustration with the lack of oversight of contract modifications (change orders): 'The philosophy in that agency is, if you run over a budget, just do a change order . . . there are so many of them, you can't even keep track of them.' This statement described precisely what happened. The Authority modified all three contracts (engineering, construction, and construction management) multiple times, including 15 modifications to the contract with Contractor C alone, escalating its value to more than three times the original bid price of $410,520 to $1,282,809. Because of these numerous modifications, Authority officials were not able to track the contract ceilings and paid Contractor C, on multiple occasions, more than the amount the contract authorized."[125]

"The Authority did not follow its own procurement policy and Federal regulations when evaluating contractor proposals and selecting its engineering contractor . . . did not involve its Engineering Committee properly. To select the most qualified contractors, the Authority's standard process includes these three steps: its Engineering Committee approves the request for proposals, reviews the proposals, and recommends a contractor to the Authority's Board for approval. However, in selecting its engineering contractor, the Authority did not seek the Committee's approval of the request for proposals nor allow the Committee enough time to conduct proper assessments of the proposals."[126]

". . . allowed one committee member's significantly disproportionate rating to be one of the decisive factors in the Authority's contractor selection process. Two of the five committee members scored the three proposals very closely; another two did not provide scores; and another gave Contractor C a perfect 100 points and the other proposals the unusually low scores of 78 and 76, respectively. This disparity is especially concerning because the rater did not justify the scores, and the Authority did not provide us the rating sheet or explanations for not providing it. Further, Authority officials did not question the validity of these extreme scores or have a process to ensure uniformity and fairness in applying the criteria. They simply tallied the three scores, allowing the third disproportionate score to propel Contractor C's rating from the lowest overall score to the highest."[127]

These are just two of several procurement and administrative issues with which the auditors had a field day. A consultant told me some time later that his firm had been retained at a cost of $250,000, with no guarantee of success, to attempt to re-float this sinking ship. Of course, by that time, the reputational damage to the agency had been painfully inflicted.

File Retention

In Chapter 42, Close-Outs, we will fully address the question of file retention; however, file retention is a critical aspect of compliance with 2 CFR, Part 200. The failure to retain all the procurement files for a project will likely lead to a deobligation of FEMA funds, if not in part, then in full.

2 CFR, § 200.334 Retention Requirements for Records

"Financial records, supporting documents, statistical records, and all other non-Federal entity records pertinent to a Federal award must be retained for a period of three years from the date of submission of the final expenditure report or, for Federal awards that are renewed quarterly or annually, from the date of the submission of the quarterly or annual financial report, respectively, as reported to the Federal awarding agency or passthrough entity in the case of a subrecipient."[128]

The retained records should contain virtually every document the local agency creates in the process of soliciting, processing, awarding, and administering its contracts for disaster-related goods and services.

There are certain important exceptions to this requirement, which we shall address in Chapter 42.

Buying from the U.S. General Services Administration (GSA)

"GSA's Disaster Purchasing Program allows state and local governments to buy supplies and services directly from all GSA Schedules to facilitate disaster preparation, response, or major disaster recovery. Purchases made in support of recovery must be in response to a Stafford Act Presidential declaration. The Federal Emergency Management Agency (FEMA) manages the list of declared disasters. State and local governments can purchase equipment and services to support natural or man-made disasters, including acts of terrorism, or nuclear, biological, chemical, or radiological attack."[129]

However, for any purchases made through the GSA schedules, the GSA price should be at least one of the three documented quotes or sealed bids, and not the only quote or bid selected.

Access to Records

"FEMA is prohibited from providing reimbursement to any SLTT (State, local, Tribal, or Territorial) government, or PNP (Private Non-Profit) organization for activities made pursuant to a contract that purports to prohibit audits or internal reviews by the FEMA administrator or Comptroller General."

Earlier in this chapter, we looked at the appeals case from the Nishnabotna Valley Rural Electric Co-operative. In that same case, the utility company was also cited for its failure to produce required records.

"Applicants must make pre-award and procurement documentation available to the awarding agency when the information is requested. FEMA sent the Applicant an RFI requesting bid solicitation documentation and all procurement or contract documentation that was not already included in the Administrative Record. In response, the Applicant mentioned that it sent out requests for proposals, but did not provide any bid solicitation documentation such as requests for proposals, invitations for bids, or cost estimates."[130] This failure was one of several which resulted in a complete deobligation of funding of $191,629.27 in tree trimming costs.

The Disaster Procurement Toolbox

Over the years, I have learned so much about disaster purchasing, far more than I ever wanted to know. As this learning process slowly unveiled itself, I began to develop some useful tools to assist local agencies in complying with the complex requirements imposed by 2 CFR, Part 200. I am not a procurement officer and do not pretend to be all-knowing about local government purchasing. However, I have accumulated a great deal of pertinent information regarding the purchasing of disaster-related goods and services.

Purchasing Department Bid Worksheet (Sample)

This form is in the support material, see Appendix, Form 40.

This is not a Federal form, and its use is not mandated by Federal rules. However, the use of this form will help to fully document procurement transactions and support procurement eligibility. This note applies to all the following forms presented here. These forms are sample forms and may need to be edited to suit the needs of the local agency and accommodate any future changes in Federal regulations.

I was meeting with a client, the city's Finance Director and the Chief Purchasing Officer, discussing the importance of compliance with 2 CFR, Part 200. The Chief Purchasing Officer stated: "They (meaning Finance) don't always tell us when Federal funds are involved in a project." Simple problem, simple solution. In real life, I would print this cover sheet form on bright fluorescent paper so it would be difficult to miss. Completing this form should be on a checklist for everyone preparing a Project Worksheet, no matter what department they might represent.

Procurement Documentation Checklist (Sample)

This form is in the Appendix, Form 41. This is not a Federal form.

In the disaster cost recovery process, checklists are a very powerful tool to help ensure that every critical step is taken to protect the eligibility of the project. This form is a "starter" form because every public agency with which I have worked does things a bit differently. However, in working with FEMA, all local agencies are held to the same strict standards regardless of agency type or size. So, each agency may want or need to modify the form to suit their particular way of doing the business of government. The secret to success with FEMA is doing the right thing consistently, and that is where a good checklist comes in handy.

Sole Source Purchase Justification Form

This four-page form is in the Appendix, Form 42. This is not a Federal form.

Sole source or non-competitive procurements are allowed only under very limited circumstances, and when allowed they must be fully documented regarding the specific conditions which required a sole source purchase. This form, when properly filled out, provides documentation to support a sole source purchase. In addition to this form, there may be additional documentation necessary to support the purchase.

This is not a FEMA form, nor is it required. However, it will provide substantial documentary support when a sole source purchase is made during a disaster response.

At the top of page 1 are two paragraphs of text which include the amounts of $xx,000. These amounts must be established by each local agency to meet its needs. These two paragraphs also provide a level of administrative oversight when a proposed purchase exceeds normal limits as established by the local agency.

The rest of page 1 and onto page 2 are check boxes to specify which conditions exist which require a sole source purchase. At the bottom of page 2 begins the narrative portion which explains in clear detail why the sole source purchase should be allowed. Following the "fill-in-the-blanks" section is where the cost reasonableness is documented, followed by the first level of authorization.

When the purchase exceeds the limits set in paragraph two, then a countersignature is required. The completed form should be attached to the other paperwork for the purchase and filed for use later, when gathering the documentation for the Project Worksheet files.

Materials Average Costing Worksheet

This form is in the Appendix, Form 43. This is not a Federal form.

FEMA regulations require that materials used for the disaster response and recovery be tracked to each location where they are used and costed out per site. This creates a massive administrative burden which most likely will fail at some point. However, FEMA will allow the local agency to use the average cost of materials if properly documented.

That is the purpose of this form: to track individual purchases of various commodities and roll them into a single average unit cost for all similar materials. In this spreadsheet, there are multiple tabs for various commodities, such as bottled drinking water, diesel fuel, plywood, sandbags, etc. Depending on the disaster, additional tabs can be created using the cut and paste feature in Excel.

As each purchase is made – in this sample case plywood for board-ups – the cost data is entered onto the spreadsheet, and with each successive purchase the average unit price will be adjusted, depending on the thickness of the plywood and the price paid, including delivery, taxes, etc. After things have settled down and all purchases for plywood are entered into the spreadsheet, then using the calculated average per sheet cost, that dollar amount should be entered into the site-specific file for later incorporation into the individual Project Worksheet file.

If additional rows are needed for more purchases, the spreadsheets can be unlocked and additional rows added using the copy and paste feature in Excel. After the final purchases are entered into each worksheet, the staff person managing that worksheet should sign and date the form. Because these costs will be represented in many different Project Worksheets, the original should be kept in a central location, and copies provided for every file where plywood was used.

Depending on the commodities being tracked, this form may be used by several different departments, or alternatively the file may be maintained in the Logistics Section of the Emergency Operations Center.

Office Relocation Expense Report

This two-page form is in the Appendix, Form 44. This is not a Federal form.

If office and workspace facilities are damaged in the disaster, there is a likelihood that some or all of the office furnishings may be destroyed, or at least require heavy cleaning before they can again be used. In either case, it is important to inventory everything damaged by the disaster so that either replacement costs or cleaning costs can be developed. This form was developed in Excel so that if there are multiple damaged facilities or multiple departments within a single damaged facility, the forms can be loaded as additional tabs in the worksheet. Using Excel's Cross-Tab reporting feature, one single consolidated cost estimate will be developed for all departments and all facilities. This is all on page 1 of 2. Page 2 is for the development of the replacement cost estimate for the damaged/destroyed office equipment. 2 CFR, Part 200 requires that the local agency consolidate its purchases to obtain the best prices.

If 4 departments have an average of 6 computers destroyed, and each department buys 6 computers, the unit price for each computer will be higher than if the local agency purchases 24 computers in a single combined purchase. Therefore, we need to consolidate similar purchases to maintain eligibility by obtaining reasonable prices for replacement items.

The additional columns are used to evaluate the possibility of leasing rather than an outright purchase of certain items, as previously mentioned in this chapter.

Price/Cost Analysis Worksheet (PUR-2)

This three-page form is given as Form 45 (see Appendix). This is not a Federal form.

The purpose of this form is to document that either, a price analysis or a cost analysis (or both) was performed in conjunction with every procurement over the Simplified Acquisition Threshold (currently $250,000) or for sole source procurements above the Federal micro-purchase threshold (currently $10,000). While the local agency may as a routine matter perform price analyses, i.e., compare multiple quotations or bids, the agency must also provide a written form which documents that the price analysis or cost analysis was performed.

Cost Analysis Spreadsheet (PUR-3)

This one-page form is given as Form 46 (see Appendix). This is not a Federal form.

The purpose of this form is to itemize and analyze each of the cost factors presented with a change order on a construction project or other procurement. Per Federal rules, the contractor or vendor must itemize the cost factors as shown on the spreadsheet. As shown on the spreadsheet, the contractor must account for their labor, equipment, and materials used for the change order. They must also break out their overhead and profit separately. This form is used in conjunction with the Price/Cost Analysis Worksheet (PUR-2). The requirement to provide this in-depth analysis for change orders must be included in the original RFP or RFQ so that the bidders are on notice regarding this requirement.

As previously stated, these are not Federal forms, nor is their use required. However, they are useful tools to assist the local agency and the purchasing staff to do a more comprehensive job of documenting their disaster-related purchases for both response and recovery operations.

In this book, there are several chapters which deserve an entire book. However, the intent of this book is to provide a broad-based overview of the entire Public Assistance program, and therefore there is a great deal of additional information which might be included, but time and space simply don't allow.

Additional Information Is Available on the Internet

The following are some of the many available resources available on the internet. The first selection is one of the most readable and understandable Federal documents ever written about disaster purchasing. Unfortunately, it was issued in early December of 2014; then, just weeks later, Title 2 of the Code of Federal Regulations, Part 200 was released, which completely changed all the citations. However, from a readability perspective, it can't be beat. It does a great job of explaining the principles of Federal regulations governing disaster procurements. The subsequent versions of this document were apparently written by someone who attended kindergarten at Harvard School of Law. While later versions of this document are correct, they're not as easily understood by the average person.

- Public Assistance Grantee and Subgrantee Procurement Requirements under 44 C.F.R. PT. 13 And 2 C.F.R. PT. 215, December 2014 https://www.fema.gov/sites/default/files/2020-07/fema_public-assistance-grantee-subgrantee-procurement-2014_field-manual.pdf
- Procurement Disaster Assistance Team (PDAT) Field Manual, October 2021, (FM-207-21-0002), https://www.fema.gov/sites/default/files/documents/fema_PDAT-field-manual_102021.pdf
- Baker Donelson, Procurement Checklist – Compliance with 2 C.F.R. Part 200, https://www.bakerdonelson.com/webfiles/Publications/Baker-Donelson-EMA-Procurement-Checklist.pdf (This document may not reflect any of the recent changes to 2 CFR, Part 200).
- Roadmap to Procurement Compliance: Procurement Disaster Assistance Team (PDAT), August 2023, https://www.fema.gov/sites/default/files/documents/fema_roadmap_procurement_compliance_checklist.pdf

At FEMA.GOV there is a staggering amount of information regarding proper procurement procedures when Federal funding is involved. When downloading information from the FEMA website or any other resource, always check to see if there are newer (or older) versions available. The last thing anyone wants to do is use a document for guidance if that document is no longer the current version.

FEMA also provides procurement training through its PDAT or Procurement Disaster Assistance Team. Information on this training should be available through your appropriate FEMA Region.

The FEMA Appeals Database is also a most excellent resource for learning about what to do and what not to do regarding procurement. When searching the Appeals Database, it usually helps to use quotation marks around the search terms to limit how many cases that will result from a query. Also be aware that searching for the term "facility eligibility" (two hits) may, and often does, provide different search results than the term "eligible facility" (one hit).

Notes

1 DHS-OIG Audit OIG-20–41, Inadequate Management and Oversight Jeopardized $187.3 Million in FEMA Grant Funds Expended by Joplin Schools, Missouri, June 19, 2020, p. 2.
2 Ibid, pp. 2–3.
3 Ibid, p. 3.

4 Ibid, p. 4.
5 Ibid, p. 4.
6 Ibid, p. 5.
7 Ibid.
8 Ibid.
9 Title 2 of the Code of Federal Regulations, Part 200, § 200.317 through §200.326, p. 123.
10 Ibid.
11 https://www.fema.gov/appeal/allowable-costs-reasonable-costs-private-nonprofit-procurement-contracting-requirements
12 Ibid.
13 Ibid.
14 Ibid.
15 Ibid.
16 Ibid.
17 Ibid.
18 Ibid.
19 Title 2 of the Code of Federal Regulations, Part 200, § 200.317 through §200.326, p. 124.
20 DHS-OIG Audit OIG-17–46-D: Minneapolis Park and Recreation Board Did Not Follow All Federal Procurement Standards for $5.1 Million in Contracts, p. 3.
21 Ibid, pp. 3–4.
22 Ibid, pp. 4–5.
23 Ibid, p. 5.
24 https://www.fema.gov/appeal/procurement-oig-audit
25 https://www.fema.gov/appeal/procurement-reasonable-costs-direct-administrative-costs
26 Ibid.
27 Ibid.
28 Ibid.
29 Ibid.
30 https://www.fema.gov/appeal/support-documentation-procurement
31 Ibid.
32 Ibid.
33 Ibid.
34 https://www.fema.gov/appeal/rural-electric-cooperative-procurement
35 Ibid.
36 Ibid.
37 Ibid.
38 https://www.fema.gov/appeal/appeals-financial-accounting-reconciliation-force-account-labor-equipment-costs-procurement
39 Ibid.
40 Ibid.
41 Ibid.
42 https://www.fema.gov/appeal/allowable-costs-reasonable-costs-financial-accounting-reconciliation-procurement-4
43 Ibid.
44 Ibid.
45 Ibid.
46 Ibid.
47 Ibid.
48 https://www.fema.gov/appeal/appeal-timeliness-support-documentation-705c
49 Ibid.
50 Ibid.
51 Ibid.
52 Ibid.
53 Ibid.
54 FEMA Disaster Assistance Fact Sheet, 9580.4 (Archived)
55 OIG-14–46-D, FEMA's Dissemination of Procurement Advice Early in Disaster Response Periods, February 28, 2014, pp. 2–3.

56 FEMA Fact Sheet: Public Assistance: Purchasing Goods Or Services Through Cooperative Purchasing Programs.
57 Ibid.
58 https://www.fema.gov/appeal/scope-work-20
59 Ibid.
60 Ibid.
61 Ibid.
62 Ibid.
63 Ibid.
64 Ibid.
65 Ibid.
66 Ibid.
67 Ibid.
68 Ibid.
69 Ibid.
70 FEMA Disaster Assistance Fact Sheet 9580.4: Emergency Work Contracting (Archived).
71 https://www.fema.gov/appeal/procurement-contracting-requirements-allowable-costs-reasonable-costs
72 Ibid.
73 Ibid.
74 Ibid.
75 Ibid.
76 Ibid.
77 Ibid.
78 Ibid.
79 Ibid.
80 Public Assistance Program and Policy Guide, Version 4, June 1, 2020, FFP 104–009–2, p. 74.
81 Ibid.
82 Ibid.
83 Ibid.
84 Ibid, p. 72.
85 https://www.fema.gov/appeal/operation-permanently-mounted-generators
86 Ibid.
87 Ibid.
88 Ibid.
89 Ibid.
90 Ibid.
91 Public Assistance Program and Policy Guide, Version 4, June 1, 2020, FFP 104–009–2, p. 82
92 Ibid, p. 83.
93 Ibid.
94 Ibid.
95 https://www.fema.gov/appeal/time-material-contract
96 Ibid.
97 Ibid.
98 Ibid.
99 Ibid.
100 Ibid.
101 https://www.fema.gov/appeal/ineligible-contract-debris-removal
102 Ibid.
103 Ibid.
104 Title 2 of the Code of Federal Regulations, Part 200, § 200.317 through §200.326, p. 129.
105 https://mccmeetingspublic.blob.core.usgovcloudapi.net/fkccfl-meet-5bc4b90069c341c6887cf9a6d63aa68b/ITEM-Attachment-001-7d508bc661f54e2ea3aca04e4b882d54.pdf, p. 124.
106 Ibid, p. 1.
107 FEMA Should Recover $10.9 Million of Improper Contracting Costs from Grant Funds Awarded to Columbus Regional Hospital, Columbus, IN, OIG-14–12-D, December 2013, pp. 3–4.
108 Ibid, p. 4.
109 https://www.fema.gov/appeal/equipment-replacement-1

110 Ibid.
111 Ibid.
112 Ibid.
113 Ibid.
114 Ibid.
115 FEMA Public Assistance Grant Funds Awarded to City of Greensburg, KS, DHS-OIG Audit DD-12–16, p. 2.
116 Ibid.
117 Ibid, p. 4.
118 https://www.fema.gov/appeal/oig-audit-reasonable-costs-support-documentation-705c
119 Ibid.
120 https://www.fema.gov/appeal/disposition-equipment
121 Ibid.
122 Ibid.
123 Ibid.
124 Ibid.
125 https://www.oig.dhs.gov/reports/2017/victor-valley-wastewater-reclamation-authority-victorville-california-did-not-properly
126 Ibid, p. 5.
127 Ibid.
128 Title 2 of the Code of Federal Regulations, § 200.334 Retention Requirements for Records.
129 https://www.gsa.gov/buy-through-us/purchasing-programs/gsa-multiple-award-schedule/schedule-buyers/state-and-local-governments/disaster-purchasing
130 https://www.fema.gov/appeal/rural-electric-cooperative-procurement

10 Insurance and Risk Management

"Predicting rain doesn't count. Building arks does."

Warren Buffett

Holy Cross School – Insurance Audit

"Holy Cross operates as a private, non-profit school with a curriculum that covers grades 5–12. Hurricane Katrina devastated the Holy Cross school buildings located in the Ninth Ward neighborhood of New Orleans. In January 2006, Holy Cross opened a temporary campus; and, in 2007, the Brothers of the Congregation of Holy Cross and their board of directors elected to relocate the campus to the Gentilly neighborhood of New Orleans. Holy Cross constructed four new buildings – an administration building, a middle school, a high school, and a central services/student center building – using FEMA funding."[1]

"Holy Cross did not obtain $48.9 million of required flood insurance coverage for its replaced disaster-damaged facilities, which is a condition for receiving Federal disaster assistance. As a result, Holy Cross does not have adequate flood insurance coverage to meet Federal regulation insurance requirements to protect it and taxpayers in future disasters."[2]

"Based on the required amount of the flood-related eligible damage assistance FEMA determined the required amount of obtain-and-maintain insurance was $52.9 million. Holy Cross should have obtained and maintained $52.9 million in flood insurance or received an exemption from insurance requirements from its state insurance commissioner. However, Holy Cross obtained only $4.0 million in flood insurance, or $48.9 million less than the required amount. Holy Cross completed construction on the high school and middle school in August 2009, completed the administration building in March 2010, and completed the central services/student center in February 2011. Holy Cross should have increased its flood insurance coverage as it completed these buildings or obtained an exemption with a certification of insurance from the Louisiana insurance commissioner."[3]

"Holy Cross officials said that they intended to file for an insurance exemption, but delayed filing because they were not certain of the process or how much flood insurance FEMA required."[4]

"However, uncertainty over how to proceed does not justify inaction given that Holy Cross started occupying its new buildings 4 years ago – more than adequate time to obtain the required flood insurance or insurance exemption."[5]

"Further, each project worksheet clearly identified the amount of flood insurance coverage that FEMA required for each building."[6]

"Therefore, FEMA should disallow as ineligible $48,879,429 for the uninsured portion of the new buildings unless Holy Cross obtains the required insurance coverage or obtains an exemption.

DOI: 10.4324/9781003487869-12

Holy Cross officials also said they 'obtained the maximum flood insurance available through the National Flood Insurance Program (NFIP) for each building; however, the FEMA obtain-and-maintain requirement sets forth substantially more flood insurance than what is available through the NFIP.'"[7]

This book could be entirely about FEMA and its insurance regulations, primarily for permanent work, Categories C through G.

In FEMA's Appeals Database, there are nearly 400 appeals cases which in one way or another deal with insurance issues. We will cover as much as possible, but insofar as this is a major source of problems within the world of Public Assistance, insurance issues will continue to evolve.

Insurance issues are the second-greatest risk factor in obtaining and retaining FEMA funding. Only improper purchasing, i.e., procurement which does not follow the requirements of Title 2 of the Code of Federal Regulations, Part 200, is a greater risk to local agencies.

In some parts of the country disasters are repeat events, and FEMA has found itself paying repeatedly for the same or very similar damages. So, FEMA has the "obtain and maintain" requirement for insurance. This limits the need for FEMA to pay for the same damages every few years, especially in those parts of the country most subject to repeated disasters.

In short, FEMA wants to get out of the disaster business, certainly on the basis of repeated damage claims. When an agency has insurance to cover the disaster damages, then FEMA does not need to pay for identical or similar damages time after time.

However, regarding FEMA and the insurance requirements of the Stafford Act, the insurance coverage the local agency needs to buy is specific to the original cause of the disaster. If the damages were caused by wind-driven rain, then that is the required insurance coverage. But if in a future disaster the damage is done by riverine flooding, then FEMA will again reimburse for the cost associated with riverine flooding if the flood insurance requirements, if any, were otherwise met.

However, government agencies and private non-profit organizations in different parts of the country will need to carefully analyze their risk if they are in areas where repetitive damages may be a potential issue. How these organizations purchase insurance may vary from location to location depending on the hazards they face and the degree to which reoccurring disasters may happen. More on this later in this chapter.

This chapter will be heavy with citations of cases from the FEMA Appeals Database, an online searchable repository of thousands of appeals reaching back more than 20 years.

The Dangers of Contracts and Agreements

There is a general caveat to keep in mind that bears repeating throughout the book. When local governments or private non-profit organizations buy insurance, sign contracts of any sort, or create internal policies, they often use "permissive" language which, in their own opinion, gives them the right or obligation to take some action under a specified set of circumstances.

However, FEMA will often read those same contracts, agreements, or policies to see how those documents specifically *prohibit* the agency from doing what they had hoped to do under the guise of the document.

We can never assume that our intent and understanding of a document will be the same as FEMA's interpretation of the same document. Furthermore, while states and local jurisdictions have the right to adopt state and local laws and regulations, those laws and regulations may never contravene the laws and regulations of the Federal government when dealing with FEMA's Public Assistance program.

Handle the Evidence with Great Care

In reading the appeals cases and audits in this book, it is important to be mindful that in some respects the information created by the applicant and shared with the respective state office of emergency management and FEMA is much like the evidence presented in a criminal trial. The outcome often depends on the correct understanding of the major AND the minor points of the laws and regulations in play. It also may depend on how clearly and effectively those points are presented at any stage of the process. The burden of effectively marshalling our case falls completely on our shoulders, even though we may be unfamiliar with the laws and regulations governing the Public Assistance process. When the local agency presents its case in a logical, cohesive, easy-to-follow style, FEMA will be more receptive to understanding the local agency's perspective, and thus be more likely to provide funding. It's all about good storytelling with great documentation to support the narrative.

Both FEMA and each respective state will provide some level of informational assistance, but we at the local level truly are carrying the heaviest load, and often carrying that load without the benefit of a comprehensive understanding of the law and regulations at hand.

The FEMA Appeals Database

When FEMA receives an appeal from an Applicant, the FEMA insurance reviewer goes to this database to look for similar cases to find guidance on how the appeal at hand should be resolved. This searchable database is a very powerful and accessible tool for local agencies making an appeal to first research how the issue has been handled in the past.

In some instances, reading a few of the available appeals may be most instructive to the local agency, and based upon the agency's reading of those appeals cases, they may decide against filing an appeal and uselessly spinning their wheels on a losing case.

Our first case is from an institute of higher education[8] in North Carolina where hurricane flooding damaged a building on campus. In this case, the school did not have the mandatory flood insurance as required by the Stafford Act,[9] when a second disaster struck the campus again two years later.

Quoting, in part, from the 2nd appeal: "When FEMA provides an applicant assistance for permanent work to replace, restore, repair, reconstruct, or construct a facility, the applicant must insure that facility against future loss. Such types and amounts of insurance must be reasonable and necessary to protect the facility against future losses from the hazards that caused the damage to the property. Specifically, an applicant must O&M *(obtain and maintain)* insurance to cover the facility for the same type of hazard that caused the damage, and which must, at a minimum, be in the amount of the estimated or actual eligible costs prior to any reductions. Applicants must insure their facilities prior to grant approval, or, if they cannot, either when the applicant resumes use of or legal responsibility for the facility or when the scope of work is complete. No applicant may receive assistance for a facility for which the applicant has previously received assistance unless all required insurance has been obtained and maintained with respect to the facility. Assistance is any form of federal grant under sections 406, 422, and 428 of the Stafford Act to replace, restore, repair, reconstruct, or construct a facility and/or its contents as a result of a major disaster."

In an interesting coda to this case, the school filed a subsequent request approximately four years after receiving the original assistance, to withdraw the original Project Worksheet and return funding in order to enable funding for the second, more damaging flood. FEMA denied the request.

The next case involves a major religious organization in New York which had several properties damaged by flooding from Hurricane Irene in 2011. "The Applicant had two insurance policies in place at the time of the disaster. The primary insurance policy was with Lexington Insurance

Company in the amount of $70 million with a deductible of $250,000. The secondary policy was with Peter Turner Insurance Company (PTIC). This policy was designed as a deductible buy-down policy, which is a supplemental policy established by the insured to cover part or all of the primary insurance policy's deductible per occurrence. The PTIC policy provided $250,000 of coverage with a $750 deductible."[10]

The applicant argued that the PTIC contract was not insurance, but rather a form of "self-insured retention." The applicant further stated that PTIC was wholly owned by the applicant, i.e., the church.

FEMA countered that PTIC was in fact a licensed and regulated insurance company in the State of New York.

Furthermore, the applicant's argument that PTIC was not an insurance company is moot, because "Even if, arguendo, FEMA did not determine that the policy between the Applicant and PTIC is 'insurance,' Section 312 of the Stafford Act still applies because it clearly states financial assistance from 'any other source' is a duplication of benefits if it is used for the same project funded by FEMA funds."[11]

There is another case which shares some administrative DNA with the previous case.[12] It is another private non-profit organization which has insurance through a "captive" or wholly owned insurer.

The old saying holds true here: "if it walks like a duck, swims like a duck, and quacks like a duck, then it probably is a duck."

The applicant in our next case is a medical provider with multiple facilities in Texas. The problems here involve a captive insurer, which the applicant claims was really a form of self-insured retention. This is a complicated case, with several legalistic nuances, none of which hold water with FEMA. The applicant argues, without success, that the captive is organized in the Cayman Islands and is not licensed to sell insurance in the United States. So, in the mind of the local agency, "this isn't insurance."

However, FEMA points out that: "The Applicant's Consolidated Financial Statement also notes that Emerald, the insurer, was incorporated in the Cayman Islands and is licensed as an insurer and regulated by the Cayman Island Monetary Authority. Accordingly, FEMA finds that Emerald operates as an insurance company and enjoys the benefits of an insurance company, as evidenced by its membership as an insurance company with the Captive Insurance Companies Members in Insurance Managers Association of Cayman (IMAC)."

Note: It is my observation in reading hundreds of FEMA appeals cases and Homeland Security audits that FEMA and the auditors can and will often dig very deep to find a rationale for denying coverage; in this particular case going to a website to find that the captive is a member of an insurance-based organization.

This case has an added dimension of scary proportions, i.e., the proration of the value of the insurance policy based upon the total face value of the policy. The applicant had an insurance policy which included both property casualty and business interruption coverages.

FEMA "noted that while the Applicant argued the adjustment of deductibles for business interruption coverage was not appropriate, the Claim Settlement Agreement (CSA) between the applicant and insurers included both property loss and business interruption claims. Accordingly, when insurance covers both, FEMA policy requires the proceeds be apportioned and deductibles will likewise be apportioned in the same manner."

In this case, the applicant probably would have been better off having a separate policy for property casualty and another policy for business interruption.

This issue of apportionment of insurance proceeds is indeed a very common occurrence in all insurance cases.

Moving from Texas to the Midwest, we next examine a case from the City of Chicago.[13] In this instance following winter storms, the applicant requested FEMA funding for plowing the runways at both O'Hare and Midway airports. FEMA declined to reimburse the City because "The provisions in the Airline Use Agreements establish that the airlines are required to pay for net operating and maintenance expenses, including costs for snow removal."[14] Hence the duplication of benefits finding.

The next case ended with a painful net result wherein the applicant was denied funding for $446,000 in roof repairs. The case involved a state university in the state where the hurricane bus often makes its destructive first stop: Florida. The state college in question had damage to two buildings on the campus. The roofs of the buildings were replaced at a cost of $823,448. However, the Risk Management Consortium to which the college belonged settled the claim for $376,346. The college in turn submitted a request to FEMA for payment of the remaining $446,102.

The Stafford Act and thus FEMA require that applicants pursue the maximum coverage under a policy. "FEMA requires the Applicant to take reasonable efforts to pursue claims to recover insurance proceeds that it is entitled to receive from its insurer(s). FEMA may limit funding if the insurance policy provides coverage that should be pursued. If the Applicant expends costs to pursue its insurance claim, FEMA offsets the insurance reduction with the Applicant's reasonable costs to pursue the claim if:

- The incurred cost resulted from pursuing insurance proceeds for FEMA-eligible work; and
- The Applicant can provide documentation to show that the incurred cost was attributed to pursuing more insurance proceeds than the initial settlement amount."[15]

Another issue arising out of this case is that the insurance consortium to which the college belonged refused to file suit on behalf of the college against its insurer "for fear of jeopardizing coverage for all members of the consortium."[16] This of course raises the question, "Who's looking out for our best interests?"

For all information and documentation that the local agency presents to FEMA to substantiate its losses – in this case, its insurance coverage and the insurance payouts – the local agency must not only provide all the pertinent data necessary to substantiate its position, but it must also EXPLAIN how the data provided supports its position for reimbursement.

In the next case, involving a Florida Public Service District: "The Applicant did not respond to FEMA's RFI (Request For Information) to explain whether all costs were presented to the insurer, and if so, to provide the insurer's response. The Applicant also did not respond to FEMA's RFI to provide the final adjuster's estimates or settlement. The insurance documents that the Applicant did provide do not show the amounts claimed by the Applicant and instead only show the payments made by the insurer. If the costs on appeal were in fact presented to the insurer, the Applicant did not provide FEMA with an explanation for why they were denied, did not demonstrate that it questioned the settlement amounts, and did not provide any further documentation from the insurer to show efforts to maximize insurance proceeds to which the Applicant was entitled. Therefore, the Applicant did not adequately explain why certain repair expenses were not covered by insurance or demonstrate that it made reasonable efforts to receive proceeds to which it was entitled. Accordingly, FEMA finds that it properly applied insurance reductions for anticipated proceeds."[17]

This case was further complicated by the fact that the district alleged that some of its expenses charged for Direct Administrative Costs (DAC) by their engineering consultant were in fact charges to increase their insurance payouts. However, the engineering consulting firm charged all expenses as "engineering services" instead of more accurately describing those expenses as "insurance recovery work" or something similar. Had the engineering firm properly described their work, some of those costs might have been eligible in the minimum, and optimally, those charges would have been evidentiary proof to FEMA that the district did make efforts to maximize its insurance recovery. Therefore, FEMA properly denied eligibility.

The next case involves a South Carolina city which suffered flooding from Hurricane Joaquin in October 2015.[18]

The applicant's building flooded to a depth of 33 inches. The heart of the matter here is that the agency knew in January of 2016 that it had additional damages but did not so inform its insurance carrier until October of 2017, nearly two years later. The insurance policy specifically stated that the agency had to report all damages within a six-month period. Because of this delay in reporting its damages, FEMA determined that the agency failed to "take reasonable efforts to recover insurance proceeds that they are entitled to receive from their insurer(s)."[19]

This case points out a common problem faced by many, if not most, jurisdictions following a disaster. The regulations must be closely followed, irrespective of the demands on agency staff following the disaster. This is particularly so for the thousands of small cities, counties, and special districts across the county. Although the agency staff may have been overburdened with work following the disaster, the documentation processes and their accompanying timelines are inviolate, and FEMA will seldom if ever issue a hall pass because the staff is overwhelmed.

In February 2001, the Nisqually Earthquake damaged portions of Lewis County, Washington. A school district in Lewis County reported damages to its gymnasium's second-floor support structure, which consisted of manufactured roof trusses.[20] Part of the second floor contained a weight room. Various engineers from the school district, the state, and FEMA inspected the damaged trusses.

Based on the inspections, the insurance company agreed to pay for only 40% of the damages, or $27,225. Allegations were made that some of the damage to the trusses was due to weights being dropped on the floor, although the district had mitigated the problem somewhat by placing rubber mats on the floor. FEMA acknowledged that some of the damage was caused by the earthquake, but the percentage of damage caused by the earthquake versus damage done by dropped weights could not be determined, and as a result the damages were ineligible.

The school district did win a small consolation prize insofar as FEMA did pay the insurance deductible of $4,851. In this case, FEMA alleged that the damage was fully covered by insurance, and therefore ineligible for FEMA assistance, other than the payment of the deductible.

Insurers Have Timelines, Too!

Another part of making reasonable efforts to maximize insurance recovery is to ensure prompt and aggressive actions in dealing with the insurance company or insurance consortium. While no one enjoys working with an insufferable autocrat, this is the time and place to be as obnoxious (within civil limits) as possible in pursuing insurance recovery. Insurers love premiums and loathe payouts. I know a fine gentleman who for 30 years worked for insurance companies. His job, as he describes it, was to "delay, diminish, and deny" insurance claims. The insurance company is a business, not a social club. Therefore, we must mobilize all available resources to obtain the maximum payments possible.

It is important to note that like FEMA, many insurers have deadlines for reporting damages. In this case from South Carolina, the local agency apparently took a laissez-faire attitude in dealing with its insurance consortium. "From October 1 to 23, 2015, Hurricane Joaquin created 1,000-year event levels of rainfall in certain regions of South Carolina. The President declared a Federal disaster on October 5, 2015. The City of Sumter's (Applicant's) Fire Department Training Facility

(Facility) was flooded with several feet of water, damaging the Facility's interior and the equipment and contents contained therein."[21]

"The Applicant filed a claim with the South Carolina Municipal Insurance and Risk Financing Fund (SCMIRF). SCMIRF completed an inspection of the damages to the Facility in October 2015 and estimated $116,068.37 in repair costs. That inspection showed the water level was 33 inches, but based on standard industry practice allowed repairs even higher, up to a 4 foot flood cut. On January 14, 2016, the Applicant's engineers identified additional damages and provided a cost estimate of $379,000.00, which reflected costs for a more extensive repair of the Facility. In February 2016, FEMA inspected the Facility and prepared Project Worksheet (PW) 457 with an estimated cost of $571,742.99 to repair the Facility and equipment, and replace contents. The PW was based on the damages and repairs identified in the Applicant's engineering estimates applied into FEMA's Cost Estimate Format (CEF)."[22]

"In March 2016, SCMIRF issued a check to the Applicant for $116,068.37 for repairs to the Facility, and a separate payment of $42,739.00 for damaged equipment. The Applicant requested clarification from SCMIRF in October 2017 regarding the amount the insurer paid, which was lower than the Applicant's engineering estimate. SCMIRF replied to the request on November 7, 2017, clarifying that the estimate was prepared based on no more than '4 feet up from the floor' in flood damages. In a March 5, 2018 letter, SCMIRF denied any further claim payments related to the disaster event. Additionally, SCMIRF noted several improvements to the Facility that were not covered by the Applicant's insurance policy."[23]

"On July 25, 2018, FEMA notified the South Carolina Emergency Management Division (Grantee) that FEMA found the Applicant's costs to repair the Facility were fully covered by insurance. Based on anticipated insurance proceeds, FEMA applied a mandatory insurance reduction to avoid duplicating anticipated proceeds, bringing total project costs in PW 457 to $0.00."[24]

"The FEMA Region IV Regional Administrator (RA) partially approved the appeal on December 3, 2019, but denied the Facility repair costs as the Applicant had not properly pursued all available insurance proceeds. FEMA found that the Applicant did not contact SCMIRF regarding any possible adjustments to the claim based on additional damages found until two years post-inspection, and 17 months after the Applicant accepted payment."

"In a letter dated January 31, 2020, the Applicant appealed FEMA's determination regarding the Facility repairs and the DAC denial. The Applicant reiterates its first appeal arguments that it had pursued the maximum insurance claims. It assert *(sic)* that it 'made reasonable efforts to recover insurance proceeds for interior damage of the [Facility] that the [p]olicy actually covered.' The Applicant emphasizes that the additional damages were the result of bacteria and mold not covered by the insurance policy."[25]

SCMIRF's October 2015 inspection accounted for damage up to 4 feet from the ground. The Applicant's engineers identified additional moisture-related damage above the 4-foot mark in a January 2016 estimate, but the Applicant did not forward this information to its provider until October 2017. The Applicant's insurance policy provides a six-month window to dispute insurance claims, starting when the insurance inspection report was completed in October 2015. It states, "[i] n the event of a disagreement between SCMIRF and the [Applicant] regarding determination of coverage and/or defense, it is agreed that the [Applicant] must appeal the coverage determination to the board of Trustees within six months of such determination."[26]

"Documentation in the Administrative Record indicates that the Applicant contacted SCMIRF in October 2017 to dispute the insurance amount paid. The Applicant states it did not dispute its insurance proceeds prior to this because its policy excluded costs to repair damages caused by mold and bacteria, and believed therefore that SCMIRF would not have adjusted the amount paid in the original claim. However, the insurance estimate developed by SCMIRF included allowances for applying anti-microbial agents to walls. In the March 2018 denial letter provided by SCMIRF, the provider does not address any mold or mildew damages as the basis for a denial and indicated that additional payments could have been made. It stated, '[h]ad the level of flooding been higher and/or the flood waters remained in the building for an extended period of time, additional wall space would have required removal but this was not the case.'"[27]

"It was the Applicant's responsibility to provide additional information and file a supplemental claim for any additional proceeds that may have been available. It did not provide the additional damage information to the insurer after its engineer's inspection, which provided results in January 2016. <u>The Applicant was aware of the disparity in the insurer's estimate and the its own within the six-month timeframe allowed to dispute it. Such a disparity in the damage descriptions and repair costs warranted that the Applicant contact its insurance provider and submit a claims adjustment.</u> Instead, the Applicant disputed the matter two years after the inspection and 17 months after accepting insurance proceeds in March 2016. FEMA finds the Applicant did not take reasonable efforts to recover insurance proceeds that they may have been entitled to receive from their insurer. As such, FEMA properly reduced funding by the anticipated insurance proceeds."[28] (Emphasis Added)

In reviewing the City's webpage, the existence of a department of risk management is not apparent, nor does a search reveal any senior appointed officials who might be identified as a risk manager. This may work well for the agency for day-to-day operations, but it presents a serious problem when the agency is unwillingly but necessarily thrust into the grinder of the Public Assistance program.

Clearly, whoever was handling the insurance issues for this case was unaware of the availability of insurance coverage for mold and mildew damage. Having an insurance policy is important, but knowing what coverage limits are afforded by the policy is equally important. When the local agency does not have such expertise available in-house, then hiring an outside insurance consultant, especially one with FEMA experience, may be critical to the cost recovery process.

Another Insurance Catch-22

This leads to another important point: insurance prorated coverage. Let's use a roof as an example. The local agency has a building, fully insured, built with a roof with a 20-year warranty. A damaging storm occurs in year 10 of the 20-year lifespan of the roof. The insurer will prorate the payment on the damaged roof at 50% because the insured has received ½ of the roof's life expectancy. However, FEMA sees this as less than a full coverage payout on a roof insured to the original value, or replacement value. This concept of prorated costs may be much more costly than the local agency had expected because FEMA will not make up the difference between the insured value and the final payout from the insurer.

This case illustrates another ongoing issue with insurance matters. FEMA may assume either the full cost recovery under the insurance policy or debit the actual insurance payment, at its option.

The final determination on how much insurance was either actually available (full coverage) or actually paid (less than full coverage) may not be determined until the project is closed out. When less than 100% of the damage is covered by the insurance, then FEMA will examine the question of how diligently the applicant pursued the insurance recovery, up to and including suing the insurance company in a court of appropriate jurisdiction.

Duplication of Benefits and Other Federal Agencies (OFA)

Shifting gears, we will now look at another aspect of the question of duplication of benefits. Insurance is the most common form of duplication of benefits. However, included in the Stafford Act[29] there is a specific exclusion for the duplication of benefits from insurance or any other source, including assistance from any Other Federal agency (OFA).

In this case, a Florida county[30] requested a Project Worksheet for repairs to State Road A1A, where Hurricane Irma caused erosion in 2017. In this case, the county and the state (Florida Department of Transportation) (FDOT) had a maintenance agreement. However, the maintenance agreement was only for landscape maintenance, not for erosion control or other work within the FDOT right-of-way.

FEMA determined first that the applicant, i.e., the county, did not have the legal responsibility to do the erosion control work, as that work was not explicitly covered under the terms of the maintenance agreement. And even if the maintenance agreement included erosion control work, the highway was a part of the Federal aid highway system and therefore ineligible work for the county. Even when, in this case, the Federal Highway Administration has no funds available for the work, FEMA cannot reimburse the costs under the duplication of benefits regulation.

In another Other Federal Agency case,[31] here involving the National Resource Conservation Service (NRCS), a Tennessee county claimed damages to five different embankments which appeared to be unimproved natural features, which are generally ineligible. FEMA noted that some of the damages were the same as those which would naturally occur over time and requested that the applicant provide information regarding the routine inspection of these embankments, including pre-disaster photographs, and reports of any work done on the embankments prior to the flood disaster.

"Although the Applicant provided pre-disaster maintenance records to try to establish the relationship between the damages claimed and the disaster, the records provide no specific information on where, when, and what pre-disaster work the Applicant conducted on three of the five facilities in question. Furthermore, the Applicant has not provided documentation to substantiate any pre-disaster maintenance to the remaining two facilities. As such, the Applicant has not provided documentation to support different conclusions than those noted in FEMA's site inspections."[32]

Additionally, and more persuasively, "FEMA policy states that if a facility is under the specific authority of another Federal agency, FEMA does not provide assistance to restore that Facility even if that Federal agency does not provide funding to restore the facility. While there are exceptions to this general prohibition (*i.e., where Public Assistance funding for emergency work is allowed*), FEMA policy clearly states that permanent work to restore roads and bridges is not eligible when restoration is under the specific authority of another agency."[33]

The prohibition on duplication of benefits also includes donations, which was dealt with in Chapter 3.

"Obtain and Maintain"

Another very common insurance-related issue revolves around the requirement to "obtain and maintain" insurance[34] once FEMA has funded permanent repair or replacement work in excess of $5,000.

In this case, a small town in Eastern Iowa had flooding in 2010. The applicant had previously received FEMA funding for flood damage at the same facility in 2008 and had failed to obtain and maintain flood insurance. This community has been a flood-mapped community since 1976.

Because this community is in a Special Flood Hazard Area (SFHA), the purchase of flood insurance should be a given. However, this is a community of less than 1,000 population, and the purchase of flood insurance may not have been in the financial cards. In this case, the lack of flood insurance cost the town over $287,000.

Now for some complexity with the obtain and maintain requirement. In this case, a Louisiana parish school board[35] suffered damages of $1,266,000 to 20 of its facilities following Hurricane Isaac. The damage was for the cleaning and remediation of mold growth from the storm.

FEMA determined that because of damages suffered in Hurricane Katrina in 2005, FEMA should reduce the reimbursement by $428,000 because the applicant had used a blanket insurance policy to meet the costs of the damage sustained in Hurricane Katrina.

A Cautionary Note on Blanket Insurance Policies

". . . if a facility that is insured under a blanket insurance policy, insurance pool arrangement, or some combination thereof, is damaged in a future similar other than flood disaster, eligible costs will be reduced by the amount of eligible damage sustained on the previous disaster. Thus, when an applicant uses one of, or a combination of, the aforementioned insurance policies, reimbursement of eligible costs, that may include deductibles, is reduced by the amount of eligible damage sustained to the same facility in a prior disaster, regardless of whether any of the costs are used to pay an insurance deductible. The International Risk Management Institute defines a blanket policy as '[a] single insurance policy that covers several different properties, shipments, or locations.'[36] FEMA expands this definition by explaining that an insurance policy is a blanket policy when it covers multiple properties to a level less than their full value."[37] (Emphasis Added)

However, because these were Category B Emergency Protective Measures, the Stafford Act does not ordinarily require the purchase of insurance for Emergency Protective Measures. Therefore, this appeal was a winner for the applicant.

But don't get your hopes up; we have a second case to consider. In this case, a town in Southern New York State[38] suffered from heavy flooding from Tropical Storm Lee in 2011. Previously in 2006, the town had experienced damaging floods for which it received FEMA assistance for the very same facility, a maintenance garage. In the previous case, there was $1,804 in costs for Emergency Protective Measures and $3,793 in permanent work, totaling $5,597.

Normally, permanent work projects of less than $5,000 do not trigger the "obtain and maintain" insurance requirement. However, in this case, FEMA had combined the $1,804 Cat 'B' work and the $3,793 in permanent repairs for a Project Worksheet total of $5,597, which did trigger the "obtain and maintain" insurance provision.

"With regard to repair of the damages caused by the 2006 flood, both mud and water had to be removed to complete the permanent repair work. Such actions were necessary to restore the facility as well as to ensure worker safety. Consequently, the cleanup work was a component of the permanent work and FEMA properly included within PW 2535. As such, eligible funding for the insurable facility exceeded $5,000.00 and the obtain and maintain requirement for flood insurance was applicable."[39]

Therefore, local agencies need to pay close attention to the "obtain and maintain" insurance requirement and take appropriate actions based on the facts in each unique case.

In the next case, a Southwest Missouri town with a population of less than 2,000 suffered from severe storms, tornadoes, straight-line winds, and flooding, which damaged the town's underground sewer lift station.[40] The FEMA Insurance Specialist determined that there should be an insurance reduction of $26,000.

However, the insurance carrier stated that the lift station was equipment rather than a facility and not covered under the policy terms.

"The Applicant's insurance policy did not explicitly or implicitly cover the lift station at the time of the disaster. As the Applicant's insurance carrier confirmed, the lift station was not listed on any of the Applicant's property schedules and was not eligible for coverage as an unnamed location.

The Applicant later obtained coverage for the lift station by scheduling it under its property policy. Since the Applicant did not receive insurance proceeds for the lift station, Public Assistance (PA) funding will not duplicate insurance benefits."[41]

This winning appeal demonstrates the necessity of close and constant communication with both FEMA and the insurers. Failure to aggressively pursue the insurance settlement is a serious detriment to full disaster cost recovery.

The next case involved a city in mid-state New York, where flooding in 2011 caused damage to a facility located in a Special Flood Hazard Area (SHFA), as designated in FEMA's flood maps. The agency had an insurance policy which included flood coverage, but the policy was not a flood insurance policy from the National Flood Insurance Program (NFIP).

The FEMA insurance specialist ordered a $30,494 reduction for no (or in this case, improper) flood insurance.

In our next case, a city, a suburb east of Seattle, had flooding in 2009. The city had blanket insurance coverage under the Washington Cities Insurance Authority, which does not meet the flood insurance requirements.

FEMA requires that property owners in designated flood zones carry flood insurance. While property owners can purchase flood insurance from private insurance companies, FEMA does not accept non-NFIP policies as proof of insurance coverage. This is because the NFIP has specific coverage and eligibility requirements that are not always met by non-NFIP policies. Additionally, FEMA may not have access to the necessary information to verify that non-NFIP policies meet their requirements.

To fully understand the issue in play here, one must go back to the origins of the Stafford Act. When the Stafford Act was pending in Congress, the number one disaster threat at the time was flooding. Consequently, the Stafford Act is somewhat "flood biased." Therefore, the mandatory requirement for flood insurance was issued through the National Flood Insurance Program. Any other insurance policy will not and does not meet the requirements of the National Flood Insurance Program, including blanket insurance policies, even if they contain some sort of flood insurance coverage. Purchasing a non-National Flood Insurance Policy is simply a waste of time when FEMA is involved and coverage is sought.

For the next case, we move to sunny Southern California, where legend says it never rains, and yet . . . here we are with a flooding incident in 2005.

This case involved two different, but related problems.[42] First, the applicant had applied for and received a waiver regarding the affordability of insurance. In this case, a California Department of Insurance _analyst_ signed the waiver. The Stafford Act only allows THE state insurance commissioner to approve such a waiver, which rendered this waiver useless for its intended purpose.

The real killer fact here is that the applicant did not have a National Flood Insurance Policy in effect. The applicant requested a time extension to get a waiver properly endorsed. However, that endorsement had not been granted at the time of the appeal decision.

Moving on to eastern Iowa, we have a major Iowa city appealing FEMA's flood insurance reduction in a complex case stemming from flooding in 2011. The city acquired a large unused industrial complex which contained 22 buildings. The city leased out 2 of these buildings to private companies.

As a result of the flooding, the local Building & Safety Department issued demolition orders for the buildings, listing the 22 separate facilities based upon the city's demolition order, which listed the 22 separate buildings.

The 22 buildings, which would normally require flood insurance of $500,000 for each building, therefore would net a flood insurance reduction of $11,000,000.

In the second appeal, the city tried to argue that there were only 8 buildings on the property, some with multiple additions. However, FEMA relied on the city's own demolition orders, which listed 22 buildings.

Of the total of 225,445 square feet contained in the buildings, only 54,781 square feet was leased out, or about 24% of the available building space.

Initially, FEMA was writing a Project Worksheet for the full 225,445 square feet with a value of $9,521,248. However, because the facility was only 24% used, the Project Worksheet was reduced to $2,313,401. The mandatory flood insurance reduction, based on the amount of space being used, was $349,825.

So, while the agency dogged one bullet in the $11,000,000 flood insurance reduction, it caught another bullet in that the total value of the project was greatly reduced to $1,963,576.

This is just another case where the city handed FEMA a proper basis for project cost reduction when it listed all 22 buildings on the demolition orders, instead of the 8 buildings which they later wished to claim.

Note: While many of these appeals cases are from 10, 20, or more years ago, they still retain relevancy in today's FEMA world. These are the underlying Federal regulations and processes which have changed little or not at all since FEMA's creation in 1979.

Flood Insurance vs. Non-Flood Insurance

While FEMA requires those agencies with facilities located in Special Flood Hazard Areas (SFHA) have the maximum flood insurance required BEFORE the flood causes damage, there is no similar pre-disaster requirement to have insurance coverage prior to a disaster for non-flood disasters, such as a tornado, earthquake, etc. However, once a disaster has occurred and FEMA assistance is provided for permanent work projects, then the applicant must have insurance covering the dollar value of the assistance provided, and the insurance must be maintained for as long as the agency owns the building. Without obtaining and maintaining such insurance, FEMA will not consider any funding for future damages should they occur. This is extremely important for those local agencies in parts of the country where disasters may cause repetitive losses. Pay me now or pay me later.

In the next case, involving a California Fair and Exhibition facility,[43] the local agency purchased a non-National Flood Insurance Policy with a high deductible.

Reading between the lines, this may have been an attempt to game the process by having the high deductible, insofar as deductibles are normally eligible for reimbursement by FEMA.

However, because this was not the required National Flood Insurance Policy, FEMA reduced the allowable deductible to $750.

The next case again involves the Nisqually Earthquake,[44] which damaged a county courthouse in Washington State. Prior to the earthquake, the county developed a plan to seismically upgrade the courthouse. This seismic upgrade would constitute an improved project, which we will discuss later in more detail.

When an improved project is funded, it is funded only based on the repair work required as a direct result of the disaster, and even if there are cost overruns, FEMA caps the Project Worksheet based on the disaster-related damages, and not on the total improved project costs.

Early on, FEMA instructed the agency to carefully track its expenses and the corresponding insurance payments. FEMA prorated the deductible and deobligated $1,130,524. The agency appealed, and during that appeal, FEMA further deducted $1,106,693 because of a duplication of benefits between the insurance recovery and the estimated costs of the approved project.

The initial costs were estimated to be $2,632,508; however, the insurance company's final pay-out was $5,315,526, which triggered this insurance reduction.

This points out an uncommon but always potential side effect of making an appeal. FEMA has thousands of employees, many of whom have years of incredible experience with the Public Assistance program. But there are also less-experienced employees who do not have this degree of experience.

Sometimes a low-level or inexperienced FEMA employee will approve a Project Worksheet which will be later be determined to be ineligible, in whole or in part, by a higher level or more experienced FEMA employee.

When a Project Worksheet is only partially deobligated, due consideration must be given to the fact that on appeal, more experienced and higher-level FEMA employees will be reviewing the appeal, and on occasion, these more senior FEMA employees will determine that more of (or the entire) Project Worksheet is ineligible and should be denied. More on this later in Chapter 41 on Appeals.

However, in this case, the appeals gods recognized through the sometimes-confusing set of facts that the deductible of $2,443,600 was an eligible cost.

The prohibition of duplication of benefits has a wide reach beyond the insurance issues in the next case, involving a New Orleans private high school.[45] The school had several of its facilities damaged in Hurricane Katrina in 2005 and was initially offered an insurance settlement of $1,069,817. The applicant sued in court and later received a total of $3,500,000 from insurance.

The applicant, as a private non-profit entity, applied for and was granted a Small Business Administration (SBA) loan of $1,500,000. $1,000,000 of the final insurance payout was earmarked to repay the Small Business Administration loan.

However, under the duplication of benefits rule, FEMA also deducted a pro-rata portion of the loan.

Enter stage left the fatal problem. The appeal of the initial FEMA insurance reduction was not filed until eight years after FEMA's letter of determination was issued. This was far beyond the 60-day window allowed for filing an appeal, and thus the appeal was denied.

Caution: Small Business Administration Loans for Private Non-Profits

For a private non-profit organization that has both organizational eligibility and specific facility eligibility, applying for an SBA loan may be a two-edged sword. If the agency, already suffering financially from the disaster damages, applies for and receives the Small Business Administration loan, it may have the duplication of benefits deductions taken, and thereby enlarge the financial hole which is already sinking the boat.

Another deadly surprise which awaits the uninitiated is the pro-ration of insurance, even when that insurance coverage nominally does not cover damaged facilities.

Perhaps this is best explained when an agency carries a blanket insurance policy which covers, for example, product liability, property casualty, business interruption, etc.

As an example, let's imagine a hypothetical large city, one which has a city-owned convention center, a marina, an airport, and an enterprise water department. This city might have a single blanket insurance policy which covers all losses up to the policy limits of $100,000,000.

However, when a disaster hits, the agency (in its own mind, but not written into the policy language), has allocated 50% or $50,000,000 of its coverage for the disruptions to its "businesses," i.e., the convention center, the marina, etc.

But because the actual dollar limits of the policy coverages are not reduced, in writing, to clear and unambiguous language, FEMA may (and probably will) elect to see the entire insurance proceeds and apportion its deduction for duplication of benefits based upon the total of $100,000,000, rather than a total of $50,000,000, which risk management would otherwise attribute to property casualty losses. This apportionment is based upon the ratio of eligible losses to ineligible losses. This torpedo can have devastating effects on the bottom line for the recovery process.

If the local agency makes use of a blanket insurance policy, it should be sure that sub-limits for each category of loss are specified to reduce the threat of a greater portion of the insurance proceeds being deducted under the duplication of benefits.

In a similar appeals case from Biloxi, MS, a large, prominent religious organization[46] requested FEMA Public Assistance of $2,890,016. The applicant also applied to the Small Business Administration for the maximum allowable loan of $1,500,000. The loan was granted, and FEMA determined that based upon the ratio of eligible to ineligible expenses, $614,653 would be deducted from the Public Assistance grant because of the duplication of funding from another Federal agency.

In this instance, the Small Business Administration loan covered both eligible and ineligible expenses, thereby inviting FEMA to make an apportionment for duplication of benefits.

I would suggest that had the loan been ONLY for otherwise FEMA-ineligible expenses, the result would have been different. But of course, all this would have to be reduced to writing in the loan documents.

However, in the heat of battle, and with no prior knowledge of the prohibition on duplication of benefits, the apparently small and insignificant details were glossed over to the applicant's detriment.

The next case takes us to a central Indiana hospital which experienced flooding in June of 2008. FEMA prepared 56 PWs for the hospital.[47] FEMA reduced the value of the PWs by $15,913,493 to reflect anticipated insurance.

FEMA met with the Regional Hospital (Applicant) on April 6, 2009, and explained that 36 percent (36%) of the $25 million insurance recovery ($9 million) would be attributable to the Applicant's business income loss due to the flood. The remaining 64 percent (64%) or $16 million would be applied to FEMA eligible damages.

The Applicant held that the Stafford Act allowed it to apply the $25 million insurance recovery exclusively to its unreimbursed business income losses.

Without either a separate business interruption policy or sub-limits within a blanket policy, the applicant was at FEMA's mercy to determine the appropriate allocation of the insurance coverage. FEMA made the apportionments in accordance with its existing policies.

In this case, filing and losing two appeals was not sufficient self-flagellation for this agency. The agency then filed a case in Federal Circuit court. "The parties' second dispute concerns the significance of proceeds the Hospital received from insurance. The statute does not allow reimbursement if the victim has another source of payment. 42 U.S.C. §5155(c). In other words, the collateral-source rule of tort law[48] does not apply to disaster relief. The Hospital's insurance covered both property losses and business-interruption losses; the Stafford Act is limited to property losses. The Hospital's insurer paid out the policy limit of $25 million without allocating between property loss and business-interruption loss. FEMA concluded that property damage represents roughly two-thirds of the Hospital's losses within the policy's scope, so it attributed approximately $16 million of the insurance proceeds to the property damage and deducted that sum from the amount otherwise payable from federal funds. The Hospital does not dispute the ratio but does contend that no deduction should have been made."[49] (Emphasis Added)

The message here is that if at all possible, the local agency should work with their insurer to allocate the paid-out loss (in writing), rather than issuing a single check with no allocation regarding where the proceeds are intended to be applied. An even better, although perhaps more costly, strategy would be to have the original insurance policy specify the apportionment of coverage before the policy is issued.

Some appeals cases are relatively simple and straightforward, while other cases are a mishmash of issues which require a full bottle of extra-strength painkillers to get through. Such is the next case involving not one, but two, different but administratively related Florida agencies:[50] a county, and the local airport located within the county. The two agencies were jointly covered by a single insurance policy which had a limit of $50,000,000. In this instance, the conjoined insurance twins were able to self-allocate the proceeds of the insurance payout with the county receiving $40,301,600 and the local airport authority received $9,698,400.

With the insurance apportionment out of the way, we are left with a commingled cluster of other issues, including 1) appeals questions, 2) Stafford Act §705(a) claims, 3) Stafford Act §705(c) claims, and 4) insurance claims. Later in the book, we will address the Stafford Act §705 claims.

As for the insurance, the applicant used some of its share of the insurance to pay for ineligible project work and eligible (FEMA-funded) projects; however, the applicant did not clearly document how the insurance money was divided between these eligible and ineligible projects. This lack of clarity left it to FEMA to make a determination regarding the duplication of benefits issues.

Quoting from the language of the appeal, "Applicants are responsible for providing 'all pertinent insurance information (policies, declarations, and [the insurer's] 'Statements of Loss').' In addition, applicants are responsible for providing not only the insurance policy, but 'all data, declarations, endorsements, exclusions, schedules, and other attachments or amendments' as well as any other documentation describing the coverage, covered items, and proof of loss."[51]

"However, the Applicant has not demonstrated that its insurance policy covered the losses in the ineligible projects. In addition, the Applicant has not provided the full insurance policy or statement of loss from its insurer, preventing FEMA from determining which losses were covered or how proceeds should be distributed."[52]

The process of tracking both the individual approved projects and the insurance payouts allocated to those respective projects must be done in an extremely granular way, carefully matching up projects, authorized costs, and the insurance payments. FEMA does not allow any allocation of costs, hours worked, or consultants' time to be performed on a percentage basis. All accounting, for everything, must be done with integers and decimal points, i.e., hours and minutes or dollars and cents

For all the information the county provided, they "still did not demonstrate how the insurance proceeds covered all claimed damages or how the Applicant apportioned the proceeds."[53]

"While FEMA will make proportional reductions based on the proceeds put toward eligible versus ineligible projects, the Applicant still must demonstrate that the policy covers all claimed losses. Without the complete information, FEMA correctly reduced assistance based on actual insurance proceeds received to avoid a duplication of benefits."[54]

The bottom line here is that no matter how experienced and arguably well-educated the risk management staff may be, this depth of detail is far beyond their normal day-to-day work processes. In reading dozens of insurance-related appeals cases, it is my considered opinion that many risk managers are skating on very thin ice when it comes to FEMA and insurance matters.

If I was in the position of hiring manger for certain administrative positions in a part of the country which is on a hurricane, tornado, or flood bus route, I would always include among the candidate interview questions, "What, if any, level of experience do you have dealing with FEMA and the Public Assistance program?" In fact, previous FEMA experience, at the local level would be one of my highly desired qualifications for prospective candidates.

The next appeal case stems from winter storms in Southern California, similar to a previous case we examined. Again, the applicant relied on a waiver which had been signed by an analyst with the state insurance commissioner's office, rather than the state insurance commissioner him/ herself.

"The Applicant petitioned the California State Insurance Commissioner for a certification that flood insurance is not reasonable and affordable for the facilities and that insurance is not needed due to the Applicant's program for self-insurance."[55] (Emphasis Added) Self-insurance is an option available only to states, not their political subdivisions.

The author of this appeal case goes on to note that "The certification must be based on the grounds of availability, adequacy, or necessity for the Applicant to receive a waiver under section 311. Affordability is not a viable argument if facilities are eligible for coverage under the federally subsidized NFIP."[56] (Emphasis Added)

"Due to the high cost of insurance, some applicants may request to insure the damaged facilities under a blanket insurance policy covering all their facilities, an insurance pool arrangement, or some combination of these options. Such an arrangement may be accepted for other than flood damages. However, if the same facility is damaged in a similar future disaster, eligible costs will be reduced by the amount of eligible damage sustained on the previous disaster."[57] (Emphasis Added)

The Danger of Swimming in an Insurance Pool

We have previously mentioned blanket policies, and now we will turn our attention to insurance pools. Dating back to the 1970s, local governments began to explore the idea of pooling their resources to create self-insurance programs. The programs allowed member governments to share the risks and costs associated with insuring their sometimes-unique risks, such as law enforcement operations, which helped to reduce premiums and improve coverage.

Eventually, these self-insurance programs evolved into what are now known as local government insurance pools. Since their inception, there are now hundreds of these pools operating across the United States. They provide coverage for a wide range of risks and are an important tool for local governments to manage their insurance needs.

Some of them have a broad base of member agencies, while others specialize in one certain type of government agency. Such is the case here, involving an insurance pool consisting primarily of colleges and universities in the State of Florida. In the Appeals Database, there are dozens of different cases dealing with these insurance consortiums. We will address only a couple of them here.

In this instance, the individual college[58] alleged that the group to which it belonged was merely a risk-sharing program with similar agencies. However, FEMA is prohibited from providing financial assistance when that constitutes a duplication of benefits because even if the funds do not come from "insurance," they come from another source which then constitutes the duplication of benefits.

Furthermore, this insurance pool had an insurance policy with a commercial insurance company for excess coverage beyond the pool's own maximum payout responsibility.

The next insurance appeals case comes from the very same insurance consortium of Florida colleges and universities we just visited.

The consortium itself had "informed FEMA that it sustained $22,774,014 in total insurable damages, and is seeking reimbursement on behalf of its member colleges of $9,451,097 of deductible costs paid by member colleges."[59]

However, the agreement between the colleges and the insurance consortium does not constitute a legal responsibility for making the necessary repairs to the various college campuses. Therefore, the consortium has no standing with FEMA to seek any reimbursement for its incurred costs.

Insurance pools in and of themselves constitute a major subclass of FEMA appeals. A search of the FEMA Appeals Database for the term "insurance pool" yields well over two dozen cases, although some of these citations will reflect back to certain key cases which are then re-referenced in other appeals.

Insurance and Eligibility May Be Related in Some Cases

Next is an insurance-related case, which more properly might be discussed regarding eligibility issues. However, it is insurance-related and therefore appropriate.

As a result of the four hurricanes that struck Florida in 2004, the Florida State Department of Financial Services, the Applicant, helped individuals process insurance claims, prioritized assistance to homeowners, and distributed educational information on structural damage prevention.

The Applicant requested FEMA assistance for costs incurred for travel and materials associated with deployment of the Applicant's employees to Disaster Recovery Centers, contract labor for staffing emergency phone lines, and for establishing an electronic communications network.

FEMA properly responded that the activities described here did not meet the criteria for emergency protective measures and thus were not eligible for Public Assistance funding.

i.   "To be eligible for reimbursement under Public Assistance, actions must:
ii. Eliminate or lessen immediate threats of significant additional damage to life, public health, or safety; or
iii. Eliminate or lessen immediate threats of significant additional damage to improved public or private property through measures that are cost effective."[60]

Facilities Under Construction

We now move on to yet another quagmire of Federal regulation regarding insurance: "the owner's responsibility."

When facilities are under construction, FEMA's go-to position is that the contractor is responsible for the project until it has been completed and accepted by the owner.

This case involved a major Southern California hospital,[61] which had contracted for the construction of a new cardiac surgery center. The facility was approximately 30 days away from final completion and acceptance by the hospital when the new project was damaged in the Northridge Earthquake.

While the fundamentals of the case are clear and simple, the unraveling process involved the interpretation of complex construction contracts and American Institute of Architects documents.

The Hospital applied for funding to conduct a structural evaluation of the building, which did have some weld failures in the steel moment frame.

The hospital tried to claim it had responsibility because, among other reasons, it had partially accepted the work because it had made partial payments for the construction. The hospital also alleged that it had purchased an "all-risk" insurance policy for the project. However, the "all-risk" policy did not include earthquake insurance.[62] And thus, FEMA properly denied eligibility for the work. Although this specific case goes way back to the late 1990s, it is a benchmark case that is still cited in newer appeals cases.

Although a contractor's responsibility for projects under construction is generally the case, I have seen two cases wherein the local government agency as owner contracted with a construction firm for a project, and was able to take on the legal responsibility for disaster damages on an unfinished construction project.

This principle is an important one for local government agencies, especially the larger cities, counties, and special districts that are often working on new facilities and remodeling existing ones. Once the construction contracts are signed and work has begun, the responsibility for disaster damage falls on the contractor absent any other special written and signed documentation to the contrary. It must always be remembered that FEMA will not assume anything unless it is reduced to writing, compliant with FEMA regulations, signed, and dated prior to the onset of the disaster.

But it is possible to transfer the risk for disaster damage to construction projects when done properly.

This next case is one of those rare instances. The appeal involves a major Southern California wholesale water agency.[63] The water project in question was damaged in 1998 winter storms and the applicant requested a $200,000 reimbursement, which it had paid as a deductible for the damages which had occurred due to the storms. FEMA, seeing that this was a project under construction, denied eligibility.

What made this case different, and ultimately eligible, was that the local agency from the project's inception had created an Owner-Controlled Insurance Policy (OCIP), which included ALL aspects of insurance for the project, including worker's compensation, general liability, and property insurance. The terms of the policy required that the project owner, not the contractor, was responsible for the various threats and hazards which might occur during the construction. Because this arrangement was created from the beginning and very specifically assigned the risks to the project owner and not the contractor, FEMA determined on appeal that the expenses were in fact eligible.

A word of caution here regarding standard American Institute of Architects (AIA) contracts. When these standard form contracts are used exclusively without additional contracts or agreements regarding insurance and risk transfer, the contractor will most likely be determined to be the responsible (and ineligible) party.

The creation of an Owner Controlled Insurance Program is best not left to amateurs. Proper authorship will require an intimate familiarity with FEMA regulations and FEMA's current Public Assistance Policy on Insurance (FP 206–086–1) (Published in June 2015).

One more related case springs from the May-August 2008 floods which damaged a major university in Eastern Iowa.[64] In this case, the university initially claimed reimbursement for a builder's risk policy. The university argued that this was a necessary expense; however, FEMA determined that the cost was an increased operating expense which was not eligible.

The university also apparently erred in requesting reimbursement for the 2008–2009 policy coverage in the 2009–2010 time frame.

Is an Insurance Appeal Worth the Time and Expense?

An important consideration should pop up any time the applicant is considering filing an appeal with FEMA. The appeal case must be worth the effort involved, or it's like hauling snow up a mountain in the dead of winter. This appeal began at $1,008 and was subsequently reduced by the university to $924. This amount of money, even if fully recovered, might not begin to cover the staff time and certainly would not begin to cover the legal fees, if any, involved in pursuing the appeal. In this and many other appeals cases, a simple cost-benefit analysis should have been performed.

Understanding the deceptively complex language of the insurance world is critical for the local agency when dealing with both the insurers and with FEMA.

I worked briefly with a California agency that had suffered the fire loss of a major recreational facility on the order of 35 to 40 million dollars. Two years after their loss, the insurance issues were still unresolved, and one of the agency attorneys had taken over the claims handling. The agency then hired a third-party insurance consultant to assist. I later spoke with one of the principals of the consulting firm who told me that the agency "had no idea how much insurance they have." The facility finally reopened 9 years later after being completely rebuilt.

It is also appropriate to assume that not all FEMA staff have the same high-level understanding of the language of insurance that their Insurance Specialists have. The case on this point springs from Cook County, IL, where a major religious group operated several schools, some of which were damaged in severe flooding in 2008.[65]

The applicant had two commercial insurance policies with a "self-insured retention" of $1,000,000 per occurrence.

Deductibles and self-insured retention are somewhat similar insofar as they both represent an amount of money paid by the insured for damages sustained; however, there are some technical nuances. But neither a deductible nor self-insured retention are insurance and neither constitutes a duplication of benefits, since they are paid BY the insured, and not TO the insured.

However, in this case, this subtle distinction was lost on the initial FEMA reviewer and the damages were denied as ineligible. Because the damages were only $545,000, well below the limit to the self-insured retention, on appeal FEMA properly determined that the damages were eligible.

However, the FEMA reviewer also noted that the applicant did not have flood insurance as required by the Stafford Act and would otherwise have to meet those requirements.

The key here is to: have staff that is fully conversant in the language of insurance; have the documentation necessary to prove the case on behalf of the local agency; and the tenacity to appeal when necessary and worthwhile; or determine that in-house staff does not have the requisite experience to be successful and reach out to a consultant with extensive prior experience with FEMA related insurance issues for guidance.

There are some disaster damages which are simply not eligible for FEMA reimbursement. There are other disaster damages which may or may not be eligible for reimbursement, depending on the individual circumstances.

The cost of business interruptions are not FEMA-eligible expenses, hence the necessity of having business interruption insurance when appropriate.

Landscaping (trees, shrubs, flowers, or grass) is generally not an eligible expense, unless the primary purpose of the landscaping is erosion control. Therefore, for those agencies and organizations where either business interruptions or damages to landscaping are important assets to protect, private insurance should be sought out.

In the next case, from central Tennessee in the spring of 2010, floods damaged two publicly owned golf courses.[66] Here the case revolved around nitpicky interpretations of the insurance policy, which, by the way, is how insurance policies are almost always interpreted. The question is: "Are the damages affecting the golf courses landscaping or are they infrastructure?" A second question revolved around the more basic question: "Are the golf courses covered locations?"

The denials of eligibility were based upon the assumption that the two golf courses were covered locations, an assumption that was faulted upon a close reading of the policy language. Neither golf course was a covered location under the terms of the policy.

In analyzing the question of whether the damages to the lawn sprinklers, piping, and control systems were covered under the policy, it appeared that they were covered items, *except* when damaged by flood. Therefore, in this case there was no insurance coverage, and the projects were indeed eligible costs.

It is a cold fact of life that no one reads an insurance policy as carefully before they sign the policy as they will when damages occur. It's easy to imagine that if you purchase insurance for a facility or risk, that it will be covered; that is, until the fine print is read.

And finally, self-insurance is currently an option only available to states.

Quoting from the Stafford Act, as follows: "Sec. 311. Insurance (42 U.S.C. 5154) (c) State Acting as Self-insurer – A State may elect to act as a self-insurer with respect to any or all of the facilities owned by the State. Such an election, if declared in writing at the time of acceptance of assistance under section 5172 or 5189 of this title [Section 406 or 422] or section 3149(c)(2) of this title) or subsequently and accompanied by a plan for self-insurance which is satisfactory to the President, shall be deemed compliance with subsection (a). No such self-insurer may receive assistance under section 5172 or 5189 of this title [Section 406 or 422] for any property or part thereof for which it has previously received assistance under this Act, to the extent that insurance for such property or part thereof would have been reasonably available."[67]

Insurance consortiums or insurance pools are insurance, not self-insurance. Self-insurance is running bare-naked through the streets without any outside help. This is generally attempted by only very large government agencies and large corporations, even when they have what is called "excess" coverage for those occasions when there may be losses exceeding some high threshold, such as $10,000,000 or $20,000,000 losses. Self-insurance does not qualify as flood insurance as far as FEMA is concerned.

I have a colleague in the southeast part of the country who attempted to get a self-insurance plan for their county. I have a copy of the letter from FEMA denying their request to become self-insured.

The last case is out of the State of Texas, where Hurricane Claudette damaged facilities of the Department of Criminal Justice. The Project Worksheets were prepared, and then obligated for $0 because the state had not complied with the insurance requirements. Title 44 of the Code of Federal Regulations §75.14 reads as follows: 44 CFR § 75.14 States exempt under this part.

"The following States have submitted applications and adequate supporting documentation and have been determined by the Federal Insurance Administrator to be exempt from the requirement of flood insurance on State-owned structures and their contents because they have in effect adequate State plans of self-insurance: Florida, Georgia, Iowa, Kentucky, Maine, New Jersey, New York, North Carolina, Oregon, Pennsylvania, South Carolina, Tennessee, and Vermont."

Adding further to this losing case is the fact that a second appeal was filed approximately seven months after the first appeal decision was rendered, clearly not within the statutory 60 days allowed for filing a second appeal.

It is my observation that many of these insurance issues are the direct result of agency risk managers, in those agencies that have a risk manager, having little or no knowledge of these Stafford Act/FEMA regulations.

For those agencies that do not have a professional risk management function, the danger is far more dire.

With FEMA, risk management and insurance are like tightrope walking without a net, at a height of 500 feet above spike-covered ground, during a thunderstorm.

With that in mind, I believe that it is in the best interests of local government agencies and private non-profit agencies to consider retaining a public adjuster firm to assist them with their insurance recovery.

I have a letter on file, given to me by a public adjuster who represented a California Central Valley jurisdiction. In this case, the agency owned a large warehouse-type building which was totally destroyed by fire. The insurance consortium of which they were members offered a settlement of $500,000. Unhappy with what they felt was a "lowball" settlement, they retained a national public insurance adjuster firm. The final result was an insurance payment of $10,000,000 for the very same loss.

For those agencies without extensive insurance expertise, consulting with an expert, while costly, may pay huge dividends. Insurance companies will strongly encourage their clients to forgo using a public adjuster when they have an insured loss, and with very good reason: public adjusters make for much larger insurance payouts.

A Review of Some Insurance Nuances

A few insurance-related nuances which, depending on the circumstances, may be important.[68]

- FEMA does not consider self-insured retentions to constitute a self-insurance plan.
- FEMA does not require applicants to obtain and maintain insurance for temporary facilities.
- The obtain and maintain requirement does not apply on projects of less than $5,000.
- States wishing to be self-insured must have a FEMA-approved self-insurance plan.
- State insurance commissioners may not waive Federal insurance requirements.
- FEMA will not accept a state insurance commissioner certification that purports to certify that flood insurance, up to the maximum amount of coverage available through a National Flood Insurance Plan (NFIP), is not reasonably available for properties insurable under the NFIP.
- FEMA will reduce assistance to an applicant by the amount of its actual or anticipated insurance proceeds. (Ultimately, it is up to the applicant to prove all facts related to insurance coverage, including what is or is not covered, and the payments therefore.)
- When a local agency spends money (on legal fees, for instance) for recovery of its costs from the insurer, those costs are offset by FEMA from its duplication of benefits deductions.
- In a case personally known to me, a large school district had an insurance policy with a deductible of $10,000 per site. In a major hurricane, ALL 500 buildings in the district were damaged, at a deductible cost of $5,000,000. Had the policy had a deductible of $10,000 per occurrence, the district would have saved $4,990,000 in deductible costs.

Insurance Strategies to Consider Before the Fact

For Public Assistance reimbursement purposes, insure local agency assets that are otherwise not FEMA eligible, and if possible do so under a separate policy to reduce the chance of FEMA apportionment between eligible and ineligible losses.

For instance, museum collections are generally not eligible for FEMA funding. If the museum has a rare and expensive collection, it should have separate insurance coverage for the collection apart from the insurance coverage for the facilities themselves. While separate policies may be more expensive, the risks should be carefully considered, especially in those parts of the country subject to repetitive losses.

Even more importantly, a much longer-term strategy would be to avoid locating new facilities in flood plains if at all possible, or requiring those facilities when built to either be elevated structures or otherwise flood-protected with permanent flood walls and robust pumping systems. Costly, no doubt, but when compared to the long-term loss potential, possibly very reasonable and prudent expenditures.

Prior to a first disaster loss, FEMA does not require agency facilities to be insured, unless the threat is from flooding, for properties in a Special Flood Hazard Area (SFHA). However, this is not an advisable strategy, insofar as many ordinary non-disaster losses will be uncovered in the case of no insurance.

Professional Damage Assessment

Consider adding "damage assessment" cost coverage to property insurance policies.

- This will enable faster damage cost estimating, which is usually done at local expense,
- Provide a ready report for FEMA to establish the Damage Description and Dimensions, and

- Provide a ready challenge when FEMA's cost estimate comes in below the agency's actual or estimated cost, which is often the case.
- Having outside insurance paid, engineers and estimators preparing the damage estimates will free up the local building and safety inspectors for other disaster-related work.
- Having professional damage and cost estimators will create an impression with FEMA that the agency is really on the ball regarding disaster cost recovery savvy.

Forgo Federal Assistance on High-Value/Low Damage Ratio Properties

It may seem counterintuitive to walk away from FEMA funding on certain projects, but in some cases that may be the best strategy of all. Consider an agency with a public facility, recently built, with a value of $50,000,000. If the eligible damages on the facility are slight, let's say $500,000 or 1% of the facility cost, the agency will be required under the Stafford Act to obtain and maintain insurance for as long as the agency owns the building. With a $500,000 loss, at a 75% FEMA cost share, the net payout from FEMA will be $375,000.

No insurer will write a policy for $500,000 on a $50-million-dollar facility. Therefore, the agency will have to buy millions of dollars of insurance to cover the $375,000 they received from FEMA. Over the years, the cost of commercial or pool insurance will most likely far exceed the $375,000 benefit originally received.

Furthermore, receiving this "lowball" damage payout may affect future damage claims under the Public Assistance program. This is especially true for agencies in Tornado, Hurricane, or Flood Alley.

Each disaster and each individual loss will change the financial calculus and determine the most appropriate path forward into the recovery.

One Notable Instance of an "Obtain & Maintain" Exception

". . . pumping stations do not fall within the category of 'insurable facilities or property' as defined in and in accordance with Public Assistance policy. The SIR (site inspection report) and pictures of the site show the pumps surrounded by a fence-like structure and located on pier-like structures over water. The pumping stations therefore do not meet the definition of a building, which is, a walled and roofed structure, other than a gas or liquid storage tank, that is principally above ground and affixed to a permanent site, as well as a manufactured home on a permanent foundation. In addition, the pumping stations do not meet the definition of equipment, which FEMA policy defines in part as personal property or, property other than real property, to include moveable machinery. The pumping stations are similarly neither contents, nor vehicles according to FEMA policy. As such, the obtain and maintain insurance requirement does not apply."[69]

A Bottom Line on Insurance

Throughout the book, we will see instances of other counterintuitive regulations which can sometimes be confusing at best. We should always proceed with the understanding that FEMA's interpretations of regulations may be at odds with how we see the same set of facts, if in fact we even know what the regulations state. We should recognize that FEMA and its staff do this work every day of the year, while for us it is hopefully a once-in-a-lifetime event. If we do not know the regulations, we will be completely at the mercy of FEMA's take on the facts. We may also waste incredibly valuable time pursuing an appeal which has little chance of success, while ignoring other "easy winner" projects.

As with all costs and losses incurred by the local agency, the complete burden of proof rests upon the local agency to provide the total documentation, both written and photographic, necessary to establish the cost or loss. The local agency must not only provide all the pertinent data but also explain how the data supports the local agency's costs and losses due to the declared disaster. Think of it as telling a compelling and richly detailed story about the costs and losses which resulted from the disaster.

As for insurance: "Applicants have the burden to not only provide the documentation, but to also explain where the work was excluded and why its insurer denied those costs, and to submit them to FEMA for funding . . ."[70]

If the local agency fails to provide a compelling narrative and support that narrative with the complete and appropriate data, FEMA may easily come to the wrong conclusions and deny funding. This is the case for all aspects of our dealings with FEMA.

Notes

1 FEMA Should Recover $48.9 Million for Inadequate Insurance Coverage for Holy Cross School, New Orleans, Louisiana, OIG-14–10-D.
2 Ibid.
3 Ibid.
4 Ibid.
5 Ibid.
6 Ibid.
7 Ibid.
8 https://www.fema.gov/appeal/insurance-18
9 Prohibited Flood Disaster Assistance (42 U.S.C. 5154a)* (a) General Prohibition – Notwithstanding any other provision of law, no Federal disaster relief assistance made available in a flood disaster area may be used to make a payment (including any loan assistance payment) to a person for repair, replacement, or restoration for damage to any personal, residential, or commercial property if that person at any time has received flood disaster assistance that was conditional on the person first having obtained flood insurance under applicable Federal law and subsequently having failed to obtain and maintain flood insurance as required under applicable Federal law on such property.
10 https://www.fema.gov/appeal/duplication-benefits-3
11 Ibid.
12 https://www.fema.gov/appeal/duplication-benefits-insurance
13 https://www.fema.gov/appeal/duplication-benefits-0
14 Ibid.
15 Public Assistance Program and Policy Guide, Version 4, June 1, 2020, p. 93.
16 https://www.fema.gov/appeal/duplication-benefits-2
17 https://www.fema.gov/appeal/direct-administrative-costs-management-costs-project-management-and-design-services
18 https://www.fema.gov/appeal/insurance-direct-administrative-costs-management-costs
19 Ibid.
20 https://www.fema.gov/appeal/ineligible-damage
21 https://www.fema.gov/appeal/insurance-direct-administrative-costs-management-costs
22 Ibid.
23 Ibid.
24 Ibid.
25 Ibid.
26 Ibid.
27 Ibid.
28 Ibid.
29 Code of Federal Regulations Title 42/Chapter 68/Subchapter III/§ 5155 (a) General prohibition: The President, in consultation with the head of each Federal agency administering any program providing financial assistance to persons, business concerns, or other entities suffering losses as a result of a major

disaster or emergency, shall assure that no such person, business concern, or other entity will receive such assistance with respect to any part of such loss as to which he has received financial assistance under any other program or from insurance or any other source.

30 https://www.fema.gov/appeal/other-federal-agency-legal-responsibility
31 https://www.fema.gov/appeal/result-declared-incident-other-federal-agency
32 Ibid.
33 Ibid.
34 Stafford Act § 311, 42 U.S.C. § 5154; 44 C.F.R. § 206 Subpart I.
35 https://www.fema.gov/appeal/insurance-15
36 https://www.irmi.com/term/insurance-definitions/blanket-policy
37 https://www.fema.gov/appeal/insurance-705c-4
38 https://www.fema.gov/appeal/timeliness-insurance
39 Ibid.
40 https://www.fema.gov/appeal/insurance-13
41 Ibid.
42 https://www.fema.gov/appeal/epicc-ahmanson-senior-center
43 https://www.fema.gov/appeal/insurance-deductible
44 https://www.fema.gov/appeal/king-county-courthouse
45 https://www.fema.gov/appeal/appeal-timeliness-duplication-benefits
46 https://www.fema.gov/appeal/small-business-administration-loan
47 https://www.fema.gov/appeal/insurance-0
48 The **collateral source rule** "is intended to ensure that the right of an injured party to be fully compensated for all his or her damages is protected, even if in some instances it entails that party obtaining double recovery from both the insurer and the wrongdoer." Lawrence D. Miller, Plaintiff and Respondent, V. Mitchell D. Ellis, Court of Appeal of California, First District, Division Three, https://casetext.com/case/miller-v-ellis-4
49 United States Court of Appeals For the Seventh Circuit No. 12–2007, Columbus Regional Hospital, v. Federal Emergency Management Agency, p. 10.
50 https://www.fema.gov/appeal/appeal-procedures-insurance-705a-705c
51 Ibid.
52 Ibid.
53 Ibid.
54 Ibid.
55 https://www.fema.gov/appeal/insurance-waiver-2
56 Ibid.
57 44 CFR § 206.253 (b) (2) Insurance requirements for facilities damaged by disasters other than flood.
58 https://www.fema.gov/appeal/duplication-benefits-insurance-6
59 https://www.fema.gov/appeal/2nd-appeal-florida-community-college-risk-management-consortium-fema-1539-dr-fl
60 https://www.fema.gov/appeal/assistance-insurance-claims
61 https://www.fema.gov/appeal/cardiac-surgery-center-seismic-upgrade-eligibility
62 Stafford Act: Sec. 406. Repair, Restoration, and Replacement of Damaged Facilities (42 U.S.C. 5172) (4) Special Rule – In any case in which the facility being repaired, restored, reconstructed, or replaced under this section was under construction on the date of the major disaster, the cost of repairing, restoring, reconstructing, or replacing the facility shall include, for the purposes of this section, only those costs that, under the contract for the construction, are the owner's responsibility and not the contractor's responsibility.
63 https://www.fema.gov/appeal/eastside-reservoir-project-insurance-deductibles
64 https://www.fema.gov/appeal/insurance-7
65 https://www.fema.gov/appeal/insurance-1
66 https://www.fema.gov/appeal/insurance-reduction
67 *Stafford Act > Title III > § 311, 42 U.S.C. § 5154c.*
68 FEMA Recovery Policy FP 206–086–1, Public Assistance Policy on Insurance, Effective June 29, 2015.
69 https://www.fema.gov/appeal/duplication-benefits-insurance-9
70 https://www.fema.gov/appeal/private-nonprofit-procurement-net-small-project-overrun-insurance-705c

Part 2
Roles and Responsibilities

11 The Role of the EOC and Departmental Operations Centers

The Emergency Operations Center (or EOC) is the nerve center for the disaster response and all its derivative assignments. EOCs are generally organized along the lines of the Incident Command System, or ICS.

Within the Incident Command System structure, there are five main groups or sections: 1) Management, which provides overall leadership and management for the EOC; 2) Operations, which manages all of the various incidents, damage sites, and the provision of survivor services; 3) Planning, which organizes the work of the EOC and specifically provides action plans for each shift within the EOC; 4) Logistics, which obtains and oversees all the resources needed for the disaster response activities, including personnel, equipment, supplies, and materials; and 5) Finance & Administration, which tracks EOC costs, oversees damage assessments, provides budget transfers for the resources being procured by Logistics, and tracks time and expenses within the EOC.

Some local agencies have added a sixth section to their EOC structure, e.g., Recovery. Sometimes this involves disaster cost recovery, but other times it focuses on community-wide recovery rather than just disaster cost recovery.

The Incident Command System: Yes? No? Maybe?

While the Incident Command System is a flexible and powerful tool for the management of disaster incidents, it is of only modest use at best for tracking disaster response and recovery costs. Using certain Incident Command System forms for disaster cost tracking is like taking a 20-year-old car and entering it in the Indianapolis Memorial Day 500 Race. The used car was not built for Formula 1 racing, and some Incident Command System forms were simply not designed for non-fire disaster response cost tracking.

One of the most powerful elements of the Incident Command System is that the organizational structure can be rapidly scaled up or down depending on the size and complexity of the incident(s). Incident Command System accomplishes this by limiting the "span-of-control." When the size of an Incident Command System element maxes out at seven, that element is split in two, and tasks are reassigned for the new structure. A fully staffed out Incident Command System structure will have top heavy layers of management compared to the numbers of "worker-bees." This is easily sustained in the short time frames in which the Incident Command System normally operates. However, for an administrative process such as disaster cost recovery, where the timelines are not as "life-and-death" critical as during the response, such top-heavy management is not fiscally sustainable, nor are there typically enough trained and experienced people available to support this type of staffing.

Many agencies use certain Incident Command System forms to attempt to capture response cost data, but these agencies do not realize that these same forms have structural deficiencies which

DOI: 10.4324/9781003487869-14

make them ill-suited for the purposes of disaster cost recovery. There will be more about this later in the book, including suggested forms which, when properly used, completely meet the cost tracking requirements.

For the most part, very little of the actual disaster cost recovery process takes place in the EOC. However, the EOC is where the organization for disaster cost recovery begins if there are no pre-existing plans, policies, and procedures. If there are plans, policies, and procedures which do exist, the EOC is where they will be reviewed and put into action.

When Should We Activate the EOC?

In some cases, disasters are growth event(s), meaning that the first day or the first week of problems are not of such a magnitude that a Presidential disaster declaration is warranted or expected. However, as the days and weeks pass, it keeps raining or flooding, and finally the disaster has reached a point where the local and state officials are simply unable to cope without either Federal assistance and/or Mutual Aid.

In other cases the disaster is a rapid-onset event, such as a tornado or earthquake, in which case the EOC will likely be fully activated from the first moments of the disaster.

I looked at Presidential disaster declarations for a recent two-year period, 2020 through 2021. In this timeframe, 105 Presidential major disaster declarations were issued. However, the average time lag between the onset of the disaster and the Presidential declaration of a major disaster was 62 days. So, in some cases, even when the disaster was a significant event from the first moments, the Presidential disaster declaration lagged significantly, leaving local agencies in limbo as to whether their employees should be fully documenting their disaster response activities or not.

For those agencies that choose NOT to activate their EOC early in the process, it now becomes a serious job of "catch-up" to generate, find, and organize days' or even weeks' worth of response activities and the appropriate documentation. In some cases, response or repair work was done early on, but there are no written reports or photographs to document the costs and work activity, and without full and proper documentation, the work is almost never eligible.

Therefore, the very best time to activate the EOC is when problems first start to arise, even if at the beginning the problems are relatively minor.

Without being facetious, the EOC should be activated every chance you get. In a disaster, the EOC is a strange and stressful environment. Frequent activation throughout the normal calendar year provides for valuable experience in working in an EOC in periods of less than maximum stress. When I worked for the City and County of San Francisco, it was the practice to activate and manage public events on a regular basis via the EOC. In some years, the San Francisco EOC was activated on a monthly basis for events other than disasters. The EOC was activated for New Year's Eve, the famous Bay-to-Breakers foot race, any championship playoff game whether the game was in the City or not, Fleet Week, and of course for any real emergencies or disasters. The frequent schedule of activations provided a very high comfort level for all staff, and the year-round series of activations provided all with an opportunity to get real EOC experience.

EOC Activation Is a Key Action

When an emergency arises and if it looks like the situation will develop into a major disaster, the local agency should start thinking strategically about the event(s) unfolding in terms of two bellwether actions. First, the agency should make a proclamation of a local disaster. Second, the local agency should activate the EOC, if only to a low-level activation initially, retaining the option to move to full activation if the situation requires it. Failure to **both** make the local disaster proclamation **and** activate the EOC sends a political message to higher levels of government that the event is not of such a magnitude to require state or Federal assistance.

Even if the local jurisdiction or non-profit does not have the authorization under law or regulation to proclaim a local emergency, I recommend that the agency does so to contribute to the preponderance of evidence that the event is of a magnitude to overwhelm local authorities. The proclamation of a disaster, although perhaps meaningless under the law, nonetheless sends a strong public message to both higher levels of government and to the members of the community, or the agency's clients.

Levels of EOC Activation

An EOC activation does not have to be an "all-or-nothing" event. Some EOC activations are very low-level, with perhaps only 3–4 people involved, and then only for limited hours. The level of EOC staffing is on a sliding scale, growing as an event develops. I have been in EOC activations where the day shift was all hands on deck, but the night shift was lightly staffed to monitor the pulse of events and prepare for the next full day shift.

Some will argue that activating the EOC for events other than disasters will cost the agency money. Indeed, it will cost something, even for a very low-level EOC activation. However, the cost for NEVER activating the EOC except for a catastrophic event will be massive. Staff at all levels in the EOC will be uncomfortable, they will have no idea of what they should be doing, they will often waste time and energy doing otherwise non-productive tasks, or worse, they will fail to work on important tasks necessary for a successful disaster cost recovery process. The EOC is like a bicycle: If you've never ridden one before, learning how to ride, especially when someone's shooting at you, will be a non-starter.

Initial EOC Tasks

In the EOC, there are certain important finance and disaster cost recovery-related functions which should take place almost from the moment the lights in the EOC are turned on.

First, someone needs to set up and monitor the tracking of all persons working in the EOC. While the time for some employees working in the EOC may not be reimbursable, the employees' time may still be used as part of the local cost share. There will be more on this later.

Normally, FEMA pays 75% of the total eligible costs for a project. The remaining 25% of those costs must be borne either by the respective state and the local jurisdiction, or in some states, entirely by the local jurisdiction. Therefore, an accurate tracking of employees' EOC time is important and valuable.

Second, someone in the EOC must take responsibility for tracking, amalgamating, and reporting the various components of disaster damage afflicting the agency. No single local government function is better qualified to do this than the Finance department. There will be more on this in the chapter on Damage Assessment.

The Finance and Administration Section should also be monitoring the "Overtime Burn Rate," the calculations necessary to determine the current fiscal state of the agency vis-à-vis its "Blue Sky," or normal budget allocations. Later in this book, there is an Excel spreadsheet which can perform this important function to provide the "cash-on-hand" status for agency spending based upon the overtime burn rate estimate.

Third, many of the first responders will not have the best (or even the necessary) forms for tracking their time, equipment, materials, and activities. In some instances, the field personnel will not have **any** forms for tracking their labor, equipment, and materials, other than their day-to-day forms which, as we have seen, may be next to useless for compliance with FEMA's documentation requirements. Someone from the EOC Finance & Administration Section may have to distribute the proper forms to field crews and show them the proper way to fill them out. This may involve some early-morning "tailgate" meetings with field personnel to get this important function on track.

Fourth, once the disaster response phase is winding down, photographic evidence of the damage done will assume a significant role in the disaster cost recovery process. Usually, no single department or division is responsible for ensuring that there are enough detailed photographs for every incident or damage site, but the photo documentation or lack of it may make or break a project's eligibility.

Because the photo documentation will have such an important role in the coming weeks and months, the Finance Section Chief may want to organize a group of potentially pre-screened and pre-registered volunteers or other agency staff to take sets of pictures for every incident or site. Because some incidents or sites may be dangerous or off-limits, additional photos may be needed later, when circumstances have normalized and are no longer a safety threat. There is a chapter in this text on both pre- and post-disaster photography.

Field Documentation Teams: One Possible Solution

Medium- to large-sized agencies may want to consider the approach used by one of my West Coast training clients. They are putting together Field Documentation Teams (FDT) of their own employees, employees who would ordinarily not be part of the first-response efforts. The first responders for this county-wide water agency say they do not have the time (nor, I would say, the inclination) to fully document their field response activities. So, this agency is training non-field personnel to shadow the field crews, to document the work being done, and the workers, equipment, and materials used while performing emergency work. Most importantly, these FDTs will take photographs of the damage before the work begins, **and** the work as it is being done, **and** again when the work is finished. This should provide the agency with excellent records upon which to base their Public Assistance claims for reimbursement. In smaller jurisdictions, this same effort could be performed by CERT (Community Emergency Response Team) members or police or fire auxiliaries and volunteers who have been properly trained in the process.

Fifth, in some disasters, Mutual Aid[1] will play a significant role during the response phase of the disaster. To ensure that the staff of the providing Mutual Aid agencies know how to properly document their time, equipment, and materials, the Finance & Administration Section Chief may want to send one of the staff to work at the "Staging Area."[2] To ensure that each Mutual Aid crew has the appropriate tracking forms and knows how to use them properly.

Once the disaster occurs, it is too late to take certain actions which could a) increase facility eligibility; b) ensure that the agency's purchasing program complies with 2 CFR, Part 200; and c) provide for some costs, such as food, lodging, and overtime pay for certain disaster responders. Each of these and other easy-to-accomplish tasks were discussed in greater detail in the previous chapters.

Typically, when the EOC is activated, the focus of activity is on the Operations Section and what's going on out in the real world, outside the EOC. The foremost focus is never on financial issues. Therefore, the Finance Section Chief will have to work diligently to maintain an awareness of what each of the other EOC Sections is doing, and how these things will affect the agency's financial status in general and disaster cost recovery in particular. This may entail sending a "representative" from the Finance & Administration Section to regularly check in with each respective EOC Section to keep tabs on those activities that have a financial impact.

Periodically, during an EOC shift, there will be status briefings. The Finance & Administration Section Chief should always have "talking points" to share with the other Sections on matters of importance for the disaster cost recovery process.[3]

One area of special concern is that the Logistics Section may want to "buy" certain disaster equipment resources, such as generators, pumps, light sets, etc. However, the Federal procurement rules are more easily complied with when these equipment resources are rented rather than outright purchased. FEMA generally only reimburses for the time the equipment is used for the disaster response, and usually this results in a pennies-on-the-dollar reimbursement for equipment purchased rather than rented. The Finance Director may want to have a policy in place requiring their approval for any capital equipment procurements. This caution generally does not apply to consumable supplies.

What the EOC Does Not Do and Should Not Do

Relative to disaster cost recovery, there are some tasks that should not be done in the EOC.

The EOC should not attempt to track the time for all field and support staff except for those working in the EOC, unless the agency is a small agency with very few employees.

Generally, each individual department will track its own employees' time, as well as the equipment and supplies they use. The EOC Finance & Administration personnel often will not know the appropriate terminology that the utility, facilities, or roads and bridges personnel use daily. There may be an exception to this for smaller agencies.

The Finance & Administration role in the EOC is a bit different from that of the other four EOC sections. The other sections are wholly consumed with responding to and resolving all outstanding disaster incidents, supporting the need for survivor's services, and restoration of essential municipal services and the damaged infrastructure.

The Finance & Administration Section, on the other hand, is more forward-focused. First, the section must get a rapid and as-accurate-as-possible tally of ALL damages, both public and private, in the community. This is necessary to obtain both a gubernatorial disaster proclamation and a Presidential disaster declaration. The Presidential disaster declaration is critical, for without that, there won't be a penny of Federal assistance.

Second, during the chaos, the Finance Director will have to perform accounting legerdemain to paint a clear and accurate picture of how the disaster has affected and will continue to affect the local budget for the remainder of the budget year, and possibly into successive budget years.

Third, the lack of contemporaneous documentation, both in written reports and still photographs, will bedevil the disaster cost recovery process in the months and years ahead. So, the Finance & Administration Section needs to ensure that the necessary and complete documentation is being created, properly organized and filed for future use.

For all other EOC sections, Management, Operations, Planning, and Logistics will pretty much disappear within a few days when the response is over. The Finance & Administration Section at that point will just be starting what in some cases may be a yearlong -to decade-long struggle to recoup the eligible disaster losses from FEMA and in some cases other Federal agencies as well.

EOC Close-Out and Transition to Disaster Cost Recovery

Typically, within a few days of the disaster onset, or a few weeks in all but the very worst disasters, EOC staffing will be reduced to clean-up and close-out staff, except for the disaster cost recovery team.

The Finance & Administration Section will then morph into the disaster cost recovery team. Some, but perhaps not all, of the EOC Finance & Administration team will transition to the disaster cost recovery team, and some staff not in the EOC Finance & Administration Section will be assigned, possibly unwillingly, to the disaster cost recovery team.

This moment of transition is a critical phase in which much of the important momentum for disaster cost recovery can be lost forever due to a lack of clear direction and ambiguous marching orders.

This should be the time where the Finance Director, fully supported by the senior city or county administrators, sets up an organizational meeting of all involved departments and divisions to formally move into the disaster cost recovery phase of overall community recovery. This meeting should not be a review of the current post-disaster status or a litany of the damages suffered; rather, it should light up the pathway to the next phase: the financial aspects of disaster cost recovery.

In this meeting, attendees should be given explicit expectations of the support needed by the disaster cost recovery team to recover as much money as possible under FEMA's Public Assistance program, as well as all other aspects of Federal post-disaster aid from other agencies. The disaster cost recovery team cannot be cast adrift at this time. It cannot recover the losses without broad and consistent support from all departments and divisions.

It is a given that many exhausted staff will want to beg off from attending "just another staff meeting." But nothing could be further from the truth. The local agency is about to enter the deep, uncharted, and often stormy seas of disaster cost recovery. This is an experience that many, if not most, agency employees have never experienced, nor have they ever imagined an administrative process so riddled with hidden explosives, trip wires, and ticking time-bombs.

For many agencies, this is like moving from "Pop Warner" football to the Super Bowl overnight. Absent previous disaster cost recovery experience, no one is prepared for this administrative onslaught.

The Department Operating Center or DOC

DOCs or Department Operations Centers are very similar in structure and function to the EOC.

In larger jurisdictions, the EOC may simply not be large enough to contain the EOC functions and the functions of each department, which may have many people working in disaster response roles. So, some departments may set up their own DOC to manage their disaster response activities. This is typically done by Public Works, Facilities, Utilities, and Roads and Bridges or some combination thereof, depending on the size and organization of a specific jurisdiction.

The DOCs will manage their own response activities under EOC direction and report those activities and issues back to the EOC as though they were co-located in the EOC.

When the EOCs are activated, the DOCs may or may not be activated. Similar to smaller-scale events, especially those in which a Presidential disaster declaration is not expected, the agency may elect to only activate one or more of the DOCs, but not the EOC.

DOCs are not just for departments or divisions with field activities. At the City of San Francisco, the Controller's Office had its own DOC so that the Controller could more effectively manage its role in the EOC, as well as manage the disaster cost recovery process. One Saturday, the Controller's DOC staff came into work, and we did a "full-scale" exercise where we set up every workstation, checked the computer and phone systems, opened up the tracking forms, and generally got the feel of how we would actually operate during a disaster.

Notes

1 Mutual Aid may be either paid or unpaid Mutual Aid, depending on the written agreements in place. In either case, when properly documented for eligible work, the cost of the Mutual Aid may either reimbursed by FEMA or counted as part of the local cost share.
2 The "Staging Area" is a physical location within the ICS where responding Mutual Aid resources first report in the disaster affected jurisdiction. A resource in the staging area is on active duty and should be ready to leave the staging area within 5 minutes of being given an assignment.
3 See Form 13 in the Appendix, EOC Finance and Administration Talking Points for the Planning Meeting.

12 The Local Agency Finance Department's Role

From the very first moments of a disaster, the local agency's Finance Director/Department will have to work diligently to get ahead of events, as they work in the EOC Finance & Administration Section.

If the event appears to be a major disaster and there is the possibility that the President will sign a major disaster declaration, then every effort needs to be made to ensure that all field responders are properly tracking their time, hours of equipment use, and the materials which they use to save lives, protect the public health, and to preserve improved property and the environment.

If, in the early stages of the disaster response, it is not evident that this will be a major disaster declaration, the recommended practice is to still collect all response costs, including labor, equipment, and materials, as a precaution against forever losing these important cost records if and when the President signs the Presidential disaster declaration. In some cases, the Presidential disaster declarations are made retroactive to a date before everything went to hell in a handbasket.

There are two FEMA documents that the F&A Section Chief should be aware of early on. The first is the Virtual Joint Preliminary Damage Assessment Preparation Checklist for the Public Assistance Initial Damage Assessment.[1] This four-page checklist is a very useful tool for staff performing damage assessments. It is also a great preview of the depth and breadth of documented information that FEMA will require to process the Project Worksheets when the disaster cost recovery gets to that stage of the Public Assistance process.

The second document the F&A Section Chief should be aware of is the PDA (Preliminary Damage Assessment) Narrative Report.[2] This is also a FEMA form, and the local agency may never see it. However, the local agency needs to provide the information requested on this form to round out the full impact and scope of the disaster. While there are certain damage and dollar-loss thresholds which must be met to qualify for a Presidential disaster declaration, there are other factors FEMA evaluates when recommending a disaster for the Presidential disaster declaration.

These factors in determining whether a Presidential disaster declaration is warranted include:

- The severity of the disaster: What is the extent of the damage, how many people are affected, and what is the need for immediate assistance?
- The impact on the community: How has the disaster affected the critical infrastructure, such as roads, bridges, hospitals, and utilities?
- What state and local resources are readily available, including personnel, equipment, and supplies?
- Is there a request from the governor for a Presidential disaster declaration?
- What are the cost-sharing requirements, including any state participation?
- What is the potential for future disasters in the same area?

DOI: 10.4324/9781003487869-15

- Is this event one of national significance, and what will the effects be on the economy, public health, and national security, if any?

Many of these questions are answered in whole or in part by the PDA Narrative Report when making a recommendation to the President for a major disaster declaration. To see how FEMA evaluates these additional factors, see the Preliminary Damage Assessment Report at Example Form 69 in the Appendix.

Although much of the initial damage assessment is performed by building and safety inspectors, architects, and/or licensed civil engineers, none of these groups of officials, no matter how well qualified they may be in their specific profession, have the financial and accounting skill set needed to perform the sort of comprehensive analysis and organization of data necessary to prepare the full damage picture for the local leadership, the state office of emergency services, and FEMA.

While the F&A Section Chief generally does not have the skill necessary to perform many of the components of the damage assessment, they will be able to pull the disparate numbers together in a meaningful way to demonstrate the need for outside disaster assistance when it is truly warranted.

The F&A Section Chief will also have to apply their expertise to the reports which will justify the need for Immediate Needs Funding, Expedited Funding, or a Community Disaster Loan, which will be discussed in Chapters 16, 17, and 18.

With the initial activation of the EOC, the senior appointed and elected leadership will almost immediately expect an 'Overtime Burn Rate'[3] analysis. The Burn Rate analysis can be an important financial document for the local agency. First, it provides a real-time estimate of the regular and overtime hours worked by staff on a department-by-department basis. This can be a useful tool in evaluating how well the agency's time tracking process is working. In a hypothetical situation, where the Excel spreadsheet estimates that the overtime for the Public Works department should be $27,500 per day, but the actual records only show that $18,900 dollars was spent, there is a problem. The problem results because the reported data does not closely match the estimate. Similarly, if the overtime is coming in substantially over budget, a problem may also exist with the labor cost tracking process.

When the state and/or FEMA see overtime estimates which consist of a single digit followed by a trailing stream of zeros, they can easily imagine that the estimate is in fact a SWAG (silly wildly approximate guess), and they will discount its veracity and suppose that the local agency may be economically adrift in a sea of reported overtime hours.

Use of the Overtime Burn Rate Estimator, while a rough estimate, will still be an order of magnitude more precise than any SWAG. Realistic and more precise estimates will also be an important component of justifying the application for Immediate Needs Funding previously mentioned.

The local agency budget cycle may have an impact on how the disaster is perceived by both the state and FEMA. For an agency that has a July 1 to June 30 budget year and has a disaster occurring early in the budget year, the local agency in theory should have cash on hand. However, if a disaster hits in May or June, the budget may be mostly expended, and will leave the agency with more of a cash flow problem than might otherwise be the case.

Following a disaster, it is clear that the local agency will have to do a comprehensive assessment of the damage suffered by its facilities, its infrastructure, and the sometimes-massive amounts of disaster-related debris. What is not always clear is that the local agencies, cities and counties, and tribal nations must also conduct a comprehensive damage assessment for all private-sector damages.

Counties generally must also collect the damage assessment data for all its cities and special districts, including all schools. The county must also collect the damage reports for all otherwise eligible non-profit agencies within the county's boundaries. There will be more on this in Chapter 20, The Local Damage Assessment Process.

Failure to gather and report ALL of the damage within the jurisdiction may result in a failure to qualify for a Presidential disaster declaration, even when the state has enough damage to qualify.

Although the local jurisdiction must gather ALL of the damage information from within its borders, each privately owned home or business, including rental housing, will be responsible for filing their own respective applications for Federal disaster assistance to the extent to which they may be eligible.

Notes

1 See Form 1 in the Appendix.
2 See Form 2 in the Appendix.
3 See Form 3 in the Appendix.

13 Hired Guns and Consultants

"All too many consultants, when asked, 'What is 2 and 2?' respond, 'What do you have in mind?'"
Norman Ralph Augustine, Former Secretary of the Army

FEMA's Public Assistance program is a complex and daunting process, at best. At its worst, it's a large and growing hole in a boat owned by a local government or eligible private non-profit agency. The boat is sinking, and someone forgot to bring the lifejackets.

However, there may be some hope available in the form of disaster cost recovery consulting firms. These firms range in size from the largest accounting and consulting firms in the world to much smaller mom-and-pop or solo practitioner firms. As a former law professor of mine was fond of saying, "You pays your money and takes your chances."

Some of these firms are financially focused, with very large practices that reach far beyond the disaster cost recovery process. In fact, for many of these firms, disaster cost recovery is only one of many different areas of their practice. Other disaster cost recovery firms started out as engineering consultants, and as the number of disasters increased, they realized there was big money in arriving on the scene after a major disaster and throwing lifejackets to their engineering clients who did not know where else to turn for assistance in working through the Public Assistance process.

The first and most important thing to recognize is that these are professional firms seeking to make a profit in assisting local agencies with their disaster cost recovery efforts.

However, there are several very important things that NONE of these firms can provide after the fact. For instance, if the local agency wants to pay their employees some form of premium or hazard pay for their disaster response work but the agency does not have a proper pre-disaster pay policy in place, absolutely no one can fix this problem once the disaster has occurred. As discussed in Chapters 2 and 3, these policies must be in place before the disaster occurs.

A disaster cost recovery consulting firm can obviously assist in preparing such policies for the next disaster. But not for the present one.

Furthermore, if the local agency does not have effective procedures in place to track the labor, equipment, and materials used in disaster response, these consultants cannot create such records after the fact.

However, a good consultant can assist the local agency and help it avoid many basic mistakes in the Public Assistance process. Perhaps most importantly, they can provide a counter-perspective to what FEMA personnel are saying.

If the local agency anticipates the need for a disaster cost recovery consultant, a much more effective strategy, following the requirements of Title 2 of the Code of Federal Regulations, Part 200, is to hire a disaster cost recovery consulting firm BEFORE a disaster strikes so that they may

DOI: 10.4324/9781003487869-16

work with the local agency to put the required policies and procedures in place as a pre-condition to having such costs fully eligible for Public Assistance.

Still More Consultants

Consultants love disasters, as disasters often bring in additional work. Beyond specialized disaster cost recovery consultants, there are consulting engineering firms with a variety of specializations. There are also attorneys who are consultants specializing in the practice of law. However, very few attorneys are knowledgeable specialists in FEMA's Public Assistance program. There are some, but they are rare exceptions. Additionally, many Project Worksheets will require a historic preservation consultant, an environmental consultant (of varying sub-specialties), and/or an archeologist, etc. Searching FEMA's Appeals Database for the word 'consultant' or 'consultants' yields over 300 appeals cases in which a consultant of one stripe or another is mentioned.

Hiring a Consultant: Pros and Cons

First, let's look at the advantages and disadvantages of hiring a disaster cost recovery consulting firm. Some of these pros and cons will apply to all manner of consulting firms, but our initial focus will be on disaster cost recovery consultants.

In a series of seven different appeals covering 18 separate Project Worksheets, a county in New York State was denied funding for Direct Administrative Costs (DAC) (which will be addressed in Chapter 32), project coordination, and the consultant's travel expenses.

"From October 27, 2012, to November 9, 2012, Hurricane Sandy caused damage throughout the State of New York. During the incident period, Nassau County (Applicant) mobilized its Department of Sheriff and Corrections (Department) to undertake emergency protective measures on behalf of its citizens. The Department's Corrections Division prepared, packaged, delivered and serviced approximately 26,000 meals to first responders, displaced residents, and county workers. The Department's Enforcement Division installed warning and hazard blockades, performed search and rescue, assisted in placement of vulnerable populations, provided emergency first aid, secured shelters, nursing homes and hospitals, and protected improved property. The Applicant later applied for and received FEMA Public Assistance (PA) funds to cover the associated expenses."[1]

"The Applicant hired project management contractors, including ███████████ ██████████████, *(the contractor)* to assist with the administration of the PA grant for repairs to the Facility. ███████████ (*the consultant's*) employees often traveled to the Applicant's jurisdiction and worked on multiple projects over the course of a day, billing period, and trip. They also kept records of time spent working on each project task, assigning different codes to different projects, tasks, and categories of tasks."[2] (Redactions and Clarification Added)

"During administration of the projects, ███████████ (*the consultant*) utilized a methodology to allocate travel expenses across multiple projects (Expense Allocation Methodology), described in a Memorandum dated January 8, 2013 (Expense Analysis Memo). Specifically, ███████████ (*the consultant*) calculated an hourly travel expense rate for each of its employees per billing period by dividing the employee's total travel expenses by the total number of hours the employee worked on Applicant-related projects during the billing period. ███████████ (*the consultant*) then multiplied an employee's travel expense rate for the billing period by the number of hours billed to a specific task by that employee, in order to allocate travel expenses to each project on a pro rata basis."[3] (Redactions and Clarification Added)

"By letter dated January 6, 2017, FEMA informed the Applicant that as a general matter, many of ███████████ (*the consultant's*) travel expenses associated with direct administrative and project coordination tasks were not eligible for reimbursement as DAC (*Direct Administrative Costs*), as they were indirect costs."[4] (Redactions and Clarification Added)

"The RA (*Regional Administrator*) also rejected the Applicant's reliance on the OMB (U.S. Office of Management and Budget) regulation at Title 2, Code of Federal Regulations (2 C.F.R.) § 200.405, since 2 C.F.R. § 200.110 expressly excludes all disasters declared prior to December 26, 2014 from the allocation principles codified in 2 C.F.R. § 200.405."[5]

"Indirect costs are defined as 'costs a grantee or [applicant] incurs for a common or joint purpose benefiting more than one cost objective that are not readily assignable to the cost objectives specifically benefitted.' An applicant may not assign costs to a PA project as DAC if those costs constitute indirect costs or if similar costs incurred for the same purpose in like circumstances have been allocated to indirect costs. Travel and per diem costs for contractor employees that work on eligible PA projects are eligible as direct costs if such costs can be and are attributed to individual projects. While FEMA reimburses travel expenses that can be attributed to specific projects, travel expenses allocated to multiple PWs in proportion to the hours worked are not eligible as DAC."[6]

"Direct costs are those that can be 'identified separately and assigned to a specific project,' such as staff time to conduct an initial inspection, prepare and submit PWs, and make interim and final inspections of the project. By contrast, 'costs a grantee or subgrantee incurs for a common or joint purpose benefitting more than one cost objective that are not readily assignable to the cost objectives specifically benefitted' are indirect costs. Travel expenses related to one specific PW qualify as DAC, while travel expenses 'related to general support and not directly tied to one specific project' are indirect costs. Indirect costs are not reimbursable as DAC. More pertinently, an applicant cannot allocate expenses to every task for all PWs in proportion to the hours worked on the task, and then claim such expenses as DAC."[7] (Emphasis Added)

"Here, the Applicant claims certain travel expenses that its contractors incurred as DAC and/or contract costs, despite its acknowledgment that ███████████ (*the contractor's*) employees worked on several PWs over the course of each trip at issue. Specifically, the Applicant seeks pro rata allocations of travel and lodging expenses across multiple PWs, based upon the hours worked on a given PW during the course of a given trip. The Applicant believes it is entitled to reimbursement for the hourly travel expense rate for a given employee multiplied by the number of hours that employee billed for each PW in a given billing period, since it does not attempt to claim a pro rata share of travel expenses for hours spent on indirect tasks."[8] (Redaction Added)

"However, as noted, a pro rata allocation of expenses across every task for all PWs on the basis of hours worked on the task does not make such expenses eligible for reimbursement as DAC. Since the travel expenses at issue benefitted more than one PW, they are indirect costs."[9]

These same conditions and arguments are present in all seven of the appeals and all 18 of the individual Project Worksheets.

With this set of appeals, I would argue that the consultant either knew or should have known that such a methodology, while perhaps generally acceptable in their other consulting work, would constitute ineligible expenses under the rules in force at time for Public Assistance. This particular consultant, as noted on their website, is a "privately owned engineering and construction firm . . . in water, environment, transportation, energy and facilities." Apparently for them, disaster cost recovery is not the major thrust of their professional practice. This goes directly to the issue of finding a proper match between the local agency's disaster cost recovery needs and the experience and capabilities of any given consulting firm. Being a licensed professional engineer does not automatically make one an expert in FEMA's Public Assistance program.

It may be appropriate when hiring a disaster cost recovery consultant to specify, in great detail, how their work and their time is accounted for. For instance, have the contract for the consultant specify that they break out direct costs, which are reimbursable by FEMA, separate and distinct from those costs which are contractor overhead costs, and separately, any indirect costs, which may be applied to multiple Project Worksheets. In this way, the local agency has more detail on those costs which are accruing.

Any consultant hired may quickly learn to tell the client what they perceive the client wants to hear in lieu of the hard facts of a particular case or Project Worksheet. This is always a delicate dance between the client and the consultant.

And to be fair to knowledgeable and experienced consultants doing their best, sometimes a client may absolutely insist on doing things the consultant knows will clearly result in problems down the road. In almost every case, the more the client knows about the Public Assistance program, the more effectively a consultant can perform their duties while working in a supportive and collaborative environment.

Many, if not most, disaster cost recovery consultants will attempt to hire former FEMA employees and former state disaster assistance employees. While many of these new hires may have *some* disaster cost recovery experience, it does not always follow that they will

Table 13.1 Hiring a Consultant: Pros and Cons 1

Advantages of Hiring a Consultant	Disadvantages of Hiring a Consultant
Expertise and Specialization: Consulting firms typically have specialized knowledge and expertise in specific areas. They may provide insights and solutions that may not otherwise be readily available.	**Dependence on External Expertise:** When relying too heavily on consulting firms, an organization may become dependent on this external expertise versus developing in-house capabilities.

Table 13.2 Hiring a Consultant: Pros and Cons 2

Advantages of Hiring a Consultant	Disadvantages of Hiring a Consultant
Objective Perspective: Consultants offer an external and neutral perspective to help identify issues and opportunities that might be unrecognized by internal staff who are too close to the situation. This is very similar to hiring an attorney and hiring the right attorney. If the issue is an intellectual property matter, a tax lawyer would be of little use.	**Lack of Agency-Specific Knowledge:** Consultants may lack deep knowledge about your organization, which can make it difficult for them to fully understand your unique needs and challenges. A consultant that normally services large agencies (with a population greater than 500,000), for example, might not be a good fit for a small jurisdiction of less than 50,000 population.

Table 13.3 Hiring a Consultant: Pros and Cons 3

Advantages of Hiring a Consultant	Disadvantages of Hiring a Consultant
Cost Efficiency: Hiring a consulting firm can be more cost-effective than hiring full-time employees with the similar expertise, particularly when considering that the disaster cost recovery process will probably go on for at least several years.	High Cost: Consulting firms can be expensive, and the full cost of hiring a consultant may not be worth it, particularly if there is not a good match of the local agency needs with the consultant's expertise.

have the sometimes-specialized experience required for a specific Project Worksheet. As an example, a former state employee, while nominally working in the state's office of emergency management, may have spent most of their time working with Hazard Mitigation. This is great experience and knowledge, but it does not necessarily follow that they are intimately familiar with procurement regulations, since states generally can follow their own procurement regulations versus having to fully comply with 2 CFR, Part 200. Similarly, if the local agency has complex insurance issues to deal with, then it would be appropriate to seek out a cost recovery consultant with extensive experience in insurance matters. Disaster cost recovery can be like any other profession. For instance, there are family practice doctors, and then there are cardiologists, internists, orthopedic surgeons, etc. The right consultant should be hired according to the unique needs of the local agency vis-à-vis the nature and extent of the damages they have suffered.

It is not inappropriate to insist on detailed work and experience histories of the staff the consultant proposes to assign to the local agency. Furthermore, if and when additional staff may be assigned, these employees should first be vetted for their qualifications by the local agency.

More Good News and Some Bad News

There is some good news and some bad news regarding hiring a cost recovery consulting firm. Some of the costs may be eligible for FEMA reimbursement, up to a point. The bad news is that FEMA will almost never cover the full cost of these services.

First, FEMA will reimburse those costs that are eligible at 75% of what FEMA considers reasonable fees. What FEMA considers a "reasonable" fee will frequently be less than what the consultant charges.

Secondly, FEMA very closely scrutinizes the consultant's invoices and compares the hourly rates charged for a given task against the work performed. For example, a consultant may charge $AAA for a specific task. FEMA may determine that the task should have been performed by a member of the consultant's staff with lower qualifications. In other words, the consultant should not charge the rate for a senior project manager if the work, in FEMA's expectation, could be effectively performed by a junior staff person.

In some appeals cases, the reader will find that the top end for a senior cost recovery consultant should not exceed $155.00 per hour. If the consultant charges the local agency $195.00 per hour, the $40.00 per hour difference is borne by the local agency. And the $155.00 per hour rate is typically reimbursed at 75%, or $116.25 per hour, a total difference of per hour of $78.75 for the senior cost recovery consultant.

And if FEMA determines that the specific task performed should have been done by a $95.00 per hour staffer, then the deficit is even greater. FEMA then reimburses $95.00 per hour at 75%, which equals $71.25, but the consultant has charged $195.00 per hour. So, the local agency is now paying $195.00 per hour but only being reimbursed $71.25, a net out-of-pocket expense of $123.75 per hour. Therefore, any time a disaster cost recovery consultant is hired by a local agency, someone at the local agency must be very attentive to the entire billing process and ensure that the appropriate level of consultant staff is performing a given task. And this, given the complex nature of the Public Assistance process, is not easy.

To put some perspective on this, the average hourly salary for a CPA (Certified Public Accountant) in New York City or San Francisco hovers currently around $50.00 per hour. In this light, who wouldn't want to be disaster cost recovery consultant and possibly make three times that amount?

There is a very old audit of a South Dakota school district which apparently has been rescinded, but was spot on regarding the issues of accountability, ethics, and conflicts of interest. However,

Table 13.4 Hiring a Consultant: Pros and Cons 4

Advantages of Hiring a Consultant	Disadvantages of Hiring a Consultant
Accountability: It may be difficult for the local agency, particularly those without recent disaster cost recovery experience, to properly define: 1) a scope of work, 2) clear deliverables, and 3) precise timelines. Especially without a defined scope of work, FEMA may have difficulty in determining if the consultant's costs are reasonable.	**Ethical Concerns:** There have been instances of unethical behavior or questionable practices by consulting firms, which can result in FEMA deobligations. **Potential for Conflicts of Interest:** Consulting firms providing a wide range of services to a local agency, i.e., disaster cost recovery services and engineering services, could represent a conflict of interest and result in lost funding.

I do recall some of the essential details of that audit, if only because at the time the amount in question was quite substantial.

An elementary school district in South Dakota suffered extensive damages due to heavy rainstorms, at least some 20 years ago. The district hired a consultant to assist them, and the consultant determined that the level of damage was such that the schools should apply for the 50% rule, i.e., the damage was so great that it would be less expensive to replace the school buildings rather than repair them. The district did apply for replacement, rather than repair, and FEMA approved the Project Worksheets.

Fast Forward: The Department of Homeland Security, Office of the Inspector General conducted an audit and found that the 50% rule had been miscalculated and that the school district should have to repay some $20,000,000, because the buildings, per the auditors, should have been repaired rather than replaced.

It is of interest that the consultant hired by the school district to determine the level of damage was later the same firm engaged to provide services as the construction manager. Clearly the consultant had a conflict of interest. The consultant was able to charge a much greater fee for completely rebuilding the schools, rather than merely repairing them.

While this may not happen often, it is nonetheless something of which the local agencies should be cognizant. This also occurred many years ago, when much less attention was paid to procurement issues than is the case now. Today, if a consultant has a hand in preparing a Request for Proposals or an Invitation for Bids, they are by regulation forbidden to submit a proposal for the work in which they had a preparatory role.

For some disaster cost recovery consultants, the last thing they want to do is to train local agency staff in how to manage the disaster cost recovery process on their own, without any further need for a consultant. However, this could be an integral part of engaging a cost recovery consultant. The local agency, of course, must want to learn, and not merely pay a consultant every time a disaster occurs.

Many years ago, while working in Los Angeles County, the County hired a consultant to draft a plan template which could be used by any of the 88 cities in the county. When the final product was unveiled, it became apparent that the consultant had structured the plan in such a way that while the plan was freely available, it was so complex that each city would have to hire the consultant to customize that plan to that specific city. Quite counterproductive, and a waste of time and money. In a similar vein, a county contracted with a consultant to develop an online disaster alerting system, again with the proviso that it would be in the public domain and generally available. However, the client isolated the source computer code in such a way that they would have to be repeatedly hired to make use of the program.

Table 13.5 Hiring a Consultant: Pros and Cons 5

Advantages of Hiring a Consultant	*Disadvantages of Hiring a Consultant*
Flexibility: Consultants should be able to adapt to the organizational and program needs and provide resources and provide support for both the short-term and long-term aspects of the disaster cost recovery process.	**Loss of Control:** When consultants are hired, the local agency loses some control over projects and decision-making to external experts. However, the local agency, not the consultant, is ultimately responsible in the same way that if there is a problem with income taxes, the taxpayer, not the tax preparer (CPA) is normally responsible for the owed taxes.

Table 13.6 Hiring a Consultant: Pros and Cons 6

Advantages of Hiring a Consultant	*Disadvantages of Hiring a Consultant*
Training and Knowledge Transfer: Some consulting firms offer training and knowledge transfer to internal staff, enabling agency employees to learn new skills and best practices.	**Incomplete Knowledge Transfer:** Consultants may bring valuable knowledge and recommendations, but they may not always effectively transfer this knowledge to local agency staff. This makes it difficult to maintain improvements going forward.

Table 13.7 Hiring a Consultant: Pros and Cons 7

Advantages of Hiring a Consultant	*Disadvantages of Hiring a Consultant*
Speed and Efficiency: Consulting firms are typically experienced professionals who can execute tasks more efficiently than inexperienced or understaffed local agency personnel.	**Time-Consuming:** Hiring a consultant can be time-consuming: 1) because of the requirements of 2 CFR, Part 200, 2) the time and effort necessary to explain the local agency's existing internal processes, and 3) fully integrating the consultant's staff with local agency personnel.

With the understanding that the disaster cost recovery process will unfold in what seems to the local agency to be a slow-motion video, the relative speed and efficiency of bringing a cost recovery consultant on board will be important. The sooner a consultant is on board, the sooner they can begin providing a recommended strategy and putting procedures into play. However, hiring a cost recovery consultant may only be done in compliance with Title 2 of the Code of Federal Regulations, Part 200, or eligibility may be forfeited. The following cases, one from Florida and the other from Massachusetts, illustrate the perils involved in on-boarding consultants of all types.

In Chapter 9: Procurement, we saw how the City of Key West lost all funding for their cost recovery consultant because of improper procurement.

FEMA does permit local agencies to have pre-disaster (aka pre-positioned, or ID/IQ (indefinite delivery, indefinite quantity)) contracts in place for disaster related services, but those contracts must be in full compliance with both 2 CFR, Part 200, and the local agency's own procurement rules, whichever is more restrictive.

Following is an appeals case which we will also examine later in the book for additional issues regarding Direct Administrative Costs or DAC, and ineligible work.

The second case comes from Massachusetts, where a major religious organization ran afoul of Title 2 of the Code of Federal Regulations, Part 200. This organization used an out-of-state "buy group," in this case, the Houston-Galveston Area Council of Governments (HGAC) buy group, improperly. This case has multiple issues, so we will only deal at this point with that portion dealing with the hiring of the cost recovery consultant. Actually, this is one of four nearly identical cases involving this same agency and very similar or identical issues. Furthermore, although this applicant is a private non-profit organization, exactly the same requirements of 2 CFR, Part 200 apply equally to all non-Federal, non-state government agencies.

"Severe storms and tornados on June 1, 2011 damaged the Roman Catholic Bishop of Springfield's (Applicant) Cathedral High School/St. Michael's Academy Middle School building (Facility), which is part of a 35 acre campus owned by the Applicant, a private nonprofit (PNP). FEMA determined 99.3 percent of the Facility was eligible for FEMA funding, as the school provided critical educational services."[10]

"The Applicant also hired Witt O'Brien's (Witt) to provide direct administrative services for all of the Applicant's emergency and permanent work projects resulting from the disaster. The Applicant utilized the Houston Galveston Area Council of Government (HGAC) to obtain Witt's services, by executing a purchase order with Witt under a preexisting contract with HGAC, under its cooperative purchasing program known as HGAC-Buy. The contract was available to the Applicant as an end-user of HGAC-Buy. In PW 250, FEMA initially awarded $6,773.70 in direct administrative costs (DAC)."[11]

Procurement Noncompliance and Reasonable Costs

"Applicants must comply with federal procurement regulations and an applicant's own procurement standards, both when soliciting services, and when choosing a vendor to provide administrative services. PNPs must conduct procurement transactions in a manner that complies with the following Federal standards: (1) provide free and open competition; (2) conduct all necessary affirmative steps to ensure the use of minority businesses, women's business enterprises, and labor surplus area firms when possible; and (3) maintain records sufficient to detail the history of the procurement. These records will include, but are not limited to: rationale for the method of procurement; selection of contract type; contractor selection or rejection; and the basis for the contract price. PNPs must perform a cost or price analysis in connection with every procurement action in excess of the simplified acquisition threshold, including contract modifications, and the method and degree of analysis depends on the facts surrounding the particular procurement situation. In addition, an applicant must avoid purchasing unnecessary items and accordingly, solicitations for services must have a clear and accurate description of the technical requirements of the service, and such descriptions must not contain features which will unduly restrict competition."[12]

"Here, the Applicant's contract award to Witt was a noncompetitive procurement. The Applicant executed a contract with Witt through the HGAC-Buy program. HGAC received 13 proposals and the Applicant claims it selected Witt after reviewing the pricing, capability to effectively perform the work, and ability to timely provide the services needed. The Applicant/HGAC did not base the procurement of Witt's services based on the Applicant's specific needs. Rather, the HGAC advertisement was for an infinite quantity of services, the SOW was broad and exceeded the services ordered and received by the Applicant, and was done before the Applicant procured HGAC's services. This is because the advertisement was not specific to the Applicant; it was instead based on services that could be provided to users nationwide, which unduly restricted competition. As noted above, the requirements for free and open competition prohibited the Applicant, or its agent, from entering into a sole sourced contract, which the HGAC contract with Witt amounted to."[13]

Because of the procurement noncompliance associated with Witt's contract, FEMA had discretionary enforcement authority to award reasonable costs or to disallow all costs. . . . Here, the RA elected to award certain costs determined to be reasonable. In reducing the rate to $132.90 per hour, the RA looked at several PA grants in other disaster declarations, including Witt's contract with the State of Vermont, which is what FEMA ultimately used as a comparison to establish labor rates in this project. This was due to the fact that the Vermont contract provided for similar services, in the same timeframe, with common staff, in FEMA Region I, and with a comparable contract size.

In this, and in most cases, it is likely that the agency was still on the hook for the full invoiced rate from the consultant even though FEMA may have reimbursed substantially less than was originally billed for services.

Consultants may (and should) bring with them best practices to share with their clients. In a perfect world, a consultant would fully train the client so that the client has a much-reduced future need for the consultant's assistance. Alas, the world is quite far from perfect, and the client may need to carefully observe what the consultant does and learn not only from the client's mistakes, but also from the consultant's valuable expertise.

Often, however, the client/local agency's staff is quite stuck in the mud of doing things as they have always done them, e.g., not particularly well, hence the need for consultants. The disaster cost recovery process should be, right after monetary recovery, about change management. This is especially true for those communities across the country which are subject to repetitive disasters year after every other year. Particularly in the U.S. Southeast, where hurricanes are a yearly occurrence in one state or another, and often in multiple states at the same time. Yet these same states, their counties, and their cities, towns, and villages actively resist changing their day-to-day administrative practices to be better positioned to financially recover from a disaster. This is one reason why consultancy is such a thriving business.

This case from Florida is a perfect example. "In 2005, rain and wind from Hurricane Wilma damaged several buildings in the Florida City Farmers Market complex. The Applicant requested assistance from FEMA to repair several buildings. FEMA prepared PWs 6552 and 6655 to repair metal roofing, ceiling tile, insulation, and flashing on Buildings 10 and 12 of the complex for

Table 13.8 Best Practices

Advantages of Hiring a Consultant	Disadvantages of Hiring a Consultant
Best Practices: Consultants often bring best practices and in-depth knowledge of FEMA's Public Assistance program to the job.	**Resistance to Change:** Employees within the organization may resist the changes recommended by a consultant. Consultants should always be hired with an eye on change management. If the local agency had strong pre-disaster policies and effective documentation processes in place, they probably could get through without hiring a consultant. Hence, some level of change will be required if the local agency is to avoid similar problems in another disaster. **Temporary Solutions:** Some consulting firms may focus on short-term solutions rather than long-term sustainability. The consulting firm should be hired 1) to assist the local agency in its cost recovery process, and 2) to aid the agency in better repositioning itself for future disasters.

Table 13.9 Problem Solving and Creation

Advantages of Hiring a Consultant	*Disadvantages of Hiring a Consultant*
Problem Solving: Consulting firms are typically hired to assist the local agency in recovering its disaster losses. Because they do this 52 weeks a year, they are normally very well-qualified and may be able to provide insights and shortcuts of which the local agency is unaware.	**Problem Creation:** This particular issue probably occurs more often with consultants other than specialists in disaster cost recovery. When the local agency hires an engineer, particularly an engineer that is not fully versed in the Public Assistance process, the engineer's report and recommendations may cause problems because of the "facts" they report or the opinions they express.

$1,725 and $22,018 respectively. PW 6552 cited roof leakage from rusty flashing that caused damage to 756 square feet of ceiling tile and insulation. PW 6655 cited damage to two overhead doors, 1,778 square feet of metal roofing, 168 square feet of ceiling tile, and 15.6 square yards of carpet. The Applicant hired ACAI Associates Incorporated (the consulting engineer) to complete an assessment report of the two structures in July 2008, over two years after the disaster. This report recommended an increase in the scope of work and additional costs for repair to both buildings for a total of $914,101."[14]

"The Applicant included the ACAI Associates (consulting engineer's) report detailing the damage and scope of repairs to both structures. This report cited damage to the buildings from long-term exposure and delayed maintenance following the 2005 storm.

The FEMA Regional Administrator denied the request of $914,101 because the Applicant did not take any steps to prevent further damage to the two structures and was requesting funds to upgrade systems and utilities not damaged by the storm."[15]

While the engineer is bound by their professional codes and standards of practice and might have been remiss had they failed to mention these facts, in hindsight the local agency might have been better off not hiring a professional who was duty-bound to present ALL the facts. This is not to suggest any impropriety of any sort, but why actively seek trouble and then pay handsomely for it? There seems to be little rationale in seeking out a professional who will argue against our version of the facts.

In a different case from the Pacific Northwest, the facts are slightly different, but the case orbits around an engineer report. "During the declared December 2007 flood event, the Chehalis River flooded and a portion of its bank adjacent to the China Creek sewer main eroded, exposing a 10-foot length of the pipe. Based on the recommendation of a geotechnical specialist, FEMA obligated PW 1062 on March 21, 2008, for $25,159 for the restoration of support and cover to the exposed length of pipe. The approved scope of work included the installation of a 14-foot-long sheet pile wall."[16]

"The Applicant's consultant observed significant erosion along a 100-foot-long section of the river bank and recommended stabilizing the entire length of eroded bank to eliminate the threat of additional erosion, which could further threaten the sewer line. In April 2008, the Applicant entered into a contract for the armoring of a 100-foot section of bank and the construction of a rock and log jam groin based on its consultant's recommendation."[17]

"On May 30, 2008, the Applicant submitted a first appeal stating that it had completed the emergency bank stabilization and requested FEMA fund the actual project cost of $169,778. The Applicant submitted a memorandum dated May 5, 2008, from its consultant that states that the bank had eroded to within less than five feet from the sewer pipe, creating a hazard of exposure and pipe failure for the entire 100-foot length of riverbank. The consultant had considered a sheet pile alternative as recommended by FEMA, but determined that it was not feasible due to the high risk of additional bank collapse. <u>The Regional Administrator denied the appeal because the Applicant had not demonstrated that there was an immediate threat of damage to the pipe."</u>[18] (Emphasis Added)

"While the Applicant's consultant states that the bank eroded to within five feet of the pipeline, the Applicant did not provide any documentation to support that statement. The appeal references as-built drawings; however, the Applicant did not submit the drawings in support of the appeal."[19]

In this case, it might appear that the consulting engineer only did half the job. The engineer made a statement and then apparently failed to back it up with any evidence, substantial or otherwise, to clearly establish that the project had been improperly scoped out. In all fairness to engineering consultants, perhaps the city did not specify in the terms of the contract what it needed and expected from the engineer in terms of a favorable report.

Any consultant who does not have extensive experience working in and with FEMA's Public Assistance program is at a serious disadvantage, because they do not truly understand that normally accepted engineering conditions and standards may be completely useless in the context of the Public Assistance program. In some cases these normally accepted professional standards may hurt the clients. This again in no way is to suggest or recommend any subterfuge or malfeasance of any sort. However, as I have previously stated, working within the Public Assistance program can be much like doing good tax planning. There are things that can be done to improve less-than-ideal situations if the local agency has knowledgeable staff, or hires fully qualified and experienced consultants to assist them in proper planning for disaster cost recovery.

However, when bringing on additional consultant staff, each new person should be vetted regarding their documented qualifications, the level(s) of tasks to which they will be assigned, and the anticipated duration of their engagement with the local agency.

Risk mitigation should be central to the engagement of any consultant. Consultants should always bring to the table extensive knowledge and experience to not only help deal with the current set of disaster issues, but also avoid leading a client local agency into treacherous waters. To illustrate this concept, there is a series of 13 different appeals which cover 25 different Project Worksheets from devastating floods which affected Cedar Rapids, Iowa, in 2008.

"Heavy rainfall between May and August 2008 resulted in severe flooding that caused extensive damage in the City of Cedar Rapids (Applicant). As a result of the flooding, the Jones Golf Course Clubhouse was inundated with water, damaging the building and contents. FEMA prepared PW 10267 for $279,091.00 using the Cost Estimating Format (CEF) to perform repairs on the clubhouse. Included in the project costs were $2,654.00 in Direct Administrative Costs (DAC). After the Iowa Homeland Security and Emergency Management Division (Grantee) reviewed

Table 13.10 Scalability

Advantages of Hiring a Consultant
Scalability: Consultants should be able to quickly adapt to the changing demands of the Public Assistance program.

Table 13.11 Risk Mitigation

Advantages of Hiring a Consultant
Risk Mitigation: Consulting firms can help identify and reduce potential future risks which exist in part because the agency does not have the appropriate policies and procedures for disaster cost recovery.

the Applicant's documentation of actual costs, FEMA closed out PW 10267 for $286,620.25 and increased the total eligible DAC to $49,824.90 ($47,170.90 more than estimated in the CEF) based on the Grantee's recommendation."[20]

"FEMA reduced the eligible DAC claimed by the Applicant's contractor, Adjustors International, to $8,010.55 ($2,407.60 less than claimed) due to insufficient documentation to support consultant's rates in excess of $155 per hour which the Applicant is appealing. The other DAC reductions, which are reduced for the same reason, are not appealed."[21]

"In addition, the Applicant submitted a claim for Project Management (PM) costs from its consultant, *(a different contractor)* Base Tactical, for $94,924.25. The Grantee determined that the PM costs were excessive and unreasonable and recommended 7% of project repair costs, $12,559.03, as a reasonable PM cost. This cost represents an $82,365.22 reduction which the Applicant did not appeal."[22]

"Of the $286,620.25 in total project costs, the following breakdown of expenses is provided: $178,388.81 for actual work performed at the Jones Golf Course Clubhouse; $45,847.51 for engineering/design costs; $49,824.90 for total DAC; and $12,559.03 for PM costs."[23]

First Appeal

"The Applicant submitted its first appeal for PW 10267 to the Grantee on July 20, 2012. With the appeal, the Applicant requested reimbursement of $2,407.60 for DAC that were charged at an hourly contract rate above $155. The Applicant asserted that the contractor's project manager rate of $285 per hour was eligible because the Applicant followed a proper procurement process, in accordance with federal regulations, and awarded the contract based on fair market value. Further, the Applicant claimed that the project manager's review and oversight of consultant staff required 'special skills,' referencing OMB Circular A-87, Attachment B, paragraph 32. The Grantee forwarded the Applicant's first appeal to FEMA with letters supporting the Applicant's request on September 10, 2012."[24]

"Upon receipt of the Applicant's first appeal, the FEMA Region VII Regional Administrator (RA) issued a request for information to assist in its analysis of the eligibility of the DAC claimed. The requested information included:

- Professional designation or title of employee performing task;
- Specific description of each task performed and the associated cost (i.e., site identification, kick-off meeting, immediate needs, preliminary cost estimate, data collection & dissemination, travel expenses, etc.) because the project phases were too broad and did not substantiate specific work activity;
- Justification for each task why specific staff or skills were required to accomplish the work"[25]

"On November 21, 2012, the RA *(Regional Administrator)* denied the first appeal with a letter explaining that the Applicant's request for $2,407.60 in contract cost was not eligible for reimbursement as the Applicant had not justified the $285 per hour rate."[26]

"FEMA's records indicate that the Applicant submitted funding requests for DAC related activities performed by Adjusters International *(the consultant)* for 458 PWs totaling approximately $2,399,295. Given the Applicant's contract for services with Adjusters International *(the consultant)* included project management, indirect cost activities, consulting and insurance adjusting services *(other services),* and the number of PWs that Adjusters International *(the consultant)* charged against, it is incumbent upon the Applicant to provide sufficiently detailed and descriptive documentation to demonstrate that the tasks performed were, in fact, eligible DAC directly attributable to a specific PW."[27]

"The documentation provided by the Applicant in this case lacks sufficient detail to discern the specific tasks or work performed by Adjusters International (the consultant). Without such information, FEMA cannot determine eligibility and reasonableness of cost. The consultant's spreadsheet details the specific tasks that were performed."[28]

In all these cases, the spark that set off the explosion which followed was that the consultant charged $285.00 per hour for at least one of its employees. This is akin to waving a red flag at an enraged bull or throwing blood in the water to find a shark. This is what turned a "routine" appeals case, if there is such a thing, into a feeding frenzy. All 13 cases are nearly identical, and every one of the cases mentions this $285.00 per hour fee. Furthermore, and this is where the bear was poked with a very sharp stick, in 7 of the 13 appeals, the total dollar amount in question was less than $420.00 for any one of the appeals, including one for $33.00 total. The combined total for all 25 Project Worksheets in the 13 appeals cases was $20,932.00. The bear was indeed angry and deobligated ALL DAC previously approved, in the amount of $197,508.62. So, for appealing less than $21,000 in DAC, the agency lost nearly $198,000 dollars. However, all the deobligations were done by the book for reasons of improper procurement.

Later in the book, we shall again see more issues involving the City of Cedar Rapids and their floods of 2008. This is one of those gifts that truly keeps on giving.

First, the consultant hired for a particular task or set of tasks must be fully qualified for the assignment. Hiring an inexperienced consultant, or worse, a consultant with wrong or insufficient qualifications, may be deadly. Having a consultant on board may give the local agency a sense of comfort and security, that "all things will work out well." As illustrated in the case histories in this chapter, the reader can see that having a consultant on board doesn't always produce the ideal outcome.

Second, while the consultant may have some very experienced staff listed on their proposal, the local agency must insist and ensure that those same highly qualified personnel are on the job with the local agency, and not dozens or hundreds of miles away providing services to other clients. However, the consultant's most senior experts will not need to necessarily be on the job every day of the week. It may be sufficient for them to be present at weekly meetings (at least very early on in the process) to ensure that things are moving ahead as planned. As shown in some of the cases in this chapter, FEMA will raise questions when the higher-priced staff are doing work which may reasonably be done by lower-cost, but still experienced, consultant staffers.

The great thing about consultants is that they usually have extensive networks and can reach out, if needed, to bring in someone with special expertise on as needed basis. Once again, caution must be exercised to ensure that the consultant is not "packing on" and bringing in staff to generate billing when such expertise is not needed.

Table 13.12 Core Competencies

Advantages of Hiring a Consultant
Core Competencies: When the local agency hires a consulting firm, it can return some staff to their normal day-to-day job responsibilities. However, few consultants can work fully independently of local staff.

Table 13.13 Access to Networks

Advantages of Hiring a Consultant
Access to Networks: Consults typically have extensive professional networks that they can access to fully support their work for the local agency.

It is very important to understand that FEMA will very closely examine the billing statements and all supporting documentation to determine what consultant costs are reasonable and necessary for the level of work being performed. Generally, FEMA sees disaster cost recovery consultants as an unnecessary and costly expense for them. However, for many local agencies overwhelmed by the disaster and the cost recovery process, the right consultant can be a godsend, albeit an expensive one.

Disclaimer

And please let me hasten to explain that I generally do not do disaster cost recovery consulting. I am a sole practitioner and trainer. I have no staff to provide the level of support which local agencies normally would need following a disaster. I never seek out this work. I have on a few occasions performed what I refer to as "handholding" and "compass pointing" to provide very limited support to existing training clients. Typically, when one of my clients does need such a broad spectrum of support I will provide them with a list, without any recommendations, of qualified disaster cost recovery consultants. I always advise clients that they must perform their own due diligence in selecting a disaster cost recovery consulting firm.

Another note on consultants. Virtually every local government uses consultants for a variety of tasks, particularly engineering consultants for the normal ongoing facility and infrastructure work that is the essence of what local government does to provide safe buildings and properly functioning infrastructure of all types. These consultants know which side of the bread to butter.

If, following a disaster, the local agency hires a consultant to determine that damage was disaster-caused, then that is what the consultant will write. FEMA on the other hand, often makes a very different evaluation, frequently at odds with what the engineering consultant's written report states. Spending good money on these types of reports when the damage was truly pre-existing, or deferred maintenance significantly contributed to the disaster, is an exercise in futility.

When an engineering consultant is hired, they will sugarcoat their opinion to avoid creating hard feelings with an otherwise good client. FEMA, on the other hand, has an uncanny ability to see through the smoke and mirrors and will often simply disregard or give short-shrift to these consultant opinions, particularly when a site inspection reveals the true facts, or when the local agency has only an after-the-fact consultant's opinion and cannot support their damage claim with their own regular inspection and maintenance reports.

Red Flag Warning

In researching this book, I have read scores of appeals cases which involved a consultant of type or another. In the process I have learned to "read between the lines" a bit on some of these cases. I have seen very small jurisdictions, and larger ones too, file multiple appeals for similar situations, and dozens of appeals focused on Direct Administrative Costs or DAC, all of which were denied for various violations of Federal regulations. This appeals case is from West Virginia, and the town of Richwood, population less than 2,000. "During the incident period June 22 through June 29, 2016, the City of Richwood (Applicant) experienced catastrophic flooding. FEMA prepared multiple Project Worksheets (PWs) including PW 986, which FEMA wrote for $398,853.00 (reflecting straight-time and overtime labor costs and direct administrative costs (DAC)) to address Category B emergency protective measures claimed for Incident Command Structure (ICS) team activities from June 22 through October 29, 2016. However, FEMA denied all costs for PW 986 on August 13, 2019, determining the length of time the ICS team was operational (four months and seven days) could not be justified when compared to the length of time taken by other emergency operations teams from nearby jurisdictions, and by the State Police and the West Virginia Department of Homeland Security and Emergency Management (Grantee). FEMA's Determination Memorandum cited to a State Auditor report that found Applicant mismanagement and misuse of FEMA funds and expressed concerns about the ICS team structure, actions, conduct, and how members were paid:"[29]

". . . the Applicant deviated significantly from its standard practices, did not act with prudence in its responsibilities to the public and the Federal Government, did not provide documentation that tracked time charged to specific eligible activities performed, has not substantiated its need to continue ICS responsibilities more than two months after other [Emergency Operation Centers] in the area had discontinued, and has not provided documentation that would negate the findings of the State Audit Report."[30]

"According to the Applicant's consultant, the ICS team was comprised of 22 temporary full-time employees. However, the documentation provided by the Applicant does not show ICS team members performed eligible emergency work. For example, job descriptions for the Floodplain Administrator and Safety Director and for the Incident Commander positions mention safety-related concerns, but the Applicant did not provide documentation describing specific eligible measures that employees in these positions, or any other position, performed to eliminate or lessen immediate threats to public health or safety. The documentation the Applicant submitted also could not be used to track hours of eligible work that may have been performed. For example, the Applicant indicates the ICS team addressed basic needs for food and supplies, but it provided no documentation FEMA could use to track the work. Additionally, it appears that food distribution costs were covered elsewhere; FEMA wrote PW 223 for the food distribution center to cover costs for temporary employees for both regular and overtime hours, to reimburse for rental equipment, and for contract services for work completed as of September 2, 2016, and work to be completed from September 3, 2016 to December 31, 2016."[31]

"Regarding cost reasonableness, the Applicant has not demonstrated that the ICS team performed eligible work, or that it could adequately document the hours and costs tied to specific activities. Further, a letter to the Internal Revenue Service acknowledged liberties taken in hiring 'with the thought that the [Applicant] would be reimbursed by FEMA for any and all expenses incurred,' demonstrating that the Applicant incurred costs that were inconsistent with the Federal grant process and thereby unreasonable."[32]

Direct Administrative Costs and Management Costs

"Per FEMA policy, if the Applicant incurs administrative costs that it tracks, charges, and accounts for directly to a specific eligible project, the costs may be eligible as DAC."

"Here, a proprietary program (presumably the consultant's program) tracked DAC on a proportional basis. Costs were not identified and separated into specific projects as required under FEMA policy. The Applicant did not tie the claimed DAC to a specific project; therefore the DAC is ineligible."[33]

Conclusion

"FEMA cannot determine that the Applicant's ICS team performed eligible emergency work and finds the Applicant did not document reasonable costs for eligible emergency work, did not follow federal grant requirements, and did not tie claimed DAC to a specific eligible project. Accordingly, the appeal is denied."[34]

In this case and others, it would appear that the consultants did not provide proper advice to the client. Arguably, this particular client may have never heard of ICS (the Incident Command

System) before the disaster, and it appears to have been at the instigation of the consultant that the city hired nearly two dozen people to staff the Emergency Operations Center.

Be very wary of consultant recommendations to apply for and/or appeal DAC (Direct Administrative Costs), which are at the very best up to 5% of the total of a Project Worksheet. The big secret is that the consultant will charge for preparing an appeal, and then when the appeal is denied, they will gladly charge a second time to file the next appeal. This is in a world where 5 out of 6 appeals are denied, according to FEMA's own data available on the FEMA website.[35]

An Expensive Consultant May Be Well Worth the Money in Some Cases

After procurement, insurance issues are the greatest risk faced by the local agency in its dealing with FEMA. We are required by Federal regulation to obtain the maximum possible insurance settlement, or FEMA may make deductions against the funds with which they would otherwise reimburse the local agency. One type of consultant that may be especially useful in this regard are public adjusters. These are essentially hired guns who will meet the insurance company at high noon and shoot it out on behalf of the local agency. As with all consultants, the firm selected must be experienced, ethical, and pass a rigorous screening by the local agency. However, in some cases, they will work what may appear to be a miracle. Following is a letter in my own files from one such firm. It speaks for itself.

"We are writing to thank you for the fine job that your firm did in handling our claim that resulted from a fire that destroyed a building that we owned on 9th and Park. The building was an old packing house, typical of packing houses that were built in the 1940's and the 1950's throughout the Central Valley. We were part of a PEPIC (Public Entity Private Insurance Pool), and our broker and the PEPIC representative suggested that the maximum due us should have been the $500,000 that was in our policy's schedule of values."[36]

"When Gregg *(the consultant)* first met with us, he told us that our broker and our JPA representative were wrong and underscored the importance of presenting a claim that represented what we actually had before the fire. Your firm spoke at our City Council meeting and fielded questions from the general public. You were hired."[37]

"There were hurdles to overcome during the process. They included the insurance company's consultant leaving out large portions of the building, the insurance company's failure to recognize code issues, and the insurance company's undervaluation of many of the building's elements. They suggested that a building with similar utility, at a much lower cost to replace than the type of building that existed, was the way to go and the basis on which we should be compensated."[38]

"You and your team coordinated the services of a forensic engineer to prepare detailed plans from employee descriptions and photographs and then created a reconstruction estimate that you presented to the insurer. You were able to get the insurance company to acquiesce to your position regarding building values and you helped to navigate the many policy conditions that the insurance company attempted to interpret in their favor. ***You negotiated a settlement in our behalf of over twenty times their original proposal!***"[39] (Emphasis Added)

"Looking back, we made the right decision. It is clear that we would not have done as well had we not retained your firm. Your knowledge of these types of structures, coupled with your expertise in loss adjusting, assured consistency to our small town as administrations changed and through the tragic death of our City Administrator, you kept things on track."[40]

"We would again like to express our congratulations on a job well done. We are happy to recommend your services to others in need."[41]

Not in every case will such an astonishing result be the outcome, but clearly, in this case, the local agency greatly benefited by hiring this consultant.

The Bottom Line on Consultants

Consultants can be truly beneficial to a local agency or private non-profit if and only if their disaster costs run into hundreds of thousands of dollars or millions of dollars. Any benefit of using a consultant where the level of losses is relatively small will be overwhelmed by the consultant's fees.

Lawyers are consultants, too. However, most lawyers are not seasoned experts in Federal regulations, particularly those Federal regulations governing the Public Assistance process.

It is critical to hire the right consultant to suit the needs of the local agency and the disaster that caused such damage.

As disasters continue to increase in size, frequency, and complexity, many more firms will seek to enter this marketplace. Caveat Emptor: let the buyer beware. Following the terrorist attacks on September 11, 2001, there was a sudden profusion of so-called terrorism experts. Literally, people who couldn't spell "terror" were now advertising themselves as terrorism experts. To be sure, there were some cognoscenti who really were terrorism experts, but their numbers were absolutely overwhelmed by all the johnnie-come-latelys who smelled money, Federal money, in the air. The local agency should always perform its due diligence in vetting and then hiring qualified consultants.

Timing is very important when hiring a consultant.

- Before the event

  - This is the ideal time to set up a properly procured contract with an experienced and reliable consulting firm on an ID/IQ (indefinite delivery/indefinite quantity) basis.

- Before the scope of work is signed off

  - It is not recommended to hire an engineering consultant AFTER projects are formulated and scopes of work are signed off. Consulting engineers will almost always recommend more work than FEMA has approved. While some of their suggestions may be appropriate, even advantageous, attempting to change a scope of work after the fact, or worse, making unilateral changes to the scope of work will almost always end up badly for the local agency.

- Not after the 60-day window has closed

  - Hiring a consulting engineer AFTER the 60-day window has closed for notifying FEMA of new damages is futile in almost every case.

- Before signing a contract, determine that the engineering form has real FEMA experience.

  - Consulting engineers usually can talk the talk. But they must also be able to walk the walk. If the engineering consultant does not have significant experience with FEMA and the Public Assistance program, they may create many more problems than they solve. In many cases, a consulting engineer's professional opinions may be at odds with FEMA's position on a particular repair. The local agency must then decide whether they want the Federal money or a happy engineer. Take the money and run!
  - Additionally, the consulting engineer will almost always have one eye on their book of business. They may see the local agency's predicament as an opportunity to add to their monthly billing, regardless of whether it is truly in the local agency's best interest.
  - Consulting engineers will always, as they should, advise clients to repair damage and include the latest codes and standards, even if the local agency has not officially adopted those codes and standards, which means FEMA will probably not fund the upgrades required by those codes and standards.

Performing Due Diligence in Hiring a Cost Recovery (or Any Other) Consultant

The local agency has solicited bids with free and open competition in accordance with all parts of 2 CFR, Part 200. Now in the process of reviewing and scoring the bids, there remains one additional option for checking and rating the bidding consultants. That is to go to the FEMA Appeals Database and search (within quotation marks) for the names of the consultant companies to see what, if any, issues may have cropped up in their dealings with other agencies. The absence of a consultant company's name does not necessarily mean that all is well; however, those consultants who have pushed the edge too far may be mentioned, and that should trigger additional probing as part of the due diligence process. In my research for this book, I have discovered a few consultants that I would place on a "No Fly" list. Certainly, some of the few consultants with potential black marks should be given demerits in the overall bid rating process.

Contract Issues

For an agency with little recent experience with disasters, the process of hiring a consultant can be fraught with danger. At some point, the local agency must develop a trusting relationship with the consultant. But until then, per the Russian proverb, "Trust but Verify." In negotiating the contract, the "low" bidder may be anything but. In one documented case, the city and the consultant signed a contract for a not-to-exceed amount of $105,000.

"The contract contained a clause that stated that the total contract value was not to exceed $105,000." Then, 108 days later, "This contract was modified on May 12, 2017, when Mayor Baber signed a contract modification that raised the maximum contract value from $105,000 to $210,000.60." Then, 75 days later, "On July 26, 2017, another contract modification was signed by Mayor Baber that raised the maximum contract value from $210,000 to $315,000."[42] Clearly, this was a "bait-and-switch" tactic. This represents a 300% contract overrun within 6 months and 3 days. Even if everything else was running perfectly, these increases would attract FEMA's undivided attention. The lesson here is that if the deal looks too good, it is probably bad.

Total Monies Paid to Simmons Consulting (Consultant #2)

"In an examination of all source documents that were made available to the Auditor's office, it was determined that Simmons Consulting invoiced the City of Richwood for $122,375.56 for services provided from January 25, 2017 until August 19, 2017. However, Simmons Consulting received $221,759.79 in check payments from the City of Richwood, which is $99,384.23 above what Simmons (the consultant) invoiced."[43]

Another note which should be of keen interest is that the original consultant in this case had recently left FEMA and set up his own consulting firm. This contract was his first as a new consultant. No local agency should hire a first-time consultant; the waters are too deep and too cold for the inexperienced. Even if they claim to have former FEMA experience, they might have worked there for years . . . but not necessarily in Public Assistance.

Some Final Thoughts

All consultants are in business to make money. Some are quite ethical; others are less so. In reading hundreds of appeals cases, and in reading between the lines of these cases, it is easy to see how some consultants, both disaster cost recovery and engineering consultants, have their clients' best interests at heart. In other cases, however, it appears the client's best interests conflict with the consultant's best interests.

A complicating factor in all this is politics. Consultants, particularly local engineering firms, are very adept at cultivating new business and they may be part of a regular foursome on the golf course, with the mayor and/or city/county manager. These established relationships sometimes cloud the best judgments and lead down a path which results in some way with a violation of Federal regulations, and then the subsequent deobligation of FEMA funds.

Hiring the right consultant can be a very smart move for a disaster-affected community. Hiring the wrong consultant, or improperly hiring the consultant, can bring down an unholy Armageddon of catastrophic problems.

Notes

1 https://www.fema.gov/appeal/direct-administrative-costs-project-management-costs-1
2 Ibid.
3 Ibid.
4 Ibid.
5 Ibid.
6 https://www.fema.gov/appeal/insurance-direct-administrative-costs-management-costs
7 https://www.fema.gov/appeal/direct-administrative-costs-project-management-costs-1
8 Ibid.
9 Ibid.
10 https://www.fema.gov/appeal/private-nonprofit-appeal-procedures-immediate-threat-procurement-dac-reasonable-costs
11 Ibid.
12 Ibid.
13 Ibid.
14 https://www.fema.gov/appeal/denial-additional-funds
15 Ibid.
16 https://www.fema.gov/appeal/bank-erosion
17 Ibid.
18 Ibid.
19 Ibid.
20 https://www.fema.gov/appeal/direct-administrative-costs-14
21 Ibid.
22 Ibid.
23 Ibid.
24 Ibid.
25 Ibid.
26 Ibid.
27 Ibid.
28 Ibid.
29 https://www.fema.gov/appeal/allowable-costs-and-reasonable-costs-direct-administrative-costs-and-management-costs
30 Ibid.
31 Ibid.
32 Ibid.
33 Ibid.
34 Ibid.
35 https://www.fema.gov/about/openfema/data-sets/fema-public-assistance-second-appeals-tracker
36 Letter taken from the author's private files.
37 Ibid.

38 Ibid.
39 Ibid.
40 Ibid.
41 Ibid.
42 West Virginia State Auditor, Public Integrity Fraud Unit, Report of Investigation, City of Richwood, March 29, 2019, https://www.wvsao.gov/SpecialInvestigation/Default, pp. 106–107.
43 Ibid, p. 107.

Part 3

During the Event

14   The Proclamation and Declaration Processes

When a disaster is imminent or has just occurred, the very first step in the disaster cost recovery process is making a local disaster proclamation.

Although the proclamation will likely be made by a local official other than the Finance Director, the quality and comprehensiveness of the proclamation may significantly affect the entire local agency, particularly the Finance staff.

There are many reasons to make the local disaster proclamation. First, in many states, making a disaster proclamation will invoke certain statutory exemptions, which enable the local government agency to take expedited response actions, and in some cases will reduce specified liabilities.

Second, the making of the proclamation sends a powerful message to both the community and the media that these are difficult times, and the support and cooperation of all is needed.

Thirdly, the proclamation sends a similar message to higher levels of government regarding the problems which the local agency is currently facing. This is particularly important insofar as ultimately the state must, if conditions are met, make the request to the Federal government for various levels of Federal assistance from FEMA and other Federal agencies as may be appropriate.

If a disaster proclamation is not made at the local level, little or nothing will happen regarding the provision of response services and ultimately recovery financing from other levels of government.

In making the disaster proclamation, the finance department should always be consulted, because the Finance Department has access to important information which both the state and Federal governments will need as they determine the need for a Gubernatorial disaster proclamation and the Presidential Disaster Declaration as appropriate.

Following is the text of the letter from then-California Governor Jerry Brown to the President requesting a Presidential declaration of disaster for the Valley Fire in Lake County, California. I consider this a classic good example of a disaster proclamation and will explain it paragraph by paragraph to emphasize the importance of each element in this example, defining the most significant elements which should be included in any disaster proclamation, local or state. As we shall see, some of the elements of this document would not necessarily apply in a local disaster proclamation but are included here for the sake of completeness.

The Letter From The Governor Requesting a Presidential Disaster Declaration

OFFICE OF THE GOVERNOR

September 21, 2015
The President
The White House
Washington, D. C. 20500
Through: Robert J. Fenton, Jr.

DOI: 10.4324/9781003487869-18

Regional Administrator
Federal Emergency Management
Agency Region IX
Oakland, California, 94607–4052

Dear Mr. President:

I very much appreciate your concern and personal call last week regarding California's wildfires.

Pursuant to Section 401 of the Robert T. Stafford Disaster Relief and Emergency Assistance Act, 42 U.S.C. Sections 5121–5207 (Stafford Act), and Title 44 of the Code of Federal Regulations Section 20636, I hereby request you declare a major disaster in the State of California as a result of the Valley Fire burning in Lake, Napa, and Sonoma Counties.

In the preceding paragraph, the Governor cites the legal authorities, an important first step.

The Valley Fire began in Lake County on September 12, 2015, burning 40,000 acres in less than 12 hours and quickly spread through Lake, Napa, and Sonoma Counties. Given this fire's rate of spread, size, and intensity, scientists consider it to be a "megafire," which behaves differently than typical wildfires. Megafires expand quickly and unpredictably, thriving on dead trees, dry vegetation, and wind conditions. Winds propel burning embers far ahead of the existing fire, accelerating fire growth at a pace that is very difficult to control. Four years of extreme drought have parched our landscapes and created millions of dead trees that have increased vulnerability to these types of fires.

Presently, the Valley Fire continues its path of destruction. It is already considered the fourth most destructive fire in California's history, devastating several communities and key parts of rural Lake County. As of the date of this letter, the Valley Fire has burned over 75,111 acres and is only 69 percent contained. It has destroyed 1,238 homes and threatened over 7,600 single residences and 150 nonresidential properties. More than 19,300 residents were issued mandatory evacuation orders necessitating the opening of 18 shelters in Lake and Napa counties. Presently, several hundred residents remain in eight shelters.

Due to the fire's rapid rate of spread through rural and isolated communities, many residents had little time to flee and some required rescue by firefighters and local law enforcement.

Tragically, the Valley Fire has taken three lives and seriously injured four firefighters. Several residents remain unaccounted for, and our emergency responders anticipate the number of fatalities could grow.

The devastation and disruption caused by the Valley Fire is extraordinary. Thousands have been made homeless by the fire. Thirty schools were closed, and many remain closed. Major roads were damaged or destroyed. The fire destroyed nearly 1,000 utility poles causing the loss of power to thousands of residents. Five local power plants were disabled. Many essential drinking water systems have been completely destroyed. and numerous others are running on emergency back-up power. Additionally, over 25,000 feet of fiber lines burned, destroying critical infrastructure used in public safety communications such as radio towers, state intercom radio systems, and numerous law enforcement vaults and towers.

> *In the preceding five paragraphs, the Governor explains the depth and breadth of what has happened with this fire to date.*

This is the third fire to significantly impact Lake County within the last three months. On July 29,2015, the Rocky Fire burned 69,438 acres and destroyed 43 residences. A few weeks later. on August 9, 2015, the Jerusalem Fire burned 25,118 acres and destroyed six residences. Shortly after these fires were contained, but before the debris and destruction could be removed, the Valley Fire began, decimating the towns of Cobb and Middletown and nearly destroying several other communities in the county.

On September 13, 2015, I declared a State of Emergency as a result of the Valley Fire under the California Emergency Services Act. The Office of Emergency Services activated our Slate Operations Center as well as the Inland and Coastal Regional Operations Centers. The State's Emergency Operations Plan was implemented, and all necessary state assets were deployed. including the California National Guard. Lake, Napa, and Sonoma counties also activated their local Emergency Operations Centers. All three counties declared local emergencies and Napa and Lake Counties further declared a local public health emergency due to the toxic contaminants of the fire.

> *In the preceding paragraph, the Governor provides a much larger picture of how the county, the region and the state have recently suffered from other recent fires.*

The State of California, local governments, community-based organizations, and volunteers have taken extraordinary steps to respond to the Valley Fire. More than 4,500 firefighters were deployed to fight the fire, including California National Guard members. In addition, 35 law enforcement agencies and more than a dozen emergency managers from neighboring counties have been deployed to assist with the response through the State's Mutual Aid system. The California Department of Social Services is assisting with shelter operations and is providing accommodations to individuals with access and functional needs. The Department of Social Services is also coordinating with Lake County to assist in identifying long term solutions for displaced residents. The American Red Cross, Salvation Army, and Voluntary Organizations Active in Disaster are providing support to the community and disaster survivors. The University of California Davis's Medical Reserve Corps activated to care for large or burned animals.

Huge amounts of wreckage and debris must be expeditiously removed to eliminate the immediate: threat to lives, public health, and safety. Fast debris removal is also necessary to enable community rebuilding and economic recovery of impacted communities. It is estimated that there are more than 1,500 properties within a 100 square mile radius that require major debris removal, each averaging 100 tons of debris that must be removed. Debris hazards, including asbestos, heavy metals, structural debris, ash, concrete foundations, and metals pose a public health and safety concern and threaten the health of the local environment.

> *In the preceding paragraph, the Governor outlines some of the major problems that need to be faced to restore normalcy.*

While we have initiated preliminary damage assessments, many residents remain homeless or displaced and have not been available to provide specific insurance information to the assessment teams. We expect that some portion of the disaster survivors have insurance coverage: however, we anticipate many have no insurance coverage or are under-insured. According to American Community Survey, 61 percent of the total residents in Lake County have mortgages and presumably are required to have insurance coverage. The Department of Insurance identified 12 insurance carriers reporting a total of 1,268 property claims to date, of which 538 are considered a total loss. This number of total loss claims is less than half the number of destroyed homes. This information did not distinguish between owner-occupied and rental properties.

> *The Governor explains some of the issues with housing and insurance, which may be addressed if the President signs a declaration.*

Even for those residents who have insurance coverage, major challenges remain to recovering their lives. Lake County is isolated and generally rural and has very little available rental or temporary housing to accommodate homeowners during the rebuilding process. As a result. many of these residents will need to seek temporary housing a long distance from Lake County. This relocation will add undue hardship for families with schoolchildren or whose jobs are in the affected area. Additionally, some victims may permanently relocate outside of Lake County, further hindering the community's ability to recover.

Lake County's unemployment rate is 8.3 percent, which is well above the State's average, and the County has few major employers. Additionally, in the five most impacted cities in the County, one fourth to one-half of the residents rely on Cal Fresh, the State's food assistance program. Given the lack of available housing and hotels within Lake County, the Office of Emergency Services is establishing base camps to house first responders and emergency management personnel who are supporting local officials, freeing up the limited amount of temporary housing and hotels to shelter disaster survivors.

A breakdown of Individual Assistance Program demographics is presented directly below:

Table 14.1 Economic Statistics for Lake County, CA residents in 2015.

	Population*	Average of Persons Below Poverty Level*	Median Household Income	Percent Elderly (over 65 yrs*)	Percent Disabled**	Percent Pre-Disaster Unemployment***
National		15.4%	$53,046	14.5%	12.6%	5.4%
California	37,253,956	15.9%	$61,094	12.9%	10.6%	6.2%
Lake County	64,665	25%	$36,548	19.8%	19.4%	8.3%

*   2009–2013 U.S. Census
**   2004 U.S. Census
***   Bureau of Labor

> *With these two paragraphs and the table, the Governor outlines the day-to-day challenges which the county's population faces even in normal times and why this community would benefit from a Presidential disaster declaration.*

California has suffered multiple disasters in the past year, which have severely impacted its resources. In October 2014, California received a Presidential Major Disaster Declaration for the South Napa Earthquake and has received ten Fire Management Assistance Grants to battle fires in the state. I have also proclaimed state of emergencies for four storm events throughout the state in the past 12 months. Additionally, there have been 69 major fires and over 5,345 fire starts in California since January 2015. The acreage burned this year is nearly triple the acres burned in 2014. Presently, over 11,000 firefighters are battling five active fires that are burning nearly 400,000 acres, displaced thousands, and resulted in injuries and loss of life. To protect lives and property from this increased fire threat, State government has provided over $200 million in emergency funding for additional wildfire fighting in the last two years.

The past four years of extreme drought have also impacted the State's resources. The State has contributed more than three billion dollars in funds and capital investments responding to the impacts of the drought. These resources provide funding for immediate relief to impacted communities and established emergency programs to protect drinking water supplies, provide emergency food aid, fund emergency housing needs, support devastated farming communities, and protect endangered fish and other animals from the drought. In addition to increasing the State's firefighting capacity and budget, I have proclaimed four states of emergency for wildfires in just the last twelve months, including a statewide declaration of emergency on July 31, 2015, due to numerous fires that were raging simultaneously. Additionally, the drought conditions and the burned topography have created a dangerously high probability of floods, debris flow, and mudslides with the slightest amount of precipitation.

> *These two paragraphs lay out the recent history of disasters in the state and how these disasters have made the state's response more problematic and justify a Presidential disaster declaration.*

I have determined this incident is of such severity and magnitude that an effective response is beyond the capabilities of the state and affected local governments and supplemental federal assistance is necessary. I am specifically requesting all individual Assistance Programs for Lake County, including the Individuals and Households Program, Transitional Sheltering Assistance, Disaster Case Management, Disaster Unemployment Assistance, Crisis Counseling and Disaster Legal Services, Hazard Mitigation statewide; and any other Stafford Act disaster assistance programs that may be appropriate for the declared counties. I am also requesting U.S. Small Business Administration disaster loans and funds from the U.S. Department of Agriculture Emergency Loan Program.

> *In this paragraph, the Governor requests specific forms of Federal disaster assistance which will be needed to finish the response and move into the recovery process.*

I certify for this major disaster the State and local governments will assume all applicable non-federal shared costs as required by the Stafford Act. I have designated the Director of the California Governor's Office of Emergency Services, Mark Ghilarducci, as the Slate Coordinating Officer for this request. Mr. Ghilarducci will work with FEMA in continuing to assess damages and may provide more information or justification on my behalf.

> *In this paragraph the Governor turns to the affirmations which are Federally required and assigns a member of his staff as the State Coordinating Officer.*

Thank you very much for considering this request.

Sincerely,
Edmund G. Brown

Enclosures:

OMB No. I 660-0009/FEMA Form 010-0-13[1]
A: Individual Assistance
B: Public Assistance
C: Requirements for Other Federal Agency Programs
D: Historic and Current Snowfall Data

> *The endnote (1) at the end of the chapter, provides a URL to the FEMA form which may provide guidance useful in preparing a local disaster proclamation. Although the local agency may never see this form, it is important to know what information FEMA needs to justify and process this request.*

State Per-Capita Indicators for Receiving FEMA Public Assistance

To obtain Federal disaster assistance from FEMA and other Federal agencies, the state and its respective counties must show minimum levels of damage to initially qualify for a Presidential disaster declaration. These amounts vary from state to state based upon the state's population.

For the Federal Fiscal Year 2023–2024, the state per capita indicators are:

Table 14.2

Fiscal Year (FY)	Statewide Indicator	Countywide Indicator	Small Project Minimum	Large Project Threshold
2023	$1.84	$4.60	$3,900	$1,037,000*

* The $1,037,000 Large Project Threshold also applies to unobligated projects in incidents declared on or after March 13, 2020, per the Simplified Procedures Rule published August 3, 2022.

Wyoming, with a population of 580,000 people, has a minimum damage level of $1,076,200. California, on the other hand with a population of approximately 40,223,504 has a minimum damage threshold of $74,011,247.

Then, each damage-affected county within a respective state must meet a per-capita indicator of $4.60. These dollar amounts, $1.84 and $4.60, are annually adjusted by the Consumer Price Index at the beginning of each Federal Fiscal Year.

Therefore, it is possible that even when a state meets its per capita threshold of $1.84, one or more counties that suffer damage from a disaster might not qualify for the Presidential declaration if each of them does not have at least $4.60 per capita of damage.

So, at the county level of government, it is extremely critical in disasters that the county track and report ALL the damage it suffered to meet the $4.60 threshold. Each city and each other unit of local government, including all special districts, school districts, and eligible private non-profit organizations should be reporting their damage to their respective county.

Some special districts and school districts may have facilities in two or more counties. In these cases, these special/school districts must report the damage incurred to the DIFFERENT respective counties where the facility is physically located.

In some cases, a school may report their damages to the local board of education or to the school district main office, but neglect to also report to the appropriate county.

Therefore, the burden is on the county (if it wants the Presidential disaster declaration) to affirmatively contact each and every unit of local government and every otherwise eligible private non-profit (think Boys and Girls Clubs, food banks, battered women's shelters, etc.) to determine if they suffered damages and what the dollar loss estimates are. We will discuss this more in Chapter 20, The Local Damage Assessment Process.

The State Per Capita Indicators Are Only Part of the Story

In addition to the hard dollar amounts, FEMA may consider other factors in making a recommendation to the President for signing the disaster declaration.

"FEMA considers the following factors:

- The estimated costs of assistance;
- Localized impacts at county, city, and tribal government levels;
- Insurance coverage in force;
- Hazard mitigation measures that contributed to the reduction of damages;
- Recent multiple disasters within the prior 12 months at the state and local level; and
- Available assistance programs of OFAs. *(Other Federal Agencies)*

In addition to these primary factors, FEMA may consider other relevant factors."[2]

Case Study: Hurricane Isabel and Alexandria, VA

"After Hurricane Isabel in September 2003, the State of Virginia was granted an expedited major disaster declaration, and the City of Alexandria was designated eligible for Categories A and B along with many other applicants. A request was made for Categories C thru G that included Alexandria. Alexandria was not designated for C thru G because its estimated damages did not meet the per capita threshold of $2.77. The City was evidently not sent a denial letter. An appeal was filed by the City on June 22, 2004, claiming that it had sufficient damages to be eligible and that misinformation from FEMA resulted in the late appeal."[3]

Note: Alexandria, Virginia is an independent city not located within a county.

In this case, due to a technicality, i.e., no denial letter was sent, the city was granted the appeal, and was eligible for Public Assistance permanent work, Categories C through G.

So even in the very earliest hours of a disaster, the Finance Department of a local government agency or private non-profit will be called upon, ready or not, to participate in jump-starting the disaster response and recovery of the community. We shall see that being involved with the disaster proclamation process is only one of many other tasks which will require the specialized knowledge and expertise of finance professionals from the first hours of the disaster's onset. We will see later in the book how we can extract language from the local proclamation to explain and justify our requests for Project Worksheets and how to similarly justify the labor, equipment, and materials used for the disaster response and recovery.

Notes

1 https://www.fema.gov/sites/default/files/documents/fema_presidential-declaration-request_fema-form_010–0-13_2022.pdf
2 FEMA, Disaster Operations Legal Reference, Version 4.0, September 25, 2020, pp. 3–16 to 3–17.
3 https://www.fema.gov/appeal/permanent-work-late-appeal

15 Debris Monitoring and Debris Management

Debris Management: A Force to Be Reckoned With

In the Pantheon of disaster cost recovery, the most important demigods are financial accounting and recordkeeping; insurance and risk management; damage assessment; eligibility; procurement; and debris management. Each of these elements can have a significant positive impact in their own way on the local agency's ability to effectively recover from a disaster. Each of these elements, improperly handled, can produce a cataclysmic financial disaster.

Debris management is a complex and multi-layered process which, as with the other key elements, reverberates through these other key elements within the Public Assistance program. Full cost recovery for debris management depends on good financial accounting and record-keeping, proper handling of insurance issues, thorough damage assessment, documented legal responsibility for eligibility, and 2 CFR, Part 200-compliant procurement to be successful. We will also address other already-familiar topics, such as dealing with the environmental and historic issues which can also bedevil otherwise good debris management and debris monitoring plans.

First of all, there were two very useful and informative books published by FEMA on debris management and debris monitoring: the Public Assistance Debris Management Guide, FEMA-325, July 2007, and the Public Assistance Debris Monitoring Guide, FEMA 327, October 2010. Both excellent books, however, are now archived by FEMA. But for someone who needs to work on developing debris management or debris monitoring plans, or issue an RFP for the same contracts, these two books are well worth reading to get a good grounding in the processes involved. The remaining available current resources are the Public Assistance Program and Policy Guide, June 1, 2020, and the current edition of the Disaster Operations Legal Reference, Version 4.0, September 25, 2020.

This book will attempt to do this topic justice; however, please note that like some other chapters, debris management itself is quite worthy of its own book. My own debris management cost recovery instructor's training manual is 1½ inches thick.

There are many ways to approach debris management and debris monitoring, and we shall begin with the timelines.

FEMA classifies debris management as Category 'A' work, Emergency Work. Nominally, all emergency work must be completed within 6 months of the date of the Presidential Declaration, unless the state (the Recipient) or FEMA authorizes and extension of time. Should the local agency require a second time extension, that must be granted by FEMA.

The rationale for debris clearance is that the work is being done to reduce or eliminate an immediate threat to life safety, the public health, or a threat to improved property. FEMA expects the local agency to aggressively pursue the clean-up of disaster debris. If the local agency dawdles in

DOI: 10.4324/9781003487869-19

its clean-up efforts, FEMA may rationalize that this work isn't important to the local agency and deny additional time extensions. Later in the chapter, we will discuss having pre-disaster contracts in place to facilitate a rapid clean-up. Should the local agency have to take the time to issue an RFP (Request for Proposals) and then go through the normal processes of awarding sealed bid contracts, time will slip away, and it will appear as though the local agency is not in a hurry to complete the debris clean-up work.

The debris clean-up process may be further delayed when some of the debris is located in or near wetlands, navigable waterways, debris removed from private property, or where there are other environmental or historic preservation issues.

"Although debris removal is usually statutorily excluded from NEPA (*National Environmental Protection Act)* review, FEMA must ensure compliance with other Federal laws, regulations, and EOs (*Executive Orders*) prior to funding the work. Accordingly, FEMA must ensure that the Applicant's debris removal operations avoid impacts to such resources as floodplains, wetlands, federally listed threatened and endangered species and their critical habitats, and historic properties (including maritime or underwater archaeological resources if waterways are impacted). The Applicant must stage debris at a safe distance from property boundaries, surface water, floodplains, wetlands, structures, wells, and septic tanks with leach fields. Additional coordination may be necessary for debris removal from waterways, stump removal, and the use of fill. The Applicant should contact the applicable Federal, State, Territorial, and Tribal regulatory agencies to ensure compliance with requirements and permits for debris-related operations. Upon completion of debris removal and disposal, site remediation may be necessary at staging sites and other impacted areas."[1]

Although debris management is excluded from a NEPA review, there are many other Federal, state, and potentially local regulations which require close attention to and compliance with all other applicable regulations. Violations of any of these may result in a FEMA deobligation of funds.

Debris Management and Debris Monitoring Planning

There are few areas within the Public Assistance program more complicated than debris management and debris monitoring. Debris happens with every disaster and is often one of the most obvious signs of that disaster. As the reader will see in this chapter, the eligibility of debris is a very fragile commodity and can be easily forfeited for many different reasons, some of which have nothing to do with the debris itself. Having pre-disaster debris management and monitoring plans, along with pre-disaster contracts for both operations, is critical to the financial recovery of the local agency. Without these plans and contracts, debris is truly a daunting process and a fiscally life-threatening event.

Therefore, beyond the importance of having an Emergency Operations Plan, there are few if any other plans (except disaster cost recovery plans) more important than a debris management plan and a companion debris monitoring plan. Debris plans, for management and monitoring, cannot be effectively developed in isolation in the local agency, regardless of the agency size. Not all public agencies have the same departments, nor do they all provide the same services. But to the maximum extent possible, debris should be an "all-hands" evolution. Effective debris management will involve the active and consistent best efforts of many different players within the local agency regardless of its size and how many (or how few) employees are available to work on it.

Because debris is such an immediate and overwhelming aspect of almost every declared disaster, it will be one of the most important things upon which the community will judge its elected officials and its employees. However, without an effective set of debris plans, the debris will linger longer and cost far more than would otherwise be necessary with good working plans.

The following study cites the importance and cost benefits of having a pre-disaster debris management plan. "Disaster debris management operations make up a significant portion of recovery expenses. The following study aims to examine how the presence of a plan makes disaster debris management effective and efficient. Ninety-five counties in the United States who received major disaster declarations between 2012 and 2015 were surveyed to examine the quality of their debris management processes. Forty-nine of these counties had debris management plans while forty-six did not. Statistical tests were conducted to address discrepancies in the effectiveness and efficiency of the debris management processes between the two groups. Such tests suggest that counties with pre-disaster debris management plans were more effective. These counties recycled almost twice as much disaster debris as counties without plans and received over three times as much Public Assistance from the Federal Emergency Management Agency (FEMA). Counties with plans also reported higher levels of perceived preparedness for future debris challenges than counties without plans. Overall, counties with pre-disaster debris management plans were partially more efficient than counties without plans. They removed more cubic yards of debris per day, but there were no statistically significant differences between the two groups in the volume of debris removed per dollar."[2]

"On average, counties with debris management plans recycled 20.56% more debris than counties without debris management plans."[3]

"Furthermore, the mean of FEMA PA funding is $109,111,253.90 more for counties with debris management plans than it is for counties without them."[4]

Faster clean-up, more money, more recycling, what's not to like?

Debris Management Is a Team Sport

Following is a table showing various typical city/county departments and their potential role(s) in debris management and debris monitoring.

Debris Management is an "All-Hands" function for many local agencies. All these relationships depend on the size and structure of the local government. Many agencies will not have some of these functions, while a limited number of agencies will have additional functions not listed here.

Developing a good working debris management plan takes time, and it should; there are complex issues to be dealt with, and a faulty debris plan may be no better than no plan at the end of the day.

There are some debris management firms which will prepare a debris management plan under contract. However, there are some things to be aware of in this regard:

1) If a contractor develops a debris management plan for a local agency, they may be prohibited under 2 CFR, Part 200 from bidding on the contract.
2) The contractor may intentionally insert some loopholes which, if left undiscovered, could result in massive change orders once the contract is activated.
3) I have seen some debris plans, so-called "Concept of Operations" plans, which are perfectly useless for actually cleaning up and disposing of debris.
4) Debris management or monitoring plans will be very agency-specific regarding the types of potential disaster threats the community faces and the classes of debris which will need to be dealt with; therefore, a generic or one-size-fits-all plan will probably be quite useless when a disaster occurs.

Table 15.1

Airport	In some communities, airports are one of the few public facilities with large tracts of open acreage which can be used for a Temporary Debris Reduction Site (TDRS).
Animal Control	Unfortunately, pets are victims too. They and feral creatures will need to be removed.
Building & Safety Department	Some structures in the jurisdiction may have to be demolished.
Business Licenses	There may be dozens or even hundreds of sub-contractors working on the debris clean-up.
City Attorney, County Counsel	There will be permits to be gotten and contracts to review.
City/County Auditor	Debris contractor invoices should be audited before payment. They will, under the best of circumstances, contain many errors.
City Manager, County Judge, Parish President, etc.	The Buck Stops Here.
Code Enforcement	There may be a need to involve code enforcement officers for certain aspects of private property clean-up.
Economic Development	Failure to quickly clean up after the disaster will have a negative impact on businesses.
Emergency Management	The emergency manager will be called upon for expertise which they may or may not have relative to debris clean-up.
Environmental Issues	Environmental issues will be front and center with FEMA and should be with the local agency as well.
Finance Department	Finance will face a heavy workload to manage all the documentation, the invoices, and the accounts payable functions.
Geographic Information Systems (GIS)	Maps of debris locations and the disaster (storm's) path.
Harbor, Port, or Marina	If the local agency has any "water" functions, they will be deep in the soup, coordinating with Federal and state agencies involved in the clean-up.
Health & Human Services Municipal Health Services	Environmental health issues will have to be addressed before operations begin, and continuously during operations, and again at final closure of the Temporary Debris Reduction Site(s) (TDRS).
Historic Preservation	Temporary Debris Reduction Sites cannot be located on or near a historic site without extensive consultations and permitting.
Human Resources	The agency may need to hire additional staff just for debris operations.
Mayor & City Council	Once again, The Buck Stops Here. The elected officials will be harshly judged if the debris clean-up struggles.
Parks & Recreation	Unfortunately, in some densely populated cities and towns, parks do offer large open space areas where a Temporary Debris Reduction Site may be located.
Planning/Community Development	Official notices regarding the debris clean-up will have to be mailed to residents when they are not living in their home of record. Residents will also have to sign and file with the local agency a Right-of-Entry document, which indemnifies all levels of government from damage claims during the clean-up.
Police	A very large Temporary Debris Reduction Site may require some level of traffic control in the interest of public safety.
Public Information Officer (PIO)	This individual will be tasked with one of the most demanding jobs associated with debris clean-up, i.e., presenting the agency's debris messages to the public and the media. The PIO will be charged with attempting to manage public expectations, which will almost always be greater than any possible reality.

(Continued)

Table 5.7 (Continued)

Public Transit	Normal transit routes may have to be shifted depending on where the Temporary Debris Reduction Sites are located.
Public Utilities, (Water, Sewer, etc.)	The Temporary Debris Reduction Site will probably need water for operations. Depending on where the site is located, erosion control and site drainage may also be needed.
Public Works	In many jurisdictions, Public Works will be the department in charge of the entire debris clean-up operations, leaning heavily on other departments for support.
Purchasing/Procurement	The debris management and monitoring contracts are the heart and soul of the disaster clean-up.
Risk Management	If Private Property Debris Removal (PPDR) is permitted by FEMA, then every homeowner will have to be contacted for their debris insurance coverage information.
Roads and Bridges	There will very likely be damage caused to local roads from all the heavy trucks and equipment operating on streets that were never designed for that kind of heavy traffic. Documentation of the good condition of the roads before the disaster is absolutely necessary for filing a claim for such damage.
Technology & Communications	Depending on who is doing the debris monitoring, Wi-Fi support may be necessary. It may be provided by the contractor, but that must be addressed in the initial contract.
Towing & Lien Sales	Abandoned vehicles and vessels may need to be stored and possibly sold if they remain unclaimed.
Utility Billing	Depending on the local agency, Utility Billing might also be involved in obtaining the Right-of-Entry waivers and debris clean-up insurance claims.
Departments and employees not otherwise listed	Should the local agency decide to do its own debris monitoring, many employees will have to be press-ganged into helping staff all the required monitoring positions.

When developing a debris management or monitoring plan, it is important to note that some debris is not eligible for FEMA funding, and certain costs almost always arise during the debris clean-up which are not eligible.

A Useful Resource

The U.S. Environmental Protection Agency (EPA) publishes a useful and comprehensive guide to disaster debris planning. It obviously has an environmental tilt, but it does have an extensive bibliography and links to other plans and planning resources. It can be found at: https://www.epa.gov/sites/default/files/2019-04/documents/final_pndd_guidance_0.pdf.

Some Good News, Some Bad News

The good news is that a search of the internet will yield many debris management plans from state and local agencies across the country, which may be used as starting points for developing a debris plan for other local agencies.

The bad news is the same. There are many debris plans available from agencies across the country, which may or may not share the same hazards and risks as other agencies. Those other agencies may not have the same available resources, including the staff and departments featured in these internet-available plans.

Some years ago, I reviewed a debris management plan for a Northern California agency, which had been recently adopted by its city council. To say that it was a half-baked plan would be generous in the extreme. There were many problems, but the standout red-flag warning was that in this plan for a California agency were references to Pennsylvania. Obviously, the creator of that plan could not even do a proper search and replace to eliminate such a glaring warning that the plan in question was probably deeply flawed and most likely quite useless in a real debris event.

When one does an internet search for complex planning documents, such as a debris management plan, often the results are worth the amount paid. Exactly worth nothing. In conducting internet-based research for debris management plans, I found plans of approximately 100 pages through 350 pages. Clearly, some plans offer more than others. Many plans contain a hefty dose of now-archived FEMA references, and at least one plan offered HGAC (Houston Galveston Area Council of Governments) as a viable resource for debris contractors. Later in this chapter, we will see how at least one county in Texas had an expensive adverse audit finding precisely because they used HGAC as a procurement resource.

Ineligible: Construction and Demolition Debris

Generally, building material debris resulting from the repair or reconstruction of eligible facilities is not FEMA-eligible. The hauling and disposal of such debris should be covered under the terms of the contracts for the building repair work. If the repairs are done by the local agency's own personnel, then the load documentation and receipts for the disposal must be kept for inclusion in the "Scope of Work" approved by FEMA.

If the local agency is approved for private property debris removal, the public must be advised that any repair or reconstruction debris must not be mixed with the other disaster debris. If homes are destroyed by the disaster, that debris is of course eligible. The problem comes when a FEMA debris monitor documents instances of homeowners mixing obviously-new building material scraps with disaster-caused debris. This may give FEMA the justification it needs to de-obligate previously approved private property debris removal.

Ineligible Debris-Related Costs

Some of the following costs are quite likely to arise, but for the most part they are not FEMA eligible.

- Loss of landfill service life: The service life of a landfill is often foreshortened by years due to the extraordinary influx of disaster debris.
- Certain tipping fees: "Landfill tipping fees usually include fixed and variable costs, along with special taxes or fees assessed by the jurisdiction in which the landfill is located. Eligible tipping fee costs are limited to the variable and fixed costs that are directly related to landfill operations, such as recycling tax. The components of tipping fees that are not directly related to landfill operations, such as special taxes or fees related to other government services or public infrastructure, are ineligible as part of the tipping fee."[5]
- Waived dump fees for residents & businesses: If the local agency waives its normal and customary fees for residents (and/or businesses) who are cleaning up their own properties, in the absence of private property debris removal approval from FEMA, these costs are not eligible expenses.
- Increased operating costs (i.e., extra dump hours, fuel costs, etc.): Should the local landfill extend its operating hours, FEMA treats these as increased operating expenses and therefore ineligible costs.
- "Debris from an eligible applicant's unimproved property or undeveloped land"[6];

- "Debris from a facility that is not eligible for funding under the Public Assistance program, such as a Private Non-profit cemetery or Private Non-profit golf course or"[7];
- "Debris from federal lands or facilities that are the authority of another federal agency or department."[8]
- Road damage by debris haulers: This is often claimed but almost never granted. As previously mentioned, the heavy trucks and equipment used for debris clearance will tear up the local roads, which weren't designed for the intense traffic from debris operations. While additional damage caused by permitted work is eligible, the problem is that very few jurisdictions can prove that their streets and roads were in excellent condition prior to the disaster. Although the debris operations may have contributed to the road damage, it is almost never the sole cause of road damage; therefore the damage is ineligible.

Debris-Related Road Damage Denied

This case is from Texas, following Hurricane Rita in 2005: "Jefferson County, Texas was struck by Hurricane Rita on September 23, 2005. After the hurricane, the Applicant removed and disposed of an estimated 2,500,000 cubic yards of vegetative and other debris. The clean-up and removal were accomplished, in part, with the use of dump trucks, front end loaders, bulldozers and other heavy equipment. As part of its debris management plan, the Applicant established three temporary debris collection sites. The largest of the debris collection sites was established at the Beaumont Municipal Airport located at 455 Keith Road, Beaumont, Texas 77713. Seven roads, Boyt, Lawhorn, Johnson, Labelle, Willis, South League and Steinhagen, served as major thoroughfares to and from the debris collection sites. Each of the identified roads is a county road, built and maintained according to county specifications and standards. The Applicant claims that the pooling of water from the hurricane, combined with the use of heavy trucks and equipment to remove the debris from the roads and abutting ditches and the use of heavy equipment to transport the debris over county roads to the debris collection sites resulted in damage to the identified roads. The Applicant has submitted seven PWs for damage caused to the county roads leading to the debris collection sites. The total amount claimed for the seven PWs is $173,162. A review of the PWs reveals that the actual amount at issue is $197,337. At the request of the Applicant, two FEMA/State inspector teams visited the sites and reviewed the claimed road damages. Both teams found the claimed damages were not disaster-related and therefore were ineligible. FEMA requested additional documentation, including road maintenance records, to support the appeal. The Regional Administrator denied the first appeal because the Applicant did not provide additional information or documentation sufficient to support its claim."[9]

Delayed Debris Clean-Up May Be Costly

This case comes from Iowa, where the county government was delayed in completing its debris clean-up. "From June 1 through August 31, 2010, Warren County Secondary Roads (Applicant) experienced severe storms, tornadoes, and flooding which deposited silt on Arthur Street. On October 18, 2010, FEMA obligated Version 0 for $119,964 to remove silt from the road and ditches. **The emergency work completion deadline was January 29, 2011, but the Applicant did not start work until August 24, 2011 and completed work on January 9, 2012.** The Applicant submitted a time extension request on December 27, 2011, but it was misplaced by the Grantee. The Applicant submitted another time extension request on February 8, 2013, which was denied by Region VII. The Applicant requested a Large Project Closeout for $29,166 in actual debris removal costs on September 23, 2013."[10] (Emphasis Added)

There was apparently a process breakdown at some point; on appeal, the county stated: "The quarterly report indicated that the PW (*Project Worksheet*) was Category C and listed the work completion deadline as the permanent work deadline instead of the emergency work deadline."[11]

Further delays were caused because: "The Applicant's second appeal letter, dated September 27, 2013, reiterates the first appeal and adds that a <u>Right of Entry (*ROE*) required for the disposal of the silt on private property took 'a couple of months' to obtain.</u>"[12] (Emphasis Added)

This county, located in south-central Iowa, is a smaller county with approximately 52,000 residents and no doubt with limited financial resources. However, the county's delay in promptly cleaning up the debris sent an unwitting back-channel message to FEMA: "This debris isn't a bad problem, or we would have cleaned it up sooner." When FEMA provides funding for emergency work, it expects that the "emergency" work will be treated as though it was a true emergency that presented an immediate threat to life safety, the public health, or improved property.

Debris Qualifications

FEMA defines debris removal to be in the public interest when necessary to:

- "Eliminate an immediate threat to lives, public health, and safety;
- Eliminate immediate threats of significant damage to improved public or private property;
- Ensure the economic recovery of the affected community to the benefit of the community at large; or
- Mitigate the risk to life and property by removing substantially damaged structures and associated appurtenances as needed to convert property acquired using FEMA hazard mitigation program funds to uses compatible with open space, recreation, or wetlands management practices."[13]

To qualify and document the need for debris clearance, there must be at least one of three conditions met:

- "A determination by the state, county, or municipal government's public health authority or other public entity that has legal authority to make a determination that disaster-generated debris on private property constitutes an immediate threat to life, public health, and safety, or is necessary to ensure the economic recovery of the community; or
- If a threat to improved property, the basis of the determination that the removal of disaster-generated debris costs less than the cost of potential damage to the improved property; or
- If necessary, for economic recovery, the basis of the determination by the state, county, or municipal government that the removal of debris is necessary to ensure economic recovery of the affected community to the benefit of the community at large."[14]

Furthermore, the debris removal must meet the general eligibility requirements:

- "The debris must have been generated by the major disaster event;
- The debris must be located within a designated disaster area on an eligible applicant's improved property or rights-of-way; and
- The debris removal must be the legal responsibility of the applicant."[15]

Additionally, the debris must not be the result of deterioration, deferred maintenance, negligence, or a failure to take appropriate precautions to prevent further damage, i.e., using a plastic tarp to prevent rainfall from further damaging a structure with disaster-caused roof damage.

Fortunately, claims of pre-existing root causes for debris are seldom raised, unlike when streets and roads or facilities are damage-claimed.

There is an idiosyncratic twist for some disaster debris clean-up. "Extracting water and clearing mud, silt, or other accumulated debris from eligible facilities if the work is conducted expeditiously for the purpose of addressing an immediate threat (if the work is only necessary to restore the facility, it is Permanent Work, not Emergency Work)."[16]

Therefore, regardless of whether the clean-up for permanent work is done by force account labor or even volunteers, the workers' time and equipment should be tracked separately from other Category A debris clearance work done under contract.

Another nuance which is important to FEMA, and therefore should be important to the local agency is the difference between "debris clearance" and "debris removal." "Debris Clearance is the clearance of debris to allow passage only. It does not include hauling or disposing of the debris. Debris clearance is often referred to as 'cut and toss' or '(*cut and push.)*' Debris Removal includes hauling and disposing of debris at a temporary or final disposal site."[17]

Emergency Access Debris Clearance

When the debris blocks public safety access routes, i.e., access for police, fire, and emergency medical response, then emergency debris clearance is eligible, but only to the extent necessary to provide emergency access. This may include some private roads. However, the local agency must submit thorough documentation of the debris clearance work and provide the necessary rights-of-entry waivers for private property.

Documentation Requirements

At a minimum, the local agency needs to provide complete documentation regarding the debris for which it will claim reimbursement, including the following:

- "Estimated debris quantities by type (required for all uncompleted work);
- Photographs of debris impacts, if available; *(Really Important)*
- Location of temporary reduction sites and permanent disposal sites (required);
- Copies of permits for reduction and disposal sites (required);
- Quantities of debris removed, reduced, disposed, and recycled (by type) with load tickets to support quantities (required if contracted, FEMA reviews a representative sample);
- Tower logs (required if contracted, FEMA reviews a representative sample);
- Documentation to substantiate legal responsibility (required);
- The basis of the immediate threat determination (required); *(by the local or state public health officer)*
- Location(s) of debris (required); and
- Documentation to substantiate the debris was deposited by the incident and was not pre-existing (e.g., waterway soundings that show pre-and post-incident levels) (required)."[18]

Note that all these items are required, or required if requested, which really means "Required, unless the money isn't important."

GIS (Geographic Information Systems) to the Rescue

If the local agency has GIS capabilities, or a GIS department, these people will need to be fully integrated into the entire disaster response and recovery effort, and especially integrated into the debris management function. Under most circumstances, the availability of GIS will be a huge step in documenting the debris problem, especially when supported by either still or video images.

I have in my files a copy of an email from a FEMA staffer requesting the geolocation of 800 burned trees prior to removal for debris clearance. GIS, if the local agency has it, will play a major role in disaster cost recovery.

Note that random surveys to find debris are not an eligible expense; however, when debris is found that portion of the debris survey can be eligible, so detailed recordkeeping is important.

GIS maps should identify the overall area of debris impact, as well as local areas of intense concentration of debris. Vehicles and vessels should also be mapped, since these typically have a higher unit cost for removal.

Debris-Related Insurance Issues

FEMA is constantly on the alert for anything that has the slightest whiff of a "duplication of benefits," and that includes debris operations.

This primarily presents an issue when the local jurisdiction is granted approval for private property debris removal (PPDR). Some homeowners insurance policies will have coverage for the removal of disaster debris. When this is the case, then the local agency must make good-faith efforts to recover the insurance payments and provide FEMA with a credit for the funds recovered from homeowners.

This process of collecting insurance proceeds from people whose homes and lives have been destroyed will surely not be popular with the locals; however, it must be done, or FEMA will impute a percentage of insured homes and make that deduction from what it would otherwise reimburse the local agency.

Generally, for businesses, FEMA's position is that businesses, including apartments, rental homes, and privately held mobile home parks, will carry debris insurance and are therefore not eligible for FEMA funding. However, FEMA does rarely approve very limited commercial property debris removal in the most extreme cases.

Commercial Property Debris Removal

"On June 27, 2007, heavy rain caused flooding throughout the city of Marble Falls, Texas. FEMA prepared PW 3385 to cover the Applicant's debris removal costs. One aspect of the debris removal project involved collecting debris in roll-off containers. FEMA denied \$62,585 for the cost of containers that the Applicant placed on private commercial properties because debris removal from private commercial property is generally not eligible for reimbursement. FEMA also denied \$19,898 profit for the Applicant's debris removal contractor. FEMA determined that the Applicant did not submit sufficient information to demonstrate that the contractor's unit prices did not include profit."[19]

First Appeal

"The Applicant filed its first appeal on January 31, 2008. The Applicant contracted with its pre-disaster garbage collection contractor to remove debris caused by the major disaster. The Applicant explained that it opted to place containers throughout heavily impacted parts of the city so volunteers and the public could dump debris into the containers. The Applicant acknowledged that 'some business generated debris was included within total volumes (but) no containers were placed for the sole benefit of the business venture(s). . . .' The Applicant asserted that because the cost of the containers was reasonable and was a necessary part of the debris removal activities, it is eligible for FEMA reimbursement. The Applicant also argued that $19,898 of the invoice it received from its contractor covered the contractor's profit and overhead; therefore, the costs are eligible for FEMA reimbursement. On March 28, 2008, the Regional Administrator denied the appeal because the Applicant was not eligible for the cost to remove debris from private commercial property. In addition, the Regional Administrator denied the Applicant's request for reimbursement of its contractor's profit and overhead because unit prices included in the contract may already reflect a profit mark-up."[20]

Second Appeal

"The Applicant argues that because it had completed its debris removal activities before it became eligible for financial assistance from FEMA, it was not aware of the requirement for FEMA to approve in advance debris removal from private property and FEMA should not penalize it for its failure to comply with the advance approval policy."[21] (Emphasis Added)

"The Applicant placed roll-off containers throughout the community to allow residents to remove disaster-related debris from their homes and properties. FEMA reimbursed the Applicant the cost to remove debris that citizens placed in roll-off containers that were located on public property. **However, the Applicant placed roll-off containers on private commercial properties that were not immediately adjacent to residential areas. It appears that the roll-off containers that were placed on private commercial property were for the use of the commercial property owners.**"[22] (Emphasis Added)

This case illustrates still another wildcard in the disaster cost recovery process. The local agency does work, especially debris clean-up and other emergency protective measures BEFORE the President signs the disaster declaration. The big question of "will there be any Federal assistance?" is yet unanswered when the work is begun, and sometimes the work will be completed and paid for before the Presidential disaster declaration is signed. Do Federal rules apply in these cases? Generally, YES. Therefore, the safest play from a cost recovery perspective is to treat all disasters as potential Federally declared disasters. This also applies to the tracking of force account labor and the equipment and materials that may be used to do the work. Play it safe and document and follow all the relevant rules every time, Presidential declaration or not.

The Initial Paperwork . . . Don't Worry . . . There's Lots More Paperwork Later

There are many reasons debris management costs may be denied or deobligated, but perhaps the most frequent reason cited is a lack of proper documentation. Even in a relatively small disaster, debris management work will cause the creation of thousands of documents. Collecting, filing, and tracking of these thousands of documents will take time and cost money, not all of which is reimbursable by FEMA. Yet without these critical documents, FEMA will reduce or eliminate payments for debris management costs.

To put this into perspective, if there is a disaster which generates one million cubic yards of debris, and the carrying capacity of a truck is 15 cubic yards, then clearing the debris will require 66,667 truck trips if all the debris is the same. If the debris is a mix of different classes of debris, then it is likely there will be more truck trips. This means that there will be about 70,000 trip tickets, one for each load transported from the pick-up site to the temporary debris reduction site (TDRS) or the landfill for final disposal. There will also be nearly 3,000 pages of "Tower Logs," plus hundreds or thousands of "Roving Monitor Logs." With all this paper, what could possibly go wrong?

The Load Ticket

This one-page form is linked in the Appendix, Form 47.

<u>This is a FEMA form, and its use is required for every load picked up and hauled.</u> Notice the sequential numbering at the top right of the form. This form has only a couple of optional fields (in some cases we may not need the GPS coordinates), but most are required for proper load documentation.

Many, if not most, of the firms providing debris monitoring services may have their own proprietary electronic system, including the forms. However, if the local agency plans to use its own force account labor, just the logistics of printing and distributing all the forms will be a challenge. Consider the fact that any load hauled without a debris ticket is an ineligible load.

The Truck Certification Form

This two-page form is linked in the Appendix, Form 48.

<u>This is a FEMA form, and its use is required for every contractor's (or sub-contractor's) truck hauling debris.</u> There may be hundreds of these vehicles of various sizes and configurations. Some will have their own claw cranes for loading. Some will have sideboards, and some will not. Some will have solid tail gates, and some will not. Furthermore, FEMA will periodically recertify some of the trucks to ensure that the truck operators are not gaming the system. For instance, once their truck is first certified, a driver may then install a false bottom which will reduce their load capacity and trip cycle time, which will make them more money at the expense of the local agency and FEMA. The truck placard issued at the time of certification must always be posted during operations.

Figure 15.1 A depiction of the type of heavy equipment which will be involved in the debris clean-up process.

The Tower Monitor Log

This one-page form is linked in the Appendix, Form 49.

This is a FEMA form, and its use is required at either the TDRS (Temporary Debris Reduction Site) or the landfill, where the debris contractor will set up a high platform where the tower monitor works. The job of the tower monitor is to inspect every truckload entering the site to determine what percentage of a full load the truck is carrying. This is a continuous full-time job, as each truck must be logged in with a percentage of capacity logged in for each truck. Hand-loaded trucks have a lower percentage of capacity rating than mechanically-loaded trucks. Trucks without sideboards or solid tail gates are rated at a lower percentage of rated capacity.

The Roving Monitor Report Form

This one-page form is linked in the Appendix, Form 50.

This is a FEMA form, and its use is required. For debris removal costs to be FEMA-eligible, the local agency must provide continuous monitoring of the debris clean-up activities, both at the sites where the debris is collected and loaded, and at the TDRS (Temporary Debris Reduction Sites) or landfill site(s). The purpose is to affirmatively account for every load of debris collected, hauled, and processed before final disposal. Absent these forms, FEMA cannot determine if the money paid for the work done is reasonable.

The Daily Issue Log

This one-page form is linked in the Appendix, Form 51.

This is a FEMA form, and its use is required. Assume that there will be issues to be resolved; FEMA does. The work of debris clearance is a large, multifaceted, environmentally significant operation being performed by local agency staff members, who in most cases are inexperienced in massive debris management operations. On the other hand, the contractors are professionals out to make a buck any way they can, and they do so with no remorse. There are so many different competing agendas in debris management that some things must inevitably go wrong.

Also understand that FEMA is closely watching the debris operations and will have its own professional monitors continuously on site checking on both the local agency monitors or the professional monitors and the contractors. The job of the FEMA monitors is not to tell the local agency about problems. Their job is to report back to FEMA that there are problems. Based upon their own in-house monitor's reports, FEMA will then have a reasonable basis for denying some, if not all, of the agency's funding for debris management.

Monitoring Appeals Case

This is an older but still current appeals case from Oklahoma. It has multiple issues, but for the moment we will only address the monitor-related problems. "McCurtain County is located in southeastern Oklahoma, bordering the state of Arkansas on the east and the state of Texas on the south. The county covers approximately 1,900 square miles and has a population of 33,400 (2000 census). Weyerhaeuser, a wood products company, is the largest employer in the County. The Ice Storm of December 2000 hit McCurtain County particularly hard. The president declared a major disaster for Oklahoma on January 5, 2001, making federal funds available to assist State and local officials with debris removal operations. The Federal share for this disaster was initially 75% but increased to 100% on March 13, 2001. The 100% Federal cost share was effective until July 6,

2001. If debris operations were conducted beyond July 6, 2001, the Federal cost share would revert back to 75%. McCurtain County awarded a contract to DRC to remove and dispose of eligible debris at $12.40 per cubic yard on January 18, 2001. DRC contracted with a number of local haulers to accomplish much of the work. Debris removal operations were conducted from January 18, 2001, to July 6, 2001. The County requested $13,969,852 for debris removal activities. FEMA approved $12,182,900. The amount in dispute was $1,786,952."[23]

"The State and FEMA conducted an Applicants Briefing for McCurtain County applicants on January 10, 2001. FEMA conducted a Kick-off Meeting (*now the Recovery Scoping Meeting or RSM*) with County Commissioners on January 29, 2001. At the meeting, FEMA stressed that only debris on public rights-of-way was eligible, that debris on private property was not eligible for reimbursement, and that the County had to monitor all contractor crews."[24] (Emphasis Added)

"The Public Assistance Coordinator (PAC) conducted a follow-up meeting with the County Commissioners on February 5, 2001, after a few days of monitoring the debris removal operations. The purpose of the meeting was to reiterate eligibility guidelines and the need for monitoring and to develop a strategy for debris removal operations."[25]

"The County published the McCurtain County Commission Guidelines for the Removal of Eligible Ice Storm Debris (Guidelines) on February 22, 2001. The Guidelines included debris eligibility requirements and the County inspector's (monitors) responsibilities."[26]

"The County and FEMA agreed in March that both would provide monitors for each work crew to ensure that only eligible debris was removed. Most of FEMA monitors were equipped with global positioning systems and digital cameras to document debris removal activities. Starting in March, FEMA and County officials met daily to assign work crews and monitors throughout the County."[27] (Emphasis Added)

"Early in the debris removal process FEMA monitors observed contractors removing debris from outside the County rights-of-way, from private property, and removing otherwise ineligible debris. Pursuant to the Guidelines, FEMA monitors did not direct any of the contractors efforts. When the FEMA monitors observed contractors removing ineligible debris, they would document the location where the activity was performed, and the estimated amount of the ineligible debris removed in their daily reports. They would inform the County monitors and the PAC (Public Assistance Coordinator) assigned to the County, who then would inform the County Commissioners."[28] (Emphasis Added)

"In its second appeal, the County comments on the qualifications of FEMA monitors and how the monitoring was conducted. The County also states, since FEMA monitors refused to interact with County monitors, they sat in their vehicles day after day for months watching and allowing the County to continue in a manner that was unacceptable to them; all the while writing secret reports deobligating the activities of the county monitors."[29] (Emphasis Added)

The appeal case continues: "The information in our files does not support these statements. FEMA monitors documented ineligible debris removal activities (clear cutting rights-of-way and removing debris from private property) as early as January 30, 2001. This information was routinely shared with State and County officials, including County Commissioners. In addition, FEMA provided comprehensive set of data to the State on December 4, 2001, that described in detail the reasons for denying some of the County's claims for reimbursement."[30]

It is important to understand that the FEMA monitors are there to protect the interests of the Federal government, not the local agency. It is the job of the local agency to protect its own interests and ensure that its debris monitors, whether contract or force account labor, are well trained and consistently tracking debris clean-up operations and providing accurate documentation of the work done. In no other way will the costs for debris management be eligible.

Upselling the Debris Clearance Work

The local agency must understand that both the prime debris contractor and its sub-contractors are aggressively looking for opportunities to "upsell." Every hauler is potentially looking for more debris to haul; this is how they make money. The drivers don't care if a debris pile is on private property, commercial property, or somewhere else; if they haul it, they get paid more. This puts a burden on the local agency to closely monitor where the trucks are working and to ensure that only FEMA-approved debris from FEMA-approved areas is picked up and hauled. FEMA most will likely deny or deobligate any funding for ineligible debris, but the local agency will still have to pay for it out of its own funds.

The In-House Paperwork and Justification for Debris Clean-Up

Once the crisis phase of the disaster has passed and the clean-up needs to begin, the local agency must create a paper trail to document and justify the need for the debris clean-up itself. If the presence of the debris presents a threat to life safety and/or the public health, the local public health officer should make a finding that life safety and/or the public health is endangered by the debris. It is important that this finding be written and signed by the Public Health Officer, not by a deputy or any other local government official. This is particularly true if the local agency is applying for debris clearance of private property.

FEMA takes the life safety/public health aspects of debris clearance quite seriously. The following article came out of the Camp Fire, which destroyed the Town of Paradise and over 14,000 homes in 2018.

"Board Gets Bombshell: Supes Learn FEMA Won't Let Residents Live on Burned-out Land

Residents will no longer be able to live on properties with burned structures until they are cleared. All the folks who've moved into trailers on their burned-out properties since the Camp Fire will very likely – and likely very soon – be told they must move. Again. It's not a pleasant prospect, but the consequences could be dire. 'I hate to be the messenger on this after everything . . .' County Chief Administrative Officer Shari McCracken informed the Board of Supervisors late in Tuesday's regular meeting (Jan. 29). 'FEMA has said we are not eligible as a county, nor is the town [of Paradise], for debris removal [money] if we allow people to live on properties with structural fire debris on it.' A hush came over the room as audience members and supervisors alike exchanged looks of confusion. The board had just spent nearly two hours discussing a set of ordinances regarding emergency, short-term shelter. Public comments had been heard. After two of those speakers questioned being denied temporary power permits in recent days, Supervisor Bill Connelly asked staff to explain. That's when McCracken dropped the bombshell that quieted the room. 'FEMA, in re-evaluating our request for public assistance for debris removal, has determined that the town's ordinance and the county's ordinance could make us ineligible for the $1.7 billion in debris removal money,' she explained. 'The only way FEMA can pay for debris removal is if there are imminent health risks. We negate saying it's imminent if people are living there.' The announcement made the public's pleas earlier in the meeting for faster action more relevant and more urgent, prompting the board to shift gears before taking a vote to ease restrictions on ag (*agricultural*) land and types of structures that will be allowed."[31]

The finding of an immediate public health threat by the local public health officer is of critical importance.

Yes, More Paperwork, Much More

Debris management is an environmental nightmare, in so many ways. Even when there are no pre-existing environmental or historic preservation issues at hand, there are the work-specific environmental challenges. Debris sitting on the ground is a problem. As the debris is collected and loaded, it will create dust, noise, and exhaust pollution from the equipment used. At the Temporary Debris Reduction Site (TDRS) or landfill, there is more of the same: dust, noise, equipment exhaust fumes. No one wants to live near a TDRS, which may require, depending on the volume and composition of the debris mix, 10 to 100 acres of open land. In heavily urbanized regions, there will be very few suitable locations where a TDRS can be located. Otherwise, the local agency will face substantially longer, and more costly, haul routes to a TDRS location where there are few neighbors to raise hell with local officials for putting the TDRS in their backyard.

Any and all of the environmental and historic preservation issues which are present, either pre-existing or situational, will require planning and permits for operations from the appropriate local, state, and Federal agencies. This is planning and permitting that takes time and costs money. And when debris is collected and hauled before the necessary permits have been issued, that same debris may become ineligible. Often the local agency is between the proverbial rock and the hard spot. Clean up the debris now, knowing that the costs may be ineligible, or leave it lying around and end up putting up with the valid complaints of the citizenry. Of course, pre-planning and issuing pre-event contracts is the one alternative which will reduce or eliminate many of these problems.

Temporary Debris Reduction Sites (TDRS)

"Establishing and operating a temporary *(debris reduction)* staging site necessary for debris separation and reduction is eligible. The cost to lease property is eligible. Additionally, if the terms of the lease require that the Applicant restore the leased property back to its condition prior to the Applicant's use, the costs related to that restoration are also eligible as part of the Category A project. If leased, the Applicant must provide the lease agreement."[32]

Any lease for property on which to situate a temporary debris reduction site should include pre-use environmental testing to ensure that there are not already contaminants on site that would increase the final clean-up costs. If the TDRS location is government-owned property, pre-use testing should still be done as a cost-preventative measure against the final site clean-up.

Another True-Life Tale

Following the Tubbs Fire, which burned more than 5,600 homes in Santa Rosa, CA, in 2017, the city began the debris clean-up process. After properties were cleaned, environmental testing showed that there were traces of naturally occurring lead and arsenic contained in residential lots. When the homes had been built there decades earlier, such testing was not required, and following the fire, those naturally occurring substances further complicated the clean-up.

A second issue arising from the Tubbs fire was that the extreme heat of the fire destroyed the gaskets of 5,600 water meters, which were buried but still exposed to the intense heat from the fire. The gaskets contained benzine, which the heat drove out of the gaskets and into the surrounding soil. Yet another quite unexpected debris/environmental complication.

Debris Work Without Environmental and Historic Issue Permits

"Between September 14–16, 2020, Hurricane Sally caused strong winds and torrential rains resulting in extensive damage throughout Alabama. The City of Creola (Applicant), in Mobile County, performed vegetative debris removal citywide between September 16, 2020 and January 18, 2021. The Applicant requested $20,487.50 in Public Assistance (PA) funding for the debris removal, which included burning debris in a burn pit and involved the use of a backhoe to disturb the ground up to 3 feet deep in a 50-foot by 50-foot area around the site. FEMA subsequently requested information from the Applicant regarding GPS coordinates, location names, and dates of debris burning. In response, the Applicant provided the GPS coordinates of the burn site, work dates, and a work schedule of its employees."[33]

"In its Environmental and Historic Preservation (EHP) review, FEMA found that the project did not comply with the section 106 consultation requirements of the National Historic Preservation Act (NHPA), because work took place before interested stakeholders could be consulted and the work was not covered by the Alabama Programmatic Agreement."[34]

"On May 5, 2021, FEMA issued a Determination Memorandum denying the request for $20,487.50. FEMA stated that the Applicant did not obtain a burn permit until after the debris removal operation and subsequent burning of the debris had started. Additionally, the Applicant did not allow FEMA the opportunity to coordinate and consult with the Advisory Council on Historic Preservation and the Choctaw Nation, the impacted Indian Tribal Government, as mandated by the NHPA and Executive Order 13175, Consultation and Coordination with Indian Tribal Governments."[35] (Emphasis Added)

First Appeal

"On June 28, 2021, the Applicant appealed the decision, and provided a timeline of the events leading up to the debris removal. The Applicant stated it acquired the title to the real property where the burn took place by deed dated December 31, 2003. Nothing in this deed reflected any historical, environmental, or archeological significance to the property. The area had undergone various cycles of construction and was operated as a dirt pit by previous owners. The Applicant noted that while FEMA designated the burn site as a historical location (which the Applicant did not concede), disturbance occurred years before it ever acquired the property. As such, the Applicant argued the property in question does not meet the legal definition of historic property."[36] (Emphasis Added)

"The Applicant commenced and completed the vegetative debris removal and burning without affording FEMA the opportunity to perform its required EHP review. If the removal and burning of debris are activities with the potential to affect historic properties, FEMA is required to identify in consultation with the State Historic Preservation Officer (SHPO) and/or the Tribal Historic Preservation Officer (THPO) whether any properties exist within the area of potential effect and, if they do, collaboratively determine the effect of the debris removal on identified properties."[37]

The appeal was denied for lack of the necessary issued permits prior to the commencement of work.

From the City of Creola and the Town of Paradise, we see just two examples of the complications which abound in the world of debris management. Further and potentially very delaying issues will arise when the local jurisdiction is near a wetland, a waterway, a navigable waterway, or the debris is a watercraft, whether the watercraft is in the water or ashore.

Ineligible Debris

"Debris removal from the following is ineligible:

• Federally maintained navigable channels and waterways;
• Flood control works under the authority of the Natural Resources Conservation Service (NRCS). Flood control works under the specific authority of NRCS are those that are part of the Watershed and Flood Prevention Operations (WFPO) Program under PL 83–566;

- Agricultural land; and
- Natural, unimproved land, such as heavily wooded areas and unused areas.

Removing debris to restore the pre-disaster capacity of engineered facilities may be eligible as Permanent Work if the Applicant can substantiate the pre-disaster capacity and maintenance of that facility."[38]

Debris in Waterways

Debris in waterways is a compound/complex situation. There are waterways, navigable waterways, and non-navigable waterways, including flood control works and natural waterways. If this book was only about debris management, we would have the time and space to go into each of these situations, each of which involves the participation of one or more Federal agencies and possibly a state agency or more. For any of these situations, the best currently available resources are those two volumes cited on the first page of this chapter. Be forewarned that these FEMA publications are periodically revised and updated, so always look for the current version.

The important thing from a disaster cost recovery perspective is that the failure to fully engage all relevant Federal, state, and local agencies will put any debris clearance activities at risk of deobligation or denial. Getting the appropriate permits will take time and waiting for consultations with these various oversight agencies may interfere with the need to promptly clean up the debris.

I am currently working with a West Coast water agency, and that agency under state law has a very limited working window, which runs from June 15th through October 15th of any given year. They have several projects affected by the need to get a sign-off from FEMA for Federal agency review. If they proceed with the work to prepare for the winter rainy season, they may be risking denial or deobligation. Therefore, they may have to wait for months until all the permits are issued before proceeding with the work to maintain eligibility. Because of these delays, the agency will have to request an extension of time for this Category A emergency work from FEMA, because while the agency waits for FEMA approval for the environmental and/or historic preservation issues, the clock is still ticking on the original 6-month emergency work timeline.

Some, but not necessarily all, of the pertinent agencies include the U.S. Army Corps of Engineers, the U.S. Coast Guard, the National Resource Conservation Service, the Environmental Protection Agency, the National Marine Fishery Service, and the U.S. Fish and Wildlife Service. Additionally, state, regional, and tribal nation agencies may also have to be involved in the consultations prior to beginning the work.

Debris: Vehicles and Vessels

While we are at the water's edge discussing debris, it is appropriate to briefly mention the removal of vessels from waterways and from dry land.

"For FEMA to reimburse an applicant for the removal of vehicles and vessels, the applicant must provide supporting documentation for its funding request. As with other types of debris removal, the removal of debris from waterways must be found to be in the public interest. In addition to establishing legal responsibility, the applicant must demonstrate one of the following:

- There is a threat to life, public health, and safety, based on a determination by the state, county, or municipal government's public health authority to make such a determination; or
- There is significant threat of damage to improved property, based on a determination by the state, county, or municipal government that the removal of disaster-generated debris from a

navigable waterway is cost-effective (debris removal is cost-effective if the cost to remove the debris is less than the cost of potential damage to the improved property); or

- Removal of debris is necessary to ensure economic recovery of the affected community to the benefit of the community at large, based on a determination by the state, county, or municipal government."[39]

For vessels: "The primary issue is the question of who bears the responsibility to remove such a vessel. Under federal law, it is the duty of the owner, lessee, or operator of a sunken craft to immediately remove it from navigable channels; failure to do so is considered abandonment of the craft, after which the craft is subject to removal by the United States. The owner, lessee, or operator is strictly liable for the full costs of removal."[40] (Emphasis Added) In such cases, the local agency may be thrust into the role of fee collector, working to locate the owner of a vehicle or vessel, and then trying to collect the costs for removal and disposal of the abandoned vehicle or vessel.

"In cases where the craft is considered abandoned, USACE has primary responsibility for the removal of sunken vessels or other obstructions from federally maintained navigable waterways under emergency conditions. USACE will remove a vessel using its emergency authorities only if the owner, operator, or lessee cannot be identified or cannot affect removal in a safe and timely manner."[41]

The U.S. Coast Guard (USCG) has primary responsibility for removing – destroying, if necessary – abandoned barges greater than 100 tons, and sunken or abandoned vessels "threatening to discharge" hazardous substances or that pose a threat to the public health, welfare, or environment."[42]

USACE and USCG have a Memorandum of Agreement under which the two agencies work together to determine if a sunken vessel either poses a threat to navigation or a pollution threat to public health and safety. If the agencies determine that the threat is to navigation, the USACE will remove the vessel. USCG will remove the vessel if it determines that its removal is essential to abate a pollution threat; otherwise, USCG will remove the oil and other hazardous substances while leaving the vessel in place.[43]

Coordination between FEMA, the USACE, and the USCG may be challenging and result in delays in the debris clearance efforts.

In October of 2006, 14 months after Hurricane Katrina, I visited Plaquemines Parish in Louisiana and was allowed to sit in on the weekly disaster recovery meeting. At the top of the agenda that morning was the issue of 3,500 abandoned automobiles remaining on private property in the Parish. According to Louisiana state law, the Louisiana Highway Patrol must first post a vehicle to be towed with a 30-day notice prior to towing. However, the private homes had been abandoned, and there was no one available to sign the Right-of-Entry waiver required by FEMA prior to any government official entering the property. Therefore, the Louisiana Highway Patrol could not go onto the property to post the notice on the vehicle. Without the vehicle posting, the Parish could not tow the vehicle. The Parish was clearly between a rock and a hard place. This is just one of the post-disaster conundrums which bedevil local authorities. They can't tow the vehicle without breaking the law, and if they break the law, they won't be eligible for reimbursement. One possible solution in such a case would be to have a "disaster-abandoned vehicle abatement law" which would eliminate the need for posting prior to towing. There would also need to be a "presumption of abandonment" regulation to eliminate the need for the Right-of-Entry waiver required by FEMA. Both regulations would have to be approved by the elected governing body prior to the disaster. In some cases, the state might also have to pass some enabling legislation to keep everything on the up-and-up.

Public Property Debris Management

The debris damage assessment is challenging and so very important as an element of the disaster cost recovery process. Most local agency employees have little debris damage assessment, unless of course they have previously experienced a major disaster.

Ideally, the local agency will have a debris damage assessment plan. Such a plan should have maps of discrete areas within a jurisdiction. Such a map will be useful in assigning debris damage inspectors, tracking those areas already surveyed, and those remaining to be inspected.

The plan should also have a standard form for specifying the locations and make-up of the disaster debris. A sample disaster debris survey form is provided in the Appendix, Form 52. This is not a FEMA form, nor is it required to be used. However, in the absence of a local agency form, this may be an excellent substitute. Because it is an Excel form, the daily tallies of all the debris surveyed may be rapidly accounted for using Excel's Crosstab reporting feature.

When preparing a Project Worksheet for approval, FEMA will want to know the quantities and various classes of debris caused by this disaster, so the previously mentioned form will be a great resource for managing this mass of data.

Removal of Debris from Public Parks and Recreation Areas

"Removal of debris from parks and recreational areas available for public use is eligible when it affects public health or safety or proper utilization of such facilities. Trees frequently constitute a large part of debris in these areas. Stump removal is not eligible unless it is determined that the stump poses a hazard."[44]

Debris clean-up is generally eligible for all public property. However, for those communities on or near a shoreline or river, the specter of environmental issues is always lurking in the shadows. Waterways themselves will usually fall under the jurisdiction of one Federal agency or another, so close coordination with FEMA, the respective state, and applicable other Federal agencies will be necessary.

Sedimentation: Clogging Up the Process

One area, however, where local agencies almost never win at this game of debris roulette is with sedimentation of reservoirs and waterways. To be eligible for FEMA funding, the local agency must definitively document that "X" amount of sediment filled in a dam or reservoir as a direct result of the disaster. The most effective way to do this is with a bathymetric survey, where licensed professionals take soundings (depth readings) to determine the pre-disaster levels of sediment contained in the reservoir or waterways.

Alternatively, in some cases where the water and debris levels are not constant, readings may be taken at bridge or culvert abutments, where "foot" marks are painted. These marks should be shown in measured levels, usually in one-foot increments. The pre-disaster debris or sediment level can then be compared to the levels existing immediately after the disaster. This will constitute irrefutable evidence of the damage done by the disaster at that location.

However, this may be one edge of a very sharp two-edged sword if the photograph also shows erosion or other conditions which would be contributory factors in a bridge, culvert, or roadway failure.

As mentioned in the first two paragraphs of this chapter, debris eligibility on public property is not usually the problem. The problems come from the lack of full documentation, improper purchasing, failure to properly monitor the debris contractor, etc.

Commingling of Household Trash with Debris

A challenge faced by many communities when doing debris clean-up is the commingling of regular household trash with the disaster debris. Part of this can be traced back to the lack of debris plan elements addressing this issue. Another part of the problem may be the lack of integration of the Public Information Officer to get the word out to the community that mixing regular household trash with disaster debris may threaten the cost eligibility for private property debris management. In either case, FEMA is alert to instances of commingling of household and commercial trash with disaster debris. Commingling can result in deobligations of funding.

One of the most common reasons for denial or deobligation of debris funding is that the local agency, or the contractors themselves, cross the line and commingle public property debris with private property debris. This is a major challenge for local agencies, i.e., how to keep the public from creating a problem with debris management that need not exist. This is one area to which FEMA pays very close attention.

This case comes from Florida and exposes another way to "commingle" debris. "From October 3 to October 19, 2016, Hurricane Matthew produced severe storm conditions in communities along the east coast of Florida, including Flagler County (Applicant), which experienced extensive debris accumulations as a result. In response, the Applicant engaged in significant debris removal efforts. FEMA documented the Applicant's private property debris removal (PPDR) in Project Worksheets (PWs) 989 and 990 but did not obligate any funding for the work due to the pending eligibility determination at issue in this appeal."[45]

"On December 21, 2016, the Applicant submitted a PPDR request letter through the Recipient, asking FEMA to approve reimbursement of debris removal costs.[4] The request included: a determination from the Applicant that removal was in the public interest, with a supporting rationale from the County Health Officer and County Fire Rescue Chief; an attachment identifying the specific neighborhoods/homeowner's associations requiring debris removal; documentation supporting the Applicant's legal authority to remove the debris; and a statement agreeing to indemnify the federal and state government from any claims arising from debris removal."[46]

"On February 7, 2017, the FCO denied the request, finding the Applicant did not provide all information required by FEMA's policy guidelines when seeking reimbursement for PPDR costs, despite repeated attempts by FEMA to obtain this information. Although the FCO did not specify what information was missing, he did state that the Applicant had "not substantiated where debris removal meets the requirement of being in the public interest.'"[47]

Now on to the important commingling issue: "On November 30, 2017, the RA denied the first appeal because the Applicant did not formally request or obtain approval from FEMA prior to commencing PPDR, contrary to Public Assistance Program and Policy Guide (PAPPG) requirements. The RA also noted that FEMA subsequently requested documents in an RFI that could validate the Applicant's eligibility after-the-fact given that FEMA was unable to view the debris initially, but the Applicant did not provide photos or other visual evidence of the debris at issue from prior to its removal. Further, the RA stated that the PPDR load ticket summary was **commingled** with other work in the attachment to the submitted response."[48] (Emphasis Added)

In this case, the debris paperwork was commingled instead of the debris itself. The net result was the same. Without a definite "trail of breadcrumbs" for FEMA to follow as they analyze the paperwork, FEMA cannot determine if the work done was eligible and if the costs for the work were reasonable.

Private Property Debris Removal (PPDR)

Private property debris removal may be one of the most emotional and frustrating aspects of the entire debris removal process. First, the community pressure on the local government agency to "do something" about the debris will be intense and universal. Once the initial shock of the disaster passes, the community will be up in arms about this. However, on the other hand, it will seem that FEMA is strongly pushing back not in fact, but in process. There are many hoops which the local agency must jump through before FEMA will approve <u>and pay for</u> private property debris removal.

The linchpin for getting private property debris removal approved is a finding by the appropriate public health authority that an immediate threat to life safety or the public health exists by the presence of the disaster debris. Only the public health authority may make this finding, not any other elected or appointed official. And it may not be a deputy to the public health officer, unless of course the public health officer is out of jurisdiction and a properly appointed deputy is serving in their stead.

Next, the local agency must document that it has the legal authority to perform private property debris removal. This is not an easy hurdle to overcome. FEMA's Appeals Database is littered with failed appeals from local agencies that thought they had the legal authority, when in fact they did not.

This case on PPDR comes from Florida, where their warm weather and low taxes are counterbalanced by their tons of hurricane debris. "Hurricane Frances (FEMA-1545-DR-FL) struck Florida on September 4, 2004, causing damage to trees and structures in the City. The City had a pre-positioned contract with Grubbs Emergency Services, LLC, to remove debris from roadway rights-of-way and public facilities within the City. Project Worksheets (PWs) 4917 and 5130 were prepared for a total of $664,561.70 to fund eligible debris removal expenses for the period of September 8–24, 2004. Expenses associated with ineligible debris removal, including debris hauled from private roads, Federal-aid roads and unspecific load locations, and for debris hauled by trucks whose truck certification papers were not available for review at the time the PW was written, were deducted prior to obligation."[49]

"The City submitted its first appeal on July 22, 2005. It stated that its contractor invoiced a total of $1,817,206 associated with PW 4917, and that FEMA reimbursed $541,873. It also mentioned PW 5130, but did not provide specific monetary figures associated with this PW. <u>It included resolutions passed by the City Council that waived procedures and formalities to ensure the safety and welfare of the community. It stated that removing debris from private roads was essential to reduce threats to life, health and safety of the citizens of the City.</u>"[50] (Emphasis Added) In this case, the city council resolutions were passed *AFTER* the storm, which meant that they were not in force when the storm hit. Too Little, Too Late.

FEMA's position on PPDR is: "FEMA regulations authorize assistance for debris removal when it is in the 'public interest' (see 44 CFR§206.224(a)) and the work is performed by an eligible applicant who has legal responsibility to do so. Generally, debris removal from private property is not eligible for Public Assistance funding. In order to be eligible, an applicant must show that it meets the preceding criteria and that it has obtained right-of-entry/hold harmless agreements from property owners. If these criteria have been met, FEMA will determine eligibility on a case-by-case basis."[51]

"The basis for the denial of the City's first appeal was the issue of legal responsibility. The City must demonstrate that it took steps, through its legal processes, to gain legal responsibility for debris removal on private property. <u>The documents provided by the City regarding garbage collection and trash pick-up do not establish legal responsibility for removing storm-related debris.</u> There is nothing in the City's Article V or trash pick-up documents that specifically addresses the responsibility for removing storm-related debris. <u>But rather, these documents relate to routine garbage and trash removal, without reference to extraordinary circumstances.</u>"[52] (Emphasis Added)

"The City's Resolutions 195, 199, and 202, declare states of emergency and empower the City of Palm Beach Gardens to 'waive the procedures and formalities otherwise required of the political subdivision by law pertaining to certain actions that can be taken to ensure the health, safety, and welfare of the community.' The City's Executive Order No. 02–2004, dated September 9, 2004, directs the City to remove all vegetative debris within the City on both public and private property. The Executive Order states that the city manager declares and requires that 'City debris removal crews and contractors shall enter into any and all streets and rights-of-way within the City, both public and private, to remove vegetative and other debris.' This order was enacted after the disaster and does not specify the circumstances in which the City would take legal responsibility to remove debris from private property."[53]

"We required eligible applicants to show that they had adopted an ordinance that addresses the abatement of public health nuisances on private property, and taken action under that ordinance, as evidence of their legal responsibility to remove debris from private property. <u>Typically, nuisance abatement ordinances require local governments to adhere to due process requirements, such as providing notice to property owners of a violation and an opportunity to be heard on the violation.</u> If the property owner does not comply with an order to abate the nuisance, the local government is authorized to take actions to abate the nuisance and bill the property owner for costs incurred or place a lien against the property. The City did not meet this standard."[54] (Emphasis Added)

"The third requirement for private property debris removal is obtaining right-of-entry/hold harmless agreements from property owners or relevant homeowner's associations prior to commencing debris removal work on private property. These agreements indemnify the Federal government from any claim arising from the removal of debris, in accordance with 42 U.S.C §5173(b). The City has not provided evidence that it obtained such agreements."[55]

For a private property debris removal ordinance to be effective, it must clearly and unambiguously state the purpose and intent of the ordinance is to clean up disaster debris to protect the health and safety of the residents and limit further damage to private property. Any references to ordinary nuisance abatement or regular trash pick-up will be a serious problem which may result in denial of costs. FEMA generally does not and will not accept any combination of state laws and or local ordinances which make general and usually vague references to trash, or health and safety, etc., Many local agencies have tried, and many have failed. The language must be quite specific.

In another relevant case, again from Florida, FEMA states: "The Applicant's second appeal argues that the combination of State statute and local ordinance establish the legal responsibility of Martin County to remove debris from private property. However, the authorities provided to the Governor by State statute during emergency declarations and general statements regarding innate responsibilities to safeguard life and property do not translate to the specific legal responsibility of Martin County to enter private property to remove disaster-related debris. Fla. Stat. §252–36(5) (I) authorizes the Governor to use of forces to assist private citizens in cleanup and recovery operations when proper permission from private property owners has been obtained. <u>However, this statute does not explicitly provide the Applicant with the legal responsibility to enter private property to remove disaster-related debris. And, although State statute states that it is a political subdivision's innate responsibility to safeguard the life and property of its citizens, the statute does not explicitly state that it is the County's legal responsibility to remove debris from private property.</u>"[56] (Emphasis Added)

The argument continues: "We required eligible applicants to show that they had adopted an ordinance that addresses the abatement of public health nuisances on private property, and taken action under that ordinance, as evidence of their legal responsibility to remove debris from private property."[57]

I have in my collected files an ordinance from a different Florida county for private property debris removal, which runs almost 100 pages. Notably, besides the state authorities and local rules, the ordinance also includes the name of every private road in the county. Just for the sake of completeness.

Right-of-Entry Waiver and Insurance Information Request

Always, for private property debris removal, the local agency must collect signed right-of-entry (ROE) waiver forms before any government officials may enter onto private property for debris removal activities. Typically, a request for debris removal insurance information is also included in the same document, or at least the form is available at the same time that the homeowner is signing the right-of-entry form. A sample sixteen-page right-of-entry form is available in the Appendix, Form 53. There are many different ROE form versions available on the internet, many of them only two or three pages long. This form came from a county which had suffered from a massive fire, so it reflects fire debris-related issues. For hurricanes, tornadoes, or flooding disasters, the focus may be slightly different. These forms will vary from state to state due to the differing state laws which may apply.

Private Property Debris Removal: Improper Request

Not only must the local agency request pre-approval for clearing debris from private property, but they must also follow the prescribed procedure for making that request, as we can see in a second look at the case from Flagler County, Florida.

"The Applicant initially requested PPDR approval on October 13, 2016, through a mission request on EM Constellation (EMC), a web-based platform administered by the Florida Division of Emergency Management (Recipient) to track and coordinate requests for emergency assistance. The EMC request sought 'approval from [the Federal Coordinating Officer (FCO) for [a] first pass of debris pickup on private roads for access by emergency responders,' with 'resources needed until' 5 p.m. on October 13, 2016. Other than basic contact information, the record does not reflect that the Applicant provided any additional information with this entry."[58]

"According to the Applicant, when it did not receive approval to commence PPDR, its staff continued to repeat the request to the Recipient and FEMA in intergovernmental conference calls and meetings. Eventually, on October 25, 2016, the Applicant commenced PPDR without FEMA's prior approval."[59]

"On December 21, 2016, the Applicant submitted a PPDR request letter through the Recipient, asking FEMA to approve reimbursement of debris removal costs. The request included: a determination from the Applicant that removal was in the public interest, with a supporting rationale from the County Health Officer and County Fire Rescue Chief; an attachment identifying the specific neighborhoods/homeowner's associations requiring debris removal; documentation supporting the Applicant's legal authority to remove the debris; and a statement agreeing to indemnify the federal and state government from any claims arising from debris removal."[60]

"On February 7, 2017, the FCO denied the request, finding the Applicant did not provide all information required by FEMA's policy guidelines when seeking reimbursement for PPDR costs, despite repeated attempts by FEMA to obtain this information. Although the FCO did not specify what information was missing, he did state that the Applicant had 'not substantiated where debris removal meets the requirement of being in the public interest.'"[61]

"The PAPPG (*Public Assistance Program and Policy Guide*) requires a specifically detailed written request and FEMA approval prior to the commencement of PPDR, and the Applicant admits that it did not comply with these requirements. The Applicant instead asks FEMA to view its EMC entry as a satisfactory written request and to find that it complied with the spirit of the PAPPG's requirement to obtain prior approval, given numerous, ignored verbal requests for approval (as well as other mitigating circumstances, such as its small size, lack of experience, urgent needs, and comprehensive PPDR request, after-the-fact). However, none of the Applicant's requests for prior approval conformed to the PAPPG requirements, as they did not include documentation demonstrating a public interest justification, establishing the Applicant's legal responsibility for PPDR, or indemnifying the federal government from resulting claims. Therefore, per FEMA policy, these requests do not excuse the lack of prior approval, nor do they satisfy the PAPPG's requirements for PPDR eligibility."[62] (Emphasis Added)

"Finally, the Applicant provides photos, videos, and other documentation, and resubmits its original December 21, 2016 PPDR request package, to help FEMA gauge eligibility after-the-fact. However, applicable FEMA policy does not provide for after-the-fact validation of PPDR eligibility absent prior approval as required by the PAPPG."[63]

It is easy to understand the deep frustration at a process which is at the same time both vague (to non-users) and complex. Yet, we have no other options other than to discover the process and closely follow it.

What is amazing to me is that given the frequent nature of hurricanes in Florida (or tornadoes, flooding, or other disaster du jour in any other state), the state legislature in all its infinite wisdom has not yet passed a statewide law mandating that local agencies (cities and counties) have a state-mandated legal responsibility for debris removal when life safety, the public health, or improved property is immediately threatened. Such a law could have saved Florida cities and counties millions of dollars in lost FEMA reimbursements over the past 20+ years.

Debris Removal from Private Roads

FEMA treats private property and private roads equally; both are considered private property for purposes of debris removal. In this case, yet again from Florida, the city removed debris from private roads without FEMA approval before beginning the work. "In September 2004, strong winds, heavy rains, and flooding from Hurricane Frances generated large amounts of storm-related debris throughout the City of Boynton Beach (Applicant). The Applicant used force account and contracted labor to remove, haul, and dispose of a total of 274,974.4 cubic yards of debris. FEMA addressed the debris removal in Project Worksheets (PWs) 7884 and 7889. During a review of the PWs, FEMA determined that the Applicant removed 7,337 CY debris and 16,766 CY of debris from private roads as documented in PW 7884 and PW 7889 respectively, and reduced costs accordingly."[64]

"In January 2006, the Grantee forwarded a first appeal to FEMA Region IV. In November 2006, FEMA Region IV issued a decision determining that the Applicant was not legally responsible for removing debris from private roads. Therefore, pursuant to 44 C.F.R. § 206.224(c), the Applicant was not eligible for Public Assistance (PA) reimbursement for costs associated with such work."[65]

". . . the Applicant asserted it was responsible for providing and ensuring continuous access of 'life safety services, water, and sewer operations' within its jurisdiction. As evidence that it was legally responsible for debris removal on private roads, the Applicant cited to Section 10–22 of the City of Boynton Beach Code of Ordinances, which states, '[a]ll refuse, garbage, trash of all types, vegetative trash, recycling, construction and demolition material accumulated in the City shall be exclusively collected, conveyed, and disposed of by the City under supervision of the Director of Public Works.'"[66]

"In a September 22, 2010 letter, the Region IV Regional Administrator (RA) concluded that, while the Applicant demonstrated it had legal authority to provide refuse and trash services, it failed to demonstrate it was legally responsible for removing debris from private roads following Hurricane Frances. In addition, the RA determined that the Applicant failed to show that the debris was so widespread it constituted a health and safety threat or that removal would benefit the general public, not just individuals. As such, the appeal was denied."[67]

"FEMA determines eligibility of debris removal from private roads by analyzing whether the applicant is legally responsible for such work, the work reduced an immediate threat to life, public health and safety, and the applicant provided to FEMA rights-of-entry and hold harmless agreements from the private property owners or Homeowners' Associations (HOAs), as a condition of receiving Federal funding."[68]

"The Applicant argues that Article II of the City of Boynton Beach Code of Ordinances establishes its legal responsibility to remove disaster-related debris. In part, Article II reads, '[a]ll refuse, garbage, trash of all types, vegetative trash, recycling, construction and demolition material . . . shall be exclusively collected, conveyed and disposed of by the City under the supervision of the Director of Public Works.' Article II defines 'refuse,' 'garbage,' 'recycling,' and 'construction and demolition material.' Article II does not define 'trash of all types,' but it defines each type of trash individually (i.e., yard trash, bulk trash, and noncombustible trash). None of the definitions provided in Article II appear to include disaster-related debris. Moreover, in Section 10–24 of the ordinance, 'placement of household garbage in a loose and uncontained manner on the roadside, swale, or other locations adjacent to the roadway with expectation of collection' is strictly prohibited. Refuse of all kinds must be placed in containers approved by the Director of Public Works in order to be collected. Article II further mandates that material intended for disposal must be placed in the container with the lid of the container closed, and the container must be placed within three feet of the curb or edge of the pavement. These requirements imply the City only collected and removed refuse that was contained in a City-approved container in a fixed location, not debris scattered onto private roads by a disaster."[69] (Emphasis Added)

While the city's trash disposal ordinance may work perfectly for the regular weekly trash pickups, it completely fails the test for disaster-caused debris. FEMA regularly looks to the adopted local codes and ordinances of government agencies and finds wonderful ammunition with which to fire fatal rounds into the heart of local agencies' best arguments for eligibility. A very apt phrase from over 500 years ago describes the situation perfectly: "Hoist with his own petard."[70] (Modern translation: Blown up with his own bomb.)

The case continues: "Article II only gives the Applicant authority to collect and transport refuse under specific circumstances. Article II does not give the Applicant legal responsibility to enter private property for the purpose of removing disaster-related debris, as required by FEMA policy guidance. In addition, Article II does not provide a process by which the Applicant would legally enter private property to remove debris, nor has the Applicant demonstrated how it followed any such process."[71]

In this case, even the footnotes of the case seem intent in "piling on" even after the death knell has rung, i.e. Footnote number "[21] Disaster-Specific Guidance #8, Debris Removal from Roadways in Private or Gated Communities, at 2. In fact, the only process outlined in Article II restricts the Applicant's ability to pick up refuse placed in a City-approved container located within three feet of the curb or edge of the pavement and, at minimum, three feet from any obstruction that may interfere with routine collection. As such, the intent of the ordinance seemingly restricts the Applicant's responsibility to enter private property to remove disaster-related debris."[72] (Emphasis Added)

Private Property Debris Removal: Insurance Recovery

Some private residences have included in their homeowner policies insurance coverage for the removal of disaster-caused debris. For FEMA this can represent a duplication of benefits. If the insurance company pays, then FEMA will not. Therefore, the responsibility of the local agency is to determine which homeowners have this coverage, and then to collect this money from either the homeowner themselves or their insurer. It can be a challenging task to locate property owners whose homes may have been destroyed and are now living with relatives, possibly in another city, town, or county. Further, the aggrieved homeowner will not be in a mood to pay for debris removal in the best of circumstances. The local agency must make a good faith effort to determine which private homes were covered for debris removal. This may mean utilizing the local media and direct mailing to the affected property owners. If the local agency cannot either find or recover the insurance moneys, it must make the good-faith effort to do so and fully document those efforts as a hedge against a FEMA deobligation.

Typically, in conducting the survey for debris-removal insured homeowners, the local agency will combine that with the request to sign the Right-of-Entry waiver required by FEMA to indemnify the Federal, state, and local governments against any claims of damage which may be alleged to have occurred by presence on the property:

"and the state must agree that debris removal from public and private property will not occur until the landowner signs an unconditional authorization for the removal of debris."[73]

Private Property Debris Removal and the accompanying challenges attached thereto are a situation where the Public Information Officer (PIO) may be worth their weight in gold. An effective PIO will create information bridges between the agency and the property owners to clarify what types of debris will be collected and what the collection schedules will be. When the debris is significant, the agency should have a dedicated PPDR hotline and web page. Obviously, the web page can be set up in advance and a simple plan outline created for the "Disaster Debris Hotline." Some of these functions may be coordinated at a county, regional, or state level, which greatly reduces administrative burden at the local level. On the State of Florida's Hurricane Ian recovery website, there is even a feature to "locate your boat." (https://iandebriscleanup.com/)

Self-Help Debris Removal and Container Monitoring

While we're talking about private property debris, the topic of roll-off bins enters the discussion. In some cases, when private property debris removal is approved, the local agency may set up locations where multiple roll-off bins are located so that homeowners themselves can clean up their properties.

However, this can lead to deobligations when the bins are not constantly monitored to prevent the mixing of debris classes, i.e., green waste mixed with white goods mixed with construction and demolition debris, etc. Additionally, the site monitors should require persons using the sites to prove the location of their residence to eliminate debris disposal by private businesses or out-of-area residents.

An appeals case from California is straight on point in this regard. This case, as so many appeals cases are, is multi-faceted, so we will focus on the issue at hand. "On August 24, 2014, an earthquake and subsequent aftershocks caused widespread damage throughout the City of Napa (Applicant). In response to the disaster the Applicant instituted a debris collection program and requested assistance from the Federal Emergency Management Agency (FEMA) to fund costs incurred related to debris collection, transportation, and disposal. Upon creation of the debris collection program, the Applicant set up sites throughout the city for the collection of disaster related debris. To perform this work the Applicant contracted with Napa Recycling and Waste Services (NRWS). NRWS typically provided a single 30 cubic yard bin per collection site. When the bins were full the citizens piled the rest of the debris on the ground surrounding the bin. This led NRWS to perform extra work and incur extra costs by having to load the debris from the ground into bins before removal. NRWS was already employed by the Applicant before the disaster to perform routine garbage and waste disposal for the city. However, following the disaster, the Applicant significantly modified the contract with NRWS to include the disaster recovery work under a new scope of work."[74] (This represents a separate procurement problem, i.e., a cardinal change.)

"Initially, the Applicant placed 8 ½ inch x 11-inch signs at the locations stating, 'earthquake debris only.' Once the number of sites was reduced from the high of 14, down to 2, round the clock security was implemented by the Applicant and carried out by the Security Enforcement Alliance (SEA), a private security firm. SEA employees were directed to log the name, phone number, and address of each person depositing debris at the sites, as well as the type of debris deposited. They were also directed to ask whether the debris was 'earthquake debris only.' Prior to the disaster the Applicant contracted with SEA to provide security at functions throughout the city. The Applicant then significantly modified the original SEA contract to include monitoring the debris drop off sites as part of a new scope of work."[75] (This is yet another procurement problem.)

"FEMA issued a Determination Memorandum denying all costs for nearly a dozen reasons including that: <u>1) there was no way to identify if the debris collected was eligible, that is, related to the earthquake; 2) there was inadequate monitoring of the debris collection sites;</u> 3) the Applicant had not established that the debris program was necessary to ease the threat of public health and safety risks; 4) there was no competitive cost solicitation; and 5) the Applicant used a time and materials (T&M) contract beyond the allowable timeframe of 70 hours."[76] (Emphasis Added)

First Appeal

"On August 28, 2015, the Applicant filed its first appeal with the Grantee challenging FEMA's denial of $1,533,754.02 in costs for debris removal. The Applicant responded to the issues in FEMA's Determination Memo by arguing, among other things, that an analysis showed that the vast majority of the debris was consistent with earthquake-related damage; 94 percent of the debris could be validated as residential debris; the debris collection sites were adequately monitored; the city monitored its contractors and the self-hauling residents; and the debris removal was necessary to eliminate an immediate threat to public health and safety. The Applicant further argued that the city paid its contractors reasonable rates in compliance with previously established procedures; the T&M contract costs were reasonable; and the small amount of commercial debris collected does not justify FEMA's denial of 100 percent of costs."[77]

"However, the Applicant acknowledges that until September 1, 2014, when the number of sites was reduced to two and the Applicant began using SEA security personnel at the remaining collections sites, it did not have any continuous monitoring in place. The Applicant performed interspersed spot checks, but there is insufficient documentation to demonstrate that this would have satisfied FEMA's monitoring requirements. This was the only type of monitoring at any of the sites between August 25-September 5, 2014. Without monitors the Applicant would be unable to determine who was dropping off debris at the locations and unable to determine whether that debris was disaster related. Therefore, up until September 6, 2014, the Applicant clearly failed to satisfy necessary monitoring requirements."[78]

"While FEMA policy does not require monitors to be certified professionals it notes that they should have experience working on construction sites and that they should be able to estimate debris quantities, differentiate debris types and follow all safety procedures. The SEA monitors may have been able to guard the sites and require those dropping off debris to fill out the log book; however, the Applicant has not demonstrated that the SEA employees monitoring the debris collections sites had the experience or skills to adequately perform the task for which they were contracted, including experience working on construction sites and skill in estimating debris quantities or discerning debris type. In fact, the Applicant notes that only one drop off was turned away – a clean load of dirt. Through an analysis of this process it is clear that the Applicant did not employ qualified monitors for the debris sites and as such did not satisfy FEMA policy."[79]

Commercial/Rental Property Debris Clean-Up

While debris removal from private property is not an everyday occurrence, debris clearance from commercial properties is even more rare. FEMA's position is that businesses are expected to carry the necessary business insurance coverage, including disaster debris clearance.

"Hurricane Zeta caused flooding, high winds, and storm surge throughout portions of Mississippi from October 28–29, 2020.[1] The disaster created debris in the City of Diamondhead (Applicant). On November 16, 2020, FEMA met with the Mississippi Emergency Management Agency (Recipient) to review the Preliminary Damage Assessment (PDA). During this PDA visit, the Applicant met with the Recipient and FEMA."[80]

"On December 1, 2020, the Applicant authorized the expenditure of funds for commercial debris removal and disposal along its streets, where debris had been pushed to the public right-of-way from commercial entities, faith-based organizations, and property owner's association properties. The Applicant removed this commercial property debris from January 8–20, 2021."[81]

"FEMA approved the Applicant's Request for Public Assistance on January 26, 2021. The Applicant, the Recipient, and FEMA conducted an exploratory call on February 3, 2021, and Recovery Scoping Meetings on February 12 and 19, 2021. The Applicant's contractor reached out to FEMA regarding commercial property debris removal (CPDR) on February 22, 2021, and FEMA advised that the CPDR request needed to be submitted to FEMA. On March 31, 2021, the Applicant submitted its CPDR request to FEMA. The Applicant stated approval of CPDR would be in the public's interest and support economic recovery for commercial entities already negatively impacted by the COVID-19 pandemic. On April 21, 2021, FEMA denied the Applicant's CPDR request on the basis that the Applicant did not obtain the required pre-approval from FEMA prior to removing the debris from commercial property."[82]

"The Applicant submitted its first appeal letter to the Recipient on June 24, 2021, requesting approval of CPDR costs totaling $78,895.05 for debris removal and monitoring."[83]

First Appeal

"The Applicant submitted its first appeal letter to the Recipient on June 24, 2021, requesting approval of CPDR (Commercial Property Debris Removal) costs totaling $78,895.05 for debris removal and monitoring. The Applicant stated that it recalled raising concerns, during the PDA (*Preliminary Damage Assessment*) on November 16, 2020, about debris fronting commercial properties in close proximity to residential homes. The Applicant stated that, as it recalled, the Recipient advised during the PDA that, 'if this commercial debris was to come across [its] desk, it would be denied,' and FEMA added no comments, which ended the conversation. The Applicant contended that FEMA's inaction to clarify statements made by the Recipient amounted to an endorsement of the Recipient's statements and a failure to offer programmatic guidance, on which the Applicant relied to its detriment by believing CPDR work would not be eligible for Public Assistance (PA) funding."[84] (Emphasis Added)

"The Applicant elaborated that FEMA did not deem the Applicant eligible for PA until 90 days after the disaster, the exploratory call on February 3, 2021 did not take place until after the Applicant had already removed the debris, and communication channels were limited prior to the major disaster declaration."[85]

"The FEMA Region IV Regional Administrator denied the appeal for CPDR work completed without the necessary pre-approval from FEMA, noting that CPDR is limited to extraordinary circumstances and requires that the Applicant meet the requirements for debris removal and receive FEMA approval prior to commencing work. FEMA concluded that the Applicant did not demonstrate that it was unable to access the applicable policy documents or that it requested additional information from FEMA regarding eligibility or the proper process to request CPDR. Despite the Applicant's assertion of receiving erroneous advice during the PDA, FEMA emphasized that FEMA policies regarding CPDR are clear and must be followed to be eligible for PA reimbursement."[86] (Emphasis Added)

"Removal of debris from commercial properties, such as industrial parks, golf courses, cemeteries, apartments, condominiums, and trailer parks, is generally ineligible because commercial enterprises are expected to retain insurance that covers debris removal. In very limited, extraordinary circumstances, FEMA may provide an exception. In such cases, the applicant must meet the requirements of the approval process, and FEMA must approve the work prior to the applicant removing the debris. Removal of debris placed on the public rights-of-way from commercial properties is ineligible unless it is pre-approved by FEMA. As part of the approval process, applicants must submit a written request to FEMA identifying the specific properties or areas of properties where debris removal activities will occur, FEMA then engages with the recipient and applicant to review the request and conduct site inspections, and FEMA must determine that CPDR at each property is eligible."[87]

"The Applicant did not submit a written request identifying specific properties where debris removal would occur or obtain approval of such work from FEMA prior to conducting CPDR. Without meeting the approval process requirements for CPDR and obtaining FEMA approval prior to removing the debris, the requested CPDR work remains ineligible for PA funding."[88]

Once again, we have a case where the debris clean-up was essentially completed even before the President signed the disaster declaration. This is not necessarily an unusual circumstance. As we saw earlier in the book, many disasters do not receive a Presidential disaster declaration for weeks or even months after the disaster has wrought havoc.

Utility Right-of-Way Clearance

Great care must be taken when requesting the trimming of trees and other vegetation for debris removal, i.e., "right-of-way" clearance. Here is another view of a previously cited case which illustrates this issue. "From January 19 to 26, 2010, a severe ice storm with high winds damaged the Nishnabotna Valley Rural Electric Cooperative's (Applicant) electric distribution system. FEMA prepared 11 Project Worksheets (PWs) for conductor replacement. The Applicant hired a contractor to trim trees and vegetation in the right-of-way for the conductor replacement work. Between December 10, 2013 and March 14, 2014, FEMA issued eleven determination memoranda to notify the Applicant that tree trimming is maintenance, and is therefore not eligible."[89]

"To be eligible for Public Assistance, an item of work must 'be required as the result of the emergency or major disaster event.' 'Generally, costs that can be directly tied to the performance of eligible work are eligible' for funding. In formulating the PWs, FEMA approved conductor replacement and determined that it was required as the result of the disaster event. The Applicant claimed that the trimming of trees and vegetation was necessary to complete the approved conductor replacement work, even though it was not mentioned in the PW scope of work. The Applicant explained that the trimming of trees and vegetation for construction was different from the trimming of trees and vegetation for maintenance, which the Applicant regularly performed. To support its claim, the Applicant provided industry handbooks that state all vegetation should be removed from the right-of-way to erect poles and string conductors and noted this practice aligns with Occupational Safety and Health Administration regulations that require tree trimming to maintain minimum safety distances between the crew and extension arms holding a live conductor. The Applicant also submitted documentation to support that the costs were directly tied to the performance of eligible work. FEMA finds that the Applicant has demonstrated that in this instance additional trimming, beyond normal maintenance, was necessary to clear vegetation for equipment access and crew safety to complete the eligible conductor replacement scope of work."[90] (Emphasis Added)

However, this was only a symbolic victory, because in the end, the work eligibility was torpedoed by the agency's failure to follow Federal procurement regulations. "While tree trimming may be required in furtherance of conductor replacement work, the Applicant did not follow the Federal procurement standards prescribed in 2 C.F.R. Part 215 (*the regulations in effect at that time*) in contracting for those services. Specifically, the Applicant did not use a suitable contract type with required contract provisions, provide procurement documentation, perform a cost or price analysis, and demonstrate efforts to utilize small businesses, minority-owned firms, and women's business enterprises. When an applicant fails to comply with procurement regulations, FEMA has the authority to take an enforcement action, which can include awarding reasonable costs. However, without the quantity of debris removed, FEMA could not determine if costs incurred were fair and reasonable, should it consider this discretionary enforcement option appropriate. As such, the Applicant's appeal is denied."[91]

This appeals case is not uncommon. There were multiple issues involved, any one of which would result in a denial of eligibility. In researching literally hundreds of appeals cases, it is very often the case that the appeal involves multiple issues issues in the same appeal. It only takes a failure on a single issue for the entire appeal to go up in flames. What is most amazing to the author is that so many agencies file appeals which on their face are dead-bang losers. When reading these appeals, it becomes quite obvious that these agencies, or their hired consultants, have little to no understanding of the impenetrable mess which they have created.

The Debris Contracts Paperwork

Following Title 2 of the Code of Federal Regulations (2 CFR), Part 200 the local agency must retain all paperwork incident to the advertising, scoring, and issuance of the contracts for both debris management and debris monitoring. The retained documents must include both the winning and losing bids in the event that FEMA has questions regarding the procurements. If the debris clean-up is for less than $250,000 i.e., the current Federal Simplified Acquisition Threshold, then the documented quotations must be retained in the files in lieu of the sealed bids.

As previously mentioned in Chapter 9, Disaster Procurement, not only is it important to have properly awarded debris management and debris monitoring contracts, but the invoices must match the basis upon which the contract was issued. That is, if the contract is a unit price contract, the work must be invoiced on the basis of unit prices, and not as a Time & Materials contract.

The contract, or job orders under a contract, must be crystal-clear regarding the areas within the local jurisdiction where debris is to be picked up and what areas are off-limits for debris clean-up.

If necessary, the contract or job orders must specify what classifications of debris are covered and which are not. For instance, a contract which may be for abandoned motor vehicles should not also mention abandoned watercraft, as watercraft removal may be under the jurisdiction of either the U.S. Army Corps of Engineers or the U.S. Coast Guard, and therefore ineligible for FEMA funding.

Time and Materials Debris Removal

Although we discussed Time & Materials (T&M) contracts in the previous chapter, it is important to repeat that information because T&M contracts are very frequently used in the early stages of the disaster clean-up. There are specific restrictions on T&M contracts, and the failure to adhere to those restrictions may well cost the local agency hundreds of thousands of dollars or more. "T&M contracts do not provide incentives to the contractor for cost control or labor efficiency. Therefore, use of T&M contracts is only allowed if <u>all</u> of the following apply:

- No other contract type was suitable;
- The contract has a ceiling price that the contractor exceeds at its own risk; and
- The Applicant maintains a high degree of oversight to obtain reasonable assurance that the contractor is using efficient methods and effective cost controls."[92] (Emphasis Added)

The following is one of my favorite appeals cases, which I use regularly in training because it is completely on point and clearly illustrates the inherent danger of filing an appeal.

"On August 25, 2005, high velocity winds generated from Hurricane Katrina produced large amounts of vegetative debris throughout the Village of Key Biscayne. FEMA approved two Project Worksheets (PWs), in the amount of $739,214 for village-wide debris removal operations."[93]

"The Applicant entered into a T&M contract with All Florida Tree and Landscape, Inc. (contractor) from August 26 through September 27, 2005, to remove hazardous trees, tree limbs, and stumps within its jurisdiction. FEMA prepared PW 385 in the amount of $208,522 to document the contract costs for this work."[94]

"During project closeout, FEMA determined that the work performed under the T&M contract extended beyond the initial 70-hour period (*then allowed by FEMA*) that FEMA allows for emergency debris clearance. It was also determined that the contractor's equipment rates were unreasonably high when compared to established FEMA equipment rates for applicant owned equipment. FEMA allowed the contractor's equipment rates for the first 70-hours of emergency debris clearance but adjusted the rates – for five (5) different pieces of equipment – to match FEMA equipment costs for the remainder of the contract. <u>This resulted in a reduction of $37,817 with adjusted total funding of $170,705.</u>"[95] (Emphasis Added)

"<u>In a letter dated September 22, 2010, the Regional Administrator denied the first appeal for $37,817</u> **and advised that the remaining funding of $170,705 on PW 385 would be deobligated**. The Regional Administrator stated that the Applicant did not fully comply with Federal procurement regulations at 44 CFR §13.36, Procurement when it entered into the T&M contract. The Regional Administrator explained that the Applicant did not demonstrate that other contract types were not suitable; that the terms of the T&M contract did not include a ceiling price; and that a cost/price analysis was not conducted in connection with the contract."[96] (Emphasis Added)

"In the absence of a contract with a defined scope of work and documentation to quantify the amount of debris the Applicant's contractor removed, FEMA cannot calculate eligible costs for debris removal services nor compare the contract with other contracts from surrounding jurisdictions."[97]

In this case, the local agency would have been far better off to have not appealed this case, which cost them an additional $170,705. Appealing an adverse Determination Memo (DM) is a high-risk enterprise because:

1) It will take valuable staff time and money to pursue the appeal.
2) Average chances of prevailing on a first appeal are 50%.
3) Average chances of prevailing on the second appeal are 33%.
4) Without truly knowing what is at stake, the local agency may be sailing an already-sinking ship into a bad storm.

Using a "Buy-Board" or Piggybacking a Debris Contract

As previously mentioned in Chapter 9: Disaster Procurement, the use of a "buy-board" or a piggyback contract for debris is a simultaneously very attractive and an extremely high-risk venture.

The following case is another of my training favorites because it raises unusual but nonetheless very valid questions about disaster procurement and debris management.

"Hays County is located on the Edwards Plateau situated between Austin and San Antonio, Texas, and is part of the Austin-Round Rock metropolitan area. The County has a population of about 195,000 and covers 680 square miles. From May 4 to June 19, 2015, the County received significant rainfall causing the rivers and creeks to overflow. The Blanco River, with a flood stage of 13 feet, crested at over 40 feet, washing away more than 400 homes and 2 main bridges. The President declared the major disaster on May 29, 2015."[98]

"On September 9, 1966, the State of Texas created the Houston-Galveston Area Council (HGAC) as a regional planning commission. HGAC, a political subdivision of the State of Texas, is a voluntary membership organization of local governments in a 13-county region surrounding Houston. According to its website, HGAC strives to make the government procurement process more efficient by providing competitively priced contracts for goods and services to help its members achieve their purchasing goals. The County used HGAC's procurement services to procure two contracts, one to perform debris removal and the other to monitor the debris removal."[99]

"The County did not always comply with Federal procurement standards. Specifically, the County used a shared services agreement with HGAC to procure two contracts totaling $1.5 million that did not fully meet Federal requirements. When advertising for the debris removal contract, HGAC unreasonably restricted competition by not allowing smaller contractors to compete for the work. For both debris-related contracts, HGAC's procurement practices also did not take the specific steps that Federal regulations require to provide opportunities for small and minority businesses, women's business enterprises, and labor surplus area firms to bid on federally funded work when possible."[100]

"The County also awarded two smaller contracts totaling $367,191 without taking the federally required affirmative steps or including all required contract provisions. In response to our audit, however, the County revised its procurement policies to comply with Federal requirements. The County also canceled one of the contracts and plans to resolicit bids for more than $200,000 of disaster work."[101]

"Federal regulations encourage grant recipients to use shared services to foster economy and efficiency. Nevertheless, the use of these shared services does not relieve the grant recipient or subrecipient of its responsibility to comply with Federal procurement requirements. Therefore, FEMA should disallow as ineligible $1,473,045 for the two contracts that Hays County awarded using HGAC's procurement services."[102]

HGAC's Procurement of the County's Debris-Related Contracts

"The County awarded two contracts, totaling $1,473,045, using procurement services provided by HGAC's Disaster Debris Clearance and Removal Services program. One contract was for debris removal ($916,046) and the other for monitoring debris removal ($556,999). HGAC made the following claims on its website:

* HGAC "has handled all the procurement issues";
* "The program provides End Users with a procurement process based on the latest FEMA policies to limit the entities exposure to potential non-reimbursement following a presidential disaster declaration"; and
* "The Program can save you time and money associated with the procurement process and can help maximize eligible FEMA reimbursement."[103] (Emphasis Added)

"However, the problems we identified do affect eligibility for Federal grant funds. HGAC's requirements for debris removal contractors overly restricted competition; and, in soliciting bids for both contracts, HGAC did not take all the affirmative steps that Federal regulations require to provide opportunities for disadvantaged businesses when possible."[104]

"Restricting Competition – HGAC's restrictions prevented otherwise qualified contractors from participating in the County's debris removal contract . . . . HGAC required its prospective debris removers to have performed three debris removal projects requiring the removal of at least 1 million cubic yards of debris. For this disaster, though, the County needed to remove a much smaller volume of debris – about 150,000 cubic yards. Therefore, HGAC's requirements prevented smaller companies from competing for the federally funded work. It is important to note that HGAC's requirements would not be overly restrictive if its procurement services for debris removal were available only to customers requiring the removal of large volumes of debris. However, HGAC's procurement service is available to any governmental entity nationwide needing debris removal, regardless of project size. To comply with Federal regulation, HGAC needs to restrict its contractors to only large debris removal projects or provide its customers with a lower-volume option."[105]

Affirmative Steps Not Taken

"According to 2 CFR 200.321(a), non-Federal entities must take all necessary affirmative steps to assure the use of small and minority businesses, women's business enterprises, and labor surplus area firms when possible."[106]

"Texas officials said the County concluded normal procurement rules did not apply because of the 'emergency/exigent period at the time the contract was awarded' and 'that HGAC was merely a vehicle to access (*a*) repository of vendors quickly.' We disagree. Although FEMA classifies debris removal as 'emergency work,' the need for debris removal does not constitute exigent circumstances unless the debris poses an immediate threat to life and property. For example, pushing debris from blocked roadways to allow emergency vehicles to pass is exigent work, but normal debris removal is not. The County took proactive measures by using its employees and equipment to push debris from roadways. The remaining debris work posed no immediate threat and, therefore, did not warrant the County's circumvention of Federal procurement standards."[107] (Emphasis Added)

In this case, the county unwittingly used an improper method of procurement, and HGAC unintentionally failed to comply with two different aspects of 2 CFR, Part 200 compliance. HGAC was badly embarrassed, but Hays County stood to lose $1.473 million dollars from this audit.

Debris Management Alternatives

There are alternatives for debris management via the U.S. Army Corps of Engineers (USACE), which come with some caveats; caveats which need to be carefully studied to determine which, if any of them, are suitable for the local agency and the community's needs.

"USACE Mission Capabilities – DFA Missions (Direct Federal Assistance)

- Right of Way (ROW) Debris Removal – Removal, reduction, and disposal of debris from the public right of way and other public property, such as parks and schools.
- Emergency Clearance – A roadway clearance mission generally requires moving debris to the median or side of the ROW to allow for emergency traffic.
- Private Property Debris Removal (PPDR) – Removal, reduction and disposal of debris from private property, when directed by FEMA.
- Demolition – Removal, reduction and disposal of residential or commercial structures.
- Debris Removal from Drainage Structures – Removal, reduction, and disposal of debris from natural streams, reservoirs and engineered channels.
- Waterway/Wet Debris – Removal, reduction and disposal of debris from coastal waters where the debris impedes navigation or produces a hazard to safety.
- CDM – The Contaminated Debris Management (CDM) Mission results from a detonation that creates general construction debris, and the like, that is contaminated with a hazardous material or a chemical, biological, radioactive, nuclear agent;
- Dead Animal Carcasses – Removal of dead animals is considered debris location of the carcass determines the type of debris:
  - on the road – right of way debris;
  - on private property – PPDR;
  - in the water – waterway debris"[108]

"FEMA may require certification from the state or local government health department, HHS, or the U.S. Department of Agriculture (USDA) that a threat to public health and safety exists. When few in number, smaller animal carcasses (e.g., rodents, skunks, or possums) do not usually pose an immediate threat to public health or safety. Removal and disposal of these carcasses is ineligible. when another Federal agency has authority to provide assistance for carcass removal and disposal. NRCS has authority to remove animal carcasses and to provide technical assistance to the Applicant under its EWP program. The USDA's Farm Service Agency may provide assistance for farmland debris cleanup. The EPA and USCG have authority to provide technical assistance and to remove animal carcasses contaminated with oil, hazardous substances, pollutants, or contaminants."[109]

USACE: Caveat #1

It is, however, important to know that USACE debris removal runs on a tight schedule, particularly for private property debris removal, when that is approved by FEMA. If, for example, the schedule is for "white goods" or "white metals" (household appliances) to be picked up on Tuesdays, and the homeowner does not have their white goods at the curb on Tuesday, the white goods will not be picked up on a subsequent day, and so on. This strict schedule provides a true economy of operation; however, the schedule does not consider that some homeowners will not receive the information in timely manner, or that a homeowner may be staying with relatives in a different town or county, where the debris pick-up schedule is not available. Therefore, there may be added costs, to be borne by the local agency, for picking up 'straggler' debris. On the other hand, if the USACE is doing emergency roadway clearance to allow emergency vehicle traffic safe access to the community, a strict schedule should pose fewer problems for the community.

USACE: Caveat #2

Another caveat is that this DFA, or Direct Federal Assistance and will still have a local agency cost share, nominally 25%, unless the disaster is so severe that the President provides 100% funding for a limited time.

The local agency may also use Mutual Aid and/or its own force account labor debris management operations.

Debris and Other Federal Agencies (OFA)

FEMA does not pay for debris removal where other Federal agencies have that responsibility. This is particularly important for "water communities" near a coastal or riverine area, i.e., those with waterways, navigable or not, wetlands, and similarly situated water features. A close reading of the current editions of the Public Assistance Program and Policy Guide and the Disaster Operations Legal Reference is highly recommended in these instances.

For debris removal, and only for debris removal, FEMA, not the Federal Highway Administration, has been responsible since 2012 for the clean-up of debris on federal highways. The repair or reconstruction of "on-system" (Federally supported) highway repairs still remains under the purview of the Federal Highway Administration.

Debris Environmental Not-So-Incidentals

Recapture of Refrigerants: As a routine matter, all refrigeration white goods, i.e., refrigerators, air conditioners, and freezers, will have to have their refrigerant gases extracted and properly disposed. This must be explicitly included in the debris management contract and properly documented to be eligible for FEMA reimbursement.

Unclear or Incomplete "Scopes-of-Work"

The following are two examples of incomplete or unclear "scopes-of-work" which resulted in an adverse audit finding in DHS-OIG Audit Report Number DD-07–04 for the City of Houston. However, on appeal, the City was able to get a partial reinstatement of deobligated funds.

"Based on the recommendations contained in the OIG audit report, FEMA deobligated $524,715 under PW 759 and $200,000 under PW 761. Of this amount, $155,493 was for costs Garner incurred for decontaminating flooded automobiles before removing them from the garage after the storm. The questioned costs related to towing approximately 150 cars from the garages to the garage ramp and then washing mud and contaminants from the cars before towing them offsite. The OIG's audit report stated, 'the work was outside the scope of eligible work as described on the project worksheets.' The Applicant argues that Garner performed the questioned work to ensure that contaminants from the garages were contained and not spread throughout the city. The Applicant also argues that it was necessary to remove the vehicles in order to clean the garages and the cost of this work was a necessary component of the contract."[110]

"FEMA prepared PW 759 to cover the costs of removing silt, mud and other debris from the garages. Although the PW did not specifically refer to cleaning out automobiles, the contaminated vehicles had to be removed from the garages before the garages could be cleaned. It is also clear that the vehicles had to be cleaned before they were moved offsite because otherwise contaminates would have spread to the relocated sites. These types of expenses are eligible emergency protective measures under section 403 of the Stafford Act. Therefore, the $155,493 of costs for this work is eligible."[111]

The second issue from out of left field dealt with costs for confined space rescue work.

"FEMA deobligated $29,624 in questioned costs that the OIG characterized as 'Rescue Standby' in the Garner invoices and an additional $6,675 of standby expenses that were billed by Eagle. The Applicant contends the workers at issue in the context of these two sets of questioned costs were in fact implementing the safety plan contained in PW 759. The Applicant's appeal notes that, the PW 759 scope of work required that a safety plan be provided and that, 'the safety plan shall be site-specific for confined space access'. . . . the City Fire Marshal determined that the garages became 'confined spaces' due to the lack of ventilation. Upon that determination, both the Fire Code and OSHA required (the City) to develop a plan and a means to evacuate any personnel who might be overcome by fumes or lack of oxygen in the confined space. The means chosen was 'Rescue Standby' which was the term used for a certified group of confined space rescue personnel who were required to be on-site during all working hours."[112]

"In summary, the Applicant argues that the salaries of the Garner and Eagle workers who were at the work site in the event that a need might arise for evacuation were actually working at the site and are eligible for reimbursement pursuant to Paragraph 7(F) of Response and Recovery Policy 9525.7, Labor Costs-Emergency Work, dated July 20, 2000. Based on the information provided, the questioned expenses are eligible for reimbursement and FEMA will re-obligate $36,299."[113]

The adverse audit finding and the initial FEMA deobligations could have been avoided had the scope of work been more thoughtfully prepared. In fact, for a city such as Houston, which has a world-renowned labyrinth of underground structures in the downtown area, there should be a debris removal and decontamination plan, or at least a clean-up checklist for the massive underground complex. This would equally apply to any city with government-owned underground parking facilities or subways.

Burning of Debris

In some parts of the country, green waste, i.e., vegetative debris, may be reduced by chipping before hauling to a landfill. In other parts of the country, open pit burning is allowed, obviously with the necessary permits in place prior to burning. However, burning is not a universal option, particularly in heavily urbanized parts of the country and those with severe air quality issues.

Household Hazardous Waste

The local agency may want to conduct household hazardous materials collections. However, laying a strong legal basis and having a health officer-approved plan in place prior to operations are both critically important.

This audit and the following appeals case derive from an audit performed by the Department of Homeland Security-Office of the Inspector General performed on the Los Angeles County Department of Public Works following the Northridge Earthquake in January of 1994.

"The Department of Homeland Security Office of Inspector General (OIG) audited $29.1 million in projects FEMA approved for the Applicant. In OIG Audit Report Number DS-05-06, dated July 3, 2006, the OIG questioned $373,300 for the collection and disposal of HHW because it determined that these activities were not directly related to the disaster. FEMA de-obligated the funds based on the OIG's recommendation. The Acting Regional Administrator sustained this determination on first appeal in a letter dated January 8, 2009. . . The Applicant submitted a second appeal letter on March 16, 2009, to the State. The Applicant provided copies of Form 303 Household

Hazardous Waste Collection, information that lists the types and quantities of HHW collected at each location and the number of participants at each location as supporting documentation."[114]

One of the issues in this case is that when the auditors compared the documentation regarding the number of participating households, there were fewer households participating in the post-disaster collections than in pre-disaster collection events.

"The Department claimed $373,300 for 3 of 28 program events that took place in fiscal year 1994, the year of the disaster. Department records supporting these events identified the number of participants and volume of waste collected; additionally, the records showed that the cost and number of participants were consistent with the other 25 events conducted during the fiscal year. Furthermore, the Department conducted 14 events before and after the disaster with no indication that the frequency of program events or the quantity of household hazardous waste increased due to the disaster. In fact, an event scheduled 6 days after the disaster had the third lowest number of participants and the sixth lowest quantity of hazardous waste collected during the fiscal year."[115]

The message here is that the local agency must clearly demonstrate the need for the response activities. In this case, the need for household hazardous waste "round-ups" were not directly caused by the declared disaster and thus did not address issues of an immediate threat to life safety and/or the public health because of the disaster.

Hazardous Materials (Industrial-Strength)

Debris which is a hazardous material, or debris which has been contaminated by hazardous materials, represents yet another wild-card for the local agency.

Any of these classes of debris can be contaminated and turned into hazardous waste and thereby require special handling, extra personnel safety, or other environmental restrictions, in addition to requiring disposal at a properly licensed and regulated facility, thereby substantially increasing costs to the local agency and FEMA. Those classes of debris which are marked with an asterisk are usually considered hazardous materials by their very nature and use.

- Construction and Demolition * (asbestos, lead paint)
- E-waste
- Garbage
- Hanging Limbs
- Hazardous Materials *
- Hazardous Leaning Trees
- Household Hazardous Waste *
- Infectious/Medical Waste * (biological)
- Orphan tanks * (oil, gases, chemicals)
- Private Property Debris
- Putrescent Waste * (biological)
- Sand/Soil/Mud
- Stumps
- Vegetative
- Vehicles * (batteries, fuel, and oil)
- Vessels * (batteries, fuel, and oil)
- Wet Debris
- White Goods * (refrigerants)

It is important to remember that FEMA, other Federal agencies, and state regulatory agencies will be fully engaged in ensuring that all the necessary permits have been issued prior to the beginning of the clean-up work, except when that work is determined to be a true emergency and an immediate threat to life safety and the public health, such as a leaking tanker truck, railroad car, or similar immediate threat. Failure of the local agency to successfully navigate the permits process may result in deobligation of costs.

Obviously, some of these classes of debris are more toxic than others, but all represent potential threats to environmental quality. The classes of debris are important to FEMA because of 1) the environmental issues attached to the various classes of debris; 2) the relative costs associated with each of the different classes of debris. Therefore, at the local level we need to ensure that not only are all debris loads documented with the proper forms, but that the debris is handled by classes and, when hazardous materials of any level of toxicity, are properly disposed.

Hazardous Materials Debris Regulatory Requirements

"Removal and disposal of pollutants and hazardous substances are eligible. Eligible activities include:

- Separation of hazardous materials from other debris;
- Specialized procedures for handling and disposing of hazardous materials;
- Control or stabilization of the hazardous material;
- Pumping water contaminated with the hazardous material; and
- Clean-up and disposal of the hazardous material.

Testing for contaminants in water, air, or soil necessary to ensure elimination of the immediate threat is eligible. "[116] *(See the PAPPG for details.)*

The local agency must comply with Federal, state, and local government environmental requirements for handling hazardous materials. Before handling or disposing of hazardous materials, the local agency should contact the appropriate Federal or other agencies to obtain required permits, notify agencies of hazardous materials storage, and to coordinate the creation of any required facility-specific Emergency Response Plans for spills, safety, and proper handling.

Additionally, appropriate certified hazardous waste specialists should handle, capture, recycle, reuse, or dispose of hazardous materials. When providing PA (Public Assistance) funding for work involving the handling of hazardous materials, FEMA must ensure compliance with the Resource Conservation and Recovery Act (RCRA).

It is important to note that the workers who handle hazardous materials must all be properly licensed or certified by the appropriate level of agency. Failure to use only properly licensed and certified hazmat specialists can result in a FEMA deobligation for the cost of the work performed. The debris management contract should further state that any work performed by unlicensed or improperly licensed workers will result in non-payment of invoices. The contract should also require that the contractor will provide the licenses and certifications for every hazmat worker upon commencement of the contract, and for each time that a new employee is added to the contract.

Demolitions

"Demolition of unsafe private structures that endanger the public may be eligible as emergency work when the following conditions are met:

- The structures were damaged and made unsafe by the declared disaster;
- The applicant certifies that the structures have been determined unsafe and pose an immediate threat to the public;

- The applicant establishes legal responsibility based on statute, ordinance, or code to exercise its authority to demolish the unsafe structure;
- The applicant obtains rights of entry; and
- The applicant indemnifies the federal government from claims arising from the demolition of the structures."[117]

"Demolition of private structures requires approval prior to work. The structures must be found to be unsafe due to the imminent threat of partial or complete collapse. FEMA will consider whether there are more cost-effective alternative measures to eliminate threats to life, public health, and safety posed by disaster-damaged, unsafe structures, including fencing off unsafe structures and restricting public access, when evaluating requests for demolition."[118]

"Local governments must agree to hold the federal government harmless and free from damages due to performance of the work. Demolition work also requires state or local certification that the structure is unsafe, as well as having an authorized local official condemn the structure in accordance with state and local law. Demolition costs are also eligible for permanent work assistance when the work is required in support of eligible repair, replacement, or reconstruction of a project."[119]

"While the Stafford Act authorizes demolition separately from debris removal, there are situations in which the distinction is a fine line. For example, in the implementation of the Expedited Debris Removal pilot program after the southern tornadoes in the spring of 2011, FEMA followed a policy of one wall standing:

If a damaged structure only had one wall left standing, it would all be considered debris and the cost of knocking over the standing wall would be considered eligible under the pilot debris program. If a structure had more than one wall standing, it would not be considered debris and it would have to be separately authorized and funded as demolition, which was outside of the purview of Expedited Debris Removal."[120]

"This is also a relevant distinction in terms of eligibility. Debris removal may be authorized when FEMA determines it to be in the public interest, which includes an economic recovery rationale, in addition to protection of health and safety. However, demolition is only authorized as an emergency protective measure where there are immediate threats to life and property and the unsafe structures endanger the public. FEMA has no authority to fund demolition activity that only addresses economic recovery."[121]

However, not all demolition work is eligible, even when a demolition is approved by FEMA. "Ineligible work associated with the demolition of private structures includes, but is not limited to:

- Removal or covering of concrete pads and driveways except for structures in a FEMA-funded buyout program; and
- Removal of slabs or foundations that do not present a health or safety hazard, except for structures in a FEMA-funded buyout program through the HMGP (*Hazard Mitigation Grant Program*), (the removal of Substantially Damaged structures and associated facilities acquired through HMGP may be eligible as Category A, Debris Removal).

This is another appearance of an appeals case from Cedar Rapids, Iowa, following the 2008 flooding in that state. "FEMA prepared PWs 6957, 10339, 10459 and 10436 to reimburse the Applicant for eligible costs associated with the demolition of private structures that were made unsafe as a result of the flooding that occurred in 2008. FEMA advised the Applicant on March 31, 2010, that the removal of concrete slabs from these damaged structures would only be eligible for Public Assistance funding if testing determined that the slabs contained hazardous material as a direct result of the declared disaster. FEMA also advised the Applicant that these determinations would be made on a case-by-case basis."[122]

First Appeal

"The Applicant appealed FEMA's guidance on May 14, 2010. The Applicant contended that its pre-existing local codes and ordinances require concrete slabs and foundations be removed as part of its demolition operations. On January 31, 2011, the Regional Administrator determined that the removal of slabs and basement walls of damaged structures built prior to 1979 would be eligible for reimbursement because they most likely contained asbestos, which would present an immediate threat to public health and safety. However, the Regional Administrator determined that FEMA would require testing for the presence of asbestos in concrete slabs of damaged structures that were built after 1979. If tests determined that asbestos was not present, the removal of the concrete slabs would not be eligible for Public Assistance funding."[123]

Second Appeal

"In its second appeal, submitted April 1, 2011, the Applicant contends that FEMA had determined that all costs associated with the removal of concrete slabs, foundations, and basements are ineligible. At the request of the State and the Applicant, FEMA convened a teleconference with representatives of the Applicant on November 17, 2011, to discuss the subject appeal. During the call, the Applicant reiterated that the removal of concrete slabs, foundations, and basements is required by its codes and ordinances as part of any demolition work. The Applicant informed FEMA that it did not test the slabs for asbestos due to the large number of properties that needed to be demolished."[124]

"I have reviewed the information submitted with the appeal and have determined that the Applicant has not demonstrated that the concrete slabs of the damaged structures, built prior to or after 1979, presented an immediate threat to public health and safety. The Applicant has not demonstrated the presence of asbestos in the slabs or that such presence would create a public health and safety threat requiring removal of the slabs. All costs associated with the removal of concrete slabs, foundations, and basements on PWs 6957, 10339, 10459 and 10436 are ineligible for Public Assistance funding. Accordingly, I am denying the second appeal."[125]

RACM (Regulated Asbestos Containing Materials)

In the procurements for both normal debris removal and structure demolitions, Title 2 of the Code of Federal Regulations, Part 200 must be complied with. In this case, the local agency introduced a prohibited geographic requirement which created an issue that resulted in a partial deobligation of funding.

"In June 2008, severe storms and flooding impacted the Applicant and caused extensive damage to the Sinclair Warehouse Complex (Sinclair). The Sinclair Complex is the former location of the Wilson-Sinclair/Farmstead Foods food processing plant. The Applicant purchased the site in 2007 and leased portions of the facilities for use as commercial warehouse and office space. Due to its proximity to the Cedar River, the Sinclair Complex experienced high velocity flooding and significant inundation from flood waters. After the flood, local building officials determined that the damaged facilities at the Sinclair Complex were unsafe, pursuant to Cedar Rapids Municipal Code, and issued a notice and order to demolish the structures in December 2009."[126]

"The Applicant requested FEMA assistance for demolition and disposal of Regulated Asbestos Containing Material (RACM) debris from Sinclair. FEMA prepared PWs 10433, 10445, 10523, 10524, and 10525 to document disaster-related damage and eligible work at the facility. The Applicant prepared a Request for Bids (RFB) on December 31, 2009, for demolition and disposal of the RACM debris from Sinclair. In the RFB, the Applicant specified that the debris was to be disposed of at the Cedar Rapids/Linn County Solid Waste Agency Landfill Site Number 1(Site No. 1). Site No. 1 is 1.5 miles from Sinclair. The original RFB did not contain an estimate of the quantity of debris. In addendums to the RFB, the Applicant estimated the debris at 100,000 tons and later at 65,000 tons. The Applicant also amended the RFB to reduce the requirement on performance and payment bonds from 100 percent to 75 percent of the contract price."[127]

"On January 15, 2010, the Applicant received 11 sealed bids. Unit prices ranged from $65 per ton to $173 per ton for removal and disposal of debris. Demolition and utility disconnects were bid as separate line items. The Applicant considered the lowest bid to be non-responsive to its RFB because the contractor proposed to take the debris to an alternate landfill approximately 90 miles from Sinclair to Milan, Illinois. The Applicant rejected all bids and rebid the project on March 5, 2010, and maintained the requirement for disposal at Site No. 1. Prior to the second bid, the Solid Waste Agency reduced its tipping fee from $120 per ton to $90 per ton. In response to the second RFB, the Applicant received ten bids, ranging from $117 per ton to $135 per ton, which also included the cost for demolition in addition to debris removal and disposal. The Applicant awarded the lowest bid to D.W. Zinser Company (Zinser) at $117 per ton, which included demolition, removal, and disposal of the RACM debris at Site No. 1."[128]

"In a letter dated June 15, 2011, FEMA stated that the Applicant's procurement process violated several regulations. FEMA determined that the Applicant's requirement to dispose of the debris at Site No. 1 constituted a geographic preference restricted by 44 CFR §13.36(c)(2). FEMA also stated that reducing the debris estimate from 100,000 tons to 65,000 tons may have influenced competition, violating 44 CFR §13.36(c)(1). Additionally, FEMA determined that the Applicant's action to reduce the performance and payment bond requirement from 100 percent to 75 percent violated 44 CFR §13.36(h)(2). FEMA limited reimbursement to $65 per ton for removal and disposal of debris, based on the lowest price per ton in the initial bid proposals, from Rachel Contracting (Rachel)."[129]

As it turned out, the requirement to use a specific landfill for disposal of the demolition debris did not constitute a prohibited geographic preference. However, it still led the agency down the path to deobligation.

"Applicants are generally prohibited from using geographic preferences for contractors pursuant to 44 CFR §13.36(c)(2), which states that, '[g]rantees and subgrantees will conduct procurements in a manner that prohibits the use of statutorily or administratively imposed in-State or local geographical preferences in the evaluation of bids or proposals, except in those cases where applicable Federal statutes expressly mandate or encourage geographic preference.' This term is not defined in 44 CFR Part 13, but generally applies to location-based preference given to contractors in the bidding process, and not to a specification within the contract such as the landfill. Therefore, the Applicant's requirement for contractors to use Site No. 1 in its RFB is not a prohibited geographic preference."[130]

Reasonable Costs and Scope of Work

"The Applicant rejected the first round of bidding because it considered the lowest bid (Rachel) to be non-responsive due to its proposal to use the Milan Landfill rather than Site No. 1. The Applicant claimed that it was required to dispose of debris 'in a landfill operated by an agency created by agreement between the City of Cedar Rapids and Linn County,' which is Site No. 1. The Applicant then re-bid the project; however, this procurement action indicated that the estimated quantity of demolition debris was 65,000 tons as opposed to the original estimate of 100,000 tons. The Applicant intentionally bid the project at almost half the estimated debris quantity in order to allow contractors to avoid acquiring performance and payment bonds for the higher contract cost of the higher quantity of debris. Because the Applicant underrepresented the scope of work to facilitate bidders' ability to obtain a performance bond, it did not comply with Federal procurement requirements. Specifically, 44 CFR §13.36(d)(2)(i)(A) states that sealed bidding is feasible when 'A complete, adequate, and realistic specification or purchase description is available.' In addition, 44 CFR §13.36(d)(2)(ii) (B) states when sealed bids are used, 'The invitation for bids, which will include any specifications and pertinent attachments, shall define the items or services in order for the bidder to properly respond.' Soliciting bids on a scope of work intentionally represented as approximately half of the estimated quantity does not fulfill the requirements to provide a complete, adequate and realistic specification and does not properly define the services to be procured."[131]

"Though the contract for $117 per ton was not properly procured due to the intentional underrepresentation of the debris tonnage, FEMA may evaluate reasonableness of costs pursuant to 44 CFR §13.43, Enforcement. 44 CFR §13.43(a)(2) states in relevant part that 'If a grantee or subgrantee materially fails to comply with any term of an award, whether stated in a Federal statute or regulation . . . the awarding agency may . . . Disallow (that is, deny both use of funds and matching credit for) all or part of the cost of the activity or action not in compliance.' Because the scope of work approximately doubled the specifications that were stated in the original bid, and the Applicant did not re-compete the contract, FEMA is not able to determine whether the requested cost of $117 per ton is reasonable for the actual scope of work of the project. Generally, such an increase causes unit costs to decrease. Therefore, the rate that FEMA determines to be a reasonable cost for this project was the original lowest bid of $65 per ton."[132]

"As indicated by the Applicant and the State in the second appeal, the $65 per ton figure does not include the cost of demolition, and the line-item cost for demolition associated with this bid was $1.3 million. As the demolition of the damaged structures is eligible work, the additional cost for demolition not included in the per tonnage rate is an eligible cost. The Applicant also requested additional funding for monitoring costs it claimed it would have incurred by using the farther landfill associated with the original lowest bid. The request for additional monitoring costs is not eligible because these costs were not actually incurred by the Applicant."

"For reasons set forth in this response, the unit cost above the previously approved $65 per ton for debris removal is not substantiated as reasonable and is therefore not eligible for funding. While the requirement to use Site No. 1 does not constitute a prohibited geographical preference, the Applicant's procurement practices did not otherwise comply with Federal procurement regulations because the applicant procured its contract based on an intentionally inaccurate representation of the scope of work."[133]

In this case, the agency appeared to be gaming the system, and that effort came back to bite them. While they had to pay $117 per ton, they were only reimbursed $65 per ton for their failures to fully comply with 2 CFR, Part 200.

Recycling and Recycling Revenue

Most states and local jurisdictions have some sort of recycling laws and ordinances. These same regulations may require that disaster debris be recycled to the maximum extent possible. This of course will add time to the process and increase the costs.

"If the Applicant receives revenue for recycling debris, FEMA reduces PA (Public Assistance) funding by the amount of revenue received. The Applicant may deduct costs for administering and marketing the sale of the salvageable materials from the fair market value. If a contract allows the contractor to take possession of salvageable material and benefit from its sale to lower bid prices, there is no salvage value to be recovered at the end of the project. Therefore, the Applicant has no further obligation to FEMA."[134]

This issue must be addressed in the debris management plan and the corresponding contract(s) for debris clearance: 1) to ensure that the issue is resolved at contact time, and 2) to document for FEMA that there is no residual income from recycling, if that is the case.

Debris Monitoring for Contracted Debris Removal

"FEMA requires the Applicant (the local agency) to monitor all contracted debris operations to ensure that the quantities and work claimed are accurate and eligible. This includes documenting debris quantities by types, quantities reduced, reduction methods, and pickup and disposal locations. If the Applicant does not monitor contracted debris removal operations, it jeopardizes its PA *(Public Assistance)* funding for that work. The Applicant may use force account resources (including temporary hires), contractors, or a combination of these for monitoring. It is not necessary, or cost-effective, to have Professional Engineers or other certified professionals *(i.e., certified arborists)* perform debris monitoring duties. FEMA considers costs unreasonable when associated with the use of staff that are more highly qualified than necessary for the associated work. If the Applicant uses staff with professional qualifications to conduct debris monitoring, it must document the reason it needed staff with those qualifications. FEMA provides training to the Applicant's force account debris monitors (including its temporary hires) upon request."[135] (Emphasis Added)

"Eligible activities associated with debris monitoring include, but are not limited to:

- Field supervisory oversight;
- Monitoring contracted debris removal at both the loading and disposal sites;
- Compiling documentation, such as load tickets and monitor reports, to substantiate eligible debris; and
- Training debris monitors on debris removal operations, monitoring responsibilities and documentation processes, and FEMA debris eligibility criteria."[136]

True-Life Tales

Following yet another massively destructive fire, a Northern California agency was involved in its debris management. A large part of the debris was thousands of burned trees, still standing but so fire-damaged that they presented a safety threat. The agency bid and awarded both debris removal and monitoring contracts. The monitoring contract was originally bid at $600,000, a not-to-exceed amount. However, the Public Works Department, which was overseeing the work, had already approved $300,000 in change orders, and the agency (Auditor-Controller's office) expected the total amount to increase to a total of $1,500,000 for the monitoring alone. Because the Public Works department had approved the $300,000 in change orders, the agency attorney opined that the agency was on the hook for the approved contract overruns, even though the original contract amount was far exceeded. This is a real-life story, probably with no happy ending. The root cause may have been a substantial underestimating of the scope of the work. This of course goes back, at least in part, to having a well-defined and comprehensive debris management plan in place before a disaster occurs.

Alternative Procedures for Debris Removal

"The Applicant may elect to participate in the Alternative Procedures for debris removal and receive reimbursement for straight-time for the Applicant's budgeted employees that conduct debris removal activities. The Applicant opts-in by including straight-time in their debris removal (Category A) project claims."[137]

As with many things FEMA, there is both a carrot and a stick approach to participating in the PAAP (Public Assistance Alternative Procedures) Debris program.

"Upon the declaration of a major disaster or emergency by the President authorizing FEMA to provide debris removal assistance, FEMA provides eligible PA subrecipients within the declared area the opportunity to participate in the alternative procedures for the debris removal pilot program. It includes:

1. A sliding scale for determining the federal share for removal of debris and wreckage based on the time it takes to complete debris and wreckage removal;
2. Use of revenue from recycled debris without offset to the grant amount as program income;
3. Reimbursement of force account labor both for regular time and overtime wages for the employees of state, tribal, or local governments, or owners or operators of PNP facilities performing or administering debris and wreckage removal; and
4. A one-time cost share incentive to a state, tribal, or local government to have a FEMA-reviewed debris management plan accepted by the FEMA Administrator, in addition to at least one prequalified debris and wreckage removal contractors before the date of the major disaster declaration."[138]

For an agency that has both the plans and contracts, or at least pre-qualified contractors, it is possible to get a fast start on clearing debris. However, if the agency must develop a debris management plan and/or solicit bids and then award a contract, the first 30 days may be a complete loss; perhaps most of the first 90 days will be lost depending on how quickly the agency can turn a bid into a working contract. Note that the clock starts running not when the President signs the disaster declaration, but when the incident period begins. This time differential may be days, but more often it will be weeks for many disasters. Also note the bottom row of the table: "Federal dollars will NOT be provided for debris removal after 180 days (unless an extension is authorized by FEMA HQ)." This is not a time extension approval issued by the state or even the FEMA Region, but by FEMA Headquarters in Washington. This may prove to be a very heavy lift.

The next point is that recycling revenue may or may not represent a bonus to the local agency. If the value of recycled materials is included as an incentive to the contractor, then there is no direct cash benefit to the local agency.

The third point regards the matter of straight time pay for force account labor. If the disaster is a large-scale event, then there will likely be little debris clearance done by the local agency's own employees, other than the 'cut and push' earlier described for emergency road clearance. So that advantage may be moot.

The last point would only apply if the local agency meets both conditions: 1) having a FEMA-reviewed plan (note: this is not a FEMA approval), and 2) having at least one pre-qualified contractor.

The most important thing here is that unless the local agency already has both a debris management and a debris monitoring plan, and both contracts in place PRIOR to the disaster, the PAAP Debris program may not work – certainly not work as well as one might hope.

First, the sliding scale may be enticing, as is illustrated in the following table.

Table 15.2 Public Assistance Alternative Procedures Pilot Program for Debris Removal

Debris Removal Work (Days from Start of Incident Period	Federal Cost Share
1–30	85%
31–90	80%
91–180	75%
Federal dollars will NOT be provided for debris removal after 180 days (unless an extension is authorized by FEMA HQ	

Source: Public Assistance Alternative Procedures Pilot Program for Debris Removal, Version 5, June 28, 2017

The real danger hidden here is that the local agency opts into the program merely by including the straight time hours for its own force account labor. Someone on the front lines who does not understand the full ramifications of including straight time labor could create a very serious problem for the agency by this simple act. It does not take an official act by the elected governing body, nor even a signed statement by a senior official.

The PAAP program is a little bit of carrot, and a lot more stick. Remember, in the SRIA (Sandy Recovery Improvement Act) of 2013, the principal reason that Congress passed the legislation was "(1) reducing the costs to the Federal Government of providing such assistance."[139]

For those local agencies that play an 'A' game every day and have all their ducks lined up in a row, the Alternative Procedures may be worth pursuing. For all other agencies, a well-considered analysis of their abilities to perform well under extreme duress should be in order. Furthermore, there is still very limited experience with the PAAP program to provide a sufficient basis for making an informed decision.

Closing Thoughts on Debris

I was fortunate some years ago to be invited to New Orleans to make a presentation on disaster cost recovery. As we were gathering in the lobby, a lady came up to me and said that she wanted to attend my session, but her boss had instructed her to attend a different program. However, she was quite emphatic as she recommended to me to share with my group that her parish, St. Tammany Parish, had audited their debris management invoices, and found that 40% of them contained errors. Had these invoices been paid, that would be money down the drain if FEMA were to audit the same invoices and find that they were paid in error. The parish would have little recourse against the contractor but would not be reimbursed by FEMA for those defective invoices.

This chapter on debris management is another of what I call the 800-pound gorillas of disaster cost recovery: those areas within the Public Assistance program wherein lie the largest percentage of errors made by local agencies and therefore result in the greatest financial losses suffered by those same agencies: Disaster Accounting; Insurance; Damage Assessment; Eligibility; Procurement; and Debris Management. There are many other areas, some of which we have yet to explore, but these six are all runaway trains looking for a gasoline tanker truck parked across the railroad tracks.

Notes

1 Public Assistance Program and Policy Guide, Version 4, June 1, 2020, FFP 104–009–2, p. 101.
2 Crowley, J. February 20, 2017. *A Measurement of the Effectiveness and Efficiency of Pre-disaster Debris Management Plans*. University of Hawaii at Manoa, Department of Urban and Regional Planning, p. 1.

3 Ibid, p. 5.
4 Ibid.
5 Public Assistance Program and Policy Guide, Version 4, June 1, 2020, FFP 104–009–2, p. 106.
6 Source: Disaster Operations Legal Reference, Version 4.0, September 25, 2020, pp. 5–50–5–51.
7 Ibid.
8 Ibid.
9 https://www.fema.gov/appeal/documentation-0
10 https://www.fema.gov/appeal/debris-removal-71
11 Ibid.
12 Ibid.
13 Disaster Operations Legal Reference, Version 4.0, September 25, 2020, pp. 5–49–5–50.
14 Ibid, pp. 5–60–5–61.
15 Ibid, pp. 5–50.
16 Public Assistance Program and Policy Guide, Version 4, June 1, 2020, FFP 104–009–2, p. 111.
17 Ibid, p. 115.
18 Ibid, p. 100.
19 https://www.fema.gov/appeal/debris-removal-private-businesses
20 Ibid.
21 Ibid.
22 Ibid.
23 https://www.fema.gov/appeal/debris-removal-4
24 Ibid.
25 Ibid.
26 Ibid.
27 Ibid.
28 Ibid.
29 Ibid.
30 Ibid.
31 https://www.newsreview.com/chico/content/board-gets-bombshell/27644851/
32 Public Assistance Program and Policy Guide, Version 4, June 1, 2020, FFP 104–009–2, p. 106.
33 https://www.fema.gov/appeal/ehp-and-other-compliance-0
34 Ibid.
35 Ibid.
36 Ibid.
37 Ibid.
38 Public Assistance Program and Policy Guide, Version 4, June 1, 2020, FFP 104–009–2, p. 100.
39 Disaster Operations Legal Reference, Version 4.0, September 25, 2020, pp. 5–56.
40 Ibid.
41 Ibid, pp. 5–57.
42 Ibid.
43 Ibid.
44 Ibid, pp. 5–59.
45 https://www.fema.gov/appeal/debris-removal-private-property-9
46 Ibid.
47 Ibid.
48 Ibid.
49 https://www.fema.gov/appeal/debris-removal-private-property-6
50 Ibid.
51 Ibid.
52 Ibid.
53 Ibid.
54 Ibid.
55 Ibid.
56 https://www.fema.gov/appeal/debris-removal-private-property
57 Ibid.
58 Ibid.
59 Ibid.
60 Ibid.
61 Ibid.

62 Ibid.
63 Ibid.
64 https://www.fema.gov/appeal/debris-removal-73
65 Ibid.
66 Ibid.
67 Ibid.
68 Ibid.
69 Ibid.
70 Hamlet, Act 3, Scene 4.
71 Ibid.
72 Ibid.
73 Disaster Operations Legal Reference, Version 4.0, September 25, 2020, pp. 3–7.
74 https://www.fema.gov/appeal/reasonable-costs-debris-removal-monitoring
75 Ibid.
76 Ibid.
77 Ibid.
78 Ibid.
79 Ibid.
80 https://www.fema.gov/appeal/private-property-debris-removal-1
81 Ibid.
82 Ibid.
83 Ibid.
84 Ibid.
85 Ibid.
86 Ibid.
87 Ibid.
88 Ibid.
89 https://www.fema.gov/appeal/rural-electric-cooperative-procurement
90 Ibid.
91 Ibid.
92 Public Assistance Program and Policy Guide, Version 4, June 1, 2020, FFP 104–009–2, p. 82.
93 Ibid.
94 Ibid.
95 Ibid.
96 Ibid.
97 Ibid.
98 DHS-OIG Audit, OIG-17–77-D, FEMA Should Disallow $1.5 Million in Grant Funds Awarded to Hays County, Texas, June 22, 2017, p. 2.
99 Ibid.
100 Ibid, p. 3.
101 Ibid.
102 Ibid.
103 Ibid, p. 4.
104 Ibid.
105 Ibid, pp. 4–5.
106 Ibid, p. 5.
107 Ibid, p. 6.
108 https://www.usace.army.mil/Missions/Emergency-Operations/emergency_support/debris/#:~: text=USACE%20Mission%20Capabilities%20%20%2D%20DFA%20Missions&text=Emergency%20 Clearance%20%E2%80%93%20A%20roadway%20clearance,property%2C%20when%20 directed%20by%20FEMA.
109 Public Assistance Program and Policy Guide, Version 4, June 1, 2020, FFP 104–009–2, p. 128.
110 https://www.fema.gov/appeal/audit-report-number-dd-07-04
111 Ibid.
112 Ibid.
113 Ibid.
114 https://www.fema.gov/appeal/household-hazardous-waste

115 DHS-OIG Audit DS-05–06 Audit of Los Angeles County Department of Public Works.
116 Public Assistance Program and Policy Guide, Version 4, June 1, 2020, FFP 104–009–2, p. 116.
117 Disaster Operations Legal Reference, Version 4.0, September 25, 2020, pp. 5–72–5–73.
118 Ibid, pp. 5–73.
119 Ibid.
120 Ibid.
121 Ibid, pp. 5–74.
122 https://www.fema.gov/appeal/demolition
123 Ibid.
124 Ibid.
125 Ibid.
126 https://www.fema.gov/appeal/regulated-asbestos-containing-material-racm-demolition-and-debris-re-moval
127 Ibid.
128 Ibid.
129 Ibid.
130 Ibid.
131 Ibid.
132 Ibid.
133 Ibid.
134 Public Assistance Program and Policy Guide, Version 4, June 1, 2020, FFP 104–009–2, pp. 105–106.
135 Ibid, p. 107.
136 Ibid.
137 Ibid, p. 101.
138 Disaster Operations Legal Reference, Version 4.0, September 25, 2020, pp. 5–48–5–49.
139 Division B – Sandy Recovery Improvement Act of 2013.

16 Immediate Needs Funding

Immediate Needs Funding

"Immediate Needs Funding (INF) is a variation of the advanced funding FEMA typically provides based on a completed scope of work memorialized in a PW in cooperation with the recipient, (*i.e., the state*), and subrecipient *(i.e., the local agency)*. With Immediate Needs Funding, funding is provided, however, for 'urgent needs' requiring payment within the first 60 days after a disaster declaration, in a manner that avoids burdening applicants 'during peak crisis operations' with completion of the ordinary PW scope of work process."[1]

Eligible work typically includes debris removal, emergency protective measures, and removal of health and safety hazards. Immediate needs funds can be used for such expenses as temporary labor costs, overtime payroll, equipment, and material fees.

How Does the Immediate Needs Funding process Work?

If a disaster is declared and the State thinks damage costs warrant the need for immediate cash flow, the State may request Immediate Needs Funding on behalf of local agencies. Up to 50% of the Federal share of emergency monies will then be placed in the State's account. Because this money can be made available in advance of normal procedures, paperwork and processing times are reduced and you can receive emergency funds faster.

What Does the Local Agency Need to Do?

- If Immediate Needs Funding is available in the state, each eligible local agency has the choice of whether to request funding.
- Immediate Needs Funding is usually based on a percentage of eligible emergency work identified during the Preliminary Damage Assessment (PDA). It is important to assist the Preliminary Damage Assessment team by informing them about the emergency work and helping to estimate the agency's needs.
- When a Preliminary Damage Assessment occurs and the damages are not identified or no immediate needs are noted, the agency may have the opportunity to request expedited handling of its emergency work when officially filing the Request for Public Assistance (RPA).
- If a Preliminary Damage Assessment does not occur, the local agency may still be eligible to receive Immediate Needs Funding. The state will determine eligible applicants and cost estimates. The local agency should notify the state of the interest in Immediate Needs Funding and be prepared to provide information to estimate the immediate needs.

DOI: 10.4324/9781003487869-20

- Whether a Preliminary Damage Assessment has been performed or not, the State will assess the need for immediate cash flow in the area. If the state determines a need, they will apply to FEMA for Immediate Needs Funding on behalf of the local agencies. Each local agency should assist the state by conveying its interest in Immediate Needs Funding and explaining the immediate needs. This may be accomplished at the Applicants' Briefing.
- If the state determines that Immediate Needs Funding is warranted, local agencies will follow the state's formal procedure for making an Immediate Needs Funding request. The state will notify each agency of this process; typically, they will have each local agency send a letter of request to a designated state official. The state will also notify each local agency of the deadline to request Immediate Needs Funding.
- A completed Request form must be submitted before FEMA can release any Immediate Needs Funding monies. The local agency should return the completed form as soon as possible, in person, by mail, or fax.
- If Immediate Needs Funding is approved by FEMA, the state will contact each local agency about how to access Immediate Needs Funding monies.

What Do Local Agencies Need to Know?

- Immediate Needs Funding is designated for costs such as overtime payroll, temporary employee payroll, equipment expenses, the use of applicant-owned equipment or equipment rental, materials purchased or used from inventory, and payments to contractors for work performed.
- Upon Immediate Needs Funding approval by FEMA, PWs will be prepared by PA staff to obligate this funding.
- Although the recommended Immediate Needs Funding amount is determined by site, each local agency may use Immediate Needs Funding money for any eligible emergency work that requires payment within the first 60 days. Immediate Needs Funding money is not available for permanent work; emergency work with environmental or historic considerations or hazard mitigation projects; or projects that will not be completed in 60 days.
- As the actual emergency work PWs are received, the Public Assistance Coordinator (PAC) will adjust the funding for these projects to account for each Immediate Needs Funding advance.
- If the total actual emergency work costs are less than the amount of Immediate Needs Funding received, the remaining Immediate Needs Funding balance will be offset against the permanent work projects. No permanent work projects will be obligated until the Immediate Needs Funding advance is reimbursed. This is important to note because the funding for all permanent work, i.e., Categories C-G will be held up until a reconciliation of Immediate Needs Funding is completed.
- The Public Assistance Coordinator will use an Immediate Needs Funding Reconciliation Sheet to track the Project Worksheets (PWs) as they are used to offset the Immediate Needs Funding monies. After all Immediate Needs Funding monies have been offset against the actual PWs, the Public Assistance Coordinator will forward a copy of this sheet to the local agency. Keep this sheet with the other project documentation to be available for future funding questions and/or audits.
- If a reconciled project is within the small-project threshold, then it will be included in the small-project validation procedure. If the cost is above the threshold, the project will be classified as a large project and actual cost documentation will be reviewed.
- Each local agency is responsible for maintaining all documentation needed to support the projects that receive Immediate Needs Funding.
- The Public Assistance Coordinator and Applicant Liaison can answer any specific questions concerning Immediate Needs Funding.

The availability and application of Immediate Needs Funding will be very dependent on the circumstances of each disaster. In 2013, the Rim Fire damaged a large area in the Sierra Nevada Foothills in California. Although the fire began on August 20th, 2013, and lasted until September 8th, 2013, the Governor of California did not request a Presidential disaster declaration until October 8th, 2013. The request was initially denied, and then on December 13th, 115 days after the fire broke out, the President signed a disaster declaration. At this point, a request for Immediate needs funding became an exercise in futility insofar as Immediate Needs Funding must be used within 60 days, which at this point had long passed.

In Chapter 11, in the section "When Should We Activate the EOC," we saw that for the years 2020 and 2021, excluding all Covid-19 cases, the average time between the onset of a disaster and the date of the Presidential disaster declaration was an average of 62 days. In these cases, where the Presidential declaration isn't signed for months after the onset of the disaster, there is little or no room for the implementation of Immediate Needs Funding.

Note

1 FEMA, Disaster Operations Legal Reference Version 4.0, September 25, 2020.

17 Expedited Funding for Emergency Work

Expedited Projects for Emergency Work

Although the keyword in the title for this funding resource available from FEMA is "expedited," in this case "expedited" is a relative term. The local agency may apply for Expedited Funding within 60 days of the Recovery Scoping Meeting (RSM) and FEMA will make an effort to fund the request within 90 days of the receipt of the request. At the maximum time windows, this puts the "expedited funding" no closer than five months, presuming that a Presidential disaster declaration is signed on day one of the disaster. If the Presidential disaster declaration is signed months after the disaster occurs, expedited funding may be available after the emergency work is completed. However, this may still be better than receiving the funding a year or more after the disaster.

FEMA may provide expedited funding for emergency work projects (Categories A or B) that meet or exceed the Large Project threshold. Prior to August 2022, the Small Project/Large Project line of demarcation was less than $140,000. However, in early August, this line was increased to $1,037,000. The regulation governing this limit may or may not change in the future.

FEMA provides funding for Expedited Projects at 50% percent of the Federal share of the estimated project cost. Thus, when a local agency has a request for $1,037,000 in expedited emergency work funding for which FEMA would ordinarily pay no less than 75%, the amount eligible for Expedited Funding would be $388,875.

A request for Expedited Projects funding must be submitted to FEMA within 60 days of the Recovery Scoping Meeting date. To support the request, the local agency must provide enough information for FEMA to validate that both the work and costs are eligible.

That said, in some extreme cases, expedited funding may be received within days, particularly if the local agency has extremely knowledgeable and very well-organized staff or consultants to assist in the application, and the severity of the disaster warrants it.

The local agency must provide the following information, grouped by the Applicant's regular operational periods.

When the emergency work has an increased Federal cost share for a limited timeframe, the local agency needs to separate work expected to be completed within the increased cost share timeframe from work anticipated to be completed after the increased cost share period:

A detailed description of the work and documentation to substantiate that the work is eligible. This includes:

- Description of immediate threat;
- Detailed description of work activities;
- Work locations; and

DOI: 10.4324/9781003487869-21

- Additionally, for debris:

    a. estimated quantities by type of debris documented with photographs or video,
    b. temporary staging and disposal locations, with
    c. copies of permits and reduction methods.

Added documentation is required, including:

- Insurance documentation, if any

The following <u>estimated costs</u> based upon:

- Force Account labor or Mutual Aid labor, documented by:

    - Number of personnel;
    - Average hours per day;
    - Average days per week;
    - Average pay rate;
    - Lodging and per diem rates; and
    - Mutual Aid Agreements.

- For Force Account Equipment:

    - Amount of equipment by type;
    - Average hours per day;
    - Average days per week; and
    - Hourly rate

- For rented equipment:

    - Rental agreements with pricing

- For contract work:

    - Request for proposals, bid documents, contracts;
    - If bids have not yet been received, the Applicant may submit a unit price estimate; and
    - Debris monitor information.

FEMA estimates the work based on cost information provided by the Applicant. If the Applicant does not provide sufficient cost information, FEMA may use average historical pricing. For contracted work, FEMA uses the unit cost from the contract if it determines the costs are reasonable; however, this is only for the purpose of expediting funding based on an estimate.

FEMA will review the local agency's procurement for compliance and will address any noncompliance prior to final reconciliation and closeout of the project. And this is a dangerous curve to navigate at any speed, because if the local agency has not followed <u>both</u> its own purchasing regulations <u>and</u> the Federal Regulations found in Title 2 of the Code of Federal Regulations, Part 200, then the local agency is at great risk for a partial or total denial of Federal funding.

FEMA will provide the Federal cost share for the remaining 50 percent of the project cost once the Applicant provides all the documentation required to support the estimated project cost for a non-Expedited Project.

The local agency should be aware that if it cannot fully and properly document these costs, it may not be eligible to receive additional FEMA funding for any other work until a satisfactory reconciliation is completed.

A former employee of the largest city on the West Coast told me that her city, unable to properly account for all the $75,000,000 which it received following a disaster, had to write a check for $30,000,000 to FEMA to square their account.

The expedited funding option, when available, allows the local agency to provide estimates or summaries of their costs, rather than finely detailed and complete documentation prior to receiving funding.

Immediate Funding, Expedited Funding – What's the Difference?

Expedited Funding and Immediate Needs Funding are cousins, if not fraternal twins. Both provide a faster way to put money into local agencies in extreme situations. Following is the explanation from the Disaster Operations Legal Reference, Version 4.0, September 25, 2020:

"Immediate Needs Funding" (INF)

"Immediate Needs Funding" (INF) is a variation of the advanced funding FEMA typically provides based on a completed scope of work memorialized in a PW in cooperation with the recipient and subrecipient.

With INF, funding is provided, however, for "urgent needs" requiring payment within the first 60 days after a disaster declaration, in a manner that avoids burdening applicants "during peak crisis operations" with completion of the ordinary PW scope of work process. If payments made with these funds are not made within sixty days, they may be taken back. This means the check is written and is in the mail within sixty days.

Expedited Payments

"In 2006, Congress amended the Stafford Act to require that FEMA provide 'expedited payments' for debris removal.

These payments are required to be not less than 50 percent of the initial estimate of the federal share of assistance to be provided not later than 60 days after the estimate and not later than 90 days after the applicant applies for debris removal assistance.

Although FEMA already provided advance payments for debris removal under federal grant rules for advance payments such as INF, Congress clearly expects FEMA to provide funding even more quickly for debris removal."[1] (Emphasis Added)

True-Life Tales: Expedited Funding

This story is told through the kindness and generosity of Steve Hynes of Deloitte and Melissa Shirah, the Florida Division of Emergency Management Recovery Bureau Chief. Following the Surfside Condo collapse, Steve was the Deputy State Coordinating Officer at the scene.

"On June 24, 2021, at approximately 1:22 a.m. EDT, Champlain Towers South, a 12-story beachfront condominium in the Miami suburb of Surfside, Florida, partially collapsed, causing the deaths of 98 people. Four people were rescued from the rubble, but one died of injuries shortly after arriving at the hospital. Eleven others were injured. Approximately thirty-five were rescued the same day from the un-collapsed portion of the building, which was demolished ten days later."[2]

Out of this disastrous event came a remarkable and successful response, a collaboration between the State of Florida, Division of Emergency Management (FDEM) and FEMA. The result of this joint effort was that within 8 hours and 25 minutes of the request for Expedited Funding, Florida (as the applicant) received approximately $20,500,000 for its costs associated with the emergency response efforts at the collapsed condominium building.

This was not an out-of-the-blue request, insofar as FDEM had been carefully nurturing a collegial relationship with FEMA to include its Region IV office and numerous field staff. This goes to the issue of ongoing preparations for disasters both within and outside of any single agency.

The Bottom Line for Advanced Funding

Although disasters all have common elements, each disaster is different. In some cases, advanced funding, either expedited funding or immediate needs funding, is not appropriate.

Notes

1 Disaster Operations Legal Reference, Version 4.0, September 25, 2020.
2 https://en.wikipedia.org/wiki/Surfside_condominium_collapse

18 Community Disaster Loan Program

Community Disaster Loans (CDLs)

"Although a distinct loan program distinct from the Public Assistance program, organizationally, FEMA manages the CDL program out of the Public Assistance Branch of the Recovery Division."[1]

"The Stafford Act authorizes FEMA to make CDLs to help local governments that have incurred significant revenue losses due to a presidentially declared major disaster if necessary, for a local government to perform its governmental functions."[2] (Emphasis Added)

"Community Disaster Loans may not be used for work eligible under the PA program but are discussed here because they are used for local governmental operations and administratively managed within the PA program."[3] (Emphasis Added)

The Community Disaster Loans Program for local governments began in 1970 as a program of community disaster grants. In 1974, Congress replaced the grant program with a program of Community Disaster Loans.

Eligibility

FEMA may make Community Disaster Loans available to any local government that:

- Is located within the area declared eligible for assistance;
- Suffers a substantial loss of tax or other revenues resulting from a major disaster;
- Has demonstrated need for financial assistance to perform its governmental functions; and
- Is not in arrears with respect to any payments due on previous loans.

FEMA will consider whether the local government is responsible for providing essential municipal operating services to the community and whether it maintains an annual operating budget. In addition, state law must not prohibit the local government from incurring indebtedness resulting from a federal loan.

Loan Amount

The loan amount is based on need. No loan may be greater than $5 million and otherwise may not exceed:

- 25% of the annual operating budget of the local government for the fiscal year in which the disaster occurs; or
- 50% of the annual operating budget for the fiscal year in which the major disaster occurs, if the disaster-related revenue loss is 75% or more of the local government's annual operating budget.

DOI: 10.4324/9781003487869-22

Loan Applications and Loan Administration

The local government must submit its application through the state, which then must certify to FEMA that the local government is legally qualified to assume the proposed debt under state law.

FEMA's regulations do not consider a tribal government as a local government wanting to directly apply to FEMA or a tribal agency applying through the tribal government and not the state. The applicant must justify its application based on need and develop it from financial information contained in its annual operating budget.

If FEMA approves the loan, the applicant and FEMA will execute a promissory note, and FEMA will disburse Community Disaster Loans funds according to the loan schedule in the promissory note.

Loan Terms

The interest rate on the loan is equal to the rate for five-year maturities as determined by the monthly U.S. Treasury Schedule of certified interest rates on the date the promissory note is signed. FEMA may approve the loan in only the fiscal year in which the major disaster occurred or the following fiscal year, and FEMA may approve only one for any local government for a single disaster. The standard loan term is five years; however, FEMA may extend the loan based on the local government's financial condition.

Use of Funds

The Community Disaster Loan recipient may only use Community Disaster Loan funds for existing governmental functions or to expand those functions to meet disaster-related needs.

Local governments may not use Community Disaster Loan funds for capital improvements, for the repair or restoration of damaged facilities, or as the non-federal share of any federal program.

Loan Cancellation

The Stafford Act mandates the cancellation of all or any part of a Community Disaster Loan if the local government's revenues during the three fiscal years after the disaster are insufficient, as a result of the disaster, to meet its operating budget. FEMA regulations set forth the specific requirements for demonstrating the insufficiency of revenues to meet the local operating budget.

The local government must apply for loan cancellation through the governor's authorized representative (GAR) to the FEMA Regional Administrator (RA) prior to the expiration of the loan. The Assistant Administrator for Recovery will make the determination whether to cancel all or any part of the Community Disaster Loan, and any amount canceled becomes a grant. The local government must still repay any portion of the loan that is not canceled.

The existence or cancellation of a Community Disaster Loan has no effect on any other Stafford Act grant or assistance, except that a local government may not be eligible for additional Community Disaster Loans if it is in arrears on required Community Disaster Loan repayments.

FEMA may, however, use another (Federal) agency's funds awarded to an applicant to offset a delinquent loan from grant funds.

In the aftermath of Hurricanes Harvey, Irma, and Maria, Congress appropriated additional funding for the Community Disaster Loan program.

In the Supplemental Appropriations legislation, Congress set aside the provisions of Stafford Act §419(c)(1) with regard to debt forgiveness for Community Disaster Loans made to Puerto Rico and the U.S. Virgin Islands, and localities within their jurisdiction, following Hurricanes Irma and Maria.

"That notwithstanding section 417(c)(1) of the Robert T. Stafford Disaster Relief and Emergency Assistance Act (42 U.S.C. 5184(c)(1)), loans to a territory or possession, and instrumentalities and local governments thereof, may be canceled in whole or in part only at the discretion of the Secretary of Homeland Security in consultation with the Secretary of the Treasury."[4]

For information regarding a Community Disaster Loans type program in Puerto Rico and the U.S. Virgin Islands, please see the "Disaster Operations Legal Reference, Version 4.0," dated September 25, 2020.

Notes

1 Disaster Operations Legal Reference, Version 4.0, September 25, 2020, pp. 5–122.
2 Ibid.
3 Ibid.
4 Ibid, pp. 5–126.

19 Mutual Aid

Figure 19.1 Depiction of an ICS (Incident Command System) Staging Area.

Mutual Aid – Legal Responsibility – University of Alabama[1]

At issue: $513,367.00

This is a complicated appeals case which will make your head hurt while reading it. The cast of characters include a 1994 Mutual Aid Plan, a 2004 Emergency Operations Plan, various local government agencies, and the University, a state agency.

The underlying principle here is that often local government agencies will create plans or agreements with language they perceive to be permissive, i.e., language which will allow a certain action or set of actions to be taken, in this case in the event of an emergency. However, FEMA may

DOI: 10.4324/9781003487869-23

read the very same documents to find language within the document which, in FEMA's interpretation, prohibits the same action or set of actions.

In brief, the City of Tuscaloosa was hit by an F4 tornado in April 2011 which, among other things, destroyed the Tuscaloosa Emergency Operations Center. The University, relying on the language of both the 1994 Mutual Aid plan and the 2004 Emergency Operations Plan, had its police officers provide services off-campus to the community. FEMA initially denied the application for funding, because the language of the 1994 Mutual Aid plan stated in Paragraph 5: "No party to this agreement shall be required to pay any compensation to any other party to this agreement for services rendered hereunder." (Emphasis Added) This clearly makes the Mutual Aid ineligible. We shall revisit this case again in detail later in the book.

In the second appeal, the University changed its tune and said that it provided aid under the terms of the 2004 Emergency Operations Plan. However, the University was not a signatory to that agreement, which would have otherwise made the Mutual Aid eligible.

Ultimately, FEMA honored a legal opinion from the Attorney General of Alabama, who stated that the University Police, under Alabama law, were authorized to provide assistance to off-campus jurisdictions with or without reference to a Mutual Aid agreement. Thus FEMA did approve this second appeal, but it was a close call and dependent on the cooperation of the State's Attorney General.

Mutual Aid for emergency response is a coordinated effort between different governmental organizations, private non-profit agencies, and individuals to provide assistance and support.

Mutual Aid takes different forms depending on the specific emergency and the resources available.

It can be formal or informal, and involve local, statewide, and interstate partnerships, and may be organized through pre-existing agreements or coordinated for the response to a specific emergency.

Mutual Aid can involve individual personnel and teams and will often include equipment.

There is no single government agency that has so many available in-house resources that it can categorically state that it would never need Mutual Aid. Mutual Aid can provide a surge capacity for both emergency responders and their specialized equipment.

Mutual Aid may be either formal or informal; however, FEMA only recognizes and reimburses formal Mutual Aid, which is generally arranged through the respective states.

Many states have intrastate Mutual Aid agreements, particularly for law enforcement and fire and emergency medical services. In some states there are also other Mutual Aid agreements; California for one has a Public Works Mutual Aid Agreement and another agreement for Emergency Management personnel to assist with staffing Emergency Operations Centers in major events.

There is also EMAC, or the Emergency Management Assistance Compact. "EMAC has been ratified by U.S. Congress (PL 104–321) and is law in all 50 states, the District of Columbia, Puerto Rico, Guam, the U.S. Virgin Islands, and the Northern Mariana Islands. EMAC's members can share resources from all disciplines, protect personnel who deploy, and be reimbursed for mission-related costs."[2]

The Emergency Management Assistance Compact is activated through the respective state or territorial offices of Emergency Management.

Intrastate Mutual Aid is also coordinated through the respective state's offices of Emergency Management.

Mutual Aid provided outside of the official state emergency management agencies (i.e., informal Mutual Aid) is generally not reimbursable by FEMA, so this involvement of the state office of emergency management is critical.

When local emergency personnel, i.e., fire, law, emergency medical services, emergency management, and others, determine the need for Mutual Aid, they must contact the state for a "Mission Request" number or other official stamp of approval.

The fire service and law enforcement use Mutual Aid on a regular basis, year in and year out. However, most other forms of Mutual Aid, i.e., animal control, public works, building inspectors, and others seldom use Mutual Aid; therefore, those unfamiliar with the administrative aspects of Mutual Aid may struggle to provide the necessary documentation for getting reimbursed.

Some fire departments also participate in "automatic aid" agreements to supplement their ability to respond to rare but potentially serious events which can tax a department's ability to respond to a major incident safely and effectively. However, Mutual Aid and automatic aid are different administrative animals and need to be treated as such.

A best practice for all is to have Mutual Aid agreements in place before they are needed. FEMA has allowed post-dated agreements to be signed, but being an active participant in Mutual Aid on a regular basis is strongly encouraged for operational, administrative, and cost recovery reasons.

Because of the varying nature of the work they do, there are differences in the Mutual Aid agreements for the fire service, law enforcement, and other groups.

The Mutual Aid Nuances

Mutual Aid may be free to the requesting party or may stipulate that the Mutual Aid is paid for by the requesting agency. Clearly, this issue must be crystal-clear before requesting and providing Mutual Aid.

However, in the case of Mutual Aid provided at no cost, the value of the Mutual Aid services provided may be used by the receiving agency as a part of their local cost share, typically 25%, absent any state participation in the cost sharing. We discussed this previously in Chapter 3 on Cost Recovery for Volunteers and Donations.

Mutual Aid must be coordinated and approved by the respective state to be FEMA-eligible. Another critical element is that Mutual Aid can only provide emergency work. (FEMA Category A or B). Mutual Aid performed for permanent work (FEMA Categories C through G) is not eligible for reimbursement.

The reimbursement for Mutual Aid may be handled in one of two ways. Mutual Aid provided by the state may be reimbursed directly to the state by FEMA. But this Mutual Aid must involve state employees and/or state equipment.

When Mutual Aid is provided by one local agency (providing agency) to another local agency (receiving agency), then the reimbursement for the Mutual Aid must be paid by the receiving agency to the providing agency. When this is done, the receiving agency then applies to FEMA for reimbursement of the Mutual Aid costs in accordance with the terms of the existing Mutual Aid agreement.

Caveats

Two local agencies may not "exchange" Mutual Aid forces quid pro quo as a way around the approved Mutual Aid process. Furthermore, if one state agency sends "Mutual Aid" to another state agency, this is not considered Mutual Aid and is not reimbursable because the employees are from the same agency, i.e., the state.[3]

It is important to know the business details of who and what will be covered under the terms of the Mutual Aid agreement. See Form 14 in the Appendix. I developed this form based on some real-world situations which created misunderstandings among local agencies in a series of California wildfires.

Using Form 14, based on the boxes checked it will be clear to both the sending and receiving agencies what will be and what will not be reimbursed. At the very top, the page is divided into two columns, one for <u>Mutual Aid for hire (paid Mutual Aid)</u> and <u>mutual assistance (unpaid Mutual Aid)</u>. Some of the boxes in either the left or right columns are blocked out because these items, such as pay, are predefined by the type of Mutual Aid.

Note: This is not a FEMA form. However, FEMA will generally honor our written agreements if they provide clear and unambiguous language regarding the terms of the agreements. The wages, benefits, and costs for equipment and supplies must be reasonable, necessary, properly procured, and used for bona fide disaster response work.

Worker's Compensation may be covered by either state law or by the Mutual Aid agreement itself. The terms of coverage must be very clear to both the providing and receiving agencies from the outset, as Worker's Compensation costs could be a real financial wildcard in the event of injury to personnel.

Similarly, property casualty insurance must be abundantly clear to both parties. Disasters are by definition high-risk events, and injuries to personnel and damage to equipment often occur.

Mutual Aid Wildcards

I was working on a very large wildfire when Emergency Manager Mutual Aid was involved. The providing agency assigned a Fire Battalion Chief to assist in the receiving agency's Emergency Operations Center. The Emergency Operations Center was working a 12-hour shift and generally closing during the night. FEMA regulations state that FEMA only reimburses for hours worked on disaster-related activities. However, the Battalion Chief was assigned to work a 24-hour shift at his home agency, and this did not change when he was assigned to Mutual Aid. The sending agency expected to be reimbursed by the receiving agency for all 24 hours. However, they refused to pay because the Battalion Chief was only working 12 hours in the EOC.

In another instance of miscommunication, a Mutual Aid person checked themselves into a local hotel and then requested reimbursement. However, the receiving agency was providing bunks for sleeping arrangements at the base camp with all the other Mutual Aid forces.

Both instances show a lack of clear understanding and agreement between the providing and receiving agencies, which leads to a lot of sour grapes later. In fact, if left unaddressed these issues can develop into longer-term problems. At another very large fire where I volunteered, in which more than 10,000 homes were destroyed, the Emergency Operations Center was staffed by a paid Incident Management Team (IMT),[4] in part because of recent problems with Mutual Aid, and many agencies were reluctant to again provide mutual aid.

On another occasion, a colleague sent me some language from his state's Mutual Aid Agreement which he felt was problematic. Indeed, it was a problem. The language specified that the Mutual Aid agreement was only for "declared" disasters.

Local governments and governors may <u>"proclaim"</u> a disaster; however, only the U.S. President may <u>"declare"</u> a disaster. Therefore, in this case the Mutual Aid agreement was only for Presidentially declared disasters, which made it ineligible for FEMA reimbursement. To be eligible for FEMA reimbursement, we must follow the same rules for either a "proclaimed" or "declared" disaster.

In a most unusual Mutual Aid case, an Illinois city arranged for Mutual Aid with a private energy utility, a Fortune 500 company.[5] The city could find no nearby source for government-to-government Mutual Aid and turned to the private company to assist them with restoring the city's electrical utility system. Unfortunately, the Department of Homeland Security auditors found that the contract was a form of a cost plus a percentage of costs (CPPC) contract, which is expressly prohibited by FEMA. Additionally, the invoices included paid breaks for the utility's workers. FEMA regulations only allow actual work time to be reimbursed, not rest breaks or mealtimes.

Clear and Well-Written Plans

All of this leads to the need for clear and comprehensively well-written Mutual Aid agreements, proper documentation of the work done, and costs incurred while performing Mutual Aid.

Be cautious of overly broad or loosely defined conditions in these agreements. Understand that FEMA will probably look at them from a very different, and often highly legalistic, point of view.

Cost Tracking

It is important that Mutual Aid forces provide written documentation that contains the same degree of detail and completeness that we should expect from our own employees. Mutual Aid forces from other agencies may not have the training or experience necessary to make this happen.

Therefore, I recommend that a member of the Emergency Operations Center, Finance & Administration Section be dispatched to the Staging Area to provide all incoming Mutual Aid crews with the forms which we will require for complete documentation of both disaster-related work done, including photographs, and detailed written reports of the work done.

On another occasion, I was assisting an agency with their disaster cost recovery startup work. This was a few days into the disaster, and this particular agency, over the first three weeks, had 80 Mutual Aid building inspectors assisting with the post-earthquake safety inspections.

Initially, the Mutual Aid building inspectors requested reimbursement of their incidental expenses, meals, mileage, etc. and they were reimbursed through the Building and Safety Department's Petty Cash account, which quickly ran out of money.

The reimbursement requests were then sent over to the Finance Department. It turned out that since these were all state employees, the state was reimbursing these expenses as well as covering their pay and benefits.

In effect, these Mutual Aid employees may have been trying to "double dip"; i.e., get reimbursed by both agencies, local and state. Clearly if FEMA had seen this, any reimbursements by the local agency would have been disallowed since the state had the responsibility and had already made the reimbursement payments.

As a result of these experiences and observations, I created a series of forms to better document the time and costs associated with Building & Safety Mutual Aid. These same forms can be adapted to cover other forms of Mutual Aid, other than fire and law, where there is much less experience in tracking these costs, and tracking forms may not be readily available.

Toolbox: Building Inspector Work, Time, and Expense Tracking Forms

Form 15 in the Appendix is a daily expense report. I recommend that this form be printed on a 5" x 8" envelope and one envelope be given to each Building Inspector on each day they work. The applicable data must be filled in and any receipts stuffed into the envelope. The message should be simple: "No Envelope, No Reimbursement." At one major fire disaster, we picked up a couple of boxes of envelopes at Staples and printed them on the fly on the photo copier for daily distribution to the inspectors.

Form 16 in the Appendix is an Excel spreadsheet (not a FEMA form) for use if the agency does not have such a form already. This form covers all the transportation, lodging, and feeding expenses a Mutual Aid building inspector might incur while on an assignment. It covers up to 2 weeks of time for each inspector.

Form 17 in the Appendix is another Excel spreadsheet (not a FEMA form) for tracking the daily roster of ALL Building Inspectors, not just Mutual Aid inspectors. Each different day that an inspector works should be logged in this form, each different day on another row. This form provides for tracking both regular time and overtime, because for the receiving or host agency, the local building inspectors time will only be reimbursed for the overtime, while for the Mutual Aid inspectors, both regular and overtime will be reimbursable.

Column J asks for the SAP (Safety Assessment Program) Certificate number. To be eligible for FEMA reimbursement, the person must be a licensed building inspector or a registered engineer or architect who has received the necessary training to perform post-disaster inspections.

Column K asks for the number of inspections performed on a given day. This is because an inspector may perform 15–25 inspections in a typical day. But sometimes an inspector may only list one or two properties inspected with a note that these inspections were of multi-unit apartments or condominiums. FEMA may look at daily productivity figures to determine that there is a reasonable value for the costs incurred.

This is a very wide spreadsheet, and for those with access to only a single screen, Columns L, M, and N carry the name and agency data across the screen for ease of use.

In Columns V and W, there is room to enter the appropriate local General Services Administration (GSA) per-diem rates and the Federal mileage rate, which will then be computed into the rest of the worksheet. These columns should be hidden in the working version of the spreadsheet.

The use of this form will provide a running summary of both the work performed and the costs associated with all the building inspections, both locally provided and Mutual Aid provided.

It is a best practice to also have someone from the Finance & Administration Section assigned to the Staging Area to ensure that before Mutual Aid forces are released to return to their home base, all the necessary paperwork is properly completed. As difficult as this may be, it will be far easier to get the paperwork done before the Mutual Aid crews are released. Once the Mutual Aid crews are home, all bets are off.

However, if additional documentation is needed to prepare the Project Worksheets, Form 18 in the Appendix is a form letter (not a FEMA form) to request additional documentation. Like many of the other non-state and non-FEMA forms, this is only an example form. However, in the event of a disaster, the forms supplied with this book will be a great place to start if your agency doesn't have similar forms.

Form 19 in the Appendix is a worksheet (not a FEMA form) for tracking each arriving Mutual Aid crew and their respective equipment. This form is based on Incident Command System Form 211 but contains specific details that are not available on the Form 211.

Form 20 in the Appendix is Memoranda of Understanding between a state and the local agency for Mutual Aid building and safety inspectors.

Mutual Aid-Supplied Equipment and Materials

Does the current Mutual Aid agreement include language which describes the parameters and process for claiming damage to mutual-aid supplied equipment and materials?

Does the Mutual Aid agreement spell out what usual and customary equipment and supplies are normally expected with the provision of Mutual Aid, i.e., does an ambulance or paramedic rescue unit come fully stocked and ready for service?

Individual and Team Qualifications

Most states have standards of training and performance for firefighters and law enforcement officers, so typically these individuals can work on an effective basis in any part of the state. But what, if any, qualifications are spelled out for other departments and their employees sent to provide

Mutual Aid? For instance, rural county animal control officers may have considerable training and experience in handling livestock, whereas urban area animal control officers may not have the same level of training and experience. Therefore, Mutual Aid requests should carefully spell out any specific special requirements needed to safely and effectively meet the disaster-affected agency's needs.

Recordkeeping

In general, the requirements for recordkeeping and documentation for Mutual Aid should be similar, if not identical, to those requirements for the agency's own employees. Failure to supply FEMA with the proper documentation for Mutual Aid expenses could result in denial of funding for the work done.

There is an excellent case on this exact point out of South Carolina.[6] This case arose out of Mutual Aid provided for the response to Hurricane Florence in September 2018. The applicant requested reimbursement for $1,339,189 for Mutual Aid costs, but with insufficient documentation. FEMA denied $257,573 of those requested costs. The applicant appealed and subsequently FEMA issued a Request for Information (RFI). "In its RFI response, the Applicant explained that many departments did not submit activity logs and that documentation was inconsistent."[7]

FEMA denied the appeal and deobligated $425,203 in funding for 16 of the Mutual Aid agencies. *(This is one of those cases where the hole in the sinking boat got even larger upon appeal.)*

The applicant filed a second appeal and added another $94,672 in costs that it had missed the first time around. This time, however, the applicant did the work, got it right, and FEMA approved the $520,076 of requested funding.

The point of this case lies in the following quotation from the case: "Mutual aid work is subject to the same eligibility criteria as contract work, and the Requesting Entity must provide a description of the services requested and received, along with documentation of associated costs (e.g., labor, equipment, supplies, or materials) to FEMA. To be eligible, costs must be adequately documented and directly tied to the performance of eligible work."[8] This all shows the importance of having and following good documentation procedures for all workers, including Mutual Aid.

There is an interesting case out of Illinois following a series of tornadoes and heavy rains. In this case, the city's electrical system was heavily damaged, and the city invoked a Mutual Aid agreement with a private for-profit company to assist the city in restoring its electrical system.

FEMA paid the city $11.4 million in emergency and permanent repair costs. Shortly after, the Department of Homeland Security auditors issued the audit, which contained questioned costs of $3,020,000. One of the findings related to how FEMA classified some of the repairs as permanent work (FEMA Category F). Mutual Aid when done for permanent work categories is not a reimbursable expense. However, for much of the work for utility systems, there is no difference in how a temporary repair is made when compared to permanent restoration work. The critical thing here is to be sure that utility system repairs are properly categorized to ensure their eligibility. In this case, there was $2.4 million of Mutual Aid time which could have been eligible. However, the city also claimed $940,000 of its own force account straight time labor, which would have been ineligible as overtime, but would have been eligible for permanent work. It appears that one way or the other the city would lose some money.

Another of the auditor's findings dealt with a prohibited cost-plus-a-percentage-of-costs, (CPPC) contract. The profit was not the issue as much as how it was charged. In theory, if the contract had specified a fixed dollar amount as "overhead and profit," this would not have been a problem.

Yet another aspect of the audit dealt with the Mutual Aid contractor paying its employees under the terms of its contract with union electrical workers. Under the contract terms, when an employee works 16 hours in a single day, they also receive 8 hours of regular time. In this manner, some employees were paid 24-hour days for 11 consecutive days of work. This would be a red flag to both FEMA and the auditors.

The point here is that pre-existing contracts notwithstanding, even when properly procured they may not stand up to close scrutiny when they appear to contravene FEMA and other Federal regulations.

Notes

1 https://www.fema.gov/appeal/legal-responsibility-6#appeal_analysis
2 https://www.emacweb.org/
3 Mutual Aid Agreement – University of Texas Medical Branch at Galveston.
4 An IMT or Incident Management Team is a trained group of firefighters, law enforcement officers, and emergency managers who work together on large incidents as an element of Mutual Aid. As a team, they provide management at disaster incidents and sometimes in Emergency Operations Centers when local officials are overwhelmed and unable to effectively manage the incident. This particularly happens when local officials are also disaster victims themselves.
5 OIG Audit Report DD-10–04 Labor Costs – City of Springfield, IL.
6 https://www.fema.gov/appeal/mutual-aid-agreements
7 Ibid.
8 Ibid.

20 The Local Damage Assessment Process

Figure 20.1 Chat GPT Generated depiction of Mutual Aid Building Inspectors.

Damage assessment is one of the more challenging aspects of the Public Assistance process because there are so many issues to understand and work through. The topic of disaster damage assessment is worthy of its own book; in fact, FEMA has published at least three books to assist local government agencies in developing and carrying out an effective and efficient damage assessment process. They are: 1) "The Damage Assessment Operations Manual: A Guide to Assessing Damage and Impact," April 5, 2016, 2) "The Local Damage Assessment Toolkit" (Undated), and 3) the FEMA "Preliminary Damage Assessment Guide," August 2021.

However, the intent of this book is not to develop a damage assessment program in and of itself, but to discuss how the damage assessment program furthers or hinders the goal of kick-starting the community's disaster recovery, specifically how to recover the costs associated with what is loosely, and many times incorrectly, called damage assessment.

DOI: 10.4324/9781003487869-24

Injuries and Fatalities

While injuries and fatalities are not a concern in a strictly financial sense, they do contribute to the larger picture of the havoc wreaked by the disaster. They draw attention to the community and how the disaster has affected the area. Fatalities should only be counted when confirmed by the local coroner's office, whether that is part of the local law enforcement organization or a standalone coroner's office. A high fatality count or a large number of injuries may trigger the need for Mutual Aid for those important services, and any Mutual Aid costs will need to be tracked.

The First Appeals Case

To get off to a quick start, let's review a case out of Florida following yet another damaging hurricane.

"From October 7–19, 2018, Hurricane Michael caused damage throughout the State of Florida. The Gadsden District Schools (Applicant) claimed that high-speed wind, wind-driven debris, and water inundation caused damage to five permanent buildings and three portable buildings at the Gadsden Technical Institute Campus (Facility). FEMA prepared Project Worksheet 729 to document the Applicant's estimated $490,777.37 in damage. FEMA conducted two site inspections, on May 30, 2019, and June 4, 2019. The Site Inspection reports noted that the Applicant reported damage to building roofs, roofing insulation, interior ceilings, lighting, floors, and walls. However, the project's scope notes and comments indicated eligibility concerns based on a review of photographs. FEMA noted many photographs did not correlate with the damages described by the Applicant. For instance, many photographs showed only partially damaged components, such as sections of a room's ceiling tiles, even though the Applicant described damages to the entirety of the component, such as all of a room's ceiling tiles."[1] (Emphasis added)

"Because of FEMA's concerns regarding the claimed damage, FEMA issued two Requests for Information (RFIs), on November 26, 2019, and March 11, 2020, seeking information and documentation to substantiate the reported damage including damage descriptions and information regarding the pre-disaster condition of the Facility. On November 11, 2019, the Applicant responded with documents, including site maps of the Facility, and building layouts. On January 13, 2021, FEMA issued a Determination Memorandum, approving $215,570.86 of the requested $490,777.37 in Public Assistance funding, but denying the remaining $275,206.51, finding that the Applicant had not provided supporting documentation demonstrating that the claimed damage to the Facility was a direct result of the declared incident."[2]

"To determine eligibility of damage claimed, FEMA may request a variety of documentation including photographs, detailed descriptions, drawings, sketches, and plans of disaster-related damage, as well as documentation supporting pre-disaster condition. It is the applicant's responsibility to demonstrate that the requested work is required to address damage caused directly by the disaster and for providing documentation to support its claim as eligible. Where preexisting damage exists, the applicant must provide documentation allowing FEMA to distinguish that damage from any disaster-related damage. The applicant must not only produce its own records but must also clearly explain how those records should be interpreted as relevant to support the appeal."[3] (Emphasis Added)

"For example, FEMA requested clarifying information for 152 claimed damage line items, equating each to a specific component, quantity/dimension (e.g. '9 each of 2'x4' lay in fluorescent lighting'), room and building number, identifying missing and conflicting information, and asking for clarification, such as why the entire ceiling needed to be replaced, and documentation, such as photographs or sketches. However, the Applicant provided only 36 additional photographs, identified by building number, but without room numbers or the clarifying information requested."[4] (Emphasis Added)

"FEMA also considers evidence of regular maintenance or preexisting issues. The Applicant's assertions and documentation do not substantiate the pre-disaster condition of the Facility. As the Applicant acknowledged, the insurance evaluation pre-disaster photographs do not address the pre-disaster conditions of the damages claimed, nor do they correlate with Site Inspection photographs, or damage photographs provided by the Applicant. Instead, the photographs show building exteriors from a distance, without sufficient detail to indicate the Facility's pre-disaster condition. The Engineering Report only speaks to potential damages from the disaster, not the Facility's pre-disaster condition."[5] (Emphasis Added)

"For example, the log shows a request dated September 24, 2018, due to a leak in the Building 14 ceiling, was completed October 7, 2021."[6] (Emphasis Added)

This is a three-year-plus gap between the time of the maintenance request and the corrective maintenance being performed. I consider this type of information to be highly prejudicial to the applicant's assertion that the damage was exclusively caused by the disaster. In this instance, the information shows that the applicant's property maintenance program is slow at best. This time delay would indicate that there are a great many more pending maintenance issues in the pipeline for the applicant, and the applicant struggles with its maintenance program.

"Further, the Applicant's maintenance policies provide maintenance and operations guidance and procedures, but do not explain or verify that the maintenance actually occurred. These documents do not indicate the pre-disaster condition of the Facility to help distinguish between the work required as a result of the disaster versus any preexisting damage."[7]

All of this goes toward establishing that: 1) for the damages to be eligible, they must have been caused by the declared disaster and not be a pre-existing condition; 2) the written damage assessment reports and photographs must clearly show that prior to the disaster the facility was in good repair and regularly maintained; and 3) the photographs must connect with and illustrate where the damages are claimed to have occurred.

A technique which should be seriously considered for organizing photographs is to create a "photo map" for each facility. Either a drawing or an aerial photo of the facility would be marked up with all exterior photos numbered with the photo number in an icon □, and all interior photographs numbered in a different-shaped icon ○. Accompanying the map or drawing would be a list of all the photos in alphabetic or numeric order to show the precise location of the damage identified by each photo.

All this work performed in analyzing and organizing the damage information will take a great deal of time and must be done in a professional manner. If the information the local agency submits to prove its damages is disorganized or incomplete, FEMA will not take the time to organize it for us, nor guess what the missing data might tell them about the damages.

Taken in sum, counting the actual damages is only the very first step in a demanding process to prove beyond the shadow of a doubt that the claimed damages were caused by the disaster and only by the disaster, and not a lack of maintenance.

With that in mind, we will move forward with the damage assessment process as it applies to disaster cost recovery.

However, for a moment, we will step back and return to the Introductory chapter and *The Language of Public Assistance*. FEMA only reimburses the local agency for the process of "Safety Assessment." For FEMA, "safety assessment" refers to the task of inspecting facilities to determine whether they are safe and healthy to occupy. The product of a safety assessment typically is an official notice posted at the facility indicating whether or not it is safe to enter and occupy.

FEMA DOES NOT PAY for damage assessments. A damage assessment in FEMA's world is an inspection to determine what the damages are and how much it will cost to restore the facility to its pre-disaster use and function. Usually, the final product of a damage assessment is an estimate of the costs to repair and restore the facility.

Therefore, it is critical that when building inspectors or licensed engineers or architects evaluate a building for "safety" their timecards and field work reports accurately convey that they were performing a safety assessment, NOT a damage assessment.

If the timecards and work records of inspectors do not clearly spell this out and mistakenly misuse the terms "safety assessment" and "damage assessment," then there's an excellent chance that their inspection time will be disallowed.

The inspectors must be crystal-clear on the difference between these two terms and use the terms appropriately to account for their time while performing inspections.

In this next case, the appeals process might have been avoided altogether had the local agency used the proper inspection forms. "In October 2016, Hurricane Matthew caused high winds and intense rainfall throughout the State of South Carolina. As a result, the City of Beaufort (Applicant) conducted emergency protective measures out of an Emergency Operating Center, including executing evacuations, and responding to police, fire, and medical calls."[8]

"In addition, the Agency determined building inspections conducted by the Applicant's contractor, SAFEbuilt Carolinas, Inc. (SAFEbuilt), from October 11 through November 29, 2016, exceeded the dates that established an immediate threat, and that the claimed inspections could not be clearly tied to conducting safety inspections in accordance with FEMA policy."[9]

The applicant argued that "the safety inspections were conducted for the purposes of determining if the buildings were safe to enter and how the Applicant determined which buildings to inspect. FEMA noted the inspection reports/support documentation should be organized in a manner that allowed FEMA to validate the hours claimed by the inspectors. The forms provided with the appeal did not appear to be assembled or referenced in a manner that supported the costs, and the forms provided are ones used for seismic inspections, rather than for safety evaluations of buildings after windstorms and floods. FEMA also asked for an explanation regarding the invoice references as 'Building Inspections' and 'Building Official Services' which appeared to reference other tasks authorized by the contract – and as such FEMA requested a copy of the contract."[10] (Emphasis Added)

"In the first appeal decision, the Regional Administrator (RA) noted that the invoices from SAFEbuilt reference tasks completed as 'Building Inspection' and 'Building Official Services' which could relate to other services in the contract. The Applicant argues this assumption is unwarranted, as the Applicant's normal operations related to Building Official Services were suspended during the Hurricane, and time spent on those services were separately invoiced. In contrast, the invoices submitted to FEMA were for safety inspections of structures in the City, despite any mistakes in the language on the invoices. The Applicant acknowledges that the wrong forms were used but the information needed was still captured on the forms. Last, the inspection reports were organized by inspector and by day and FEMA policy does not require a different method of organization."[11] (Emphasis Added)

"FEMA reviewed the Applicant's documentation of claimed safety inspections and found them to support eligibility. Specifically, they show whether a structure was inspected, whether it was characterized as restricted use or unsafe, the building name and address, any overall hazards and/or structural hazards, along with any commentary explaining any notations of a hazard. They are organized by inspector and then by date. There is no other information or description of work on the inspection reports that would indicate work other than safety inspections being conducted; the mere use of a preprinted form is not enough to determine the Applicant's contractor performed and billed for ineligible work during the early days of the disaster. In addition, FEMA has matched the corresponding inspection reports to the invoices to verify the amounts charged. Based on the information provided, FEMA finds the work and costs eligible for reimbursement."[12]

Furthermore, all inspectors must be licensed or certified as either inspectors, architects, or the appropriate type of engineer for their time performing inspections to be eligible for reimbursement by FEMA. As a routine practice, each inspector (including Mutual Aid or contract inspectors) should provide a copy of their license or certificate as appropriate.

Little of this has to do directly with the financial offices of an agency, except that the financial pain will be great when FEMA disallows funding for the failure to know and follow the regulations, in this case, for properly conducting and describing safety and damage assessments.

Public Assistance Damage Assessment

Damage assessment is the process of measuring the depth and breadth of all dollar losses, the displacement of residents and businesses, and the losses to the utility and transportation infrastructures from a natural or man-made disaster.

Although the local government agency will not have a direct role in the financial recovery for private homeowners, businesses, and private for-profit utilities, the damage assessment conducted by the local agency must tally all these disparate costs to reach the per-capita loss threshold for the state and each affected county to determine whether the damage is FEMA-eligible or not.

Finance-Driven Concerns for Damage Assessment

As previously mentioned, if the local government agency is a city or a county, then the agency does not only report its own range of damages for facilities, roads, and any public utilities, but it must also collect the damage estimates from any sub-agency within its jurisdictional limits. Therefore, if a city contains a school district, a private utility, and/or a Boys & Girls Club (or other eligible non-profit) then it must collect the damage estimates for those agencies and report those damages to their respective county, to assist the county in meeting its per-capita damage threshold. (Currently in Federal Fiscal Year 2023–24 set at $4.60 per capita.) Each Presidentially declared county must have its population multiplied by $4.60 per capita to qualify for Public Assistance.

Similarly, for a county, it does not only collect the damages which it has suffered, but it must also have the damage estimates for each city within the county, including all the sub-agencies within the county and all its cities, and each city's respective sub-agencies.

Not all the damages suffered will be FEMA-eligible. At this point that does not matter. What is needed is the gross damage estimate necessary to reach the county's $4.60 per capita cost to qualify if there is a Presidential disaster declaration signed.

The failure to reach the (current) $4.60 per-capita damage indicator usually eliminates the entire county as a FEMA-eligible applicant, even if some cities in the county exceed the per-capita threshold. However, in extreme cases, there may be some wiggle room on this.

Financial Impact Reporting

While the county per-capita number is an important threshold which generally needs to be met to trigger Federal disaster assistance, FEMA can and does consider other factors concerning how the disaster has affected the community. Several of these other factors are mentioned in Chapter 14. If a community has been hit repeatedly with a series of disasters in recent months or the last few years, the President may sign a disaster declaration even though the $4.60 per capita was not met. Similarly, if the community has a very high percentage of unemployment or other like challenges, a Presidential declaration may be issued. However, these are not common occurrences. In any case, either the Emergency Operations Center, Finance and Administration staff, or the local agency finance director will want to monitor and report all factors which may support receiving a Presidential disaster declaration. The Stafford Act, the Federal law which authorizes the Federal government to provide disaster assistance, states that FEMA will pay no less than 75% of the cost of eligible work. However, in some extreme cases, the President may authorize FEMA funding at 90% to 100% for a limited time. These "enhanced" funding levels are quite dependent on the extreme peril affecting the declared counties. The more information about the extreme financial impact a jurisdiction experiences and is reported will help move toward a higher funding level when the totality of circumstances warrant.

The reporting of these financial stresses and complications for both extraordinary levels of damage and extreme impacts on local agency revenue streams may be contributing factors for enhanced levels of Federal assistance and should be treated as important elements of the overall damage assessment for the local agency.

Disaster Unemployment Assistance

Local agency finance officials should also be aware of and report on the effects on local businesses. One form of Federal disaster assistance is the Disaster Unemployment Insurance program administered by the U.S. Department of Labor.

"Disaster Unemployment Assistance (DUA) provides financial assistance to individuals whose employment or self-employment has been lost or interrupted as a direct result of a major disaster and who are not eligible for regular unemployment insurance benefits.

Disaster Unemployment Assistance Eligibility

When a major disaster has been declared by the President, DUA is generally available to any unemployed worker or self-employed individual who lived, worked, or was scheduled to work in the disaster area at the time of the disaster; and due to the disaster:

* no longer has a job or a place to work; or
* cannot reach the place of work; or
* cannot work due to damage to the place of work; or
* cannot work because of an injury caused by the disaster.

An individual who becomes the head of household and is seeking work because the former head of household died as a result of the disaster may also qualify for DUA benefits."[13]

This single benefit, although not administered through the local agency, may make a huge difference in the overall recovery of the community.

Complications in Sub-Agency Damage Assessments

There are some exceptions and complications involved with the damage assessment process. First, there are some cities in the country which are freestanding and separate from a county. Some of these cities are Baltimore, Maryland; St. Louis, Missouri; Carson City, Nevada; Alexandria, Virginia; Richmond, Virginia. These cities are most likely treated as a separate county regarding the county per-capita damage levels.

Second, there are also some cities, for example Denver, CO and Houston, TX, which have a physical presence in multiple counties. In these cases, the city must report its damage to the respective county wherein the facility is located.

In some cases, particularly with school and utility districts, the entity may have facilities located in multiple cities and possibly also in some county unincorporated territory. As with cities that lie in multiple counties, these districts must report the damage on a city-by-city basis. For example, a school district may have suffered 15 million dollars in damage, but that damage is divided up among 4 different cities, with damages of 2 million, 3 million, 4 million and 6 million dollars respectively.

Although each school is most likely to report their damages to the local school district, and/or perhaps to the county or state board of education, there is no reliable guarantee that the report of this damage will ever get to the appropriate county. As a result of such underreporting, a county might miss its per-capita indicator, even though neighboring counties may all be declared FEMA-eligible.

While this process of tracking the costs for private property owners, businesses, special districts, etc. may be costly, it is absolutely necessary; all these costs, along with the losses to public property, help add up to meet the county's per-capita number.

Initially, of course, most of the effort going into what we generically refer to as "damage assessment" will be costs for "safety assessment," which, when properly documented, will be FEMA-eligible expenses.

Damage Assessment Cost Tracking

When a major disaster strikes a community, the local agency can reasonably expect to have a massive surge in demand for safety inspections for public facilities, private homes, businesses, and the utility and transportation infrastructures.

In 2014, Northern California was struck by the Napa Earthquake. I assisted a city in the region with its initial disaster cost recovery efforts. This city had four full-time building inspectors on staff. However, due to the reports of damage across all sectors, in the first three weeks following the earthquake, the city had 80 Mutual Aid building inspectors who worked for some part of that three-week period to help the city cope with the sudden and overwhelming demand for building inspections.

Each of these Mutual Aid building inspectors had to be supported, paid for their time, and in most cases, provided lodging, meals, fuel, and either mileage fees or auto rental costs.

Note: These same expenses must also be covered for the damage assessment phase once the safety assessments have been completed. Even though the damage assessment costs are not FEMA-eligible expenses, good business practice dictates that these costs be tracked to quantify the total cost of the disaster for local government officials.

The local agency does not need precise and detailed loss estimates for private sector damages. Those costs are for private property owners and their insurers to deal with. And in some cases, private property owners, particularly businesses, will apply to the Small Business Administration (SBA) for loans, but again that will be between the SBA and the property owner.

The local agency will need the total of the damages for each individual damage site as well as the overall total for the jurisdiction.

Post-Safety Inspection Building Inspections I

After the safety inspections have been completed, additional inspections at damaged properties will for the most part NOT be eligible for FEMA reimbursement. For example, as a part of the safety inspection, if the inspector orders the removal of the electric meter because of dangling exposed wires, that cost would be eligible. However, the cost for a reinspection prior to reinstalling the electric meter would not be an eligible cost, since at that point there is no present threat to public safety, even though the original cause of the damage was a disaster.

In yet another appearance of an appeals case from Cedar Rapids and the Iowa floods of 2008 is specifically on point regarding these "post-safety inspection" inspections.

"In May 2008, severe storms and flooding caused damage throughout the State of Iowa. The President declared a major disaster (FEMA-1763-DR-IA) on May 27, 2008. Due to the extensive flooding, the disaster incident period did not close until August 13, 2008. The Applicant had multiple facilities inundated with flood water. The Applicant's Code Enforcement Division (CED) was overwhelmed by the number of building and structural inspections necessary to protect the health and safety of the inhabitants of the flooded area. The flood affected 7,198 properties, 5,390 of those were residential. FEMA prepared PW 4675 to document the Applicant's claimed cost of $978,621 for demolition and emergency building inspections. During final review, FEMA determined that $530,192 was ineligible because the inspections were not necessary to address an immediate threat to life and public health and safety in accordance with Disaster Assistance Policy (DAP) 9523.2, Eligibility of Building Safety Inspections Supporting Emergency Work dated January 28, 2008."[14]

"On August 1, 2012, FEMA requested additional information related to the nature of the inspections. Specifically, the cost associated with each type of inspection performed, the purpose of the re-inspections performed, a copy of the Linn County public health declaration, legible timesheets, and travel documents supporting the expenses being requested. FEMA received the additional information from the Applicant on August 21, 2012."[15] (Emphasis Added)

"The Applicant did not provide information on the cost by type of inspection as requested, therefore, FEMA is unable to determine the specific types of inspections that were done and the cost of those inspections. In the Contractor's letter to the City of Cedar Rapids dated June 4, 2009, it states that under Contract Resolution 0575-07-08 Flood-Related Expenses, the Contractor's staff performed inspections once repair work was completed, progress inspections of homes that had been flood-damaged, and re-inspections following debris removal from the structure to re-assess the structure for life safety. Based on that information, the inspections are not eligible for funding since they are part of the Applicant's normal permit and inspection process and are not safety inspections."[16] (Emphasis Added)

Post-Safety Inspection Building Inspections II

For FEMA, these "post-safety inspection" building inspections and reinspections are an "increased operating cost" and not eligible for FEMA funding. In another appeals case, this one from post-Katrina New Orleans, the city lost on appeal for $2,512,000. Of note is one particular line from the appeal, which states: "FEMA also determined that the Applicant did not have the legal responsibility to inspect the interior portion of the structures."[17] This may have been a quirk in the New Orleans Building & Safety Code, which did not give explicit authority and responsibility for making interior inspections; however, it would be important that each city and/or county have this authority specifically provided for in their local building and safety codes.

Therefore, it is critical that all building and safety inspectors, be they staff, contract, Mutual Aid, or volunteer, carefully document the type of inspection they may be performing. Because if FEMA cannot determine which are eligible inspections and which are not eligible inspections, they will simply deny all inspection costs for lack of proper documentation. In fact, in an ideal situation, the inspectors would have one set of forms for safety inspections, and a different set for all other types of building inspections.

Damage Assessment Wildcards: Building and Safety Officials

First and foremost are the Building and Safety officials who, like many other public officials, are used to doing things their way and not having to answer to a higher authority in matters routinely under their purview. For instance, when a building official signs a building demolition order for an unsafe and unstable structure, that pretty much is the end of the story, unless the building is damaged in a disaster, and FEMA then has a large say in the matter. There are a few issues which, by law, FEMA must address, particularly the environmental and historic issues. It is not FEMA's position to dictate to local officials how to do their job, but if the job isn't done in accordance with Federal regulations and Executive Orders, FEMA simply won't pay for it.

In this appeals case, local officials demolished a number of structures without first giving FEMA a chance to inspect and approve the demolitions. The town did not also fully address the environmental and historic concerns prior to the demolitions.

"From August 26 to September 10, 2012, flood water and wind driven rain from Hurricane Isaac damaged 18 privately owned residential structures in the Town of Jean Lafitte, Louisiana (Applicant). The Applicant verified that the structures were unoccupied, condemned the structures, and completed demolitions without giving FEMA notice. The demolitions took place from mid-September until early November 2012."[18]

"On April 1, 2013, the Applicant sent a letter to the Louisiana State Historic Preservation Officer (SHPO) requesting a National Historic Preservation Act (NHPA) Section 106 review for 15 of the properties. The Applicant stated that ten of the properties were mobile homes, none were more than fifty years of age, and the other five were wooden structures of no architectural or historical significance."[19]

"FEMA's EHP staff subsequently reviewed the demolition site and found discrepancies related to procedural compliance. They reported that no contact or consultation with FEMA or SHPO occurred; the affected properties were not identified in the context of historical districts; the level of effect on historical districts was not assessed; there was no consultation between FEMA EHP, the Governor's Office of Homeland Security and Emergency Preparedness (Grantee) and the Applicant to resolve any adverse effects; and a NHPA Section 106 review was not completed, contrary to FEMA's programmatic agreement with the State of Louisiana."[20]

The town appealed the denial of funding. "The Regional Administrator denied the appeal on February 3, 2015, finding no indication the structures were unsafe as a direct result of the disaster such that partial or complete collapse was imminent. Based on photographic documentation, the RA found no visible loss of structural integrity in 17 of the 18 structures and that the residences were upright with their exterior walls and roofs intact. The RA also noted that the 18th structure, a small wooden shed, could have been temporarily fenced off to protect safety. The RA also found that the Applicant completed the demolition work prior to FEMA inspection or approval, and EHP staff were not afforded the opportunity to conduct a review, contrary to DAP9523.4."[21]

In another appeals case, the issue of demolitions has again arisen with a different twist. "FEMA prepared PWs 6957, 10339, 10459 and 10436 to reimburse the Applicant for eligible costs associated with the demolition of private structures that were made unsafe as a result of the flooding that occurred in 2008. FEMA advised the Applicant on March 31, 2010, that the removal of concrete slabs from these damaged structures would only be eligible for Public Assistance funding if testing determined that the slabs contained hazardous material as a direct result of the declared disaster. FEMA also advised the Applicant that these determinations would be made on a case-by-case basis."[22]

"The Applicant appealed FEMA's guidance on May 14, 2010. The Applicant contended that its pre-existing local codes and ordinances require concrete slabs and foundations be removed as part of its demolition operations. On January 31, 2011, the Regional Administrator determined that the removal of slabs and basement walls of damaged structures built prior to 1979 would be eligible for reimbursement because they most likely contained asbestos, which would present an immediate threat to public health and safety. However, the Regional Administrator determined that FEMA would require testing for the presence of asbestos in concrete slabs of damaged structures that were built after 1979. If tests determined that asbestos was not present, the removal of the concrete slabs would not be eligible for Public Assistance funding."[23] (Emphasis Added)

"The Applicant informed FEMA that it did not test the slabs for asbestos due to the large number of properties that needed to be demolished."[24]

In the closing comment, the FEMA reviewer states: "I have reviewed the information submitted with the appeal and have determined that the Applicant has not demonstrated that the concrete slabs of the damaged structures, built prior to or after 1979, presented an immediate threat to public health and safety. The Applicant has not demonstrated the presence of asbestos in the slabs or that such presence would create a public health and safety threat requiring removal of the slabs."[25]

Note: Although FEMA generally honors local building codes and standards for repair and reconstruction, it does not do so for the demolition of foundations, slabs, or basements, unless the local agency can establish that these are a threat to health and safety.

It is interesting that the city would not pay to test at least some of the concrete slabs, yet the city wanted FEMA to pay for the demolition, which would be considerably more expensive than testing. It is also easy to understand that the city would want to clear the concrete slab "scars" from the neighborhoods to promote general community recovery. However, this is generally not an eligible expense unless health and safety issues can be established. Local jurisdictions are completely free to do as they wish regarding disaster cleanup, repair, and restoration. However, FEMA is under no obligation to pay for work which is determined by regulation to be ineligible. Public Assistance is a fully discretionary program, and to be eligible for Federal funding, local agencies must comply with all Federal regulations regarding disaster assistance.

Damage Assessment Wildcards: Conflicting Inspection Reports

Each local agency must make an effort to present its case for claimed damage in the simplest, yet most comprehensive and easy to understand manner. We want to assiduously avoid the fog which often surrounds claimed damaged. Every time that FEMA issues a Request for Information, we run an increased risk of a partial deobligation or outright total denial of funding. In the next case, this "fog of disaster" completely surrounds a Texas hospital group, which suffered a loss of $14,569,505 divided among 10 different facilities, due to questions of pre-existing damage and deferred maintenance, as demonstrated by three different roof inspection reports. Although the following case represents only one property, the facts are similar for all ten of the properties in question.

"From August 23 to September 15, 2017, wind-driven rain from Hurricane Harvey impacted the roof of Medical Office Building 740 (Facility), located in Beaumont, Texas. The Facility is owned and maintained by Baptist Hospitals of Southeast Texas (Applicant), a Private Nonprofit. The Facility's roof has a total surface area of 24,738 square feet."[26]

"The Applicant hired Zero/Six Consulting (Zero/Six) to inspect and assess various properties, including the Facility. On March 5, 2018, Zero/Six published a report finding that rainfall from the disaster overwhelmed the Facility's 'building envelope systems . . . allowing for water infiltration beyond the building envelope, damaging both building systems and the building interior.' Zero/Six found that more than 50 percent of the roof had been compromised and recommended completely replacing the roof. It also recommended replacing metal roof flashings, remediating interior areas damaged by water infiltration, and repairing a damaged window."[27]

Next, "The Applicant's insurer hired Envista Forensics (Envista) to inspect and assess various properties, including the Facility." "In general, Envista found evidence of pre-disaster deterioration in roof assemblies, and reasoned that these conditions had allowed for water intrusion, accumulation, and retention. Consequently, Envista determined that, for many of the Applicant's properties, 'where moisture is currently present in the affected roof assemblies, some of that moisture has been present since before [the disaster] and their respective contributions cannot be quantified.' Referring specifically to the Facility, Envista disagreed with the Zero/Six recommendation that the roof required replacement."[28]

"The Applicant's insurer also hired In-Line Forensics, Inc. (In-Line) to estimate disaster-related repair costs for the Applicant's properties. On August 24, 2018, In-Line issued a report detailing the estimated costs of repair, based on Envista's determinations. In-Line noted Zero/Six's recommendation to replace the roof and restore interior spaces at the Facility. However, as Envista did not substantiate disaster-related damages to the Facility, In-Line did not include any estimated costs for the Facility in its report."[29]

So, we now have four different written post-disaster inspection reports, including FEMA's own report written by a Site Inspector (SI), each with its own perspective on the nature and extent of the damages and their causes. This plethora of reports gives FEMA the perfect opportunity to pick and choose its set of facts as presented in these four different reports. It must be remembered that any report issued by an insurance company will have a pre-established conclusion, i.e., that the roofs were old and not properly maintained. These facts contribute to what might be a worst-case scenario in terms of proving that the roof damage was exclusively caused by Hurricane Harvey.

And this is not an isolated single case. I have on file another similar case, also from Hurricane Harvey, from a charter school which claimed roof damage from the storm. Once again there were conflicting facts (?), or at least conflicting opinions all dressed up as facts, which contributed to the failure to obtain FEMA assistance for roof replacement at an estimated $900,000.

Damage Assessment Wildcards: Lack of Regular Maintenance and Maintenance Records

This is one of the most important and deepest secrets surrounding FEMA's Public Assistance program. The damage assessment process does not begin once the disaster occurs; it theoretically starts 3 to 5 years BEFORE the disaster occurs, although you will never find this statement in any documentation anywhere.

When FEMA observes reported disaster damage, they are also very much looking at each instance of claimed damage for pre-existing damage and deferred maintenance issues. Typically, in these situations where there are indications of pre-existing damage or deferred maintenance, FEMA will issue a Request for Information (RFI) to collect additional data about pre-existing damage and instances where the lack of routine inspections and routine maintenance were contributory factors when the damage occurred.

There are no specific Federal regulations which require the local agency to provide detailed photos of claimed damage; however, it is absolutely in the local agency's best interests to do so to prove that the damage exists, and that it was caused exclusively, or at least substantially, by the storm.

For this reason, it is a best practice (but more often honored in the breach) to take photos anytime there is sufficient advance warning to do so. It's virtually impossible to argue with a good set of Before & After photos showing the facility or site both before and immediately after the disaster which caused the damage.

Similarly, for those public agencies that own and operate any sort of dam or retention basin, it is critical to take depth soundings in these water storage facilities if it is anticipated that a storm will cause substantial increased sedimentation. However, the measurements taken must be taken and certified by someone with documented expertise, such as a registered engineer or bathyologist.

In this case from North Carolina, the importance of pre-disaster conditions is clearly spelled out.

"On July 27, 2013, severe storms produced heavy rainfall which resulted in the flooding of the Reddies River in North Carolina. In the town of North Wilkesboro (Applicant), the Reddies River is dammed and creates a reservoir that supplies water for the North Wilkesboro Water Treatment Plant (Plant) and the water for the town. Storm-generated sediment deposited in and around the Plant's raw water intake adversely impacted the flow of water through the intake. The Applicant requested $639,080.00 in Public Assistance funding to remove approximately 9,832 cubic yards of sediment it claimed was deposited in the reservoir as a result of the storm during a four-day period of July 27–30, 2013. In December 2013, FEMA prepared a Public Assistance Determination Memo to document the Applicant's initial request. Within the Determination Memo, FEMA noted that the official incident period established for the event was July 27, 2013 (i.e., one day only). FEMA also indicated that it would not approve funding to dredge the entire reservoir because the Applicant had not provided the information required to establish the amount of sediment that existed previously, which was necessary to determine the amount deposited as a direct result of the event; and had not substantiated that it maintained the reservoir on a regular basis."[30]

"At issue is whether the Applicant provided sufficient documentation to demonstrate that sedimentation resulting from the event caused immediate threats at other areas of the Applicant's reservoir, necessitating emergency debris removal. Here, FEMA determined that debris generated by the event posed an immediate threat of clogging or damaging the area immediately surrounding the water intake structure; therefore, removal of that debris is eligible as emergency work under Category A."[31]

"However, it (the applicant) provided no data or specific explanation to support that removal of the additional quantity as estimated by its engineer ameliorates any immediate threat to the intake mechanism caused by the event in question. Moreover, the Applicant did not offer any documentation to indicate that it has completed the removal work funded by FEMA in PW 23 or initiated any action to dredge sediment from other areas claimed to have been impacted by the event."[32]

"Although FEMA prepared a Category 'A' Project Worksheet to address the initial funding request, FEMA also considered whether the Applicant's claim for sediment removal qualified for additional assistance under permanent work criteria, specifically Category 'D' – Water Control Facilities. Stafford Act § 406 authorizes FEMA to fund the restoration of damaged public facilities, including the restoration of reservoirs to their pre-disaster capacity. To fund this work, FEMA requires documentation from an applicant to substantiate a reservoir's pre-event capacity, active use, and maintenance history."[33]

". . . the Applicant must demonstrate that it routinely clears out the reservoir (i.e., the facility) for it to be considered "an actively used and maintained facility.""[34]

"In response to the Final RFI, the Applicant submitted a copy of the Project Status Report as proof that it completed a project to dredge the reservoir four years prior to the incident, in 2009, together with a letter from the Applicant's engineer dated September 15, 2013. This is a singular example of prior maintenance but does not establish that the Applicant performed routine clearance of the reservoir. In fact, according to the letter, the Applicant's engineer stated that prior to the dredging in 2009, no sediment removal had been performed for 'many, many, many years [and] at the time of the dredging project, the Town was having difficulty getting water to its water plant intake because of the excessive sediment that had built up behind the dam.'"[35]

"PA funding to restore a reservoir is contingent upon the Applicant's ability to produce maintenance records or surveys to establish the pre-disaster capacity. According to FEMA guidance, the pre-disaster level of debris in a reservoir is of particular importance to determine the amount of newly deposited disaster-related debris or sediment. Although the Project Status Report mentions the total quantity of material dredged in 2009, it neither delineates from where the sediment was removed, nor does it provide the resulting capacity of the reservoir. Absent specific documentation to illustrate that the Applicant performed regular clearance of the reservoir and records to establish its pre-event capacity, FEMA cannot distinguish the amount of disaster-deposited sediment from sediment that accumulated prior to the event. Consequently, due to the inadequacy of the information provided, there is no compelling basis to support increasing the amount of funding previously awarded by FEMA."[36]

The cost of regular dredging of a reservoir is an expensive proposition which few water agencies can afford. However, if the agency has a regular (annual or bi-annual) maintenance program whereby some part of the reservoir system dredged EVERY year, and after a period of some years the entire system has been dredged and otherwise maintained on a specified repeating cycle, this will go a long way toward demonstrating an effective maintenance program which would ameliorate any finding of deferred maintenance.

Damage Assessment Wildcards: Whole-System Utility Damage Inspections

"Random surveys to look for damage are not eligible costs; however, if disaster-related damage is discovered or evident during such a survey, FEMA may pay for inspections to determine the extent of damage and method of repair."[37]

In this case from Florida, the applicant is denied funding for multiple reasons, any of which would be a fatal flaw. "This is in response to your letter dated May 27, 2008, which transmitted the referenced second appeal on behalf of the Florida Department of Transportation (Applicant). The Applicant is appealing the Department of Homeland Security's Federal Emergency Management Agency's denial of funding for inspections of bridges, signs, and lighting systems in Broward, Indian River, Martin, Palm Beach, and St. Lucie counties, collectively known as District Four."[38]

"Following Hurricane Wilma, the Applicant conducted structural safety inspections of bridges, signs, and lighting systems throughout District Four. On June 13, 2006, FEMA prepared PW 9146 for $1,950,000. On August 15, 2006, FEMA determined that the work was not eligible for Public Assistance funding because the work was the responsibility of the Federal Highway Administration (FHWA) and because damage surveys are not eligible for FEMA reimbursement."[39]

"The Applicant filed a first appeal dated August 13, 2007, stating that the inspections were not eligible for reimbursement under FHWA Emergency Relief (ER) funding, but the work was eligible for Public Assistance reimbursement because the inspections were performed as emergency protective measures to establish if the condition of the facilities posed an immediate threat to public safety."[40]

"The Regional Administrator noted that the inspections were performed throughout an eight-month period during which time the roadways remained opened to the traveling public, indicating that there was no immediate threat to public safety. Consequently, the Regional Administrator concluded that these inspections were, in fact, damage assessments used to determine the location and nature of work necessary to make repairs to the damaged facilities." (Emphasis Added)

So, this was really a futile attempt to recover costs for which there was no recourse. Count 1) This involved Federal Highway Administration roads, therefore ineligible work; Count 2) Because of the time delay and the fact that the roads were all still open, there was no immediate threat to health or safety, therefore ineligible work; Count 3) This work was in reality a damage assessment and not a safety assessment, therefore ineligible work.

This particular appeal case also points out a familiar phenomenon, that of multiple failings in a single appeal. Very often the local agency makes multiple errors or omissions in how they perform work or document the work which has been performed. It's not enough to get some of the process right; we must get almost everything right – certainly all of those things which are FEMA's 'go-to' reasons for deobligating costs.

Damage Assessment Wildcards: Lack of Urgency for Emergency Protective Measures

Disasters are awful, completely awful. People's lives are shattered; financial crises ensue at the personal, businesses, and local governmental levels. After the initial "honeymoon" period following a disaster, that time when the whole community pulls together, apathy and emotional overload will set in. It becomes easy to put things off. The delaying of certain emergency actions, which by definition imply a need for speed, may not play well with FEMA timelines. If certain work is classified as emergency work and then delayed without good reason, it may become difficult to meet the six-month initial timeline for completion. In the following case, the local city delayed hiring extra building inspectors and as a result were denied FEMA funding.

"This letter is in response to your letter dated May 19, 2008, which transmitted the referenced second appeal on behalf of the City of Port Neches (Applicant). The Applicant is appealing the Department of Homeland Security's Federal Emergency Management Agency's (FEMA) denial of contract costs for building inspections."[41]

"As part of its recovery actions following the landfall of Hurricane Rita, on September 24, 2005, the Applicant enlisted contractors to perform building inspections of residential and commercial properties. The contractors conducted 1,100 inspections from October 13, 2005, through January 6, 2006, at a cost of $65,400. FEMA determined that these costs were ineligible for reimbursement."[42]

"The Applicant argued in its first appeal, submitted June 7, 2006, that it was necessary to hire contractors because it employs only one building inspector. The Applicant argued that it could not meet the demands for inspections following the disaster using force account labor. The Applicant also stated that the use of contractors was necessary to protect public health and safety."[43]

"However, the contractors began working 19 days following the hurricane's landfall and continued to work for 12 weeks. An immediate threat was not present. In addition, the Applicant submitted its second appeal 17 months after the regulatory deadline established by 44 CFR §206.206(c)."

So, this agency plodded along and allowed considerable time before beginning "emergency safety inspections." Additionally, they were apparently in no hurry to file an appeal within the 60 days provided in the regulations.

One potential mitigating factor in the "late" hiring of building inspectors could have been the time necessary to allow proper procurement as required under Title 2 of the Code of Federal Regulations, Part 200. However, if that was the case, the issue was not raised in the appeals case . . . not that it would have mattered, having filed the appeal 15 months too late.

Therefore, one possible pre-disaster procurement that a local agency might want to pursue is the awarding of a contract for emergency safety inspections, or alternatively arrange a Mutual Aid memorandum of understanding with other regional cities or counties to provide inspectors when needed following a disaster.

Another possible scenario that might be imagined here is that local officials thought that the disaster would be a good opportunity to hire some local contractors to perform the inspections, thus employing local people at (they might have hoped) Federal expense. The appeals case is completely silent on this. However, in some appeals and certainly in some audits, the actions of local officials are referred to the United States Attorney's office for prosecutorial review. It won't be the first time, nor will it be the last.

Timelines

The previous case of the City of Port Neches makes a good segue to the matter of timelines. It should be understood that the local agency's concept of an important timeline and FEMA's concept of timelines may be significantly different. In the previous case, the city failed to "timely" hire (per FEMA) building inspectors.

In all cases, the initial timeline for safety inspections is six months from the date of the Presidential disaster declaration. When that time is insufficient due to the massive nature of a disaster, then an extension may be granted. However, extensions are not automatic, and they are never verbally approved. A local agency staff member may verbally request an extension, or a state or FEMA staff member may verbally approve an extension, but any form of verbal request or approval of a request is never honored. All requests and approvals must be signed (by both parties) and in writing PRIOR to the initial six-month deadline expiring.

We will later discuss how important it is for the local agency to have some method of closely tracking each and every deadline attached to the Public Assistance program. There are many such deadlines, and they can be different for every project, as well as for the disaster at large. Failure to effectively manage all the timelines can (and usually does) result in a painful deobligation of funding for projects. While in many cases tracking all these deadlines is not the responsibility of the Finance Department, an agency failure to effectively manage the timelines will definitely come home to roost with the Finance Department.

In this case from Texas, we will see the penalty for a late "Damage Inventory" (or List of Projects) submission. "During the ***incident period of February 11–21, 2021***, Texas experienced severe winter storms. The City of Glenn Heights (Applicant) submitted a Request for Public Assistance. The ***Recovery Scoping Meeting occurred on August 3, 2021***, making the 60-day deadline for the Applicant's submission of disaster-related damages to FEMA October 2, 2021. On December 17 and 23, 2021, FEMA emailed the Applicant to inform it that the time to submit projects had expired and advised the Applicant to either request a late Damage Inventory or withdraw the Request for Public Assistance. On ***February 17, 2022, the Applicant requested that FEMA approve a 60-day extension to submit a late DI (Damage Inventory) request due to extenuating circumstances, including staff turnover, sick leave for staff due to COVID-19, and the ongoing response to the COVID-19 pandemic.*** The Applicant stated that it anticipated damages would be uploaded to FEMA's grants management system within 30 days. FEMA denied the request for a late DI submission, noting that the deadline for the DI was October 2, 2021, and finding the Applicant had not demonstrated an extenuating circumstance that would have prevented it from timely identifying damages. The Applicant received notification of FEMA's determination on May 6, 2022."[44] (Emphasis Added)

Note: In this disaster, 163 days elapsed between the end of the disaster event period for purposes of the Federal declaration and the Recovery Scoping Meeting. The applicant had an ADDITIONAL 60 days after the Recovery Scoping Meeting to submit their Damage Inventory, or a total of 223 days, nearly 8 months, in which to collect all the damages.

In the first appeal, "The Applicant reiterated arguments previously raised, as well as stating that it lost key staff members who had direct knowledge of the FEMA grant submission process and required deadlines. The Applicant requested $147,104.86 for costs associated with emergency work, such as staffing and operating an Emergency Operations Center and staffing a warming shelter."[45]

"FEMA found that the Applicant did not provide documentation which would allow FEMA to validate and quantify the reported damage or the claimed emergency protective measures until 11 months after the RSM."[46]

"The Applicant's deadline to identify and report damages was October 2, 2021, 60 days after the Recovery Scoping Meeting (first substantive meeting). On February 17, 2022, 198 days after the RSM, the Applicant requested permission to submit late damages."[47]

In this case 198 days, or more than 6 ½ months late may seem a bit extreme to ask for leniency, but I have reviewed another case where the local agency was merely 7 days late, and the same denial followed.

How Does FEMA Look at Damage?

It is worth noting that FEMA has its own "Site Inspection" report forms tailored to various types of public infrastructure. Most run several pages long, and there are different forms for:

- Debris
- Bridges
- Culverts
- Road & Low Water Crossings
- Dams & Reservoirs
- Levees & Irrigation
- Pumping Facilities
- Sediment & Retention Basins
- Buildings, Vehicles & Equipment
- Utilities
- Beaches
- Mass Transit
- Parks, Recreation, Cemetery, etc.

Each of these forms has questions particular to the type of damage which might be possible, and each of the forms have a full set of questions regarding insurance and environmental and historic issues which FEMA must consider as it funds Project Worksheets. These forms are for FEMA's Site Inspector's use, and it is likely that the local agency may never see these forms, or only see them in passing. What is important to know is that FEMA is actively looking for these "Special Consideration," along with any signs of pre-existing damage and/or deferred maintenance.

The Essential Elements of Information

FEMA also provides to the local agency forms called "Essential Elements of Information," or EEIs. These forms are to be filled out for each project, or in some cases groupings of similar projects, to determine some basic information regarding the damage and the work necessary to repair or restore the damaged facility. There are seven different two-page, one for each category of damage, Categories A through G. These are among the many different required forms the local agency needs to fill out as part of the Project Worksheet application process. These forms provide a preview of the breadth and intensity of the documentation required by FEMA for Project Work-sheet approval and obligation.

Thus far, we have mainly looked at building-related issues; however, almost all other possible damages, i.e., roads, bridges, public utilities, and improved natural features" are treated in a very similar manner, following most of the same principles which have been so far discussed.

Let's take a brief look at successful damage documentation from a Minnesota appeals case.

"Between March 12 and April 28, 2019, Minnesota experienced severe winter storms, straight-line winds, and flooding that impacted several counties, including Freeborn County. Freeborn County Highway (Applicant) requested Public Assistance to repair twelve roads (Facilities) dam-aged by the declared disaster. FEMA did not conduct site inspections because the Applicant indi-cated that the work was 100 percent completed at the time of the Recovery Scoping Meeting. The Applicant submitted invoices, maintenance records, and photographs of the damage to the Facili-ties, but FEMA was unable to determine whether the Facilities sustained damage directly due to the disaster or whether the damage was due to a lack of maintenance."[48]

"As noted by the Applicant, the 'Damage Description and Dimensions' page of Grants Man-ager/Grants Portal breaks down the individual sites with starting and stopping GPS coordinates and indicates how much gravel was used to repair the roads along those coordinates. The Appli-cant supported this information with its 'Contract Work Summary,' showing the materials and corresponding invoices, the labor summary, and the cost validation spreadsheet. Additionally, the Applicant provided photographs of the Facilities showing flooded sections which are labeled with site names and GPS coordinates. These photographs show standing water on and rutting of the roadway surface, as well as water overtopping the road and running off the opposite side. These photographs also show road closure and traffic guidance signs to prevent traffic and additional damage to the roads following the disaster. ***Finally, the Applicant submits its 'Road Cost Ledger,' showing the breakdown of work done to maintain the roads prior to the disaster.*** This document shows when the work was done and on which road, what materials were used, and the labor, equip-ment, material, and other costs."[49] (Emphasis Added)

Roads and bridges (FEMA Category C) are the largest single cost to FEMA and are worthy of reviewing a couple of roads and bridges appeals cases. In the Appeals Database, there are over 1,000 cases, nearly half of all appeals cases, which include roads, bridges and culverts.

The first case is from Florida. "From September 4 to October 18, 2017, Hurricane Irma caused damage throughout Florida, including Okeechobee County (Applicant). The Applicant sustained roadway damage, embankment erosion, or a combination of the two at three culvert crossings: NW 190th Road, NE 48th Avenue, and NE 304th Street (Facilities). The Applicant requested Pub-lic Assistance through the Florida Division of Emergency Management (Grantee) for repairs to the Facilities. FEMA prepared Project Worksheet 2832 to document the damage, scope of work for repair (replacement of embankment fill material and roadway repairs), and project cost of $57,204.86."[50] (Emphasis Added)

The Applicant developed plans for repair, which added work outside the approved scope of work – specifically culvert replacements at NW 190th Road and NE 48th Avenue, and culvert and additional roadway repairs at NE 304th Street – and requested that FEMA fund its actual repair costs of $1,519,081.00.[51] (Emphasis Added)

Notice here that the applicant is requesting a 2656% cost increase. To FEMA this level of cost increase is a flaming red flag. Not a great start for an appeal.

The appeals case continues: "On September 5, 2019, the Applicant appealed, asserting that the project cost estimate was incorrect and did not include all related costs. The Applicant stated that the approved costs were only an estimated cost for engineering services to inspect and estimate the extent of roadway damages."⁵² (Emphasis Added) This statement indicates a total lack of understanding between the County and FEMA.

"On February 28, 2020, FEMA issued a Request for Information seeking documentation to demonstrate that the three culverts were damaged by the disaster as well as information that upgrades and improvements completed by the Applicant were disaster-related or required by codes and standards. On April 27, 2020, the Applicant replied, providing four bridge inspection reports for the NE 304th Street bridge culvert and a post-event inspection for that site. The Applicant explained that it could not locate additional information related to maintenance records, inspection reports, or pictures, and did not provide any information regarding the improvements.⁵³ (Emphasis Added)

Now for the killer cyanide capsule. "For the NW 190th Road and NE 48th Avenue sites, FEMA found that the administrative record lacked sufficient documentation to demonstrate that the culverts were damaged by the event and required replacement. Further, the SIRs (*Site Inspection Reports*) noted that the Applicant had stated that it planned on replacing the culverts as a maintenance issue. Post-disaster pictures did not indicate that the culverts were damaged as a result of the event, and the Applicant did not provide documentation to establish the culverts' pre-disaster condition. For the NE 304th Street site, FEMA reviewed the bridge inspection reports and found that many of the deficiencies corrected as part of the scope of work completed by the Applicant were for preexisting damages that would not be eligible for reimbursement."⁵⁴ (Emphasis Added) This single comment alone would completely kill this case, because FEMA will NEVER fund repairs which were already planned.

"FEMA reviewed the pre-disaster inspection reports and finds that there were preexisting deficiencies to the culvert and the roadway. Notably, the February 2017 report indicates asphalt settlement in the roadway where the claimed damage occurred, which indicates that the roadway damage was due to preexisting deterioration that was exacerbated by the disaster, but the damage was not solely a result of the disaster. Accordingly, the additional work to repair the damage is not eligible for assistance."⁵⁵

FEMA has heard of this new thing called Google Maps and does not hesitate to use it in making its eligibility determinations.

In an appeals case from Montgomery County, Iowa, we can see a typical case of deferred maintenance coupled with pre-existing damages. "From March 12 – May 16, 2019, severe storms and flooding caused damage throughout Iowa. The Montgomery County Road Department (Applicant) requested Public Assistance funding to address damage to its 250th-Grant TWP Bridge (Facility). The Applicant claimed severe scour produced by flooding and ice blocks caused the Facility to settle and requested funding to remove and replace two steel reinforced concrete piers. FEMA created Project Worksheet (PW) 1015 to document work and estimated costs of $1,458,024.00 associated with repairing the Facility."⁵⁶

"FEMA subsequently issued a Determination Memorandum finding that the Applicant had not demonstrated disaster-related damage to the Facility or provided information to FEMA to allow the Agency to determine the claimed work was the result of the declared incident. FEMA noted that documentation from a May 12, 2017, inspection observed cracking, leaching, and deterioration, and the inspection had recorded the Facility's substructure condition rating at 4, equating to poor condition that may involve deterioration or scour. Although the Applicant provided pre- and post-disaster inspection reports, the Applicant did not demonstrate or provide supporting documentation that it repaired or maintained the Facility on a routine basis prior to the event."⁵⁷

"The Applicant provided documentation of pre-disaster Facility maintenance, including: (1) an invoice for debris removal dated November 2010, performed after a prior disaster; (2) a photograph, invoice, and plan drawings for installation of revetments completed in July 1999; and (3) spot painting performed in 1952."⁵⁸ (Emphasis Added)

"The Applicant's pre-disaster records document that it performed routine biennial inspections of the Facility between 2009 and 2017. However, those same records identified preexisting damage and deterioration of the Facility's substructure and channel, including erosion and scour. Furthermore, the Engineer's Letter explains that the Facility had very high scour potential and foundation material had a tendency to deteriorate over time, especially near the surface, and become scourable. The Applicant acknowledges there was preexisting damage to the Facility, but counters that its documentation showed it did not need to perform repairs prior to the disaster. However, the absence of plans to repair does not demonstrate the Facility's pre-disaster condition, particularly in light of the documentation showing deterioration. Further, the Applicant did not provide documentation of any repair or maintenance work completed after revetment installation in 1999 and FEMA-funded disaster debris removal in 2010. Accordingly, FEMA is unable to distinguish between preexisting deterioration and disaster-related damage."⁵⁹

Note: The case does not state the age of this bridge, but it appears that it was last painted (spot painting) in 1952, presumably some years after it was built. In any case, it was probably more than 70 years old, and an internet search indicates that the county is now funding its replacement in 2024.

Another aspect of proper documentation of disaster losses comes in a case from Puerto Rico. "From September 17 to November 15, 2017, Hurricane Maria caused severe damage throughout Puerto Rico. Strong winds and wind-driven debris damaged a 16-story reinforced concrete building and adjacent parking structure (Facility) located in San Juan. The Facility is owned and maintained by the Puerto Rico Retirement and Adjudication System (Applicant).⁶⁰

The Applicant requested Public Assistance funding for the restoration of the Facility and its contents. On July 31, 2019, FEMA inspected the Facility and subsequently developed Project Worksheet (PW) 6574 to document the restoration. FEMA awarded $6,895,216.68 in Public Assistance funding for the project. ***However, FEMA could not validate the eligibility of the Applicant's claim for the Facility's contents, comprising more than 1,600 individual items, including office furniture, computer equipment, electronics, and others.*** In order to proceed with the restoration of the Facility, FEMA separated the contents from PW 6574 and placed them under Damage Inventory (DI) number 423939."⁶¹ (Emphasis Added)

"In a Determination Memorandum dated April 13, 2021, FEMA denied PA funding for estimated costs totaling $1,833,000.00 for DI 423939. FEMA determined that the Applicant had not provided documentation 'demonstrating that the claimed contents and equipment were present in the Facility at the time of the disaster and/or . . . were damaged as a result of the disaster.'"⁶²

FEMA issued a Request for Information regarding the removal and disposal of the disputed items from the Facility. FEMA also requested an explanation of remarks from the post-disaster inspection report that depicted some of the disputed items as "Seized, Pending Seizure, or Transferred Equipment."⁶³

"FEMA found that the Applicant's pre-disaster purchase orders, invoices, and receipts did not show that the disputed items were present in the Facility at the time of the disaster."⁶⁴

"The Applicant states that the Declaration documents were used 'to regulate the transfer and disposal' of disputed items. The Amendments show the transfer of office furniture, electronics, etc. to various agencies, e.g., the Musical Arts Corporation, the Miguel Such Vocational School, and others. The Applicant acknowledges this purpose on second appeal. However, though this documentation shows the transfer of the listed items from the Applicant to another entity, neither the Declarations nor the Amendments demonstrate the location of the items prior to or during the disaster, the presence of disaster-related damage, or the property's ultimate disposition. FEMA cannot determine, based only on the Applicant's assurances, that the listed property was present in the Facility, was damaged by the disaster, and was then turned in and disposed of. Moreover, FEMA is not able to find that the listed items were damaged beyond repair as the Applicant claims. Each Declaration form is marked 'Capitalizable,' indicating that the property had salvage value at the time it was declared surplus."[65]

"Perhaps more importantly, the Applicant has not presented a single, definitive list of the 1,600-plus disputed items. The administrative record contains several spreadsheets purporting to serve this purpose, including the inspection report noted by the Recipient. However, the lists vary significantly, in terms of both total dollar value and the details of the individual items listed. These discrepancies are not addressed in the Applicant's appeal letter or in the supporting documentation."[66]

"FEMA acknowledges that the Applicant's post-disaster photographs demonstrate loss to the Facility's contents. However, the photographs do not enable the verification of eligible damage to specific items and, given the issues above, FEMA is unable to substantiate the Applicant's claim of eligible damage to disputed content items using the other available documentation."[67]

This case demonstrates the challenges of requesting reimbursement for supplies and small equipment. No one tracks, on a daily basis, the use of and location of the hundreds or thousands of small items which may be contained in a disaster-affected facility. However, there is one alternative method in Chapter 8: Pre- and Post-Disaster Photo Documentation.

The Importance of Photo Documentation for Damage Assessment

Although we discussed this in detail in Chapter 8: Pre- and Post-Disaster Photo Documentation, this one concept is so important that it begs to be repeated. Good pre- and post-disaster photo documentation is one of the most important things a local agency can do in defending its claims for damage reimbursement.

All field staff should be made aware of the importance of photo documentation and instructed to take photos (everyone has a digital camera these days) when they arrive at the scene of an incident before they begin work. One member of each work crew should be designated as the photo documenter and have a primary task to first take a quick set of snapshots to create an undeniable record of the damage and problems from the incident.

In addition to documenting the problems and associated damage, the photos can act as a continuing record of a work crews activities. In the heat of battle, it is a major challenge to get employees to keep a proper written record of the "Five Ws": the who, what, where, when, why, and how long. However, at the end of their shift, employees can review their photo record of the day's activities and create a viable account of their work.

Hidden in the metadata of each digital photo is the date and time, as well as the GPS coordinates and compass direction of the shot. After the fact, these are very powerful data to validate the problems encountered, the work done to resolve the problems, the labor, equipment, and materials used.

Caution: Risk Management Photographs

A routine part of a risk manager's job, or this may be done by the insurer themselves, is to take photographs of the local agency's insured facilities. These photos will generally be insufficient for the purposes of FEMA documentation.

Often, they are taken at enough distance to capture the entire building in a single frame. This distance is too far back usually to see the closeup details of damage. There will almost never be pictures taken of any facility or equipment which is not insured. Thus, a water pump station, which consists of the pump, electrical components, and usually a sheet metal shed to protect the pump from the elements, will likely not be photographed. Roads, which constitute the single largest Public Assistance damage category, are very seldom photographed because they are almost never insured.

So, even if the risk manager claims to already have "lots of pictures," it's a safe guess that they are not of the quality and quantity we may need for documenting disaster damage.

Damage Assessment Process Overview

Now that we have seen some of the issues that may arise out of the damage assessment process and how they might affect eligibility for FEMA reimbursement, let's look at an overview of what the process does and how it works. Following that discussion, we will go to the "Damage Assessment Toolbox" to look at some useful non-FEMA forms and spreadsheets which will help to manage the process and the data generated by the damage assessments.

The damage assessment process should provide a comprehensive picture for:

- the type, scope, severity of the disaster,
- the impact on the local government,
- the justification of a disaster declaration,
- any additional resources which may be required,
- the impact on people and the community,
- emergency public information,
- any possible hazard mitigation projects.

To provide this information, the damage assessment gathers information on:

- the number of persons injured, confirmed fatalities, and reported missing,
- the number and location of damaged public structures, and the dollar loss estimate,
- the number, location, and estimate dollar loss for damaged roads, bridges, and culverts,
- the estimated numbers of homes and businesses damaged and the cost of private property damage,
- the number or percentage of homes and businesses without water, power, or other utilities, and estimated time offline,
- the amount of dollar loss for all utilities, public and private,
- the number of people in shelters,
- the additional number of people displaced and in need of housing,
- the estimated damages to school districts, special districts, and private non-profits,
- the estimated damage to agricultural operations,
- the estimated financial impact on local agency revenues in the short, medium, and long terms.

How the Damage Assessment Process Unfolds and What This Means to Finance

Initially, in most cities and counties, Fire Department and Law Enforcement officers will drive on pre-determined routes in the first few minutes after the disaster event has passed to check on certain "high value" or critically needed facilities, such as hospitals, key government buildings, major hazardous sites, such as an oil refinery or chemical plant, and schools, if they were in session at the time. The purpose of this "windshield survey" is to determine whether these facilities need immediate assistance, or if they are safe, operational, and able to support the general disaster response and recovery.

During this initial timeframe, the Finance and disaster cost recovery team should be gathering agency budget data and revenue impact data to support the local request for the gubernatorial proclamation and hopefully a Presidential disaster declaration. The Finance and disaster cost recovery team should also be setting up the forms and tools necessary to compile the various damage reports which will filter into the Emergency Operations Center over the next hours, days, and weeks. We will see those tools at the end of this chapter.

The damage assessment process is not always a smooth operation. It will start out herky-jerky and slowly improve until either the process is done (if and when there is a long delay in receiving the Presidential disaster declaration) or until the 60-day window which follows the Recovery Scoping Meeting has elapsed. However, the continued need for additional damage assessment may go on as damage sites may have to be revisited to validate scopes of work.

Additionally, the damage assessment process is usually a layered series of inspections and reinspections as each inspection has a particular purpose. For instance, a building inspector visits a damaged local agency facility and determines that the building is structurally safe, does not have flooding, and does not have resultant mold growth. The inspector tags the building and reports it as safe. However, the building has no (pick one or more) water, electricity, internet, elevator, etc., which makes the building safe, but unoccupiable. This means that there will have to be subsequent reinspections (which may not be FEMA-eligible) when each utility is restored. Yet another inspection will have to be conducted when the insurance adjuster (if the property was insured) comes out for their survey. And so, it goes. A single facility may need several inspections after the initial safety inspection. For businesses and homeowners in the community, a similar scenario will play out with likely more inspections.

It is important to understand that not all building inspections are eligible for reimbursement, even when properly documented. "The costs of building inspections are eligible as Category B costs, if necessary, to establish whether a damaged structure poses an immediate threat to life, public health, or safety. The following inspections are not eligible under the Public Assistance program because these inspections go beyond the scope of a safety inspection:

- To determine if the building was substantially damaged beyond repair under the National Flood Insurance Program (NFIP);
- To determine if the building should be elevated or relocated; or
- To determine if the repairs are needed to make the building habitable."[68]

For a moment, let's look at the management of the inspectors and inspection teams. In almost all disasters, the Building & Safety Department or its equivalent function will almost assuredly be overwhelmed and require the assistance from either Mutual Aid inspectors, contractors, and/or volunteer inspectors whose day jobs are licensed architect or registered civil engineers. In the smaller and more rural communities, these additional resources may be difficult to come by. In such cases, a viable resource may be EMAC, or the Emergency Management Assistance Compact (https://www.emacweb.org). Through EMAC, most types of Mutual Aid may be arranged. EMAC is part of emergency management programs in all 50 states and many of the U.S. territorial jurisdictions. As with most resources, EMAC does take time to activate, mobilize, and arrive on scene. In those cases where there is sufficient advance warning, EMAC may be contacted through the state office of emergency management to ramp up the Mutual Aid for early arrival on scene.

Mutual Aid Cost Factors

There are two basic formats for Mutual Aid: Mutual Aid for hire, and no-pay Mutual Aid.

In the first instance, in addition to paying for the travel, lodging, meals, on-scene transportation, and incidentals, the local agency agrees to cover the cost of the inspector's salary and benefits.

In the second scenario, the inspector's home agency agrees to cover their wages and benefits, or the inspector is a volunteer. The American Institute of Architects is just one of several professional organizations which participates in disaster responses across the country. Another key resource is the American Public Works Association.

A third Mutual Aid scenario is to request Mutual Aid inspectors from the state office of emergency management, and/or the state Department of Transportation, for roads, bridges, and culverts. The advantage of having state employees performing Mutual Aid is that the state itself may apply directly to FEMA for reimbursement of costs related to safety inspections. Depending on the nature and extent of the damage, this may represent a substantial reduction in the local agency's cash flow. A downside of having state-registered engineers conduct the safety inspection is that they usually are not fulltime professional building inspectors, and buildings which they inspect may need a "clarifying" inspection performed at a later date. I know this from personal experience during my response to the 2014 Northern California (Napa) Earthquake.

However, in almost all cases, the city or county will be struggling to account for and pay for all of the travel, local transport (rental vehicles or mileage), lodging, food, and incidentals for these Mutual Aid building inspectors. Depending on the damages suffered in the disaster, there may also be a sizeable contingent of civil engineers inspecting the roads, bridges, and culverts for damage. Depending on the Mutual Aid arrangements, the cost of some or possibly all the inspectors' wages and benefits will be added.

All these inspectors must fully document their time with the "Five Ws" AND their inspection reports with details regarding the results of each different inspection site. As previously mentioned, they MUST describe in detail that this was either a safety inspection or a damage inspection. Without this critical piece of data, all may otherwise be lost.

Computerized Building and Safety Programs – Or Not

Many cities and counties have incorporated computerized building inspection software programs into their day-to-day operations. The question here is, "Do those systems have the capacity to handle 10, 20, or 30 times the normal the normal level of building inspection requests?" This is an important question to ask the next time the program needs to be updated or replaced.

Agencies relying on a pen-and-paper system for normal operations will need a sudden and massive reorganization of how they take inspection requests, how they assign the inspections, and how they compile and report each day's inspection reports.

When I worked with a small city following the Napa Earthquake, the Building & Safety Department struggled with the data it was collecting. Each evening when the inspectors returned with their day's reports, two regular staff members would arrive at work, and work until 2 or 3 o'clock in the morning to enter the data into spreadsheets to be ready for the next day's inspections and the daily damage reports for management.

As mentioned previously in Chapter 7, in the sub-section "Slow and Inaccurate Damage Assessments Will Delay Federal Assistance," the inability to rapidly collect and process damage information can lead to a substantial delay in receiving a Presidential disaster declaration. The worst case from the period studied was 183 days between the onset of the disaster and the signing of the Presidential declaration. The financial consequence is that not one dollar of Federal funding flows into the local treasury until the Presidential declaration is in place. Actually, the delay will be longer than that because after the President signs the declaration, THEN and only then will Congress vote to make the appropriation which will provide the cash for the Disaster Relief Fund.

Effective Tracking of Inspection Requests

A major challenge in large-scale disasters is the effective tracking of inspection requests. Although power and telephones may not be working immediately after a disaster, the requests for safety inspections will somehow manage to arrive at City Hall, and to minimize costs and save time, the local agency needs to have a process in place for receiving, prioritizing, and conducting safety inspections.

A slightly different scenario occurred in Hurricane Katrina, when some Urban Search and Rescue (USAR) teams were searching flooded residential areas of New Orleans. Some of these teams failed to properly mark and track the homes which they had inspected during their search for victims. Consequently, the next day, some properties had to be re-searched. And still the inspected homes were not properly tracked and were searched for the third time for victims. Meanwhile, some victims sat on the roof of their homes awaiting rescue while other homes were searched repeatedly.

I saw the very same sort of scenario play out during the Napa Earthquake. Some properties had 3, 4, even 5 different requests for inspection. Part of this can be attributed to the normal confusion which attaches itself to the disaster response. However, an effective tracking system would go a long way toward reducing the number of add-on requests once the initial request has been made.

If the existing inspection request tracking system, either pen and paper or electronic, cannot handle the load, then a simple spreadsheet may have to be quickly put together to handle the data overload.

From a financial perspective, the danger is that FEMA will only pay for one safety inspection. If additional safety re-inspections are flagged at certain addresses, FEMA may deny funding for those add-on safety inspections.

What Constitutes Damage, and Why Does Finance Care?

Generally, FEMA classifies damage into one of four categories:

- **Destroyed:** Total Loss, Permanently Uninhabitable
- **Major:** Uninhabitable, Extensive Repairs Which Will Require More Than 30 Days To Complete
- **Minor:** Uninhabitable, Repairs Which Can Be Done In Less Than 30 Days
- **Affected:** No Structural Damage, Habitable Without Repairs

Affected Structures may be safe to occupy, but not habitable due to the loss of utilities or road access.

As earlier mentioned in this chapter in the case of the City of Beaufort, SC, using the wrong forms can be a problem. The problem may be overcome, but in that case there was a considerable waste of time and money to file and pursue two appeals which could have easily been avoided by using the correct forms.

The forms which were incorrectly used for that disaster bear discussion. Although the appeals case does not mention which "incorrect" forms were used, it is probable that the forms were available from the Applied Technology Council (ATC), an organization in California with roots dating back 50 years. The Council's work focuses on the structural integrity of facilities, particularly but not exclusively in regard to seismic activity. The Council's methodology for post-earthquake inspections is included in its Rapid, Detailed, and Fixed Equipment Checklists, i.e., the ATC-20 series. They also have similar products for wind and flooding events.

The issue which may arise when using the ATC-20 forms is that they classify damaged structures differently than FEMA does. Whereas FEMA has four classifications of damage, the ATC-20 series uses one of three classifications, "Safe," "Restricted Use," and "Unsafe." These classifications work well within the ATC-20 system, but do conflict with FEMA's four damage categories. However, an ATC-20 inspection properly done is clearly a Safety Assessment, and it is not likely to be mistaken for a damage assessment or damage estimate. Nonetheless, it is best to use the proper forms, especially if there are FEMA staff who are unfamiliar with the ATC-20 methodology.

Substantial Damage Inspections

For damage assessment in mapped flood hazard areas, an additional aspect presents itself: the Substantial Damage Estimate. This program, a part of the National Flood Insurance Program (NFIP), applies to both residential and non-residential buildings.

"When buildings undergo repair or improvement, it is an opportunity for floodplain management programs to reduce flood damage to existing structures. More than 21,000 communities participate in the National Flood Insurance Program (NFIP) by adopting and enforcing regulations and codes that apply to development in Special Flood Hazard Areas (SFHAs). Local floodplain management regulations and codes contain minimum NFIP requirements that are not only for new structures, but also for existing structures with proposed 'substantial improvements' or repair of 'substantial damage.'"[69]

"Local officials in communities that participate in the NFIP must determine whether proposed work qualifies as a substantial improvement or repair of substantial damage (referred to as an 'SI/SD determination'). If work on buildings constitutes SI/SD, then structures must be brought into compliance with NFIP requirements for new construction, including the requirement that lowest floors be elevated to or above the base flood elevation (BFE). Meeting this requirement can also be accomplished by demolition followed by construction of new buildings that meet the NFIP requirements on the same sites or by relocating buildings to locations outside of the Special Flood Hazard Area (SFHA). In some cases, after a disaster, communities have worked with owners to buy damaged homes in order to demolish the buildings and preserve the land as open space."

"The NFIP defines SI/SD as follows: 'Substantial improvement (SI) means any reconstruction, rehabilitation, addition, or other improvement of a structure, the cost of which equals or exceeds 50 percent of the market value of the structure (or smaller percentage if established by the community) before the "start of construction" of the improvement.' This term includes structures that have incurred 'substantial damage,' regardless of the actual repair work performed.

Substantial damage (SD) means damage of any origin sustained by a structure whereby the cost of restoring the structure to its pre-damaged condition would equal or exceed 50 percent of the market value of the structure before the damage occurred. Work on structures that are determined to be substantially damaged is considered to be substantial improvement, regardless of the actual repair work performed."[70]

When a disaster occurs, FEMA and local officials conduct damage assessments to evaluate the impact on buildings and infrastructure. FEMA uses the Substantial Damage Estimate (SDE) as a tool to assess the extent of damage caused by natural disasters or emergencies. The Substantial Damage Estimate is a determination made by local government officials, building inspectors, or FEMA representatives to assess whether the cost of repairing a damaged structure exceeds a certain percentage of its pre-disaster value.

They consider factors such as structural damage, foundation issues, electrical and plumbing systems, and other relevant components. By comparing the estimated cost of repairs or replacement to the pre-disaster value of the structure, they can determine if it meets or exceeds the substantial damage threshold. The Substantial Damage Estimate is used to determine whether a structure has incurred significant damage and whether it should be repaired, rebuilt, or demolished based on applicable regulations and codes.

For example, if the Substantial Damage Estimate is 50%, a structure would be considered substantially damaged if the estimated repair costs exceed 50% of its pre-disaster value. When a structure is determined to be substantially damaged, it may trigger specific requirements or regulations, such as mandatory upgrades to meet current building codes or potential limitations on rebuilding in certain areas. It can also affect eligibility for certain types of assistance or insurance claims.

If a building is located in a Special Flood Hazard Area, it does not matter whether the disaster was a flood or other disaster; the Substantial Damage Estimate program will be involved. FEMA provides several tools, job aids, and a manual: the Substantial Improvement, Substantial Damage Desk Reference, FEMA P-758, May 2010.

The Substantial Damage Estimate process applies to both publicly owned facilities and private structures. Particularly in the case of older structures built long before current building codes were adopted, there may be a substantial cost to repair/rebuild older structures to bring them into full compliance with modern building codes.

Damage Assessment Archive

As the process of conducting both safety and damage assessments moves forward, the agency needs to consider how it will organize and retain all the inspection reports and other files for future reference. Many of the reports will go into the files for supporting the application for individual Project Worksheets. Over time, many different individuals in many separate departments and outside organizations, i.e., FEMA, the state, consultants, engineers, and insurers may need to review the files.

In this digital age, there are many different cloud storage programs and services available; it's just a matter of selecting one which will best suit the local agency's needs.

In some cases, the local agency may already have an electronic document management system, in which case a determination needs to be made if the system is adaptable enough to meet the rigors of the Public Assistance process. If the system is flexible enough, then all that remains is to create the user defined fields, such as the 'DR' or disaster number, the Project Worksheet number, etc.

In the following paragraphs, I will describe a system for comprehensive file management which will provide ease of use and full access as necessary for everyone who needs to view the inspection files, in addition to all the myriad other documents which will make up the Project Worksheets.

In any case, this illustration, which I call the 'wagon wheel' diagram, demonstrates how one single file structure would work, providing the maximum amount of flexibility while maintaining a strong organizational structure. This diagram is used in conjunction with a two-page form, Form 37 in the Appendix. Consider this form (37) a fax cover sheet, which matches title for title the contents of the wagon wheel diagram, and the check boxes on the Filing Assignment Checklist. The titles on either sheet indicate filing groups for the various types of documents that may be necessary to properly document our damages and everything we do going forward to support the application for a Project Worksheet.

This is a one-size-fits-all filing system. For instance, there is a folder for Survivor's Services, i.e., shelters, mass feeding, etc. There is another folder for Private Non-Profits, etc. If one or more of these sub-folders do not apply, it is simply left unused. Do not delete the sub-folder; just leave it empty.

As seen on the Filing Assignment Checklist (Form 37) each of the major categories, or file folders, has sub-categories or sub-folders as shown on the form. Rather than heap the task of

Project Worksheet File Structure

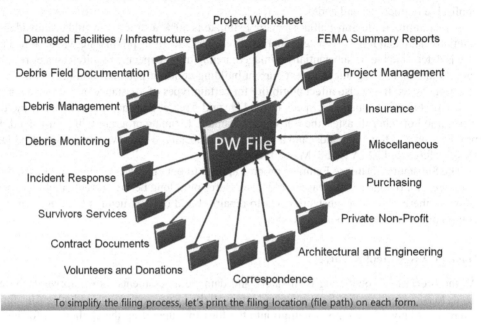

Figure 20.2 Sample diagram of the 'Wagon Wheel' filing structure for disaster cost recovery.

organizing and filing upon an existing staff person, the local agency can hire a temporary worker to fill this function.

Form 38 in the Appendix is a sample of the labels used to identify and track each single document. These labels essentially provide a serial number, along with other pertinent information, to assist in filing, tracking, and recovering individual documents for the cost recovery process.

In this scenario, a knowledgeable disaster cost recovery staff person can take a document or stack of similar documents, i.e., field work reports, check the appropriate boxes on the form and clip the 'fax' cover sheet to the documents to be scanned and hand them off to the temporary worker, who can then scan the individual records.

Using a Fujitsu Scan Snap scanner that can scan both sides of a document, in color, and convert the scan into an Adobe Acrobat format, the temporary worker can scan hundreds of documents in a single day. The chances of misfiling a document can be further reduced by printing the final file location at the bottom of the forms. Filing errors may also be reduced by printing all the Public Works forms on a light orange paper, and Facilities forms on a light blue, etc. Just color-coding forms will help reduce filing errors and quickly identify the departmental source of a document.

Immediately prior to scanning, a label (see the sample form in the Appendix, Form 38) is placed on each face of the document. The labels are printed in Arial font, 12-point type, which is a machine-readable font. The label is scanned along with the document, leaving a trail of breadcrumbs to follow should a document be misfiled. In this manner, a single document once scanned and filed can always be found.

The right to upload files needs to be closely controlled, and in this system, files should never be deleted. However, using Adobe Acrobat, Professional Edition, obsolete files can be identified with a stamp or label to indicate the document has been superseded or voided. Similarly, the right to view files can also be controlled as needed.

This filing system was originally set up in Windows Explorer. However, today there are many different cloud-based file sharing programs, such as DropBox, SugarSync, etc., which will also serve this need.

Once a user goes into a first-level sub-folder, there are additional levels of sub-folders so that documents may be sorted based upon the day of the week or any other valid sort criteria.

This filing system, as developed, covers virtually every category of information which may be needed at any point in the disaster cost recovery process.

Later in the book, we will see that there are certain documents which should be a part of EVERY Project Worksheet file. These include copy of the labor bargaining unit agreement which spells out the terms of the pay and benefits to which an employee is entitled when force account labor is involved. Another common document requirement is to have a copy of the local and state proclamations and the Presidential disaster declaration in every Project Worksheet application package.

Uploading these documents is simplified by loading each respective "common" document into its respective file location BEFORE releasing the file program for general use. In this manner, every time that the file's skeletal structure is replicated, these common documents are also recreated in the new filing package.

By uploading the common files to the system before it is released for general use, many filing errors can be eliminated and the amount of time needed to build complete Project Worksheet greatly reduced.

Who Is Doing Safety or Damage Assessments?

While I worked for the City of San Francisco, I developed and circulated a survey to the various departments requesting information about how they saw their role in safety/damage assessments. I asked the following questions:

- My department would conduct a structural inspection of our facilities <u>to determine if the facility was safe to use</u> after an earthquake.
- My department would conduct a structural inspection of our facilities <u>to determine the cost to repair or rebuild</u> a facility after an earthquake.
- My department would conduct a <u>non-structural inspection</u> of our facilities (i.e., damaged ceiling tiles, hanging light fixtures, etc.) to determine the cost to repair or rebuild a facility after an earthquake.
- My department would conduct an inspection of our properties and facilities to determine the cost of debris removal after an earthquake.
- My department would conduct inspections of infrastructure (underground utilities, etc.) on our properties to determine the cost to repair or rebuild them after an earthquake.
- My department would conduct inspections of infrastructure throughout the City (underground utilities, roads, bridges, transit infrastructure, etc.) to determine the cost to repair or rebuild after an earthquake.
- My department would create a list of our damaged vehicles to determine the cost to repair or replace them after a major earthquake.
- My department would track the expenses if one (or more) of our facilities was damaged and we had to relocate to a temporary building.
- My department would create a comprehensive inventory of all damaged furnishings (cubicles, bookshelves, file cabinets, etc.) and damaged technology (computers, copier/printers, telephones, etc.) so we could get FEMA reimbursement for our losses.
- My department would be involved in providing temporary housing to displaced persons following an earthquake.

In all the responses I received, what was most interesting was the number of departments which (according to the responses) assumed they would have an active role in conducting various elements of the safety/damage assessments. This more than likely would lead to a duplication of efforts, although under emergency circumstances, it is easy to understand that each department would want to have some role in the assessment of their own facilities. Therefore, under these conditions, safety/damage assessment training might not be limited to the usual suspects, i.e., everyday building inspectors and road/bridge engineers.

One possible way to speed up the tally of all damage would be to use voice dictation to enumerate all individual items of damage, and then to send those tapes out for transcription by someone who works as a medical transcriber. This would probably involve setting this up prior to a disaster and involve some level of training for both the recorder and the transcriber, who will most likely not be familiar with some of the terminology used by the person making the recording. A similar process is sometimes used within the context of insurance work.

Damage Assessment of Debris

Debris is one of the first costs the local agency will bear following the disaster, and sometimes the most important cost when damage to buildings and infrastructure is limited. In all cases, it is important that the debris portion of the damage assessment be thorough on a jurisdiction-wide basis. Even when there are challenges in accessing cut-off portions of a city or county, maximum efforts should be made to discover all eligible debris damage.

The Safety Assessment/Damage Assessment Toolbox – Part 1: Public Damage

Finally, we get to the Damage Assessment Toolbox. This is a collection of forms for tracking and managing the data which in some cases is absolutely required for proper documentation, and in other cases is convenient for managing the people and the process.

There are two different groups of Excel spreadsheets and Adobe Acrobat forms. In the first group are forms for conducting damage assessments of publicly owned facilities, equipment, and contents. The second group is used for tracking private property damage in the community. In any given disaster it is unlikely that an agency will use all of these forms, but they are provided so that the local agency may pick and choose the forms to best suit their needs at the moment.

In either case, all the forms are identified by a number, generally indicating the sequence in which the form will be used, although in some cases this may vary and some of the forms may be used concurrently with other forms.

Important Notes

These forms ARE NOT FEMA FORMS: neither are they forms from any state or any other government agency, unless otherwise noted. Each of these forms was specifically designed to assist in tracking damages for disaster cost recovery purposes. Readers may choose to modify the forms as they see fit to better suit the needs of their own agency. HOWEVER, these forms, particularly those in Excel, have been painstakingly created, sometimes with complicated programming, which if altered may ruin the form and provide incorrect data.

If a local agency uses these forms, they should make them available on a shared computer drive, but before releasing them for general use, they should be locked and password-protected to prevent others from modifying them to protect the integrity of the calculations in the spreadsheets.

I have had agencies attempt to modify the forms "to better suit their needs," and in the revision process they have left out some critical elements which rendered the form useless for its intended purposes. The local agency may already have similar forms, and the use of these forms is not required. These forms are included for those agencies which may not have good disaster cost recovery forms.

Toolbox: Facility Initial Damage Report (DA-I-1) Form 26 in the Appendix

Working with the Forms in their numbered order, we first come to the Facility Initial Damage Report (DA-I-1). This is what I refer to as a "FLASH" form, a form designed to get a "quick and dirty" assessment of the integrity and functionality of a given facility, much like how a paramedic does a rapid triage of a patient, i.e., they make a rapid assessment of the following: breathing rate, respiration rate, capillary refill rate, ability to follow simple commands.

The point here is to rapidly sort those local government facilities which can be used for the disaster response, and those which are damaged but in a static condition, and those facilities which are themselves in a deteriorating condition and in need of some response activity, such as fire suppression or pumping of a basement. On this form, not every box needs to be filled out, but obviously the more information available, the clearer the picture of this facility will be.

At a minimum, the agency should have one of these forms filled out for every significant facility the agency may need for its response. Next on the list should be those facilities which would be nice to have. We will see in the next form, the Facilities Damage Reporting Status (DA-I-2), how the Facility Initial Damage Report and the Facilities Damage Reporting Status can be joined to ensure that all critical facilities get inspected in priority order.

Toolbox: Facilities Damage Reporting Status (DA-I-2(A, B, C)) Forms 27 A, B, and C in the Appendix

This form has evolved over the years and now consolidates three different forms into a single form for tracking: 1) the local agency facilities themselves, 2) the initially estimated damages to those facilities, and 3) rough approximations of the total losses based on a) facility damage, b) lost furnishings and supplies, and c) possible temporary relocation costs. All this information combined will provide a more complete and consistent early estimate of the total damages suffered, not just the facility damage itself.

General Notes for This Spreadsheet and Its Three Tabs

The spreadsheets contain rows for 500 entries, which should be enough for all but the largest of local government agencies. A competent Excel user will be able to add additional rows should that be necessary. Any changes, additions, or deletions of individual facilities should only be made on Tab #1. Once entered there, they will automatically populate the next two tabs of the worksheet. At the bottom of Tab #1, there is validation data which must be set up for each individual local agency depending on the services they provide and their organizational structure. With Tabs #2 & #3, the blue-shaded cells should be locked and data for those blue-shaded cells transferred from Tab #1. The clear cells are for data entry. In Tab #2, the yellow, green, and red shading is driven by Excel's conditional formatting feature.

The Master Facilities List – Tab #1

Looking at the form, starting from the extreme left, is the "Initial Inspection Status." When the safety inspection report is received and entered into the spreadsheet, the column turns green, using

Excel's conditional formatting feature. A quick glance shows the inspection work done, and that which remains.

- Column B indicates the pre-assigned priority for inspection.
- Column C contains the facility name.
- Column D connotates the use or function of the facility. In rows 23 and 24, the use indicated is "Tenant." This is important because in many cases, tenant-occupied buildings may not be FEMA-eligible or are only partially eligible.
- Column E is the street number.
- Column F is the street name.
- Column G is the City name, because in some cases, particularly for water departments, there may be reservoirs or pump stations outside the city or county limits.
- Column H indicates the year the facility was built. This is important because structures more than 50 years old must be considered for any historic implications. However, age is only one indicator of historic status. Sometimes an owner will build an iconic and beautiful structure which, even as it is completed, will be considered a historic structure. Examples of such buildings are the Walt Disney Concert Hall (Los Angeles, California, completed in 2003); The National Museum of African American History and Culture (Washington, D.C., completed in 2016). The threshold for historic consideration may vary from agency to agency.
- Column I is a primary inspection assignment; typically, this will be the Building and Safety department; however, in some jurisdictions, it could be Facilities or another department.
- Column J indicates the date of the completed inspection.
- Column K shows the FEMA damage classification, either "Destroyed," "Major," "Minor," or "Affected."
- Column L shows the ATC-20 Seismic (or ATC-45 for flooding) inspection status, if needed.
- Column M shows the initial dollar damage estimate, which in this case may simply be a ballpark rough estimate of magnitude, rather than a more precise dollar estimate based on an analysis of the building components.
- Column N says Yes or No to the question of historic facility status, solely in this case based on an age calculation.
- Column O concerns any initial environmental or hazardous materials concerns.
- Column P inquires about insurance coverage for the facility.
- Column Q asks if the facility is only used by the local government agency or if other entities use some of the space.
- Column R is concerned with the percentage of facility occupancy when some portion of the facility is leased, rented, or donated to any other agency or organization, whether they are another government agency, a private non-profit, or a for-profit entity. The percentage of occupancy by the owning agency can affect the facility's overall eligibility, as will be discussed in Chapter 26: Eligibility.
- Column S is a placeholder for the estimated replacement cost of the facility.
- Column T should reflect the insured value of the structure.
- Column U asks for the total square footage of the facility.

All these different factors may later play into the facility's eligibility; rather than wait for a disaster, much of this data can be gathered in advance to smooth out the damage assessment process once a disaster hits.

The data from columns B through F are then carried over to the next two tabs in this spreadsheet.

Facilities Damage Reporting Status – Tab #2 (Damage Reporting Status)

The purpose of this tab of the spreadsheet is to track the status of the various inspections which may occur at a facility.

Columns B through F are automatically transferred from the first tab.

- Column G tracks the ATC-20 (or ATC-45) inspection status.
- Column H tracks the FEMA damage category: Destroyed, Major, Minor, or Affected.
- Column I is for tracking the status of the facility's mechanical systems, if any.
- Column J is for tracking the facility's overall utility status.
- Column K is for the report on the building's furnishings.
- Column L tracks the status of the computer systems.
- Column M is for the status of the telephones.
- Column N is for the assignment of a damaged site to the Damage Inventory/List of Projects.
- Column O tracks the line Project Worksheet number, if known.
- Column P is for the assignment of a damage site to a department for preparing the application and/or managing the project one approved by FEMA.

Toolbox: Disaster Loss Estimation Form (DA-I-2-(C)) Tab #3

The purpose of this form is to provide an early rough estimate of the complete span of damages at a single facility, including the physical losses to the building itself; a furnishings estimate, based upon the facility's square feet of floor space; and the estimated costs of temporarily relocating the facility for a period of time.

As with the previous form, the first columns of data, Columns A through F, transfer from the first tab. If data is entered in Tab #1 for the facility square footage and structure replacement value, then these two additional data sets will also transfer from Tab #1.

On Tab #3, data only needs to be entered into five columns.

In Column I, enter the estimated percent of damage for each facility.

In Column N, enter the daily operating budget. This number may be extracted from the annual budget for the cost of utilities, maintenance, and operating supplies, such as janitorial products.

In Column O, enter the anticipated number of days, not weeks or months, the relocation may last.

In Column P, enter the estimated cost per day for the displacement, including rent, utilities, and maintenance.

In Column Q, enter the estimated number of days of the displacement. Note: the functional downtime and the displacement time may be the same in some cases.

Often when damage occurs to a facility, the damage estimate is based exclusively on the actual physical damage to the building and frequently does not account for the losses to the building furnishings and supply inventory. Although the temporary relocation will probably be tracked on its own Project Worksheet if approved by FEMA, as will the losses to furnishings and supplies, this spreadsheet provides an overview of the totality of the loss for each facility, and the total estimated losses for the agency.

Toolbox: Office Furnishings and Equipment Damage Report DA-I-5 (A and B)
Forms 28 A and B in the Appendix

As we saw in the Puerto Rico appeals case earlier in this chapter, FEMA may require extensive documentation to prove that damaged office equipment and supplies were in fact owned and used by the local agency immediately prior to the disaster and located in the damaged facility.

Furthermore, Title 2 of the Code of Federal Regulations, Part 200 requires in § 200.318 General procurement standards (d): "The non-Federal entity's procedures must avoid acquisition of unnecessary or duplicative items. Consideration should be given to consolidating or breaking out procurements to obtain a more economical purchase. Where appropriate, an analysis will be made of lease versus purchase alternatives, and any other appropriate analysis to determine the most economical approach."[71]

The Office Furnishings and Equipment Damage Report addresses this section of Title 2 of the Code of Federal Regulations regarding the consolidation of replacement purchases of equipment and supplies to obtain the most economical prices.

The first page deals with those items which are commonly found in offices and are likely to be damaged or destroyed when buildings are damaged in a disaster. The second page is for tallying those often-unique pieces of equipment for which there are likely to be only one in each office or function. For instance, a specialized automotive computer used by fleet maintenance for diagnosing engine problems, or an MRI machine in a hospital.

With this form, in the second column from the right there are spaces for the Room #, the Floor, and contact information. Once a department or division has completed this Excel form, using Excel's Cross-Tab reporting, each individual form can be easily and quickly rolled up into a single consolidated form for the entire agency. This is one of many damage assessment forms which can be filled out by general office staff, rather than by an inspector.

Toolbox: Office Relocation Expense Report (DA-I-6(A)) Forms 29 A and B in the Appendix

This form is for use only when the local agency has had a facility be so badly damaged that it must temporarily relocate the office or workspace. All temporary relocations must first be approved in writing by FEMA; and they are for a 6-month period as an emergency protective measure. Any initial extension of time for the relocation must be approved by the state. Should a second extension be required, that will depend on FEMA approval of the extension.

To prepare the request for a Project Worksheet to cover the cost of a temporary relocation, this form assists the local agency to quantify its needs for space and equipment, as well as the space itself and the utilities, etc.

The first page breaks out the specific items and the number of those items needed. The second page with the six columns to the right is for doing the analysis required by FEMA to determine if it is less expensive to purchase outright or to lease the equipment for the duration of the relocation.

Under 2 CFR, Part 200, FEMA requires that contracts break out any delivery and set up charges separately from the lease or rental cost per month, with a separate breakout for the tear down and removal costs. By using a standard form such as this, FEMA will see that the local agency is well-organized and understands the procurement requirements involved.

Toolbox: Disaster Damage Documentation Checklist (DA-I-7) Form 30 in the Appendix

This form is a sample checklist, and the actual checklist for any agency may be different, and FEMA may change its documentation requirements in the future.

As indicated by the right-most of the three columns, not all the documentation of disaster damages will come from the inspectors themselves. Varying by disaster, many other departments or divisions will play a key role to substantiate the disaster-caused losses. The importance of using a checklist is that during the immediate aftermath of the disaster, when staff at all levels is very stressed-out, it is easy to overlook some important bit of information that may later be crucial to proving our case for disaster-caused damage.

Toolbox: Post Disaster Vehicle Damage Report (DA-I-8) Form 31 in the Appendix

When I worked for the City of San Francisco, we began a project which we thought would be an easy topic to handle, e.g., vehicle damage caused by a disaster. Four months later, we realized it was much more complicated than we first thought. FEMA will pay for damage to vehicles caused directly by the disaster. But it does not pay for damages caused by operator error while responding to a disaster. Therefore, we must carefully document both the nature and extent of vehicle damage and how the disaster was the direct cause of that damage. Additionally, FEMA only reimburses the local agency based on the vehicle's or equipment's Blue Book value.

This form is essentially a checklist to ensure that the agency has all the required documentation to prove the loss. Furthermore, such damaged vehicles must be stored until such time as FEMA can inspect them, before repairs are made or the vehicle is sold.

There is a good reason FEMA is so strict on all aspects of the Public Assistance program, including vehicle replacement. This is the headline from an article in the New York Daily News from February 19, 2019.

"NYC Admits Defrauding FEMA Out of Millions After Superstorm Sandy: A hurricane of lies about city-owned Department of Transportation vehicles supposedly damaged by Superstorm Sandy has resulted in a $5.3 million settlement with the feds."[72] This wasn't the first time someone tried to defraud FEMA, and it won't be the last.

The Safety Assessment/Damage Assessment Toolbox – Part 2, Private Damage
Toolbox: Initial Damage Estimate Tally Sheet (DA-X-1) Form 32 in the Appendix

The purpose of this form is to compile on a single form the initial damage picture for the local agency. It gathers information in a way that corresponds with how local and state officials need to present their case for either a gubernatorial proclamation or a Presidential declaration. This information will change rapidly in the first hours and days after a disaster. Successive copies of this form should be kept together in a binder, with the front sheet always the most recent tally. This form may need to be amended to account for the specific disaster and how the local agency operates.

Toolbox: Damage and Needs Assessment Summary (DA-X-2)

The Damage and Needs Assessment Summary is a multi-page form for tracking damages at a high level, both internally and across the community. One California county uses this form for both its internal departments and all of its individual cities, special districts, and private non-profits. The county uses Excel's Cross-Tab feature to regularly update the overall county damage picture on a regular basis.

Again, the convention for this form is that the shaded cells are locked and require no data entry. In the section on the front page labeled "Public Damages," the data populating all the shaded cells is derived from the subsequent pages. As damage (by FEMA Category (A-G)) is entered on Pages 3 through 8, the damage is tallied by category and posted on Page 1. On Page 2 of the form, the data summaries from the remaining pages are posted back to Page 2 in the appropriate boxes.

Although the damages reported will trickle in over the hours, days, and weeks after the disaster, as the data is entered on the next available line on a page the spreadsheet will automatically sort it by type and category. If the local agency is using this form to collect its own damage information and that of its sub-agencies, it is critical to ensure that the form is locked and password-protected to maintain the integrity of the data and the calculations.

Pages 3 through 12 require some forced choices when entering damage data. This is not a perfect solution, but given the need to aggregate damage into some definable and standard groupings forced choices are required.

Toolbox: Disaster Impact Financial Summary (DA-X-3) Form 34 in the Appendix

The purpose of this form is to begin the process of acquiring financial data necessary to warrant either the gubernatorial proclamation or the Presidential declaration. Once again, this is a sample form which the local agency may want to modify to better suit its needs or the conditions wrought by the disaster.

The form is divided into sections, such as the Emergency Operations Center, Building & Safety, Economic Development, etc. Copies of the form should be made and distributed to the appropriate departments as needed. As with all disaster-related forms, the information will change over time, and old copies should be retained for research and historical purposes.

Toolbox: Property Damage Report (DA-X-5 (A-D)) Form 35 A-D

This is an alternate way to track property damage to structures. However, this version does not include any public or private infrastructure. I developed this form some years before I developed the Damage and Needs Assessment Summary. It is a simpler but also less inclusive tracking of the damages which have occurred.

With this form, as with many of the other forms in this book, red-shaded cells indicate there is a problem with the data entered. The data is either incomplete as entered, or it conflicts with other information already entered.

Toolbox: Tracking and Documenting Building Inspections

In Chapter 19 on Mutual Aid, Forms 14 through 18, found in the Appendix, may be used to track and manage Mutual Aid building inspectors and other inspectors.

The Other Part of Damage Inspections: Annual Inspections

As we have seen in numerous appeals cases, reporting disaster damage is one thing, but proving that the damage was caused by the disaster may be another matter entirely.

To prove that the damages reported were caused completely by the disaster, FEMA often requests substantial written and photographic evidence to support the local agency's contention that this damage was disaster-caused, and not the result of deferred maintenance or that it was pre-existing damage.

While there is nothing in FEMA regulations which specifically requires this written and photographic documentation, we must provide substantive proof, and these two forms of proof are the easiest with which to prove our case when the documentation does exist.

FEMA typically will ask to see the inspection plans and the inspection reports. They often also ask for regular maintenance reports which would be completed when maintenance work is completed.

Inspection reports with little or no substantive information or which are merely noted with a check mark often do not provide enough details to be considered proper documentation.

Providing enough information to satisfy FEMA's requirements may be a Catch-22 situation, but it is not FEMA's intent or responsibility to restore our facilities to brand-new condition. I am familiar with cases where the local agency had plans pending to tear down and replace certain structures before the disaster hit. They saw the disaster as a gift from heaven, and that FEMA would pay for the project and thereby save them money. This is not in the cards for the Public Assistance program. This might occasionally happen through an oversight, but it is an uncommon happenstance.

Many times, when denied Public Assistance funding, the local agency will then begin a lengthy appeals process to get the project funded. In more cases than not, this is a losing proposition and a waste of time and money for both the local agency and FEMA.

The secret is to find or create a building or facility checklist which will provide the type of information to support our damage claims by documenting the pre-disaster conditions. There are scores of building inspection templates available online; however, they are often focused on fire and life safety and a healthy building environment, and they do not often address the types of issues for which FEMA is looking.

I have found one form online from the Government of the Northwest Territories of Canada for Roof Inspections. Naturally, in Northern Canada, all property owners are concerned about the watertight integrity of their roofs. This form is included in the Appendix, Form 36 as an example of what an inspection plan for roofs should be. For other local agency assets, such as roads, culverts, bridges, utilities, etc., each inspection form would contain different information appropriate to the type of facility being inspected.

Other resources for inspection forms would be the respective state departments of transportation, various utility commissions, the state commissioner of dams, and possibly the American Public Works Association. However, when I spot-checked the American Public Works Association website for this kind of inspection form, I did not see the type of documents that I would have included in this book. The publications I did find are more disaster response-oriented than disaster cost recovery-oriented.

In the hundreds of appeals cases I researched in preparation for writing this book, I was astounded by the number of cases where the local agency stated they did not have any formal inspection or maintenance program or procedures. This is a big tip-off to FEMA that the damage suffered was either pre-existing or at least partially a result of deferred maintenance. In any case, without a program and procedures, it's difficult to otherwise prove our case.

In this appeals case, we go to an Ohio township. "From February 5 to 13, 2019, severe storms caused flooding and damage throughout Perry Township, Ohio *(One of 26 townships of this name in Ohio.)(Comment Added)* (Applicant). FEMA formulated Grants Manager Projects (GMP) 104094, 104120, 104218, 106653, 104123, 104223, and 133856 to address repair work to the Applicant's roads, ditches, and culverts (Facilities). The Applicant informed FEMA that it did not have a formal road maintenance policy and that repairs were based on recommendations made by its Trustees that inspected the roads."[73]

"For GMP 133856, FEMA requested supporting documentation to verify that work was completed and costs, and to develop the project's damage description and dimensions, scope, and cost. For the other projects, FEMA expressed concern about the eligibility of claimed damages because site inspections and photographs taken to verify site conditions indicated damages such as road surface erosion, rock loss and ditch damage that may have occurred over time from other causes. FEMA requested supporting documentation, including construction plans, maintenance records, material invoices, photographs, inspection reports or other information, demonstrating that the Applicant regularly maintained ditches running along the road sites, and that roads and culverts were regularly maintained and in good condition prior to the disaster. The Applicant commented for GMP 133856 in FEMA's Grants Portal that the work was done by Trustees whose time was not recorded as they cannot charge for labor and that it had already provided maintenance records."[74]

"While logs and photographs are not required in order to receive FEMA assistance, they may be helpful to demonstrate that the damage was directly caused by the incident. The Applicant provided activity logs for work done on roads and undated photographs claimed to show regular maintenance. The logs show the Applicant 'hauled stone' on 3 of the 14 roads on January 16, 2019, but the Applicant did not provide activity logs FEMA requested that would show maintenance for the five years preceding the declared event. The information on these logs and the undated photographs do not provide sufficient detail to confirm the performance of normal maintenance activities and distinguish between pre-existing damage and damage caused by the incident. ***In addition, the Applicant acknowledged it does not have a formal written road maintenance policy, and that repairs are based on recommendations made by the Trustees (along with temporary workers) that inspect the roads.*** Accordingly, the Applicant has not established that work to repair the damages to the Facilities was a direct result of the declared disaster."[75] (Emphasis Added)

In contrast, in this final case on damage assessment, we look at a case from Kansas. "From May 4 to June 21, 2015, severe storms with heavy rainfall caused flooding in numerous areas in eastern Kansas, including Lowe Township (Subrecipient) in Washington County. The President issued a major disaster declaration on July 20, 2015. The Subrecipient submitted a request for Public Assistance on August 7, 2015, to repair flood damages to its roads."[76]

"On June 9, 2016, FEMA issued a Public Assistance Determination Memorandum notifying the Subrecipient that the project was ineligible for grant funding. FEMA found the Subrecipient failed to document pre-disaster maintenance of its culverts, which would enable verification of disaster-related damages. Additionally, FEMA found the Subrecipient failed to demonstrate that the culverts were damaged beyond repair, as photographs taken during the site visits did not show flood damage to the terrain surrounding the restored culverts, or physical damage to the unrestored culverts. FEMA reduced funding for PW 353 to $0.00."[77]

On appeal: "The Subrecipient argued: (1) the area had experienced three times the normal amount of rainfall during the incident period, thus the storms were the cause of damages; (2) it completed most of the restorations prior to FEMA's involvement in the project; (3) FEMA based its decision on an examination of site photographs, which was unreasonable; (4) it did not have the resources to conduct the deliberate culvert inspections that would satisfy FEMA's documentation requirements; and (5) the culverts were 95 to 100 percent blocked with debris and damaged beyond repair. The Subrecipient submitted documentation with the appeal, including written statements from contractors hired to repair the culvert sites, annual budgets for fiscal years (FYs) 2013 to 2015, and invoices (with corresponding cancelled checks) showing expenses and payments for culvert repairs."[78]

"On first appeal, FEMA determined the Subrecipient did not demonstrate pre-disaster maintenance of the culvert sites. The determination was based in part on an examination of the annual budgets, finding they did not contain enough detail to determine the specific type or location of maintenance work completed in a given Fiscal Year. ***However, close scrutiny of the budget data shows the Subrecipient apportioned all expenses into one of two categories: 'general' or 'roads.' This indicates the priority the Subrecipient places on public road maintenance; indeed, maintenance of road networks is one of the primary historical reasons a township exists as a subdivision of local government in Kansas. For each year represented, the Subrecipient never allocated*** *__less than 40 percent of its total budget to its roads.__*[79] Thus, in this case, the local agency was able to prevail in its appeal.

There are no magic numbers or fixed criteria in play here. Each Project Worksheet application will be evaluated based on its own merits and the documentation provided to make the case. Clearly, the safest possible way to prove that damages were caused directly and only by the disaster is to have thorough pre- and post-disaster photographic documentation, well-written regular pre-disaster inspection reports, and a formal written maintenance plan. Anything less than this all depends on the local agency's risk appetite. The failure of a local agency to properly document its damages is frankly not a concern of FEMA's. If we want Federal funds, we must play by Federal rules.

For the sake of inclusiveness, there are seven checklists for the information which FEMA may require for various aspects of the Public Assistance program, including a one-page checklist for documentation to support a damage claim. These checklists were extracted from the first edition of the Public Assistance Program and Policy Guide, issued in January 2016, but some of these are not available in the current edition (2020) of the Guide. I would characterize these lists as samples or "starter" lists, as some FEMA requirements may have changed in the past seven years, and the circumstances of each agency and each disaster may vary. They are in the Appendix, Form 36 (A-G).

Notes

1 https://www.fema.gov/appeal/result-declared-incident-42
2 Ibid.
3 Ibid.
4 Ibid.
5 Ibid.
6 Ibid.
7 Ibid.
8 https://www.fema.gov/appeal/force-account-labor-overtime-labor-costs-force-account-labor-emergency-labor-support
9 Ibid.
10 Ibid.
11 Ibid.
12 Ibid.
13 https://oui.doleta.gov/unemploy/disaster.asp
14 https://www.fema.gov/appeal/building-safety-inspections
15 Ibid.
16 Ibid.
17 https://www.fema.gov/appeal/electrical-safety-inspections
18 https://www.fema.gov/appeal/debris-removal-construction-and-demolition
19 Ibid.
20 Ibid.
21 Ibid.
22 https://www.fema.gov/appeal/demolition
23 Ibid.
24 Ibid.
25 Ibid.
26 https://www.fema.gov/appeal/result-declared-incident-9
27 Ibid.
28 Ibid.
29 Ibid.
30 https://www.fema.gov/appeal/direct-result-disaster-debris-removal-soil-silt-rock

31 Ibid.
32 Ibid.
33 Ibid.
34 Ibid.
35 Ibid.
36 Ibid.
37 Disaster Operations Legal Reference, September 2020, pp. 5–58.
38 https://www.fema.gov/appeal/safety-inspections
39 Ibid.
40 Ibid.
41 https://www.fema.gov/appeal/building-inspections
42 Ibid.
43 Ibid.
44 https://www.fema.gov/appeal/application-procedures-2
45 Ibid.
46 Ibid.
47 Ibid.
48 https://www.fema.gov/appeal/result-declared-incident-33
49 Ibid.
50 https://www.fema.gov/appeal/result-declared-incident-11
51 Ibid.
52 Ibid.
53 Ibid.
54 Ibid.
55 Ibid.
56 https://www.fema.gov/appeal/result-declared-incident-23
57 Ibid.
58 Ibid.
59 Ibid.
60 https://www.fema.gov/appeal/result-declared-incident-40
61 Ibid.
62 Ibid.
63 Ibid.
64 Ibid.
65 Ibid.
66 Ibid.
67 Ibid.
68 Disaster Operations Legal Reference, Version 4.0, September 25, 2020, pp. 5–68.
69 Substantial Improvement, Substantial Damage Desk Reference FEMA P-758, May 2010, pp. 1–1.
70 Ibid.
71 2 CFR, Part 200, §200.318(d)
72 https://www.governing.com/archive/tns-nyc-lies-to-fema-storm-sandy.html
73 https://www.fema.gov/appeal/appeals-result-declared-incident
74 Ibid.
75 Ibid.
76 https://www.fema.gov/appeal/roads-direct-result-disaster
77 Ibid.
78 Ibid.
79 Ibid.

21 The FEMA Preliminary Damage Assessment

The damage assessment process can be a major stumbling block for a disaster-affected agency. Damage assessment is seldom done by the agency and therefore there is little organizational experience or administrative capacity for the process.

A hypothetical local agency may normally have 150 building and safety inspections to perform in an average week and is structured to meet this need, with an appropriate number of qualified inspectors, and possibly a digital system for tracking both the inspection projects and the building inspector's time.

Fast-forward to a disaster, and possibly a 10-, 20-, 30-, or more fold increase in the number of requested inspections. The building inspectors are instantly overwhelmed and they themselves may also be victims, or close associates of victims, which layers on incredible stress. Additionally, the agency building inspection computer program may be under-capacity for the task at hand.

I was a member of a Mutual Aid Disaster Cost Recovery team sent to assist a local agency in California after a relatively minor but nonetheless damaging earthquake some years ago. One of the other Mutual Aid-providing agencies was a very large California city which had written its own building inspection software app for use on an iPad. They loaned the smaller agency several iPads to improve their capacity to perform and better manage post-earthquake safety inspections. After a couple of days, the iPads were returned. The process of learning a new computer program and integrating it into their existing system was too much for the stress-ladened agency to handle in the midst of the crisis.

How might the local Department of Building and Safety cope with this massive increase in demand for services, particularly when the roads may be damaged and in many cases strewn with impassible debris?

This sets the stage for this chapter on the Preliminary Damage Assessment (PDA) process.

First of all, FEMA provides little useful information on how to manage these substantial challenges at the local level. From the Federal perspective, this is not their job. Nor would local agencies want the Federal government telling them how to do their business. However, this does leave an often-substantial gap between what we normally do as a local agency and what Federal regulations require we do after a disaster.

FEMA does provide the "Preliminary Damage Assessment Guide.'" However, this book focuses largely on how FEMA, working with state and local authorities, performs the "Preliminary Damage Assessment" rather than on how the locals should organize themselves and the damage assessment process for their locality. This is not a failing by any means. There are so many different building and safety departments, to say nothing of road and highway departments or utility departments, that it would be quite impossible for FEMA to propose a single standard system for use at the local level.

DOI: 10.4324/9781003487869-25

I recommend that local Building & Safety officials and those responsible for all roads and utility infrastructure be familiar with the Preliminary Damage Assessment Guide, but it will not provide them with a clearly defined damage assessment process, which is truly and entirely a local responsibility.

First and foremost, there must be a clear understanding of what the Preliminary Damage Assessment is and is not.

As previously stated, the local agency is responsible for creating the "Damage Inventory," which is also called by various other names depending on the state. In California, the list is called the "List of Projects"; in Nebraska the list is called the "Red Book"; in Texas, it is called the "Damage Assessment Report" or the "Disaster Damage Assessment." ' So, depending on which state, territory, or tribal nation you work in, there may be a different name for what FEMA refers to as the "Damage Inventory."

Regardless of what the list is called, it is the exclusive responsibility of the local agency to prepare the roster of all damage sites, response activities, and costs for sheltering and feeding disaster survivors.

FEMA DOES NOT look for damage. FEMA merely validates the damages the local agency has reported.

Typically, the Preliminary Damage Assessment is FEMA's and the state's chance to view the damages firsthand. There will be additional site inspections as the process continues, but the purpose of the Preliminary Damage Assessment is to verify that the damages are as severe and/or widespread as reported by the local agency. Both FEMA and the state will use the information gathered and verified during the Preliminary Damage Assessment to estimate their personnel and equipment resources to be engaged to support the locals during the disaster recovery.

Usually, a Preliminary Damage Assessment team consists of the appropriate representatives from the local agency, FEMA personnel, and state Office of Emergency Services staff. They will normally travel together in a van or small bus to visit the sites selected by the local agency.

With the Preliminary Damage Assessment team, local agency personnel should be prepared to visit the worst of the damage sites and a representative sampling of less-damaged facilities, possibly including some homes and businesses, depending on the scope of the damages.

The local agency should assign a responsible local official to guide the Assessment team. Appropriate level staff should also be a part of the team, i.e., a building inspector when the team visits damaged buildings; a road engineer when the team visits sites of road damage; and a utilities engineer when the team visits damaged utility infrastructure, etc.

Also note that besides FEMA, there may be representatives from other Federal agencies depending on the types of damages wrought by the disaster, and whether there are notable environmental or historical issues.

It is of critical importance that the local staff assigned to the Preliminary Damage Assessment team NOT make any gratuitous statements which might endanger the eligibility of a potential project. Making a statement such as, "We were going to tear down that building next year" would be fatal to funding. Although that may have been the case before the disaster, the threatened structure might now be needed due to extensive damage to other structures.

It should be the job of the staff assigned to tour with the Preliminary Damage Assessment team to make every reasonable effort to convey how seriously damaged the community is, if necessary. This is the first solid opportunity to 'sell' FEMA and the state on how much the local agency needs outside assistance to recover from the disaster.

The following is a small version of the Preliminary Damage Assessment Narrative Report. A full-size version is available in the Appendix, Form 2. While this is a FEMA form, for its own use, it bears some study, because staff can learn from it the kinds of information FEMA is seeking.

In fact, it's probably a good idea to have a pre-meeting with the local agency staff assigned to the Preliminary Damage Assessment team to assign talking points for each of the specific items of information FEMA needs to complete the form.

Having information prepared beforehand will make the inspection go faster and more likely to have a favorable outcome.

Every time that FEMA must request additional information, whether it is for the Preliminary Damage Assessment or later for a Project Worksheet, the process gets slowed down, and the money moves further away from the local agency, if only for a time. But our job in disaster cost recovery is to get the most money we are entitled to, and eligible for, in the least amount of time.

PDA NARRATIVE REPORT

City	County	State	Date	Page	Local Government Official/Contact No.

1. Event type (i.e., flood, wind-driven rain, and tornado) and description of damage trends observed (i.e., water contamination).

2. Identify issues related to sewer backup (i.e., insurance, damage to sewer lines, and normal sewer backup).

3. Identify areas with utilities out; include projected date of restoration.

4. Identify areas of concentrated damages.

5. Identify remote areas.	6. Identify major inaccessible areas and reasons (i.e., mudslide, landslide, and roads out).

7. Describe types of structures surveyed (i.e., brick, wood frame, foundation, basements, etc.).

8. Describe prevalence of damage to manufactured homes or mobile home parks.

9. Number of businesses impacted.	10. Names of major employers impacted (i.e., description and number of employees).
11. Other factors that impact tax base (i.e., vacation and tourism properties damaged, permanent exodus of population from disaster area, loss of use of commercial areas, and loss of production base).	12. Describe agricultural impact, if applicable (i.e., loss of crops and livestock).

13. Are there currently shelters open?

Figure 21.1 Sample of FEMA's PDA Narrative Report.

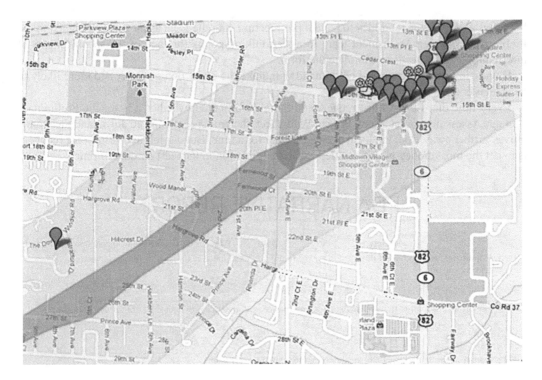

Figure 21.2 Hypothetical depiction of a GIS generated map of a tornado's path and the resulting heavily damaged areas.

A member of the local staff should be designated, ideally before a disaster, as the local agency damage assessment coordinator. This may or may not be the local agency emergency services coordinator or director, or another mid-level to senior level staff person with a well-rounded knowledge of the local agency. He or she should be actively supported by building inspectors, road and bridge engineers, utility staff and, if needed, financial staff, risk management personnel, and so on.

One of the questions FEMA personnel will ask is: "What are your priorities for recovery?" This is an important question, because if we as the local agency don't have established priorities, neither will FEMA nor the state. Setting priorities is our job and must be done before the recovery process can move ahead. However, the question of priorities may not be an instant answer; it may involve meetings with both the local elected officials and other stakeholders within the community. To the extent possible, this is a question which should be discussed and decisions made before the Preliminary Damage Assessment takes place.

To put it another way, all damages need a knowledgeable and effective spokesperson on the team to ensure they get the attention that should be due to each category of damage.

The Preliminary Damage Assessment team from the local agency may not be a unified and collegial group. Each member of the team will represent certain "interests," i.e., "damages." But those "interests" must not create friction that could otherwise disrupt the team or convey to either FEMA or the state that this group is more trouble than it's worth.

It is a good idea to integrate the local agency's GIS staff if they have one. GIS people are experts at conveying data and visual information in an integrated manner that can be much more powerful than either data or visual information alone. One of the most effective damage assessment presentations I have ever seen was a GIS map similar to the following illustration. This image maps the destruction caused by a tornado; it shows the tornado's path and the location of the structures which were damaged or destroyed. This is a near-perfect way to convey information and get a Preliminary Damage Assessment off to a great start.

In this example, the broad path of a tornado is shown running from lower left to upper right, with the most significantly damaged facilities shown with pins. This example clearly shows the extent of the tornado's path in the community and provides an excellent overview of the damage.

The following case out of Florida provides some interesting insights into the damage assessment process and the appeals process which often follows denials of funding. This particular case fails on three different fronts.

"In 2005, Hurricane Wilma caused a large amount of debris to be deposited on the roadways throughout Broward County, Florida. Following the storm, the Broward County School Board (Applicant) conducted dry bus runs to survey its bus routes and bus stops for debris and unsafe conditions. The dry bus runs were conducted by force account labor in buses owned by the Applicant. The force account labor did not, nor were they expected to, remove, eliminate, or lessen the amount of debris found on the roadway. FEMA obligated Project Worksheet (PW) 8296 in the amount of $432,153.11 to fund costs associated with the force account labor used to conduct the dry runs. At final inspection, FEMA determined that the dry bus run activity was ineligible for Public Assistance (PA) funding as the work related to a damage assessment and was not cost effective. FEMA de-obligated PW 8296 entirely and denied an additional $9,716.15 in costs claimed at final inspection."[1]

"In its first appeal dated June 23, 2011, the Applicant requested $441,869.16 for costs associated with dry runs that it conducted after Hurricane Wilma. The Applicant asserted that the dry runs ensured that the bus routes and stops were safe for driver and student occupation."[2]

"Here, the Applicant submitted a second appeal dated August 9, 2012. The Grantee submitted its written recommendation, with the Applicant's second appeal attached, to FEMA in June 2014, two years after FEMA's first appeal determination."[3] (Emphasis Added)

This is yet another case where the local agency (the applicant) timely filed an appeal, but the state delayed in forwarding the appeal to FEMA. The case notes: "Neither the Stafford Act nor 44 C.F.R. provides FEMA authority to grant time extensions for filing second appeals."[4]

The discussion continues: "The Applicant used the dry runs to confirm the existence or non-existence of debris and hazardous material, not lessen or eliminate such hazards. Accordingly, the dry runs cannot be classified as an emergency protective measure. FEMA classifies the Applicant's activity as a survey of damage. Damage surveys are not eligible for Public Assistance because the Applicant's administrative allowance covers this type of work."[5]

Furthermore, "The Applicant failed to demonstrate that it was legally responsible for removing debris or hazardous material present along the bus routes or restoring the roads to an operable condition."[6]

The case continues: "Regarding PW 8296, lessening or eliminating the immediate threat would have resulted in the removal or movement of the hazard, rather than singularly identifying whether a hazard exists. The work performed by the Applicant did not result in the removal or movement of the hazard, nor, as it was explained in the Grantee's letter dated June 17, 2014, was it intended to result in such movement or removal. Because the work was not necessary to remove or lessen the immediate threat, the work fails the first prong of the allowable cost requirement; therefore, it is ineligible for PA funding."[7]

The case goes on further to drive another nail in this coffin: "Even if, arguendo, FEMA determined that the work was eligible as an emergency protective measure, the costs associated with the work are not reasonable. The Applicant used 1,232 buses, carrying two employees each, to survey a total of 123,200 miles of road. The surveys were conducted during a 72-hour period and each force account laborer was paid an overtime rate. At final inspection, FEMA determined the costs associated with the dry runs were not reasonable as the extent of the activity was not necessary to accomplish the Applicant's intended outcome – ensuring the roads and bus routes were free of debris and hazards."[8]

So, this one appeals case lost on three different counts: 1) a late filed appeal; 2) ineligible work (conducting a damage survey without legal responsibility); and 3) unreasonable costs. Any one of these findings would have been fatal.

And yet, there is still one more problem to be reckoned with: "FEMA obligated Project Worksheet (PW) 8296 in the amount of $432,153.11 to fund costs associated with the force account labor used to conduct the dry runs."[9] Someone at FEMA, who we might suspect was substantially inexperienced, initially approved the Project Worksheet in the first place. However, at the core, the local agency relied on FEMA's approval of work that shouldn't have been done, in a manner which was inappropriate, and at an unreasonable cost. The late filing of the appeal was just a coup de grace.

From a Finance Officer's perspective, there is little to do about safety and damage inspections, at least until the invoices come rolling in and FEMA denies funding because procedures were not followed, the documentation was inadequate, or there was a lack of pre-disaster inspections and corresponding maintenance work was done.

The real problem is that neither the staff in the building and safety department, nor most emergency managers, have any idea these issues exist or that they will mercilessly clobber the local agency's efforts to be awarded FEMA funding to restore the community.

This case from North Dakota should help to clarify the purpose of the Preliminary Damage Assessment. "Heavy rains in June 2007 caused flooding in Ransom County (Applicant). While conducting a Preliminary Damage Assessment (PDA) of the county, the PDA team noted that floodwater had overtopped the road, causing erosion to the road's surface. They also noted internal damage to a rusted corrugated metal pipe (CMP) culvert, as well as erosion to the steep road shoulders at both ends of the 5x40 foot CMP. The team recommended that repair of the CMP should include extending both ends of the CMP by 6 feet. In September 2007, the Applicant repaired the damaged road, removed trees and fences, added fill to flatten the slope of the shoulders and replaced the underlying culvert with a 5x80 foot CMP at a contract cost of $24,953. A project officer visited the repaired site and determined that replacement of the culvert was ineligible as the damage was not a result of the declared event. The State prepared PW 398, for $72.50 for gravel on the road surface and fill for the eroded shoulders. FEMA obligated the PW on February 28, 2008, for $0 because the estimated cost was below the $1,000 regulatory threshold. On May 6, 2008, the Applicant submitted a first appeal claiming that the damage to the culvert was caused by the declared disaster and that the PDA established the eligibility of the work. On June 12, 2008, the State forwarded but did not support the appeal because it was an unapproved improved project. The Regional Administrator (RA) denied the appeal on November 17, 2008, and explained that although there was evidence of damage to the culvert, there was no evidence to support that the damage was caused by the disaster. The RA also clarified that the purpose of the PDA is to quickly assess damage and evaluate the impact of the disaster, not to establish final determinations on specific projects' work and cost eligibility. On January 29, 2009, the Applicant filed a second appeal claiming that the culvert damage and required scope of work was documented in the PDA, and that the FEMA Project Officer's Site Inspection documented damage to the culvert. The State supported the second appeal but did not transmit it to FEMA until October 12, 2010. The Applicant submitted no new documentation with the second appeal that demonstrates that the disaster caused the damage to the culvert. Furthermore, the second appeal was not transmitted to FEMA within the regulatory timeframe."[10]

This case was lost on multiple counts. 1) the appeal was filed after the deadline; 2) the approved project costs were below the prevailing $1,000 small-project threshold in effect at that time; 3) there was insufficient documentation to establish that the damage was caused by the disaster. The local agency unilaterally made a change in scope on the project.

So, while the Preliminary Damage Assessment team visits damage sites and reviews the claimed damages, this in no way is a final determination of anything, i.e., eligibility, costs, scope of work, etc.

Notes

1 https://www.fema.gov/appeal/damage-surveys
2 Ibid.
3 Ibid.
4 Ibid.
5 Ibid.
6 Ibid.
7 Ibid.
8 Ibid.
9 Ibid.
10 https://www.fema.gov/appeal/culvert-replacement

22 Other Federal Agency Funding

Figure 22.1 Chat GPT generated depiction of a USACE project. Note: In reality the work will be mainly done by contractors, and not military personnel.

Section 312(a) of the Stafford Act prohibits the use of Federal disaster assistance to pay an entity twice for the same disaster loss. Most notably, the duplication of benefits applies to any insurance payments which are received, or which should have been received under a policy. We also saw in Chapter 3 that the same prohibition on duplication of benefits applies to donations received for work which is FEMA-eligible. For private non-profits, duplication of benefits also applies to loans

DOI: 10.4324/9781003487869-26

received from the Small Business Administration, and FEMA may make a deduction of grant funding similar to those made for insurance payouts.

The prohibition on duplication of benefits also applies to situations where disaster-caused damages are or may be eligible for funding from any other Federal agency.

There are many Federal agencies that provide disaster assistance which falls under the duplication of benefits rule. Some of the major Federal agencies are:

The U.S. Small Business Administration (SBA), which provides low-interest loans to non-profits affected by disasters. These loans may be used to repair or replace damaged property, inventory, and equipment. The SBA may also provide Economic Injury Disaster Loans (EIDL) to small businesses under certain circumstances.

The U.S. Army Corps of Engineers (USACE) plays a significant role in emergency response and recovery efforts, particularly in relation to flood control, coastal emergencies, and infrastructure repair. They may also be responsible for tasks like temporary emergency power, debris removal, and temporary housing.

The U.S. Department of Agriculture (USDA) offers aid to farmers, ranchers, and rural communities affected by disasters. This includes emergency loans, financial assistance, technical support, and resource conservation programs intended to restore agricultural operations and protect natural resources.

The U.S. Department of Health and Human Services (HHS) coordinates medical and public health response efforts during disasters. They provide support for healthcare facilities, medical supplies and equipment, and emergency medical services. HHS also assists with public health monitoring, disease control, and mental health services.

The U.S. Department of Housing and Urban Development (HUD) offers various programs to assist with housing needs after a disaster. This includes grants for home repairs, temporary housing assistance, and community development block grants to support long-term recovery efforts.

Through the CDBG program (Community Development Block Grant), the Department of Housing and Urban Development provides one of the very few grants which may be joined with FEMA Public Assistance grants without triggering a duplication of benefits ruling.

Additionally, certain Federally supported housing programs may not be eligible for HUD funding, and therefore may be eligible for FEMA funding. This is a highly technical area, very much outside the scope of this book. In such cases, the assistance of an experienced and well-qualified consultant may be recommended.

The U.S. Department of Transportation (DOT) assists with transportation-related aspects of disaster response and recovery. They support the restoration of roads, bridges, and public transportation systems. The Federal Department of Transportation includes the Federal Highway Administration and the Federal Transit Authority.

The U.S. Environmental Protection Agency (EPA) plays a role in disaster response by addressing environmental hazards and ensuring the safety of air, water, and land in affected areas. They coordinate with local authorities to assess and manage hazardous materials, contaminated sites, and other environmental concerns. We will later see how the EPA may also play an oversized role for those projects involving environmental issues.

These are some of the other Federal agencies which may provide Federal assistance following a disaster:

- The Department of Defense
- The National Institutes of Health
- The National Oceanic and Atmospheric Administration

These and many other Federal agencies may also play important roles in other aspects of disaster response and recovery, particularly in supporting the National Response Framework (NRF) as a part of the ESFs or Emergency Support Functions. Information that a Federal agency is involved in the disaster response, however, does not necessarily mean that they will also be providing financial support in the form of grants or loans.

Much More Federal Aid Not in This Book

Additionally, but outside the scope of this book, some of these agencies and many others also provide disaster assistance to individuals and families under the "Individual Assistance" (IA) program. All Federal aid benefits provided under the "Individual Assistance" program are made directly between an individual or family and FEMA, generally through tele-registration, which relieves the local government agencies from having to deal with yet another set of problems.

This chapter is particularly important to local agencies, both governmental and private non-profit, because although FEMA is the primary Federal agency to respond to a disaster, many of these other agencies may be involved and the question of duplication of benefits will arise. This is important because damage to roads, bridges, and waterways, as well as environmental issues, play an oversized role in many disasters.

Although FEMA is a primary grant provider, any time that another Federal agency's turf is encroached upon, the duplication of benefits issue arises from the grave as surely as a zombie at midnight.

Therefore, the local agency must have a game plan for applying for Federal funding. Do not waste valuable time applying to FEMA for work which is clearly in the domain of another Federal agency. Examples of this are manifest: on-system Federal-aid roads; distribution of food cards; debris removal from Federal waterways, etc. Close to 10% of all appeals listed in FEMA's Appeals Database relate to a duplication of benefits of one sort or another, be it insurance, donations, or other Federal agencies (OFA). It seems that even when there is just the faintest smell of a duplication of benefits, the available funding may be in mortal peril.

Alternatively, if the local agency chooses to apply to FEMA for funding even though there may be an "Other Federal Agency" issue possible, then also apply to that other Federal agency to protect the project's funding potential, it is not uncommon that FEMA will not issue a "Determination Memo" (DM) until after the deadline has passed to make an application to the other Federal agency. The reverse also applies: if making an application to the other Federal agency, also file an application with FEMA for the same project. Clearly, this is time-consuming; therefore, for some small projects the local agency may forego the dual filing process.

Other Federal Agency Case History #1

"On August 4, 2020, heavy rains, strong winds, flooding, and tornadoes from Tropical Storm Isaias impacted the State of New Jersey. Gloucester County (Applicant) requested $214,785.93 in Public Assistance funding for contract costs to repair a section of Auburn Road. However, on April 1, 2022, FEMA issued a Determination Memorandum denying funding because the road was classified as a major collector Federal-aid highway by the U.S. Department of Transportation, which falls under the Federal Highway Administration's (FHWA) Emergency Relief (ER) program. FEMA found, therefore, that Auburn Road was not eligible for PA funding."[1]

"Federal-aid routes are not eligible for permanent work funding even if the Federal Highway Administration (FHWA) 'Emergency Relief' program is not activated or if the program is activated but FHWA does not provide funding for the work. Similar to permanent work, emergency repair of Federal-aid highways is also ineligible if FHWA has the specific authority to provide assistance."[2]

"Even though FHWA did not provide funding for the work under its ER program, it remains ineligible for PA funding. Importantly, it would still be ineligible as emergency work because FHWA has the authority to repair a major collector Federal-aid highway under its ER program, and emergency repair of a facility is ineligible if another federal agency has the specific authority to provide assistance for the facility."[3]

Other Federal Agency Case History #2

"As a result of tornadoes, severe storms, and flooding occurring June 12, 2010, through July 31, 2010, debris logjams formed in Locust Creek. Locust Creek is a natural stream that is located in Pershing State Park in Linn County, Missouri. At the Applicant's request, FEMA prepared PW 605 in the amount of $392,592 to remove 39,259 cubic yards of vegetative debris from the channel and banks at two locations in Locust Creek.

FEMA directed the Applicant to contact the U.S. Department of Agriculture's Natural Resources Conservation Service (NRCS) for assistance as the NRCS is the responsible Federal agency for watershed impairments through its Emergency Watershed Protection Program (EWP). EWP eligible activities include, but are not limited to, providing financial and technical assistance to remove debris from stream channels."[4]

"In a November 5, 2010, email, NRCS affirmed the Applicant's eligibility for EWP assistance. However, the NRCS stated that it had no EWP funds available in 2010 for such projects. NRCS stated that EWP funding was only available for projects that would avoid loss of life, and that the logjams did not meet that criterion. On November 19, 2010, FEMA denied funding for PW 605 because funding for debris removal from natural streams is within the authority of the NRCS."[5]

"On January 31, 2011, the Supervisor of the Parks District advised the Applicant via email that 'the location of the logjams in Locust Creek pose no direct threat of loss of life, and that there are no dwellings, habitation or developed areas in this section of the floodplain as it is mainly forested wetlands and agricultural fields.' The supervisor also advised that 'all camping areas are well above the floodplain,' and that the 'logjams pose no threat to loss of life there as well.'"[6]

"The NRCS indicated it did not have funding available for logjams in Locust Creek. Lack of funding does not alter an agency's authority, and therefore does not then constitute eligibility for Public Assistance funding. Further, the NRCS found that the logjams in Locust Creek did not pose a threat to lives or property since the Locust Creek area consists of forested wetlands and agricultural fields. The logjams therefore did not qualify for emergency funding from NRCS under the EWP program."[7]

Other Federal Agency Case History #3

"Severe storm surge from Hurricane Isaac during the incident period August 26 to September 10, 2012, damaged 119 Coastal Reference Monitoring System (CRMS) sites. The CRMS is a mechanism to monitor and evaluate the effectiveness of various wetland restoration projects by collecting data at 391 different sites. Damaged items included PVC pipes, boardwalk boards, staff gauges, and warning signs and posts. The CRMS sites were funded by the Department of the Interior's U.S. Geological Survey (USGS) through a cooperative agreement with the Louisiana Department of Natural Resources to monitor, conserve, restore, create, and enhance vegetated wetlands in coastal Louisiana. The agreements were entered into pursuant to the authority of the Coastal Wetlands Planning, Protection and Restoration Act of 1990 (CWPPRA). State responsibilities for the

CRMS sites were transferred from the Office of Coastal Restoration and Management within the Louisiana Department of Natural Resources to the Coastal Protection and Restoration Authority (Applicant) in 2009.

FEMA prepared Project Worksheet 1557 to document repair of the 119 CRMS sites for $214,319.43. FEMA found the work to be ineligible because it was the responsibility of another federal agency and the CRMS sites lacked regular maintenance plans. FEMA wrote PW 1557 for zero dollars.

"PA funding is not available when another Federal agency has specific authority to restore facilities damaged or destroyed by an event which is declared a major disaster."[8]

"Further, a June 26, 2015 letter from the U.S. Army Corps of Engineers (USACE) provides that 'if the Federal and State sponsors of an existing CWPPRA project submit a request to restore infrastructure constructed with CWPPRA funding that was damaged or destroyed by a storm event, the Task Force has the discretion to approve or disapprove the request.' While FEMA has not consulted with the Department of the Army regarding this project, this letter reflects the discretionary authority of USACE and the Task Force, under the CWPPRA, to approve or deny project work to repair disaster related damage. Accordingly, FEMA finds that pursuant to the plain language of CWPPRA, the responsibility for this proposed work rests with another federal agency."[9]

"Stafford Act Section 312 specifically prohibits applicants from receiving duplicate financial assistance and makes applicants liable for benefits available from another source, including contracts. The cooperative agreement that covers the CRMS sites requires the Applicant and USGS to assume maintenance responsibilities for the expected life of the project, through 2019. The USGS is required to reimburse the Applicant for 85 percent of such costs for the CRMS sites, subject to the availability of funding. The cooperative agreement notes that the signatories are each responsible for their respective cost shares."[10]

Interplay Between Duplication of Benefits and Legal Responsibility

These two concepts are sometimes closely intertwined with each other. If the local agency does not have the legal responsibility for repairing damages or other disaster-related work, the work is not FEMA-eligible, whether or not another Federal agency may have responsibility.

When the local agency does have legal jurisdiction, and another Federal agency does not have responsibility, duplication of benefits can still occur because of insurance or donations issues.

In the final case history on this topic, we will see that although the local agency does have some legal responsibility under a contract, their part of the work did involve a duplication of benefits.

Other Federal Agency Case History #4

"Flooding along the Mississippi and Illinois Rivers from February 24 – July 3, 2019 caused levee breaches and embankment failures along the Nutwood Drainage and Levee District's (Applicant) levee system (Facility). The Applicant requested Public Assistance funding to purchase soil/borrow materials to repair the damage. FEMA issued a Determination Memorandum on February 25, 2021, stating costs were ineligible because the Applicant did not provide sufficient documentation supporting the $444,480.00 cost estimate and did not demonstrate that the claimed costs were reasonable."[11]

"The Applicant participates in the U.S. Army Corps of Engineer's (USACE) Rehabilitation and Inspection Program (RIP). The Cooperation Agreement between the Applicant and USACE states USACE constructed the Facility and that USACE would repair the Facility pursuant to its statutory authority to assist in the repair or restoration of flood control improvements threatened or destroyed by floods. <u>The Cooperation Agreement also states that the Applicant would remain responsible for providing lands, easements, and rights-of-way, including suitable borrow material for the project.</u> However, FEMA does not provide assistance for a facility under the specific authority of another agency, even if that federal agency does not provide funding for costs to restore the facility. Therefore, the Facility is not eligible for PA funding because USACE has specific authority to perform the Facility repairs and the responsibility for the provision of borrow material are stipulated in the agreement between USACE and the Applicant under that authority."[12]

So, in this case, although the local agency was not responsible for actually doing the repairs, it nevertheless remained ineligible for the costs to provide the soil material required for the project at a loss of nearly $450,000.

It is therefore important and quite necessary that once the damage information is collected, staff evaluate each damage site or potential project to determine which Federal agency, if not FEMA, is likely to be the appropriate Federal agency from which to request disaster assistance.

The reality is that new, inexperienced, and low-level FEMA employees may not be fully aware of all the nuances involved in FEMA funding and therefore may verbally, if not tentatively approve in writing, a project which will fall under the umbrella of another Federal agency.

A Federal Crossfire: It's Just a Shrimp Boat

Local agencies may often find themselves in the middle of a battle between two or more Federal agencies, with no input whatsoever, and subject to whatever decision is reached by the 'gods' in the Federal heavens.

My good friend Jesse St. Amant, who was then the Director of the Plaquemines Parish Office of Homeland Security and Emergency Preparedness, told me this story while I was on a trip to observe the recovery 14 months after Hurricane Katrina.

A shrimp boat had washed ashore during Hurricane Katrina and came to rest in the middle of a local street. FEMA, according to Jesse, would not touch the boat (for debris removal), because boats fall under the purview of the United States Coast Guard. The U.S. Coast Guard would not get involved with removing the boat because the boat was on dry land, and the Coast Guard's jurisdiction ends at the water line. Jesse said with a straight face, and I quote, "One night the most amazing thing happened: the boat spontaneously burst into flame." Now it was merely debris, and arguably eligible for debris removal from the public right-of-way.

Notes

1 https://www.fema.gov/appeal/other-federal-agency-5
2 Ibid.
3 Ibid.
4 https://www.fema.gov/appeal/debris-removal-locust-creek
5 Ibid.
6 Ibid.
7 Ibid.
8 https://www.fema.gov/appeal/legal-responsibility-other-federal-agency-duplication-benefits-0
9 Ibid.
10 Ibid.
11 https://www.fema.gov/appeal/other-federal-agency-6
12 Ibid.

23 FEMA Authorized Repair versus Replace (The 50% Rule)

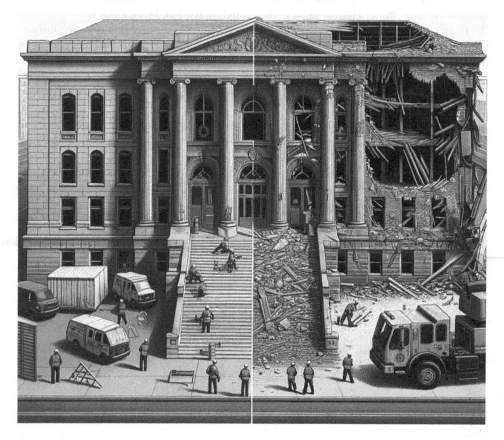

Figure 23.1 Depiction of the question, "Repair or Replace."

Repair versus Replacement

In the Public Assistance program, when a facility (either a building or a component of infrastructure, such as a section of piping) is more than 50% damaged, FEMA can authorize that the facility be demolished and rebuilt. There is sound financial logic in such a decision. Repairing a heavily damaged or destroyed facility can end up costing more than replacement. This is especially true

DOI: 10.4324/9781003487869-27

for older facilities, where replacement parts may not be readily available and might even have to be custom-made. Furthermore, as facilities age, they become more fragile (especially mechanical systems), and this can lead to additional damage when trying to tie newer materials into older materials or systems.

However, the problem with the 50% rule arises when making the calculations to determine the actual percentage of damage compared to the pre-disaster value of the facility. Understanding the 50% rule and then using the arithmetic involved in making the "more than 50% damage" calculation is not universally understood by local agencies, in some instances by FEMA contractors, and amazingly, again in some cases, by FEMA staff itself.

First, apparently neither few people at FEMA nor their contractors know how to properly make the mathematical calculations necessary to determine if the facility is truly damaged more than 50% or not. The author has seen appeals and Homeland Security audits from different FEMA Regions where similar mistakes were made. There are six different Department of Homeland Security, Office of the Inspector General audits, and as many as 222* appeals cases dealing with the Repair or Replace issue.

* (The number of appeals cases varies depending on the search terms used to find these appeals cases, i.e.,

- '50% rule' (15 appeals)';
- '50 percent rule' (27 appeals)
- 'repair or replace' (135 appeals);
- 'repair vs. replace' (24 appeals);
- 'repair vs replace' (1 appeal).), or
- 'repair versus replace' (20 appeals)
- Another variable is to search the Appeals Database under the heading of "Repair vs. Replacement," which yields nine different cases, some of which may be included in the previous categories.

This Department of Homeland Security audit dates from 2014, and improvements have been made since then, but this goes to the root of the problem. "FEMA's Public Assistance program provides financial assistance to recover from a wide variety of events, including hurricanes, earthquakes, tornadoes, floods, tsunamis, and terrorist attacks. FEMA obligates an average of $10 billion in Disaster Relief Funds annually, with the majority being for Public Assistance grants. Much of these funds are for the repair or replacement of damaged facilities. One of the most important recovery eligibility decisions FEMA makes following a declared disaster can be whether to fund the repair or replacement of damaged buildings. Generally, FEMA will replace a facility if the estimated cost to repair it exceeds 50 percent of the estimated cost to replace it. For this calculation, repair estimate is the numerator and replacement estimate is the denominator. FEMA uses its '50 Percent Rule' to calculate this percentage."[1] (Emphasis Added)

Results of Audit

"Applying FEMA's 50 percent repair or replace rule correctly can be very difficult and susceptible to error, misinterpretation, and manipulation. Our audit results have demonstrated that millions of dollars are at risk from incorrect 50 percent repair or replace rule decisions. In fiscal years 2012 and 2013, we recommended FEMA disallow over $100 million of costs that resulted from questionable 50 percent repair or replace decisions in five audits. In those audits, FEMA made the replace decisions based on collective 50 Percent Rule estimates of $31 million for repairs and

$50 million for replacements (based on FEMA's application of its policy). Due to various problems we identified, we ultimately recommended that FEMA should have paid $226 million to repair facilities, instead of $327 million to replace them."[2]

"Implementing the 50 percent repair or replace rule involves complicated estimates that attempt to apply sometimes ambiguous rules, often with incomplete damage descriptions and limited information on the building's pre-disaster design."[3]

"Issues/Weaknesses Related to FEMA's 50 Percent Rule

The weaknesses in FEMA's existing policy illustrate how susceptible 50 percent repair or replace rule calculations are to error or manipulation. They also point to the inadequate training and experience of those who perform and review the calculations. In analyzing the results of previous audits, we identified 11 specific issues/weaknesses with FEMA's implementation of its 50 percent repair or replace rule. We believe that addressing these issues will make FEMA's decisions to repair or replace facilities less costly and more fair and consistent.

Those issues include:

1) inclusion of 'soft' costs;
2) omission of building elevation in replacement;
3) inclusion of building elevation in repair;
4) use of 'conceptual' cost estimates;
5) inaccurate/incomplete cost estimates;
6) inclusion of code triggered whole building upgrades in the repair;
7) inclusion of Emergency Protective Measures in the repair;
8) absence of formal training/standard qualifications;
9) insufficient independent review;
10) insufficient supporting documentation; and
11) decisions made without thorough assessments."[4]

"FEMA Should Reconsider the '50 Percent Rule' Threshold and Formula

Overshadowing these issues is the 50% threshold itself. The replacement threshold is, by definition, much lower than cost effectiveness dictates. Also, such a low threshold can motivate applicants who incur relatively minor disaster damage to exaggerate the repair costs of structurally sound buildings, while minimizing the replacement costs, in an effort to reach the 50% threshold. Also, with such a low threshold, relatively minor mistakes can lead to erroneous decisions. In addition, the current '50 Percent Rule' calculation does not include all costs associated with the repair or replacement of a damaged facility. This results in a ratio that does not accurately compare the complete costs for either option."[5]

The audit continues, and this is where the complications set in, with complex formula for determining whether to either repair or replace the facility.

"Specifically, the numerator of the fraction includes only the direct costs of repairing the disaster damage, referred to as 'hard' costs, and may include costs associated with the current codes and standards that apply to the repair of damaged elements only. The numerator does not include costs associated with the following:

a. upgrades and other elements triggered by codes and standards;
b. design associated with upgrades;

c. demolition of entire facility;

d. site work;

e. applicable project management costs;

f. contents; and

g. hazard mitigation measures.

The denominator of the fraction is the cost of replacing the facility based on its pre. disaster design, design capacity, and according to applicable codes and standards currently in effect. These codes and standards may relate to structural elements such as mechanical or electrical systems, or the size of a structure. The denominator does not include costs associated with the following:

a. demolition;

b. site work;

c. applicable project management costs;

d. contents; and

e. hazard mitigation measures."[6]

"Only direct construction costs, or 'hard' costs, can be included in the numerator or denominator of either the repair or the replacement costs. 'Soft' costs include the costs for project management, architectural fees, cost escalation, and profit."[7]

This is not an easy task in any case.

The Good News, The Bad News

The good news for local agencies is that the application of the 50% rule does not happen very often. The bad news is that when it does go wrong, it is usually a very expensive problem, often with a multimillion-dollar audit finding.

Replacement Funding Denied

This case comes from Alabama following a 2018 tornado. In reading between the lines of this complex, multi-faceted case, it might be assumed that the school was pushing for the replacement of a nearly-50-year-old building.

"From March 19–20, 2018, severe storms and tornadoes damaged Jacksonville State University's (Applicant) Wallace Hall (Facility), a two-story structure that houses the Applicant's nursing school. The Facility is a concrete block structure, built in 1973, and has a metal sloped roof with steel trusses installed over the original flat roof in 1983. Immediately following the disaster, the Applicant coordinated with EDT Forensic Engineering and Consulting (EDT) and LBYD Engineers (LBYD) to inspect the Facility for damages. EDT identified damages to a portion of the roof and made repair recommendations, and LBYD observed "minor exterior damage to [the] façade and signs of roof damage."[8]

"<u>The Applicant demolished the Facility's interior finishes, including the abatement of all asbestos containing materials (ACM), prior to FEMA's inspection on June 8, 2018.</u> Because the Facility had been gutted, the site inspector could not observe damages firsthand and relied on the Applicant's recounted description of damages. The Applicant did not provide photographs of interior damage taken prior to demolition and ACM abatement."[9] (Emphasis Added)

"The applicant is responsible for providing documentation to support its claim as eligible and show that work is required to address damage caused by the disaster, and where preexisting damage exists, to distinguish that damage from the disaster-related damage. FEMA could not observe damages to the Facility's interior finishes after the demolition and the Applicant did not provide photographs of interior damage taken prior to demolition. The Applicant has not established the existence or extent of eligible interior damages to the Facility that are a direct result of the disaster. Additionally, the Applicant neither provides documentation to distinguish ACM abatement damages from disaster-related damage nor argues that ACM abatement is necessary due to disaster-caused damage."[10]

"The Applicant's description of the Facility's predisaster condition does not distinguish preexisting concrete damage from disaster-related damage. The Applicant has not provided documentation demonstrating repairs to the Facility's steel frame and concrete slab are required as a result of the disaster."[11]

"Using estimates which only include eligible work, the cost to repair the Facility does not exceed 50 percent of the replacement cost. The repair estimates provided by the Applicant include costs and quantities related to repair or replacement of items beyond damages shown to have been caused as a direct result of the disaster. Additionally, the Applicant's proposed calculation based on insurance proceeds includes costs, such as soft costs, which FEMA does not include in the 50 Percent Rule calculation. After removing soft costs and costs for the demolition of undamaged elements and repair and replacement of items not damaged by the disaster, FEMA validated costs of $2,693,249.16 for repair and $8,376,915.00 for replacement. Based on these validated costs, the 50 Percent Rule yields a ratio of 32.2 percent. Accordingly, the Facility is not eligible for replacement."[12]

Another Boogie Monster Hiding Under the Bed

Perhaps the most insidious temptation attaching itself to a replacement project when approved by FEMA is the perfectly irresistible temptation to make improvements beyond what might be provided for in upgrades mandated by application of the current codes and standards. No one wants to replace exactly what existed prior to the disaster. There are always some minor, and sometimes major, enhancements the occupants of a building would change if they could. And the rebuilding after a disaster seems to be the perfect time to slip in a few unauthorized tweaks. These "unauthorized tweaks" can destroy all the funding made available for the facility's replacement.

Fairfield, CT and the Penfield Pavilion: $4,340,054.11 Up in Smoke

"From October 29 to November 9, 2012, Hurricane Sandy produced storm surge impacting the State of Connecticut, including the Town of Fairfield (Applicant). FEMA developed Project Worksheet (PW) 680 to capture damages to the Applicant's Penfield Pavilion (Facility), a 16,756 square foot single-story structure surrounded by 10,811 square feet of wooden decking."[13]

"FEMA calculated that the cost to repair the Facility exceeded 50 percent of the cost to replace it, and on December 17, 2015 approved and awarded a replacement scope of work (SOW) for PW 680 in the amount of $4,340,054.11. The SOW stated that the Applicant must return the Facility to 'its original design, function, and capacity within the original footprint, meeting all appropriate Codes and Standards.' The SOW included a new foundation for the Facility, elevating the lowest floor to at least 15.5 feet, or 2.5 feet above Base Flood Elevation."[14]

"On April 18, 2016 and June 30, 2016, the Connecticut Department of Emergency Services and Public Protection (Grantee) transmitted the Applicant's SOW change requests. Among other changes, the Applicant sought to salvage part of the Facility by removing it for foundation repairs before returning it, regrade and steepen the pitch of the parking lot, install a new patio replacing the existing exterior wooden deck, and install fill in the project site to establish a new intermediate grade plane under and around the building."[15]

"The Grantee and the Connecticut Department of Energy and Environmental Protection (CT DEEP) requested technical assistance from FEMA on June 1, 2016, as to whether the revised SOW would comply with National Flood Insurance Program (NFIP) regulations. FEMA responded by letter on August 9, 2016, expressing concerns that the SOW may not comply with local and NFIP regulations, and that by commencing the revised SOW without FEMA approval, not elevating the lowest floor to 15.5 feet, and conducting work outside FEMA's environmental and historic preservation (EHP) review, the Applicant had materially violated the terms and conditions of PW 680."[16]

"The Applicant replied on October 28, 2016, acknowledging that construction had commenced on February 29, 2016, but stated that the work was within the approved SOW. The Applicant completed construction on its revised SOW without FEMA approval, and on November 28, 2018, FEMA issued a Determination Memorandum disallowing all costs (*$4,340,054.11*) for PW 680, pursuant to Title 44 Code of Federal Regulations (44 C.F.R.) §13.43, stating the Applicant had violated the terms of the award by completing a revised SOW without prior FEMA approval and the project was no longer eligible for Public Assistance (PA) funding."[17] (Emphasis Added)

In the first appeal, the Town argued: '. . . that had it not continued construction on the revised SOW, its contracts would have expired, thereby increasing its costs, and the damaged facility would continue to present a public safety hazard and result in a loss of income to the town.'"

"On June 20, 2019, the Regional Administrator for FEMA Region I denied the appeal, finding that the Applicant violated the terms and conditions of the PA grant award by changing the SOW without FEMA approval. FEMA specified that the changes to the SOW included not raising the lowest floor of the Facility to 15.5 feet, not fully demolishing the Pavilion, regrading the parking lot, constructing a new patio, and installing large amounts of fill. FEMA also found that the project was ineligible because the Applicant initiated the work on the revised SOW without affording FEMA the opportunity to conduct an EHP review, including a floodplain management review, as required by Executive Order 11988, rendering the project ineligible for PA funding."[18]

"Applicants must obtain the prior approval of FEMA for any revision of the scope or objective of the project. FEMA policy cautions applicants not to assume that such costs can be reported at the end of the project and that the additional funds will be approved automatically. Where an applicant materially fails to comply with any term of an award, including failing to obtain FEMA's prior approval for a SOW change, FEMA may disallow all or part of the grant award."[19]

In an October 2021 newspaper article, the Town's First Selectwoman, Brenda Kupchick: "said she thinks the town should have hired a construction manager to handle the project, instead of commissioning a building committee like the town did. That way, she said, that company's insurance would pay if something is not built to proper specifications. Then, they're on the hook for it, because they are supposed to be a professional company making sure things are done appropriately," she said.[20] "In this case, we don't have that because we had a building committee of appointed members of our community."

The town could have hardly done worse, exchanging a "building committee" arguably made up of local citizens for a professional and well-experienced disaster cost recovery consultant.

One other point on this appeals case. The town was fighting with fluff, when it argued that any delay would "result in a loss of income to the town." Increased operating expenses and lost income are simply not ever eligible under the Stafford Act. To raise this argument in an appeals case simply puts FEMA on notice that the local agency has very few clues about how the Public Assistance process works.

If this instance of changing the scope of work on a "replacement" project were the only case, it would be a sober warning to avoid this pitfall in the Public Assistance program. In fact, this problem is endemic to "replacement" projects. Local government agencies appear to have near-total susceptibility to throwing monkey wrenches (plural) willy-nilly into the gears.

Culvert versus Bridge

Even when a project is not a matter of "repair versus replace," the local agency can still find itself painted into a corner with no escape available. This case from Killington, Vermont, may be typical of so many other Public Assistance appeals cases. Background on why the town (population less than 1500) would change the scope of work may be found in this quotation from Wikipedia: "Killington's voters have twice voted to secede from Vermont and join the state of New Hampshire, 25 miles to the east. The movement stems from what some residents perceive as an inequity in taxes sent to the state of Vermont, for services received."[21] Apparently, there's a different drummer leading the parade in Killington, Vermont.

"From August 27 to September 2, 2011, Tropical Storm Irene caused flooding in the town of Killington, Vermont (Applicant), damaging the Stage Road culvert beyond repair. The Applicant requested Public Assistance through the Vermont Division of Emergency Management (Grantee)."[22]

"On August 22, 2012, FEMA prepared Project Worksheet (PW) 3076 for construction of a replacement box culvert, awarding a total amount of $137,403.18. A standard condition of the PW was that any change in the scope of work (SOW) would require prior approval from FEMA to ensure completion of any Environmental and Historic Preservation (EHP) reviews."[23]

"The Applicant built a bridge at the same location rather than a replacement culvert but did not receive prior approval from FEMA before beginning construction. On August 13, 2015, the Grantee submitted a closeout request on behalf of the Applicant, requesting $262,914.91 for construction of the bridge. This amount reflected a total project cost of $398,914.91, minus a $136,000.00 grant the Applicant received from the state."[24]

On February 8, 2018, FEMA Region I issued a Determination Memorandum deobligating all funding for the project. FEMA Region I found that the Applicant violated a condition of the award by constructing the bridge without receiving prior approval from FEMA. Although FEMA's July 27, 2012 EHP review stated that the approved SOW fell within a Programmatic Allowance, it did not apply for construction of a bridge. Construction of the bridge instead of the culvert would have required FEMA to proceed with the National Historic Preservation Act (NHPA) consultation process. Because no such review was done prior to the bridge being completed, FEMA deobligated all funding."[25]

"The Applicant appealed in a letter dated April 6, 2018, arguing that it told three different FEMA project specialists in May and June, 2012, that a bridge needed to replace the culvert to comply with Vermont codes and standards. In addition, the Applicant noted that the EHP review done on July 27, 2012, found that no historical properties were affected, thus, no further NHPA review was necessary. Finally, the Applicant argued that the Public Assistance Guide allows grantees, rather than FEMA, to approve improved projects like the bridge."[26]

"The RA (*Regional Administrator*) noted that while the Public Assistance Guide allows Grantees to approve improved projects, the Grantee is still required to obtain approval from FEMA for any change in the pre-approved predisaster configuration of a facility. In addition, because the Applicant did not obtain prior approval for the change in the SOW, FEMA could not conduct the requisite NHPA consultation process. This was a failure to comply with a term of the award, and therefore, FEMA was authorized to recover all funding per 44 C.F.R. § 13.43."[27]

This makes a very important point. Telling either the state or FEMA that a change is needed in the scope of work does not work. All communication must be in writing. Period. Reliance on verbal communication of any sort is a torpedo that has sunk not only ships but entire navies. In fact, any form of communication other than a formal letter containing the correct information plants the seeds of risk, ruin, and recrimination for the local agency. On the obverse side of the coin, NEVER accept any form of verbal approval from the state, FEMA, or any other state or Federal agency that may be involved in the application or execution of a Project Worksheet. The FEMA Appeals Database is strewn with reported instances where the local agency alleges that they told FEMA something or FEMA told the local agency something. All for naught. Verbal communications are a poison, and once ingested, death will result sooner or later.

FEMA Giveth and FEMA Taketh Away

In this case, the FEMA initially approved a preplacement for a damaged structure, then later determined that the initial approval was in error and deobligated the replacement funding which left the local agency high and dry.

"During the incident period from October 26 through November 8, 2012, Atlantic Highlands Harbor's (Applicant) Restroom/Office building (Facility) was damaged by floodwater from Hurricane Sandy storm surge and collisions from floating boats and docks. FEMA initially approved the Scope of Work (SOW) to repair the Facility, but later determined the Facility eligible for replacement under the 50 Percent Rule and obligated Project Worksheet (PW) 4229 for $82,544.86. FEMA obligated four additional versions of the project including an Improved Project to add a second floor with two offices and storage, block walls instead of wood frame, and flood doors. In January 2020, FEMA adjusted costs to account for building elevation and state historic preservation requirements and increased the total eligible amount to $712,687.83, but was not able to validate the Applicant's bid proposal as reasonable as it included improvements deemed unnecessary for restoration or code compliance."[28]

"On April 29, 2020, FEMA issued a Request for Information asking the Applicant to provide a copy of the Floodplain Management ordinance that governs substantially damaged structures, and the Substantial Damage Determination for the Facility. The Applicant's response included ordinances, a State of New Jersey-Department of Environmental Protection Permit, the Substantial Damage Determination and FEMA Form 90–91 demonstrating that FEMA found that the repair cost was greater than 50 percent of the replacement cost (and the Facility thus eligible for replacement)."[29]

"In a letter dated August 5, 2020, the FEMA Region II Regional Administrator denied the first appeal. FEMA found that while it had previously adjusted eligible replacement costs to include omitted compliance and elevation costs, it had not re-evaluated replacement eligibility. FEMA re-estimated repair and replacement costs and found that repair costs were only 24.76 percent of the replacement cost; therefore, the Facility was no longer eligible for replacement. Instead, FEMA found that the Facility was eligible for repair and elevation only. Consequently, FEMA deobligated $191,439.22, thus reducing the eligible project amount to $521,248.61."[30] (Emphasis Added)

The Trojan Horse Redux

If a local agency receives authorization from FEMA to replace rather than repair a facility, the offer should be embraced with all the suspicion that would be attached to a New Age Trojan Horse. The "gift" of replacement, at least in FEMA appeals cases, often holds the seeds of self-destruction . . . sometimes if only because the locals, elected and appointed, cannot resist tampering with the FEMA-approved scope of work.

The Repair versus Replace Toolbox

This is a very small toolbox, but sometimes good things come in small packages.

This two-page form is in the Appendix, Form 54. This is NOT a FEMA form, and its use is NOT required.

However, this form was developed following an example found in a FEMA audit which dealt with the question of "repair versus replace" (DHS-OIG Audit DD-13–04, *FEMA Improperly Applied the 50 Percent Rule in Its Decision To Pay for the Replacement of the Martinsville High School, Martinsville, Illinois, p. 6)*. In fact, the first page of the form is taken directly from the audit. The second page simply does the math for you by disregarding those costs which are not allowed under the current rules.

If others persist in chasing after this once-in-a-lifetime opportunity, show them the money.

At the end of the day, the important thing to know is that this doesn't happen too often, but if it does happen, it could turn out to be a financial fiasco. A recommendation when presented with this "gift" is to retain a truly experienced advisor to assist you in the process. This should be an advisor with both the experience and authority necessary to successfully marshal the project through every stage of the process.

Notes

1 DHS-OIG Audit FEMA's Progress in Clarifying its "50 Percent Rule" for the Public Assistance Grant Program, August 2014, p. 3.
2 Ibid, p. 5.
3 Ibid.
4 Ibid, p. 7.
5 Ibid, p. 14.
6 Ibid, p. 19.
7 Ibid.
8 https://www.fema.gov/appeal/result-declared-incident-repair-vs-replacement
9 Ibid.
10 Ibid.
11 Ibid.
12 Ibid.
13 https://www.fema.gov/appeal/change-scope-work-environmental-and-historic-preservation-compliance
14 Ibid.
15 Ibid.
16 Ibid.
17 Ibid.
18 Ibid.
19 Ibid.
20 https://www.ctinsider.com/news/article/Future-for-Fairfield-s-Penfield-Pavilion-16566526.php
21 https://en.wikipedia.org/wiki/Killington,_Vermont
22 https://www.fema.gov/appeal/scope-work-historic-preservation-705c
23 Ibid.
24 Ibid.
25 Ibid.
26 Ibid.
27 Ibid.
28 https://www.fema.gov/appeal/repair-vs-replacement
29 Ibid.
30 Ibid.

24 Developing the Damage Inventory, AKA 'The List of Projects'

Figure 24.1 Chat GPT Depiction of typical disaster caused damages.

Developing the Damage Inventory

Per FEMA regulation and policy, it is exclusively the local jurisdiction's responsibility to provide a list of all damages for which Public Assistance will be sought.

Neither the Public Assistance Program and Policy Guide, Version 4, June 1, 2020, nor the Disaster Operations Legal Reference, Version 4.0, September 25, 2020, specifically mentions the term

DOI: 10.4324/9781003487869-28

"Damage Inventory" by name, although this is the term commonly used for this compiled list of damages. In various parts of the country, the Damage Inventory may also be known as: the Damage Assessment Report; Damage Survey Report (DSR); Damage Assessment Inventory; Damage Catalog; Damage Enumeration; Damage Report; Impact Assessment; the List of Projects; the Red Book, etc.

It's important to note that while the name for the process and the resulting list can vary across different organizations, regions, and emergency management practices, the purpose of the list is to assess and document the extent of damages prior to making the application for individual Project Worksheets after a Presidential disaster declaration is made.

When initially compiling the list of damages, the dollar amount of the damage is not nearly as important as the fact that a damage site (or cost center, such as a shelter or feeding operation) is in fact listed. Both FEMA and the state realize that obtaining detailed and more accurate dollar costs is a time-consuming process. They also understand that the dollar value of initial damage reports will inevitably increase over the short- to mid-term.

A fundamental rule for conducting a damage assessment is when in doubt, and if there is a likely possibility of damage, place the site or facility on the list. This is especially true if an area of suspected damage is inaccessible or underwater. There are appeals cases, where the jurisdiction could not reach some areas within the jurisdiction for weeks and even months because of standing floodwaters.

This is absolutely critical: Within 60 days of the first substantive meeting with FEMA, generally the Recovery Scoping Meeting, all damages must be on the list and submitted to the state. In most cases, the failure to report damage within this 60-day window will most likely result in a denial of eligibility.

There is no penalty for removing a damaged site from the list at any time, even after the 60-day window has closed. But after 60 days, with very few exceptions, nothing may be added.

In this 60-day window, final costs are not needed. In fact, in most cases, costs may be estimated by an order of magnitude because this is a planning tool for FEMA, the state, and the local jurisdictions, and not a precise working estimate at this early stage of the Public Assistance process.

The difficulty of conducting a damage assessment and creating a damage inventory lies in the fact that this is a task which seldom needs to be done, and most jurisdictions have no established methodology for conducting a proper damage assessment which provides the data to populate the damage inventory.

Most local agencies, especially disaster "first-timers," have little appreciation for how much detailed data FEMA will require to validate damages as eligible. At the local level, we can easily put together a basic list of damaged facilities and infrastructure, in addition to those costs incurred for emergency response activities. However, FEMA will quickly come back requesting additional information. A sampling of this need for documented information can be derived from the "Essential Elements of Information" or EEIs.

If those staff members working on damage assessment carry a copy of the respective EEI for the type of damage they are reporting, they can begin to see the depth and breadth of FEMA's need for documented details, especially the need for pre-disaster photographs that show that the facility or unit of infrastructure was in sound condition prior to the disaster and therefore, the disaster damage being reported was caused by, and only by, the disaster at hand.

There are seven different EEIs, each corresponding to a FEMA Category of Work, A-G: Category A, Debris; Category B, Emergency Protective Measures; Category C, Roads, and Bridges; Category D, Water Control Facilities; Category E, Facilities; Category F, Utilities; and Category G, Parks, Recreation, and Miscellaneous. While these EEIs have some common elements, they also have unique questions relative to the type of damages they may incur.

The EEIs are available from the Grants Portal and are also in the Appendix Forms, Forms 39A through 39G. Initially, it is not a requirement to use the EEIs in generating the basic list of damages; however, FEMA will require the EEIs to be filled out early in the process.

The Damage and Needs Assessment Summary Form (DA-X-2) or Form 33, which was introduced in Chapter 20, can serve as a template for gathering all the damage sites into a single form. One of the advantages of this form is that it will automatically gather various damage sites into the proper damage categories, regardless of when the damage is reported.

In the first days following a disaster chaos will reign supreme, and keeping track of all the damages will challenge the most organized of agencies. Therefore, the agency should have some semblance of a damage assessment plan in place to avoid wasted time and the chance that some damages will be overlooked in the first 60 days.

Following the Napa Earthquake of 2014, while I was assisting a local agency, I passed by a building which looked remarkably like a fire station; however, it appeared to be empty. Indeed, it was a fire station, which had been taken out of service because of financial troubles affecting the city before the earthquake. The station did not appear to be damaged, but there was also no record of anyone inspecting the building for damage. Had the building been damaged, it would have gone unreported. Even though it would likely be ineligible because it was vacant, the city would have wanted to know that damage had occurred.

So, the local agency should have a current list of all its facilities to use as a benchmark to determine that all facilities received at least a passing glance for any disaster-caused damage.

FEMA and the state will request that the damage inventory be arranged by damage category. This is good administrative practice in any case as certain of the damages, such as debris cleanup, will have much in common with other debris sites, and little in common with the other categories of damage.

A good practice when amending the damage inventory is to never remove a line item, but rather to simply redline it. First, it takes time to reorder the damage inventory when deletions are made, and second, it may cause some administrative confusion at either the state level or FEMA, which can result in some damage sites being dropped off the list.

When submitting a revised damage inventory, it should be clearly marked as a revised list and state that all previous lists are obsolete.

All damage and all potential damage should be listed on the damage inventory, even if the local jurisdiction suspects that some of the damage may be ineligible due to pre-existing damage, or a lack of documentation to support a regular inspection and maintenance program. The Presidential disaster declaration is based in large part on the totality of damage caused by the disaster, and not on the amount of eligible damages. Regarding damages or potential damages, if in doubt, add them to the damage inventory before the 60-day window expires.

Grouping Damage Sites into Categories

It is my experience that the process of grouping damage sites into categories is both an art and a science. I worked with a client who had a large camping facility destroyed in a fire. The camp consisted of 70 camp tents (elevated platforms), a kitchen and dining hall, a laundry facility, a theater, men's and women's restrooms, camp store, water treatment plant, wastewater treatment plant, and other miscellaneous buildings.

The initial FEMA representative wanted to group all the damages into one large project, including the kitchen/dining hall, the water treatment plant, and the wastewater treatment plant, each of which would require specialized knowledge and differing levels of engineering.

The next FEMA representative wanted to separate out the water and wastewater plants into one project and group the other various buildings into groups, depending on the type of structure and each structure's need for utilities.

How any local agency's grouping of its projects is done may vary from one FEMA representative to the next. These shifting sands may result in additional work for local agency personnel.

There is no single magic formula for how projects are grouped, although there are some guidelines found in the Public Assistance Program and Policy Guide on pages 61–63.

From the local agency perspective, the grouping of damages into projects may depend on how the agency does its procurement and what staff is available for managing the projects.

The process of grouping damages into various projects is a two-step process with a first grouping of Category A, Debris Management work, and all of Category B, Emergency Protective Measures. The second step is a more detailed sorting of permanent work projects (Categories C through G), factoring out projects which have environmental and historical issues, are in special flood hazard areas, or involve ineligible work, etc.

While this sorting and grouping might appear to have little to do directly with disaster cost recovery, it is in fact an important part of the process. The damage inventory must be complete and eventually finely detailed. Work which appears to be ineligible for any number of reasons should be put on a back burner to avoid wasting time, and money, in pursuing a lost cause. In my review of hundreds of appeals cases, one fact stands out as an homage to futility. Without doing detailed research, of all 2400+ appeals cases, I would conservatively estimate that at least one-half, if not two-thirds, of all second appeals cases fail not for a single reason, but for multiple reasons. That is, the appeal fails because of a procurement problem, but would have also failed for a lack of documentation, or would have failed because of an untimely filing, or would have failed because of no legal responsibility, etc. Some agencies are so far down the rabbit hole they do not know which way is up, and they waste precious time and money pursuing an appeal which fails on multiple counts. In my research I found an Ohio county[1,2] which filed 21 second appeals totaling $4,277,323, all of which were lost, many because of pre-existing conditions.

Another important aspect of the Damage Inventory is that it will serve as a document for sorting out the priority for the repair and reconstruction of local agency facilities and infrastructure. No government agency has unlimited tax revenue, and in a significant disaster, the totality of the damages is likely to overwhelm the agency's available reserves. Even with a very high success rate in getting Project Worksheets funded, there will not usually be sufficient funding to fully restore all the damages. The priorities will of course be partially political, and the elected and senior appointed officials will need the best information possible to obtain a clear picture of the nature and extent of the damages and what funds may be available to deal with the losses. All of this should naturally involve the agency Finance Director and their staff.

This case from Florida illustrates how the Damage Inventory, with the appropriate supporting documentation, saved the day and brought home over $500,000 in funding previously denied by FEMA.

"Florida experienced flooding and damage as a result of Hurricane Irma from September 4 – October 18, 2017. Seminole County (Applicant) requested $697,180.18 in Public Assistance (PA) to repair damage to its culverts, roads, fencing along roads, shoulders, ditches, and signage along roadways (Facilities), which were repaired using Force Account Labor (FAL) and Force Account Equipment (FAE). On January 23, 2020, FEMA denied this request in a Determination Memorandum (DM), stating that it could only verify costs in the amount of $3,059.41, which were below the FEMA minimum project threshold, and therefore, the entire project was denied. FEMA noted the Applicant had not responded to two Requests for Information (RFIs) the Agency had issued to obtain missing information and documentation. Therefore, FEMA found that because the Applicant had not provided documentation that supported the claimed damages or the performance of eligible work, it was unable to validate all claimed disaster-related damages, work, and costs for this project."[3]

First Appeal

"The Applicant submitted its first appeal to the Florida Division of Emergency Management (Grantee) on March 27, 2020, contending that the requested repairs should be eligible for PA funding. The Applicant requested $697,180.18 in costs and argued that due to confusion at the project development stage, FEMA may not have properly reviewed the documents submitted by the Applicant. It asserted that it had provided the requested damage information to FEMA and the documentation showed that the damages listed in the DM were fully documented as required by law and FEMA policy."[4]

"The FEMA Region IV Regional Administrator denied the first appeal in a March 3, 2021 decision. FEMA noted it is an applicant's responsibility to demonstrate costs are directly tied to the performance of eligible work, and reasonable and necessary to accomplish eligible disaster-related work. FEMA determined, however, the Applicant had not provided documentation or clarifying information to verify the eligibility of claimed damages, work, and costs."[5]

Second Appeal

"On April 30, 2021, the Applicant submitted its second appeal and revised the amount in dispute to $547,067.66. The Applicant states that it presented a damage inventory (Damage Inventory) to FEMA on December 22, 2017, which outlined 253 potential projects. In support of its appeal, the Applicant provides the Damage Inventory, various spreadsheets and charts including a 'Damages and Scope of Work' chart (to document what work was performed at each site, what materials/labor and equipment were used, and what supporting documents correspond to each site), as well as a 'Cost Summary' chart, which further explain previously provided documents, and tables clarifying which documents supported which projects."[6]

"In its second appeal submission, the Applicant provides the Damage Inventory that lists each claimed site associated with this appeal, with locations and damage descriptions. It also submits the Damages and Scope of Work chart, which includes an itemized list of disaster-related damage locations, damage descriptions (consistent with information previously provided), the scope of work performed, as well as a catalogue of documentation provided to support disaster-related work. The list detailing the supporting documentation for each site, which the Applicant included in the chart, helps explain how the voluminous documentation provided relates to each site in order to allow FEMA to verify the eligibility of disaster-related damages and work."[7]

"The Briar Cliff Drive site serves as an example of how the documentation supports the Applicant's claim. The Damage Inventory specifies that at 214 Briar Cliff Drive, the hurricane caused damage that required emergency repair of the roadway for about 1 mile through repaving, placing 6 inches of asphalt base material and 1.5 inches of asphalt pavement. The Damages and Scope of Work chart details that the road at that site was inundated with flood water, causing potholes that needed to be filled and repaired, which resulted in the repair of said potholes with asphalt. The chart goes on to specify the force account labor, equipment, and materials used for the work, as well as the documentation that supports the eligibility of the work performed at the site (i.e., a site inspection form, Google Earth images, and work orders). The pre-disaster Google Earth image of the site does not show damage, but the post-disaster image shows multiple areas of roadway damage and subsequent repairs consistent with the disaster-related work detailed in the Applicant's supporting documentation."[8]

"The Applicant has demonstrated that the work and associated costs to repair the Facilities, are eligible. Accordingly, this appeal is partially granted in the amount of $546,471.40."[9]

Notes

1 https://www.fema.gov/appeal/result-declared-incident-45
2 This is a rural county of 457 square miles, with a population of less than 16,000 people.
3 https://www.fema.gov/appeal/result-declared-incident-allowable-costs-and-reasonable-costs
4 Ibid.
5 Ibid.
6 Ibid.
7 Ibid.
8 Ibid.
9 Ibid.

25 Interpreting Contacts, Policies, and Memoranda of Understandings

"There are different sources of uncertainty. Some are a result of contract terms that are inherently subjective. Terms such as 'reasonable,' 'material' and 'could reasonably be expected to' are always going to be subject to differing interpretations at the margins."

Charles M. Fox

Interpreting Contracts and Agreements

If the Public Assistance process is anything, it is a quasi-legal contractual process every step of the way. Understanding and adhering to many different types of contracts and agreements is the heart and soul of Federal disaster assistance. In some cases, even one slip-up can doom a project to deobligation and failure. Data at all stages of the cost recovery process must be properly documented in a clear and straightforward manner to ensure eligibility. The following list is a start, but may not be an all-inclusive list of contracts and agreements which might have an adverse effect on the eligibility of a proposed project:

- Damage Description and Dimensions
- Scope of Work
- Codes and Standards
- Environmental and Historic Issues
- Insurance Policies
- Mutual Aid Agreements
- Procurement from Buy Groups
- Private Property Debris Authority
- Disaster Services Performed by Private Non-Profits
- Leases
  - Facilities and Equipment Leased to Others
  - Facilities and Equipment Leased from Others

Defects or contradictions in any of the documents may result in ineligibility of the project.

First of all, although it may be assumed, it still must be said that for most documents, the lack of a proper signature is a catastrophic failure. This applies to almost all documents required in support of a claim for damages and the ensuing Project Worksheet. For this, there are very few exceptions.

DOI: 10.4324/9781003487869-29

Comprehensive Damage Documentation

The Damage Description and Dimensions must be thorough and complete to the maximum extent possible. This means not only looking for the obvious damage, but also considering what damage may be hidden from plain sight. High-quality endoscopes are available online for less than $50.00. They enable the user to see inside walls and other hidden places by punching a tiny hole in a wall or entering a machine through a small opening. When additional but unseen damage is suspected, this is a great solution to determine if hidden damage exists, without tearing out the walls.

Once all the damage is discovered, the next important task is to list EVERY single item of damage. Because if some items are left off the DDD (Damage Description and Dimensions), we cannot expect that they will be included in the Scope of Work, and therefore will be ineligible for reimbursement.

One Case of Delayed Damage Reporting

"As a result of the Loma Prieta earthquake (DR-845), the City of San Carlos (subgrantee) contends that several roof trusses in the San Carlos City Hall (facility) were damaged. The subgrantee did not identify the facility as disaster-damaged when the joint Federal/State inspection team visited the City of San Carlos on November 8, 1989. In January 1997, FEMA received from the grantee, the Governor's Office of Emergency Services (OES), the subgrantee's Final Inspection Report (FIR) which identified only one Disaster Survey Report (DSR) in the amount of $3,553 for the repair of curbs, gutters, and sidewalks in areas unrelated to the location of City Hall. By letter dated January 29, 1997, FEMA advised OES that it considered the subgrantee's application for this disaster closed. Subsequently, by letter dated February 25, 1997, OES forwarded the subgrantee's request for a FEMA/OES joint inspection of the facility. This request was prompted by the subgrantee's discovery of damaged roof truss members in November 1996 when it began renovating the facility. FEMA denied the subgrantee's request because of its "extreme lateness" and noted that it had closed the subgrantee's application for this disaster on January 29, 1997."[1]

First Appeal

"The subgrantee appealed FEMA's denial of its request for a site inspection in a letter dated March 2, 1998. In its appeal, the subgrantee stated that it did not discover the damage until November 1996 because it was 'hidden above the ceiling, which did not appear to be damaged.' In support of its appeal, the subgrantee submitted photographs of the damages with its first appeal, together with a letter from the construction manager noting that the seismic event did not cause any 'taletale signs of structural damage' and the damage 'could be considered latent' and 'very difficult to discover.'"[2]

"In its response, FEMA noted that it is the subgrantee's responsibility to identify and report damages during the initial site inspection or within 60 days thereafter. FEMA found that the subgrantee's failure to discover the damage until it began renovating the facility approximately 7 years after the disaster event does not constitute an extenuating circumstance beyond the subgrantee's control. FEMA concluded, therefore, that an extension of the regulatory time for reporting additional damage was not warranted. The appeal was, therefore, denied pursuant to Title 44 of the Code of Federal Regulations (44 CFR), section 206.202(d)."[3]

In this case, it should be noted that the ceiling in the area where the damage was alleged to have occurred was a T-bar drop-in ceiling. Therefore, if a staff person had gotten a ladder and lifted up just one ceiling tile, with a flashlight they would have seen the damaged part of the structure. After a disaster occurs and the initial search for damage is complete with no obvious damage to report, then it's time for a second and more thorough investigation.

Scope of Work as a Contract

Once a project is formulated and the scope of work is signed, it is an immutable contract which the local agency then violates at its great risk. Depending on how one searches FEMA's Appeals Database, there are currently 906 cases involving "Scope of Work" and another 211 cases involving "SOW," the common acronym for Scope of Work. Therefore, perhaps as many as 46% of all appeals cases somehow involve problems relating to the scope of work.

If the local agency unilaterally changes <u>anything</u> in the scope of work without first notifying FEMA in writing and then waiting for FEMA's written approval, it runs a substantial risk that FEMA may deobligate some or all of the approved work.

"From June 15 – July 12, 2018, severe storms, heavy rainfall and widespread flooding impacted Brown County, Minnesota. The Brown County Drainage Authority (Applicant) claimed disaster-related damage to 48 sites along its system of drainage ditches. At sites 16–23, FEMA approved a Scope of Work (SOW) to replace a total of 632.4 cubic yards (CY) of embankment fill along 630 linear feet of the drainage ditch. <u>However, the Applicant subsequently placed 4,166.9 CY of rip rap along 2,500 linear feet. After completing the work, the Applicant submitted a request to FEMA for the costs of the additional repairs; it also requested a change in repair method, from fill material to rip rap, as hazard mitigation.</u> In a Determination Memorandum, FEMA denied funding for the additional work, finding that the Applicant had not demonstrated that damages to the additional ditch length were a direct result of the disaster; it also found that the Applicant completed work in excess of the SOW without approval."[4]

First Appeal

"The Applicant filed its first appeal in a letter dated February 24, 2021. The Applicant contended that the work was necessary to restore the ditch to its predisaster condition. The Applicant stated that the additional 1,870 feet of damages claimed to sites 16–23 were 'concealed by water and vegetation during FEMA site inspections and discovered upon repair of the initial bank slumps.'"[5]

"On August 6, 2021, the FEMA Region V Acting Regional Administrator denied the appeal, finding that the Applicant did not request a SOW modification <u>prior to performing the work</u>, stating 'it appears the Applicant was aware of the additional damages and its planned scope modifications prior to initiating the work,' and that '[b]ecause the Applicant initiated and completed work outside the approved SOW without receiving FEMA approval, the additional work is not eligible for PA funding.'"[6] (Emphasis Added)

Byzantine Complications in an Already-Complex World

Very often in appeals cases, the unilateral change made by a local agency in a scope of work is compounded by issues related to codes and standards and/or environmental or historic considerations. However, no matter the reason(s), the local agency simply cannot instigate any changes in a scope of work without first noticing FEMA and receiving a written approval, if one will be forthcoming.

Often the process of requesting a change in the scope of work from FEMA will necessitate the halt of repairs or construction, which are usually costly. At that point the local agency must do some math and make a determination as to whether to wait for approval and endure the associated costs or proceed with the change and suffer the consequences of deobligation.

Insurance Documents – What's in Them, or Not

No one, except for insurance attorneys, reads every word in an insurance policy. The language of insurance is not readily intuitive. The language is dense and riddled with special meanings, all of which goes to how important it is. Many local agencies, especially smaller agencies, often know that insurance is important, but they know little else. In some cases, they do not even have a single staff member who has the collateral job description of Risk Manager. Those that do have a designated risk manager, or even a department of risk management, still usually have very little experience with FEMA and its approach to insurance issues. FEMA, on the other hand, has staff with a great deal of insurance experience. It's another case of David and Goliath, except in this case, David doesn't have his slingshot.

The time to deal with insurance issues is before a disaster strikes. Once a loss occurs (the disaster), everything becomes set in stone for that particular event. The local agency must, as a matter of course, provide FEMA with the insurance policies, the insurance adjuster's loss reports, and all other related insurance documents. FEMA will decide how much money we should expect to receive from an insurer and make the appropriate deductions to account for the prohibition on duplication of benefits. As daunting a task as it may seem, the local agency must be more insurance-educated to avoid the sometimes-staggering losses, both from the insurers and FEMA's deductions for duplication of benefits.

This next case is one of those "skin of their teeth" cases where the local agency faced three issues: insurance and its deductibles, a late filing of an appeal, and a '705c' issue, which will be addressed in more detail in Chapter 41: Appeals and Arbitration. Here we will only briefly address the insurance part of this appeal, in which the local agency did prevail.

"On September 3, 2004, Hurricane Frances caused damage to 182 of Broward County School Board District's (Applicant) schools and administrative buildings. FEMA obligated Project Worksheet (PW) 5548 in the amount of $227,469.24 on September 30, 2005, to address minor damage at those facilities. During the closeout process for PW 5548, FEMA approved a cost overrun of $3,095.42 to increase the project's eligible amount to $230,564.66, but noted that it needed additional documentation itemizing the project costs by facility in order to complete a review of prior damages and verify the Applicant's compliance with prior insurance requirements. On October 24, 2013, FEMA placed the project's closeout process on hold to submit a request to the Florida Division of Emergency Management (Grantee) for that additional documentation. After receiving no response, FEMA applied an insurance noncompliance reduction of $230,564.66 in PW 5548, Version 1 on October 10, 2014. On October 22, 2015, FEMA reinstated the $230,564.66 insurance noncompliance reduction in PW 5548, Version 2 after receiving the requested documentation. However, FEMA reduced that amount by $14,865.66 pursuant to Title 44 of the Code of Federal Regulations (44 C.F.R.) § 206.253 because the Applicant used blanket coverage to meet its insurance requirements associated with its prior losses sustained in FEMA-955-DR-FL and FEMA-1306-DR-FL. On January 26, 2016, the Grantee uploaded a notification to FloridaPA.org reflecting the determination in Version 2, and sent an email advising the Applicant to view the notification package on FloridaPA.org."[7]

First Appeal

"The Applicant submitted its first appeal on February 5, 2016, requesting that FEMA reinstate the $14,865.66 in prior loss reductions applied in Version 2. The Applicant argued that the Robert T.

Stafford Disaster Relief and Emergency Assistance Act (Stafford Act) § 705(c) prohibits FEMA from recovering the funds at issue because all three prongs of the subsection were satisfied, and that any issues related to the Applicant's compliance with insurance requirements should have been addressed more than 10 years ago when FEMA prepared Version 0. The Applicant also emphasized that it received no insurance proceeds for PW 5548 because the project costs did not reach the insurance deductible amount, and that the restrictions on reimbursement of insurance deductibles described in FEMA policies issued in 2008 and 2015 do not apply retroactively to this disaster. Lastly, the Applicant asserted that FEMA incorrectly classified its insurance policy as blanket coverage, and improperly applied the prior loss reductions as a result."[8]

"According to PA policy in effect at the time of the disaster, eligible costs for insurable facilities may include deductibles. However, if a facility insured under a blanket insurance policy, insurance pool arrangement, or some combination thereof, is damaged in a future similar other than flood disaster, eligible costs will be reduced by the amount of eligible damage sustained in the previous disaster. Thus, when an applicant uses one or a combination of the aforementioned insurance policies, reimbursement of eligible costs is reduced by the amount of eligible damage sustained to the same facility in a prior disaster, regardless of whether any of the costs are used to pay an insurance deductible. The International Risk Management Institute defines a blanket policy as '[a] single insurance policy that covers several different properties, shipments, or locations.' FEMA expands this definition by explaining that an insurance policy is a blanket policy when it covers multiple properties to a level less than their full value."[9] (Emphasis Added)

"Here, the Applicant's insurance policy constitutes blanket insurance coverage because it insured multiple properties under shared coverage limits set at amounts below the properties' total insured value. Moreover, the Applicant's insurance policy did not separately itemize or break down the coverages and premiums for each of the insured properties. While PW 5548 only addressed minor damage below $5,000.00 for each of the Applicant's 182 facilities, FEMA previously placed insurance requirements on 10 of those facilities that sustained damage exceeding $5,000.00 in FEMA-955-DR-FL or FEMA-1306-DR-FL. In PW 5548, the repair costs for those 10 facilities amount to $14,865.66. Accordingly, the RA correctly determined that FEMA was required to reduce eligible costs by $14,865.66 pursuant to 44 C.F.R. § 206.253(b)(2) for eligible damage sustained at 10 of the Applicant's facilities in previous disasters because the Applicant used blanket insurance coverage to insure its facilities."[10] (Emphasis Added)

They Lost, But Still Won This Round

The FEMA reviewer of this particular case concluded that, "While FEMA erred in initially approving the $14,865.66 in costs without implementing the required regulatory prior loss reductions, Stafford Act § 705(c) prohibits FEMA from recovering the costs at issue because all three conditions of the subsection are satisfied. Accordingly, $14,865.66 in previously awarded funds will be reinstated."[11]

Absent the provision Section 705c provision in the Stafford Act, this case would have been a loser for the district. However, in either case, win or lose, the amount in question was less than $15,000. However, the principles still remain and in other cases, the 705c argument does not prevail due to other issues.

The important message here is that knowing what insurance the local agency has, what it covers, and what it doesn't cover are critical elements of information in the successful pursuit of Public Assistance funding. When an insurance policy does not allocate the coverages for each covered facility, nor apportion the percentage of the premiums paid to individually covered facilities, this lack of specificity provides FEMA with a great opportunity (from FEMA's perspective) to make whatever insurance allocations it deems appropriate, regardless of the unwritten intent of the agreement between the local agency and its insurer(s).

Legitimate Differing Interpretation of Legal Documents

One of my "bits" when doing training is to hold up a gold coin (chocolate wrapped in gold foil), a fifty-cent piece which has the bust of President John F. Kennedy on one side. The other side has the American Eagle emblem. I ask one participant to tell the class what they see. Then I flip the coin and ask another student to tell what they see. Both see the same coin, but they see very different images. Thus it is with FEMA and the local agencies. At the local level, contracts and agreements are written and read from a perspective of permissiveness. "How does this agreement or contract allow us to do something?" FEMA, on the other hand, reads the very same document from the perspective of "How does document this prohibit a certain course of action?" Or more precisely, "Does this document expressly permit or require a certain course of action?"

Procurement and Buy Groups

Throughout the course of this book, we have seen cases where the local agency used the services of well-meaning and professional buy group(s), or purchasing network(s), to quickly avail themselves of disaster-related services, from debris clearance to cost recovery consulting. Unfortunately for many of these well-meaning local agencies and buy groups, the procurement goes ballistic, and the local agency loses some, or all, of the Public Assistance it so desperately needed for disaster response and recovery. We have seen, in the arguments put forth by these local agencies, their rationalizations for why they didn't need to follow, or in some cases were exempt from, Federal procurement regulations. FEMA is very much a rules-based agency, and generally the rules are quite clear and must be followed. The problem of course is that many agencies have never seen the rules, much less developed a strong understanding of what they mean and how FEMA applies them.

Extreme caution must be used when evaluating the option of using a buy group: not only to determine the lowest price, but also to know that ALL elements of Title 2 of the Code of Federal Regulations were met in soliciting proposals and awarding contracts.

An Unusual Case Which Came Up a Winner

"From September 17 to November 15, 2017, Hurricane Maria caused severe damage throughout Puerto Rico. Asociacion Frailes Capuchinos, Inc. (Applicant) requested Public Assistance (PA) funding to repair the San Francisco Chapel (Facility), which was originally constructed in 1756. FEMA prepared Grants Manager Project 121002 to document the Applicant's request and identified disaster damage to the temple, offices, and residential areas of the Facility."[12]

"With its project application, the Applicant submitted a certified copy of the minutes of a meeting that occurred in 1905, where the Third Order of St. Francis of Assisi (Franciscan Order), the owner of the Facility, granted perpetual use of the Facility to the Applicant via usufruct[13] (1905 Agreement). The 1905 Agreement allowed the Applicant to make improvements and modifications to the Facility at its own expense, but established that, '[t]he repairs to be made in the church and in the adjoining cloister will be paid for by the [Franciscan Order].' The Applicant also provided a certified copy of the minutes from an October 30, 2010 meeting, in which the Franciscan Order ratified and confirmed the assignment made in 1905 in all its terms and conditions. The Certification of Record from the 2010 meeting (2010 Agreement) stated that all conservation expenses and improvements of the Facility will be made by the Applicant without right of compensation, thereby allowing the Applicant to continue to use the Facility in perpetuity."[14]

"On December 3, 2021, FEMA denied the project, stating that the Applicant had not established legal responsibility for repairs of the Facility. FEMA stated that the documentation provided did not include clauses that made the Applicant responsible for structural repairs or those repairs necessary in case of fire, hurricane, earthquake, or any other disaster."[15]

First Appeal

"The Applicant submitted its first appeal, dated January 30, 2022, which included a certified sworn statement that detailed the chronology of how it came into possession of the Facility. The Applicant also provided a copy of a private contract of assignment of rights (Assignment of Rights), dated September 23, 2021, in which the Franciscan Order assigned ownership of the Facility to the Applicant for $1.00 and acknowledged that the Applicant has enjoyed continuous and uninterrupted possession of the Facility since 1905. The Applicant stated that it has had legal responsibility for the Facility without interruption since 1905 and provided maintenance records and other documentation of repairs it had performed to the Facility over the years."[16]

"On December 23, 2022, the FEMA Region 2 Regional Administrator denied the appeal, finding that the Applicant had not established that it had legal responsibility for repairs to the Facility at the time of the declared incident. FEMA stated that, since the 2010 Agreement does not address responsibility for disaster-related repairs, under Puerto Rico law, the Applicant, as usufructuary, would be responsible for performing ordinary repairs, and the Franciscan Order, as the owner, would be responsible for extraordinary repairs."[17]

"On February 21, 2023, the Applicant submitted its second appeal, presenting new information that it is in the process of formalizing the registration of the title in the Property Registry of Puerto Rico, including information documenting its request for a time extension until its legal claim is completed."[18]

"The Recipient claims that, for more than 20 years, the Applicant has been in possession of the Facility as owners, which is defined in Puerto Rico law as 'acting as the true owner by means of its actions or by the acts performed in relation to the property.'"[19]

"Here, the written agreement regarding legal responsibility for the Facility is contained in the Certification of Record from 2010 that ratified the original agreement from 1905, which establishes that the Applicant is legally responsible for 'all expenses of conservation and annexes' in perpetuity. There is nothing in the agreement that limits or defines conservation expenses; rather than being limited by specific definitions, the term 'all conservation expenses in perpetuity,' can reasonably be understood to mean a wide range of expenses associated with caring for the Facility, including repairs from natural weather events, such as a hurricane."[20]

In this case, after two appeals, the private non-profit prevailed, apparently with some history on its side. However, I know of one West Coast agency in a similar situation. In this instance, the city's public library buildings are owned by the city itself but operated by an independent library board. The "free" use agreement was established in the late 1800s, and without clear and convincing documentation regarding the legal responsibility for disaster-caused damages, the preceding situation might not turn out the same.

Private Property Debris Removal Redux

As we previously saw in Chapter 15: Debris Monitoring and Debris Management, the ability of the local agency to conduct post-disaster private property debris removal hinges on its pre-disaster policies and ordinances. Absent these critical documents, Private Property Debris Removal (PPDR) is next to impossible to achieve. The language must be clear, specific, and inclusive of those activities which may be a part of PPDR.

The following language is taken from a West Coast city's residential trash hauling contract. **"Provision of Emergency Services**. <u>Contractor shall provide emergency services at the City's request in the event of major accidents, disruptions, or natural calamities. Emergency services may include, but are not limited to: assistance handling, salvaging, processing, composting, or recycling materials; and disposing of Solid Waste.</u> Contractor shall be capable of providing emergency services within twenty-four (24) hours of notification by the City or as soon thereafter as is reasonably practical in light of the circumstances. Emergency services which exceed the Contractor's obligations shall be compensated in accordance with Article 9. If Contractor cannot provide the requested emergency services, the City will have the right to take possession of the Contractor's equipment for the purposes of providing emergency services."[21] (Emphasis Added)

While it might be possible to imagine that the underlined language in the preceding paragraph would give the local agency the responsibility for conducting PPDR, FEMA would almost certainly find that this language in no way provides a legal basis for the responsibility for PPDR.

I have in my private files a set of ordinances from a Florida county which does provide explicitly for PPDR, including the name of every street in the county where PPDR might occur following a disaster. And then beyond the specific authority for PPDR, there is also the question of the proper procurement of a contract for debris removal services, along with another contract for debris monitoring services.

Disaster Services Provided by Private Non-Profits

Following disasters, many private non-profit organizations will step up to provide desperately-needed services for the survivors, including providing shelter, mass feeding, crisis counseling, pet rescue and care, etc. However, for the local agency to be able to either claim the value of these services against the local cost share or be able to reimburse those providers for their costs, there must be a signed agreement between the local agency legally responsible for providing those services and the non-profit provider. The legally responsible local agency must nominally direct that such services be provided. If the private non-profit, for example a local church, simply opens a shelter without an agreement, their good works are not countable among the donations received, nor can the local agency reimburse them with the expectation of themselves getting reimbursed by FEMA.

The careful attention to detail when documenting donated labor, equipment, and supplies is highlighted in this case from Pendelton, OR. "From February 5–9, 2020, severe storms, flooding, landslides, and mudslides impacted portions of Oregon, including the City of Pendleton (Applicant). From February 9 to April 28, 2020, the Applicant conducted debris removal activities in the area of two mobile home parks within the Applicant's Riverside community (Mobile Home Parks). The Applicant used force account labor (FAL) and force account equipment (FAE) to remove and dispose of debris at a claimed cost of $174,400.36. Additionally, volunteers and businesses provided time, equipment, and supplies to assist in removing debris from locations in and around the Mobile Home Parks at a claimed cost of $36,024.54. The Applicant submitted a written request for FEMA Public Assistance (PA) funding for the FAL and FAE debris removal activities. The Applicant also requested PA funding for the donated resources to offset the non-Federal share of PA funding for emergency work projects. FEMA prepared Grants Manager Project (GMP) 150503 to document the request for FAL and FAE and GMP 150694 to document the request for donated resources."[22]

"In a Determination Memorandum (DM) issued in April 2022 for GMP 150503 (the project involving FAL and FAE to dispose of debris), FEMA determined that the Mobile Home Parks were commercial properties, and the Applicant removed the debris from these commercial properties without receiving prior approval from FEMA. FEMA further noted that the documentation provided from the Applicant's accounting supervisor did not constitute a determination from a public health official or public entity with the legal authority to make a determination that disaster-generated debris on private property in the designated area represented an immediate threat to life, public health, or safety or to the economic recovery of the community-at-large. FEMA also concluded that the Applicant did not demonstrate the claimed activities would benefit more than a limited group of people (the affected residents of the Mobile Home Parks) versus the community-at-large. FEMA therefore denied the Applicant's request for $174,400.36."[23]

"In a DM issued in April 2022 for GMP 150694, FEMA determined the donated resources claimed by the Applicant related to debris removal activities in the commercial Mobile Home Parks. FEMA found, however, that the Applicant did not submit a written request to FEMA identifying the specific properties or areas of properties where private property debris removal activities would occur prior to performing the work. Thus, FEMA denied the Applicant's request to offset its non-Federal cost share for the $36,024.54 in claimed donated resources."[24] (Emphasis Added) This amounted to a total loss of $210,424.90.

First Appeal

"The Applicant submitted its appeals for GMPs 150503 and 150694 on June 20, 2022. The Applicant contended it did not physically remove property out of the commercial Mobile Home Parks, but rather homeowners within the park piled debris along public rights-of-way (ROW), which the Applicant then picked up and hauled away, and other residents in the area took debris to a staging area to be similarly hauled away by the Applicant. In support of its claim that the debris removal benefited the community-at-large, the Applicant explained that the debris was scattered all over the Riverside area, both within and outside of the Mobile Home Parks, and streets had silt and debris scattered on them, blocking access to roads connecting the Applicant with other cities and not allowing residents to access work and get groceries."[25]

"For the donated resources in GMP 150694, FEMA concluded that the Applicant neither identified volunteer work performed on public versus private or commercial property to distinguish potentially eligible portions of work nor substantiated that the claimed donated resources included only work on public ROWs and did not include debris removal activities on private property. Because the Applicant did not demonstrate the donated resources were used only on public ROWs and the Applicant did not submit a written request to FEMA identifying specific areas where private property debris removal would occur prior to performing the work, FEMA found the donated resources ineligible for PA funding."[26]

"An applicant may use the value of donated resources to offset the non-Federal share of its eligible emergency work projects, provided the applicant tracks the resources and work performed, including a description, specific locations, and hours. When an applicant uses donated resources for ineligible emergency work, the value of those resources are not eligible as an offset to the non-Federal share. For donated labor, applicants should provide the name of the individual, days worked, the hours worked, the location of the work, and the work performed. For donated equipment, the applicant should provide the type of equipment, size and capacity information, location, days, and hours the equipment is used, the equipment operators' names, the schedule of rates, and who donated each piece of equipment. The Applicant is responsible for providing documentation to support its claim as eligible and to clearly explain how those records support the appeal."[27] (Emphasis Added)

For Better or Worse: The Language of Leases

Lastly, we come to the issue of facilities either leased/rented to or from a third party, be it a private for-profit entity, a private non-profit entity, or another governmental entity, be it local, state, or Federal.

The specific terms of the lease must clearly establish which party to the lease is legally responsible for repairing disaster-caused damage. Absent such precise language in the lease, FEMA has the option to interpret the lease as it sees fit.

As we saw earlier in the case of a Texas county with 21 different appeals stemming from a ground lease with the U.S. Army Corps of Engineers (USACE), each appeal was denied because the lease specifically because of a hold harmless clause.

"In the past, FEMA has denied PA funding to restore facilities located on land owned by the USACE, in particular when the instrument leasing the USACE land to a different party includes provisions that identify risks to the facility and hold the Federal Government harmless. On their face, hold harmless clauses do not apply to federal grant assistance programs such as the FEMA PA program. However, FEMA considers hold harmless provisions when evaluating the inherent level of risk and as evidence of the state or local government's awareness and acceptance of risk. FEMA reviews each project on a case-by-case basis and determines eligibility using the terms of the legal instrument. If the governing legal instrument includes language that clearly holds the applicant responsible for any flood damage that occurs to its facilities due to USACE actions or inactions, and/or any other causes specified in the legal instrument, FEMA will deny PA funding for the project because inclusion of such language indicates that the risk of damage is great, and that the owner of the facility is aware of and has assumed it, should damage occur. Here, the second appeal review centers on section 10 of the lease between the USACE and the Applicant. The lease reads:

"The United States shall not be responsible for damages to property or injuries to persons which may arise from or be incident to the exercise of the privileges herein granted, or for damages to the property of the lessee, or for damages to the property or injuries to the person of the lessee's officers, agents, servants, or employees or others who may be on said premises at their invitation or the invitation of any one of them, arising from or incident to the flooding of said premises by the Government or flooding from any other cause, or arising from or incident to any other governmental activities on the said premises."[28]

"The language plainly states that the United States shall not be responsible for damages that arise due to flooding, whether a result of actions by the Federal Government or because of any other cause."[29]

In another case, also out of Texas, the City of Galveston was held to be not legally responsible for storm-related damages on private property.

"On September 13, 2008, heavy rain, wind, and storm surge from Hurricane Ike damaged beaches in the City of Galveston (Applicant). Afterwards, the Applicant sought FEMA Public Assistance funding to repair punctured and deflated beach geotextile tubes and eroded sand dunes. FEMA representatives prepared several Project Worksheets (PWs) for the repair of the Applicant's damaged facilities, including several geotextile tubes. However, FEMA did not prepare a PW for the geotextile tube at Beachside Village Beach (Facility). FEMA determined that the Facility was ineligible because the City of Galveston was not legally responsible for this portion of the geotextile tube."[30]

"After later learning that a PW could be prepared to cover omitted damages, the Applicant began to aggregate documentation to prove its ownership of the Facility through easement ownership of the property upon which it was placed. On March 22, 2012, the Applicant sent a letter to the Grantee requesting a new Project Worksheet be written for the work performed to repair the Facility. The Grantee forwarded this request to FEMA on May 1, 2012. On July 3, 2012, FEMA denied the Applicant's request, asserting that the documentation provided 'clearly' demonstrated that the Beachside Village HomeOwners Association (HOA), not the Applicant, had legal responsibility for the Facility."[31]

"Title 44 of the Code of Federal Regulations (C.F.R.) § 206.223(a)(3) specifies, to be eligible for financial assistance, a project or item of work must be the legal responsibility of an eligible applicant at the time of the disaster. Based on the documentation provided by the Applicant, it did not have the legal responsibility for the repairs to the Facility at the time of the disaster. Specifically, the Agreement states the Applicant has 'no obligation to enhance, maintain, repair or replace' the Facility. In addition, the Agreement provides that if the Facility is destroyed by a storm or other natural disaster, the Applicant had no obligation to seek funds from FEMA or from private contributions to repair or replace the Facility. Further, as indicated in the RA's first appeal decision, the easement governing this appeal merely grants access on the individual land owner's property for the purpose of construction on the project and has a termination clause in the event a disaster destroys the project. On June 27, 2014, FEMA hosted an appeal meeting with the Applicant. During this meeting, the Applicant indicated it had not reimbursed the HOA for work to repair the damage to the Facility nor had the Applicant established a timeline for when it would. Moreover, the Applicant acknowledged that reimbursing the HOA was discretionary, rather than a mandatory legal responsibility as required by 44 C.F.R. § 206.223(a)(3)."[32]

Final Thoughts on Writing and Interpreting Agreements, Contracts, and Leases

Generally, when any of these documents are written, little attention is paid to the possibility of Armageddon, nor even to run-of-the-mill lesser disasters. As members of the human species, we do not like to dwell on possible misfortunes. But dwell on it we must if we are to position our agencies to be able to better recover our disaster costs.

No one can, nor will they, wholesale revise every agreement or contract to which they are a party. However, going forward, it would be so easy to include "boilerplate" language as one of a contract's standard clauses, clauses which provide the local agency with the necessary legal authority to respond to and recover from a disaster. Furthermore, as these contracts and agreements come up for renewal/renegotiation, such standard provisions should be added into the revised documents. Then over time, the agency will have substantially more legal authority than before the revisions were made.

FEMA will generally honor our pre-existing legal authorities and policies, but only if they are properly drawn up, properly adopted, and consistently adhered to over time, so long as there is no clear conflict with Federal policy or regulation otherwise prohibiting such legal authority.

A great deal of this of course often depends on getting the agency's legal counsel, be they contractor or employee, on board and supportive of the need to create agency-friendly documents. Focusing on these issues is not paranoia; it is effective risk management and good stewardship of the public interest.

If within the purview of the local agency there are no qualified specialists in FEMA law and regulation, then it is highly recommended to consult with an attorney who does have such expertise. An internet search for "FEMA + Lawyers" will yield the contact information for such expertise; however, as with all internet-based information, "Caveat Emptor."

And one final thought. Staff of the local agency should <u>always carefully read</u> the terms and conditions which may be incorporated into a contract, lease, or agreement by other parties to the agreement. This is where some companies slip in contract provisions which will significantly alter the nature of the agreement, as we saw earlier when a debris contractor added terms which changed an otherwise well-drawn-up contract into a cost plus a percentage of cost, or CPPC, contract.

Notes

1 https://www.fema.gov/appeal/san-carlos-city-hall
2 Ibid.
3 Ibid.
4 https://www.fema.gov/appeal/change-scope-work-result-declared-incident
5 Ibid.
6 Ibid.
7 https://www.fema.gov/appeal/appeal-timeliness-insurance-705c
8 Ibid.
9 Ibid.
10 Ibid.
11 Ibid.
12 https://www.fema.gov/appeal/legal-responsibility-40
13 "Usufruct is the right to use and benefit from a property, while the ownership of which belongs to another person. The person who enjoys the usufruct is called the usufructuary. The usufructuary shall maintain the property as a responsible owner and shall not cause damage to or diminution of the property, except where the property is subject to natural depletion over time." (https://www.law.cornell.edu/wex/usufruct)
14 Ibid.
15 Ibid.
16 Ibid.
17 Ibid.
18 Ibid.
19 Ibid.
20 Ibid.
21 https://www.cityofpaloalto.org/files/assets/public/v/1/public-works/recycle/business-recycling/green-business-profiles/second-amended-and-restated-agreement-for-solid-waste-recyclable-agreement.pdf
22 https://www.fema.gov/appeal/private-property-debris-removal-donated-resources
23 Ibid.
24 Ibid.
25 Ibid.
26 Ibid.
27 Ibid.
28 https://www.fema.gov/appeal/legal-responsibility-30
29 Ibid.
30 https://www.fema.gov/appeal/legal-responsibility-8
31 Ibid.
32 Ibid.

Part 4
Submitting for Reimbursement

26 Eligibility

This is another of several 800-pound gorillas swinging through the pages of this book. And this chapter on eligibility is one of those massively important concepts within the Public Assistance program. Understanding eligibility can make or break a local agency's best efforts to get the maximum recovery of disaster-related costs from FEMA.

A question that I'm occasionally asked is, "Is there a single list of what is eligible or what is not eligible?" The correct answer is an emphatic "No," there is no list anywhere which definitively lays out what is or is not eligible.

There are four fundamental principles of eligibility, but once those four are met, then it becomes a matter of nuances, facts, and filters, which we will examine at some length because of the importance of eligibility in qualifying projects for FEMA funding.

Let's be very clear. One of FEMA's responsibilities is to provide Federal financial assistance to eligible local governments and private non-profit agencies when, and only when, those entities meet ALL the requirements in the:

- Stafford Act;
- Title 44 of the Code of Federal Regulations, Part 206;
- All environmental and historic preservation regulations;
- Title 2 of the Code of Federal Regulations, Part 200;
- the terms set forth in the Federal-State Agreement which is signed for each different disaster;
- terms set forth in each approved Project Worksheet;
- And there are additional Federal regulations which may apply; however, these are the major ones on which we will focus.

The Federal government's position is quite clear. Local agencies of all stripes must follow the regulations, or FEMA will either deny funding, in whole or in part, or take previously awarded funding back.

Unlike in criminal law, where the accused is innocent until proven guilty, the damages suffered by local agencies do not exist for FEMA's purposes, until we prove that the damages were caused directly by the disaster and there were no contributions, or at least be de minimus contributions to the damages from pre-existing damage or from deferred maintenance. This is why the damage assessment process and the resulting documentation provided therefrom is so important for passing through the gauntlet of eligibility.

Before we talk about the fundamental building blocks of eligibility, let's talk about situations where the local agency has affirmatively walked away from eligibility, although at the time they signed the agreements that was probably the farthest thing from their mind.

DOI: 10.4324/9781003487869-31

In this set of appeals for 19 different Project Worksheets, a single Texas county lost at least $8,000,000 in FEMA funding because they built structures and facilities on land which they leased from the U.S. Army Corps of Engineers.

The lease for the use of land owned by the U.S. Army Corps of Engineers (USACE) is very clear and specific for the acceptance of the risks of flooding involved in these cases.

"Here, the second appeal review centers on section 10 of the lease between USACE and the Applicant. The lease reads:

The United States shall not be responsible for damages to property or injuries to persons which may arise from or be incident to the exercise of the privileges herein granted, or for damages to the property of the lessee, or for damages to the property or injuries to the person of the lessee's officers, agents, servants, or employees or others who may be on said premises at their invitation or the invitation of any one of them, arising from or incident to the flooding of said premises by the Government or flooding from any other cause, or arising from or incident to any other governmental activities on the said premises.

The language plainly states that the United States shall not be responsible for damages that arise due to flooding, whether a result of actions by the Federal Government or because of any other cause."[1]

The second appeal analysis continues: "As noted above, <u>FEMA has consistently denied PA funding to restore facilities located on land owned by the USACE, in particular when the instrument leasing USACE land to a different party includes provisions that identify risks to the facility and hold the Federal Government harmless.</u> Here, the governing legal instrument (the lease) includes language that clearly holds the Applicant responsible for flood damage that occurs to its property (i.e., the Facilities) from any cause, whether the result of USACE action or not. FEMA finds that the Applicant was aware of and assumed an inherent level of risk associated with operating the Facilities within Addicks Reservoir. Therefore, FEMA will not provide PA funding for the Facilities."[2] (Emphasis Added)

Were this a single case, that would be the end of that. In fact, local agencies do enter into these leases or use agreements for the advantage of creating public facilities without having to first purchase expensive land. It's a good deal . . . until there's a disaster.

In the list of these 19 separate second appeals, three of the appeals listed no dollar value because early on, FEMA officials recognized the issue of legal responsibility and did not even bother to work up a cost estimate.

This situation might be compared to a pre-nuptial agreement: everything is fine, until it isn't. However, as we work our way through eligibility, we shall see that there are a great many other ways to lose eligibility.

Local agencies should view eligibility as a chain. One weak or broken link, and the chain fails or is at the edge of failure, with resulting adverse financial consequences.

Eligibility Management

However, eligibility is also a "manageable" concept; that is, the local agency can take some affirmative actions to reduce questionable eligibility, and to "enhance" eligibility to increase the ability to receive more FEMA funding than would otherwise be possible absent these proposed affirmative actions. These optional but advisable affirmative actions will be pointed out throughout the chapter.

It is very important to understand that not everything is eligible, and most losses won't be paid at 100% or even at the 75% Federal share. There are simply some costs and expenses which are not eligible for FEMA reimbursement.

If the local agency has someone on staff who understands this complex world of eligibility/ineligibility, it will be possible to focus agency resources on pursuing the most likely costs for damages to be reimbursed and not waste valuable staff time and financial resources on dead-bang eligibility losers.

As I was researching and organizing this complex chapter on eligibility, I grouped various aspects of eligibility and ineligibility into 35 different groups where related issues made sense. The challenge to organizing all this information is that in a sense, eligibility is like walking along a tightrope; one misstep, and it the ground will jump up at us. In other words, eligibility is like a checklist where every box must be checked to maintain eligibility. One missed check box, and the eligibility vanishes forever.

In a revisit to a case we earlier examined in the Procurement Chapter, the New York State local agency lost $268,217 for otherwise eligible work because of a lack of recordkeeping and purchasing violations. This is yet another appeals case with multiple failure facets.

"From September 7–11, 2011, Tropical Storm Lee caused flooding damage to the Susquehanna Apartments – North Shore Campus, a multi-family housing complex with five, two-story buildings owned and operated by the Binghamton Housing Authority (Applicant) in Binghamton, NY."[3]

"In response, the Applicant used its own Force Account Labor and contracted with Homer C. & Sons General Contractors (Homer Gow) and Keystone Associates, Architects, Engineers and Surveyors, LLC (Keystone) for campus repairs and associated project management. Repair work was initiated within a week of the disaster declaration and largely completed by January 6, 2012, although Keystone continued to coordinate with FEMA and contractors to review invoicing and design through July 2012. Force Account Labor (FAL) work was documented in employee timecards containing brief descriptions of tasks, such as 'flood,' 'security,' or 'snow removal.' For all other work, the Applicant's contractors issued purchase orders and invoices with descriptions of tasks, dates, employees, and costs based on the time and materials (T&M) involved."[4]

"There were 31 Homer Gow purchase orders totaling $589,955.10 and 6 Keystone invoices totaling $68,792.85. The Applicant claims that the Keystone invoices were based on a pre-existing, written, and competitively bid contract, dated February 2011. The Homer Gow purchase orders, however, were based solely on oral-agreements, including an agreement not to exceed $25,000.00 for any individual order."[5]

In this case, the work was apparently eligible for reimbursement. But the local agency requested to apportion its Force Account Labor based on the work its crews performed alongside its two contractors. The descriptions of the work performed were described as "flood," "security," or "snow removal," without any other specifics, including the apartment number or address, or what the specific disaster-related damages were. Descriptions such as these are completely useless for FEMA's required documentation. In this case, either of these issues, i.e., no documentation or purchasing, would be sufficient to result in a denial of funding, as happened in this case. Here, the eligibility chain was broken by a failure to properly document the Force Account Labor. Absent the lack of documentation, the eligibility chain would have also been broken by the procurement violations which we have previously discussed.

In another case from Texas, which is actually a side show in a much larger appeals case involving over $8,327,546 for utilities restoration, the local agency claimed $8,499.87 for providing water, ice, and personal supplies to employees in the field.

(That's right: $8,499 divided by $8,327,546 is .001%; that's what we're arguing about here. Sometimes there's no nit too small not to pick.)

Anyway, the case continues: "Title 44 C.F.R. § 206.223(a)(3) requires work to be the legal responsibility of an eligible applicant in order to be eligible for PA funding. An Applicant must demonstrate legal responsibility by providing documentation for the work claimed. Although the

Applicant argues that, as a standard operating procedure, it provides water and ice at its office and that reimbursement of water and ice for employees working in the field is a natural extension of its office policy, it offered no documentation to establish it was legally required to do so. The Applicant also acknowledged its union contract typically required employees to provide their own personal supplies, and that it could not substantiate through documentation, that it was legally obligated to pay for the supplies. As the Applicant has not demonstrated it had legal responsibility to provide water, ice, and personal supplies, the costs are ineligible for reimbursement."[6]

The moral of this story is that the local agency must have its policies in place before the disaster to be eligible for reimbursement of this type of expense. The principle is what is at stake here. This could have just as easily been a questioned amount of a hundred thousand dollars or more.

The Building Blocks for Eligibility

With all that out of the way, let's look at the four building blocks for eligibility: 1) the applicant (local agency); 2) the facility; 3) the work; and 4) the cost.

These four criteria are the relatively easy part, and can be readily dealt with.

First, the applicant must be eligible. This typically includes all state and local government agencies, i.e., individual states, cities, counties (parishes), special districts, including school districts, towns, villages, Native American tribes, U.S. Territories; and certain private non-profit agencies. A more complete list is available in the Public Assistance Program and Policy Guide under the heading 'Applicant Eligibility.' This may seem cut and dried, but it does get complicated for certain private non-profit agencies, which we will get into in a bit.

The next building block for eligibility is that the facility must be eligible. While this may appear obvious, it can be complicated. For instance, a local road that is not the responsibility of the Federal Highway Administration may be disaster-damaged and still not be eligible because of pre-disaster deterioration of the road surface. In a different scenario, a local agency owns a building, but leases it to a for-profit enterprise. This makes the building ineligible, because it is not used to provide services of a governmental nature. We will look at this more in the appeals cases to follow. Another frequent stumbling block for facility eligibility is that the local agency rents space for a Police Substation in a commercial district. The facility is disaster-damaged; however, the facility is ineligible, because the building's owner, not the city, is normally responsible for repairs. We will look at this in an appeals case. However, the building's contents, when damaged, may be eligible when properly documented.

Third, the work itself must be eligible. Snow removal is a good example of disaster-related work which is usually ineligible. The following language is from the PAPPG:

"Snow-related activities, including snow removal, de-icing, salting, snow dumps, and sanding of roads and other eligible facilities, is only an eligible emergency protective measure when a winter storm results in record or near-record snowfall. FEMA authorizes snow assistance by county based on a finding that the county received record or near-record snowfall or meets the contiguous county criteria as described below. FEMA evaluates Tribal lands either as part of a requested county or separately."[7] "FEMA generally considers near record as being within 10 percent of the record snowfall."[8]

The fourth eligibility building block is that the cost of the work must be reasonable. This is another complicating factor. FEMA works across the country and often uses national averages for costs. In some parts of the country, this is sufficient. However, in other parts of the country these "average" costs do not come close to the actual costs, particularly in a post-disaster environment when both labor and materials become scarce and costs increase. These Federal cost principles can be found in Title 2 of the Code of Federal Regulations, Part 200. It is important to note that there are contractors and suppliers who will take every advantage to make extra profit during disasters. The Federal regulations are, in part, written to minimize these exposures.

For Private Non-Profits, the pathway to eligibility is different because FEMA must first determine whether the Private Non-Profit owns or operates a facility that provides an eligible service to determine whether the Applicant is eligible. We will look at this in more detail later.

Furthermore, for most emergency work (Categories A and B) done by local governments, evaluating facility eligibility is not necessary. However, local agencies must be aware that what they consider emergency work and what FEMA considers emergency work may be two different stories. From FEMA's perspective, emergency work, Categories A and B work, is the work done to directly save lives; protect public health and safety; protect improved property; or eliminate or lessen an immediate threat of additional damage.

From the local agency perspective, however, the fact that a tornado blew the city hall off its foundation may constitute a local emergency. But the destruction of the city hall in and of itself is not an emergency if there is no immediate threat to life safety, public health, or improved property. It most assuredly is a problem to be dealt with, but it is not a life-threatening situation which would warrant shortcuts in the Public Assistance process.

Administrative Expenses Not Generally Eligible

There are some administrative expenses for work on specific Project Worksheets which are eligible, and these will be dealt with in Chapter 32, 'Direct Administrative Costs' or DAC. The following costs, however, are not a part of these Direct Administrative Costs.

These are certain administrative actions which the local jurisdiction may take as necessary steps to put the community on the path to full recovery; however, some of these costs will not be eligible for FEMA reimbursement. Although they may be important to the local agency and the community, they simply are not eligible expenses. In general, the purchase and distribution of food vouchers, gasoline cards, bus passes (with rare exception), cash vouchers, debit cards, or direct payments to survivors are ineligible. Neither the cost of obtaining these cards or vouchers nor the expense of having staff distribute them are eligible. If volunteers distribute these items, then the volunteer's time is not eligible to be used as part of the local cost share. However, it may be important to fully track the time of employees to account completely for the total cost of the disaster, but their time is ineligible.

Ineligible: Loss of Revenue

Another disaster-related ineligible expense is the loss of revenue from normal income streams, including the fees paid for local agency enterprise functions. This appeals case is from Florida:

"Toll collection operations on the Florida Turnpike were suspended during mass evacuations pursuant to the Governor's orders of a State of Emergency for seven separate disasters and one emergency declaration in 2004 and 2005. The Applicant seeks to recover a total of $51,309,400, for uncollected toll road revenue. FEMA denied this funding because loss of revenue is not an eligible cost under the Public Assistance Program. The appealed PWs and amounts are:

Disaster Project Worksheet Amount Appealed

- FEMA-1539-DR-FL (Charley) 7205 $3,071,400.00
- FEMA-1545-DR-FL (Frances) 9428 $14,446,700.00
- FEMA-1551-DR-FL (Ivan) 3797 $7,838,500.00
- FEMA-1561-DR-FL (Jeanne) 6453 $6,853,600.00

- FEMA-1595-DR-FL (Dennis) 1602 $464,300.00
- FEMA-1602-DR-FL (Katrina) 1472 $1,758,500.00
- FEMA-1609-DR-FL (Wilma) 9213 $155,421,600.00
- FEMA-3259-EM-FL (Rita) 150   <u>$1,454,800.00</u>

                   Total $51,309,400.00"[9]

Ineligible: Increased Operating Expenses

Another issue frequently seen in the appeals cases are appeals for increased operating expenses. In this case from Missouri, the local agency provided electric power to the community, albeit at an increased cost.

"In January 2009, severe winter storms in the State of Missouri caused icing on power lines and trees. Heavy ice accumulation caused trees and power poles to break. The Applicant lost commercial power from January 27, 2009, to February 25, 2009, and requested assistance from FEMA for the cost of force account labor and equipment use to supply power from its backup electrical substation. The Applicant had Mutual Aid agreements with the cities of Higginsville and Farmington for personnel to operate generators in this substation. FEMA prepared PW 414 for $545,528 in May 2009. The project costs were reduced to $320,818 to reflect credit from the Southwestern Power Administration and sales revenue from customers. Upon review, the expenses in PW 414 were found ineligible because the Applicant obtained power from an alternate source, and such costs are ineligible as indicated in the Public Assistance Guide (FEMA 322), pages 54–55, dated June 2007."[10]

The case continues: "<u>The Applicant was not powering generators specifically at hospitals or other health and safety facilities, but instead turned-on power for citywide service at a backup electrical substation. The Applicant did not provide any documentation differentiating power costs for critical facilities versus citywide service.</u> This substation also produces electricity far above the standard rate set by Southwestern Power Administration, the area's regular electric utility service. The costs for operating the backup generators and force account labor for this work are not eligible as an emergency protective measure. Therefore, the cost of obtaining electrical power from an alternate source, the Applicant's backup power substation, is considered an increased operating expense and ineligible for Public Assistance Program funding."[11] (Emphasis Added)

Arguably, had the city only provided power for critical facilities, they might have made a claim for Category B emergency protective measures. By providing electrical power for the entire city, they substantially changed the outcome.

Initial claims and appeals for increased operating expenses are more common from hospitals, which in disasters obviously have greatly increased operating costs due to a surge of disaster victim patients. Only with very rare exceptions are these costs eligible.

As a footnote to the Covid-19 response, many local government agencies and particularly hospitals received FEMA Determination Memos stating that their claims for costs represented "increased operating costs," even when the tasks undertaken were complete outliers to their normal work activities.

Ineligible: Tax (Re)Assessments

Following disasters when there is significant damage to private property, both residential and commercial, the property owners will file claims with the local agency to have their property reassessed to a lower level while they rebuild, which in some case may take years. The process of making the reassessment is an ineligible expense, as would the resulting loss of revenue from taxes on those properties. This same principle also applies to other administrative tasks performed by the local agency, including those building inspections performed after the initial Safety Assessment.

Damaged Debris Haul Roads

Another "automatic" ineligible is the loss of useful service life. This occurs primarily in two areas, roads and landfills, and may apply to other areas as well. During the debris cleanup process, there are many trucks, wheel loaders, etc., running on local roads that were not designed for such heavy traffic. FEMA's position is that any such road damage was not caused directly by the disaster and is therefore ineligible unless the local agency can prove otherwise.

The next case is from California, following another of that state's devastating wildfires.

"From October 8–31, 2017, wildfires caused extensive damage to communities in northern California, including Sonoma County (Applicant). After submitting an initial scope of work for Project Worksheet (PW) 263, the Applicant submitted additional damages for consideration on June 21, 2018. The Applicant asserted that Private Property Debris Removal (PPDR) operations damaged 32 of its roads (Facilities) and requested an additional $21,365,500.00 in funding. The Applicant stated the increased traffic by trucks hauling debris associated with PPDR operations, conducted by private contractors to clear lots and haul debris, contributed to raveling, rutting, cracking, potholes, and road edge damages to the Facilities. The Applicant provided FEMA with a spreadsheet identifying approximately 754 roadway sections as having suffered at least one form of damage. To support its claim, the Applicant submitted pre- and post- disaster photographs of the claimed damaged Facilities, road maintenance records, and a 2017 Pavement Management Program Final Report."[12]

The appeal goes on: "FEMA may provide PA funding to a local government for the repair of a public facility damaged by a major disaster. To be eligible, work must be required as a result of the declared incident. If an applicant damages property while performing eligible emergency work, the damages may be eligible for repair as part of that respective project if the damage was unavoidable and due to severe conditions resulting from the incident. The applicant is responsible for providing documentation to support its claim as eligible and show that work is required to address damage caused by the disaster, and where pre-existing damage exists, to distinguish that from damage from the disaster. Appeals must contain documented justification supporting the applicant's position."[13] (Emphasis Added)

"The county's 2017 Pavement Management Program Final Report revealed that the Applicant's road networks were in 'poor' condition, with a network (Pavement Conditions Index) PCI of 48. The postdisaster photographs provided by the Applicant showed substantial deterioration of the Facilities, which the Applicant claims were damaged as a result of the increased traffic and heavy loads stemming from the PPDR operations. The pre- and post-disaster photographs show similar deterioration, making it challenging to differentiate between the predisaster condition of the Facilities and any damages caused by the PPDR operations. Although the post-disaster imagery from the FEMA Site Inspection Report sampling showed damage to the roads, the damage is consistent with normal wear and tear that is attributable primarily to deferred maintenance and the deteriorated conditions of the Facilities at the time of the disaster. The predisaster maintenance records provided by the Applicant do not establish that the Applicant performed repairs to correct the Facilities' deficiencies. Here, the Applicant's documentation makes no distinction between pre-existing conditions and damages that were caused while performing PPDR work."[14]

FEMA's "go-to" argument in the appeals cases I reviewed is that the roads had pre-existing damage and/or deferred maintenance. If a claim of road damage from disaster-related operations is to be made, the documentation regarding the pre-disaster condition of the roads must be convincingly in the local agency's favor. Without analyzing all 2,348 appeals cases on file, my assumption would be that nearly 100% of these "roads damaged by disaster work" cases would fail on appeal.

Ineligible: Non-Emergency Work

As previously discussed, certain administrative tasks are not eligible for funding. In this case from Florida, we see yet another example: "Following Hurricane Opal, the Florida Department of Business and Professional Regulation (DBPR), the subgrantee, formed two task forces to provide public assistance to residents of the declared disaster areas of Bay and Walton Counties. According to the subgrantee, these task forces were deployed to protect disaster victims from contractor and consumer fraud in the aftermath of the hurricane by conducting public seminars and meetings with local building officials; appearing on or producing material for the broadcast media; distributing brochures and pamphlets; handling and investigating questions and reports regarding this threat; posting warning information on transportation routes; and conducting a public information and assistance campaign."[15]

"FEMA maintains that the work performed by the task forces does not constitute essential emergency measures. For public assistance information to be eligible for FEMA funding, it must directly eliminate or alleviate an immediate threat to public health or safety. Relevant emergency measures in a situation such as this may include structural analysis to determine the integrity of buildings so as to avert immediate threats to life and property. Conversely, warning that work may be performed which would result in unsound structural integrity, or directly confronting unlicensed contractors, such as in this situation, would not be eligible. The immediate threat to personal and property safety would be an unsound structure, not an unlicensed contractor. An example of dis-seminated information eligible for funding may be literature concerning unsafe drinking water. If drinking water were tainted such that use would present an immediate threat to the health of a community, public assistance campaigns and documents would be valid examples of emergency measures provided for under Section 403. Information dealing with fraud or contractual issues is not eligible because it does not directly address an immediate threat."[16]

It would be reasonable then that public information dealing directly with health and safety issues could be eligible; however, limiting the information only to issues of disaster-related health and safety might be a real challenge in this era of woke communications.

Ineligible: Certain Costs Related to File Restoration

Eligible activities associated with the recovery of files include, but are not limited to: recovery of damaged paper copies, stabilization of damaged paper copies, sanitizing damaged copies (when mold is present), photocopying/scanning damaged copies, and recovering data from damaged hard drives.

However, some file recovery activities are ineligible, such as work done to: establish new data-bases, manually enter data, scan files into computers to create digital files, and to decipher damaged hard copies.

Ineligible: Projects Costing Less Than $3,900 (in 2024 Dollars)

This low-end threshold may rise each new Federal Fiscal Year. The strategy when faced with a series of below-the-threshold damage sites is to combine similar types of projects into a single project when possible; i.e., all broken water pipes from different locations. However, depending on the staff from FEMA, this approach may or may not fly.

Ineligible: Costs for a Letter of Map Agreement (LOMA) or Letter of Map Revision (LOMR)

Facilities located in a Special Flood Hazard Area (SFHA) are areas that are subject to inundation during a 100-year flood, a flood which has a 1% chance of occurrence in a given year. If the local agency believes that its property was incorrectly identified on a Flood Insurance Rate Map (FIRM) as located within the Special Flood Hazard Area, it may request a Letter of Map Amendment or Letter of Map Revision from FEMA within 6 months of the declaration. However, costs incurred in requesting a Letter of Map Amendment or Letter of Map Revision are ineligible for PA funding.

Ineligible: Alternate Projects, Depending

In some cases, the local agency may opt to request an Alternate Project, which may allow greater flexibility in restoring a damaged facility. However, there are rules governing the use of alternate project funds. In this case from Texas, we see such an issue:

"Tropical Storm Allison produced severe flooding during the period of June 8–9, 2001, causing damages to non-structural elements and essential mechanical, electrical and plumbing (MEP) systems, and to equipment in the Speech and Hearing Institute (SHI) Building at the University of Texas Health Science Center at Houston (UTHSCH). FEMA informally delivered the draft Project Worksheet (PW) #551 to UTHSCH and the state on September 26, 2002, wherein $4,063 in emergency work was determined eligible and $158,930 in permanent repairs (less insurance of $27,925) was determined ineligible because UTHSCH did not intend to make repairs. In addition, UTHSCH was advised that an improved or alternate project would not be eligible absent a legal responsibility to repair the damaged building."[17]

"The relationship is one of Landlord (TIRR) *(The Institute For Rehabilitation and Research)* and Tenant (UTHSCH). Nothing in the lease agreement or any other document produced by UTHSCH supports the position that UTHSCH owned SHI at the time of the disaster and presently. As a Tenant assigned repair responsibility by the lease agreement, UTHSCH is eligible for FEMA funding to repair the damaged facility. It is not eligible to use that funding for a different purpose at another location by electing the improved or alternate project option. Its responsibility is limited to the leased location. FEMA therefore processed PW #551 with no eligible funding for permanent repairs. Further, FEMA states that UTHSCH's request for an improved project should be denied."[18]

"FEMA determined in the first appeal that UTHSCH was a Tenant with repair responsibility by the lease agreement. FEMA now also acknowledges UTHSCH's intention of reinstating the predisaster functions and use conducted at SHI at a different location. However, in the lease agreement provided to FEMA, the lease expires December 31, 2002. On that date UTHSCH would no longer have legal responsibility for the leased premises making UTHSCH ineligible for permanent work funding once the lease expired on that date (44 CFR § 206.223(a)(3)). Further, as documented in PW #551, TIRR indicated that they would demolish the leased premises, build an office/parking facility and would not hold UTHSCH to their legal responsibility of making repairs to SHI. In addition, while improved projects allow for significant change from the pre-disaster configuration (e.g., a different location) (Public Assistance Guide p. 85), UTHSCH only had repair responsibility for the leased premises (as stated in the lease agreement). Therefore, an improved project at a different location is not an option for UTHSCH."[19]

In a case dealing with an Alternative Procedures Project, FEMA denied funding because of the local agency's late request for the use of funds.

"On October 7, 2017, Hurricane Nate impacted Escambia and Santa Rosa counties in Florida with storm surge and rainfall causing flooding and other damage. The President signed an emergency declaration on October 8, 2017, with an incident period of October 7–11, 2017. On May 22, 2018, the Florida Division of Emergency Management (Grantee) elected to participate in the Public Assistance Alternative Procedures for Direct Administrative Costs (PAAP-DAC) program for the disaster. FEMA obligated PW 4, a category B project for emergency protective measures, in the amount of $426,708.30. The period of performance (POP) for PW 4 ended on October 8, 2018. On July 30, 2018, FEMA obligated Project Worksheet (PW) 5, a category Z project, to reimburse DAC (*Direct Administrative Costs*) associated with PW 4 in the amount of $21,420.45. On August 20, 2019, the Grantee requested FEMA deobligate $20,348.25 from PW 5 and allow the Grantee to use the funds in accordance with PAAP-DAC policy on 'use of excess funds.' FEMA wrote PW 7 on October 4, 2019, to document this request. On April 30, 2020, FEMA issued a Determination Memorandum denying the Grantee's request as untimely. FEMA found that the deadline to submit the request was April 6, 2019, 180 days after the latest period of performance (POP) for PW 4, and the Grantee made its request on August 20, 2019."[20]

"The Robert T. Stafford Disaster Relief and Emergency Assistance Act authorizes FEMA to provide funding for management costs to applicants based on an estimate, if the applicant elects to participate in the alternative procedure program. PAAP-DAC policy permits excess DAC funds to be used for any costs otherwise eligible, if the applicant identifies the excess funds and submits the request to use the funds to FEMA within 180 days of the latest project Period of Performance."[21] (Emphasis Added)

Once again, the specter of critical deadlines results in a denial of otherwise eligible funding and points to the importance of knowing, and carefully tracking, these timelines.

Often Ineligible: Beach Sand Replenishment

Per Title 44 of the Code of Federal Regulations, beach re-sanding is not eligible except under certain circumstances.

"(j) Beaches.

(1) Replacement of sand on an unimproved natural beach is not eligible.
(2) Improved beaches. Work on an improved beach may be eligible under the following conditions:

   (i)   The beach was constructed by the placement of sand (of proper grain size) to a designed elevation, width, and slope; and
   (ii) A maintenance program involving periodic renourishment of sand must have been established and adhered to by the applicant."[22]

Please refer to the PAPPG, Chapter 8: Permanent Work Eligibility for further details on this complex topic. For documentation purposes, FEMA will require the engineered beach design plans and thorough documentation of the regular re-sanding of the beaches in question, including invoices for contracted work, or complete records of the labor, equipment, and materials used if done by force account labor.

An addendum to any discussion on beach repair may include the placement of dune grass. However, this is only eligible under the following conditions.

"Placement of dune grass on an emergency dune or berm is only eligible if it is required by permit and is an established, enforced, uniform practice that applies to the construction of all emergency berms within the Applicant's jurisdiction, regardless of the circumstance. The Applicant must include the grass placement cost in the dune or berm construction cost when evaluating cost-effectiveness. Any maintenance of the dune grass after the initial installation is ineligible."[23]

Repair Versus Replacement: Often Ineligible

When a facility is damaged more than 50% of its pre-disaster value, FEMA, for good reason, may authorize the local agency to tear down the damaged facility and replace it with a new one of the same size and function.

Often, this is truly a Trojan Horse situation. While the authorization to tear down and replace is not all that common, it is often a deadly undertaking by the local agency.

Although it is listed here in the Eligibility chapter, this was dealt with in much greater detail in Chapter 23, Repair Vs. Replace, aka The 50% Rule.

Codes and Standards Upgrades: Often Ineligible

Similarly to Repair vs. Replacement, Codes and Standards, because it is such a misunderstood aspect of the Public Assistance process, will be dealt with in greater detail in its own chapter, Chapter 34. However, we will now mention some of the common aspects regarding this issue.

First, according to the PAPPG, "Emergency repair or stabilization of an eligible facility is eligible as Emergency Work if it eliminates or lessens an immediate threat. Work performed under an exigent circumstance that restores the pre-disaster design and function of the facility in accordance with codes and standards is Permanent Work, not Emergency Work."[24] (Emphasis Added)

"FEMA provides PA funding to restore facilities based on pre-disaster design and function in conformity with current applicable codes, specifications, and standards."[25]

However, this is not all cut and dried because: "The Applicant needs to provide documentation to support the eligibility of code or standard upgrades, including, but not limited to, the requirement to apply the codes or standards and to support that they were formally adopted, implemented, and uniformly applied."[26]

Ineligible: Unreasonable Costs

Unreasonable costs come in many different colors.

First, costs may be unreasonable simply because the local agency paid too much for a given service or goods purchased. A classic example of this comes from my time assisting a local California agency following the 2014 Napa Earthquake. A metal building owned by the local agency was damaged from the violent shaking of the earthquake, and a hole in the side of the building opened up. The building was used as a Fire Department training facility, and the Fire Department issued a repair order to a local contractor to make a temporary repair to secure the building. The contractor covered the hole with two sheets of 4' x 8' plywood and used 10 each of 2" x 4" x 8' wood studs to support and brace the plywood sheets. The invoice total was $4,150.00. This was clearly an exorbitant price, even considering the work was done on a Sunday at overtime rates. In my files I still retain a copy of this invoice.

Following a disaster there are always plenty of businesses that are willing to charge (and overcharge) for work performed or goods provided, even despite local- and state-issued anti-price gouging laws. In this case, we simply rejected the invoice and sent it back to the Fire Department to renegotiate a reasonable cost.

If FEMA had ever seen this invoice, it would have set off alarms all the way to Regional Headquarters and invited intense scrutiny of all purchases.

A second way for costs to be determined to be unreasonable is to provide insufficient documentation to enable FEMA to determine the appropriateness of the questioned costs. In my files, I have a copy of a Materials Summary worksheet from a large West Coast agency, which lists numerous different items which were in high demand, sometimes almost unattainable, during the early days of the Covid-19 pandemic. The line items list "alcohol" without spelling out what type of alcohol, the strength of the alcohol, the quantity of alcohol per container, the number of containers per case, etc. Such a Materials Summary Worksheet would be denied absent additional clarifying details.

In this same document, there were purchases listed for KN-95 face masks. Over a number of procurements, the agency purchased 48,000 masks at an average unit price of $3.76 per mask. A reasonable cost under the circumstances. However, they, again over several purchases, purchased an additional 8,500 masks at an average cost of $49.56 per mask. Clearly, in light of their own previous purchases, an unreasonable price for KN-95 masks. This sort of error could trigger intense scrutiny of all their Covid-related purchases. If they were lucky, FEMA would have paid $3.76 per mask for all 56,500 masks, leaving them with a per mask deficit of $45.80, or $389,300 for the lot.

A third way for costs to be presumed unreasonable is for the local agency to have a purchasing policy which does not conform to the requirements of Title 2 of the Code of Federal Regulations, Part 200 (2 CFR, Part 200). Absent full compliance with both the local purchasing policy AND 2 CFR, Part 200, FEMA will presume the costs to be unreasonable even when the contract prices are competitive when compared to the prices paid for the same goods or services by other local agencies during the same time frame. For FEMA, the failure to follow 2 CFR, Part 200 is generally presumptive that the costs were unreasonable.

Still another way for costs to be determined to be unreasonable is to have the associated labor and equipment charges be out of sync with the numbers of materials used on a project. Earlier in the book, I cited the case of Mariposa County, CA, where the costs seemed to be out of sync with the amount of roadway repaired, probably because most of the materials were taken from stockpiles, but not recorded and charged out to the job.

It is important to be aware that both the auditors and FEMA love to comparison shop when conducting an audit or file review. They will look at the prices paid for similar goods or services provided to neighboring jurisdictions and compare those prices to the prices paid by the local agency, often with dramatic results showing the local agency paid too much under the circumstances.

"FEMA calculated an average per pole cost by computing an average cost for similar work done under seventeen different Project Worksheets conducted by eight other electrical cooperatives during the same wildfire disaster. FEMA examined the costs of 1,321 poles and the average cost per pole was $2,428.81, while the Applicant's claimed average contract cost per pole was $4,669.81."[27]

In all fairness, "the Applicant's (cost) analysis was significantly higher than what was done by FEMA, but also included a higher number of three-phase lines and transformer/meter poles."[28]

Ineligible by Contract

As mentioned at the beginning of this chapter, local agencies will sometimes either lease or be granted a "use permit" to construct facilities on land which is not theirs. It does not matter whether the owner is the Federal government, a state government, other local agency, or a private party; one must closely read the terms of the lease in its entirety to determine in disaster damages who will be the party with legal responsibility to make repairs, and indeed if those repairs will be eligible for Federal disaster assistance, either from FEMA or any other Federal agency.

Once again, back to the Napa Earthquake of 2014. The local agency whom I was assisting owned a large building, which was under lease to another governmental agency. The building suffered some damage; however, the damage was all "cosmetic" and not "structural." The terms of the lease clearly specified that the repair of structural damage was the responsibility of the lessor (the local government agency). However, cosmetic damage was the responsibility of the tenant. In this case however, the tenant (an 800-pound gorilla in that community) insisted that the lessor make the repairs which would cost around $100,000. The local agency did make the repairs, but they did so knowing that they would not be eligible for reimbursement because of the language of the contract.

In another personally known case, this one Covid-related, a client wanted to have its leased office buildings deep cleaned according to the Centers for Disease Control's recommendations. They inquired whether this would be an eligible cost. I requested that they send me a sampling of their leases, which they did. In one of the three I reviewed, the language was very specific in stating that the owner of the building was responsible for cleaning for any "biological" contamination. Therefore, if the local agency had contracted for the cleaning, it would not have been eligible for that building.

Very early on in the Public Assistance process, FEMA will request information regarding the ownership of a damaged facility, and if not an owned facility, a copy of the lease or rental agreement to determine which party bears the legal responsibility for making repairs.

Similarly, when the local agency owns a facility and rents or leases all or some portion of the building to another party, FEMA will again want to have a copy of the rental or lease agreement to determine the legal responsibility for making the repairs.

This matter of renting or leasing a local agency-owned facility to a third party carries with it another potential risk for denial or deobligation of funding. Let's take a concrete example. Let's say the facility is 20,000 square feet, and the agency uses 8,000 square feet for its own offices, and rents or leases the remaining 12,000 square feet to one or more third parties. In this case, because the local agency uses less than 50% of the building, the entire building is ineligible for Federal Assistance.

If the local agency used 11,000 square feet for its own offices and leased the remaining 9,000 square feet of space to a third party, then the building would be eligible if damaged, but at a reduced rate based upon the square footage leased; in this example, it would be 55% eligible.

I once taught a class in a modern four-story steel-frame, glass-clad building. The agency used two floors for its own offices and two floors were leased out, making the facility ineligible. Should they take over a few hundred square feet for more office space, that building would become eligible: at a reduced rate, but still better than no eligibility at all.

Unfortunately, when leases and rental agreements between local government agencies and third parties are drawn up, these issues are simply frequently not recognized or considered. This is not something that is taught in law school, so the local agency attorney is most likely unaware of the financial consequences lurking in the dark and mysterious language of the "fine print."

The Saga of Safeco Field

There are many twists and permutations in the eligibility world. This is a case from the Pacific Northwest: "This is in response to your August 11, 2003, letter transmitting the above referenced second appeal submitted by the Washington State Major League Baseball Stadium Public Facilities District (PFD) to the Department of Homeland Security's Federal Emergency Management Agency (FEMA). The applicant is requesting reimbursement for repair of Safeco Field and the adjacent parking structure, and for safety inspections ($472,766.52). Damage to the facilities occurred during the Nisqually Earthquake on February 28, 2001."[29]

"44 CFR § 206.223 states that to be eligible for assistance, an item of work must be the legal responsibility of an eligible applicant. The FEMA Chief of Staff responded to the first appeal in a letter dated February 28, 2003, and determined that the PFD was not legally responsible for repairs. Although the PFD owns the ballpark, it leases the ballpark to the Baseball Club of Seattle (Club). According to terms of the Operations and Lease Agreement and the Project Closeout and

Settlement Agreement, the lessee (the Club), not the PFD, is legally responsible for the earthquake repairs. The lease states that the PFD may use funds from the Excess Revenues Fund to reimburse the Club for repair costs, but reimbursement is required only when funds are available." (Emphasis Added)[30]

"Article 7.1 of the lease agreement states that, "the Club is solely and exclusively responsible for all Major Maintenance and Capital Improvements during the Operating Term." "Notwithstanding the foregoing provisions of this Article 7.1, the Parties' obligation to repair or rebuild the Ballpark following Catastrophic Damage shall be governed solely by the provisions of Articles 7.6 and 7.7." "The damage to Safeco Field and the parking structure does not meet the definition of 'Catastrophic Damage' as defined in Article 7.6."[31]

In this case, while the Public Facilities District (PFD) was responsible under terms of the lease to pay for the damage, the District itself did not perform the repairs and thereby was not eligible for reimbursement.

The Bottom Line on Leases and Rental Agreements

When a lease or rental agreement is drawn up, it is critical that it include very specific language of responsibility for making disaster damage repairs. The usual contact language which often covers "repairs and maintenance" or similar language is insufficient. The language must clearly and specifically assign responsibility for making repairs for ***disaster-caused damage***. For FEMA, it does not matter to which party this responsibility is contractually assigned. If the local agency leases a building with what is often known as a "triple-net" lease, even then I would request specific language be added to cover the repair of disaster-caused damages. Alternatively, the language may specify that the landlord is fully responsible for the repairs for disaster-caused damages, both cosmetic and structural.

* It should become a standard practice for local agencies that either rent to or from third parties to periodically update and renew these leases and rental agreements. At renewal time, this is the perfect opportunity to include this important language into the agreement as a hedge against future disasters. This is Eligibility Management 101.

The Damage Assessment Role in Eligibility

Earlier in this chapter, in the section entitled "Damaged Debris Haul Roads," we saw that additional damages incurred while performing eligible work *is* eligible; however, it still must be proven eligible; that is to say, there was no pre-existing damage or damage as a result of deferred maintenance which substantially contributed to these new damages.

Another case where the damage assessment plays a significant role in proving disaster damages is the water business. Many water agencies have dams and reservoirs for water storage, flood control, and hydro-electric power generation. When originally constructed, these dams and reservoirs were built to engineered specifications regarding how much water, generally measured in acre feet, each facility would contain. However, in the normal course of nature, sedimentation occurs and reduces the structure's capacity, and eventually all dams and reservoirs if not maintained would silt up and be unable to store any water. It is a common occurrence for water agencies, following a major storm with its natural sediment flows, to request that FEMA fund a dredging operation to restore the capacity of the dam or reservoir. However, FEMA will only pay for removing the sedimentation which occurred as a direct result of the declared storm, not all sediment deposited outside of the declared storm period.

To prove that a substantial amount of sediment was deposited by a storm, the local agency must provide some proof of how much sediment the storm deposited. Agencies will often attempt to prove this with an engineering study measuring the water flow and levels of sediment believed to be carried by the storm flow. This is simply a waste of time and money. There is one surefire way to measure increased sedimentation. A bathymetric survey uses various technologies to measure the depth of a dam or reservoir BEFORE the storm, or relies on a very recent bathymetric survey which incontrovertibly demonstrates the pre-storm levels of sediment measured against the sediment levels immediately after the storm. Absent a reliable bathymetric survey, the local agency's hopes for reimbursement are tied to a wish and a prayer, neither of which are FEMA-eligible.

The 60-Day Window for Submitting the Damage Inventory

Typically, the day of the Recovery Scoping Meeting, where FEMA representatives visit the local agency's offices (also possibly virtually) begins a 60-day window for the local agency to submit its Damage Inventory (or List of Projects, etc.). This 60-day window is inviolate; it is seldom extended unless under the most extreme of circumstances. Agencies will claim that their employees weren't familiar with this deadline, or more recently "there were staff shortages due to Covid-19," or "my dog ate the list." Regardless, if damages are not timely reported, they are dead on arrival on day 61 or later. I have seen cases where local agencies have missed the deadline by days, sometime weeks, and even years. With FEMA, late is late, and late is ineligible.

"The Applicant's deadline to identify and report damages was October 2, 2021, 60 days after the (Recovery Scoping Meeting) RSM/first substantive meeting. On February 17, 2022, 198 days after the RSM, the Applicant requested permission to submit late damages. The Applicant acknowledged that its request was untimely. The reasons cited by the Applicant in its second appeal to justify the untimely submission include 'turnover in its emergency management team, extended sick leave for several employees, [and] unforeseeable issues due to COVID-19.' However, these general descriptions do not provide enough detail to demonstrate they constitute extenuating circumstances beyond the Applicant's control, for instance, that the Applicant had insufficient resources to timely submit the identification of damages due to COVID-19 related issues. Therefore, neither the Applicant nor Recipient demonstrated the existence of extenuating circumstances that were beyond their control to justify the delay."[32]

Ineligible: Damage Surveys

Conducting a damage assessment is the responsibility of the local agency and is not eligible for FEMA funding. This statement stands in direct counterpoint to the eligibility of Safety Assessments, which are, when properly documented as such, eligible for reimbursement. However, this nuance is commonly misunderstood; reasonably so, since many people use "safety assessments" and "damage assessments" interchangeably.

This case evolves out of the 2013 Rim Fire in California. "From August 17 to October 24, 2013, a wildland fire (Rim Fire) that began in the Stanislaus National Forest raged through Tuolumne County and burned more than 257,000 acres of land. The Rim Fire threatened parts of the electrical power distribution system operated by Hetch Hetchy Water and Power (HHWP) within Tuolumne County, California. HHWP is a public utility owned by the San Francisco Public Utilities Commission, which is a department of the City and County of San Francisco (Applicant). The Rim Fire caused electrical arcing among two 230kV transmission lines (Lines 5 and 6) causing them to disengage from the power source. Before the transmission lines could be re-energized, HHWP followed certain state and industry safety precautions which included performing an assessment of the electrical system. HHWP work crews visually inspected the affected transmission towers and lines and communicated their observations to a contractor, who then conducted a detailed damage survey and issued a report to HHWP. According to the contractor's report, no fire damage was observed on the lattice towers or conductors, while the tower insulators appeared to be contaminated with ash from the Rim Fire. An insulator was removed and sent off for further testing. The result of the testing was that no heat damage was detected on the insulator. The contractor's report recommended washing/cleaning the insulators for long-term operating reliability."[33]

"FEMA formulated PW 77 to document the Applicant's overall request for Public Assistance (PA) for surveys of various portions of HHWP's power distribution system. In the Scope of Work for Lines 5 and 6, FEMA documented the visual inspection performed by HHWP work crews, as well as the results of the testing performed on the representative insulator from inside the burn perimeter. FEMA determined there was no damage to the transmission lines and towers at Lines 5 and 6 as a result of the Rim Fire. All of the work described in the PW was determined to be ineligible for PA funding and PW 77 was obligated for zero dollars."[34]

"The record does not reflect an immediate threat to life, public health or safety posed by the presence of ash on the insulators. While the contractor's report states that washing/cleaning the insulators is recommended to minimize the risk of flashover, the purported threat is general in nature and the recommendation is couched in terms of maintaining 'long-term operating reliability.' While the Applicant's assertion that such activity was required by industry standards and federal and state regulations may be true, it does not establish the existence of an immediate threat for the purposes of PA eligibility. Accordingly, the Applicant's work to survey and clean the insulators is ineligible as emergency work."[35]

"Pursuant to Stafford Act § 406, PA *(Public Assistance)* funds may be available to a state or local government for the repair, restoration, reconstruction or replacement of a public facility damaged or destroyed by a major disaster. Per FEMA policy, the owner of a facility is responsible for determining the extent of damage. Surveys for damage are not eligible for PA funding. Some examples of ineligible survey costs are general surveys for eligible facilities; video inspection of sewer lines; bridge inspections to determine the possibility of damage; and pier inspections to determine the possibility of damage. However, when disaster-related damages are discovered, inspections performed by an engineer to evaluate the necessary 'type and extent' of repairs are eligible."[36] (Emphasis Added)

But only for those locations where the damage was discovered.

Ineligible Damage: Failure to Protect from Further Damage

This is another interesting case out of Texas, where the agency lost eligibility in part because it failed to protect its property from ADDITIONAL damage after the storm passed. We won't cite all the issues, just the one that's on point here.

"From August 23-September 15, 2017, the State of Texas, including the City of Port Aransas (Applicant), was impacted by high winds, severe storms, and flooding from Hurricane Harvey. The Applicant requested Public Assistance (PA) funding in 2017 for damages resulting from storm surge and wind-driven waves that overtopped the Charlie's Pasture Bulkhead, damaging sidewalks and curbs and washing out sections of the bulkhead and large quantities of fill at the base and under the sidewalks as well as native soil from the Nature Preserve behind the bulkhead (collectively Facility). On November 26, 2019, the Applicant notified FEMA it identified additional claimed land erosion damages and thereafter provided additional damage inventory (DI) items and requested the project be revised to include additional land erosion damage to the Facility. In May 2020, the Applicant requested an expedited Category B, emergency work project (installation of a temporary sheet piling bulkhead) as a preventative measure to stop land erosion occurring adjacent to an increased breach in the Facility's bulkhead. The Applicant began work on a temporary bulkhead in October 2020. On March 12, 2021, FEMA obligated $6,732,446.04 to repair the Facility damages originally identified in 2017."[37]

The case continues: "The Applicant acknowledged it did not enact temporary protective measures until May 2020. This acknowledgement is further supported by the documentation showing the Applicant did not begin to install a rip rap barrier until July 2020, a temporary steel bulkhead until October 2020, or a permanent concrete bulkhead until January 2021. Regardless of the Applicant's argument regarding the reasons for its delay (e.g., permitting issues), the Facility was unprotected from continuing land erosion for an extended period of time post-disaster. Thus, the Applicant has not demonstrated that the additional claimed land erosion damages are a direct result of the declared incident, rather than its failure to protect the Facility from further damage." (Emphasis Added)

There were other issues involved, but this is evidentiary proof that eligibility is at best a tricky issue to be reckoned with.

Ineligible: No Formal Maintenance Program, No Maintenance Reports

Not having a formal maintenance program and not making and keeping maintenance records is probably one of the greatest eligibility-killers of all time. There are literally hundreds of cases in the Appeals Database. And unfortunately, the Finance Department has very little to do with correcting these shortfalls.

In my sometimes-fevered imagination, I can see some of these real-life true statements as lines from a popular situation comedy.

"A narrative prepared by the City Engineer for the appeal acknowledged there were holes in the CMP (corrugated metal pipe) when the event occurred."[38]

"The Applicant stated Parks, Facilities Maintenance, and Streets inspect, monitor and maintain infrastructure, but the process is not formalized, so there are no maintenance records."[39]

"The Applicant informed the site inspector that the roof did not leak in regular rain storms, and only leaked during wind driven rain events."[40] (Emphasis Added)

"The Applicant appealed, arguing that it would not be practical to repair bridges after every storm, this specific disaster made the bridge unsafe, and, therefore, the damages were disaster related rather than a result of lack of regular maintenance."[41]

This case from Illinois is very typical of many cases in the Appeals Database. "From February 24 – July 3, 2019, severe storms and floods impacted Illinois. The Green River Special Drainage District #3 (Applicant) requested Public Assistance (PA) to repair 24 drainage ditch embankment sites along the Green River Ditch and Bakers Drainage Ditch (Facilities). FEMA created Project Worksheet (PW) 802 to document the work and estimated costs of $373,973.00 associated with repairing the Facilities. FEMA conducted a site inspection and documented its findings in a Site Inspection Report (SIR) that included photographs showing unclassified fill, erosion, blowouts, sloughing, and scouring. FEMA issued an initial request for information (RFI), asking for pre-disaster maintenance records demonstrating that the Facilities had been routinely maintained. In response, the Applicant provided information that did not indicate work specific to the Facilities in question, but included work/materials not observed at the Facilities, work performed at other locations, and work performed after the incident period. On October 23, 2020, FEMA denied the Applicant's request for Public Assistance to repair the Facilities because it could not determine whether the damage to the Facilities was disaster-related and the Applicant did not support its claim that the damages were a direct result of the declared event."[42] (Emphasis Added)

"The Applicant also acknowledged that it did not have predisaster survey data, maintenance plans, or activity logs documenting regular maintenance. FEMA sent another RFI requesting information showing: the predisaster capacity of the Facilities; documentation establishing a routine maintenance schedule/program; and evidence of repairs, maintenance, inspections, and monitoring. The Applicant replied that it could not provide drawings, design documentation, written or documented routine maintenance plans, nor the other information requested. The FEMA Region V Acting Regional Administrator denied the appeal on August 6, 2021, finding that the Applicant did not distinguish between pre-existing damage and damage caused by the incident, nor establish the predisaster capacity of the Facilities or the performance of maintenance on a regular schedule. Thus, the Applicant failed to demonstrate that claimed damages to the Facilities were a direct result of the declared disaster."[43]

A great portion of America still consists of smaller and rural communities with low operating budgets, and staff that do their jobs as well as they know how, but they do not generally have the resources and training necessary to meet the frankly staggering requirements imposed by the Stafford Act and subsequent regulations and policies. Nonetheless, these are the administrative requirements which must be met to qualify for Federal disaster assistance.

Eligibility Hazard: No Pre-Disaster Photos

As we have previously discussed, photos of facilities of all types are a very important tool for proving to FEMA that the facility was in good condition prior to the disaster. While there are no specific regulations requiring the submission of photographs, using good photos is simply the best way to prove the existence of disaster damage and that the disaster was the root cause of that damage. A side-by-side comparison is practically irrefutable evidence of the damage and its cause.

This appeals case from Florida illustrates the point. "From September 14–28, 2020, Hurricane Sally caused strong winds, torrential rain, and tidal surge resulting in extensive damage throughout the state of Florida. Escambia County (Applicant) requested Public Assistance (PA) funding to repair damage to a corrugated metal pipe (CMP) culvert and adjacent road. The Applicant claimed the culvert sustained front slope erosion and that the adjacent road experienced cracking due to disaster-related surface water flooding and high-velocity water flows. FEMA prepared Grants Manager Project (GMP) 179321 to capture the damage and associated repair costs to the road and culvert (Facility) estimated at $283,245.00.

On April 20, 2021, FEMA conducted a site inspection. The Site Inspection Report (SIR) documented scour and erosion to the road and culvert. The SIR included post-disaster photographs showing front slope erosion, a decayed downstream headwall, fatigue cracking, and a 72-inch reinforced concrete pipe under the railroad overtaken by vegetative debris. On May 5, 2021, a licensed professional engineer working on behalf of the Applicant, prepared a Preliminary Engineering Assessment (PEA) of the Facility. The PEA indicated that erosion on the front slope of the embankment was undermining the pavement."[44]

"FEMA's SIR and the Applicant's PEA both noted damage to the Facility, including front-slope erosion, a decayed downstream headwall, fatigue cracking along the roadway and a 72-inch reinforced concrete pipe under the railroad overtaken by vegetative debris. This type of damage raised questions as to the cause of this damage. FEMA requested additional documentation from the Applicant to establish the damages were a direct result of the disaster. **However, the Applicant did not provide documentation that tied the damage to the disaster, such as technical assessments or predisaster photographs or maintenance records to support its claim.**"[45]

Eligibility Hazard: No Photos of Damages . . . Or Bad Damage Photos

In almost all cases, disaster damage photos are a must-have. This case from Alabama perfectly amplifies this necessity.

"Hurricane Sally caused damage in the State of Alabama from September 14–16, 2020. Most Pure Heart of Mary Parish (Applicant), a house of worship and Private Nonprofit (PNP), reported damage to its church building (Facility) as a result of the disaster. The Applicant sought Public Assistance (PA) funding for repairs to address wind and water damage to the Facility's interior and exterior, including mold remediation, and roof damage. FEMA prepared Grants Manager Project 183645, in the amount of $150,000.00, to document the Applicant's claim for costs of repairs."

This again is a case with multiple issues, so we will only address that of proper documentation. "Here, the Applicant provided a document, labeled 'Exhibit B' (previously referred to as the DDD *(Damage Description and Dimensions))* in its second appeal request that states 'wind driven rain infiltrated into the wall cavity creating mold growth in the interior of the church. Mold remediation required.' The document lists items and activities that may be associated with mold remediation such as tearing out drywall and insulation and applying an anti-microbial agent. It also included its insurance adjuster's report, which includes some of the items listed in Exhibit B along with cost estimates; however, the quantities are not the same in each document and it is unclear in the insurance report which items are specifically related to requested mold remediation work. As noted in the first appeal response, the Applicant has not provided documentation, such as work contracts or invoices, or other information such as whether the work is complete, who performed the work, the extent of damage, or photographs indicating pre- and post-disaster condition that would allow FEMA to determine an eligible scope of work and costs or verify the requested work was required due to an immediate threat resulting from the declared incident. As such, the work is not eligible for PA funding as emergency protective measures." (Emphasis Added)

The Bottom Line on Photographs

In sum, clear, well-organized pre- and post-disaster photographs of claimed damages are critical as evidence in documenting for FEMA the realistic picture of damages suffered. It is very much worth noting here the insufficiency of "insurance" photos. These photos generally do not provide enough details about the pre-disaster conditions, nor the specific disaster-caused damages claimed by the local agency.

On the other hand, if the agency does not have a well-documented maintenance program, or if indeed there is pre-existing damage, then why bother?

Eligibility Hazard: Pre-existing Damage (Except Minor*)[46]

When the local agency does have disaster damage which was exacerbated by pre-existing damage, this will indeed be a steep and slippery mountain to climb. We must remember that although this is, we hope, a once-in-a-career experience, the staff members at FEMA do this work 365 days a year. Many FEMA staff develop a "nose" for pre-existing damage. The Stafford Act was never intended to repair or replace local facilities and infrastructure when the local agency chose, albeit under economic stress, not to properly maintain its property.

If there is a substantial and very costly project which does in fact have pre-existing damage, it may be appropriate to consider hiring an experienced and well-qualified consultant to prepare the Project Worksheet. This will be an algebraic equation with the cost of the damage; the percentage contribution of the pre-existing damage; the cost of the consultant; and other factors to determine if a project is worth pursuing at all. There clearly are projects which simply do not pencil out, and pursuing them will be a significant and frustrating waste of time and already-scarce money.

Eligibility Hazard Deferred Maintenance (Except Minor*)[47]

Much the same may be said when deferred maintenance plays a contributory role in disaster damage. This appeals case from South Carolina is spot-on. "Hurricane Florence produced heavy winds and rainfall across portions of South Carolina and was declared a major disaster on September 16, 2018. The Conway Hospital (Applicant), a Private Nonprofit medical provider, reported damages after the storm to parking lots and buildings it owned and maintained, including damage to its Conway Medical Center roof. FEMA prepared Project Worksheet (PW) 142 to document damages to the Applicant's property."[48]

"FEMA conducted a site inspection on December 13, 2018, at which time the site inspector observed no damage but noted that the Applicant was hiring a licensed roof contractor (Tremco) to inspect the roof. The site inspector identified the roof as having been built in **1982** and noted that the Applicant informed the site inspector that the roof did not leak in regular rainstorms, and only leaked during wind driven rain events."[49] (Emphasis Added)

"The RA (Regional Administrator) concluded that the roof system was deficient prior to the disaster, citing documentation of observed deterioration, ongoing issues with leaks, and the Applicant's decision to continue implementing spot repairs instead of replacing the roof despite knowing it was out of code."[50]

"Before making an eligibility determination, FEMA considers each of the following: the age of the building and building systems; evidence of regular maintenance or pre-existing issues; and the severity and impacts of the incident."[51]

In this case, the roof was installed in 1982, and the damaging storm was in 2018, a span of 36 years. This is at the far edge of any roof's life expectancy, and in most cases would be a red flag, even with a strong and effective maintenance program. In many cases, I see aged infrastructure and facilities, which even if well-maintained are already near or even well past the end of their economic life, which makes any argument for a Project Worksheet an iffy proposition.

Ineligible: Disaster Debris . . . Sometimes

There are nearly a dozen ways, maybe more, to have debris removal (generally eligible) declared ineligible because of actions or inactions by the local agency. We dealt more exhaustively with debris management (removal) and debris monitoring (required) in Chapter 15, Debris Monitoring and Debris Management. But here we will discuss spinning gold into straw; i.e., losing eligibility once it's approved, or removing debris which is simply never eligible under FEMA's rules.

Ineligible: Debris Removal

There are four situations where debris removal is not an eligible expense. These are debris removal from: 1) Federally Maintained Navigable Channels and Waterways; 2) NRCS (*Natural Resource Conservation Service)* Flood Control Works; 3) Agricultural Land; and 4) Natural, Unimproved Land. In the first two conditions, this is a matter of another Federal agency (OFA) having jurisdiction. In some cases, local elected and senior appointed officials may not understand this and order the debris removed, but FEMA simply will not reimburse these expenses. In the second two situations, again, local officials may order the removal of debris; however, this is completely at risk for the agency.

The following case from Florida is illustrative of this issue. "From September 4 to October 18, 2017, Hurricane Irma caused damage in Florida. Collier County (Applicant) performed debris removal operations throughout multiple waterways, including the reduction/chipping of debris. FEMA prepared Grants Manager Project 42430 and Project Worksheet (PW) 7373 to document the project. The PW notes that the Applicant also performed work under a grant from the Natural Resources Conservation Service (NRCS) separate from this project, but 'per the Applicant, no sites or work duplicate any NRCS-funded work.'"[52]

"On November 16, 2020, FEMA issued a Determination Memorandum (DM), partially approving Public Assistance (PA) in the amount of $7,502,231.88; however, FEMA denied $470,133.60, stating that FEMA cannot duplicate funds provided by another federal agency, NRCS. FEMA explained that debris removal from the Palm River and Port Au Prince Canal was the legal responsibility of the NRCS, so it was not eligible for PA. FEMA cited to minutes from an October 15, 2020 meeting attended by FEMA and the Applicant, stating that locations funded by the NRCS include Port Au Prince Canal and the Palm River."[53]

"Here, FEMA provided PA funding for the Applicant's waterway debris removal. The NRCS also provided federal funding for this work, including for work in the Palm River and Port Au Prince Canal. The NRCS grant covered work performed during the period of July 2, 2018, to April 8, 2019, and stipulates that the NRCS does not reimburse costs incurred prior to the signing of the agreement. The Applicant requested that FEMA reimburse costs for debris removal from the Palm River performed on June 20 and June 21, 2018, which was before the NRCS award took effect. Since the NRCS did not reimburse costs incurred prior to July 2, 2018, PA funding does not constitute a duplication of benefits and costs associated with debris removal from the Palm River are eligible. The Applicant also requested that FEMA reimburse costs for debris removal from the Port Au Prince Canal, but this work occurred during the project period of the NRCS grant. FEMA previously notified the Applicant through the November 16, 2020 DM (*Determination Memo*) that FEMA cannot duplicate funds provided by another Federal agency. However, the Applicant has not provided documentation verifying NRCS did not provide assistance for the work at the Port Au Prince Canal. Therefore, the costs associated with the work at that site are ineligible."[54]

Ineligible: Debris Removal from Private Property (If Not Approved by FEMA)

I have a West Coast client city, population over 300,000, that has 300 Homeowners Associations. Absent the necessary enabling legislation, following a disaster most of the city's residential neighborhoods would be ineligible for debris removal paid for by FEMA. Private Property Debris Removal (PPDR), unless pre-approved by FEMA, is ineligible. This topic was discussed in great detail in Chapter 15 but is included here in eligibility because even if approved by FEMA, the eligibility could still be jeopardized by a lack of proper documentation and other issues, including damaged roadways, unreasonable costs, and procurement errors.

Ineligible: Removal of Debris Placed on Public Right-of-Ways from Commercial Properties Unless Pre-Approved by FEMA

There is an additional risk which is quite important. If Private Property Debris Removal is approved, care must be taken that commercial debris is not mixed with the debris from homes. Were FEMA to discover that these two classes of debris were mixed, that could invalidate, in whole or in part, the debris that was otherwise eligible for clearance.

Ineligible: Removal of Materials Related to the Construction, Repair, or Renovation of Either Residential or Commercial Structures

This is another chance that otherwise eligible debris removal might be denied obligation if FEMA finds re-construction debris mixed in with other classes of debris. Following disasters, residents and businesses alike will begin to rebuild their damaged property as soon as possible, even before the debris management program gets started. The challenge for local officials is to get community cooperation to avoid mixing construction debris with disaster-caused debris.

Total Right-of-Way Debris Clearance (Limited Allowed)

"The Applicant may need to clear its ROW (*Right-of-Way*) to obtain access to repair a utility. It is the Applicant's responsibility to maintain its ROW. FEMA may fund limited clearance of incident-related debris from the ROW to enable access to the facility. Additionally, if trees in the vicinity of the facility were damaged by the incident and an arborist confirms that the trees cause an immediate threat of further damage to the facility (e.g., overhead power lines), FEMA may provide PA funding to remove those trees. Any further clearance of debris in the ROW is ineligible for FEMA funding."[55]

Ineligible: Certain Landfill and Tipping Fee Components

"Landfill tipping fees usually include fixed and variable costs, along with special taxes or fees assessed by the jurisdiction in which the landfill is located. Eligible tipping fee costs are limited to the variable and fixed costs that are directly related to landfill operations, such as recycling tax. The components of tipping fees that are not directly related to landfill operations, such as special taxes or fees related to other government services or public infrastructure, are ineligible as part of the tipping fee. When providing PA funding for tipping fees, FEMA removes any ineligible components."[56]

This next case deals with compound issues; however, we will focus on only the Tipping Fee issue. "On September 28, 2016, the President declared Hurricane Hermine a major disaster. The disaster, which had an incident period of August 31 through September 11, 2016, deposited 2,674.35 tons of construction and demolition (C&D) debris within Pasco County (Applicant), blocking the egress and ingress of the general public. The Applicant also documented that, post-disaster, 14 trees were leaning or falling over on hiking and walking trails. Since the damages posed an imminent public health and safety threat, the Applicant hired contractors to complete debris removal, monitoring, and disposal."[57]

"In June 2018, the Applicant requested an amendment to PW 334 to address a change to the scope of work (SOW) and to correct missing debris disposal fees, materials, and direct administrative costs (DAC). The Applicant stated that it hired a consulting firm, Metric Engineering, Inc. (Metric), in July 2017 to review all projects for this disaster. As a result of the review work associated with the DAC, Metric identified missing debris disposal costs."[58]

"FEMA thereafter transmitted a Request for Information (RFI), asking for additional documentation that supported the requested costs. For instance, FEMA requested the Applicant explain how it calculated the tipping fees' reimbursement, as Ceres' (*the contractor*) load tickets did not correlate with the Applicant-provided Report."[59]

"The Applicant responded by first clarifying the claimed tipping fees did not pertain to haul loads associated with Ceres."[60]

"Regarding the tipping fees, FEMA found that the Applicant had not produced documentation that allowed FEMA to verify the total, eligible costs of debris disposal."[61]

"Here, as the Landfill's owner (evidenced by the permit renewal identifying it as the permittee), the Applicant waived tipping fees related to this disaster for citizens, contractors, and internal departments. Instead of charging the fees, it reimbursed itself the waived fees from its General Fund, and now requests PA funding to recoup those lost costs. However, because the tipping fees represent revenue lost as a result of the disaster, they are ineligible for PA funding."[62]

Although the tipping fees are an eligible expense, they must be properly documented and correlate with all other debris-related documentation. If the local agency waives the tipping fees, then FEMA treats this as "lost revenue" and the fees become ineligible.

Ineligible: Certain Tree Trimming and Removal

Following severe storms of all types, vegetative debris poses a hazard and a nuisance to the community. However, this is an area where debris contractors can take advantage of the local jurisdiction and FEMA by performing work which is clearly outside the approved scope of work. As a result, FEMA has very explicit rules governing all aspects of "green waste" debris collection.

For much more detailed information, see the PAPPG; the Public Assistance Debris Monitoring Guide, March 3, 2021; and the now-archived FEMA Debris Management Guide (FEMA 325, July 2007), which although technically out of date will still provide very valuable information about all debris management issues including "green waste."

From the pages of the 2020 edition of the PAPPG: "Eligible vegetative debris may include tree limbs, branches, stumps, or trees that are still in place, but damaged to the extent they pose an immediate threat. These items are ineligible if the hazard existed prior to the incident, or if the item is in a natural area and does not extend over improved property or public-use areas, such as trails, sidewalks, or playgrounds."[63]

"Contractors typically charge debris removal based on a unit price for volume (cubic yards) or weight (tons). A hazardous tree or stump may be collected individually. When these items are collected individually, contractors often charge a price per tree or stump based on its size. FEMA encourages Applicants to procure branch or limb removal from trees on a one-time charge per tree basis as opposed to a unit price per limb or branch to facilitate more cost-effective operations."[64]

"FEMA has specific eligibility criteria and documentation requirements for funding these items based on a price per each item instead of by volume or weight. If the Applicant does not provide sufficient documentation, it jeopardizes its PA funding. Pruning, maintenance, trimming, and landscaping are ineligible."[65]

Ineligible: Demolition, in Many Cases

When a structure is so damaged that it presents an immediate threat to life, safety, public health, or other improved property, it may be eligible for demolition, subject to several restrictions.

First, demolition is not an eligible expense when fencing the building site is a less costly option. "The DAP9523.4 states that a 'Public Assistance Group Supervisor must concur that the demolition of unsafe structures and the removal of demolition debris are in the public interest.' Additionally, FEMA will consider alternative measures (e.g., fencing or restricting public access) when evaluating requests for demolition."[66] (Emphasis Added) Note that this level of approval must come from the Public Assistance Group Supervisor (PAGS); hence any lower-level FEMA staffer may not properly authorize such action.

Secondly, "demolition of structures owned by commercial enterprises, including businesses, apartments, condominiums, and mobile homes in commercial trailer parks, are generally ineligible as it is expected that the commercial enterprises retain insurance that cover the cost of demolition. In very limited, extraordinary circumstances, FEMA may provide an exception. In such cases, the Applicant must meet the requirements of the (PAPPG), Chapter 7: I.G. *Debris Removal from Private Property*."[67]

Third, "if a structure is condemned prior to the incident, emergency protective measures related to that structure are ineligible."[68]

Fourth, the removal of slabs and foundations that are not a health or safety hazard are generally ineligible. The removal of slabs is approved on a case-by-case basis. As we previously discussed this case in Chapter 15: Another case in point comes from Iowa. "FEMA prepared PWs 6957, 10339, 10459 and 10436 to reimburse the Applicant for eligible costs associated with the demolition of private structures that were made unsafe as a result of the flooding that occurred in 2008. FEMA advised the Applicant on March 31, 2010, that the removal of concrete slabs from these damaged structures would only be eligible for Public Assistance funding if testing determined that the slabs contained hazardous material as a direct result of the declared disaster. FEMA also advised the Applicant that these determinations would be made on a case-by-case basis."[69]

"I have reviewed the information submitted with the appeal and have determined that the Applicant has not demonstrated that the concrete slabs of the damaged structures, built prior to or after 1979, presented an immediate threat to public health and safety. The Applicant has not demonstrated the presence of asbestos in the slabs or that such presence would create a public health and safety threat requiring removal of the slabs. All costs associated with the removal of concrete slabs, foundations, and basements on PWs 6957, 10339, 10459 and 10436 are ineligible for Public Assistance funding."[70]

Lastly, demolition-related permits, licenses, and titles are generally ineligible as increased operation expenses, although the city or county may still want to track these costs to determine the full costs of the disaster, whether eligible or ineligible.

Ineligible: Eligible Work Without Proper Documentation

The lack of proper documentation of Force Account Labor, equipment, and materials, whether force account or rented, contracted, or purchased, is yet another case of turning gold into lead. This applies not only to the agency's workers but also to its volunteers performing emergency protective measures. In this case from a Texas school district, the loss is $132,715.52. "From September 7 to October 2, 2008, Hurricane Ike struck Texas with high winds, heavy rains, and storm surge. FEMA prepared and obligated Project Worksheet (PW) 4321, awarding $132,715.52 for force account labor (FAL) and force account equipment (FAE) associated with Category B emergency protective measures completed from September 13 to 26, 2008 to protect the Applicant's buildings from further damage. FEMA also included $1,312.00 in to-be-completed direct administrative costs (DAC) in the approved costs. FEMA noted in the PW that pursuant to Title 44 of the Code of Federal Regulations (C.F.R.) § 13.42, the Applicant must maintain work-related records for three years from closure and that all records relative to this PW were subject to examination and audit by FEMA and must reflect work related to disaster- specific costs."[71]

In the second appeal, "The Applicant acknowledged it did not have all the documentation requested due to a flood and change in bank ownership, but nevertheless asserted the previously provided documentation supported its appeal. However, the Applicant has not explained how the documentation provided supports the costs in dispute. Here, the Applicant provided timesheets and payroll registers which included payroll names, employee numbers, pay periods, banking numbers, check numbers, check dates, and net payment amounts for each employee, along with W-2 forms to substantiate the hourly labor amounts claimed. However, the documentation the Applicant provided does not establish the date of work with activities performed and the equipment used for each activity with associated costs. The timesheets, payroll registers, and equipment logs contain generic descriptors of the work such as transporting and patrolling but contain no details on what type of work each employee performed. For instance, the entries do not describe the 'who, what, when, where, and why, and how much' for each item of disaster recovery work nor do they demonstrate how the actions eliminated or lessened threats to lives, public health and safety, or threats of additional damage to improved property. In addition, the Applicant's documentation shows that more than 90 percent of the Applicant's claimed FAL costs are for ineligible straight-time labor costs, rather than for overtime costs. Finally, similar to the FAL and FAE costs discussed above, due to missing documentation for the claimed DAC, the Applicant did not provide documentation that establishes those costs are tied to the performance of eligible work."[72] (Emphasis Added)

Standby Time: Heads or Tails

The very use of the word "standby time" is an invitation for scrutiny by FEMA.

First, when resources, labor, or equipment are in a "Staging Area," they should not be reported as "on standby." The term "staging area" has a very specific meaning within the context of the Incident Command System or ICS. Resources in "staging" are ready to respond within a few minutes and are not considered "on standby."

However, in some cases resources are indeed on "standby," and there are regulations which must be considered as these resources are reported. This case comes out of New York State: "The Long Island Power Authority (Applicant) is a public utility that provides electrical services to customers in Suffolk County, New York. In March 2017, a severe winter storm was predicted to cause damage throughout New York, including in Suffolk County. The Applicant expected outages and in preparation, it pre-positioned electrical contractors to perform utility repair work in Suffolk County. The storm changed direction and did not hit Suffolk County as expected, and the Applicant cancelled its request for electrical crews. Some of the electrical contractors were en-route from out of state, while the contractors who had already arrived were in staging areas on standby. These pre-positioned electrical contractors did not perform emergency work as a result of the disaster."[73]

"FEMA prepared Project Worksheet (PW) 707 to document $8,933,248.50 in costs incurred by the Applicant to pre-position the electrical contractors. The Agency determined on June 20, 2018, that those costs were ineligible for Public Assistance (PA) funding. FEMA found that pre-positioned resources are only eligible if they perform eligible emergency work. Here, the electrical contractors who were pre-positioned did not perform eligible emergency work."[74]

"The Stafford Act § 403 grants FEMA discretionary authority to provide assistance essential to meet immediate threats to life and property resulting from a major disaster. Implementing this authority, 44 C.F.R. § 206.225(a) authorizes reimbursement of emergency protective measures necessary to eliminate or lessen immediate threats to life, public health, or safety, as well as threats of significant additional damage to improved property. However, costs related to pre-positioning resources for a disaster are only eligible if the resources are used in the performance of eligible emergency work. The only exceptions to this prohibition are for costs to pre-position resources for evacuating, or providing emergency medical care during the evacuation period, which are eligible even if those resources are not used."[75] (Emphasis Added)

"Here, the Applicant pre-positioned electrical contractors prior to the disaster to be ready to deal with power outages. However, the storm changed direction and the contractors did not perform emergency work. FEMA policy is clear that pre-positioning costs are only eligible if the contractors performed eligible emergency work. These electrical contractors did not. Therefore, the costs for pre-positioning the crews are not eligible. The policy does not include evacuations or providing emergency medical care during evacuations as examples, but rather they are exceptions to the prohibition because they are life saving measures."[76]

"Standby time in preparation for emergency work to save lives and protect public health and safety is eligible in limited circumstances."[77]

In another appeals case, this time from Florida, standby time was found to be ineligible. "Hurricane Irma struck Florida on September 10, 2017. The Polk County Sheriff's Office (Applicant) utilized force account labor (FAL) to perform emergency protective measures and claimed $1,023,579.49 in costs. FEMA prepared Grants Manager Project (GMP) 22698/ Project Worksheet (PW) 3314 to document the work and reimburse eligible costs. FEMA approved $783,469.38 but denied $240,110.11 in costs associated with duties which FEMA considered increased operating costs, including patrolling, inmate security, traffic control, and stand-by time."[78]

"FEMA also informed the Applicant that other work activities remained ineligible. These included: (1) detention security/support and continued and maintained security not directly associated with the transporting inmates to the temporary facility and not specifically related to inmate relocation; (2) routine patrol work not directly related to accomplishing specific emergency health and safety tasks; and (3) increased supervision activities not necessary to immediately protect lives, health, safety, or improved property. Finally, FEMA determined that stand-by staff did not exclusively perform emergency work specific to the disaster or outside of their everyday scope of responsibilities, so stand-by time is not eligible."[79] (Emphasis Added)

"According to the Applicant, some stand-by staff reported for duty before hurricane conditions became too dangerous to drive. Others staged at an operation site to be available to provide relief or were required to report to duty before/after normal shift to insure proper staffing. Most were simply on stand-by status. These staff did not exclusively perform emergency work specific to the disaster or outside of their everyday scope of responsibilities, therefore the requested stand-by time is ineligible."[80]

The term "standby" should be carefully used, and only when it truly describes the situation at hand. Further, agencies should carefully consider the both the response and financial implications when requesting Mutual Aid or placing employees on "standby."

Eligibility Reducers

The Stafford Act prohibits any duplication of benefits under the Public Assistance program.[81] A duplication of benefits may come from different directions. A reduction may come from a situation where the local agency has a facility located in a mapped flood zone. FEMA regulations require that such a facility must have a minimum amount of flood insurance purchased though the National Flood Insurance Program (NFIP). So-called "flood insurance" purchased from any other source will not satisfy this requirement. If an agency should have had flood insurance for a facility and does not, or if the agency does not have the minimum required amount of flood insurance, then FEMA will make a mandatory reduction in the amount of funding which it would have otherwise provided.

A second way to have an otherwise eligible project dollar amount reduced is because of insurance payments made to the local agency for the disaster-related damage.

A third possible reduction may present itself when the local agency has a facility that was previously damaged in a disaster and received FEMA funding. Then, per FEMA requirements, the agency should have purchased insurance for the hazard which caused the original damage. When the agency fails to purchase the insurance, often referred to as the O&M (Obtain and Maintain) requirement, that facility will no longer be eligible for reimbursement.

A fourth eligibility reducer is the "improper" receipt of donations for the repair and restoration of a facility which is otherwise FEMA-eligible. There is more about this situation in Chapter 9: Insurance and Risk Management.

Eligibility Killers: Environmental and Historic Considerations

Unlike the previous section where an agency may have eligibility reduced, a failure to abide by the environmental and historic "Special Considerations" can and often does result in a complete denial of FEMA funding.

"FEMA prepared PW 1409 to repair a dirt service road leading to the Upper Cloverleaf Reservoir. The Applicant requested an improved project to pave the dirt service road with 3-inch asphalt concrete pavement. In addition to paving the dirt road as requested, the Applicant relocated the alignment of the road in some areas and conducted minor leveling of vegetation and ground up to ten feet on either side of the newly paved road."[82]

"After a site visit on November 20, 2006, FEMA de-obligated $50,830 because the Applicant completed the improved project prior to FEMA completing its environmental review, which precluded FEMA's ability to comply with the National Environmental Policy Act (NEPA), the Endangered Species Act (ESA), or the National Historic Preservation Act (NHPA)."[83]

"The Deputy Regional Administrator denied the Applicant's appeal on October 14, 2008, because the Applicant paved 60 percent of the dirt road with 3-inch thick asphalt concrete and re-aligned the road prior to FEMA conducting its environmental and historic reviews. As such, FEMA was not able to comply with the requirements of NEPA, ESA and NHPA."[84]

Another case with historic preservation issues comes to us from a South Dakota case. "From September 9–26, 2019, South Dakota experienced severe storms, tornadoes, and flooding, resulting in a major disaster declaration on November 18, 2019. Hutchinson County (Applicant) claimed damage to the Harvey Wall Bridge (Facility) and FEMA developed Grants Manager Project 129976 to document the repair work to the facility. The claimed damage included erosion of base and subbase material on the approach road, scouring of the asphalt, erosion of the soil embankments and supporting rip rap, and damage to the abutments, footings, and guardrail. The Applicant completed the repair work on November 27, 2019, at a cost of $417,095.43."[85]

"During its Environmental and Historic Preservation (EHP) review, FEMA determined that the Applicant, in the course of its work, disturbed approximately eight acres of archaeologically sensitive ground without prior consultation with its State Historic Preservation Office (SHPO). FEMA found that the disturbances, including excavation of an adjacent area as a source for material for the project (the 'borrow pit'), creation of an access road to the borrow pit, and excavation and grading in the floodplain, were not covered under the Programmatic Allowances of the South Dakota Section 106 Programmatic Agreement. FEMA determined that the project therefore did not comply with the National Historic Preservation Act (NHPA). FEMA further determined that the Applicant violated the Clean Water Act, because it did not obtain a Construction Stormwater General Permit for the project, nor did it develop a Stormwater Pollution Prevention Plan. Finally, FEMA determined the project did not comply with Executive Order 11988, regarding floodplain management, because the project was completed before FEMA could notify the public for input or conduct an alternatives analysis, and the Applicant did not complete a hydrologic and hydraulic evaluation. For these reasons, FEMA denied funding for the project on March 22, 2021."[86]

First Appeal

"The Applicant appealed on May 18, 2021, requesting FEMA obligate $417,095.43 for the repairs to the Facility. The Applicant argued that it did not violate the NHPA, because the borrow pit was smaller than the threshold for which a permit is required. The Applicant stated it did not release any pollutants into the water during the project. The Applicant stated that it obtained a floodplain permit after it learned of the permit requirement, and that the rip rap was replaced without any disturbance to the slope of upstream or downstream banks."[87]

"FEMA issued a Request For Information (RFI) to the Applicant on September 23, 2021, seeking any documentation that could demonstrate 'the borrow pit was an approved or certified source or that the Applicant consulted with the SHPO prior to its excavation of material from the borrow pit.'"[88]

On February 1, 2022, the Regional Administrator for FEMA Region VIII denied the Applicant's appeal. FEMA stated that the Applicant completed the repair work, including the creation of a borrow pit from which materials for the work were taken, without prior consultation with the SHPO.

"The Applicant commenced and completed the repair work on the Facility without affording FEMA the opportunity to perform its required EHP review. The excavation of the adjacent borrow pit was not covered under the programmatic allowances of the South Dakota NHPA section 106 Programmatic Agreement, and the Applicant did not consult with its SHPO prior to the start of construction. The project, therefore, does not comply with Section 106 of the NHPA. FEMA cannot provide PA funding to projects that do not comply with Federal EHP laws. The Applicant's request for funding the cost of materials not sourced from the borrow pit must be denied, as they are part of the same noncompliant project."[89]

Equipment Eligibility: Two Killers

Here are two "don't even bother to apply" shortcuts regarding equipment. First, fixed mounted emergency electrical generators, such as those found at police stations, fire stations, emergency operations centers, and hospitals, are ineligible for reimbursement for the run-time hours. However, the fuel that they consume for emergency operations is reimbursable.

In an Ohio appeals case, FEMA writes: "During the incident period of June 29 through July 2, 2012, strong winds and severe storms produced extensive damage throughout Trimble Township causing downed utility lines and widespread power outages for multiple days. The Trimble Township Wastewater Treatment District (Applicant) utilized five fixed generators and two portable generators during the event to support emergency protective measures at the wastewater treatment plant, main lift station, and remote lift stations. FEMA prepared Project Worksheet (PW) 982 for $8,187 to fund the force account labor costs associated with emergency protective measures, fuel for the fixed generators, and usage of the temporary generators based on FEMA's schedule of equipment rates. Because five of the generators were fixed, FEMA did not reimburse the use of those five generators based on FEMA's equipment rates but reimbursed the fuel costs only ($3,351)."[90]

The preceding notwithstanding, the PAPPG (the Public Assistance Program and Policy Guide) on page 72 appears to have diametrically opposed language which is quoted here: "III. Applicant-Owned and Purchased Equipment. "FEMA provides PA funding for the use of Applicant-owned (force account) equipment, including permanently mounted generators, based on hourly rates."[91] (Emphasis Added)

In the second "don't even bother" situation, this same case goes on and explains that equipment maintenance and repair are also ineligible expenses. "Application of this guidance necessitates a distinction between portable and fixed generators. FEMA reimburses the use of portable generators based on FEMA equipment rates or similar set rates. <u>FEMA equipment rates include such costs as operation of equipment, depreciation, overhead, maintenance, field repairs, fuel, lubricants, tires, Occupational Safety and Health Administration equipment, and other costs incidental to operation.</u> This method of calculating reimbursement is not applicable to fixed generators or generators that are permanent fixtures because a portion of the costs included in the equipment rates, like depreciation and the other ownership components, are built into the operating and ownership costs of the facility that the fixed generator is installed to support. Accordingly, FEMA will reimburse fuel costs for fixed generators if they are used to perform eligible emergency work because those are the only increased costs incurred by the applicant as a direct result of the event. This distinction applies to fixed generators regardless of whether the generators are affixed inside a facility or to a concrete slab outside of a facility."[92] (Emphasis Added)

I have seen many cases where the local agency attempted to be reimbursed for a mechanic's time or parts and supplies, only to be rejected outright.

Ineligible: Increased Operating Costs

As previously discussed, increased operating costs are ineligible expenses; this includes fire & law response costs if not directly tied to the disaster. This case from Florida clearly illustrates this point. "Hurricane Irma, with an incident period from September 4 through October 18, 2017, caused widespread damage in Florida. During the incident period, Clay County (Applicant) closed a bridge at County Road 218 that had become impassable. As a result, emergency response times increased for the Applicant's Fire Rescue Station 14 (Fire Station 14), located on the western side of the bridge, to assist residents on the eastern side; the closest available detour to service the eastern-side residents increased the travel distance to 13.4 miles. The Applicant only had its Fire Rescue Station 15 (Fire Station 15), located on the eastern side of the bridge, to provide initial response services to that area. Because of the detour route, the Applicant augmented and redistributed the staffing of Fire Stations 14 and 15 from October 4 to November 30, 2017. FEMA developed Project Worksheet 1731 to document the Applicant's requested reimbursement of $53,479.50 for the standby time and overtime associated with the augmentation and redistribution of its emergency personnel force account labor."[93]

"FEMA concluded that the work performed by the staff was not disaster-related work to save lives and protect public property, but rather associated costs were related to operating a facility and providing a service and are considered ineligible increased operating costs."[94]

"The Applicant asserted that the staffing augmentation, in effect from September 19 (the date of the bridge closure) through December 8, 2017 (the date the bridge was reopened), represents short-term costs necessary to ensure effective response service on both sides of the bridge to accomplish emergency health and safety tasks and should thus be deemed eligible emergency protective measures. In support, the Applicant submitted a spreadsheet listing personnel overtime hours for Fire Stations 14 and 15, with an associated description of the type of work completed as 'Overtime – Disaster.' In a transmittal letter dated September 16, 2019, the Grantee expressed support for the appeal."[95]

"On October 15, 2020, the FEMA Region IV Regional Administrator denied the appeal. FEMA determined the augmented personnel at Fire Station 14 and redistributed existing personnel to Fire Station 15 were performing normal duties to support the continuation of essential services for the community."[96]

Ineligible: Transportation and Communication Costs

Another ineligible cost is for emergency transportation (other than for evacuations), and communications when lifelines are disrupted. "A SLTT (*state, local, tribal, or territorial*) government may provide emergency communication services and public transportation when existing systems are damaged to the extent vital functions of community life or incident response are disrupted. The costs of these services are ineligible for reimbursement. However, FEMA may provide short-term DFA (*direct Federal aid*) for these services."[97]

Therefore, if these needs exist within a disaster affected community, the local agency should work with the state and FEMA for the provision of these services. Should the local agency provide these services, it will be an out-of-pocket increased operating expense.

Ineligible: Certain Testing Costs for Long-Term Clean-Up Operations

When dealing with hazardous materials issues, there are some eligible costs; however, not all costs will be eligible. "Testing for contaminants in water, air, or soil necessary to ensure elimination of the immediate threat is eligible in accordance with Chapter 7: II.F. *Expenses Related to Operating a Facility or Providing a Service.* However, testing for the purpose of long-term cleanup actions is ineligible." (Emphasis Added)[98]

"The City's claim under Project 18 included $74,580 of unauthorized project costs. The FEMA *Public Assistance Guide* (FEMA Public Assistance Guide 321, October 2001, p. 24) states, that if a change in the scope of work is identified, '[t]he applicant should contact the State to ensure that proper guidelines for documenting any additional costs are followed.' Project 18 authorized the removal and disposal of debris. However, the City's final claim under the project included $74,580 of costs for personal protective equipment, water and sewer line capping, *and air monitoring*. Neither FEMA nor the State included these items in the authorized scope of work on the final version of the project worksheet. Rather, the project worksheet authorized debris removal costs based on a cubic yards per unit price. In addition, the City did not have documentation to indicate that it contacted the State to include these items in the project's scope of work. Therefore, we question $74,580 of unauthorized project costs."[99] (Emphasis Added)

However, in this case, the reason for the denial of costs was that this was work done beyond the authorized Scope of Work, and not as testing for long-term cleanup.

Eligible/Ineligible: Animal Carcasses

"Removal and disposal of animal carcasses, including interim processing, is eligible. If the removal and disposal is conducted as part of the overall debris removal operations, the work may be funded as Category A. FEMA may require certification from the SLTT (*state, local, tribal, or territorial*) government health department, HHS (*Health and Human Services*), or the U.S. Department of Agriculture (USDA) that a threat to public health and safety exists. When few in number, smaller animal carcasses (e.g., rodents, skunks, or possums) do not usually pose an immediate threat to public health or safety. Removal and disposal of these carcasses is ineligible."[100]

More Ineligibility

At this point, it may seem that there is more which is ineligible than eligible, but in fact, this ineligibility train is still adding cars.

As previously mentioned, projects with costs less than $3,900 (Federal Fiscal Year 2023–2024) are not eligible. This amount is generally adjusted each October 1st by the Consumer Price Index. In the last 20 years, this threshold has increased from $1,000 in 2004 to today's figure of $3,900.

Ineligible: Inactive Facilities

From Title 44 Code of Federal Regulations: "Inactive facilities. Facilities that were not in active use at the time of the disaster are not eligible except in those instances where the facilities were only temporarily inoperative for repairs or remodeling, or where active use by the applicant was firmly established in an approved budget or the owner can demonstrate to FEMA's satisfaction an intent to begin use within a reasonable time."[101]

This case is an audit of a California city damaged in an earthquake, conducted by the Department of Homeland Security, Office of the Inspector General: "City officials improperly claimed $2,377,185 to Project 228 to replace its Printery Building (Building), a building that the Masonic Association deeded to the City for use as a recreational/youth center and rental space. This occurred because FEMA officials' estimates and calculations were based on inaccurate documentation presented to FEMA by City officials. Specifically, City officials provided documentation to FEMA that indicated that the Building was fully occupied at the time of the earthquake."[102]

This is a lengthy audit dealing with issues related to FEMA's 50% Rule (Repair or Replace), so we will address only the inactive space issue.

"In reality, however, the Building was not completely in active use at the time of the earthquake, nor did the City have any evidence for how it intended to reoccupy the vacant portions of the Building."[103]

"City records regarding predisaster use and future plans indicated that at the time of the earthquake –

* Only 82% of the Building was occupied:
* 15,529 of the total 18,887 square feet were in active use.
* The remaining 18% of the Building was vacant and inactive:"[104]

"We therefore question $2,377,185 in ineligible, excessive costs. City officials agreed that the Building was not fully occupied at the time of the earthquake and that there was no intent to reoccupy. FEMA was unaware that a portion of the Building was not in active use at the time of the earthquake."[105]

Ineligible: Mixed-Use Facilities (Used for Less than 50% of Eligible Services)

Although this topic can be discussed later in this chapter when we discuss in greater detail issues related to Private Non-Profit agencies, this topic also might apply when a local government agency owns a facility which may be partly used by a private non-profit. This case comes to us from New York following Hurricane Sandy. "From October 27 to November 9, 2012, Hurricane Sandy caused damage to the Sixth Street Community Center, Inc.'s (Applicant) Sixth Street Community Center (Facility). The Applicant, a private nonprofit (PNP) organization, submitted a Request for Public Assistance (RPA) to FEMA for funding to cleanup and permanently repair its Facility. FEMA denied the RPA (*Request For Public Assistance*) on January 26, 2016, through the New York State Division of Homeland Security and Emergency Services (Grantee). FEMA based the denial on its findings that the Facility was primarily recreational and did not meet the criteria to be an eligible community center as described in Disaster Assistance Policy DAP9521.1, Community Center Eligibility."[106]

"In an April 13, 2015 final request for information (Final RFI), FEMA asked the Applicant to demonstrate: (1) how the Facility meets FEMA's definition of a 'community center' as set forth in DAP9521.1, (2) that the Facility's primary purpose is to serve as a community center, (3) that more than 50 percent of the Facility's space is used to support eligible activities, and (4) that the Applicant applied for and was denied a disaster loan from the Small Business Administration pursuant to 44 C.F.R. § 206.226(c)(2)."[107]

"Of particular importance to this appeal, the Applicant described its Soul Food Café (Café) as one of its eligible community center activities. The Café is an onsite kitchen and dining area that 'provides community residents with healthy affordable lunches and dinners and a friendly atmosphere for meeting and socializing as well as free internet access.' The Café serves as a venue for a weekly nutrition workshop that uses produce from the Applicant's Community Supported Agriculture program."[108]

"Through his January 8, 2016, first appeal decision, the FEMA Region II Regional Administrator (RA) determined that the Applicant sufficiently addressed all of FEMA's concerns except for satisfying the requirements that more that 50 percent of the Facility's space supported eligible activities. The RA found that the Café is a commercial enterprise that sells food at market prices and for this reason is an ineligible activity. No other activities were determined ineligible. In total, the RA found that only 2,017 SF (47.4 percent) was used for eligible activities and consequently denied the appeal."[109]

"Eligible PNP facilities include those that provide essential governmental type services to the public, such as community centers. DAP 9521.3 provides that 'Even when an organization that owns a facility is an eligible PNP, the facility itself must be primarily used for eligible services. Space is the primary consideration in determining if a facility is eligible.' It also explains that when facilities are used for both eligible and ineligible purposes (i.e., multi- or mixed-use facility), eligibility is determined by looking at the time the facility is used for eligible and ineligible services. Hence, as noted in DAP9521.1, an eligible community center must be primarily used as a gathering place for a variety of social, educational enrichment, and community service activities based on the principal of majority use (i.e., over 50 percent of total use)."[110]

"In the first appeal decision, the RA determined that the Applicant's Facility is a community based PNP organization that has provided ongoing activities and supports the Applicant's social, education enrichment, and community service activities. However, the RA determined that the Café and its allocated space were 'not used for an eligible activity as it is a commercial enterprise selling food at market prices.' PNPs often raise funds to support their programs through the sale of goods at associated gift shops, restaurants, and kiosks. FEMA regulation and policy does not designate these fund-raising type activities as ineligible. On the contrary, the appendix to DAP9521.1 provides a fictional, yet relevant, description of an eligible community center that is 'supported through weekly bingo, thrift and gift shop sales, and other fundraising activities.' Here, the function of the Applicant's Café is comparable, as it serves as a venue for social activities, supports healthy eating, and provides residents with affordable meals and free access to the internet. Moreover, volunteers staff the Cafe, and all proceeds are reinvested into community service programs. Whether the Applicant sells its food and beverages at market prices is not dispositive in determining eligibility. In this instance, the functions performed through the Café are eligible."[111]

Eligible/Ineligible: Parking Garages

A parking garage may be eligible or ineligible depending on its use. A parking garage which supports government offices, a qualified school, college or university, or a Private Non-Profit hospital, generally will be eligible for Public Assistance. However, a parking structure which is used primarily for private businesses would be ineligible.

• However, this is an opportunity in some cases for eligibility management. I had a West Coast client that owned and operated a downtown multi-story parking garage which primarily served area businesses. They were considering tearing it down and replacing it with a larger, more economical-to-operate parking garage. Because either the present or future garage would be ineligible based on its use, I recommended that they consider granting a franchise to a private company to build, own, and operate the facility, with a percentage of the revenue paid to the city. In this way, the city could eliminate a potentially ineligible property and still generate revenue.

Cautionary Eligibility: For Relocated Facilities

In certain instances, FEMA will require that a facility located in a mapped flood zone be relocated as a condition of Public Assistance funding. This can be an extremely technical matter, and working with a highly qualified consultant is strongly recommended to ensure that all goes according to plan.

"Eligible work associated with relocation includes land acquisition and construction of necessary support facilities, such as roads, parking lots, and utilities."[112]

"For land acquisition, if the facility was located on 10 acres of land at the time of the incident, and FEMA determines that 10 acres is not necessary for the operation of the facility, FEMA limits PA funding to the necessary amount of land."[113]

"In situations where the Applicant owns the facility, but not the land or the support facilities at the original location, the cost to purchase the land or build support facilities is ineligible."[114]

"When FEMA requires relocation, FEMA does not provide future PA funding for repair or replacement of the original facility or for other facilities at the original site unless the facility facilitates an open space use. For example, if the Applicant converts the original site to a park, FEMA may provide PA funding in the future for park components, such as benches, tables, restrooms, or gravel roads."[115]

If at some point the local agency wishes to sell the property acquired with any level of Federal funding, certain rules apply, and in some cases the local agency may have to repay some of the proceeds of the sale. As noted in the following paragraph, if the original land from which the facility was relocated is sold, the buyer must be made aware of the limitations of any Federal assistance for that property in case of a future disaster.

"The Applicant may sell or lease the original facility or the land on which a relocated facility was originally located. The Applicant must inform the purchaser of the property that FEMA will not provide future PA funding for repair or replacement of the original facility or for other facilities at the original site unless the facility facilitates an open pace use."[116]

"The property which the facility is relocated to, and the relocated facility itself, are subject to the real property provisions of 2 C.F.R. part 200 including disposition and reporting requirements under 2 C.F.R. §§ 200.311 and 329, respectively."[117]

These requirements may stem in whole or in part from a California case arising from the 1989 Loma Prieta Earthquake, where the city sold a property before completing the approved scope of work.

"(Audit) Summary. We concluded that since the City did not comply with grant requirements, it was not eligible to receive the $16,226,089 FEMA provided for repairs to the Ford Assembly Building under Damage Survey Report 78123. Project records showed that the City did not complete the reduced scope of work prior to the stated March 31, 2003, deadline or prior to the December 2004 sale of the building. Since the City failed to comply with the grant requirements by not completing the project within the specified deadlines and by selling the building before the project scope was completed, the project is ineligible for FEMA funding, as explained in 44 CFR § 206.204(d)(2). Therefore, as allowed by 44 CFR § 13.43(a)(2), *Enforcement: Remedies for Noncompliance*, we recommend that FEMA disallow the $15.5 million for repairs/mitigation and the $743,306 for earlier funded architectural and engineering costs, for total questioned costs of $16,226,089."[118]

Ineligible: Destroyed Collections or Individual Objects

Collections and individual works of art are ineligible for FEMA funding. However, they may be eligible for "conservation," i.e., cleaning and preserving the items. Federal funds may not be used to fully restore or replace these items.

"Collections and individual objects are artifacts, specimens, artworks, archives, public records, and other items that are often considered irreplaceable because of their artistic, educational, historic, legal, scientific, or social significance. They are nonliving and, therefore, do not include animals or plant material, and are usually one-of-a-kind. Eligible collections and individual objects may be in storage or on display in a public or PNP facility and may include items located outdoors, such as sculptures and public art installations."[119]

- This is another opportunity for eligibility management. While a museum may be eligible for FEMA funding to repair and restore the facility, its collections are not eligible. Therefore, if only limited funds are available to purchase insurance, some of that insurance should be purchased to cover the ineligible collections. The policy should very clearly specify what is insured and what is not. Furthermore, the facility itself should still be insured for liability, fire, theft, etc. If the facility is located in a mapped flood zone, then the Federally mandated flood insurance must also be purchased.

Following a disaster, if a donor(s) wishes to contribute to the total post-disaster restoration of a museum, consideration should be given to direct all donations to the restoration and replacement of damaged items or collections. The donations must clearly spell out these intentions, i.e., that the donations are not for the facility but for the contents, to avoid FEMA making a deduction for a duplication of benefits. Again, with such strategies, discussions with a well-qualified consultant are strongly advised to ensure that the insurance policies and any other supporting documents and administrative policies are precisely written and within the law.

Ineligible: Restoring a Facility to Its Original Condition When the Use Has Changed

It is not uncommon for public (and private non-profit) buildings to change use and function over time. When I worked for San Francisco, as part of our photo documentation project, we visited various city-owned buildings. One of those buildings had originally been a Masonic Lodge. It had beautiful architectural features, including wonderful wood carvings and wood-beamed ceilings. One of the large rooms, which had obviously been a meeting room, was now used as a large file room, filled with rows of filing cabinets. Were this building to be damaged, FEMA would only pay to have the room restored as a file room, without any of the beautiful woodwork or carved ornamentation.

"Pre-disaster function is the function for which the facility was originally designed or subsequently modified. For example, if the Applicant designed and constructed an administrative building, but later altered it in accordance with applicable construction codes or standards to use as a school, the pre-disaster function would be as a school. If the facility was serving an alternate function at the time of the incident, but was not altered to provide that function, FEMA provides PA funding to restore the facility either to the original pre-disaster function, OR pre-disaster alternate function, whichever costs less."[120]

This appeals case is from Mississippi. "Hurricane Katrina caused severe damage to the Hope Academy School facility in August 2005. The Applicant applied for assistance in October 2005 as a private nonprofit educational facility. FEMA prepared several Project Worksheets (PWs) in May 2006 to replace the school building because it was 65% damaged and eligible for replacement as outlined in Disaster Assistance Policy 9524.4, Repair vs. Replacement of a Facility under 44 CFR §206.226(f) (The 50% Rule). FEMA prepared PW 9724 for $991,250 to replace the facility. Upon further review, FEMA determined PW 9724 was ineligible because Hope Academy was not an accredited educational institution."[121]

"The Applicant submitted its first appeal February 3, 2009, requesting facility eligibility. The Applicant demonstrated that its facility met the eligibility criteria for elementary and secondary schools. The FEMA Regional Administrator partially approved the first appeal for $655,519 on February 22, 2009. The remaining $335,731 on PW 9724 was not approved because it was allocated to replace the Applicant's auditorium, which was deemed ineligible for Public Assistance funding because it was established as a chapel used for religious purposes."[122] (Emphasis Added)

However, on appeal, the church was able to prove that the great majority of the time the building was in fact used as a school. This appeal was a winner.

Therefore, should a local agency or private non-profit choose to use a facility for a purpose other than that for which it was originally designed and used, i.e., a warehouse becomes office space, or an assembly area a meeting room, the agency should formally repurpose and rededicate the facility to this permanent new use. In this case, it would have avoided the time and expense of filing two appeals and moved the restoration along much more quickly.

Ineligible: Flood Control Works

"Flood control works are those structures such as levees, flood walls, flood control channels, and water control structures designed and constructed to have appreciable effects in preventing damage by irregular and unusual rises in water levels."[123]

"Generally, flood control works are under the authority of USACE or NRCS and restoration of damaged flood control works under the authority of another Federal agency is ineligible. Flood control works under the specific authority of NRCS are those that are part of the Watershed and Flood Prevention Operations (WFPO) Program under PL 83–566.327."[124]

"Secondary levees riverward of a primary levee are ineligible, unless the secondary levee protects human life."[125]

This applies to publicly owned levees and flood control works. Private levees are another matter entirely, and generally not eligible for FEMA funding.

If damages arise with public flood control works, consultation with a flood control works-experienced expert is highly advised, particularly when contemplating filing an appeal.

Eligible/Ineligible: Flood Fighting

"Flood fighting activities may include, but are not limited to, sandbagging, dewatering behind a levee by breaching or pumping, or increasing the height of a levee. These activities are eligible if necessary to reduce an immediate threat to life, public health and safety, or improved property.

These activities are eligible even if they are associated with a facility that is eligible for the USACE RIP (*Rehabilitation and Inspection Program*), as USACE cannot reimburse the Applicant for flood fighting. However, they are ineligible if associated with flood control works under the specific authority of NRCS."[126]

"The repair of deliberate breaches made by the Applicant to accomplish dewatering is eligible as part of the Emergency Work Project."[127]

"Dewatering agricultural and natural areas behind levees and other water control structures is ineligible."[128]

Ineligible: No Flood Insurance When Required

As previously stated in Chapter 9, flood insurance for facilities in mapped flood zones is required to ensure full eligibility.

Ineligible: Previously Damaged and Now Uninsured Facilities

Referring again to Chapter 9, when a facility was previously disaster-damaged, received FEMA funding, and is no longer insured, the facility is ineligible for any future assistance.

Ineligible: Work Under Construction

When the local agency has hired a contractor to repair, renovate or build a facility, that work must generally be covered by a "course-of-construction" policy, which makes the contractor liable for any damage which occurs during the construction process until such time as the agency formally accepts the project as complete. There may be a rare exception if the agency establishes a carefully drawn policy which makes it, and not the contractor, liable. However, this is expert territory and must be precisely done to qualify for eligibility.

Ineligible: Most Landscaping

"On August 29, 2006, heavy rain and wind from Hurricane Katrina damaged the Bay St. Louis School District's Upper Elementary School campus, including North Bay Elementary and Bay-Waveland Upper Elementary schools. FEMA obligated Project Worksheet (PW) 11157 to address relocation of the campus for $3,536,331. At closeout, the Applicant submitted additional costs of $146,021, of which $115,814 was approved. The remaining $30,207 represented denied costs related to a sod allowance of $6,000; landscaping trees for $21,900; and two desiccant dryers and two compressors for $2,307."[129]

"the FEMA Response and Recovery Directorate Policy Number 9524.5, Trees, Shrubs, and Other Plantings Associated with Facilities, (Sept. 24, 1998), in effect at the time of the disaster, provides that 'Trees, shrubs, and other plantings, except grass and sod, will no longer be eligible under Section 406 of Public Law 93–288, as amended (Repair, Restoration, and Replacement of Damaged Facilities).'" This policy applies to "any measure taken with respect to trees, shrubs, and other plantings, except grass and sod – including but not limited to replacement, non-emergency removal for purposes of replacement, and remedial actions taken to abate disaster damage." This prohibition, which does not allow for exceptions, "applies to trees and shrubs in recreational areas, such as parks, as well as trees and shrubs associated with public facilities, such as those located in the median strips along roadways and as landscaping for public buildings."[130]

However, in what at first appears to be contradictory information but upon closer reading is not, is language from the Public Assistance Program and Policy Guide: "Grass and sod replacement are eligible if it is an integral part of the restoration of an eligible recreational facility. Vegetation replacement is also eligible if necessary to restore the function of the facility (e.g., if vegetation is a component of a sewage filtration system).[131] (Emphasis Added)

This is a second case, this time from North Dakota. "In April 1997 flood waters inundated a significant portion of the University of North Dakota's (Applicant) steam line system. The replacement of the underground steam distribution system was completed in two phases. The Phase I contract was the complete replacement of the steam line from the east end of the campus to the middle of campus. The Phase II contract completed the steam line from English Coulee west. The Federal Emergency Management Agency (FEMA) approved the scope of work in DSR 59315 that authorized the replacement of the system. FEMA obligated $25,417,125 for final closeout. In a letter dated September 30, 2005, the Applicant appealed FEMA's denial of $637,138.26 for costs associated with landscaping, engineering abatement, contracts, and change orders. In a letter dated August 17, 2006, the Regional Director upheld four of the 241 change orders and obligated $10,809 as reflected in DSR 64854. In a letter dated November 8, 2006, the Applicant appealed FEMA's denial of $484,373.07 for seeding and sod of the steam line trench and eight of the 241 contract change orders requested."[132]

"In its first appeal, the Applicant appealed FEMA's denial of landscaping costs for nearly 11 miles of trenching. The costs represent final grading, topsoil, seeding/sod, and watering. The Applicant stated that FEMA improperly applied FEMA Response and Recovery Policy 9524.5, Trees, Shrubs, and Other Plantings Associated with Facilities, dated November 25, 1997, because the policy was published after the incident period. The Applicant also argued that grass existed prior to the pipe replacement and should be replaced. The Applicant was unaware that such costs were not eligible. The Regional Director denied the landscaping costs because FEMA practice prior to and since the disaster had been to restore grass only for erosion purposes when the slope exceeded a 2:1 ratio."[133]

"The seeding and sod work was for cosmetic purposes as it did not impact essential services or the operation of the new system. The seeding and sod work is ineligible for funding under the Public Assistance Program unless there is a substantial issue of erosion. The policy prohibiting seeding and sod was developed in response to a critical report by the FEMA Office of Inspector General in 1996 and, therefore, became effective nationally prior to FEMA-1174-DR-ND. Grass and sod will not be eligible for cosmetic purposes."[134]

Therefore, it is a complete waste of time and money for both the local agency and FEMA to request eligibility for landscaping unless the landscaping is specifically for erosion control. To establish that landscaping is eligible, the local agency will have to provide engineered landscape plans which directly address erosion. Further, the agency will have to substantially document the regular maintenance of said landscaping.

Ineligible: Landslides When Site Is Unstable and There Is Pre-disaster Instability

Generally, FEMA does not reimburse for land movement. This case is from California and is representative of many landslide claims. "Landslides damaged Amesti Road in Santa Cruz County (Applicant). DSR 27263 was written in June 1998 to repair Amesti Road at an estimated cost of $469,949 with stabilization as a condition of the grant prior to obligation. The Applicant requested a time extension and revised funding for a total of $1,210,550 in December 2002."[135]

"FEMA denied the request and on October 21, 2003, the Applicant submitted its first appeal. It stated that it had been waiting for an answer regarding whether it risked Hazard Mitigation

Grant Program funding if Amesti Road were realigned through a Geological Hazard Abatement District."[136]

"The Regional Administrator denied the first appeal on July 30, 2007, stating that the landslides had damaged the road in two disasters, though no money was ever obligated to restore the road because it remained unstable. <u>In cases when a site is found to be unstable due to an identified, pre-existing condition, the Applicant is responsible for stabilizing the site. Once the site has been stabilized, the cost to restore the facility at the original site is eligible.</u>"[137] (Emphasis Added)

In a current (2023) search on Google maps, Amesti Road still shows as not fully repaired in the slide area.

If the local agency restores the integral ground to its pre-disaster condition, then repair or replacement of the damaged facility may be eligible. And once again, the issues surrounding any type of land movement will involve engineers and geo-technical experts, and working with experienced experts is well advised.

Ineligible: The Agency Does Not Have Legal Responsibility for the Work

There are different ways that ineligibility can attach itself to disaster damages.

1) As previously mentioned, the facilities are under construction, and without a carefully written contract which assigns responsibility to the local agency as owner.
2) The local agency does not own the facility.
3) The local agency leases the facility from another party, and the lease doesn't require that the tenant is responsible for disaster-caused damage.
4) The facility is owned by a qualified local agency, but it is not used for governmental purposes, such as a facility leased to a private business, an ineligible private non-profit, or a vacant facility.

In this appeals case from Texas, we can see the problems brought on by a lease. This is a multi-issue appeal, so we will focus only on the issues related to the lease itself. "In September 2008, Hurricane Ike impacted the state of Texas, including Galveston County, where the Port of Galveston (Applicant) is located. The Applicant suffered extensive damage, resulting in preparation of numerous Project Worksheets (PW), including several to address storm induced erosion at a number of piers. On July 17, 2014, the Applicant submitted a proposed project, prepared by its consultant, seeking funding for repair of Pier 14 East (Facility).[138]

"On August 4, 2014, the Federal Emergency Management Agency (FEMA) issued a request for information (RFI), stating that the Applicant had not provided any quantifiable description of the disaster related damage. It noted that the Pier 14 T-Head, which joined Pier 14 East and West on the north side, had been determined to be unsafe and closed prior to the storm, and pre-disaster aerial images of the Facility suggested that that the pier was not in active use and that the surface was already failing. Accordingly, the RFI requested documentation clarifying whether the Facility was in active use, establishing that it was properly maintained, and quantifying specific damages that were a direct result of the disaster."[139]

"In order to be eligible for PA funding, an item of work must be the legal responsibility of an eligible applicant. To meet this requirement, both the facility and the work must be the legal responsibility of the applicant. This requirement applies at the time of the disaster. Ownership of a facility is usually sufficient to establish legal responsibility for repair work, but where a facility is under a lease agreement, a tenant will be responsible if the terms of the lease specifically make the lessee responsible for disaster related damage. FEMA will sometimes approve the transfer of legal responsibility from one eligible applicant to another after a disaster, but if an eligible applicant did not have legal responsibility at the time of the disaster, the project is ineligible for assistance."[140]

"Here, the lease agreement specifically made Malin (the lessee), a for profit entity not eligible for PA, rather than the Applicant (the lessor), legally responsible for the Facility in the event that it was damaged or partially destroyed by a hurricane. The lease also made Malin legally responsible in the event that the Facility was totally destroyed, unless the Applicant later elected to terminate the agreement . . . Under the terms of the lease, Malin was legally responsible for the repair of damage to the Facility at the time of the disaster."[141]

As the reader can see from previous chapters, the eligible/ineligible issue can whipsaw work which would otherwise appear to be eligible. We will continue to see this as we move ahead in this chapter and the following chapters.

Ineligible: Mutual Aid, in Some Cases

In most cases, Mutual Aid is only eligible for reimbursement for Categories A and B (emergency) work. With the exception of utility restoration, Mutual Aid cannot be reimbursed for permanent work.

"Mutual aid resources are eligible when used for Emergency Work, emergency utility restoration (regardless of whether it is deemed Category B or F) or grant management activities [subject to the criteria in FEMA Recovery Policy FP 104–11–2, Public Assistance Management Costs (Interim)]."[142]

Mutual Aid work is subject to the same eligibility criteria as contract work; therefore, the agency receiving Mutual Aid must ensure that the agency providing Mutual Aid fully documents its emergency work in the same manner as the local agency's Force Account Labor, Force Account Equipment, and any supplies or materials used in the performance of that work.

Costs for the transportation of the Providing Entity's equipment and personnel to the declared area are eligible.

However, "Ineligible work performed by a Providing Entity includes, but is not limited to:

- Preparing to deploy;
- Dispatch operations outside the receiving State, Territory, or Tribe;
- Training and exercises; and
- Support for long-term recovery and mitigation operations."[143]

"If the Providing Entity backfills deployed personnel, overtime for backfill personnel is eligible even if they are not performing eligible work. However, straight-time for backfill personnel is ineligible."[144]

Ineligible: 'In-House' Mutual Aid

"When the Requesting Entity is a SLTT (*State, local, tribal, or territorial*) government and the Providing Entity is another division within the same SLTT government, straight-time for budgeted employees of the Providing Entity is ineligible."[145]

In this case from Texas, we can see FEMA's logic for this ruling. "This letter is in response to your letter dated October 20, 2010, which transmitted the referenced second appeal on behalf of the University of Texas Medical Branch at Galveston (UTMB) (Applicant). The Applicant is appealing the Department of Homeland Security's Federal Emergency Management Agency's (FEMA) denial of funding for labor costs incurred under a Mutual Aid Agreement following Hurricane Ike."[146]

"The Applicant is a component institution of the University of Texas (UT) System. In response to Hurricane Ike, the Applicant utilized additional personnel who were provided by several UT institutions, in accordance with the UT System Disaster Response Mutual Aid Guidebook (Mutual Aid Guidebook). The Applicant claimed contract labor costs for additional police personnel for security, chemical and biological experts to remove contaminated biological materials, and additional personnel who provided various emergency protective measures after Hurricane Ike. FEMA considered all related costs to be ineligible on the basis that all additional labor claimed by the Applicant as contract labor came from the same entity (the UT System), or the same State government. FEMA prepared five PWs documenting the full claimed amount for the services performed and obligated the PWs for zero dollars on September 30, 2009."[147]

"Disaster Assistance Policy DAP 9523.6, Mutual Aid Agreements for Public Assistance and Fire Management Assistance, Section VII(E)(2) states, 'The labor force expenses of the Providing Entity will not be treated as contract labor if the labor force is employed by the same local or State government as the Requesting Entity.' FEMA reviewed the Mutual Aid Guidebook and the post-disaster invoice contracts signed between UTMB and various UT institutions. FEMA has determined that the Requesting Entity (UTMB) and the Providing Entity (various UT institutions) are component parts of the UT System and are 'State' institutions of higher learning under Texas's Education Code. The UT component schools share the same Board of Regents, appointed by the Governor of Texas. The Board of Regents commits funding for the institutions' various programs, as well as for the associated personnel, equipment, and supplies."[148]

"Each component institution has its own budget and presumably some autonomy, as the Applicant stated, but they are each funded through the UT System's overall budget. They share the same funding sources, retirement system, insurance and benefit plans. The state-and-federally-supported UT System is the employer of the personnel in question, and therefore the Requesting Entity and Providing Entity are employed by the same State government. Therefore, the requested cost is ineligible for Public Assistance reimbursement pursuant to DAP9523.6."[149]

In attempting to review the University of Texas System Mutual Aid Plan, this was found: "Created in 2002 by a team of over 60 people including subject matter experts in finance, physical plant, security, environmental health and safety, human resources, procurement, counsel and information resources, The Disaster Response Mutual Aid Agreement MOU and Guidebook are collectively referred to as the Mutual Aid Plan."[150]

Clearly, no one at that time thought to include someone with FEMA Public Assistance experience on the team. The lesson to be learned here is "Do Not Create Policies in a Vacuum, i.e., without access to serious expertise in the Public Assistance program."

Ineligible: Other Federal Agency-Funded Work

There are disaster damages which would be FEMA-eligible if they were not already under the purview of another Federal agency, even if that Federal agency does not provide funding for the work in question. I liken these situations to being stuck in the middle of the O.K. Corral at 3:00 P.M. on Wednesday, October 26, 1881, the day of a big gunfight. In this Federal crossfire, the local agency will almost never come out unscathed.

This appeals case comes from Nashville/Davidson County, Tennessee. "On the incident period date of March 3, 2020, severe storms generated tornadoes, straight-line winds, and flooding across Tennessee. The Applicant requested $384,686.25 in Public Assistance (PA) funding for repairs to/replacements of traffic control devices at 19 site locations. FEMA prepared GMP 661784, a permanent work project, to capture the claimed work and costs. On May 2, 2022, FEMA issued a

Determination Memorandum, denying reimbursement of the $384,686.25, noting that the invoice submitted for the costs included work on federal-aid routes, which are under the authority of the Federal Highway Administration's (FHWA) Emergency Relief (ER) Program and therefore did not fall within the purview of FEMA's PA program. FEMA observed the Applicant had acknowledged that several signal locations were under FHWA jurisdiction. Additionally, FEMA stated that other sites, which may be the responsibility of the local jurisdiction to maintain, were also classified as federal-aid routes."[151]

"On July 18, 2023, the FEMA Region 4 Regional Administrator partially granted the appeal, awarding $99,446.75 in repair costs for traffic signals at 1 of the 19 site locations. FEMA denied the remainder of costs, $285,239.50, associated with the remaining 18 locations because it determined the other sites were located at intersections with federal-aid routes classified as major collectors, minor arterials, or principal arterials and thus fell under the purview of FHWA's ER Program. FEMA stated that regardless of which entity is responsible for general maintenance, the Agency was prohibited from providing PA funding for damage on FHWA routes."[152]

Here, the documentation in the record shows that the 18 sites at issue are each located at an intersection with a Federal-aid route. Therefore, the traffic control devices are road components of Federal-aid routes and are consequently not associated with eligible public facilities. Although the Applicant asserts that it is legally responsible for the repairs/replacements of the traffic control devices, the issue of whether an applicant has legal responsibility to complete repair work to facilities is different than the issue of whether another federal agency has specific authority to restore the facilities. Here, even though the Applicant states it did not receive funding from FHWA, the requested work associated with the Federal-aid routes is nonetheless ineligible for PA funding.[153]

In this case, even though the local agency had legal responsibility for the repairs, the intersections of local roads and Federal Aid roads gave FEMA reason to invoke the Other Federal Agency prohibition for a duplication of benefits, even in this case, where there was no funding available from the Federal Highway Administration.

Eligibility Enhancer: In Some Cases

In this discussion on eligibility, however, it is quite appropriate to expound on the benefits of proper photo documentation when in fact the facilities or infrastructure were in well-maintained condition prior to the disaster. Disaster-caused damage may often be difficult to distinguish from damage which was exacerbated by pre-existing conditions, a lack of regular maintenance, or simply lacks the proof of pre-disaster maintenance records. It is a very best practice to have a protocol in place either prior to a storm warning, or the beginning of the disaster season, e.g., hurricane season, winter storm season, etc., to take a pre-established set of photos of those items of infrastructure or individual facilities which would become problematic if damaged by a disaster.

One of the Very Best Chapters in the Book

In Chapters 2 and 3, we discussed the importance of pre-disaster policies to protect and preserve the local agency's eligibility. This section reprises the absolute importance of strong and clear pre-disaster policies. Properly written and consistently followed, these policies will absolutely reduce the 3D, multiphonic, technicolor migraines which any agency without these policies will surely experience.

First, the policies must meet all five criteria listed in Chapter 2. Policies not meeting these five criteria are a waste of time, and although the agency, via the policy, may be on the hook for certain expenses, i.e., employee feeding, etc., these costs will not be FEMA-eligible.

Not only will these policies help fend off denial or deobligation; in some cases they may enhance eligibility for certain expenses.

- **Compliant Purchasing Procedures:** As we saw in Chapter 9, the failure to follow the Federal procurement regulations in Title 2 of the Code of Federal Regulation often results in partial or total denial or deobligation of costs. This one policy may be worth all other policies put together.
- **Clear Responsibility for Damage in Contracts:** Developing a written and consistently implemented policy of clearly identifying the party responsible for disaster-caused damage in lease or rental agreements over time will reduce the exposure to denial and deobligation. The agency attorney should be able to develop boilerplate language which can be inserted into new contracts and contracts up for renewal.
- **Stick to the Scope of Work:** In researching this book, I have found hundreds of cases where public works staff, road engineers, project managers, and others involved with repairs, reconstruction, and rebuilding after a disaster choose to ignore the written and FEMA-approved Scope of Work. This is spitting in the eye of the devil. This happens on regular projects, improved projects, and alternate projects all the time. The agency should have a written policy that requires the staff involved to closely follow the FEMA-approved Scope of Work or suffer some defined penalty for a violation of the policy. There seems to be no other way to rein in this "cowboy" attitude.
- **Good Maintenance Policies & Regular Reports:** The agency should have a formal maintenance program with a comprehensive written schedule for maintenance at regular intervals. The failure to provide such proof to FEMA is one of the most common reasons for denial and deobligation.
- **Comprehensive Maintenance Documentation:** Time after time after time, agencies are denied FEMA funding because the so-called inspection reports contain no real information, particularly that which would defend the local agency's position that the damages in question were disaster-caused and not caused by pre-existing issues or occurred because of deferred maintenance. A √ (*Check Mark*) says nothing and conveys no meaning about the condition of a facility and might as easily have been filled out in the office without ever visiting the site.
- **Policy on Proper Photo Documentation:** No single act can better position the defense of eligibility than the presentation one good photograph which shows enough detail to be meaningful and convincing to the flintiest of FEMA personnel.
- **Paid Administrative Leave, Disaster Overtime:** FEMA will honor the local agency's disaster pay policies if and when they are properly drawn up and consistently applied, and do not otherwise violate Federal regulations and cost principles.
- **Policies Which Cover Feeding and Lodging, etc.:** Similarly, FEMA will honor local agency policies for these disaster-related expenses, when properly written and consistently applied in both Federally declared disasters and all other disasters.
- **Policy on Tracking Time of Second-Level Supervisors and Above:** The local agency should have a written policy requiring that ALL employees at all levels track their time for disaster-related activities to capture these costs as an "in-kind" match for the local cost share requirement.
- **Proper Acceptance of Monetary Donations:** FEMA's Appeals Database is littered with sad stories of agencies that happily received donations from extraordinarily generous people, only to lose the full benefit of that donation because of the issue of duplication of benefits. Policies should be in place before the disaster to anticipate this and properly accept donations in a way which minimizes the risk of a duplication of benefits.

- **Policy for the Value of Donated Resources Used for Eligible Work:** The local agency should have a formal policy for volunteer time tracking which, in addition to setting up a disaster volunteer program, should also require all volunteers to properly track their time for bona fide and eligible emergency work to capture the value of their time, and possibly equipment or supply donations. The policy should also be clear that these expenses will be a part of the local agency's cost share and not be requested for reimbursement, which would be a kiss of death.

Eligibility Reducers in Procurement

Blue Book Prices

Many agencies are surprised to find out that when they have equipment which is damaged in a disaster, FEMA only pays the "Blue Book" value for that equipment. This of course assumes that all the other criteria for equipment eligibility are met, including providing the "Pink Slip," current registration, records showing current maintenance, etc. Equipment damaged by operator error, or for any other reason other than direct damage by the disaster, e.g., a radio tower blown down by hurricane-force winds, will likely be ineligible for funding.

Following Hurricane Katrina, many New Orleans Police Department vehicles were damaged by the storm. Some of these vehicles reportedly had 250,000 to 300,000 miles on them. These cars were worth pennies on the dollar, but that's the rule. If the local agency will replace older vehicles with extremely low Blue Book values, inquiries should be made about funding the vehicle replacements as an improved project, so that the vehicles may be safely replaced with newer used vehicles, or even new vehicles.

This case stems from the Joplin, MO tornado of May 2011. "On May 22, 2011, an E-5 tornado struck the City of Joplin, Missouri (Applicant), and as a result, some of the Applicant's fire vehicles suffered significant damage, with five of the vehicles a total loss. In addition, three other fire vehicles and other pieces of fire equipment incurred repairable damage. FEMA wrote Project Worksheet (PW) 1939 for the permanent repair and replacement of fire vehicles and related equipment, for a total estimated award of $439,785.00. On September 26, 2016, the Grantee submitted a Large Project Final Accounting, in which the Applicant requested payment of $919,633.78. FEMA issued a Determination Memorandum (DM) on February 23, 2018, denying the requested funding amount. FEMA noted that per agency policy, eligible replacement costs for vehicles are based on used items of similar age, capacity, and condition. The Applicant, however, purchased new vehicles without demonstrating that similar used items were either not available within a reasonable time or distance, or not in accordance with national consensus standards. In addition, FEMA noted that the Applicant purchased additional fire equipment not included in PW 1939. Thus, FEMA determined that the PW amounted to an improved project and capped the award at the obligated amount less actual insurance proceeds, for a total of $212,829.62. The Applicant appealed, arguing that its fire department purchases only new fire and police vehicles based on public safety concerns, and that it conducted a search for comparable used vehicles but found none because its department required specific, custom upgrades to the vehicles. FEMA denied the first appeal for the same reasons as in the DM, but also found that the Applicant failed to demonstrate that any custom upgrades or new trucks were required by codes and standards. FEMA also determined the temporary used fire trucks, which FEMA funded separately under PW 1950, constituted the permanent replacement trucks for PW 1939 and in addition to denying the request for additional funding in PW 1939, FEMA also deobligated all funding in PW 1950."[154]

Like For Like vs. Least-Cost Alternatives

In most cases, the local agency must repair or replace a damaged facility to its immediate pre-disaster use and condition or the current use, whichever is the least costly option. However, when the local agency can present a less costly alternative that option *may* be approved by FEMA. But the local agency should be prepared for a fight over this, if only because some (especially newer) FEMA employees may not be familiar with this alternative. In some cases, it simply may not be worth the trouble.

Violations of Title 2 of the Code of Federal Regulations, Part 200 (2 CFR, Part 200)

Failures in purchasing are the single greatest threat to obtaining and keeping a FEMA Public Assistance grant. Local agencies must follow their own purchasing rules AND those in 2 CFR, Part 200. Failure to do so places the agency at great risk for deobligations, in some cases total deobligations. Consider the Project Worksheet as the Titanic and procurement as the ice. Enough said; that's all she wrote.

Eligible/Ineligible: Plastic Blue Roofs

In the Public Assistance Program and Policy Guide, Version 4, June 1, 2020, page 117, is the following quoted text:
    "Supplies and Commodities
The purchase of supplies and commodities required for emergency protective measures is eligible.
    Costs related to the Applicant purchasing supplies or using its own stock to perform Emergency Work are eligible and reimbursed in accordance with Chapter 6: III.5. Supplies. Examples include, but are not limited to, safety equipment, personal protective equipment, radios, power tools, sand, and tarps."[155] (Emphasis Added)
    "Purchasing and packaging life-saving and life-sustaining commodities and providing them to the impacted community are eligible. Examples of such commodities include, but are not limited to, food, water, ice, personal hygiene items, cots, blankets, tarps, **plastic sheeting for roof damage,** and generators, as well as food and water for household pets and service animals. The cost of delivering these same commodities to unsheltered residents in communities where conditions constitute a level of severity such that these items are not easily accessible for purchase is also eligible. This includes food and water for household pets whose owners are in shelters."[156] (Emphasis Added)
    Further along in the same Public Assistance Program and Policy Guide, Version 4, June 1, 2020, p. 136) is this quoted text: "Operation Blue Roof (DFA Only) (*Direct Federal Assistance*)
    Operation Blue Roof provides homeowners with plastic sheeting to cover damaged roofs until arrangements can be made for permanent repairs. The purpose of Operation Blue Roof is to protect property, reduce temporary housing costs, and allows residents to remain in their homes while recovering from the incident. Therefore, only dwellings that can be safely occupied after blue roof installation are eligible. The costs of these services are ineligible for reimbursement. However, FEMA may provide DFA for these services."[157] (Emphasis Added)
    One might suppose that as long as the local agency doesn't call their "blue roofs" by the name of "blue roofs," the work might be eligible . . . or not. I expect that the next edition of the Public Assistance Program and Policy Guide may address this apparent discrepancy. In any case, the local

agency should proceed with caution on providing roof coverings for homeowners, in blue or any other color.

Ineligible: Unauthorized Changes in the Scope of Work

Making unauthorized changes in the scope of work approved by FEMA is a very serious mistake made by many agencies. In fact, this one problem shows up in more than 37% of all second appeals cases. Simply put, this is a fatal failing in the process of repairing and reconstructing damaged facilities.

In some cases, the eligible amount for a Project Worksheet is reduced, and in other cases, the entire amount may be deobligated.

Local officials will often find themselves at odds with FEMA over how a project is to be repaired or replaced, both in terms of the materials used and how the work is done.

In all fairness, FEMA is simply looking for the absolute least costly way to restore a facility, and local officials will want to restore the facility in the best possible way. And here arises the eternal conflict between *the best way* and *the least expensive way.*

Regardless, at the local level, we must do the work per the approved scope of work, or FEMA will take away the money. FEMA considers the approved Project Worksheet, including the defined and approved Scope of Work, a legally binding contract.

Often the arguments center around the application of Codes and Standards, which the locals will insist they must follow, and FEMA says the Codes and Standards do not apply, or the local agency did not properly adopt or enforce a particular code or standard. We will discuss Codes and Standards in some depth in Chapter 34.

This appeals case comes from New York State following Hurricane Irene in 2011.

"From August 26 to September 5, 2011, heavy rain, wind, and flooding from Hurricane Irene caused damage in New York. During the event, high water levels in Cedar Pond Brook destroyed a gabion wall and embankment behind the wall. Rockland County (Applicant) requested Public Assistance (PA) through the New York Division of Homeland Security and Emergency Services (Grantee) for the cost of repairs. FEMA prepared Project Worksheet (PW) 9122 that identified the damaged facility as a 125-foot long gabion wall and embankment behind the wall. FEMA prepared a cost estimate of $153,898.00 for in-kind repairs and awarded the project on November 16, 2012. The PW stated that the Applicant was to notify the Grantee with any changes to the approved scope of work (SOW) and to also provide photo documentation of any additional damages discovered during construction."[158]

"<u>On November 21, 2018</u>, the Applicant submitted a request to change the project's SOW, explaining that the project was completed in <u>Summer 2018</u> using heavy stone fill instead of gabion baskets. The Applicant explained that in its experience gabion baskets routinely fail, and heavy stone was a more reliable solution. The Grantee transmitted the request to FEMA and included the Applicant's project proposal that it asserts was submitted to FEMA during project development, with repairs consisting of the placement of heavy stone fill with a cost estimate of $257,207.51."[159] (Emphasis Added)

"On April 24, 2019, FEMA denied the request explaining that the material change from gabions to heavy stone fill represented an improved project. Therefore, FEMA limited funding associated with the Federal share of the costs that would be associated with repairing the damaged facility to its predisaster design."

"In a letter dated February 5, 2020, the FEMA Region II Regional Administrator denied the first appeal. FEMA determined that the Applicant completed work outside of the approved SOW by restoring an additional 55 LF (*lineal feet*) of embankment and did not provide documentation to support that the additional damage was caused by the disaster. FEMA reaffirmed that the Applicant performed an improved project and limited funding accordingly."[160]

"The Applicant submitted a second appeal on May 27, 2020, asserting that the approved SOW was in error and the length of damage estimated was incorrect. The Applicant asserts that its June 5, 2012 proposal estimated the length of embankment as 240 LF and adds that it was told at the time not to worry about the differences and to proceed with the project and submit actual costs and project length when the project was designed and completed. The Applicant submitted the scope change request on November 21, 2018, showing the actual project length was 220 LF. The Applicant also explained that the change from gabions to heavy stone reduced the project cost and was better suited to the site conditions. Had the Applicant used gabions, project costs would have been higher, so it asserts the additional $47,434.10 is appropriate and reasonable."[161] (Emphasis Added)

"FEMA prepared the PW to repair 125 LF of damaged embankment, which the Applicant agreed to. PW 9122 notes that the Applicant was advised by FEMA to notify the Grantee with any changes to the approved SOW and to also provide photo documentation of any additional damages discovered during construction. The Applicant submitted its scope change request several years after the work was completed. Under FEMA policy, scope change requests are to be submitted prior to commencement, not at completion. Further, the Applicant has not provided documentation, such as predisaster pictures, inspection reports, logs or maintenance records, to demonstrate that repairing the additional length of embankment was a result of the declared incident. Therefore, the Applicant has not demonstrated that any additional reinforcement of the embankment beyond the approved area is required as a direct result of the disaster."[162]

In this case, the local agency made several errors: 1) They changed materials from gabion baskets to heavy stone; 2) They increased the length of the project from 125 lineal feet to 180 lineal feet; 3) They failed to request a change in the scope of work BEFORE commencing the work; 4) They apparently relied on verbal assurances (worse than worthless) that all would be worked out after the project's completion. The Appeals Database is chock full of similar cases, with few if any winners in the lot.

Making Changes in the Scope of Work

This is not to say that it is impossible to get a change in the scope of work approved. However, the changes must be requested at the time it becomes apparent that a change is necessary because of errors made in developing the scope of work, or additional hidden damage is discovered once the work has begun.

In some cases, this may require that work be halted for the time necessary to receive FEMA's written approval. This can be a serious matter because in stopping work, the contractor will lose money; and the project will apparently sit idle for an indeterminate time, which may be politically untenable. In such cases, hard decisions will have to be made, i.e., ignore the change of scope of work issues and suffer the financial consequences, or stop the project, which will also likely incur some additional costs.

To be abundantly clear, requesting a change in the scope of work and receiving written approval for that requested change in the scope of work is never a foregone conclusion. Once FEMA has signed off on a Project Worksheet, they will require substantial evidence to get them to make the requested change(s). But when conditions warrant, and the proper procedures are followed, FEMA does approve changes and will issue a new version of a large Project Worksheet.

However, in many cases, arguments about changes in the scope of work are mostly about differences of opinion, and differing motivations, i.e., FEMA's motivation is lower cost, and the local agency's motivation is the best job possible. Ultimately, it's all about the money.

This appeals case comes from Reclamation District #2130 in northern California. "During the incident period of January 3 – 12, 2017, severe winter storms, flooding and mudslides resulted in widespread damage in northern California. Reclamation District #2130, Honker Bay (Applicant) requested Public Assistance (PA) funding for restoration of its levee damaged from the incident. FEMA prepared Project Worksheet (PW) 778 to document the Scope of Work (SOW) necessary to repair the levee at an estimated cost of $385,000.00. The SOW consisted of placing 3,373 cubic yards (cy) (cubic yards) of unclassified fill across seven sites along the levee. In addition, the SOW identified 184.6 cy of rip rap that would be reset plus 71 cy to be replaced. The Applicant completed the work to restore the levee on September 20, 2019."[163]

"FEMA transmitted a request for information (RFI) to the Grantee on May 4, 2020 seeking, in part, a description of work completed and explanation showing how it is eligible work. Additionally, FEMA noted the Applicant completed a significant change in the SOW without notifying FEMA of the change prior to work completion as required in FEMA policy.[164]"

"The Grantee forwarded the Applicant's RFI response in a letter dated August 11, 2020. The Applicant explained it was not aware of the inadequacies of the repair work as defined in the SOW (*scope of work*) until after work was completed on October 19, 2018. Furthermore, the Applicant stated in the memorandum that the Grantee verbally notified it after an inspection of the completed work that, "[it] believed there would be no problem with funding any additional work required to restore our levee to its pre-topping condition."[165]

"FEMA responded on December 1, 2020, notifying the Grantee and Applicant that the additional work is outside the approved SOW, and constitutes an Improved Project. FEMA therefore capped project costs at the original PW estimate, pending environmental review."[166]

"The Regional Administrator (RA) for FEMA Region IX denied the Applicant's appeal in a letter dated July 26, 2021. The RA found that the Applicant neither notified FEMA of the newly identified damages requiring a change in the SOW nor substantiated its contention that the damages were a direct result of the event."[167]

Ineligible: Long-Term Medical Treatment

"When the emergency medical delivery system within a declared area is destroyed, severely compromised or overwhelmed, FEMA may fund extraordinary costs associated with operating emergency rooms and with providing temporary facilities for emergency medical care of survivors.

- Costs associated with emergency medical care should be customary for the emergency medical services provided.
- Costs are eligible for up to 30 days from the declaration date unless extended by FEMA.
- Long-term medical treatment is ineligible.
- FEMA determines the reasonableness of these costs based on Medicare's cost-to-charge ratio (a ratio established by Medicare to estimate a medical service provider's actual costs in relation to its charges).

FEMA does not provide PA funding for these costs if underwritten by private insurance, Medicare, Medicaid, or a pre-existing private payment agreement. The Applicant must take reasonable steps to provide documentation on a patient-by-patient basis verifying that insurance coverage or any other source funding including private insurance, Medicaid, or Medicare, has been pursued and does not exist for the costs associated with emergency medical care and emergency medical evacuations.

Ineligible costs include:

- Medical care costs incurred once a survivor is admitted to a medical facility on an inpatient basis;
- Costs associated with follow-on treatment of survivors beyond 30 days of the declaration; and
- Administrative costs associated with the treatment of survivors."[168]

Killer Timelines

As previously mentioned, should the local agency BEGIN work on an approved project BEFORE FEMA has completed its required environmental and historic reviews as needed, the result is often a complete deobligation of FEMA funding. We will go into detail on these issues in Chapters 30 and 31.

The POP *(Period of Performance)*

Regulations require that emergency work, Categories A & B, must normally be completed within 6 months of the date of the Presidential declaration, unless an extension of time is approved in writing. When work is done after the approved timeline has expired, that portion of the work may be deobligated.

This case is from New York State: "On April 16, 2010, the President declared a major disaster for severe storms and flooding that impacted the Village of Warwick (Applicant). As a result of the disaster, on August 26, 2010, FEMA awarded Project Worksheet (PW) 364 as a permanent work project. It approved: (1) $1,351.31 in costs associated with an exploratory investigation conducted in May 2010 to determine the full extent of damages to the Applicant's underground drainage system; and, (2) $29,366.84 in costs associated with work to be completed, installing a new concrete box culvert totaling 101 linear feet (LF) and completing road and sidewalk repairs in the vicinity."[169]

"Six years later, in July 2016, the Applicant submitted a time extension request to extend the period of performance (POP) deadline for PW 364 to December 31, 2016. The Applicant based the request on the assertion it discovered additional damages when it was preparing to complete the previously approved repairs. In conjunction with the time extension request, the Applicant also contemporaneously requested a change to the scope of work (SOW) to include work associated with extensive deterioration not initially recorded. As documented in FEMA's Public Assistance (PA) grants management database, the Applicant sought approval to construct a new concrete box culvert totaling 420 LF (an increase of 319 LF from the originally approved culvert) and install nine drainage structures."[170] (Emphasis Added)

"Here, the Applicant acknowledges that it commenced restoration work for PW 364 in the spring/summer of 2016, after the Grantee's retroactive extension to April 16, 2014. Therefore, because $29,366.84 in costs associated with permanent repair work were incurred after the latest approved project completion date, they are not eligible for reimbursement."[171]

"The Applicant first states this project was put on hold when the Applicant was forced to repair more pressing infrastructure damages caused by subsequent disasters. Therefore, it's clear that any delay in work for this reason was not due to this disaster. Furthermore, even after the Applicant repaired damages unrelated to this disaster, it still did not commence permanent repair work for this project until six years after the disaster."[172]

"Next, the Applicant states another reason for the delay in project completion was that the PW was lost within a retired Department of Public Works Supervisor's files after the Applicant transitioned to a new administration and consultant engineer. While that is unfortunate, staffing changes and human error not related to the disaster are not a basis to waive an administrative condition for assistance under section 301 of the Stafford Act."[173]

The game of Public Assistance is a game of hardball, with the exception that the ball is not made of cork and leather but rather stainless steel. There is little to no room in the law and regulations for human-related issues. These sorts of excuses, and from the Federal perspective they are merely excuses, and carry no weight, particularly where timelines are involved.

Facilities Scheduled for Repair or Replacement

"Facilities that are not yet under contract but are scheduled for repair or replacement using non-Federal funds are eligible provided that the claimed damage did not exist prior to the incident (FEMA may review procurement and contract documents to validate). If damage existed prior to the incident, only the repair of damage caused by the incident is eligible."[174]

"A facility scheduled for replacement within 12 months of the start of the incident period using Federal funds is ineligible. In such a case, the Applicant should coordinate with the agency funding the project to expedite replacement, if possible."[175]

Ineligible: Structures Demolished Prior to FEMA Inspection

Structures which are claimed to be severely damaged in a disaster and in need of repair or replacement must be "formally" inspected by FEMA prior to demolition, or the local agency runs a great risk of having funding denied or deobligated. I use the term "formally" to indicate that if FEMA visits the site for any other purpose, this may not and likely does not constitute an inspection for purposes of approving a facility demolition. The Appeals Database is strewn with the detritus of lost funding and lost appeals when a facility was demolished prior to the FEMA inspection.

This appeals case in point comes from Hurricane Katrina.

"In August 2005, Hurricane Katrina caused major flooding and damage to the Mount Nebo Bible Baptist Church's (Applicant) facility, a building located at 1720 Flood Street, New Orleans, LA. The Applicant is a private non-profit (PNP) faith-based organization. At the time of the event, the facility was a 3,753 square foot (SF), two-story brick building, providing religious activities and programs, literacy programs, clothing distribution, food and nutrition programs, teen retreats, health and wellness programs, and operating as a homeless shelter. None of the potentially Public Assistance eligible services were licensed through the state of Louisiana. Through PW 20447, issued on October 24, 2012, FEMA determined the facility was ineligible for Public Assistance funding due to lack of documentation demonstrating that it was primarily used for eligible activities."[176]

First Appeal

"The Applicant submitted its first appeal to the Grantee on March 22, 2013. With the appeal, the Applicant asserted that Hurricane Katrina caused severe damage to its facility which resulted in the facility being condemned and demolished. The Applicant also asserted that, prior to the disaster, the facility operated as a place of worship and a community center. The Applicant stated that, of the 3,753 SF, 30 percent was used for worship services and 70 percent was used for community service activities."[177]

"In a letter, dated July 11, 2013, the FEMA Region VI Regional Administrator (RA) denied the appeal because the Applicant failed to provide documentation to clearly demonstrate its facility was primarily used for eligible activities . . . The RA also noted that, by demolishing the facility prior to applying for FEMA assistance, FEMA was unable to visually confirm the Applicant's claims that the facility and its contents were damaged beyond repair due to the disaster."[178]

This case is yet another appeal which failed for multiple reasons. In fact, many of these complex cases might make for an extended "expose" article in any one of dozens of monthly magazines. The catalogue of errors made and the list of failed omissions would be a compelling story.

Ineligible: Unimproved Land

Unimproved (raw) land is not eligible for FEMA funding considering that there are no improvements on the land, and unimproved land is also not eligible for debris removal costs, insofar as there are no threats to life safety, public safety, or improved property.

Land used for agricultural purposes is similarly ineligible for FEMA funding.

However, under programs from other Federal agencies, notably the U.S. Department of Agriculture and the Natural Resources Conservation Service (NRCS), there may be some funding available. However, any of those programs are far outside the scope of this book.

Limited Eligibility: Household Electric Meter Repair

"In rare cases, to reduce the number of survivors needing shelter, FEMA may provide limited PA funding to a SLTT government to repair residential electrical meters. To receive PA funding, the SLTT government must:

- Issue a finding of an immediate threat to safety due to loss of power caused by damaged meters or weather heads;
- Request participation in this program; and
- Receive FEMA approval for each identified property.

Only residential properties are eligible for this program. Commercial properties, including apartment complexes, are ineligible. If approved, the applicable SLTT government must:

- Obtain a signed right-of-entry from each residential property owner;
- Take reasonable measures to document any known insurance proceeds;
- Contract with licensed electricians to perform electrical meter repair;
- Coordinate the work with the property owner, the power company, and the contracted electricians; and
- Be responsible for payment of the non-Federal share.

Eligible work is limited to that associated with repairing damage to items otherwise installed and maintained by a homeowner's electrician, including the weather head, service cable, and meter socket.

FEMA generally provides PA funding up to $800 per meter per residential dwelling. This amount includes equipment, materials, labor, and inspection fees to restore the meter to current local codes. It is also inclusive of limited debris clearance when necessary to access the damaged meter or weather head. Removal and disposal of the debris is ineligible. Eligible work is limited to that completed within 30 days from the declaration date unless extended by FEMA.

FEMA does not provide PA funding for repair costs if it is not safe to restore power to the residence or if other impacts would restrict the dwelling from being habitable even after power restoration.

FEMA PA and IA *(Individual Assistance) staff* coordinate closely to ensure FEMA does not fund the same work under both programs."[179]

Limited Eligibility: Electrical Conductor Upgrade to Amperage Capacity above #2 ACSR (Aluminum Conductor Steel Reinforces)

"For electrical transmission or distribution systems, determining the disaster-related damage to some components, such as poles, guys, and cross-arms, can usually be accomplished by visual inspection."[180]

"However, determining the full extent of disaster-related damage to conductors is more challenging, particularly with older systems."[181]

"A conductor (e.g., the wire) is eligible for replacement when it is stretched beyond the point where it can be effectively repaired and re-sagged to meet appropriate clearances, sag, and tension, and to meet pre-disaster reliability."[182]

"The use of #2 Aluminum Conductor Steel Reinforced (ACSR) is considered a lower cost alternative to replacing conductor with equal or lesser amperage capacity such as copper weld conductor, hard and soft drawn copper wire, smaller ACSR, and Amerductor."[183]

"If the Applicant plans to upgrade its conductor to an amperage capacity above #2 ACSR, and there is no code or standard requiring the upgrade that meets the eligibility requirements discussed in B (sic), the additional upgrades are ineligible, and the Applicant must request an Improved Project."[184]

"If the damage does not meet the criteria for replacement, only the repair of the damaged line section(s) is eligible."[185]

As one might expect, the issue of utility repairs, electric, or other utilities are highly technical matters, and if the local agency is involved in this work, qualified engineers and other subject matter experts are de rigueur.

Changing Gears I: Colleges and Universities, Animals

Within the Public Assistance program, there are some eligibility regulations which apply specifically to non-profit Institutes of Higher Education, or as FEMA refers to them, IHE.

While the medical treatment and/or replacement of animals in general are an eligible expense for many different agencies other than institutes of higher education, there are some particular restrictions on those animals sometimes found in research facilities.

"Animals housed or exhibited in an eligible facility are eligible for replacement with the same number of comparable animals if they are:

- Injured to the extent they are no longer able to function for the intended purpose;
- Killed;
- A destroyed specimen; or
- A damaged specimen that is not recoverable.

The animal is ineligible for replacement if a comparable animal is not available for purchase, or the Applicant is unable to obtain a comparable one at a reasonable cost.

Eligible animals may include, but are not limited to:

- Police animals;
- Trained and certified rescue dogs;

- Animals in museums, zoos, or publicly owned nature centers;
- Fish in fish hatcheries;
- Taxidermy specimens (animals preserved and mounted in life like representations);
- Animals used by rehabilitation facilities as part of diagnosis or treatment; and
- Laboratory animals used in an active research program.

The replacement of animals on loan to an eligible facility at the time they are destroyed is eligible if the Applicant substantiates legal responsibility. Additionally, FEMA may provide PA funding for actions taken to save the lives of these animals as a Category B emergency protective measure.

Ineligible costs associated with replacing laboratory animals include:

- The cost of reproducing a new animal with all the characteristics of the lost animal to re-establish research;
- The cost of using a laboratory to perform a breeding program to advance benchmark stock to the genetic changes lost because of the incident;
- The cost associated with surgery required to replace a surgically altered animal; and
- The cost associated with the replacement of a laboratory animal when an animal of similar genetic characteristics can be obtained at no cost from other researchers or institutions.

If the Applicant requests, and the Recipient approves, other than in-kind and exact number of replacement animals, FEMA caps the Federal share based on the estimated in-kind replacement costs."[186]

There is additional information regarding the costs involved in the replacement of animals in the current edition of the Public Assistance Program and Policy Guide, Version 4, June 1, 2020, p. 174. It should be a consideration for research institutes to include disaster-specific language in the agreement any time that animals or research specimens are loaned or exchanged to satisfy the requirement for legal responsibility to enable FEMA reimbursement.

Reagents and Specimen Collections

Reagents and specimen collections live in an "Either Or" world. They may be eligible or not, depending on the following factors. Again, as with so many issues in the Public Assistance process, this aspect may benefit greatly from the assistance of a well-qualified consultant or another researcher who has successfully navigated these treacherous shoals.

"Reagents and specimen collections are eligible for replacement based on the following criteria.

The number of units of each reagent eligible for replacement is equal to the number lost OR to the number necessary to restore basic research activity, whichever is less.

FEMA reimburses the purchase price from commercial sources or other institutions, whichever is less.

The replacement of reagents that are so unique that they are considered an outcome of a research program is ineligible.

Replacing a representative, but not necessarily a whole portion, of a specimen collection may be eligible.

To be eligible for replacement, the specimen types should be available for purchase from commercial sources or other institutions and support an ongoing eligible educational or medical program."[187]

Ineligible: Relocation of College & University Athletic Fields & Student Unions

While student unions and athletic fields may be eligible for FEMA assistance to repair or replace when severely damaged, these same facilities are not eligible for costs associated with their relocation.[188]

Changing Gears II: Private Non-Profit Organizations

As sometimes-confusing as the Public Assistance program may be for local government agencies, it can be even more so for private non-profit organizations (PNP). Virtually all local government agencies are eligible applicants. The rules are much more convoluted for private non-profits.

"Only certain private non-profits are eligible Applicants. To be an eligible PNP Applicant, the PNP must show that it has:

- A ruling letter from the U.S. Internal Revenue Service that was in effect as of the declaration date and granted tax exemption under sections 501(c), (d), or (e) of the Internal Revenue Code; or
- Documentation from the State substantiating it is a non-revenue producing, nonprofit entity organized or doing business under State law.

If the organization is not required to obtain 501(c)(3) status or tax-exempt status under applicable State law, the organization must provide articles of association, bylaws, or other documents indicating that it is an organized entity, and a certification that it is compliant with Internal Revenue Code section 501(c)(3) and State law requirements.

Additionally . . . prior to determining whether the PNP is eligible, FEMA must first determine whether the PNP owns or operates an eligible facility.

For PNPs, an eligible facility is one that provides one of the services listed below (the declared incident must have damaged the facility):

- A facility that provides a critical service, which is defined as education, utility, emergency, or medical or
- A facility that provides a noncritical, but essential social service AND provides those services to the general public.
- PNP facilities generally meet the requirement of serving the general public if ALL of the following conditions are met.
  - Facility use is not limited to any of the following:
    - A certain number of individuals;
    - A defined group of individuals who have a financial interest in the facility, such as a condominium association;
    - Certain classes of individuals; or
    - An unreasonably restrictive geographical area, such as a neighborhood within a community;
- Facility access is not limited to a specific population (such as those with gates or other security systems intended to restrict public access); and
- Any membership fees meet all of the following criteria:

- Are nominal;
- Are waived when an individual can show inability to pay the fee;
- Are not of such magnitude to preclude use by a significant portion of the community; and
- Do not exceed what is appropriate based on other facilities used for similar services.

- Certain types of facilities, such as senior centers, that restrict access in a manner clearly related to the nature of the facility, are still considered to provide essential social services to the general public.

In cases where the facility provides multiple services, such as a community center, FEMA reviews additional items to determine the primary service that facility provides.

Facilities established or primarily used for political, athletic, recreational, vocational, or academic training, conferences, or similar activities are ineligible."[189]

And this is the easy part. For much more detail on private non-profits and their eligibility and eligibility restrictions, see the current edition of the Public Assistance Program and Policy Guide.

Eligible/Ineligible: Community Development Districts and Homeowners Associations

The last section in this chapter on Eligibility deals with Community Development Districts (CDDs), which are a unique quasi-governmental feature predominantly in Florida, and in many cases also covers homeowners associations (HOAs) nationwide.

"Community Development Districts are special districts in Florida, that finance, plan, establish, acquire, construct or reconstruct, operate, and maintain systems, facilities, and basic infrastructure within their respective jurisdictions. To be eligible, a Community Development District must own and be legally responsible for maintenance, and operation of an eligible facility that is open to and serves the general public."[190]

"When a facility maintained by a Community Development District is not open to the general public or does not provide a service to the general public, the facility is ineligible."[191] HOAs by their very nature are limited to a very defined and geographically restricted membership, only open to their homeowners.

The community development districts may provide and maintain domestic water supply; sewerage, wastewater management; roads, bridges, and culverts, street lighting; public transportation including buses, trolleys, transit shelters, ridesharing and parking facilities, environmental contamination response, conservation areas, parks and recreation, firefighting services, schools and related structures, security, trash disposal, and vector control.

Homeowners Associations, on the other hand, frequently do not provide the same wide range of utilities and services found in Florida's Community Development Districts.

However, for both HOAs and CDDs, the rub is, "Are they open to the General Public?" For the most part, these districts provide their services to a specific and restricted membership, i.e., the population which resides within the district.

"From September 4 to October 18, 2017, strong winds, heavy rains, and storm surge from Hurricane Irma caused damage throughout Florida. Heritage Bay Community Development District (Applicant) is a planned unit development or a community development district (CDD) in Collier County, Florida, that was established for the purpose of constructing, owning, and maintaining property or facilities. Lakes 30A and 30B are two stormwater retention ponds (Ponds) that were constructed as part of the Applicant's stormwater management system and water control facilities and permitted through the South Florida Water Management District (SFWMD)."[192]

"Hurricane Irma caused flooding and shoreline erosion that caused rip rap to wash away into the Ponds and damaged underlying geo-technical fabric. The Applicant requested Public Assistance (PA) through the Florida Division of Emergency Management (Grantee) for the cost of repairs, which consisted of the replacement of rip rap and the damaged geo-technical fabric. FEMA created Grants Manager Project 25524 and Project Worksheet (PW) 3780 to capture the requested repairs."[193]

"On June 11, 2019, FEMA issued a Determination Memorandum, finding the Ponds were not open to or did not provide a service to the general public and, pursuant to FEMA policy, were not eligible."[194]

"Heritage Bay Community Development District (Applicant) requested PA funding for repairs to its stormwater retention ponds (Ponds) with estimated costs totaling $1,670,069.05. FEMA created Grants Manager Project 25524 and Project Worksheet 3780 to capture the work. FEMA issued a Determination Memorandum concluding the Ponds were not eligible for assistance because, when a facility maintained by a Community Development District (CDD) is not open to the general public or does not provide a service to the general public, the facility is not eligible. The Applicant appealed, asserting the Ponds met both provisions of FEMA's policy. The FEMA Region IV Regional Administrator denied the first appeal. FEMA determined that the Applicant had not provided documentation to support its assertions, and found the Ponds were not open to the general public because the Applicant's community is closed via a gated guard house and did not provide a service to the general public because the Ponds had only an indirect impact on the regional stormwater management system. The Applicant submitted a second appeal asserting that the Ponds provide a service to the general public because they accept stormwater from adjacent watersheds and public parcels via designed control structures, thus providing flood control and water quality maintenance, for the benefit of the general public."[195]

"FEMA may provide PA funding to a local government for the repair of a public facility damaged by a major disaster. Local government includes special districts, such as a CDD. Eligible public facilities include any flood control, irrigation, reclamation, sewage treatment and collection, water supply and distribution, or watershed development. However, when a facility maintained by a CDD is not open to the general public and does not serve the general public, the facility is ineligible for assistance."[196]

"Regarding the provision that a facility maintained by a CDD must be open to the general public, FEMA originally determined that the Ponds were located within a gated community with controlled access, so they were not open to the general public and therefore ineligible. The Applicant appealed, stating that the Ponds were open to the general public if access was desired or required. However, access to Heritage Bay is through a gated guard house, and the gate system is enforced to provide access to Community members, not the general public. Therefore, the Ponds are not open to the general public. Under FEMA policy, when a facility maintained by a CDD is not open to the general public and does not serve the general public, the facility is ineligible for assistance. In this case, the Ponds do not satisfy the criterion of being open to the general public."[197]

In a similar case from Nebraska, this appeals case follows: "Beginning March 9, 2019, a severe winter storm and flooding submerged roads and other infrastructure and deposited debris and caused damage to SID#5-Timberwood's (Applicant)'s roads, culvert, and boat ramp. The Applicant, a Community Development District (CDD), requested Public Assistance (PA) to address claimed disaster damage. FEMA found the repairs were ineligible because other than 425 feet of a public entrance road, its roads, culvert, and boat ramp were not open to the general public, and it did not show that work was required as a result of the declared incident. The Applicant submitted first appeals, asserting its roads, culvert, and boat ramp were open to the general public, that it performed maintenance, and that the declared incident caused the claimed damages. The Applicant responded to a Request for Information from FEMA with information to support its claims. The FEMA Region VII Regional Administrator (RA) denied the first appeals, finding that although the Applicant met the FEMA definition of a CDD, facilities maintained by CDDs must be open to or provide services for the general public to be eligible for funding. FEMA also found the repairs to the 425 feet of public entrance road were ineligible because the Applicant did not show the damages were the result of the declared incident."[198]

So, we come to the end of the chapter on Eligibility in this book. If this chapter was massive, that is because the topic of eligibility is massive and always not clear-cut.

When searching the FEMA Appeals Database, in no less than 60% of the cases does the issue of 'eligibility' arise. When searching the Appeals Database there are at least 7 different ways to look up eligibility issues: 1) Eligibility; 2) eligible facility; 3) facility eligibility; 4) general eligibility; 5) general work eligibility; 6) ineligible damage, and 7) work eligibility.

Eligibility is the linchpin around which all FEMA assistance rotates. Eligibility is often very case-specific, and sometimes an almost-unobservable fact or two can turn the tables and make otherwise eligible damage ineligible.

Our Aging American Infrastructure

Aging infrastructure may be the axel around which the eligibility wheel spins. Across the country, we see signs of aging and deteriorating roads, bridges, culverts, and buildings. It is only natural that FEMA sees the same news reports as the public and makes an assumption that, absent strong documented proof, whatever was disaster-damaged was in previously less-than-good condition and therefore ineligible for funding. This is one of the great challenges of the Public Assistance program.

In this audit, which holds the current record for the most money ever questioned ($2.06 Billion), the auditors discuss the aging water infrastructure of New Orleans. "On August 29, 2005, and September 24, 2005, the President declared major disasters in Louisiana for damages from Hurricanes Katrina and Rita, respectively. The hurricanes caused levies to breach, flooding portions of the City and surrounding parishes. In 2006, FEMA began approving projects and cost estimates for the S&W (Sewerage and Water) Board to repair sewer and water systems and the City to repair the streets associated with the water system repairs, collectively known as infrastructure repairs. As of December 2015, FEMA had approved $784.9 million in infrastructure related projects."[199]

Results of Audit

"Although FEMA attributed the damages to the water distribution system directly to the disasters, we concluded that FEMA did not have sufficient evidence to support its decision. The demonstration of direct cause is necessary for work to be considered eligible for Federal disaster assistance funding, as required by the Robert T. Stafford Disaster Relief and Emergency Assistance Act (Stafford Act) and FEMA's own policies."[200]

"New Orleans' water, wastewater and drainage systems were very old and in poor condition prior to Hurricanes Katrina and Rita. In 2003, 30 percent of the water mains were close to 100 years old, about one third were between 40 and 100 years old, and only a third were newer than 40 years."[201] (Emphasis Added)

Final Thought on Eligibility

Even more frustrating, the local agency can have eligibility confirmed and then lose that eligibility because of some action taken or a failure to complete a critical step after the Project Worksheet has been approved.

Figure 26.1 A Chat GPT depiction of Eligibility Whack-a-Mole.

The concept of eligibility is in many respects much like playing a game of Whack-a-Mole. Just when it appears that a project's eligibility is secure, someone or something changes and eligibility is again in doubt. Eligibility is one of the most important yet fragile aspects of the Public Assistance process. As the great philosopher and baseball player Yogi Berra once said, "It ain't over til it's over." And that's how eligibility is: it can turn on a dime when the local agency doesn't pay attention to the details.

Notes

1 https://www.fema.gov/appeal/legal-responsibility-36
2 Ibid.
3 https://www.fema.gov/appeal/support-documentation-procurement
4 Ibid.
5 Ibid.
6 https://www.fema.gov/appeal/reasonable-costs-legal-responsibility
7 Public Assistance Program and Policy Guide, Version 4, June 1, 2020, FFP 104–009–2, p. 238.
8 Ibid.
9 https://www.fema.gov/appeal/uncollected-toll-road-revenue
10 https://www.fema.gov/appeal/increased-operating-costs
11 Ibid.
12 https://www.fema.gov/appeal/damage-caused-while-performing-eligible-work
13 Ibid.
14 Ibid.
15 https://www.fema.gov/appeal/emergency-response
16 Ibid.
17 https://www.fema.gov/appeal/speech-and-hearing-institute-building
18 Ibid.
19 Ibid.

20 https://www.fema.gov/appeal/direct-administrative-costs-and-management-costs-alternative-procedures
21 Ibid.
22 Title 44 of the Code of Federal Regulations, §206.226 Restoration of damaged facilities.
23 Public Assistance Program and Policy Guide, Version 4, June 1, 2020, FFP 104–009–2, p. 138.
24 Public Assistance Program and Policy Guide, Version 4, June 1, 2020, FFP 104–009–2, p. 135.
25 Ibid, p. 145.
26 Ibid.
27 https://www.fema.gov/appeal/restoration-power
28 Ibid.
29 https://www.fema.gov/appeal/safeco-field
30 Ibid.
31 Ibid.
32 https://www.fema.gov/appeal/application-procedures-2
33 https://www.fema.gov/appeal/damage-surveys-0
34 Ibid.
35 Ibid.
36 Ibid.
37 https://www.fema.gov/appeal/result-declared-incident-49
38 https://www.fema.gov/appeal/deferred-maintenance-predisaster-conditions
39 Ibid.
40 https://www.fema.gov/appeal/result-declared-incident-hazard-mitigation-
41 https://www.fema.gov/appeal/result-declared-incident-12
42 https://www.fema.gov/appeal/result-declared-incident
43 Ibid.
44 https://www.fema.gov/appeal/result-declared-incident-51
45 Ibid.
46 Subject to Interpretation by FEMA
47 Ibid.
48 https://www.fema.gov/appeal/result-declared-incident-hazard-mitigation-
49 Ibid.
50 Ibid.
51 Ibid.
52 https://www.fema.gov/appeal/appeals-other-federal-agency-duplication-benefits-ehp-other-compliance
53 Ibid.
54 Ibid.
55 Public Assistance Program and Policy Guide, Version 4, June 1, 2020, FFP 104–009–2, p. 176.
56 Ibid, p. 106.
57 https://www.fema.gov/appeal/debris-removal-construction-and-demolition-debris-removal-vegetative
58 Ibid.
59 Ibid.
60 Ibid.
61 Ibid.
62 Ibid.
63 Public Assistance Program and Policy Guide, Version 4, June 1, 2020, FFP 104–009–2, p. 101.
64 Ibid.
65 Ibid.
66 https://www.fema.gov/appeal/debris-removal-construction-and-demolition-0
67 Public Assistance Program and Policy Guide, Version 4, June 1, 2020, FFP 104–009–2, p. 129.
68 Ibid, p. 128.
69 https://www.fema.gov/appeal/demolition
70 Ibid.
71 https://www.fema.gov/appeal/force-account-labor-equipment-costsfinancial-accounting-reconciliation-section-705
72 Ibid.
73 https://www.fema.gov/appeal/pre-positioned-resources
74 Ibid.
75 Ibid.

76 Ibid.
77 Ibid.
78 https://www.fema.gov/appeal/ineligible-costs-appeals
79 Ibid.
80 Ibid.
81 Duplication of Benefits (42 USC 5155) Stafford Act § 312 (b) (2)
82 https://www.fema.gov/appeal/road-repair-2
83 Ibid.
84 Ibid.
85 https://www.fema.gov/appeal/ehp-and-other-compliance
86 Ibid.
87 Ibid.
88 Ibid.
89 Ibid.
90 https://www.fema.gov/appeal/operation-fixed-generators
91 Public Assistance Program and Policy Guide, Version 4, June 1, 2020, FFP 104–009–2, p. 72.
92 Ibid.
93 https://www.fema.gov/appeal/ineligible-costs-immediate-threat-0
94 Ibid.
95 Ibid.
96 Ibid.
97 Public Assistance Program and Policy Guide, Version 4, June 1, 2020, FFP 104–009–2, p. 114.
98 Ibid, p. 116.
99 DHS-OIG Audit DA-13–10, FEMA Should Recover $8.5 Million of Public Assistance Grant Funds Awarded to the City of Gulfport, Mississippi, for Debris Removal and Emergency Protective Measures – Hurricane Katrina, p. 7.
100 Public Assistance Program and Policy Guide, Version 4, June 1, 2020, FFP 104–009–2, p. 128.
101 Title 44 Code of Federal Regulations (CFR) § 206.226(k)(2)
102 DHS-OIG Audit DS-12–07, FEMA Public Assistance Grant Funds Awarded to City of Atascadero, CA, p. 7.
103 Ibid.
104 Ibid.
105 Ibid, p. 9.
106 https://www.fema.gov/appeal/request-public-assistance-private-nonprofit
107 Ibid.
108 Ibid.
109 Ibid.
110 Ibid.
111 Ibid.
112 Public Assistance Program and Policy Guide, Version 4, June 1, 2020, FFP 104–009–2, p. 161.
113 Ibid.
114 Ibid.
115 Ibid.
116 Ibid.
117 Ibid.
118 OIG-07–26: Audit of Federal Emergency Management Agency Public Assistance Grant Funding Awarded to the City of Richmond California After the Loma Prieta Earthquake, p. 5.
119 Public Assistance Program and Policy Guide, Version 4, June 1, 2020, FFP 104–009–2, p. 175.
120 Ibid, p. 140.
121 https://www.fema.gov/appeal/private-nonprofit-eligibility-3
122 Ibid.
123 Public Assistance Program and Policy Guide, Version 4, June 1, 2020, FFP 104–009–2, p. 171.
124 Ibid.
125 Ibid.
126 Ibid, p. 114.
127 Ibid.
128 Ibid.

129 https://www.fema.gov/appeal/tree-replacement
130 Ibid.
131 Public Assistance Program and Policy Guide, Version 4, June 1, 2020, FFP 104–009–2, p. 179.
132 https://www.fema.gov/appeal/steam-line-replacement
133 Ibid.
134 Ibid.
135 https://www.fema.gov/appeal/amesti-road
136 Ibid.
137 Ibid.
138 https://www.fema.gov/appeal/direct-result-disaster-legal-responsibility-private-entity
139 Ibid.
140 Ibid.
141 Ibid.
142 Public Assistance Program and Policy Guide, Version 4, June 1, 2020, FFP 104–009–2, p. 86.
143 Ibid.
144 Ibid, p. 87.
145 Ibid, p. 86.
146 https://www.fema.gov/appeal/mutual-aid-agreement
147 Ibid.
148 Ibid.
149 Ibid.
150 https://www.utsystem.edu/offices/risk-management/disaster-response-mutual-aid-plan
151 https://www.fema.gov/appeal/other-federal-agency-8
152 Ibid.
153 Ibid.
154 https://www.fema.gov/appeal/equipment-replacement-costs-improved-project
155 Public Assistance Program and Policy Guide, Version 4, June 1, 2020, FFP 104–009–2, p. 117.
156 Ibid.
157 Ibid, p. 136.
158 https://www.fema.gov/appeal/result-declared-incident-improved-project
159 Ibid.
160 Ibid.
161 Ibid.
162 Ibid.
163 https://www.fema.gov/appeal/change-scope-work-0
164 Ibid.
165 Ibid.
166 Ibid.
167 Ibid.
168 Public Assistance Program and Policy Guide, Version 4, June 1, 2020, FFP 104–009–2, pp. 117–118.
169 https://www.fema.gov/appeal/time-limitationsextensions-0
170 Ibid.
171 Ibid.
172 Ibid.
173 Ibid.
174 Public Assistance Program and Policy Guide, Version 4, June 1, 2020, FFP 104–009–2, p. 59.
175 Ibid.
176 https://www.fema.gov/appeal/facility-eligibility-1
177 Ibid.
178 Ibid.
179 Public Assistance Program and Policy Guide, Version 4, June 1, 2020, FFP 104–009–2, pp. 126–127.
180 Ibid, pp. 177–178.
181 Ibid.
182 Ibid.
183 Ibid.
184 Ibid.
185 Ibid.

186 Ibid, pp. 173–174.
187 Ibid, p. 173.
188 Ibid, p. 130.
189 Ibid, pp. 43–44.
190 Ibid, p. 43.
191 Ibid, p. 56.
192 https://www.fema.gov/appeal/public-interest
193 Ibid.
194 Ibid.
195 Ibid.
196 Ibid.
197 Ibid.
198 https://www.fema.gov/appeal/public-interest-result-declared-incident
199 DHS-OIG Audit 17–97-D, FEMA Should Disallow $2.04 Billion Approved for New Orleans Infrastructure Repairs, July 24, 2017, p. 1.
200 Ibid, p. 3.
201 Ibid.

27 Categorizing Projects

All FEMA's Project Worksheets, Small and Large

Even as the process of completing the Damage Inventory is beginning to wind down, staff will begin the process of formulating projects. Following are the classifications or groupings of all projects:

- Small Projects (total value less than $1,037,000)
- Large Projects (total value greater than $1,037,000)
- Improved Projects (may be small or large, but funding is capped)
- Alternate Projects (may also be small or large, but funding is capped)
- Alternative Procedures & Capped Funding (may be used for a different facility than that which was originally damaged, also capped funding)

Each of these project classifications has some advantages and disadvantages, and although some of this work will be done without input from the Finance Department, the Department should be aware of these advantages and disadvantages as the project formulation moves ahead.

Small Projects

FEMA has always had small and large projects. When I began work in emergency management, the small project threshold was approximately $35,000 with a minimum of $1,000. Today (2024), the small project threshold is $1,037,000, with a minimum project cost of $3,900. This is both good and bad, depending on the circumstances. The current small project limit of $1,037,000 jumped in August of 2022 from the mid-$135,000 range to the amount of $1,037,000. These numbers will most likely change again on October 1 of 2024, and then each year thereafter.

A small projects are funded on estimated costs, and if there is a cost overrun, this is addressed at the closeout for all of an agency's small projects. This process will be addressed in Chapter 42: The Net Small Project Overrun, or NSPO.

A primary advantage of small projects, from the local agency perspective, is that the project is funded upfront, as opposed to a large project, which is funded by a pay-as-you-go methodology. This helps the local agency's cash flow position because the funds are deposited and drawn down as a project is completed. Borrowing of construction funds will be minimized for the local agency.

However, if we take a hypothetical set of 10 Project Worksheets with a nominal value of $1,000,000, the total package of Project Worksheets is $10,000,000. At close-out, if the agency has violated some regulation(s) in completing the projects, the entire $10,000,000 may be at risk of deobligation. The resetting of the small project threshold from $135,000 to $1,037,000 may be

DOI: 10.4324/9781003487869-32

a good thing or it may be another disaster, all depending on how well the local agency understands the FEMA regulations and abides by them.

In a perfect world, FEMA would like to have 95% of all projects written to be small projects. Historically, small Project Worksheets accounted for nearly 90% of all Project Worksheets written, but these same Project Worksheets accounted for less than 10% of all funds dispersed for disaster recovery. So, in the past local agencies processed a lot of paper for not so much money. However, with the small project limit now raised to $1,037,000 this data may change.

Another difference between small and large projects is that small projects generally do not have "versions" as do large projects. "Subsequent versions of PWs are not normally permitted for small projects, unless there is a considerable change in the Scope of Work."[1] This statement notwithstanding, all desired changes in the scope of work must be submitted to and approved by FEMA before the work is started in all cases.

Large Projects

Large projects are those projects which exceed $1,037,000.

A cautionary note: For a small project with a high net value that approaches the large project threshold, caution must be exercised if there are changes in the scope of work or an approved work order change moves the project from the small project classification to a large project. This will potentially affect the handling of the project and should be discussed with both the state and FEMA at the earliest possible moment to avoid serious unforeseen problems with this transition.

Case Study: Change from Small to Large Project Status

We have previously examined this case in Chapter 9: Procurement. Once again, here is another multi-faceted appeals case "In the spring and summer of 2011, warm temperatures caused significant runoff and flooding in the state of South Dakota following a winter with above-normal snowfall. On May 13, 2011, the President declared a major disaster for the state (FEMA-1984-DR-SD), with an incident period of March 11 to July 22, 2011."[2]

"The flooding caused erosion and degradation of the sanitary sewer system operated by the City of Pierre (*South Dakota*) (Applicant). The sewer system delivers sewage to the Applicant's wastewater treatment plant. A 72-foot long section of a 10-inch diameter clay sanitary sewer pipe on Missouri Avenue failed, creating a sinkhole that began developing during the disaster incident period. The sinkhole stretched due east along the sewer line (the 'East Line' to Pierre Street) from a manhole that serves as a connection point between additional sewer lines and a lift station. The Applicant used contract services, force account labor, and force account equipment to address resulting sewer backups, bypass pumping, and perform temporary repairs to the sinkhole."[3]

"The Applicant received two bids from contractors to perform permanent repairs to the sinkhole and remove and replace the sewer line, one bid for $86,000.00 and another for $160,400.00. On October 25, 2011, the Applicant awarded a contract to the lower bidder, Morris, Inc. (the 'Contractor')."[4]

"On October 26, 2011, the Applicant issued a notice to proceed to the Contractor. During excavation and repair and after the pipe was exposed, additional damage was discovered on two additional sewer lines and the manhole. On November 29, 2011, a change order was issued for work to include: (1) removal of the manhole and placement of a concrete base under the replacement manhole, (2) excavation and removal of a damaged 12-inch line to the lift station to the north (the 'North Line' to lift station), (3) excavation and removal of a damaged 10-inch line flowing into the manhole from the west and installation of a new line (the 'West Line' to Fort Street), and

(4) installation of sheet piling to protect structures and laborers. The change order amounted to $237,244.86."[5]

In this case, the Project Worksheet amount went from well under the small project threshold at that time to nearly $200,000 over the small project threshold. One of the most serious complications was that the procurement, which was appropriate for a small project, became a major stumbling block because of the cost increase. In this particular case, because of the onset of winter, the construction work could not be done under freezing conditions, and the agency was granted a waiver. This, however, was a very rare exception to the rules.

This case is just one of many in the Appeals Database where there are multiple issues, layered one upon another. The analysis of this complex case runs 18 pages.

Changes to Large Project Worksheets

"Subsequent versions are written to modify a Project Worksheet for four reasons.

- To modify the Scope of Work
- To add damaged elements
- To change the Period of Performance (time extensions)
- To modify the cost."[6]

The important thing with a request for a change in a Project Worksheet is that it will require extensive documentation no matter which of these four reasons legitimately justify the changes requested. Further, <u>FEMA must be notified at the first available opportunity that a change is requested.</u> To wait until the completion of the project to make these notifications is tantamount to financial suicide. In the scores of appeals cases I have reviewed, the local agency frequently alleges in the appeal that they were told to "wait until the project is finished and then we'll fix everything at close-out." This is WRONG, WRONG, and more WRONG. Never wait until the completion of a project to pop these surprises on FEMA. It will always go badly. If a FEMA person suggests waiting to the end to finish up these matters, ignore them; they are not giving you good advice.

Changed Scope of Work: Total Deobligation of $267,785

"From May 5, 2015, through June 22, 2015, the State of Oklahoma was impacted by severe storms, straight-line winds, and flooding. The City of Ardmore (Applicant) requested reimbursement under FEMA's Public Assistance (PA) program for replacement and repair of culverts, roads, curbs, and gutters at three sites. FEMA developed Project Worksheet (PW) 878 with an estimated cost of $130,259.81 and a scope of work (SOW) to restore the damaged facilities to their predisaster condition. FEMA reviewed the project for Environmental and Historic Preservation (EHP) compliance, and based on the approved SOW, determined the project was statutorily excluded from National Environmental Policy Act (NEPA) review. The EHP review included conditions that stated, 'any change to the approved SOW will require re-evaluation for compliance with NEPA and other [EHP] laws and executive orders' and, 'failure to comply with these conditions may jeopardize federal assistance[,] including funding.'"[7]

"On April 29, 2019, the Oklahoma Department of Emergency Management and Homeland Security (Recipient) requested that FEMA close out the large project with final reported costs of $267,785.39 in completed work, which represented a $137,525.58 cost overrun. The closeout package included an April 24, 2019 letter from the Applicant that stated that final costs were higher than estimated because the damage was found to be more extensive than originally identified and the more modest repairs in the original scope proved to be unfeasible."[8]

"In a letter dated July 12, 2022, FEMA transmitted a Determination Memorandum to the Applicant denying the full amount of $267,785.39. FEMA found that the Applicant had changed the SOW at Sites 1 and 3 without prior approval from FEMA; therefore, the work did not comply with PA regulations and policy.[9]

"In a first appeal letter dated September 15, 2022, the Applicant claimed that it was not possible to identify the full extent of the damage until it started the repair work; and the PW's SOW did not reflect the full scope of damages and the necessary repairs. Additionally, the Applicant claimed that, throughout the project, it worked closely with FEMA field staff who were fully aware of the changes to the SOW and the need for them. The Applicant claimed that FEMA staff did not express concerns about its failing to request formal approval for a SOW change and did not believe a new EHP review was necessary. The Applicant stated that any work performed was with the overt, direct, and continuous approval of FEMA personnel and it did not have specific guidance stating it needed FEMA's written concurrence to proceed with the work."[10] (Emphasis Added) In this case, because the local agency unilaterally changed the scope of work, the entire project was deobligated.

Where the Complications Set In

So far, so good. Neither small nor large projects are without potential complications of all sorts, but they are almost always less complicated than improved projects or alternate projects.

The basic premise of FEMA's Public Assistance program is to assist local government agencies to restore their damaged facilities and infrastructure to their pre-disaster use and function, and no more.

Improved Projects

An improved project, on the other hand, requests FEMA funding to improve a facility or infrastructure beyond what existed immediately prior to the disaster. In some cases this is a simple matter, but in other cases it is a hot mess.

First, FEMA funding is capped at the estimate to restore the facility to its prior condition. Any costs beyond that baseline are the responsibility of the local agency, even when there are legitimate reasons for a change in the scope of work.

Second, if the improved project in any way changes the "footprint" of the building or disturbs the ground in any manner, then the specter of historic and environmental issues must be dealt with, which almost always will cause project delays and increased costs, which were already capped.

Even if there is a legitimate reason for a change in the scope of work, the local agency is completely responsible for proving to FEMA which costs were part of the original project scope, and which costs may be related to the improvements.

An example of an improved project might be the addition of another bay to the disaster-damaged fire station headquarters to house a new piece of equipment. This will at a minimum require ground disturbance, which will trigger an environmental review of one level or another. If the fire headquarters is more than 50 years old, this will also trigger a historic review as well.

Improved projects require the advance approval of the state as the recipient. Alternate projects, on the other hand, require the advance approval of FEMA.

Alternate Projects

In some cases, when a facility or infrastructure is badly damaged, it may set off a round of thought-ful analysis: Do we really need this facility or bridge in this location at this time? This will hope-fully generate a careful and well-thought-out analysis of how the community might be rebuilt to be better than before. However, the analysis may fall short when evaluating the potential financial complications accompanying such a decision.

One of the first things that needs to be considered is that the funding for an alternate project will be based upon the costs to restore the facility to its pre-disaster condition, and then that amount is reduced by 10%. So right out of the gate, the local agency is "paying" a premium for the privilege of creating an alternate project.

A favorite example of an alternate project comes out of the Pacific Northwest, where a flood washed away four single-lane bridges over a river. The alternate project proposal was to build a new two-lane bridge at a median position from where the four bridges previously stood. Per FEMA regulations, the cost to build the new two-lane bridge would be based on the costs to restore the former four single-lane bridges. All is well so far. Hypothetically, however, if at the new site pre-liminary excavations discovered a previously unknown site of contaminated soil or Native Ameri-can artifacts were discovered, the project would have to come to a screeching halt while these issues are resolved, and the costs still remain capped.

In some cases where either an improved project or an alternate project is being considered, it may be both more cost-effective and a better use of time to complete a project as a regular small or large project and then, when the project is complete and the FEMA file is closed, to make the contemplated changes to better serve the public needs.

Alternative Procedures and Capped Funding

In January of 2013, Congress adopted and the President signed into law the Sandy Recovery Improvement Act (SRIA). In the introduction, the following text appears: "The law identifies these goals for the procedures:

- Reducing the costs to the Federal Government of providing public assistance.
- Increasing flexibility in the administration of such assistance.
- Expediting the provision of assistance to a state, tribal or local government, or nonprofit owner or operator of a private nonprofit facility.
- Providing financial incentives and disincentives for timely and cost-effective completion of projects with such assistance." (Emphasis Added)

I believe that any discussion of Alternative Procedures should always bear in mind the primary goal of the legislation, that of reducing the costs of the Public Assistance program to the Federal government. While in some cases there may be benefits to local agencies, the primary goal is sav-ing the Federal government money. While saving Federal money is a laudable goal, it is not always in the best direct interests of disaster-afflicted local governments.

The Alternative Procedures do not have universal application to the Public Assistance program. Alternative procedures are available for debris clearance and for permanent-work large projects with a value over $1,037,000. Category B, Emergency Protective Measures, and small projects are not included in the law.

Let us then address the key points for Alternative Procedures for large projects:

1) The grants are based on fixed estimates. FEMA and the local agency agree on a set amount of funding based upon the damages incurred and the work necessary to restore the facility,

including infrastructure. Should the project run over the agreed-upon estimate, the overruns will be paid by the local agency. In essence, this is a bet placed against the accuracy of the agreed-upon estimate.

2) Under the Alternative Procedures, there is no 10% reduction of funding as there would normally be for an ordinary alternate project. The local agency receives 100% of the obligated funds. This is clearly a plus, particularly if the agreed-upon estimate is spot-on accurate.

3) The local agency is allowed to create a grouping of different projects under a single Alternative Procedures grant.

4) When there is an excess of funds, i.e., construction costs are less than the agreed-upon estimate, the local agency may use the excess funds for certain limited purposes, for mitigation activities and other activities to improve future Public Assistance operations or planning, within a defined timeframe.

5) For very large projects over $5,000,000, the local agency can request an independent expert panel to validate, based on applicable regulations and policies, the Administrator's or certified cost estimate prepared by the subrecipient's professionally licensed engineers.

Use of Excess Funds

Regarding item number 4, just because there is a provision in the regulation for the use of excess funds on these Alternative Procedures projects, it does not necessarily follow that there will always, or even ever, mean that such funds will exist. FEMA constantly strives to limit the obligated funding to the bare minimum (in its estimation) necessary to restore a facility to its pre-disaster use and function. This is like planning to spend money from a winning lottery ticket before the numbers are drawn. It is definitely an enticement, but not a very statistically valid one.

From the perspective of a local government agency, obtaining a crystal-clear picture of the rules and regulations of the Alternative Procedures is a bit of a challenge, because information on the Alternative Procedures is scattered through 20 different sections of the Public Assistance Program and Policy Guide in the 2020 edition.

"Any excess funds remaining after the approved SOW is complete may be used for cost effective activities that reduce the risk of future damage, hardship, or suffering from a major disaster, and activities that improve future PA operations or planning. The Applicant must submit a proposed SOW for use of any excess funds, along with a project timeline to the Recipient within 90 days of completing its last Alternative Procedures Project. The Recipient must forward the request to FEMA within 180 days of date the last Alternative Procedures Project was completed. FEMA evaluates the proposed use of excess funds for reasonableness to ensure prudent use of funds.

FEMA also evaluates the submitted project timeline and approves an appropriate deadline for work completion, not to exceed the overall disaster period of performance."[11]

"FEMA will initiate closure of the original subaward and then prepare a new subaward to document the use of the eligible excess funds and conduct all required reviews prior to obligation. As appropriate, requirements to obtain-and-maintain insurance apply to work funded with excess funds."[12] The regulations do not specify a "period of performance" for the use of any excess funds, but there may be such a limitation included when FEMA approves the plan for the use of funds.

Important Note

"FEMA does not consider appeals on Alternative Procedures Permanent Work Projects . . . unless it is related to a cost adjustment made by FEMA after the Fixed-Cost Offer is accepted (i.e., related to insurance, noncompliance, or an audit). Any disagreement on damage, SOW (*Scope of Work*), or cost must be resolved prior to accepting the fixed-cost offer. Additionally, FEMA does not consider appeals on time extension denials for Alternative Procedures Projects."[13]

Obtain and Maintain Insurance Applies

Virtually all other Public Assistance program requirements still remain in force including but not limited to environmental and historic issues, procurement which is compliant with Title 2 of the Code of Federal Regulations, and the obtain and maintain requirement for insurance. Furthermore, the insurance obtain and maintain requirement also applies to the use of excess funds, should there be any.

Mitigation Funds Are Available

Under this program, it is possible to also get mitigation funds as a part of the grant. However, a failure to complete the mitigation work will result in a deobligation of those funds.

Use of Alternative Procedures Funds

When the Alternative Procedures project is complete, and if there are excess funds, the local agency must file a plan with FEMA designating the use of those funds for eligible purposes.

This chapter does not cover all the details regarding Alternative Procedures projects. For more information refer to the Public Assistance Program and Policy Guide, Version 4, June 1, 2020, FFP

Table 27.1 Use of Alternative Procedures Funds

Type of Work or Cost: (all work or costs listed must otherwise be eligible for PA)	Use of Fixed-Cost Funds	Use of Excess Funds
Restoration of disaster-damaged facilities and equipment	Eligible	Eligible
Alternate Projects (e.g., purchasing equipment, constructing new facilities, improvements to undamaged facilities such as shelters and emergency operation centers) in declared areas	Eligible	Eligible
Cost-effective hazard mitigation measures for undamaged facilities	**Ineligible**	Eligible
Covering future insurance premiums, including meeting obtain and maintain (O&M) insurance requirements, on damaged or undamaged facilities	**Ineligible**	Eligible
Conducting or participating in training for response or recovery activities, including Federal grants management or procurement courses	**Ineligible**	Eligible
Planning for future disaster response and recovery operations, such as developing or updating plans (e.g., debris management plans, hazard mitigation plans, pre-disaster recovery plans, emergency management plans), integrating these plans into other plans, preparedness activities, exercises, and outreach	**Ineligible**	Eligible
Salaries for PA or emergency management staff. This may include but is not limited to staff performing PA award or subaward administration, monitoring, and closeout activities for other PA disaster awards, and staff developing or updating disaster plans	**Ineligible**	Eligible
All the following are <u>ineligible</u> expenses for either Fixed Fund use or Excess Fund use: paying down debts, covering operating expenses, covering budget shortfalls, covering the non-federal cost share of FEMA projects or other federal awards, work on facilities that are ineligible due to a failure to meet previous obtain and maintain insurance requirements		

104–009–2 and the Public Assistance Alternative Procedures Pilot Program Guide for Permanent Work (Version 3) March 29, 2016, or the current version.

The following audit is from the files of the Department of Homeland Security, Office of the Inspector General and summarizes what might go wrong with an Alternative Procedures project when the local agency has what might appear to be a windfall grant. For perspective, this is a rural community of less than 7,000 population.

"On April 28, 2014, a treacherous EF-4 tornado tore a path through the City of Louisville, Mississippi, killing 10 people. The powerful storm was measured at 34 miles long, up to 3/4 miles wide, with wind speeds up to 185 mph. The City suffered catastrophic damages to residential neighborhoods, infrastructure, businesses, and other public facilities."[14]

"From the 1960s until 2009, Georgia Pacific operated a plywood facility in the City. Upon closure of the Georgia Pacific facility, the City purchased the property, including the main plywood factory building and all the supporting exterior facilities. On April 29, 2013, the City leased the facility to a for-profit entity. The lease places the responsibility for facility repairs on the City."[15]

"The Tornado destroyed the City-owned plywood facility, which was weeks away from opening. The City expected the plywood facility to provide over 400 new jobs to the community; therefore, the economic impact of losing it could have been devastating. On April 30, 2014, the President issued a major disaster declaration for certain areas in Mississippi for damages resulting from severe storms, tornadoes, and flooding during the period of April 28, 2014, through May 3, 2014."[16]

"FEMA neglected to prepare a $47.3 million project worksheet for the City's new scope of work to redesign the new plywood facility and acquire/replace/repair 11 additional facilities in accordance with the PAAP Program. As a result, the project remains unauthorized and might not comply with Federal environmental and historic preservation laws, which places the City's Federal funding in jeopardy."[17]

"For estimating replacement costs, FEMA considered the factory and each of its eight auxiliary buildings to be separate sites as follows:

Site 1: Exterior site amenities
Site 2: Main plywood factory building
Site 3: Open metal shed
Site 4: A-frame shed
Site 5: Regenerative thermal oxidizer control shed
Site 6: Safety outbuilding
Site 7: Electrostatic precipitator
Site 8: Guard house
Site 9: Concrete log conditioning kiln building

"While pre-disaster function, design, capacity, and condition determine the amount of FEMA eligible funding, a subgrantee may use this funding to complete a project with a different function, design, or capacity. FEMA refers to such a project as an alternate project. Thus, with FEMA's approval, the City would be eligible to use the $47.3 million in funds toward an alternate project without the reduction in funding required under the standard alternate project procedures.

"Subsequently, the City chose to participate in the PAAP Program and use the eligible funds toward an alternate project. The PAAP Program allows consolidating facilities into a single project with no requirement to build to predisaster function, design, or capacity. On January 27, 2015, the

City submitted its request for a consolidated fixed estimate subgrant to FEMA and its proposed scope of work, which included the following 12 projects:

Project 1: Plywood and Veneer Plant
Project 2: City Street Repairs
Project 3: Memorial Park Cemetery Enhancements
Project 4: Equipment Purchases
Project 5: Property Acquisitions
Project 6: Traffic Signal Purchase and Installation
Project 7: Ivy Park Renovation, Enhancement Expansion
Project 8: Old Armory Roof Repair
Project 9: Sidewalk Repairs
Project 10: City-owned Railroad Reconstruction/Repair
Project 11: Drainage Improvements
Project 12: Municipal Arts Center Renovation"[18]

This is from the first audit, issued in the middle of August 2016. Six weeks later, the Inspector General issued a second audit of the same community and recommended that FEMA disallow $25.4 million dollars, largely for violations of Federal Procurement regulations.

The complication with improved projects, alternate projects, and alternative procedures projects is that no one can see behind the magic screen. We cannot know what problems may exist, and in almost every case, the funding is capped. If the project was already desperately needed, and the disaster provided the "perfect" opportunity to resolve the problem, maybe, but stock up on antacids if the local agency's risk tolerance is low.

My flat-out recommendation is, if possible, to avoid requesting either an improved or alternate project, and completely avoid alternate procedures projects with capped funding. Unless the agency has staff (or hired consultants) with extensive experience in improved or alternate projects, these are relatively high-risk endeavors which may cost the agency much more than any initial estimate may predict, and in many cases will significantly delay the completion of the project, at any cost.

Small Project Validation

Small Project Worksheets may be prepared by the local agency, possibly in some cases by the state, or by FEMA. If the local agency prepares its own small projects, then FEMA will validate those projects based on established criteria.

FEMA will evaluate small projects to ensure that the estimate:

- Is prepared by a licensed Professional Engineer or other estimating professional, such as a licensed architect or certified professional cost estimator who certifies that the estimate was prepared in accordance with industry standards;
- Includes certification that the estimated cost directly corresponds to the repair of the agreed-upon damage;
- Is based on unit costs for each component of the scope of work (SOW) and not a lump sum amount; and
- Contains a level of detail sufficient for FEMA to validate that all components correspond with the agreed-upon SOW.

FEMA will also review the scope of work and cost estimate to verify only eligible items are included:

- All scope of work items in the cost estimate are required based on the agreed-upon damage description and dimensions.
- If the scope of work included ineligible items, FEMA may remove the ineligible components from the estimate.
- If the scope of work included ineligible items, FEMA may return the estimate to the Applicant to revise.

While an option for local agencies, preparation of small projects may be better left to estimating or engineering professionals. As previously mentioned in Chapter 9: Insurance, the local agency may wish to purchase a policy rider which will provide professional damage and cost estimating services paid for through an insurance policy.

For a more detailed look at small project validation, see the current edition of the Public Assistance Program and Policy Guide, or the Validation of Small Projects, 9570.6 SOP, September 1999.

Period of Performance (POP)

As previously stated in this book, all timelines are critical within the Public Assistance program, and all projects, once approved, have a specified Period of Performance or POP. Should a project be running behind schedule, it is absolutely imperative that a formal time extension be requested from either the state (first extension) or FEMA (subsequent extensions), with a full explanation of the extenuating circumstances which warrant the extension.

Work done after the Period of Performance has expired will no longer be eligible for funding. The POP also governs the timeline for requesting Direct Administrative Costs and alternate use of excess funds when those funds are available.

"On October 7, 2017, Hurricane Nate impacted Escambia and Santa Rosa counties in Florida with storm surge and rainfall causing flooding and other damage. The President signed an emergency declaration on October 8, 2017, with an incident period of October 7-11, 2017. On May 22, 2018, the Florida Division of Emergency Management (Grantee) elected to participate in the Public Assistance Alternative Procedures for Direct Administrative Costs (PAAP-DAC) program for the disaster. FEMA obligated PW 4, a category B project for emergency protective measures, in the amount of $426,708.30. The period of performance (POP) for PW 4 ended on October 8, 2018. On July 30, 2018, FEMA obligated Project Worksheet (PW) 5, a category Z project, to reimburse DAC associated with PW 4 in the amount of $21,420.45. On August 20, 2019, the Grantee requested FEMA deobligate $20,348.25 from PW 5 and allow the Grantee to use the funds in accordance with PAAP-DAC policy on "use of excess funds." FEMA wrote PW 7 on October 4, 2019 to document this request. On April 30, 2020, FEMA issued a Determination Memorandum denying the Grantee's request as untimely. FEMA found that the deadline to submit the request was April 6, 2019, 180 days after the latest period of performance (POP) for PW 4, and the Grantee made its request on August 20, 2019."[19]

First Appeal

"The Grantee submitted its first appeal on July 21, 2020, contending that FEMA erred in applying the POP of PW 4 to calculate the deadline to submit its request to reallocate excess DAC. Instead, the Grantee argues that FEMA should have applied the POP of PW 5, its category Z DAC project, to calculate the request. The Grantee asserts that PAAP-DAC Policy Version 1.1 treats Category Z projects the same as Category A-G projects, and that because the POP end date for PW 5 was October 8, 2019, its request was timely. FEMA denied the appeal on May 3, 2021. FEMA found that under the PAAP-DAC Policy Version 1.1, the applicable POP for PW 5 (the Category Z DAC project) should equal that of the latest Category A-G project, PW 4. FEMA stated that as a result, the deadline for the Grantee to submit its request was April 6, 2019, and the request was untimely."[20]

"The Grantee opted into PAAP-DAC for this disaster and had only one Category A-G PW, PW 4. The POP for PW 4 ended on October 8, 2018. This means April 6, 2019, 180 days later, was the deadline for submitting a request to use excess DAC funds. The PAAP-DAC policy defines the POP for PW 5, the DAC PW, as equal to the latest Category A-G PW POP (PW 4), or April 6, 2019. The Grantee submitted its request to use excess DAC funds on August 20, 2019, after the deadline had passed."[21]

The Public Assistance program is a game of hardball, serious money is involved, and no quarter is given, except on extremely rare occasions. This is one reason why local agencies must quickly prioritize their projects and do what is necessary within its fiscal constraints to meet these important deadlines.

Notes

1 FEMA, Project Worksheet Development Guide, July 2008.
2 https://www.fema.gov/appeal/scope-work-20
3 Ibid.
4 Ibid.
5 Ibid.
6 Project Worksheet Development Guide, July 2008, p. 61.
7 https://www.fema.gov/appeal/change-scope-work-ehp-and-other-compliance
8 Ibid.
9 Ibid.
10 Ibid.
11 Public Assistance Program and Policy Guide, Version 4, June 1, 2020, FFP 104–009–2, p. 165.
12 Public Assistance Alternative Procedures Pilot Program Guide for Permanent Work (Version 3) March 29, 2016, p. 13.
13 Public Assistance Program and Policy Guide, Version 4, June 1, 2020, FFP 104–009–2, p. 41.
14 DHS-OIG Audit: OIG-16–119-D: FEMA Improperly Awarded $47.3 Million to the City of Louisville, Mississippi, August 16, 2016, p. 2.
15 Ibid.
16 Ibid.
17 Ibid, p. 3.
18 Ibid, p. 4.
19 https://www.fema.gov/appeal/direct-administrative-costs-and-management-costs-alternative-procedures
20 Ibid.
21 Ibid.

28 Beginning the Paperwork Process

When a disaster occurs or is on the immediate horizon, operations within the local government agency will begin to rapidly shift into high gear as field emergency workers (law enforcement, fire fighters, emergency medical personnel, public works, roads & bridges, etc.) begin to prepare or in some cases immediately respond to incidents. These are the most visible aspects of the local government disaster response.

At the same time, the administrative side of the local agency should also be quickly preparing for the onslaught of recordkeeping, purchasing of disaster supplies, and opening up and staffing the Emergency Operation Center, and in some cases setting up Department Operations Centers as needed.

In events like hurricanes, riverine flooding, and severe winter storms, weather forecasters will have provided hours if not days of advance warning, including estimates of how severe the event will likely be.

First Steps for Disaster Cost Recovery

As addressed earlier in the book, the very first step is to issue a local proclamation of disaster. When properly done, this will provide information regarding the nature of the disaster, along with some preliminary or estimated damage numbers, the general economic conditions of the city or county, and of course, a request for outside assistance from the state and/or Federal government.

The proclamation will help to define which administrative actions may need to be taken next:

- If time permits before the disaster hits, refer to the Pre-Season Disaster Financial Preparation Checklist to remind employees of how important they are in enabling the city or county to recover its disaster costs. (See Form 24 in the Appendix)
- Which employees need to report to or remain at work?
- Which employees are to remain at home or return there directly?
- Advise all employees of how emergency "report-to-work" communications will be handled, i.e., local broadcast media, social media, text messages, etc.
- For those employees remaining on duty provide them with a briefing and the forms for properly tracking their time for disaster response activities. Further remind them that if they only work part of a shift on disaster activities, their records need to reflect, hour-by-hour, which disaster activities they worked on and what work may have been non-disaster related.
- What, if any, provisions for disaster pay will be implemented? (See Chapters 2 and 3 for information regarding disaster pay policies.)
- What provisions may need to be made for on-duty employee feeding? (See Chapters 2 and 3 for information regarding disaster feeding policies.)

DOI: 10.4324/9781003487869-33

- If possible, determine the potential need for various types of Mutual Aid other than law enforcement, firefighting, and/or public works, i.e., animal control officer Mutual Aid, Building & Safety inspector Mutual Aid, etc.
- Determine the need for and pre-organize individual volunteer efforts and volunteer organizations active in disasters (VOADs).
- Make sure that all field operating departments have enough of the necessary forms with which to document their labor, equipment, and the materials used. Fire and Law usually do a pretty good job with this. *However, I have also seen some very egregious errors in recordkeeping done by firefighters and police officers* that resulted in or would have resulted in deobligation for their time worked.
- Review the current budget in preparation for requests for unbudgeted disaster materials and supplies which will be needed in the coming days and weeks.
- Open the necessary forms and processes for tracking the damages. Although Building & Safety may have an existing protocol for tracking and reporting on damage, Finance still has its own separate role to play once it receives the raw data from Building & Safety.
- The same holds true for all other departments performing damage inspections: Roads & Bridges, Utilities, Facilities, disaster debris, etc. They each should have their own inspection forms, but Finance will still need to extract the pertinent data from each report and integrate that information into the overall damage assessment report.
- If the agency has a hidden "Disaster Donations" web page, arrange for that information to be activated on the city or county's home page.
- These are a sampling of pre-disaster tasks to be considered. Depending on a host of factors, i.e., intensity and full range of the damages suffered; the pre-disaster financial status of the local agency; and the range of services normally provided by the local agency, there may be more pre-event steps to be taken by the local agency for complete preparations.

All these items will have some bearing on the costs incurred by the local agency, although some of them will not be set up or managed by the Emergency Operations Center, Finance & Administration Section, or the Disaster Cost Recovery team.

Once these items have been addressed to the degree necessary, it's time to await the initial damage reports.

To Keep Records or Not?

If it appears likely that this will be a major disaster, and this threshold may vary from community to community depending on the severity of the disaster and the ability of the local agencies to timely and effectively respond, the next-higher level of government will issue either a county-wide disaster proclamation or a gubernatorial disaster proclamation.

However, in the time elapsed between an event occurrence and the local disaster proclamation, or between the local proclamation and the county or state proclamation, local emergency forces will be in a recordkeeping state of limbo. Should the field forces document their time to comply with FEMA requirements or not?

In some cases, a higher level of government may not immediately make a proclamation, and as we saw in Chapter 6, the average time between a disaster occurring and the signing of the Presidential disaster declaration for Federal Fiscal Years 2020 and 2021 was 62 days. This is a long time to be in disaster response mode without proper recordkeeping. If disaster response work is carried out without good documentation, those costs will probably be forever lost.

Therefore, the best practice is to keep comprehensive records for all response activities from the very first response calls, even if and when there is not yet a disaster proclamation. In this way, the local agency can maximize its disaster cost recovery. In any case, even if the present event is not Presidentially declared, the habit of properly documenting the employee time spent, equipment, and materials used is excellent practice for the real deal when it may occur.

The Applicant's Briefing

Once the governor has made the request for a Presidential disaster declaration and that declaration has been signed, the wheels of big government will slowly start spinning. After a few days, perhaps a week or more after the Presidential declaration has been signed, the state will hold the Applicant's Briefing. This is the first formal step in the Public Assistance process.

This (usually) in-person meeting is often held on a county-by-county basis, although these days it might also be done virtually. EVERY jurisdiction and private non-profit agency within the county should attend this important briefing where the 'rules' for this disaster will be laid out. At this meeting, officials will also lay out the available Federal grant programs available for this specific disaster. There are at last count 17 different Federal agencies that may offer some form of disaster assistance, with approximately 70 specific programs available to local governments, private non-profits, small business, and individuals and families. However, the exact programs which will be available will vary from disaster to disaster depending on a host of factors. For instance, an urban disaster probably will not have any assistance available from the U.S. Department of Agriculture. I worked on a disaster in Northern California about 10 years ago, where Small Business Administration loans were made available for private non-profits but not for small businesses. In that same disaster, Individual Assistance, i.e., for homeowners, was not part of the initial Federal aid package. The Individual Assistance program was only added weeks later, when the number of damaged homes supported that finding of need.

So, each disaster will have a unique mix of Federal programs available based on the damages done, the needs of the community, and the ability, or lack thereof, of the local government to effectively respond to the disaster and restore the community.

In some cases, the state may request that only the Emergency Services Director, or the equivalent, and the Disaster Cost Recovery team leader should attend. I disagree. I believe that every department or division that suffered damages should send a representative to this meeting. Everyone hears things differently and pays more attention to those things in their wheelhouse. Senior or deputy departmental leadership should be present at this meeting where the "rules of engagement" will be promulgated. Some departments may believe that these rules do not apply to their operations. Au contraire; the rules do apply to all and equally so.

I recommend that the attendees take a stack of business cards with them and network with everyone they can, especially FEMA and state personnel. The disaster recovery will be a long, drawn-out process, lasting for years, and on day one we cannot know who we may need to contact for some crucial information weeks, months, or years into the future.

The Applicant's Briefing is also a great time to reconnect with colleagues in neighboring jurisdictions to compare notes. Disaster cost recovery staff will need a great deal of support throughout the process, and some important support may be had among our nearby colleagues, many of whom are dealing with the same problems as we are. Already, from the first days, disaster cost recovery staff should be thinking about setting up a regular schedule of in-person (highly recommended) or virtual meetings with their colleagues in neighboring similar jurisdictions, i.e., cities meet with cities, schools meet with schools, etc., as well as less frequent but still regular county-wide meetings of all affected agencies. The disaster cost recovery process burden will be much lighter if it's shared with our colleagues, and we will learn from each other in addition to providing much-needed support.

The Recovery Scoping Meeting (RSM)

As was briefly introduced in the previous chapter on the FEMA Grants Portal, the next meeting in the disaster cost recovery process is the Recovery Scoping Meeting. However, before this meeting occurs, a Program Delivery Manager (PDMG) from FEMA will make a call to each local agency to discuss their current damage assessment picture to determine the size and scopes of the work which must be completed to return the city, county, special district, etc., to a pre-disaster status, as much as is possible with Federal assistance.

The size and impact of the disaster will enter the equation of how quickly FEMA and the state will be able to respond in force. A response to a disaster in one of the 15 states with a population of less than 2,000,000 people will administratively be far different from one of those 10 states which have a population greater than 10,000,000 people. Furthermore, the nature, distribution, and degree of the damage will also affect the level of possible response. Lastly, the region's or country's recent disaster experiences will make a difference, i.e., the 2017 epidemic of Hurricanes Harvey, Irma, and Maria, when there was not only a severe shortage of disaster response staff at FEMA but disaster debris removal contractors were playing a shell game with local agencies because they were so short of workers and equipment.

However, the tactic of delaying the Recovery Scoping Meeting should in no way be an automatic response. In those cases where the Presidential disaster declaration comes many weeks or months after the disaster, most communities will have a comprehensive well-defined list of damages and disaster response costs BEFORE the President signs the declaration. In this scenario, get the Recovery Scoping Meeting scheduled as soon as possible, for without the Recovery Scoping Meeting, the funding will not begin to flow.

The Most Important Thing About the Recovery Scoping Meeting

From the date on which the Recovery Scoping Meeting is held, the local jurisdiction has 60 days to submit its list of damages. Damages include actual damages as well as costs for immediate response activities, costs for evacuation, sheltering, and mass feeding, etc. Additional damages or costs submitted after this 60-day window will most likely be denied as ineligible unless there are extenuating circumstances. But be forewarned: FEMA is very strict about what constitutes an extenuating circumstance.

It's All in the Timing

Hypothetically, if a disaster strikes a community and the Presidential disaster declaration is made within a few days, the disaster recovery will likely (on average) initially move more quickly than a disaster which is not declared for 60 days or more.

When the disaster is not declared for many weeks or months, the local agency has a great deal of time in which to discover and report all its damages. However, when the disaster is quickly declared, the 60-day window will appear to be much shorter. Therefore, one tactic that the local agency may use to gain a few more days in which to discover additional damages is to delay (to the extent possible) the Recovery Scoping Meeting.

It is not uncommon for FEMA staff to press for early Recovery Scoping Meetings. (Remember, they also have a job to do, and their time is also important.) However, in those fast-moving situations, the local agency may want to push back, if only for a few days, the date for the Recovery Scoping Meeting.

The Other Important Thing About the Recovery Scoping Meeting

The Recovery Scoping Meeting is also critical because it sets up certain important timelines which must be adhered to at the risk of losing a project's funding. At the Recovery Scoping Meeting, the Program Delivery Manager should be able to provide the local agency with the critical dates for the various projects. In brief, Category A (Debris Management) and Category B (Emergency Protective Measures) must be completed within six months of the date of the Presidential disaster declaration. However, time extensions may be available. An initial extension may be made by the state, acting as FEMA's agent. If a subsequent extension is necessary, that must be approved by FEMA.

For Permanent Work, Categories C though G, there is an 18-month window for project completion. Again, an initial extension may be made by the state. If a subsequent extension is necessary, that must be approved by FEMA.

If the work on a project is lagging for any reason, and the work will not be completed within the appropriate timeframe, then a letter requesting a time extension must be submitted BEFORE the window closes. If a case is on appeal, or there is some other administrative action pending, **this does not stop the clock**. The original dates of performance must be adhered to in all cases unless a time extension has been granted.

FEMA carefully watches the Period of Performance (or POP). The cost for any work done after the current timeline has expired may be deducted from the amount originally obligated under the Project Worksheet.

The Bottom Line on Timelines

All timelines must be adhered to. Missing a deadline will effectively stop a project dead in its tracks, with no hope of resuscitation. This may be one of the easiest ways that FEMA may deobligate approved funding.

The Essential Elements of Information

"During the Recovery Scoping Meeting, the Program Delivery Manager will discuss documentation requirements for projects. Following this meeting and project formulation of the damages, the FEMA Program Delivery Manager will address the Essential Elements of Information Questionnaires which will be visible to the Applicants and the Recipient within Grants Portal."[1]

"The FEMA Program Delivery Manager will respond to the questionnaire using the Applicant's answers, which will generate a list of required documentation the Applicant shall be required to provide. In addition, responses to the questionnaire will open dialogue boxes within the Questionnaire that require response. The FEMA Program Delivery Manager works together with the Applicant to address these specific questions with reconciled answers."[2]

"When the Program Delivery Manager is working with the Applicant, s/he will continue to show them what types of documentation they will have to provide in accordance with Essential Elements of Information requirements. These will be listed by category and sub-category (Examples including Force Account labor, equipment, contract, materials, and rented equipment). The documentation provided is specific to the project to support the Damage Description and Dimensions, the scope of work, and the project costs."[3]

Properly filling out the Essential Elements of Information sheets is a first step in the process of providing FEMA with all the key information it needs to determine project eligibility. However, these are only the first steps, as an avalanche of paperwork will follow as the process moves ahead.

As local agency staff work on completing the "Essential Elements of Information" it is important to be aware of the questions asked about FEMA's "Special Considerations." We will address these issues in detail in Chapter 30.

FEMA by law is very tuned-in to any issues of environmental and/or historic concern. The failure of the local agency to consider the importance of the Special Considerations has often resulted in partial and even total deobligation of approved projects, even after they have been completed. FEMA considers compliance with the provisions for Special Considerations to be significant, and "deal breakers" when they are not closely followed.

File the RPA (Request for Public Assistance) On Time or Go Home Broke

Local agencies are held to strict standards regarding the timely submission of the required applications and other paperwork. FEMA, on the other hand, does not suffer any penalties when it misses its nominal deadlines. This may be unfair, but it is the way the system works.

First and foremost, following the signing of a Presidential disaster declaration is the requirement to file the Request for Public Assistance, or the RPA. "FEMA accepts RPAs up to 30 days from the date the respective area was designated. FEMA may extend the deadline for submitting an RPA if the Recipient submits a <u>request in writing</u> with justification based on extenuating circumstances beyond the Applicant's or Recipient's control."[4] (Emphasis Added) If the local agency does not timely file the RPA, the game is all over for them. There is no tomorrow without a properly filed RPA.

This case from Missouri is spot on regarding the RPA. "During the incident period of July 25–28, 2022, Missouri experienced severe storms and flooding. The President declared a major disaster on August 8, 2022. The regulatory 30-day deadline to submit a Request for Public Assistance (RPA) to FEMA expired September 7, 2022. On September 2, 2022, the Missouri State Emergency Management Agency (Recipient) sent a reminder email to the City of Maplewood (Applicant) of the upcoming September 7, 2022, deadline to submit its RPA. On October 18, 2022, the Applicant submitted a letter to the Recipient, requesting acceptance of the late RPA. The Applicant stated that it was not aware of the RPA deadline until October 5, 2022, after the September 7, 2022, deadline had passed. The Recipient forwarded the request to FEMA on October 24, 2022, recommending denial of the request."[5]

"On October 26, 2022, FEMA denied the request for a time extension for the Applicant to submit its RPA. FEMA found the Applicant's confusion of the RPA submittal deadline did not constitute extenuating circumstances beyond the Recipient's or Applicant's control."[6]

First Appeal

"In a letter dated November 21, 2022, the Applicant appealed FEMA's denial of its time extension request to submit its RPA. The Applicant described various disaster cleanup events and implied that those events pulled its staff and resources preventing it from submitting its RPA. It stated it did not understand it needed to submit an RPA to receive disaster assistance and noted that FEMA told the Applicant it should wait for further contact rather than submitting its RPA to the Recipient."[7]

"On February 23, 2023, the FEMA Region 7 Regional Administrator (RA) denied the Applicant's first appeal finding the RA did not possess the authority to grant an extension in this case because the Recipient did not request one. Further, FEMA determined the Applicant had not demonstrated that extenuating circumstances prevented the Applicant from submitting a timely RPA submission within the 30-day deadline."[8]

Second Appeal

"In its second appeal, the Applicant expands its argument concerning the communication it received from FEMA, stating that the Applicant was never informed to contact the Recipient to submit its RPA. The Applicant explained it was awaiting contact from FEMA and the deadline for submitting its RPA passed."[9]

"If an applicant wishes to seek Public Assistance funding, it must first submit an RPA to FEMA through the recipient. Recipients must submit an applicant's completed RPA to the FEMA RA within 30 days after designation of the area where the damage occurred. FEMA may extend this deadline if the recipient submits a written justification based on extenuating circumstances beyond the applicant's or the recipient's control. The recipient is responsible for providing technical advice and assistance to all eligible applicants, ensuring all potential applicants are aware of available PA, and submitting documents necessary for the award of grants."[10]

"The deadline for applicants to submit RPAs for this disaster was September 7, 2022. Here, the Applicant submitted its RPA on October 18, 2022, and the Recipient forwarded it on October 24, 2022. The administrative record includes documentation to show the Applicant received an email on September 2, 2022 from the Recipient reminding the Applicant of the September 7, 2022 RPA deadline. The Applicant asserts both lack of Recipient and FEMA communication led to confusion and, miscommunication from FEMA about the Applicant's responsibility to submit the RPA contributed to the Applicant's untimely RPA submission."[11]

"However, limited staffing and resources due to the disaster events also does not constitute extenuating circumstances beyond the Applicant's or the Recipient's control."[12]

Notes

1 https://emilms.fema.gov/is_1022/groups/66.html
2 Ibid.
3 Ibid.
4 Public Assistance Program and Policy Guide, Version 4, June 1, 2020, FFP 104–009–2, p. 36.
5 Ibid.
6 Ibid.
7 Ibid.
8 Ibid.
9 Ibid.
10 Ibid.
11 Ibid.
12 Ibid.

29 The Public Assistance Grants Portal

For decades, FEMA's Public Assistance program was strictly a pen-and-paper process, encumbered with all the problems accompanying manual processes. Now, FEMA has a new Public Assistance Program Delivery Model, also known as the Grants Portal.

As with any newly implemented system in both government and industry, there are issues which must be addressed as the program matures. Furthermore, the growth and transition are likely to continue as FEMA makes improvements and introduces new features to better automate and manage this massive grant program. Because the Portal is a moving target in terms of changes and improvements, this chapter will be a brief explanation of how the system is supposed to work, with the caveat that theory and practice do not always mesh perfectly.

First of all, what is NOT changing with FEMA:

- The laws governing Public Assistance
- The regulations governing Public Assistance
- FEMA's Policies for Public Assistance

There are certain administrative steps carried over from the old way of doing business, including filing the Request for Public Assistance (RPA) within 30 days of the Presidential disaster declaration, and the Preliminary Damage Assessment, where representatives from FEMA, and possibly the state, and definitely the local government representatives, meet to visit some of the damage sites in the local jurisdiction. These steps and others have not changed.

Therefore, most of what is addressed in this book will not likely change, as many of the laws, regulations, and policies haven't changed in over 40 years, except perhaps in some cases to become more restrictive.

What has changed for Public Assistance, in whole or in part, is the terminology, FEMA staff individual roles, some of the tools, and especially the process. FEMA sees this new way of doing business as more customer-focused; more consistent; a platform for continuous improvement; and in the end, a way to automate the process and move more money more quickly to the jurisdictions and agencies affected by a disaster.

Some of the significant new roles in this new process are the PDMG, or Program Delivery Manager, the Site Inspector, and the Consolidated Resource Center. Also new to the process is the concept of placing projects into one of three lanes, depending on the project's status:

There are new phases or steps in the Public Assistance program. They include:

- The Exploratory Phone Call, a call made by the FEMA Program Delivery Manager (PDMG) to each local jurisdiction to make an initial overall assessment and working picture of the nature and extent of the damages suffered because of the disaster.

DOI: 10.4324/9781003487869-34

- The Recovery Scoping Meeting, which is the on-site meeting for each applicant to discuss in more depth the specific damages typically suffered by the local agency, and how the local agency is prioritizing the cleanup and repair of those damages. The Recovery Scoping Meeting replaces the old Kick-Off meeting.
- The Site Inspection, where a specific inspector is assigned to visit each damage site, take damage photographs, develop the "Damage Description and Dimensions" or DDD, and write up a report which is then sent to the Consolidated Resource Center or CRC.
- The Consolidated Resource Center (CRC) is one of several offices across the country where specialists review each Site Inspection Report (SIR) and develop the Scope of Work, then make a cost estimate for the necessary funding to complete the specific project.

Another significant change is the concept of the three lanes in the Portal. Those projects (mainly emergency work) which are completed (or within two weeks of being complete) are put into the Completed Work lane, where they may be quickly funded since the costs are, or nearly are, complete.

The Standard Lane consists of those projects which have yet to be worked on but do not have any unusual aspects, or complicating factors, such as environmental or historic considerations.

The Specialized Lane is the home for large and complex projects which may also require technical expertise to deal with the environmental and/or historic aspects.

The intent here is to move the less-complex and completed or nearly completed projects through the system quickly and efficiently for expeditious funding. The Standard Lane projects are intended to move the process along more quickly than otherwise possible because of the lack of complicating factors like environmental and historic issues.

None of these changes, however, changes or diminishes the need for very detailed documentation, some of which has already been discussed in the book. Also not changed are the very specific and rigidly enforced timelines for the local jurisdiction (the applicant) to comply with various dates as specified in the regulations. The complete responsibility of the local agency to fully support its claims of damage also remains unchanged. These are a few but certainly not all of the changes, nor is this a complete list of those requirements which have not changed at all.

Look at this as the process of baking bread. We have a new stove, but for the bread to come out of the oven, we still have to mix the proper ingredients and put them in the oven.

As in the past, there is still a very substantial responsibility placed on the local jurisdiction to know and understand the laws, regulations, and policies which apply to the Public Assistance process. If we fail to take the required steps, now in the Portal instead of with pen and paper, we will have a very difficult time with our disaster recovery efforts.

There is much more to know about FEMA's relatively new approach to processing claims for Public Assistance, and FEMA does provide training. The respective states are also charged with assisting the local agencies with access to and support for using the Portal.

However, many of the states do not have sufficient staff, and many of their personnel are not fully trained in the wide range of nuances of the Public Assistance program. Therefore, I believe that for local government agencies, the best defense is a good offense. Knowing and truly understanding the regulations is the best way for a local agency to have the greatest success in pursuing their Public Assistance damage claims.

Portal Process Cautions

My life experience leading up to my career in emergency management and disaster cost recovery has had some unusual turns. As a young man, I worked for years in the private

FEMA/State/Tribal
Program Delivery Coordinator
Your point of contact
throughout the Public
Assistance process

Figure 29.1 Graphic from the PAPPG depicting a PDMG and their role in the PA program.

sector in construction, so I understand better than some the complexities of construction, both new construction and renovations and repairs. I worked as a carpenter, as an estimator, and as a project manager. These are demanding jobs which require a certain set of skills, and not everyone is equal to all tasks. These following comments are based in part on those years of experience.

There is a process gap early in the Public Assistance process that can lead to bigger problems down the road. The Program Delivery Manager (PDMG) helps the local agencies to manage each client's set of projects. The PDMG assigns Site Inspectors to visit each damage site, to take photos, develop the Damage Description and Dimensions (DDD) and write up the damage report. The Site Inspector then forwards his/her work to the Consolidated Resource Center (CRC) for development of the Scope of Work and project cost estimating.

However, the CRC can rely only on those written reports and photographs as the basis for developing the Scope of Work and the cost estimate. If either the Site Inspector misses something or the CRC misses something, the Scope of Work and the resulting cost estimate will be inaccurate and not truly representative of the work necessary to restore the facility to its pre-disaster condition. In these cases, the local agency must reject the Scope of Work and cost estimate.

Therefore, it is critical that the local agency have someone, either on staff or on contract, to closely review both the Scope of Work and the cost estimate once it is returned from the CRC. The project will then have to be re-inspected and resubmitted to the CRC for a rework. And we cannot rely on everything being properly corrected by a return inspection and trip to the CRC. The reworked project will AGAIN have to be carefully reviewed for completeness and accuracy.

As previously stated, how the new Portal system is supposed to work and how it does work may sometimes be at odds, and we should not be sidetracked if and when glitches occur.

Based on the above graphic, one might assume that once they are assigned, the Program Delivery Manager (PDMG) will remain part of the team working to restore the local community throughout the Public Assistance process. But this may not always be the case. I have a colleague in a major city in the southeast United States who reported that following a major storm, their assigned PDMG was the first of three different PDMGs assigned to their agency. For those at the front line of disaster cost recovery, this will be disheartening but should not be fatal. We will find ourselves starting all over with each new face that shows up. And faces will change at FEMA, at the state, and surprise, also at the local agency level. Change is constant, and managing this change will be our challenge.

This reality does bring up one very important thought. If you find yourself on the merry-go-round with new FEMA staff appearing more often that you would like, think of how valuable written communications and written reports will be in getting the projects back on track as quickly as possible.

What Is FEMA GO?

FEMA's Grants Portal and the FEMA GO program are related but separate components of the overall grant management system used by the Federal Emergency Management Agency.

The FEMA Grants Portal is an online platform that serves as the entry point for grant applicants and recipients to access FEMA's various grant programs. The Grants Portal provides information about available grants, application processes, eligibility criteria, and other resources to assist potential applicants, as well as allowing users to search for grants, submit grant applications, and track their application status.

On the other hand, FEMA GO (Grants Outcomes) is a distinct system within FEMA's grant management infrastructure.

FEMA GO is an online platform specifically designed for managing and tracking the lifecycle of grants awarded by FEMA. It includes functionalities for grant administration, financial management, reporting, and performance monitoring.

So, while there may some confusion about the role of the Grants Portal and FEMA GO, perhaps the easiest way to understand is that the Grants Portal is for all applicants, while FEMA GO is an interrelated program used by FEMA and the states to help manage FEMA grants.

A Look at Some Case Histories

"From December 27–28, 2018, severe storms, flooding, and a tornado impacted Jones County, Mississippi (Applicant) causing damage to the Applicant's roads and associated culverts, shoulders, ditches, and bridge wall heads (Facilities). After repairing the damaged Facilities, the Applicant requested Public Assistance funding for Grants Manager Projects (GMP) 116528 and 116533. The Applicant requested $17,053.69 for GMP 116528 and $13,228.21 for GMP 116533, totaling $30,281.90. However, FEMA found that the Applicant did not submit proper documentation to verify the costs of the force account labor (FAL), force account equipment (FAE), and materials used, and therefore, the Applicant did not demonstrate the work or costs were associated with either project. FEMA issued determination memoranda denying Public Assistance funding for both projects on February 3, 2020."[1]

"The Applicant appealed the decision to the Grantee, requesting $30,281.90 in PA. *The Applicant stated that it had difficulty gathering and uploading the necessary information and supporting documentation through Grants Portal, FEMA's Applicant-facing grants management database system.* As such, the Applicant followed up with the Mississippi Emergency Management Agency (Grantee), with documentation and a Google Drive link to handle larger files, including force account payroll checks and information, inventory for leased machinery and mobile equipment, and purchase orders."[2] (Emphasis Added)

"The Applicant submitted second appeals on March 18 and 19, 2021 for GMPs 116528 and 116533, respectively. In these transmittals, the Applicant states that it could not upload any additional documentation through the Grants Portal. It explains that the Grantee offered assistance to forward the documentation to FEMA, and that there were no objections to the Applicant's use of a Google Drive link, so the Applicant assumed that the appeals process was moving forward with FEMA possessing all provided documentation. The Grantee forwarded the second appeals and the previously submitted supporting documentation that was included in the Google Drive to FEMA with a letter of support dated March 26, 2021."[3] (Empasis Added.)

"In considering all the documentation submitted on second appeal, FEMA finds the Applicant has demonstrated the requested costs for FAL, FAE, and materials are adequately documented and directly tied to the performance of eligible work for GMPs 116528 and 116533 (i.e., restoration of the damaged Facilities)."[4]

In this case, whatever the difficulties were, they were finally successfully resolved in favor of the county. The problem may have been with the county, or with the Portal itself. The importance here is to never abandon ship; work with the state and FEMA to resolve the issues. No system is failproof forever. Therefore, workarounds are sometimes necessary.

The next case illustrates how important it is to be familiar with and effectively use the Portal.

"California Wildfires occurred between August 14 and September 26, 2020. The President declared a major disaster on August 22, 2020, and amended the declaration on October 18, 2020 to include Sierra County. The 30-day timeframe from the declaration date to submit a Request for Public Assistance was extended to November 17, 2020, due to the October 18, 2020, amendment. The Sierra County Fire Protection District #1 (Applicant) submitted a Request for Public Assistance through the California Governor's Office of Emergency Services (Grantee) via letter dated November 24, 2020. The Applicant justified the late submittal of the RPA as a series of misunderstandings and the inability to submit the RPA through FEMA's Grants Portal system. On December 23, 2020, FEMA issued a Determination Memorandum finding that the Applicant did not demonstrate an extenuating circumstance beyond its control to justify an extension of the November 17, 2020 deadline, and therefore, FEMA denied the Applicant's request."[5] (Emphasis Added)

"The deadline for applicants in the County to submit RPAs to FEMA, through Grants Portal, was November 17, 2020. The Applicant submitted its RPA in Grants Portal on November 24, 2020, seven days after the deadline. At the time of submission, the Applicant acknowledged that the request was untimely. In its appeals, the Applicant cites several cumulative factors contributing to the untimely RPA submittal, including unsuccessfully submitting documents to the Grantee, lack of volunteer staff with experience in the RPA process, volunteer staff handling concurrent fire suppression at other wildfire events, and other miscommunication errors. However, confusion on the Applicant's part, insufficient communication and coordination, and certain hardships that result from either the disaster or other events, do not constitute extenuating circumstances beyond its or the Grantee's control."[6] (Emphasis Added)

"It is the responsibility of the Grantee to ensure the Applicant is aware of the availability and requirements of the PA program. The Grantee provided the Applicant with the requirements for submitting the RPA on November 9, 2020, before expiration of the 30-day deadline. There are three different notations in the Grantee's Fact Sheet instructing applicants to submit RPAs via Grants Portal, as well as containing a link to access and register a Grants Portal account, and a link to a tutorial containing instructions for how to submit an RPA on Grants Portal. Therefore, the Applicant's attempt to submit an RPA through an erroneous method (i.e., FEMA GO) is not an extenuating circumstance beyond its control."[7] (Emphasis Added)

In this appeals case, the footnotes further expand on the local agency's (the applicant's) responsibilities in applying for FEMA Public Assistance funding. "The Applicant's lack of knowledge and lack of understanding of the Public Assistance Program are not circumstances outside of its or the Grantee's control; and hardships the Applicant encountered due to the effects of the disaster do not constitute extenuating circumstances beyond the Applicant's or the Grantee's control to warrant an extension of the regulatory RPA deadline."[8]

This means even small, rural agencies are held to the same standard as the largest cities and counties in the country. Even if the local agency relies, perhaps a great deal, on volunteers or part-time employees, they must meet the regulatory and procedural program requirements or risk losing valuable Public Assistance funding.

We Must 'Read and Heed' Communications Sent Through the Grants Portal

The Grants Portal is the system of record for applying for and managing our FEMA Public Assistance grants. In this case, we see the importance of following up on communications sent via the Grants Portal. "This (letter) is in response to a letter from your office dated February 25, 2022, which transmitted the referenced second appeal on behalf of the City of Creola (Applicant). The Applicant is appealing the U.S. Department of Homeland Security's Federal Emergency Management Agency's (FEMA) denial of $35,057.75 in costs pertaining to debris removal."[9]

The letter goes on further to say: "The Applicant viewed the Determination Memorandum denying eligibility in Grants Portal on June 28, 2021. However, the Applicant did not file an appeal until December 21, 2021. This was after the 60-day timeframe required by FEMA's regulations, making the first appeal untimely. Therefore, this appeal is denied."[10]

Chapter Closing

The intent of this book is to prepare and educate local agencies in the complete FEMA Public Assistance process, and not just about how to use the Portal. This would be like a first-time student driver sitting at the wheel of a Lamborghini. It's a great car, it's a great feeling, but can we go anywhere if we don't know how to turn the engine on, understand the rules of the road, and have some idea of where we are headed?

In this case, a full understanding of the fundamental principles of the Public Assistance program is required before we sit down at the computer and fire up the Grants Portal. Our Lamborghini will take us anywhere at 90 miles per hour, but not if we're driving in circles or lost in the fog.

Notes

1 https://www.fema.gov/appeal/force-account-labor-equipment-costs
2 Ibid.
3 Ibid.
4 Ibid.
5 https://www.fema.gov/appeal/request-public-assistance-time-limitationsextensions-0
6 Ibid.
7 Ibid.
8 Ibid, Footnote 8.
9 https://www.fema.gov/appeal/appeals-28
10 Ibid.

30 The Special Consideration Questions

Figure 30.1 Depiction of environmental work following a disaster.

Special Considerations

Every single Project Worksheet must include the "Special Consideration Questions" form (Old FEMA Form 009–0-120). Oddly, however, the Public Assistance Program and Policy Guide, June 2020 edition does not anywhere contain the term "special consideration," although there are frequent references and discussions of environmental and historic considerations. This may account for the frequent disconnect between policy and practice as perceived by the local jurisdictions.

DOI: 10.4324/9781003487869-35

FEMA's "Special Considerations Questions" form contains nine questions, each of which must be answered regardless of the type of project being requested, even when the answer is "Unsure."

When any of the questions have a "Yes" answer, the agency should be aware that the project may now stand on the edge of an abyss. On one side of the chasm is FEMA, and on the other side are one or more other Federal and state agencies which deal with environmental or historic preservation issues.

In many cases, to paraphrase Winston Churchill's famous 1939 quote about Russia, "special considerations" are a riddle wrapped in a mystery inside an enigma. The special considerations are almost always highly technical in nature, and ruled over by state and Federal bureaucrats whose concerns are frequently out of harmony with the local government agency and its disaster recovery priorities.

Be that as it may be, when the local agency suffers damage to certain facilities, there are few available options except to apply for Federal disaster assistance to restore the facility. However, as was described in Chapter 22, Other Federal Agencies (OFA) are now a part of the funding calculus, and depending on a host of factors, funding may or may not be available from either FEMA or another Federal Agency, depending on the nature and extent of the damage, and whether the damage presents an immediate threat to life safety, public health, or threatens improved property.

If the project has a high potential value, then serious consideration should be given to retaining a specialized consultant, particularly one who has very specific experience with the issue(s) at hand. Many "bread and butter" cost recovery consultants may find themselves in seriously deep water (no pun intended) in these environmental and historic issues.

It is of supreme importance to understand what the underlying issue is which applies to all Federal grants, and particularly how it applies in cases involving any special considerations.

Title 44 of the Code of Federal Regulations § 13.43 Enforcement.

(a) Remedies for noncompliance.

   If a grantee or subgrantee materially fails to comply with **any term of an award**, whether stated in a Federal statute or regulation, an assurance, in a State plan or application, a notice of award, or elsewhere, the awarding agency may take one or more of the following actions, as appropriate in the circumstances:

   (1) Temporarily withhold cash payments pending correction of the deficiency by the grantee or subgrantee or more severe enforcement action by the awarding agency,
   (2) Disallow (that is, deny both use of funds and matching credit for) all or part of the cost of the activity or action not in compliance,
   (3) Wholly or partly suspend or terminate the current award for the grantee's or subgrantee's program,
   (4) Withhold further awards for the program, or
   (5) Take other remedies that may be legally available.
   (Emphasis Added)

If we, as the local agency, do not fully comply with the terms and conditions of the approved Project Worksheet, then FEMA has the right to deny part or all the project's funding. In reviewing hundreds of appeals cases, it seems that the deobligation of all a project's funding happens more often in cases where the local agency failed to comply with the environmental and historic preservation requirements than in any other instance. And the noncompliance need not be with the grant in toto, but ANY material noncompliance with ANY part of the agreement as set forth in the approved Project Worksheet.

"Special Considerations": Insurance

This appeals case comes out of Hurricane Issac in Plaquemines Parish, LA. This is a case of compound violations also involving historic preservation, codes and standards, another Federal agency, and pre-existing damage, but the insurance issue is our concern here. "During the declared incident period of August 26, 2012 through September 10, 2012, Hurricane Isaac struck Plaquemines Parish, Louisiana (Applicant) with a 10-to-15-foot storm surge, inundating Fort Jackson (Facility), a decommissioned military fortification that was declared a National Historic Landmark (NHL) in 1960 and listed in the National Register of Historic Places in 1977. FEMA prepared Project Worksheet (PW) 1535 to document the damage and proposed repair work to the Facility. FEMA estimated disaster-related repair costs totaling $334,886.00 but found that the Applicant failed to obtain and maintain insurance, which FEMA required as a condition of the grant funding for repairs to the Facility following Hurricane Katrina. FEMA found that 15 of the 19 sites listed on the PW were ineligible as a result and awarded $16,754.00 for repairs to the remaining eligible sites."[1]

"Special Considerations": Coastal High Hazard Areas

"From October 7–19, 2018, Hurricane Michael caused extensive damage throughout Florida. The Florida Department of Environmental Protection (Applicant) requested Public Assistance (PA) to repair damage to structures located within the T.H. Stone Memorial St. Joseph Peninsula State Park (Park), including its Shop 6 Bays, Mower Shed, and Linen Shed. The Park is located within a special flood hazard area and encompasses wetland areas on a peninsula situated between St. Joseph Bay and the Gulf of Mexico. FEMA created Project Worksheet (PW) 1950 on March 10, 2020, to document the claimed work, but noted that the Applicant did not provide estimated costs, a detailed Scope of Work (SOW), contracts, or bids for the project. FEMA created a cost estimate for PW 1950 on October 26, 2020."[2]

"In May 2021, FEMA issued informal and formal requests for information (RFIs) seeking to verify the Applicant's compliance with EHP (*Environmental and Historic Preservation*) requirements. Specifically, FEMA requested that the Applicant explain:

(1) the percentage of work completed for each structure;
(2) whether replacement structures would be restored to predisaster conditions and locations;
(3) notification of any new ground disturbances;
(4) copies of drawings, construction/engineering plans, or any supporting documentation for reconstruction work;
(5) the dimensions, square footage, and materials used for replacement structures;
(6) the location of equipment and material staging;
(7) updated historic site forms submitted for the demolition of structures in the Park;
(8) elevations and any floodproofing considerations for structures below the base flood elevation (BFE);
(9) whether structures would be strengthened against flood risk in any other way;
(10) whether structures could be relocated outside of the flood zones; and
(11) whether the Applicant contacted the local Floodplain Manager or Administrator regarding replacement of structures in the Coastal High Hazard Area (CHHA)."[3]

"The Applicant responded to the formal RFI with completed work percentages for each damage inventory and explained that no additional information was available due to the Park being completely redesigned. In its informal RFI response, the Applicant stated that:

(1) the damaged structures had no historical value and would either be rebuilt to current codes and standards or not be rebuilt;

(2) updated historic site forms for demolished structures would not be required;

(3) the Shop 6 Bays would not be relocated or elevated, and all repair work was complete;

(4) both the Mower Shed and Linen Shed would be relocated;

(5) work on the Mower Shed and Linen Shed had not begun; and

(6) it was not aware of any contact with the local Floodplain Manager or Administrator regarding replacement structures in the CHHA (*Coastal High Hazard Area*). The Applicant also included design plans for the Linen Shed and a flood map of the Park."[4]

"FEMA concluded that the Applicant did not provide documentation necessary to verify compliance with applicable EHP requirements. Specifically, FEMA noted that the Applicant failed to provide documentation establishing compliance associated with the avoidance of adverse impacts within a floodplain or to historic properties. Such documentation included:

(1) confirmation of replacement structures being restored to predisaster condition and locations;

(2) notification of any new ground disturbances;

(3) supporting documentation for reconstruction work;

(4) replacement structure dimensions, square footage, and materials;

(5) equipment and material staging location information;

(6) updated historic site forms submitted for demolished structures;

(7) structure elevations and any floodproofing considerations for structures below the BFE (Base Flood Elevation); and

(8) notification of other flood risk mitigation efforts."[5]

"The Applicant submitted documentation demonstrating it incurred costs for work; however, it has not established EHP compliance associated with the avoidance of potential adverse impacts within a floodplain or to historic properties. Though it describes the work at issue as either 100-percent or 75-percent complete, the information provided by the Applicant does not clearly demonstrate what work was done or is proposed to be done. Additionally, the Applicant still has not provided information establishing: (1) any new ground disturbances; (2) reconstruction work details; (3) replacement structure dimensions, square footage, and materials; (4) equipment and material staging location information; or (5) floodproofing considerations and other flood risk mitigation efforts. Without this documentation, FEMA is unable to determine whether any Scope of Work complied with EHP requirements to prevent adverse consequences for activities within a floodplain. The Applicant directed FEMA to see its attached plans, but the Applicant's documentation does not include any plans addressing EHP considerations."[6]

"Furthermore, although the Applicant stated that updated historic site forms for demolished structures are not required, it is FEMA's responsibility to determine the effects of a potential PA (Public Assistance) project on historic properties prior to the start of construction and to provide the state historic preservation office the opportunity to concur with FEMA's findings."[7]

While this is a complex case, the lessons are clear. In this situation, the facility's location in a coastal high hazard area is immediately problematic. A great deal of documentation is required for the process to succeed. Changing the location of a facility in any environmental or historic area may trigger complications far beyond any of the benefits potentially gained by making the changes.

"Special Considerations": Coastal Barrier Resources Area

"High wind and surf associated with Hurricane Gustav damaged approximately four miles of shoreline within the County-maintained, engineered portion of St. Joseph Peninsula Beach.

Erosion removed an estimated 23.13 cubic yards (CY) of sand per linear foot of shoreline within this area, and there was also damage to existing sand fencing and sea oat plants. FEMA prepared PW 14 to document the damage and scope of work required to restore the beach to its maintained, pre-disaster design. This portion of the shoreline is located within the Coastal Barrier Resources System (CBRS) and is subject to the provisions of the Coastal Barrier Resources Act (CBRA). To be eligible for Federal disaster relief, projects located within the CBRS must be consistent with the purposes of CBRA, as set forth in 44 CFR §206.341, Policy, to: 'minimize the loss of human life, the wasteful expenditure of Federal revenues, and the damage to fish, wildlife and other natural resources associated with coastal barriers.' The Applicant submitted an engineering study that determined the beach could be restored with minimal adverse impact on the natural ecosystem of the beach, and FEMA initially determined that the project met the criteria for a CBRA exception as a 'Special Purpose Facility' under 44 CFR §206.347(c)(4)."[8]

"Pursuant to 44 CFR §206.348, Consultation, FEMA consulted with United States Fish and Wildlife Service (USFWS), as the representative for the Department of the Interior (DOI), for a determination that the project was consistent with the purposes of CBRA. USFWS evaluated the Applicant's project for beach nourishment and dune installation and determined that it was not consistent with the purpose of CBRA to minimize damage to fish, wildlife, and other natural resources. Specifically, USFWS determined that beach nourishment is likely to result in adverse effects to the federally threatened piping plover, and long-term, large-scale beach stabilization projects conflict with the protection or persistence of important natural land forms, processes, and wildlife resources. USFWS also stated that such stabilization projects have the indirect effects of increases in residential development, infrastructure, and public recreational uses. USFWS issued findings of non-concurrence with FEMA's initial determination on May 27, 2009, and November 6, 2009."[9]

"As a result of the findings of USFWS, FEMA subsequently determined that the beach restoration work was not consistent with the purposes of CBRA, and deobligated all funds for the project, in the amount of $15,113,160."[10]

"Special Considerations": Change in Pre-Disaster Conditions

Yet another object lesson in how to lose FEMA money comes from Wyoming. "From May 18 through July 8, 2011, severe storms and heavy rains caused flooding throughout the State of Wyoming. The City of Sundance's (Applicant) Cole Water Storage Tank (water tank) shifted due to excessive moisture saturating the soils around the water tank, though the water tank itself was undamaged. FEMA prepared Project Worksheet (PW) 181 to document work to stabilize the site of the water tank. The approved scope of work (SOW) involved stabilizing the existing site, by using micropiles and ground anchors to tie into an existing ring foundation wall and installing ground anchors at the lower back retaining wall for increased ground stability. The PW noted that the Applicant preferred to move the water tank to a new site, and if it did so, the estimated cost would be capped at $300,000.00 (reflecting the cost to stabilize the existing site) as an improved project. The PW also contained a comment stating that the Applicant must notify the state if there were any changes in the Scope of Work prior to starting the repairs, and failure to do so may jeopardize receipt of federal funding. In addition, the Record of Environmental Consideration (REC) for PW 181 included a condition that '[a]ny change to the approved scope of work will require re-evaluation for compliance with NEPA and other Laws and Executive Orders.'"[11]

"In 2012, the Applicant's engineers provided the Applicant with alternative sites for the water tank, noting that a Wyoming Department of Environmental Quality permit would be required prior to beginning construction and the requirement that certain sites would need a National

Environmental Policy Act (NEPA) review. In 2014, after consultation with its engineers, the Applicant determined the existing foundation was unstable and moved the water tank 3.8 miles north of the city."[12]

"On February 5, 2016, after completion of the work, the Applicant submitted an improved project request to the State of Wyoming Office of Homeland Security (Grantee). The Grantee forwarded it to FEMA, who denied the request on January 10, 2017. FEMA determined the Applicant failed to receive approval prior to changing the Scope of Work and, by moving the water tank, FEMA did not have the opportunity to conduct the necessary environmental and historic preservation (EHP) reviews, including a NEPA review. As such, FEMA deobligated all funding."[13]

Like so many other appeals cases, this case fails on two counts. The first was a change in the scope of work without notifying FEMA and receiving approval BEFORE doing the work. Second, the applicant failed to follow the requirements for the environmental issues, many of which were triggered by the decision to relocate the water tank.

"Special Considerations": Hazard Mitigation

Typically, both FEMA and the state will seek out hazard mitigation projects to reduce potential damage from future disasters. There are different types of hazard mitigation funding. The one we are concerned with here is Section 406 Hazard Mitigation, which may provide additional funding to "over strengthen" facilities to reduce the likelihood of future damage in a similar type of disaster. Section 406 Hazard Mitigation only applies to those facilities which were damaged by the disaster. Hazard mitigation projects, depending on the hazard addressed, may include elevation or relocation of damaged structures in flood hazard areas; adding hurricane ties to a damaged roof; "oversizing" of structural members for seismic resistance, etc.

However, not all mitigation projects will "pencil out"; i.e., the potential benefit gained is outweighed by the cost of doing the work. Also, some requests for hazard mitigation funding will be inappropriate because Section 406 Hazard Mitigation funds are only available for facilities which were disaster-damaged.

This appeals case comes from New Jersey. "Between August 27, 2011 and September 5, 2011, flooding from Hurricane Irene damaged major circuit breaker system components at the Borough of Milltown's (Applicant) Washington Avenue electrical substation (Facility). The Facility, which is located in a Special Flood Hazard Area, was built in 1958 and has incurred storm related damage on previous occasions. Specifically, the Applicant indicated that flood damage occurred previously, and provided documented costs for 2007, 2010 and 2011, which total $605,224.00."[14]

"On March 8, 2012, FEMA obligated Project Worksheet (PW) 2362, for $219,657.83, to repair and replace the damaged circuit breaker system components. The eligible work was 100 percent complete when the PW was obligated. Separately, FEMA awarded PW 3835, for $120,296.00, to repair and replace other damaged elements at the Facility. The total eligible funding to repair all the damage was $339,953.83."[15]

"On September 23, 2013, the Applicant applied for flood mitigation assistance, requesting $11,752,878.44, from FEMA's Flood Mitigation Assistance (FMA) program. The application details a plan to use the funding to acquire property, and design and construct a new substation located outside of the 2 percent annual flood plain."[16]

"On March 10, 2015, FEMA hazard mitigation specialists prepared a benefit cost analysis (BCA) for the requested permanent relocation. The analysis found that permanently relocating the Facility would result in $21,389,777.00 in benefits and $11,752,880.00 in costs, a benefit cost ratio (BCR) of 1.82. The BCA was recalculated on April 21, 2015, resulting in a BCR of 1.5, based on $18,940,561.00 in benefits and $12,628,840.00 in costs."[17]

In its March 24, 2015, letter to FEMA, the Grantee described the Applicant's claim that the project be converted to a permanent relocation out of the floodplain to avoid further repetitive damage to the Facility, as evidenced by the 2007, 2010, and 2011 losses. The letter provided a general description of the proposed relocation project including the scope of work for the new and the existing location. The letter stated that the Facility is the sole source of electricity for the Borough of Milltown, and the (*Benefit Cost Ratio*) BCR shows the relocation project is cost-effective."[18]

"On May 20, 2015, FEMA denied the funding request, finding the cost to relocate the Facility is not reasonable when compared with the repair cost of the current Facility. FEMA stated that Hurricane Irene inflicted $436,039.00 in total damage to the Facility, a small amount when compared with $11,752,880.00 for permanent relocation. FEMA noted that a facility must be destroyed before permanent relocation can be found eligible and defined "destroyed" as when damage exceeds fifty percent of the cost of repairing the facility. FEMA acknowledged that although the BCR is cost effective for mitigation, mitigation costs are not eligible in an improved project."[19] (Emphasis Added)

"Special Considerations": Historic Preservation

All the special considerations are cut from similar cloth insofar as they often involve other state and/or Federal agencies, typically require more time for project approval, and have similar requirements when repairing or reconstructing a facility.

This case from Minnesota involves both historic and environmental issues. "From September 22 through October 14, 2010, severe storms and flooding impacted Blue Earth County, Minnesota where the Township of Rapidan (Applicant) is located. As a result of the disaster, the Applicant's roadway, 563rd Lane, (Facility) suffered severe embankment washouts in four different locations. Noting that the damaged road was in imminent danger of collapse and presented an immediate threat to safety as a result of the river changing course and cutting into the bank of the road, the Applicant requested that the road be permanently relocated 50 feet away from the river. After conducting a site visit, FEMA agreed that it was not physically possible to repair the road in its existing location. As such, FEMA prepared Project Worksheet (PW) 1485 documenting costs in the amount of $264,341.00 to employ contract labor and equipment to relocate the road and construct it according to the Applicant's specifications and in compliance with all federal and state legal and regulatory requirements. Due to the Facility's close proximity to an archaeologically sensitive site ('the hill'), FEMA predicated grant assistance for the Facility on further environmental and historic preservation (EHP) evaluations and consultations should the Applicant deviate from the FEMA-approved scope of work (SOW). This was documented in the FEMA Record of Environmental Consideration (REC)."[20] (Emphasis Added)

"In late 2014, the Applicant requested a cost overrun totaling $354,043.22. In a December 30, 2014 email, FEMA Region V requested the Applicant explain any differences between the actual and approved costs, the source of the overrun, and documentation that linked actual costs to the approved Scope of Work. In a March 9, 2015 response, the Minnesota Homeland Security and Emergency Management (Grantee) provided additional information regarding the difference in costs, along with the Applicant's response and support documentation. Included with the response was a letter from I & S Group (Contractor), dated August 19, 2014, stating that much of the additional cost could be attributed to the original design being based on an erroneous topographic survey which caused a mid-construction redesign of the road relocation. As such, there were extra costs due to down time, digital model revision, remobilization and restocking. A December 18, 2014 letter from the Contractor stated, '[t]he final road alignment is conceptually the same as the footprint included in the PW. Disturbance of the hill was limited to the bottom one-third per direction given from FEMA to [the Applicant].' The Applicant asserted the road was moved as close to the archaeologically sensitive hill as possible without disturbing the slope or the hill. The Applicant further stated that it installed a retaining wall at the base of the hill to protect the hill from any erosion damage."[21]

"After review of these communications, FEMA determined that the Applicant moved the Facility closer to the hill than approved in the PW's Scope of Work and installed a retaining wall abutting the hill without prior approval from FEMA. As such, FEMA fully deobligated PW 1485 because the Applicant completed work not pre-approved by FEMA, which prevented FEMA's re-evaluation of the site for potential National Historic Preservation Act (NHPA) § 106 issues and consultation with Indian Tribal Governments."[22]

"Upon review of the second appeal documentation, FEMA concludes that the Applicant deviated from the approved Scope of Work, in both constructing the retaining wall and moving the Facility 50 feet beyond that which was approved by FEMA. In addition, excavation at specific locations cut into the archaeological site. This is confirmed using Google images depicting the Facility's location before the disaster and after completion of the relocation project. As such, both federal Regulation and FEMA guidance required the Applicant to notify and receive approval from FEMA prior to the start of the additional excavation and construction. Regardless of the Applicant's claim that it was instructed that it did not need to notify FEMA prior to the start of the additional work, and that it should wait until closeout to submit additional costs, there is no support that FEMA offered this advice, nor would such obviate the Applicant's need to comply with federal law and FEMA policy."[23]

"The Applicant deviated from the approved Scope of Work and encroached on an archaeologically sensitive site. Moreover, the Applicant did not request prior approval from FEMA before deviating from the approved Scope of Work as required by 44 C.F.R. § 13.30(d) and the FEMA Record of Environmental Consideration. In failing to notify FEMA prior to completing additional work, the Applicant prevented FEMA from conducting the necessary EHP reviews and consultations, in violation of Federal Regulations and the grant award's conditions. As such, the project is ineligible."[24]

For facilities, the general rule is that when a building is 50 years or older, it must have a review for historic issues, even if there is no apparent historic value present. This also applies to new buildings which by their design or use are noteworthy, such as a Frank Gehry-designed building.

Special Considerations: How to Lose $4,000,000 in One Project

"From August 27 to September 1, 2011, Tropical Storm Irene caused substantial damage to a coastal revetment in Milford, Connecticut. In response, the City of Milford (Applicant) applied through the Connecticut Department of Homeland Security and Emergency Management (Grantee) in December 2011 for a Public Assistance (PA) grant to restore the revetment to predisaster condition, with additional mitigation measures."[25]

"Upon receiving the request, FEMA initiated procedures required under the National Historic Preservation Act (NHPA) to identify and minimize the effects of federal undertakings on sites of historic significance. FEMA subsequently learned of two Native American burial grounds in the revetment's vicinity, excavated before World War II, which indicated an elevated potential for additional burial grounds and associated resources to be located in the project's area of potential effect (APE). In addition, pre-historic remains had recently been discovered in Branford, a town eight miles north, as a result of damage caused by Tropical Storm Irene. Accordingly, the State Historic Preservation Officer (SHPO) recommended archaeological monitoring during the repairs, and the Mohegan Tribal Historic Preservation Officer (THPO) requested to be notified of these efforts and be provided an opportunity to participate if necessary. With these conditions included in the project's Record of Environmental Considerations (REC), the SHPO and THPO raised no objections to FEMA's ultimate determination that no historic properties would be affected, which allowed the restoration project to move forward."[26]

"On April 5, 2012, FEMA awarded Project Worksheet (PW) 247 with total estimated project costs of $3,918,825.00. In addition to the more general condition of compliance with all federal, state, and local laws, FEMA included the following special conditions in the REC: (Record of Environmental Concerns)

[1.] <u>During all excavation, the project shall be monitored by a qualified professional archaeologist.</u> Following completion of the field efforts, the monitor shall prepare and provide to the [SHPO] a technical memorandum summarizing the monitoring efforts . . . .

[2.] <u>Prior to work beginning, the Mohegan Tribal Government shall be notified of the work schedule</u> and be provided the opportunity to monitor the project. The Tribe will also be provided with the name and contact information of the qualified professional archaeologist that will be monitoring the project."[27] (Emphasis Added)

"Between December 2013 and February 2014, the Applicant worked with the Grantee to submit its final projects accounting to FEMA for the completed restoration, with incurred costs totaling $2,070,106.02. However, the Applicant did not indicate whether it had complied with the special conditions documented in the Record of Environmental Consideration. When FEMA requested evidence demonstrating compliance, the Applicant revealed that its contractor did not enlist an archaeological monitor, and thus, the Applicant did not comply with either of the special conditions."[28]

"Here, the Acting RA (Regional Administrator) found that the decision to terminate the project in full was within the bounds of his discretion, consistent with the remedies set forth in 44 C.F.R. § 13.43, and fully supported after consideration of relevant factors and circumstances, including 1) the adverse effects to historic properties and archaeological resources, 2) the clarity with which FEMA had communicated the special conditions in the Record of Environmental Consideration, and 3) any good-faith efforts to comply with those conditions."[29]

The Special Considerations requirements are important, and they are not to be trifled with. FEMA takes this violation quite seriously, and heavy penalties are often imposed for failure to comply.

Notes

1 https://www.fema.gov/appeal/environmental-and-historic-preservation-predisaster-condition-direct-re-sult-disaster
2 https://www.fema.gov/appeal/ehp-and-other-compliance-1
3 Ibid.
4 Ibid.
5 Ibid.
6 Ibid.
7 Ibid.
8 https://www.fema.gov/appeal/beach-renourishment
9 Ibid.
10 Ibid.
11 https://www.fema.gov/appeal/scope-work-improved-project-environmental-compliance
12 Ibid.
13 Ibid.

14 https://www.fema.gov/appeal/permanent-relocation
15 Ibid.
16 Ibid.
17 Ibid.
18 Ibid.
19 Ibid.
20 https://www.fema.gov/appeal/environmental-compliance-3
21 Ibid.
22 Ibid.
23 Ibid.
24 Ibid.
25 https://www.fema.gov/appeal/environmental-compliance-5
26 Ibid.
27 Ibid.
28 Ibid.
29 Ibid.

31 The National Environmental Policy Act (NEPA)

The National Environmental Policy Act (NEPA)

Although there are many different laws and regulations concerning FEMA and environmental and historic considerations, the National Environmental Policy Act (NEPA) is one of those most cited in appeals cases, and for that reason we will explore it further.

"Section 102 of the National Environmental Policy Act (NEPA) requires Federal agencies to integrate environmental values into their decision-making processes by considering the environmental impacts of their proposed actions and reasonable alternatives to those actions. The White House Council on Environmental Quality publishes its NEPA regulations in Title 40 of the Code of Federal Regulations (C.F.R.) Parts 1500–1508. The U.S. Department of Homeland Security publishes policies and procedures for implementing NEPA and provide specific processes that FEMA must follow before funding a project. The NEPA process ensures consideration of environmental consequences of the project before decisions are made and involves the public."[1]

"Although some exemptions from these laws apply to FEMA emergency work and assistance, there is no blanket exemption for disaster assistance FEMA performs under the Stafford Act."[2]

NEPA's STATEXs and CATEXs

"Permanent Work Projects that restore a damaged facility essentially to pre-disaster design are excluded from National Environmental Policy Act (NEPA) review through a statutory exclusion (STATEX). All others require NEPA review. Many qualify for one of the Categorical Exclusions (CATEXs) under NEPA which apply to actions that typically have little or no impact on the environment, as long as there are no 'extraordinary circumstances' as defined by DHS."[3]

The Statutory Exclusions (STATEX)

- "Debris Removal under an emergency or major disaster declaration; and
- Repair, Restoration, and Replacement of Damaged Facilities (Permanent Work under the Public Assistance [PA] Program), provided the repair or replacement has the effect of restoring the facility substantially as it existed before the disaster or emergency occurred."[4]

The Categorical Exclusions (CATEX)

- "Acquisition of properties and the associated demolition and removal or relocation of structures;
- Demolition of structures and other improvements or disposal of uncontaminated structures and other improvements to permitted off-site locations;

DOI: 10.4324/9781003487869-36

- Physical relocation of individual structures where FEMA has no involvement in the relocation site selection or development;
- Granting of community-wide exceptions for flood-proofed residential basements meeting the requirements of the National Flood Insurance Program;
- Repair, reconstruction, restoration, elevation, retrofitting, upgrading to current codes and standards, or replacement of any facility in a manner that substantially conforms to the pre-existing design, function, and location;
- Improvements to existing facilities and the construction of small scale hazard mitigation measures in existing developed areas with substantially completed infrastructure;
- Actions conducted within enclosed facilities where all airborne emissions, waterborne effluent, external radiation levels, outdoor noise, and solid and bulk waste disposal practices comply with existing laws and regulations."[5]

Extraordinary Circumstances

"CATEXs do not apply when there are extraordinary circumstances present that may result in significant environmental impacts. In such a case, FEMA prepares an EA (Environmental Assessment), unless the potential impact can be mitigated below a level of concern."[6]

Extraordinary circumstances include the following:

- "Greater scope or size than customary for the type of activity;
- A high level of public controversy;
- Potential for degradation of an already-environmentally compromised area;
- Use of new or unproven technology with unique or unknown environmental risks;
- Potentially significant effect on threatened or endangered species or critical habitat, or other protected resources (e.g., archeological, historical, or cultural);
- Potentially significant effect on public health or safety;
- Potential violation of law or regulation protecting the environment;
- Potential for significant cumulative impacts when combined with other past, present, and reasonably foreseeable future actions; and
- Potential to establish a precedent for future actions with significant effects."[7]

Example of Extraordinary Circumstances

"The demolition of a building would normally fall within a CATEX; however, if that building is historic or located within a historic district, the demolition action would require an EA (*Environmental Assessment*). because of extraordinary circumstances. In another example, if the extraordinary circumstance is the presence of an endangered species, say, a bird that nests at the building, modifying the construction schedule to avoid the nesting period may mitigate the impact, removing the extraordinary circumstances so that the project, subject to the revised construction schedule, may be treated as a CATEX."[8]

This next case involved a dam repair in South Carolina. "From October 1 to 23, 2015, Hurricane Joaquin created 1,000-year event levels of rainfall in certain regions of South Carolina. The President declared a major disaster on October 5, 2015. Dam structure D-1444 (Facility) owned by Sumter County (Applicant) suffered disaster-related damage. This structure is an earthen embankment dam with a two-lane paved roadway atop it. FEMA wrote Project Worksheet (PW) 976 to reimburse the costs of repairs to the roadway atop the Facility.

The Applicant hired AECOM Technical Services, Inc. (Contractor) on April 11, 2016, to assess damage to the dam and recommend repairs. The Contractor submitted a report dated June 13, 2016 which identified damages not accounted for in PW 976 and recommended the construction of an emergency spillway to reduce the potential for future overtopping. The South Carolina Department of Health and Environmental Control (SCDHEC) reclassified the Facility from a class two to a class one dam on June 1, 2016, necessitating revisions to the repairs. The Applicant amended its agreement with its Contractor on July 22, 2016 to include the additional repairs and the recommended spillway.

FEMA and the Applicant met on August 15, 2017 to review the proposed repairs and improvements. FEMA prepared a new PW (1108, the subject of this appeal) in November 2017 with an estimated eligible repair cost of $946,421.00 for repair of the earthen dam and a Hazard Mitigation Proposal (HMP) of $603,195.00 for the emergency spillway. The Applicant initiated work on December 5, 2017, with a projected completion of July 14, 2018, later extended to September 27, 2018.

FEMA's Environmental and Historic Preservation (EHP) review raised concerns regarding the downstream and community effects of the added spillway, and on May 9, 2018, FEMA informed the Applicant that an environmental assessment (EA) was required. The Applicant submitted the EA on August 23, 2018. In a follow-up meeting on November 7, 2018, the Applicant informed FEMA that work was started prior to the preparation of the EA and was 90 percent complete.

FEMA issued a Determination Memorandum (DM) on April 3, 2019 denying costs for PW 1108, as FEMA did not comply with the National Environmental Protection Act (NEPA) because the Agency was unable to perform its required environmental reviews prior to construction, and the HMP was no longer eligible as the work was denied."[9]

"The Applicant appealed FEMA's determination for $1,662,159.39. The Applicant argued that the repair work was eligible for statutory exclusion from NEPA as the dam was being repaired to predisaster condition. The Applicant claimed it did not anticipate an EA would be required prior to work commencing. Furthermore, the Applicant claimed it received verbal permission from FEMA to commence the work once the PW was written."[10] (Emphasis Added)

"FEMA Region IV Regional Administrator (RA) denied the appeal in a letter dated June 15, 2020. FEMA noted that the SOW developed in PW 1108 did not return the Facility to its predisaster condition. The SOW for PW 1108 expanded on the SOW of PW 976 and required re-evaluation for compliance with NEPA. As a result, PW 1108 did not qualify for statutory exclusion from NEPA review and the project and HMP were ineligible as the Applicant **began** work on the Facility prior to FEMA completing its EHP review."[11] (Emphasis Added)

"Changes in the SOW may result in additional EHP compliance reviews and/or new permits. A project's SOW may impact EHP resources; EHP staff must review the SOW to determine if modifications could reduce potential impacts. Proceeding with permanent work before FEMA completes EHP reviews jeopardizes PA funding. However, a project is categorically excluded from environmental review when FEMA has found that it will have little or no environmental impact. If, however, there is potential to affect protected natural or cultural resources, it cannot be categorically excluded and will require an EA. **Finally, no approval given by field personnel outside of the obligation process can be considered legally binding.**"[12] (Emphasis Added)

"FEMA obligated PW 976 on May 17, 2016 and included a SOW without changes to the original design of the structure. FEMA included conditions in PW 976 that 'any change to the approved [SOW] will require re-evaluation for compliance with NEPA and other Laws and Executive orders.' FEMA then wrote PW 1108 to reflect changes to the SOW, repairing damages and modifying the footprint of the Facility, including adding an emergency spillway and elevation of the roadway. These changes deviated from the approved SOW in PW 976 and required re-evaluation for environmental compliance.

Because FEMA determined the work could potentially affect protected natural or cultural resources, an EA was required. This is because the proposed SOW would not meet the categorical exclusion as the improvements involve potential impacts to upstream and downstream waters. In addition, the administrative record shows FEMA informed the Applicant multiple times of the risks of beginning work prior to the obligation of their projects."[13] (Emphasis Added)

Not NEPA, But Still Deadly

This next case, although not NEPA-specific, deals with an environmental issue and introduces a specific wildcard created by an Executive Order of the Florida governor.

"In 2017, Hurricane Irma damaged Collier County's (Applicant) Stan Gober Bridge (Facility). FEMA prepared Project Worksheet (PW) 5163, approving replacement of 219 tons of riprap to restore the Facility to predisaster condition. FEMA placed a Clean Water Act (CWA) condition on the project, noting that the Applicant was responsible for coordinating with the U.S. Army Corps of Engineer (USACE) and obtaining any required CWA section 404 permit or a Letter of Determination of No Effect from USACE.

Thereafter, the Applicant transmitted various Florida orders relating to the disaster. Specifically, Florida's Executive Order No. 17–235 declared a state of emergency and suspended any statute or rule that would prevent, hinder, or delay any recovery action necessary to cope with this emergency.

Florida Department of Environmental Protection (FDEP) OGC No. 17–0989 authorized certain actions to be conducted without notice to FDEP or a water management district, namely, installation of shoreline stabilization riprap that restored locations to predisaster condition.

The Applicant relied on the Florida orders to claim that because it met FDEP requirements, it satisfied the grant's CWA condition.

However, FEMA issued a determination memorandum finding that the Applicant did not demonstrate it coordinated the work completed with USACE or that it obtained either a required section 404 permit or a Letter of Determination of No Effect from USACE. In first appeal filings, the Applicant reiterated its reliance on the Florida orders to claim it satisfied the CWA condition and asserted it had coordinated with USACE. However, the FEMA Region IV Regional Administrator determined the Applicant had not demonstrated it complied with section 404 of the CWA because the Applicant had not provided documentation it coordinated with USACE to obtain either a permit for the work to the Facility or a declaration that no permit was required.

FEMA also noted that while the Florida orders waived certain state requirements, they did not exempt applicants from Federal regulations and permitting requirements."[14] (Emphasis Added)

This situation is a deathtrap for local governments. Although governors, mayors, county judges, and other elected and appointed officials often issue orders waiving certain legal and/or procedural orders, these orders have absolutely no effect on Federal laws or regulations. Local government agencies choosing to follow these waivers do so at their own extreme risk.

A Final If Heretical and Cynical Thought

After reading hundreds of appeals cases and DHS-OIG audits, the mind may begin to have thoughts similar to a drug-induced coma. In this case, it may be that even when a particular Project Worksheet has NO relevant environmental or historical issues, FEMA staff may include the language regarding its obligation to adhere to all environmental and historic regulations and Executive Orders, because that's what they usually do.

This then provides a deobligation escape hatch when the local agency makes an unapproved and unilateral change in the scope of work. Then instead of being faced with an "improved project" which FEMA typically allows at the original cost estimate, the opportunity presents itself where the entire project may be deobligated for the failure to consider the environmental and historic issues, which may or may not exist.

Notes

1 Public Assistance Program and Policy Guide, Version 4, June 1, 2020, FFP 104–009–2, p. 221.
2 Disaster Operations Legal Reference, Version 4.0, September 25, 2020, pp. 8–1.
3 Public Assistance Program and Policy Guide, Version 4, June 1, 2020, FFP 104–009–2, p. 141.
4 Ibid, pp. 8–6.
5 Ibid, pp. 8–5 through 8–6.
6 Ibid, pp. 8–8.
7 Ibid, pp. 8–8 through 8–9.
8 Ibid, pp. 8–10.
9 https://www.fema.gov/appeal/environmental-and-historic-preservation-compliance-hazard-mitigation
10 Ibid.
11 Ibid.
12 Ibid.
13 Ibid.
14 https://www.fema.gov/appeal/environmental-and-historic-preservation-compliance

32 Direct Administrative Costs (DAC)

Figure 32.1 Depiction of a rigged street-card game.

> Appealing a deobligation of DAC "is like losing your paycheck playing a rigged game of three-card monte and then playing the same game again a week later 'cause the cards are a different color."
>
> Paraphrase of Adam McKay quote

From a strictly financial perspective, for local agencies DAC, or Direct Administrative Costs, is a game of three-card monte.

Improper procurement is the gaping chest wound of Public Assistance.

Insurance issues are the amputated limbs of Public Assistance.

DAC for local agencies is usually a bug bite compared to the total losses from the disaster.

DOI: 10.4324/9781003487869-37

After reading hundreds of appeals cases for local agencies, there appears for many agencies to be no greater waste of time and money than applying for Direct Administrative Costs, except for the waste of time and money in filing DAC appeals cases.

Most local agencies only receive reimbursements for 40 to 50% of their total disaster losses for a variety of reasons. Some work is simply not eligible. Other work was not properly documented using the 5Ws: who, what, when, where, why, and how long for labor, equipment, and materials used for disaster response activities. Other work done under contract was not properly procured. Other times, FEMA makes required deductions to avoid duplicate of benefits. Why do so many agencies chase after a mere 5% of a Project Worksheet's costs while they ignore the importance of proper procurement, or the necessity of clearly understanding how their insurance or lack thereof will affect their bottom line?

How can agencies that do not or cannot properly document their time for their disaster field workers properly document their time for DAC, which is even more restrictive in terms of the details needed to properly document staff time? The situation is even worse when the DAC is for hired consultants of every stripe, not just disaster cost recovery consultants. The local agency relies implicitly on the consultant to properly document their time in such a way as to fully document and support the necessity and reasonableness of the costs incurred for Direct Administrative Costs. The failure rate for Direct Administrative Costs appeals cases is abysmal.

This case is from the Port of Galveston, Texas. "From September 7 to October 2, 2008, Hurricane Ike impacted areas in East Texas. The Port of Galveston (Applicant) claimed that the disaster caused erosion damage to fill material beneath concrete slabs at several of its piers. FEMA developed Project Worksheet (PW) 15830 to document permanent work and costs for repairs to Pier 10, including a hazard mitigation proposal and project-related direct administrative costs (DAC). FEMA initially obligated Public Assistance (PA) funding based on estimated costs for the project but later deobligated funding to account for actual insurance proceeds received by the Applicant. On December 11, 2020, the Texas Division of Emergency Management (Recipient) submitted a large project closeout request for PW 15830 that included additional DAC."[1]

"Regarding the DAC claim, FEMA pointed to a previous first appeal decision for PW 15839, a separate project also associated with repairs the Applicant completed following the same disaster. FEMA explained that in the referenced first appeal decision, it found DAC the Applicant claimed for services performed by Beck Disaster Recovery (BDR) *(the consultant)* was ineligible due to improper contract procurement. FEMA found that the Applicant's DAC claim for BDR (the consultant's) services under PW 15830, with costs totaling $229,269.01, was similarly ineligible."[2]

"The Applicant provided a lengthy analysis of the BDR (consultant's) contract procurement process under PW 15839, asserting that it complied with federal procurement requirements. The Applicant acknowledged that the BDR contract for that project was procured through an agreement in which an entity known as the Houston-Galveston Area Council Buy Board (HGAC-Buy) acted as its procurement agent. It asserted that HGAC-Buy procured the contract competitively, receiving 13 proposals in response to the bid solicitation, and that this was 'a direct indicator that adequate price competition was not lacking.' Thus, it asserted that BDR's (the consultant's) costs were reasonable, and a cost analysis for the contract was not required. Finally, the Applicant asserted that the use of HGAC-Buy for procurement constituted 'an intergovernmental purchasing agreement' that fulfilled federal standards under Title 44 of the Code of Federal Regulations Part 13, which was in effect at the time of the disaster."[3]

"On October 14, 2022, the FEMA Region 6 Regional Administrator (RA) denied the appeal, finding that the BDR contract was not compliant with federal procurement regulations. FEMA explained that HGAC-Buy did not base the procurement of the contract on the Applicant's specific requirements. FEMA noted that the contract bid advertisement was completed before the Applicant requested HGAC-Buy's assistance and included 'an infinite quantity of services' that 'could be provided to users nationwide.' Thus, FEMA determined that the broad nature of the procurement action restricted competition for the specific requirements under PW 15830 and amounted to a prohibited sole-sourced contract. FEMA also determined that the Applicant failed to demonstrate compliance with other federal procurement standards, such as performing a cost analysis or taking steps to utilize socioeconomic procurement practices."[4]

"On first appeal, FEMA determined that the Applicant's contract with BDR (the consultant) was not competitively procured. FEMA also found that the Applicant did not perform a cost analysis for the contract or take necessary steps to utilize small businesses, minority-owned firms, and/or women's business enterprises for the administrative services at issue. On second appeal, the Applicant does not contest the substance of these determinations."[5]

"On second appeal, FEMA examined the available documentation associated with the costs incurred under the BDR (consultant's) contract. The supporting documents total almost 4,000 pages, most of which appear to be unrelated to the Applicant's DAC claim for PW 15830. However, where information is highlighted and is presumably part of the claim (e.g., highlighted job titles and task descriptions listed on employee timesheets), it often lacks detail that would directly tie any of the associated work to PW 15830. In those cases where the Applicant notes project-specific information, the task descriptions provided are not specific enough for FEMA to evaluate their eligibility. The Applicant did not provide an explanation of the documentation with its appeal letter that would substantiate its assertion regarding reasonable costs or otherwise demonstrate how the documents support FEMA's previous request in the RFI. Therefore, FEMA finds that the Applicant has not provided documentation enabling a reasonable costs determination."[6]

Conclusion

"The Applicant failed to comply with procurement standards applicable to local governments. Additionally, the Applicant has not provided information that would enable a reasonable costs determination. Therefore, this appeal is denied."[7]

As bad as this may appear, it's actually much, much worse. In total, FEMA denied 15 different appeals for Direct Administrative Costs which covered 24 separate Project Worksheets. The total denied funding was $1,257,118.82.

In another series of DAC appeals also out of Texas, FEMA denied a major hospital system $904,672.00 of DAC, this time for insufficient documentation of the work allegedly performed as Direct Administrative Costs.[8]

In this series of cases, "FEMA did not issue an RFI specifically for PW 9894, instead considering the Applicant's RFI response to another appeal with the identical issue to be part of the record. In that RFI, FEMA requested documentation demonstrating that procurement of DAC contractors was performed in compliance with federal procurement requirements; copies of executed DAC contracts including scope of work (SOW) descriptions, qualifications of contractor personnel and hourly rates; documentation identifying the specific direct administrative work performed and trackable to the PWs; and the skill levels of the personnel performing the work. The Applicant's response to the RFI described the procurement process and provided copies of its DAC contract, a sample invoice showing rates charged, and its DAC request with associated appeal documentation submitted previously. It restated previous issues and contentions and acknowledged that it could not provide documentation identifying specific DAC tasks performed by its contractors relative to its PWs (Project Worksheets)."[9]

"The FEMA Region VI Regional Administrator denied the appeal by letter dated October 22, 2019. . . Finally, the Applicant acknowledged in its RFI response that it could not provide the documentation needed to support its DAC claim."[10]

And it is interesting to note that in both of these series of DAC denials, both entities had well-known disaster cost recovery consultants on contract at the time.

In yet another series of ten DAC appeals cases, a Florida School District was partially awarded $25,450 out of $40,072.[11]

However, in the Florida schools case, the average net from the appeals was only $1,272.50 per appeal. One must question the cost of the staff time involved in putting the 20 appeals cases together. (10 appeals times 2 = 20 appeals.) If someone performed a critical analysis of the time spent to recover this money, the agency would likely be in the hole financially.

We have already seen in the previous chapter that Cedar Rapids, Iowa, lost $198,000 in already-obligated DAC after appealing a mere $21,000 in deobligated DAC.

To say that FEMA closely scrutinizes requests for Direct Administrative Costs would be a felonious understatement.

All this said, if a local agency is playing an "A" game, then requesting DAC should be an option to add onto the obligated value of the Project Worksheets.

However, in more than 25 years of experience my observation is that very few local agencies, particularly smaller agencies, play at the championship level necessary to properly document the tasks as required to qualify for DAC reimbursement. Obviously, there are also some large agencies that are not playing an "A" game of disaster cost recovery, either.

Interestingly, the Public Assistance Program and Policy Guide, Version 4, effective on June 1, 2020, only lists the term "Direct Administrative Cost" one time, in the "Terms and Definitions" section of the PAPPG.

DAC Challenges

One of the challenges of documenting time for DAC is that time spent working on multiple projects is not eligible as a direct cost. Often, local staff and/or consultants may be in a meeting where several projects are discussed. Generally, none of this time is eligible for DAC reimbursement. However, if instead of one single meeting the various projects are discussed in their own separate meetings, then arguably, that time would be eligible. There is a form in this book which will partially automate and simplify the very detailed recordkeeping necessary to track multiple meetings, their attendees, their assignments, and the associated hourly wage and benefit costs.

The five-page form may be found in the Appendix, Form 57. This is not a FEMA form, and its use is not required by FEMA. However, it can assist in providing the detailed information which FEMA requires to properly document such information.

Page 1 is the "Base Data" sheet. Staff enters the base information, which is drawn from the same database of employees presented earlier in Form 25 in the Appendix. In Form 25, there is a list of all the local agency personnel, including their full name, job title, their base pay rate, employee ID number, their overtime ratio (typically 1.5 for time and one half pay), their straight time benefit rate, and their overtime benefit rate.

The correct data for each individual employee is automatically entered on the "Base Data" sheet as an employee's name is selected from the drop-down list which appears when the Attendee's name is selected. The person preparing the documents also enters the pertinent data for each individual meeting.

Also, on page 1 of 5, where the "Activities" are listed at the bottom of the page, each cell of the spreadsheet is a drop-down list of specific tasks which are generally considered DAC-eligible tasks. If a proposed task is not on the drop-down list, there is room to add additional tasks. However, the drop-down lists have been created from those tasks which in the past have usually been allowed for Direct Administrative Costs. Use caution in adding additional tasks to the list of tasks provided in the form.

When this is done, the meeting agenda form (page 2 of 5) will be automatically generated.

On page 3 of 5, the minutes will be similarly generated, with only the specific "Notes" to be entered regarding the discussion of the items noted in the agenda.

Page 4 of 5 is the meeting assignments/deliverables record, indicating which employees may have been given tasks to complete before the next meeting.

Page 5 of 5 then produces the "Labor Cost Tracker" which is self-generated, except to enter into the far-left column whether the employee was working on straight time or overtime.

Thus, a burdensome administrative task for tracking work done on a project-by-project basis is simplified and provides a fully documented record of the meeting for a single specific Project Worksheet.

These five sheets of documentation will need to be generated for each separate meeting to clearly show that the costs are directly attributable to a single Project Worksheet, and that the costs are not "indirect costs" which are ineligible for reimbursement.

FEMA also has its own DAC tracking worksheet, found in the Appendix, Form 58. This is a FEMA form, but to my knowledge its use is not required if the local agency can otherwise properly document its Direct Management Costs. This form is more appropriately used when there are field activities which may involve the use of equipment and/or materials for a specific project.

Also, for this form, a new copy of the form should be generated for each separate activity. Do not use the form for multiple different activities on the same project or for multiple different projects.

DAC and Travel Expenses

There are a number of appeals cases where DAC has been disallowed for a consultant's travel time and expense. FEMA's rationale is that travel time and expense are indirect costs insofar as these costs usually benefit multiple projects and are thus not Direct Administrative Costs. This case from Nassau County, NY, is illustrative of this issue. "From October 27, 2012, to November 9, 2012, Hurricane Sandy caused damage throughout the State of New York. Nassau County (Applicant) hired project management contractors, including Camp Dresser McKee & Smith (CDM Smith) (the consultant), to assist with the administration of multiple Public Assistance (PA) grants. CDM Smith's (The consultant's) employees often traveled to the Applicant's jurisdiction and worked on multiple projects over the course of a day, billing period, and trip. They also kept records of time spent working on each project task by assigning different codes to different projects, tasks, and categories of tasks."[12]

"Between June 25, 2013 and September 4, 2014, FEMA obligated several Project Worksheets (PWs) to document emergency protective measures and storm-related repairs. During the period in which FEMA initially obligated these PWs, the Applicant, the New York State Division of Homeland Security and Emergency Services (Grantee), and FEMA met and discussed the division of certain CDM Smith (consultant's) disaster consulting work into the following three categories: (1) Direct Administrative Costs (DAC), (2) project management, and (3) project coordination. During administration of the projects, CDM Smith (the consultant) utilized a methodology to allocate travel expenses across multiple projects (Expense Allocation Methodology), described in a Memorandum dated January 8, 2013 (Expense Analysis Memo). Specifically, CDM Smith (the consultant) calculated an hourly travel expense rate for each of its employees per billing period by dividing the employee's total travel expenses by the total number of hours the employee worked on Applicant projects during the billing period. CDM Smith (the consultant) then multiplied an employee's travel expense rate for the billing period by the number of hours billed to a specific task by that employee, in order to allocate travel expenses to each project on a pro rata basis."[13]

"By letter dated January 6, 2017 (DAC Determination Memo), however, FEMA informed the Applicant that CDM Smith's (the consultant's) indirect travel expenses associated with direct administrative and project coordination tasks were not eligible for reimbursement as DAC. This determination rested on FEMA Disaster Assistance Policy (DAP) 9525.9, Section 324 Management Costs and Direct Administrative Costs (November 13, 2007), and the Memorandum from the Assistant Administrator, Disaster Assistance Directorate, dated September 8, 2009, (DAC Guidance)."[14]

"Direct costs are those that can be 'identified separately and assigned to a specific project,' such as staff time to conduct an initial inspection, prepare and submit PWs, and make interim and final inspections of the project. By contrast, 'costs a grantee or subgrantee incurs for a common or joint purpose benefitting more than one cost objective that are not readily assignable to the cost objectives specifically benefitted' are indirect costs. Travel expenses related to one specific PW qualify as DAC, while travel expenses 'related to general support and not directly tied to one specific project' are indirect costs. Indirect costs are not eligible for reimbursement as DAC. More pertinently, an applicant cannot allocate expenses to every task for all PWs in proportion to the hours worked on the task, and then claim such expenses as DAC."[15]

"Here, the Applicant attempts to claim as DAC and/or contract costs certain travel expenses that its contractors incurred, despite its acknowledgment that CDM Smith's (the contractor's) employees worked on several PWs over the course of each trip at issue. Specifically, the Applicant seeks pro rata allocations of travel and lodging expenses across multiple PWs, based upon the hours worked on a given PW during the course of a given trip."[16]

"However, as noted, a pro rata allocation of expenses across every task for all PWs on the basis worked on the task does not make such expenses eligible for reimbursement as DAC. Since the travel expenses at issue benefited more than one PW, they are indirect costs. Accordingly, under DAP 9525.9, the Applicant cannot allocate or otherwise assign such expenses to individual projects as DAC or contract costs. Such costs are only reimbursable as management expenses, if at all."[17]

Therefore, if a local agency is going to claim DAC, it must clearly understand that most if not all of the consultant's travel expenses will be ineligible for reimbursement, and thus borne entirely by the local agency as out-of-pocket expenses.

The Bottom Line on Direct Administrative Costs (DAC)

Another 5% of disaster financial assistance is a particularly good thing. The issue is that DAC is difficult to get, especially for local agencies that have not mastered the fundamentals of disaster cost tracking. And for those agencies, DAC may be more of an illusion than an attainable reality.

If a disaster cost recovery consultant says that their fees are reimbursable (technically, partially reimbursable), this may be true. However, if the cost recovery consultant does not properly document their time, or if their services were not procured in compliance with 2 CFR, Part 200, then pursuing DAC will be a high-risk endeavor, and quite possibly not worth the effort that it takes. Furthermore, depending on the consultant's fee schedule, those hourly rates currently above $155.00 may invite extreme scrutiny from FEMA. However, in all cases, FEMA insists that each specific task is performed by an appropriate level member of the consultant's team.

And it must be understood that not all tasks are DAC eligible, whether performed by the local agencies' own staff or the consultant's staff. If the local agency is determined to apply for DAC, then it must be intimately familiar with FEMA's Recovery Policy FP 104–11–2 in its current version.

Notes

1 https://www.fema.gov/appeal/allowable-costs-reasonable-costs-financial-accounting-reconciliation-pro-curement-13
2 Ibid.
3 Ibid.
4 Ibid.
5 Ibid.
6 Ibid.
7 Ibid.
8 https://www.fema.gov/appeal/direct-administrative-costs-and-management-costs-appeals
9 Ibid.
10 Ibid.
11 https://www.fema.gov/appeal/direct-administrative-costs-and-management-costs-0
12 https://www.fema.gov/appeal/direct-administrative-costs-project-management-costs
13 Ibid.
14 Ibid.
15 Ibid.
16 Ibid.
17 Ibid.

33 Regional (and Personal) Interpretations of FEMA Regulations

FEMA has approximately 20,000 employees on its workforce. Despite volumes of Federal laws and regulations, this means that there are somewhere in the neighborhood of 20,000 different opinions at work every day. Although the laws and regulations are generally clear and specific, there is always room for interpretation, even under our constitutional framework.

The Constitutional Framework

"Under the Constitution, Congress raises revenue and appropriates funds for Federal agency operations and programs. Courts interpret this constitutional authority to mean that executive branch officials, e.g., FCOs (*Federal Coordinating Officers*) and staff members, must find affirmative authority for the obligation and expenditure of appropriated funds. The established rule is that the expenditure of public funds is proper only when authorized by Congress, not that public funds may be expended unless prohibited by Congress."[1] (Emphasis Added)

FEMA's task, relative to the Public Assistance program, is to provide financial (and sometimes direct) assistance to local agencies when authorized to do so by the President, as evidenced by the signing of a Presidential disaster declaration. FEMA provides funding, but only when the need for that funding is in clear evidence. For local agencies, this important principle is sometimes either unnoticed or overlooked. FEMA will not provide assistance merely because the local agency says something was damaged or costs were otherwise incurred. The documentation is everything.

The local agency must prove that a) the agency itself is an eligible recipient, b) the agency is legally responsible for the work, c) the claimed damage exists, d) the claimed damage was caused by the declared disaster, e) the disaster was the sole cause of the damage, i.e., there were no other contributory factors which could have been responsible, even in part, for the damages, and f) providing financial aid for the damages themselves is not otherwise prohibited by law or regulation.

Although this language may appear to be clear-cut, it may be anything but. There are an unlimited number of variations in life and in disasters; the task of determining the correct path is not always in clear sight. Hence, we come to the variable interpretations of the regulations.

Staffing Wildcards

Disasters come in various sizes, scopes, and intensities. A disaster in Vermont needs little more than a million dollars to qualify for a Presidential disaster declaration, while a disaster in California, in mid-2023, needs approximately 70,000 million dollars to qualify for a Federal declaration. This means that a disaster in Vermont may be well within the capabilities of the FEMA Region I office to support, whereas a California disaster may require the staffing assistance provided by other FEMA regions, certainly in the very early days of the disaster. A multi-state disaster, such

DOI: 10.4324/9781003487869-38

as Hurricane Katrina, Hurricane Sandy, or similar size disaster may necessitate many, if not most, FEMA regions to lend a hand for the initial response support.

And there enters a potential problem for the local agencies. The local agency may have previous disaster recovery experience, but now has been assigned to a FEMA staffer from another FEMA region. Voila! The rules appear to be different, or at least the interpretation of those rules is different. Such is life. In the words of the poet, "Theirs not to make reply/Theirs not to reason why/ Theirs but to do and die."[2]

The good news is that many of these temporarily assigned FEMA staffers will shortly return to their home base and take their differing interpretations of the regulations with them. The bad news is that once we get a replacement staffer, we may have to start all over again, possibly with yet another interpretation of the regulations.

This is one of the most frustrating aspects of the Public Assistance program: I call it the carousel. A colleague of mine worked as a consultant for a major port following a disaster and kept a written log of every staff person, either from the state emergency management agency or FEMA, assigned to assist the port with its recovery. He was there for nearly eight years. Over that approximately 100-month time period, his list contained 111 different names. This means that every month on average, he had to deal with a changing of the guard. This rotation of support staff makes a difficult job even more so, especially considering that each of these different people may have a slightly different interpretation of the regulations and require that (otherwise) unnecessary changes be made.

This merry-go-round of continuing staff changes is not entirely a FEMA policy issue. First, when FEMA staff is temporarily assigned to another region of the country, it is natural that these employees will want to return to their own homes as soon as possible. Second, there are Internal Revenue Service regulations which require that travel and living expenses after a time become taxable as ordinary income. In a hypothetical case, if a FEMA employee is paid $60,000 per year, then their daily earnings are in the $230.00 per day range. The cost of hotels, meals, and other travel incidentals may, depending on time of year and location, be close to the employee's daily wages. To have this much money added to their annual salary represents a hefty tax increase and a powerful incentive to return home, where this travel expense tax disappears. These two factors are in addition to the normal job turnover rates experienced by any other employer. Hence, the local agencies will experience a gradual, but continual change of personnel, usually from both the state and FEMA. For some local agency that is struggling to stay afloat in choppy seas, the change of shift for the lifeguards is not an eagerly anticipated event.

Information on the IRS website confirms these issues: "Generally, your tax home is the entire city or general area where your main place of business or work is located, regardless of where you maintain your family home. For example, you live with your family in Chicago but work in Milwaukee where you stay in a hotel and eat in restaurants. You return to Chicago every weekend. You may not deduct any of your travel, meals or lodging in Milwaukee because that's your tax home. Your travel on weekends to your family home in Chicago isn't for your work, so these expenses are also not deductible."[3]

A financial administrator colleague in another state worked for an agency that had the most unfortunate track record for several years. In the 2010s, they had 8 different disasters, either major Presidential disasters or Fire Management Assistance Grant (FMAG) disasters. This colleague told me that every disaster had different rules, or at least different interpretations of the same rules.

Furthermore, not all employees at any level of government, local, state, or Federal, are equally knowledgeable, experienced, and well trained. This is true for FEMA and the respective state's emergency management agencies. Newer, and arguably inexperienced, employees may provide information or give direction which is either inappropriate or flat-out wrong.

498 Submitting for Reimbursement

Earlier, in Chapter 9, we looked at an appeals case of a regional hospital in Ohio. There were multiple problems with their appeal, and they probably wasted a great deal of time and money on pursuing it. However, having been denied satisfaction via the appeals process, they apparently felt they had not wasted enough money, so they filed a lawsuit with a district court of appeals. This is an excerpt from the court's decision in the case: "According to the Hospital, one of FEMA's employees promised reimbursement for the cost of new equipment. That promise, if made, lacks legal significance. No field employee can commit the agency to pay more than the statute and regulations require."[4]

Regional Interpretations

Some 20+ years ago there was a flood along the Red River which had a substantial impact on Grand Forks, North Dakota, but also affected properties across the river in Minnesota. In that part of the country, the Red River is the line of demarcation between FEMA Region V and Region VII. There were appeals cases, long lost to the author's memory, where similar circumstances of damage were approved in one region but denied in the other.

On a similar note, while teaching a class some years ago, I was discussing a point when one of the attendees, who happened to be a long-term FEMA employee, pointed out that in his region, the particular rule was neither interpreted nor enforced as it was written.

The Bottom Line

In dealing with both FEMA and the state, we will experience staff turnover. With those rotations of personnel will come differing interpretations of the regulations and different requests for information as the process evolves.

A recommended best practice is for the local agency to maintain a roster of these staff rotations, by name, by agency, and by dates of assignment, if only to have rock-solid information available to demonstrate to the local agency senior management and elected officials some of the serious challenges which must be faced in moving the disaster cost recovery process forward.

Note, however, that these rotations of staff from either the state or FEMA will have no bearing should the agency decide to file an appeal on a denial or deobligation. At the local agency, we are expected by FEMA to know the rules, at least as they are written, and abide by them.

This is of course the great challenge of the Public Assistance process. The local agency is responsible for knowing and understanding a great body of regulations, derived from many different statutes, which that same local agency hopes it will never need to know or use.

Few if any local government agencies are willing to operate without liability insurance; few agencies would operate without fire insurance; but many government agencies are apparently willing to run bare-naked into the face of the greatest potential loss it might ever experience with a catastrophic disaster. Knowledge of these Federal regulations is power, and without knowledge of the regulations, the local agency is relatively powerless and almost completely dependent on the advice of FEMA and the state to restore itself to its pre-disaster condition.

Notes

1 Disaster Operations Legal Reference, Version 4.0, September 25, 2020, pp. 2–19.
2 Lord Tennyson, Alfred, 1854, The Charge of the Light Brigade.
3 https://www.irs.gov/taxtopics/tc511
4 United States Court of Appeals For the Seventh Circuit No. 12–2007, Columbus Regional Hospital, v. Federal Emergency Management Agency, p. 9.

34 Building and Infrastructure Codes and Standards

Figure 34.1 Depiction of a structure needing post-disaster repairs.

Codes and Standards

"The Stafford Act authorizes FEMA to reimburse the costs of repair and replacement (*of damaged structures and infrastructure*) based on the design of the facility as it existed immediately before the disaster event but also in 'conformity with codes, specifications, and standards applicable at the time at which the disaster occurred.' Improvements and upgrades are eligible provided they are accordance with applicable standards of safety, decency, and sanitation and in conformity with applicable codes, specifications, and standards."[1]

This chapter is important because structures and infrastructure owned by local agencies are often decades old, and the minimum codes and standards required for building new structures

DOI: 10.4324/9781003487869-39

or infrastructure have changed since the original construction. FEMA provides funding for these "upgrades" necessary to comply with the newly adopted codes and standards appropriate to the type of construction involved. However, absent the proper adoption and enforcement of the applicable codes and standards, FEMA will not provide funding and the costs will have to be borne by the local agency.

Codes and Standards Eligibility Criteria

"Facility repairs and new construction may 'trigger' upgrade requirements established by codes or standards. Upgrades required by Federal or SLTT (State, local, tribal, or territorial) repair or replacement codes or standards are eligible only if the code or standard:

- Applies to the type of restoration required;
- Is appropriate to the pre-disaster use of the facility;
- Is reasonable, in writing, formally adopted by the SLTT government, and implemented by the Applicant on or before the declaration date, OR is a legal Federal requirement;
- Applies uniformly; and
- Was enforced during the time it was in effect."[2]

"A code or standard must meet **all five** criteria to be eligible for funding."[3] (Emphasis Added)

Codes and standards issues are common in appeals cases; references to codes and standards appear in nearly 10% of all appeals cases, often in mixed-bag appeals cases where several issues are at stake. From a disaster cost recovery perspective, codes and standards appeal case losses range from tens of thousands of dollars to hundreds of thousands of dollars, and sometimes into seven-figure losses. In some cases, the local agency retains the original Project Worksheet obligation amount but gets nothing for the codes and standards work, which FEMA may determine to be an improved project.

Even when the codes and standards are properly adopted, consistently enforced, and meet all other requirements, if the FEMA-approved scope of work does not specifically address the inclusion of those codes and standards, then the local agency must file a request to FEMA for a revised scope of work which includes those required codes and standards.

When citing a required code or standard, it is not sufficient to cite the code as follows: The National Electrical Code (NEC), or NFPA 70 (National Fire Protection Association). The code citation must include the exact chapter and verse of the language in the code.

"250.114 Equipment Connected by Cord and Plug.

Exposed, normally non-current-carrying metal parts of cord-and plug-connected equipment shall be connected to the equipment grounding conductor under any of the following conditions:

(3) In residential occupancies:

    e. Portable handlamps and portable luminaires

(4) In other than residential occupancies:

    e. Portable handlamps and portable luminaires"[4]

Codes and Standards Adoption

"Codes and standards must be in writing, formally adopted by the SLTT government, and implemented by the Applicant on or before the declaration date, OR be a legal Federal requirement, such as an ADA or seismic safety requirement. An appropriate legislative body or regulatory authority within the jurisdiction must:

- Approve the code or standard;
- Make it a matter of public record; and
- Formally incorporate it into the building code or other applicable ordinance.

The code or standard must apply to the facility in question. For example, if a State has jurisdiction over a particular type of work and formally adopts a code or standard related to that work, a Tribal or local government in that State does not necessarily have had to formally adopt the code or standard for it to apply to its facility. The Tribal or local government meets the above requirement if it shows that it implements the code or standard consistently."[5]

The rules for codes and standards are different for repair work versus replacement, i.e., new construction. When the facility can be restored to its pre-disaster function and capacity, only those elements being repaired require compliance with the existing codes and standards. When the facility is so damaged that FEMA authorizes a replacement facility, then the adopted codes and standards apply throughout the project. We will discuss both aspects separately.

At first glance, the application of the appropriate codes and standards may seem uncomplicated. This is simply not the case. Codes and standards, whether for buildings, roads and bridges, culverts, or other infrastructure are highly technical in nature and subject to close reading to avoid costly errors.

Moreover, the topic of codes and standards is further complicated because there are multiple codes and standards, and then there are recommended best practices, which are in FEMA's interpretation not enforceable, nor are they eligible criteria for the repair or replacement of facilities and infrastructure. Just one of the wildcards in this hand is the U.S. Army Corps of Engineers (USACE) Nationwide Permit System, which is often cited as a code and standard, but may in fact not be enforceable or eligible for FEMA funding.

This "codes and standards" case is from Missouri and illustrates the complexities in play. Like so many other appeals cases, this case contains multiple issues, so we will focus on the codes and standards issues.

"From August 2 to 14, 2013, severe storms, straight-line winds, and flooding damaged numerous water crossings (corrugated metal pipe (CMP) and box culverts, concrete slab low water crossings, and a concrete overpass) in Pulaski County, Missouri (Applicant). The President declared a major disaster on September 6, 2013."[6]

"Between October 2013 and April 2014, FEMA prepared Project Worksheets (PWs) 10, 381, 382, 383, 384, and 386 to document eligible Category C (roads/bridges) work to restore the Applicant's water crossings to their predisaster condition, with a total estimated cost of $282,546.05 for all projects. FEMA approved a scope of work (SOW) under each PW to completely replace the water crossings using force account labor, equipment, and materials, and informed the Applicant of construction permitting requirements necessary for each project."[7]

"The Applicant hired a contractor to prepare engineering reports and design plans for each recommended water crossing replacement structure. The contractor began planning for each new replacement structure to comply with construction guidelines required to receive permit authorization from the U.S. Army Corps of Engineers (USACE) under its authorities to regulate the discharge of dredged or fill material into waters of the United States. Between March and July 2015, the Applicant submitted design plans for each project to USACE for review."[8]

"USACE issued a series of jurisdictional determination memorandums, authorizing the Applicant's project designs under nationwide permits (NWPs). USACE noted that the Applicant's projects were required to comply with guidelines found in the Missouri Nationwide Permit Regional Conditions. At the request of the State of Missouri Emergency Management Agency (Grantee), the Applicant also submitted separate project designs that would restore each water crossing to its predisaster condition, which more closely reflected the items of work in the approved SOWs. In email correspondence from this time, USACE advised the Applicant such designs would not meet NWP guidelines, and would therefore not be authorized."[9]

"Because the predisaster designs failed to meet USACE permitting requirements, the Applicant submitted SOW (*scope of work*) change requests to FEMA for selected sites documented in PWs 10, 381, 382, 383, 384, and 386. The SOW change requests reflected the design plans approved by USACE, and noted increased costs for each project; the increased costs resulted from changes the Applicant claimed were necessary to 'meet current bridge design standards and [satisfy] the appropriate permits for new stream crossings.' Items of work reflected in the SOW change requests substantially upgraded the primary structure(s) at the majority of the water crossing sites (for example, replacing CMP (*corrugated metal pipe*) culverts with triple box culverts or a slab-beam bridge)."[10]

"From August 2015 to April 2016, FEMA issued a series of Determination Memoranda that denied the Applicant's SOW change requests. Generally, FEMA found that the various construction guidance and specification documents used to develop the Applicant's project designs did not meet the criteria for eligible codes and standards listed at 44 C.F.R. § 206.226(d) and described in more detail by Disaster Assistance Policy (DAP) 9527.4, Construction Codes and Standards (2008). Regarding the NWP guidelines in particular, FEMA found: (1) USACE did not mandate specific design criteria through the NWP general or regional conditions; (2) lower cost options were possible that would meet permitting requirements; and (3) the Applicant failed to demonstrate USACE had denied permits for project designs that would return each water crossing to its predisaster condition."[11] (Emphasis Added)

"Additionally, FEMA determined that for each site there were multiple alternative designs that would be less costly to construct, while still satisfying the NWP conditions. FEMA directed the Applicant to provide at least three alternative designs for each site, including proposed SOWs and estimated costs, and to identify the design with the lowest economic impact."[12] (Emphasis Added)

In cases where it may appear to FEMA that the local agency is attempting to "game" the system, FEMA may respond with what may appear to be overly burdensome documentation requests, as seen here in the previous paragraph.

"The RA (*Regional Administrator*) determined that the NWP general and regional conditions allowed for discretion in their application and therefore did not apply uniformly to all sites, and the Applicant failed to demonstrate the formal adoption of the guidelines prior to the disaster. Likewise, the industry, State, and local construction guidelines used to develop the Applicant's preferred designs were ineligible for PA funding. Finally, the RA found that the Applicant had skewed its hydrological and hydraulic analyses to favor its preferred project designs, and failed to provide alternative project designs of reasonable cost that were 'close in design to the pre-disaster [sic] configuration' of each site, and would also meet permitting requirements."[13] (Emphasis Added)

"FEMA has the authority to determine which repairs, code-mandated or otherwise, are eligible for assistance, and generally does not fund code-mandated work that does not meet all five criteria, regardless of whether the work is needed to obtain a building, occupancy, environmental, or other permit. An eligible code or standard must contain objective standards based on specific design criteria. Guidelines that offer generic guidance or merely make recommendations do not satisfy the eligibility criteria in 44 C.F.R. § 206.226(d). As stated in the RA's (*Regional Administrator's*) decision, the NWP conditions (in particular NWP General Condition 9 (Management of Water Flows) and the Missouri NWP Regional Conditions, which the Applicant identified as containing the controlling standard for development of its project designs) frequently use discretionary language and broad guidelines in describing construction practices. Where specific criteria are given, the NWP conditions frame such criteria in terms of **recommendations, versus requirements** for mandatory adherence. Insofar as the NWP conditions constitute standards for construction, they are subjective and allow for significant discretion in implementation. The NWP conditions do not meet the criteria for eligible codes and standards, therefore FEMA cannot approve the Applicant's current SOW change requests."[14] (Emphasis Added)

In the case of a set of codes and standards which are industry based, regional or state-wide, the local jurisdiction should always formally adopt these codes and standards as their own to guarantee that they will be applicable and eligible in the event of a disaster.

This next case is also a multi-issue case, and we will focus on the codes and standards issues. Here the failure to formally adopt codes and standards plays a role in this case from Tennessee. "In May 2010, severe storms, tornadoes, heavy rains, high winds, flooding, and flash flooding impacted the City of Clarksville, Tennessee. As a result, the Ultraviolet (UV) Filter Building (Facility) within Clarksville Gas and Water's (Applicant) wastewater treatment plant (WWTP) was flooded and the Facility's UV disinfection system was damaged. FEMA prepared Project Worksheet (PW) 4722 to estimate damage and associated costs to the Facility. FEMA estimated the amount of disaster damage at $2,176,377.70."[15]

"The Applicant requested a total amount of $5,720,000.00, as opposed to $2,176,377.70 originally estimated by FEMA. The Applicant attributed the additional costs to replacement, as opposed to repair, of the Facility to meet current regulatory discharge limitation standards."[16]

"... the RA (*Regional Administrator*) agreed that the predisaster UV disinfection system did not meet current regulatory requirements, and approved an improved project to install the bulk sodium hypochlorite system, contingent upon its receipt of a Grantee-approved time extension request and an accepted improved project request. However, the RA determined that additional costs to comply with an August 1, 2010 National Pollutant Discharge Elimination System (NPDES) permit were ineligible because the permit established discharge limitation standards after the disaster declaration date and the upgrades were not required to restore the Facility to pre-disaster design and capacity and capped the total eligible amount at $2,947,415.70."[17]

"However, to be eligible for PA funding, the work must be the result of the disaster event, regardless of whether the work is a necessary code or standard upgrade, meaning there must be a direct relationship between the upgrade work and the disaster damage. Stated differently, while any upgrade must comply with all applicable environmental laws, this does not necessarily mean the upgrade work is eligible under the PA Program. Moreover, FEMA does not fund work to bring into compliance facilities in violation of codes or standards at the time of the disaster."[18] (Emphasis Added)

"As required by the Clean Water Act, all municipal, industrial and commercial facilities that discharge wastewater or stormwater directly from a point source into a water of the United States must obtain an NPDES permit to ensure that the receiving waters will achieve their Water Quality Standards. Compliance with an NPDES permit does not mandate certain design or construction methods, but requires a permitee to meet certain effluent discharge limits at its facility. The Applicant states that, when the Facility was installed in 2001, the permit requirements mandated a disinfection standard of 200 fecal coliform per 100 milliliters (mL) by monthly geometric mean. However, a new NPDES permit was issued in 2007 requiring a disinfection limit of 126 E. coli per 100 mL by monthly geometric mean and 487 E. coli per 100 mL as a daily maximum, a more stringent effluent limitation."[19]

"Even if NPDES permit requirements are deemed 'codes' under 44 C.F.R. § 206.226(d), it is important to note that the disaster did not necessitate the requirements in the 2007 NPDES permit. The issuance of the NPDES permit in April 2007 compelled the more stringent effluent discharge limits. Because the UV Filter Building is part of a wastewater treatment facility, the Applicant was required to comply with the new effluent limitations, effective on June 1, 2007, and perform the necessary upgrades irrespective of whether the disaster damaged the Facility or not. Therefore, upgrading the UV system to comply with more stringent effluent limitations was not required as the result of the disaster. Consequently, costs associated with such upgrades are not eligible under the PA program."[20]

"Further, the Applicant concedes that the UV system did not meet the 2007 NPDES permit requirements at the time of the disaster in its second appeal. Environmental Protection Agency (EPA) records also show the WWTP's *(wastewater treatment plant)* effluent violated NPDES requirements immediately prior, during, and immediately following the disaster event. The second appeal provides no explanation as to why, almost three years after the permit became effective, the Facility had not been updated to comply with the 2007 NPDES permit requirements. Because work to bring facilities in violation of code into compliance is not eligible under the PA Program, upgrade work necessary to bring the UV disinfection system into compliance with NPDES permit requirements is not eligible."[21]

In general, the issue of codes and standards relative to infrastructure, roads, bridges, and culverts are complex and may require close coordination with FEMA and multiple other agencies: Federal, state, regional, tribal in some cases, and local. Frequently while sorting out the codes and standards issues, the local agency may not even begin construction work prior to receiving the approvals of all involved agencies. The codes and standards issues for buildings may be slightly less burdensome because they often do not involve outside agencies to the same degree that some infrastructure projects, particularly water related or water adjacent projects, may present.

After reading hundreds of appeal cases, it appears that there is often a disconnect between the disaster cost recovery team or department staff developing the Project Worksheets and the construction project managers who are responsible for administering the contracts and getting projects completed. These construction managers seem hell-bent on doing the project the way they think is best irrespective of the contractual language of the Project Worksheet, including a very specific Scope of Work.

When the terms of the scope of work are violated, sometimes in minute ways and sometimes in significant ways, FEMA will land very hard on the local agency for its failure to comply with the terms of the Project Worksheet, particularly the defined and approved Scope of Work. FEMA's primary option is to reduce the level of funding. If the agency is fortunate, FEMA will classify the project as an "improved project" and only pay the dollar amount initially approved. In worst cases, which may also depend on how many other violations of the terms of the Project Worksheet exist, FEMA may deny all funding for the specific project.

Although there are likely fewer inter-agency coordination issues with building restorations, that is not to say that there will never be coordination issues with outside agencies, as seen here in the next case from California.

"During the incident period of August 24 through September 8, 2014, a 6.0 magnitude earthquake and subsequent aftershocks caused damage throughout Napa County. Because there was no alternative location for 900+ students and staff, and the Napa Valley Unified School District (Applicant) was concerned about the public health and safety hazard posed by damaged suspended light fixtures and ceiling systems, it acted quickly to replace them. The Applicant requested Public Assistance (PA) funding for work to replace the damaged suspended lighting and ceiling systems at six school campuses, asserting that the California Division of the State Architect (DSA) required the complete replacement of damaged systems in accordance with code-compliant systems."[22]

"FEMA advised the Applicant of the requirement that for code upgrades to be eligible for PA funding, they must meet certain eligibility criteria. The Applicant responded with a letter from the DSA, which indicated that, when reviewing the project, it applied code requirements specified in the California Building Standards Code (CBC). FEMA advised the Applicant that the DSA letter did not establish that any written codes or standards required replacement of the systems. The Applicant submitted a second letter from DSA, which stated that based on CBC requirements, the damaged suspended ceiling and lights have to be replaced as a system, not in parts, to ensure that corrective action complies with DSA's procedure and applicable Interpretations of Regulations (IR)."[23]

"On March 9, 2015, FEMA prepared Project Worksheet (PW) 191 to document the reported earthquake damage. FEMA approved replacement for fallen suspended lighting fixtures, and repair to predisaster condition for the remaining damaged suspended lighting and ceiling systems. FEMA's PA Determination Memorandum found the Applicant failed to identify codes or standards that prohibited repair and required complete replacement of suspended lighting and ceiling systems, and designated the restoration as an improved project because the scope of work (SOW) performed by the Applicant exceeded eligible work. FEMA capped the eligible funding based on estimated costs to repair the suspended lighting and ceiling systems, and direct administrative costs, obligating PW 191 for $127,586.63."[24]

"The Applicant submitted first appeal letters dated July 1 and July 30, 2015, requesting reimbursement totaling $1,851,876.29. The Applicant asserted the suspended lighting system was no longer code compliant, and replacement was the only factory warranted repair. The Applicant indicated components to repair damaged suspended ceiling elements were no longer available and noted the DSA would not allow fabrication and testing of components to modify the outdated suspended ceiling. They had no choice but to replace the suspended ceiling which was not code compliant in accordance with DSA requirements. The Applicant attached letters from several parties involved in the project to support its claim. A consulting structural engineer cited DSA IR 25–2.13, Metal Suspension Systems for Lay-in Panel Ceilings, noting suspended ceiling grid systems could not be modified or repaired unless brought up to code."[25]

"The FEMA Region IX Regional Administrator (RA) denied the appeal on April 5, 2017. The RA determined Section 4–309(e) did not satisfy the requirement that a code or standard apply to the type of repair or restoration criterion set forth in 44 C.F.R. § 206.226(d)(1), because Section 4–309(e) triggered upgrades on the basis of structural damage and, citing the Guide and Checklist for Nonstructural Earthquake Hazards in California Schools, suspended light fixtures and ceiling systems are nonstructural building components. With regard to DSA's general authority under the Field Act to enforce the CBC, cited by the Applicant as requiring the upgrades, the RA determined, in the absence of a formally adopted code requiring the upgrades, a decision to require upgrades rested on an official's discretion and not on objective written standards."[26]

Once again, had the school district formally adopted the code requirements of the Office of the State Architect, there might have been some solid ground upon which to stand. However, this would have required incredible foresight on the part of the school administrators.

A Minefield in Quicksand

The mishmash between codes and standards and the scope of work is a bit like walking through a minefield strewn in a bog of quicksand. This is a treacherous landscape if ever there was one. Many local agencies do not have a crystal-clear understanding of what it takes to have a code or standard accepted by FEMA. The local agency through its engineers and project managers tends to see its disaster-damaged facilities as a great opportunity to make much-needed improvements, and to do so under the guise of a codes and standards upgrade. These engineers and project managers will examine the work to be done and then grasp at straws, straws which in reality do not exist, as a basis for making improvements. FEMA always plays hardball with codes and standards, with no quarter given.

Submitting for Reimbursement

A West Coast agency had a major disaster loss some years ago. This is an agency with a very liberal and progressive agenda, including a LEED (*Leadership in Energy and Environmental Design*), ordinance. The ordinance stipulates how energy-efficient (as close to zero carbon emissions as possible) standards are enforced in both new and remodeled construction projects.

In the disaster loss, some of the facilities were nearly a hundred years old, and clearly the building codes and standards had changed over the decades. This agency would not even consider replacing those destroyed facilities without making them LEED certified. However, there was a poison pill in the ordinance. I stated that the standards applied "unless doing so would be cost prohibitive." This single sentence dooms these codes and standards upgrades to oblivion. To FEMA this makes the ordinance discretionary, and therefore inapplicable.

This case, from Mississippi following Hurricane Katrina, appears to be exactly like the situation just described. "Storm surge from Hurricane Karina damaged the Applicant's water, sewer and drainage systems south of the CSX railroad tracks. In October 2005, a joint team of personnel from the Environmental Protection Agency (EPA), FEMA and the Applicant conducted damage assessments of the Applicant's water and sewer systems in this area. Following the assessments, EPA recommended replacement of all water lines, service connections, meters, meter saddles and meter pits. The City subdivided the reconstruction area into six sub-areas (1, 2, 3A, 3B, 3C, and 3D). FEMA prepared PW 10970 for $20,453,194 to replace all sewer lines, mains and connections in Area 3B to their pre-disaster design. Area 3B encompasses the area between Oaks Avenue to the eastern city limits and between the CSX railroad tracks and U.S. Highway 90."[27]

"On December 5, 2007, the Applicant submitted a Request for an Improved Project to expand the water and sewer systems to account for future demand in Area 3B. By a letter dated March 25, 2009, the Applicant submitted a request for additional funding for the costs associated with the expansion to the systems. The Applicant explained that the expansion was in accordance with local codes and standards in effect prior to Hurricane Katrina. The Applicant further explained that because so few buildings remained after the disaster and zoning determined what structures could return to the area, the City's zoning code was the only logical foundation upon which to base the capacity of public services. Furthermore, the size of the water mains was based on the fire flow requirements required by the Gulfport Fire Chief. Finally, the sewer main sizes were based on an engineering study to identify the peak flow discharge rates in order to meet the code and zoning requirements. In a letter dated August 31, 2009, FEMA determined that costs to increase the size of some water lines to meet existing fire ordinance requirements were eligible for funding. However, the letter also stated that the Applicant's ordinances did not require water and sewer line sizes to be based on comprehensive zoning plans. Therefore, the costs associated with those size increases were not eligible for funding."[28] (Emphasis Added)

First Appeal

"The Applicant appealed this determination in a letter dated November 14, 2009. The Applicant asserted that the engineering design standards are set forth by the Mississippi Department of Environmental Quality (MDEQ) and the Mississippi Department of Health (MDH) and they require the water and sewer system to be designed at peak flow in order to serve the expected population of the area."

"On May 13, 2010, the Regional Administrator denied the first appeal stating that zoning codes do not meet FEMA's requirements for eligible codes and standards. The Regional Administrator stated that applicants can obtain variances to zoning regulations, which demonstrates that they are not necessarily uniformly applied. In addition, the Regional Administrator noted that zoning codes apply to future land use and capacity, but do not apply as construction codes for the purposes of reconstructing the water and sewer lines."[29]

"The peak flow requirements are derived from the City's comprehensive zoning map, which reflect post-disaster redevelopment projections. As stated in the Regional Administrator's first appeal response, zoning requirements are subject to change and variances can be obtained. Therefore, the design criteria do not meet FEMA's requirements for uniform application by the Applicant. Furthermore, the design criteria used is for the purpose of accommodating future capacity demands. It is not a construction code requirement related to the repair or replacement of the systems." *(damaged by the disaster)*[30]

The Americans with Disabilities Act (ADA) Compliance

A common request for codes and standards upgrades centers around the ADA. Here, in a case from New Jersey, is a situation where ADA compliance was NOT funded because of failure to meet all five requirements for codes and standards upgrades.

"During the incident period from October 26, 2012, to November 8, 2012, Hurricane Sandy's high *(tides)* and straight line-winds, tidal surge and flooding caused damage in the State of New Jersey. On November 14, 2012, the New Jersey Department of Environmental Protection (Applicant) requested Public Assistance (PA) for repair costs to address damages to its public buildings at the Leonardo State Marina. The three buildings damaged included a Concession Building, an Office/Toilet Building, and a Maintenance Office Building (Facilities)."[31]

"On October 28, 2013, the Applicant requested an improved project from the State of New Jersey Office of Emergency Management (Grantee). The improved project proposed to demolish the Office/Toilet Building, Concession Building, and Maintenance Office and consolidate the three buildings into a single new structure. On August 11, 2014, the Grantee forwarded the Applicant's design plans to FEMA. FEMA responded on October 6, 2014, noting that the demolition and associated costs were not included in the scope of work (SOW), and requested a detailed SOW based on the design drawings, with a cost estimate."[32]

On May 4, 2015, the Applicant demolished the Concession Building and Office/Toilet Building. On June 25, 2015, the Grantee transmitted the Applicant's request to FEMA for: (1) a SOW change for PW 4510 to reflect additional interior and exterior building damage, including code and standard upgrades that would trigger replacement of the Concession Building and Office/Toilet Building; (2) an improved project designation to consolidate the functions of the Office/Toilet and other Facilities into a single new building; and (3) an alternate project designation for the Concession Building that would apply funding toward construction of the new consolidated services building."[33]

"FEMA prepared and sent the Applicant a Determination Memorandum that denied the Applicant's request to revise the damage description, SOW, and costs to repair the Concession Building and Office/Toilet Building . . . FEMA also noted that the Applicant demolished both structures before FEMA could reevaluate the damage pursuant to FEMA's 50 Percent Rule."[34]

In this case, the local agency compounded its problems by demolishing the building prior to FEMA making an inspection to determine if the building should be repaired or replaced in accordance with the 50% rule. (Which we discussed in Chapter 23.)

While the agency notes in this appeals case that FEMA personnel were at the site, "evidenced by at least six site visits over a period of three years."[35] None of those visits were for the specific purpose of examining the damage vis-à-vis repairing versus replacing the buildings. Hence, the agency demolished the evidence it sorely needed for FEMA to make its determination. Although FEMA can sometimes move at what may be charitably described as a snail's pace, that does not relieve the local agency from complying with ALL necessary aspects of the Project Worksheet development process. The local need to clean up and return life to normal is not necessarily reflected in in FEMA's normal workflow processes, which can sometimes appear sluggish to outsiders.

One of the pivot points in this multi-faceted case centers on ADA compliance.

"The ADA applies to restoration of damaged facilities under the Stafford Act, and requires that any building or facility that is accessible to the public or any residence or workplace containing persons with disabilities be accessible to and useable by persons with disabilities. FEMA has the authority and responsibility to determine which repairs, code-mandated or otherwise, are eligible for assistance. FEMA generally does not fund code-mandated work that does not meet all five prongs of 44 C.F.R. § 206.226(d), regardless of whether the work is needed to obtain a building, occupancy, or environmental permit. An ADA relevant repair must affect both the structural element of the facility and affect the usability or accessibility of the facility. Here, the SOW to repair the Office/Toilet Building concerns changes to mechanical and electric systems, replacing shower stalls and partitions, floor and ceiling tiles, and replacing contents."[36] (Emphasis Added)

"The Applicant argues in order to obtain a building permit and CO *(certificate of occupancy)*, it needed to comply with ADA requirements to expand the bathroom and shower area. Specifically, the Applicant contends that the Office/Toilet Building was built in 1940, and the shower and bathroom areas did not contain enough square footage, or barrier free area, to allow for ADA compliance. The Applicant argues that the NJ building code triggered ADA compliance in that no work can be taken that diminishes accessibility below that which is required by the Barrier Free Sub code and the bathrooms did not contain enough square footage, or barrier free area to allow for ADA compliance."[37]

"The Applicant demolished the buildings and as such, FEMA was unable to re-evaluate the building and estimate costs for ADA compliance. Furthermore, the Applicant requested ADA upgrades in order to obtain a CO and a building permit and those conditions, alone, without meeting the five prongs of 206.226(d), is an insufficient basis for FEMA to fund the work. The Applicant did not demonstrate that the first prong of 44 C.F.R. § 206.226(d) was met, because it failed to show ADA compliance applied to the repair work in the SOW (i.e., that expanding the bathrooms applied to the approved SOW to repair the mechanical and electric systems, replacing shower stalls and partitions, floor and ceiling tiles, and replacing contents). Accordingly, the requested ADA compliant work is not eligible for PA funding."[38]

So even ADA compliance, a Federal law, is not sacrosanct if it does not meet all five requirements for implementation of codes and standards mentioned on the first page of this chapter. Furthermore, if the facility in question had been cited for noncompliance with the ADA prior to the disaster, FEMA funding would not be available. This applies to all codes and standards issues, i.e., if the local agency has been cited, or has failed to meet mandated standards before the disaster, then FEMA will not include the work necessary to meet those deficiencies in the scope of work after the disaster.

Codes and Standards' Consistent Application

Adherence to properly adopted codes and standards must be consistent. This case from Oklahoma speaks to this issue. "During the incident period of May 5 – June 22, 2015, severe storms and straight-line winds affected the City of Norman (Subrecipient). The President declared a Major Disaster for the State of Oklahoma (DR-4222-OK) on May 26, 2015. Record-breaking rainfall resulted in flooding that damaged roads and culverts throughout the Subrecipient's jurisdiction. FEMA developed Project Worksheets (PWs) 1479, 1480, 1481, and 1482 to cover repairs to the roads and culverts at four locations."[39]

"In order for FEMA to find that a code or standard applies uniformly across similar facilities, the code or standard cannot allow selective application, it cannot be subject to discretionary enforcement by public officials, <u>it must be applied regardless of the source of funding for the upgrade work, and it cannot be applied selectively based on the availability of funds</u>."[40] (Emphasis Added)

"FEMA requested specific information regarding the size of the damaged culverts and the replacement culverts, location, installation dates, an explanation of the design and materials selection process, and maintenance records validating the use of the codes. In its response, the Subrecipient described an example of a project in which drainage pipes were replaced by two bridges and another in which a small bridge was replaced with a larger bridge. It also described a community development project in which culverts will be 'significantly upsized to meet codes,' without specifics on how they will be upgraded (i.e., material, size, or cost). Additionally, it provided an example of a subdivision project in which new developments were constructed 'in conformance with city codes,' again without specificity as to location, size, materials, or standards."[41]

"In all of the examples provided, the Subrecipient described the improvements made to other culvert projects within its jurisdiction, but based on the limited information provided, FEMA cannot ascertain whether those improvements were necessary and sufficient to meet the codes and standards . . . However, it is unclear whether the codes and standards require an H&H (*Hydrology and Hydraulics*), study for each new culvert project. The documentation provided for the other culvert projects lacked specific information about size, materials, and design frequency, and did not demonstrate that they complied with the codes and standards. Furthermore, the Subrecipient admitted that its records are not easily searchable or well documented enough to be able to validate the use of codes and standards, and that its design files have not been well preserved."[42]

In this case, although the local agency may have consistently followed its codes and standards for the work, it could not prove that it had done so. FEMA has an uncanny ability to see clearly even when everything is smoke and mirrors. Although disasters are a far cry from a criminal indictment, the preservation and presentation of documentary evidence should strive to mimic the standards to which law enforcement is held in proving guilt in a court of law.

Notes

1 Disaster Operations Legal Reference, Version 4.0, September 25, 2020, pp. 5–90.
2 Public Assistance Program and Policy Guide, Version 4, June 1, 2020, FFP 104–009–2, p. 145.
3 https://www.fema.gov/appeal/codes-and-standards-11
4 NFPA® 70® National Electrical Code® 2023 Edition.
5 Public Assistance Program and Policy Guide, Version 4, June 1, 2020, FFP 104–009–2, p. 147.
6 https://www.fema.gov/appeal/roads-appeal-timeliness-codes-and-standards-scope-work
7 Ibid.
8 Ibid.
9 Ibid.
10 Ibid.
11 Ibid.
12 Ibid.
13 Ibid.
14 Ibid.
15 https://www.fema.gov/appeal/codes-and-standards
16 Ibid.
17 Ibid.
18 Ibid.
19 Ibid.
20 Ibid.
21 Ibid.

22 https://www.fema.gov/appeal/codes-and-standards-10
23 Ibid.
24 Ibid.
25 Ibid.
26 Ibid.
27 https://www.fema.gov/appeal/expansion-water-and-sewer-systems
28 Ibid.
29 Ibid.
30 Ibid.
31 https://www.fema.gov/appeal/appeal-timeliness-scope-work-50-percent-rule-codes-and-standards
32 Ibid.
33 Ibid.
34 Ibid.
35 Ibid.
36 Ibid.
37 Ibid.
38 Ibid.
39 https://www.fema.gov/appeal/category-work-pre-disaster-condition-codes-and-standards
40 Ibid.
41 Ibid.
42 Ibid.

35 Catch 22s – Conflicting Regulations

Figure 35.1 Depiction of government 'red tape' and conflicting regulations.

Conflicting FEMA and Other Federal Regulations

This chapter on conflicting rules and regulations will be merciful in length, but not merciful in content. FEMA is a very large organization with thousands of employees, and even in much smaller organizations, with arguably less-demanding missions, it is often the case that the right hand is unaware of what the left hand is doing. And so it is here.

Some of the issues discussed in this chapter will be real, "in-print" conflicts, and some issues will be perceived because of either a lack of clarity in the regulations or a lack of understanding of the regulations.

DOI: 10.4324/9781003487869-40

First, let us look at the issue of "Like for Like" replacement versus "Least Cost Replacement." FEMA's mission is to assist in restoring damaged facilities to their pre-disaster condition, and no better.

True-Life Tales

Some years ago, I had the opportunity to speak to a group of local government financial officers in New Orleans. I was partnered with the Chief Financial Officer of a Parish School Board. He had a story from Hurricane Rita, which struck Louisiana a mere three weeks after Hurricane Katrina had devastated Southern Louisiana and Mississippi. He related that his school district had 10 campuses, each of which had a football field with the accompanying tall field lights. The powerful hurricane winds destroyed every one of the tall light poles. What had been in place were the metal poles, which are quite expensive, and his team realized that they could replace them with cast concrete poles for less money. However, when this was first proposed, FEMA initially insisted on a like-for-like replacement with the more expensive poles. Karl's team persisted, and finally FEMA relented and approved a less-costly replacement using the cast concrete poles.

In this case, it may have been that the staffer from FEMA had not yet read that far in the rule book to discover the part on "Least Cost Replacement" versus like-for-like replacement. Like-for-like is generally the goal of the Public Assistance program; however, it is possible to use least-cost replacement when that is approved in the scope of work by FEMA. But getting approval for a least-cost replacement may take some extra effort.

Hazard Mitigation Is Not an Improved Project

The local agency generally has the option to request Hazard Mitigation to increase the facility's resistance to future damage from the same hazard that caused the initial damage. This is accomplished through a qualified application for Hazard Mitigation funding when requesting a Project Worksheet. The local agency may also elect to request either an improved project or an alternate project, either of which will "improve" the pre-disaster condition of the damage facility, but the work is paid for by the local agency above and beyond the funding provided by FEMA for the disaster-caused damage.

Note, however, that Hazard Mitigation is not available for replacement projects, only for repair projects.

A Least Cost Replacement (?)

In some cases, after the scope of work has been written and FEMA approved, the local agency's engineers or project managers may determine that there is a less expensive way to effect the repair of the disaster damage. Following is a case which we previously reviewed from New York State. "From August 26 to September 5, 2011, heavy rain, wind, and flooding from Hurricane Irene caused damage in New York. During the event, high water levels in Cedar Pond Brook destroyed a gabion wall (see footnote 2 below) and embankment behind the wall. Rockland County (Applicant) requested Public Assistance (PA) through the New York Division of Homeland Security and Emergency Services (Grantee) for the cost of repairs. FEMA prepared Project Worksheet (PW) 9122 that identified the damaged facility as a 125-foot long gabion wall and embankment behind the wall. FEMA prepared a cost estimate of $153,898.00 for in-kind repairs and awarded the project on November 16, 2012. The PW stated that the Applicant was to notify the Grantee with any changes to the approved scope of work (SOW) and to also provide photo documentation of any additional damages discovered during construction."[1]

"On November 21, 2018, the Applicant submitted a request to change the project's SOW, explaining that the project was completed in Summer 2018 using heavy stone fill instead of gabion baskets. The Applicant explained that in its experience gabion baskets[2] routinely fail, and heavy stone was a more reliable solution. The Grantee transmitted the request to FEMA and included the Applicant's project proposal that it asserts was submitted to FEMA during project development, with repairs consisting of the placement of heavy stone fill with a cost estimate of $257,207.51."[3]

"On April 24, 2019, FEMA denied the request explaining that the material change from gabions to heavy stone fill represented an improved project. Therefore, FEMA limited funding associated with the Federal share of the costs that would be associated with repairing the damaged facility to its predisaster design."[4]

"In a letter dated February 5, 2020, the FEMA Region II Regional Administrator denied the first appeal. FEMA determined that the Applicant completed work outside of the approved SOW by restoring an additional 55 LF of embankment and did not provide documentation to support that the additional damage was caused by the disaster. FEMA reaffirmed that the Applicant performed an improved project and limited funding accordingly."[5]

Second Appeal

"The Applicant submitted a second appeal on May 27, 2020, asserting that the approved SOW was in error and the length of damage estimated was incorrect. The Applicant asserts that its June 5, 2012 proposal estimated the length of embankment as 240 LF (*lineal feet*) and adds that it was told at the time not to worry about the differences and to proceed with the project and submit actual costs and project length when the project was designed and completed. The Applicant submitted the scope change request on November 21, 2018, showing the actual project length was 220 LF. The Applicant also explained that the change from gabions to heavy stone reduced the project cost and was better suited to the site conditions. Had the Applicant used gabions, project costs would have been higher, so it asserts the additional $47,434.10 is appropriate and reasonable."[6]

"FEMA prepared the PW to repair 125 LF of damaged embankment, which the Applicant agreed to. PW 9122 notes that the Applicant was advised by FEMA to notify the Grantee with any changes to the approved SOW and to also provide photo documentation of any additional damages discovered during construction. The Applicant submitted its scope change request several years after the work was completed. Under FEMA policy, scope change requests are to be submitted prior to commencement, not at completion. Further, the Applicant has not provided documentation, such as predisaster pictures, inspection reports, logs or maintenance records, to demonstrate that repairing the additional length of embankment was a result of the declared incident. Therefore, the Applicant has not demonstrated that any additional reinforcement of the embankment beyond the approved area is required as a direct result of the disaster."[7]

Once again, there are two telling clues about how successful this local agency might be in pursuing an appeal: 1) They relied on someone's "verbal instruction or approval," and 2) They began the work before notifying FEMA of the changed Scope of Work. Merely notifying FEMA would be insufficient, because the local agency must receive FEMA approval before beginning the work.

When the local agency repairs or reconstructs disaster damage, there are two very different perspectives in play during the entire process which can lead to serious disagreements. FEMA's perspective has at least two elements (beyond the basic eligibility questions): 1) the cost of the work done, and 2) was the scope of work accomplished without variation from the approved scope of work? The local perspective may include: 1) how can we make this better as we repair the facility?, 2) how can we accomplish this work quickly?, and 3) how can we do this at a lower cost, if possible?

In this case, the engineers may have been proud of coming up with a lower unit cost method of repair, although the total cost was higher than the original worksheet as approved. No matter. The project at the most basic level failed because the local agency either did not timely request a change in the scope of work, or absent that, complete the job as per the approved Project Worksheet. So, realizing a less expensive way to repair the facility was for nothing, except the loss of more than $100,000.

Unlike in real life, where it is often easier to ask for forgiveness rather than permission, the reverse is true with FEMA. Always ask for permission, but never ask for forgiveness. "Forgiveness" is not a word commonly found in the FEMA dictionary.

Replacement of Used but Disaster-Damaged Police Vehicles

This is another "like for like" appeals case from Mississippi following Hurricane Katrina. "In 2005, Hurricane Katrina's high winds and storm surge destroyed eight police vehicles owned by the City of D'Iberville (Applicant). The vehicles consisted of six Ford Crown Victoria sedans (spanning model years 1995 to 2005), one 2000 Ford Expedition sport utility vehicle (SUV), and one 1999 Dodge Ram truck. Prior to FEMA preparing PW 10079, the Applicant purchased the following vehicles to replace those destroyed during the hurricane: three Chevrolet Tahoe SUVs, three Chevrolet Silverado trucks, one GMC Sierra truck, and one Dodge Ram truck. The total cost of these eight replacement vehicles was $193,240."[8]

"Using Applicant-provided insurance appraiser reports as well as a $22,246 purchase invoice for a 2005 Ford Crown Victoria, FEMA prepared PW 10079 for a total of $150,206 for the replacement costs of the six destroyed Ford Crown Victoria sedans (amounting to $133,476), the 2000 Ford Explorer SUV ($9,675), and the 1999 Dodge Ram truck ($7,055). A reduction of $78,170 was initially applied for anticipated insurance proceeds. PW 10079 was adjusted (-$16,464) in version 2 to reflect $94,634 in actual insurance proceeds the Applicant received, resulting in a total PW obligation of $55,572."[9]

"On May 31, 2011, the Applicant submitted a first appeal, which was transmitted by the Grantee to FEMA on July 26, 2011, requesting reimbursement of $43,034, (the difference between the replacement purchased amount of $193,240 and the actual insurance proceeds of $94,634 and previously obligated $55,572). The Applicant stated that it was in desperate need of police vehicles to protect its citizens in the wake of Hurricane Katrina. Because it would take weeks to order comparable vehicles, the Applicant asserted, it purchased SUVs and trucks from local dealerships – the only vehicles it could procure in the days immediately following the hurricane."[10]

"In this case, the Regional Administrator determined, the SUVs the Applicant purchased were not comparable to Ford Crown Victoria sedans and were not eligible as replacement vehicles. The Regional Administrator also referenced the 1999 version of the FEMA Public Assistance Guide to note that, although a replacement not being available within a reasonable time and distance is justification for replacing a used item with a new item, such circumstances do not justify replacing a used item with a more expensive new item. According to the Regional Administrator's decision, FEMA will fund the full cost of a replacement item only if the replacement is comparable to the original item."[11]

In this case, had the local agency replaced the damaged patrol cars with similar sedan models instead of the SUVs it purchased, it might have passed the bar and received FEMA funding. However, this is always on a case-by-case basis.

The Blue Roof Conundrum

This is a classic example of the complexity of Federal regulations and their interpretations by Federal employees. For this illustration, we revive an issue which we previously examined from a different perspective. In the Public Assistance Program and Policy Guide, Version 4, June 1, 2020, FFP 104–009–2, p. 117, is the following language: "Purchasing and packaging life-saving and life-sustaining commodities and providing them to the impacted community are eligible. <u>Examples of such commodities include,</u> but are not limited to, food, water, ice, personal hygiene items, cots, blankets, tarps, <u>plastic sheeting for roof damage,</u> and generators, as well as food and water for household pets and service animals."[12]

Fast forwarding to page 135 in the same book is the following language: "Operation Blue Roof (DFA Only) (*Direct Federal Assistance*) Operation Blue Roof provides homeowners with plastic sheeting to cover damaged roofs until arrangements can be made for permanent repairs. The purpose of Operation Blue Roof is to protect property, reduce temporary housing costs, and allows residents to remain in their homes while recovering from the incident. Therefore, only dwellings that can be safely occupied after blue roof installation are eligible. The costs of these services are ineligible for reimbursement. However, FEMA may provide DFA for these services."

Thus, we have two apparently conflicting statements in the Public Assistance Program and Policy Guide, Version 4, June 1, 2020. However, in the first case (page 117), the tarps may be only provided, and in the second case, the tarps may be only installed, but that is not clear in the regulations as written.

Conflicting Regulatory Agendas – Federal/State Requirements

Another bedeviling situation may arise because of conflicting Federal requirements and the requirements of the individual states. In the audit of the VictorValley Wastewater Authority, the agency was under the gun from a California state agency, with a threatened $10,000 per day fine for failure to meet certain water quality standards. At the same time, it was required under Title 2 of the Code of Federal Regulations, Part 200 to conduct a proper sealed bid procurement for work to replace a damaged pipeline, always a lengthy process, and following that process might have resulted in substantial fines from the state agency. Currently, the author has a California client with a similar problem, wherein the state has limited the agency's ability to work during the rainy season, versus FEMA's requirement to complete emergency work (Category A or B) within six months. In some cases there may be workarounds, such as requesting time extensions from FEMA. However, if an agency does not have a clear knowledge of the regulations and the process involved, the opportunity to take advantage of these workarounds may disappear because of time constraints.

Careful Reading of the Regulations Is Required

In some instances, certain work is FEMA-eligible and the same work under different circumstances is not eligible. The following text is taken from the Public Assistance Program and Policy Guide, Version 4, June 1, 2020.

"Parks, Recreational, Other (Category G)

Eligible publicly owned facilities in this category include:

- Mass transit facilities such as railways;
- Beaches;
- Parks;
- Playground equipment;
- Swimming pools;

- Bath houses;
- Tennis courts;
- Boat docks;
- Piers;
- Picnic tables;
- Golf courses;
- Ball fields;
- Fish hatcheries;
- Ports and harbors; and
- Other facilities that do not fit in Categories C–F.

Unimproved natural features are ineligible.

Plantings (such as trees, shrubs, and other vegetation) are eligible when they are part of the restoration of an eligible facility for the purpose of erosion control, to minimize sediment runoff, or to stabilize slopes, including dunes on eligible improved beaches.

Grass and sod replacement are eligible if it is an integral part of the restoration of an eligible recreational facility. Vegetation replacement is also eligible if necessary to restore the function of the facility (e.g., if vegetation is a component of a sewage filtration system).

Plantings required to mitigate environmental impacts, such as those required to address impacts to wetlands or endangered species habitat, are only eligible if required by a Federal or SLTT code or standard or permit that meets the specified criteria.

Long-term monitoring to ensure vegetative growth is ineligible even if it meets the requirements above.

Plantings ineligible for replacement include, but are not limited to:

- Replacement of trees, shrubs, and other vegetation;
- Replacement of destroyed crops; and
- Cosmetic or aesthetic vegetation, such as landscaping around public facilities or in median strips along roadways. This restriction applies even when the vegetation is damaged during performance of eligible work, such as when repairing underground utilities within landscaped areas."[13] (Emphasis Added)

However, language in the Disaster Operations Legal Reference may be interpreted slightly differently:

"Trees and Ground Cover

Trees and ground cover are not eligible for replacement. This restriction applies to trees and shrubs in recreation areas, such as parks, as well as trees and shrubs associated with public facilities. However, such plantings may be eligible for replacement when:

- Grass and sod replacement is an integral part of the repair or replacement of an eligible recreational facility (e.g., publicly owned sports fields); or
- They are part of the restoration of an eligible facility and are necessary to stabilize slopes, erosion control, or minimize sediment runoff; or required for the mitigation of environmental impacts."[14]

While there may be no direct conflict in these two documents, the subtleties may confuse and escape the inexperienced reader. For local agency personnel looking to justify certain work, they may gravitate towards the language that appears to provide the needed justification, although it may not.

Childcare, Yes and Childcare, No

Another potentially confusing element is childcare. The Sandy Recovery Improvement Act (Public Law 113–2 – Jan. 29, 2013) allowed the provision of childcare for victims' families. However, childcare for the children of those responding to the disaster are not eligible expenses. The allowance for childcare was made under "Other Needs Assistance" or ONA, which is part of the "Individual Assistance" that government assistance made available for disaster victims, rather than Public Assistance, which is the assistance provided to local government agencies.

Leased Equipment

The eligibility of leased equipment or facilities is definitely on a case-by-case basis. "A building may be the legal responsibility of an eligible applicant, but some or all of the contents may be the legal responsibility of an ineligible applicant. For example, the replacement of leased hospital equipment may be the legal responsibility of a contractor to the hospital. In such instances, replacement of the equipment is not eligible under the PA program. In the event of damage to a facility under construction, legal responsibility for the damage must be examined carefully as FEMA must determine which entity – eligible applicant or contractor – is legally responsible for repairs."[15]

In some cases of leased facilities, a close reading of the lease agreement will be required. "The State of South Dakota owned several railroad lines that were flood damaged in 2014. The state leased the railroad lines to a rail authority to operate the railroad. The rail authority later entered into a sublease with a private railroad operator. The lease agreements provided respectively that the lessee (the rail authority and the private operator) were explicitly responsible for the railroad's general maintenance and repairs. The agreements further provided that the state and the rail authority were not responsible for weather-related damage pursuant to a force majeure clause in the contract. Based on the terms of the leases, <u>FEMA determined the state retained legal responsibility for the disaster-related damage repairs because neither agreement contractually bound their respective lessees or expressly transferred legal responsibility of the disaster related repairs to the lessees, the rail authority, or the private corporation.</u> Absent an express transfer of legal responsibility in the lease agreement, the state, as owner of the facility, maintains its inherently legal responsibility for disaster-related damage repairs."[16] (Emphasis Added)

In the case where the local agency leases its photocopier/laser printers from an outside vendor, depending on the specific lease terms, the photocopier machines may not be FEMA eligible, but the local agency none the less may be responsible for the repair or replacement of the machines, unless otherwise provided for in the lease, particularly in the fine print, which is seldom read until there's a problem.

Repair vs. Replacement

This is another area where there is often great confusion, certainly at the local agency level and sometimes within FEMA itself, regarding the eligibility of a damaged facility to be either repaired or replaced. This is a very important distinction which we discussed in Chapter 23.

Miscellaneous Catch-22s

There are many other topics which may or may not be eligible, depending on the case-by-case circumstances. These include the replacement of books, which hinges on whether the books are library-quality books or rare books of the serious-collector variety (See the Public Assistance Program and Policy Guide, Version 4, June 1, 2020, FFP 104–009–2, p. 176.)

For universities and research facilities, the replacement of reagents and specimens may be eligible on a qualified basis. (See the Public Assistance Program and Policy Guide, Version 4, June 1, 2020, FFP 104–009–2, p. 173.)

For coastal communities, the replacement of beach sand may or may not be eligible based upon several qualifying conditions. (See the Public Assistance Program and Policy Guide, Version 4, June 1, 2020, FFP 104–009–2, p. 180.)

Private Non-Profit Agencies (PNPs) are often unique in the FEMA world, and depending on the type of PNP and the services it provides, the PNP may be eligible for FEMA funding under the Public Assistance program. We will delve into the PNP world in Chapter 37.

True-Life Tales

Some years ago, a city with which I worked had a small landslide. FEMA generally does not fund the restoration of ground which has moved. If a local agency repairs the ground, then FEMA may restore the damaged facility which sat upon that restored ground. However, in this instance, the city was a private gated community of entirely private property, roads, and homes. FEMA typically does not fund damage to private property under the Public Assistance program. However, the city (a private gated community) received FEMA funding. The funding was not to restore the slide itself, but (this is the important part) to clear a roadway because the slide had cut off homes from public emergency access. Police and fire vehicles were blocked by the slide. Thus, a very careful description of the eligible essence of the work performed provided a legitimate basis for FEMA funding, funding which would not have been available to "clear a landslide" but was available to clear the road for emergency vehicle access. In the same way a medical doctor cannot properly diagnose an illness without the proper patient information and medical tests, FEMA cannot provide funding for work or damage that's improperly described. This is the type of situation where a well-chosen and well-qualified consultant may be worthwhile.

A Final Word on Catch-22s

One more very important consideration that's already been discussed is that when performing emergency repairs, ALWAYS ensure that the work reports specifically state the work done was a temporary repair. To leave out the word temporary is to provide FEMA with the opportunity to determine that the repair was permanent and thus completed work. If the local agency has properly adopted and consistently applied codes and standards, then some work done as a temporary repair may also be eligible as a permanent repair as mandated by the codes and standards.

This chapter can only begin to touch on the breadth of possible Catch-22s. The world of the Public Assistance program continues to evolve, and what works today may not work tomorrow. However, the most important thing to understand is that the program DOES change, and we should expect that new and previously unexpected issues will arise when least expected. It may be likened to walking through a proverbial minefield: always be alert, always be aware.

Notes

1 https://www.fema.gov/appeal/result-declared-incident-improved-project
2 A gabion basket is a wire box-like structure filled with large stones and used to retain soil or to protect an embankment.
3 Ibid.
4 Ibid.
5 Ibid.

6 Ibid.
7 Ibid.
8 https://www.fema.gov/appeal/replacement-police-vehicles-improved-project
9 Ibid.
10 Ibid.
11 Ibid.
12 Public Assistance Program and Policy Guide, Version 4, June 1, 2020, FFP 104–009–2, p. 117.
13 Ibid, p. 179.
14 Disaster Operations Legal Reference, Version 4.0, September 25, 2020, pp. 5–85.
15 Ibid, pp. 5–24.
16 Ibid, pp. 5–28.

36 Local Agency Self-Inflicted Gunshot Wounds

"We have met the enemy, and he is us."

Walt Kelly, "Pogo," 1971

Self-Inflicted Gunshot Wounds

If this book had only one chapter, this would be the one.

For all the failings of FEMA, reality-based or imaginary, the number of FEMA's faults would drown in the Mariana Trench of local agency apathy, ignorance, and failure to act in their own self-interest. As the cartoon character Pogo once said, "We have met the enemy, and he is us."[1]

Almost all the difficulties that local agencies face when dealing with FEMA would be much less debilitating had the local agency taken any number of steps before, during, and after the disaster to be better prepared for disasters and the disaster cost recovery process.

Note: Some of items listed in this chapter are more fully addressed in their respective chapters, but are included here for the sake of completeness, and for those readers that may not read every chapter in the book. This book frequently contains some repetitive material, however this is intentional and due to the serious importance of the material as it contributes to the success of the program.

First, the Federal government, in the personage of FEMA, has very different perspectives and goals following a disaster. For the local agency, the disaster is up close and personal. For FEMA, the disaster is another day at the office. This is a legitimate difference in perspectives. The locals affected by the disaster are typically experiencing a wide-ranging spectrum of emotions and losses. For both state and Federal employees, no matter the Federal agency, the disaster response is their job. Because their homes, lives, and businesses are not affected, state and Federal employees simply cannot put themselves into the locals' shoes. The locals are in a high and steady state of stress. Even considering a lack of empathy, it would not do to have those who have arrived to help in the recovery operating in a similar state of high emotion.

Even more importantly, the goals of the Feds and the locals are radically different. The locals want and need to restore their community to some semblance of normalcy as quickly as possible; they are partially blinded by emotion to the fact that what was lost may have taken decades to build at a lower historical cost than will be possible now.

The Feds, on the other hand, have arrived to assist the local communities rebuild, BUT only when ALL the conditions embodied in Federal law and regulation have been met. Feds from any agency can only provide disaster relief funding when conditions are specifically within the guidelines established by Congress. The Federal government may be our Uncle Sam, but it is not our uncle, with the concomitant willingness to give a little extra or forgive minor or major flaws.

On the contrary, the Federal government, as represented by all its agencies, has historically been and will continue to be sought out by criminals and fraudsters seeking personal enrichment. As a

DOI: 10.4324/9781003487869-41

result, Federal agencies in general, and FEMA in particular, must have a healthy dose of skepticism about any request for Federal funding. We as the local agencies must be prepared to prove, beyond the shadow of a doubt, that our claimed disaster damages were caused by the specific disaster, and that there was no contribution, or at least only a de-minimis contribution, to the damage because of pre-existing conditions or deferred maintenance.

In the same way that I cannot merely walk into a bank and ask for a large sum of money without a solid business plan, a good credit history, and references, the local agencies must be prepared to provide all the necessary documentation, including a plethora of photographs, to warrant the approval and funding of Project Worksheets.

Another critically important fact is that the normal recordkeeping processes of many local governments simply do not meet the normal everyday recordkeeping processes of the Federal government. And the smaller the agency, the more likely this is to be true. The business practices and normal documentation requirements for a small jurisdiction in any part of the country would not, should not, and cannot normally measure up to Federal standards. As a species, humans like to keep things simple; it helps us to manage our lives and get the most out of what we have. On the other hand, the complex body of regulations helps FEMA "simplify" their work, and thus a conflict naturally emerges when, under great stress, locals have to up their game to recover from the disaster. At the local level, we cannot continue to do business as usual and expect that such a level of performance will be acceptable to FEMA.

Stability and Then a Rapid Shifting of Gears

For government officials at any level, constancy and stability are generally hallmarks of efficient government administration. Following a disaster, however, a high premium is placed on the ability to flex, pivot, and innovate in a manner that would be completely unacceptable for normal government operations. But the elected and senior appointed officials who have spent a career seeking stability and constancy are thrust unmercifully into a role for which many of them are not well-prepared, perhaps not even capable. And all this is evolving under layers of stress unimagined just a few days ago. But flex, pivot, and innovate we must to recover from the disaster. Disaster planning and preparation must be a normal part of the organization, or it will be extraordinarily difficult to achieve an acceptable level of recovery.

To this end, and as difficult as it may be, local officials must be prepared to realize that they may be in deep, deep water and need outside professional assistance. This will not be the case in all disasters. In fact, the calculus of this equation will be different for each agency in each disaster. Typically, smaller agencies will reach this point of need sooner than a nearby large agency which has more available experienced staff and internal resources. However, the "X" to be solved for in the equation will have to include the financial resources needed to fund such assistance.

Perhaps the most important key to success in generating organizational and political support is to monetize the effects of a disaster. The local agency's emergency manager, in compliance with standard disaster planning tenets, should have developed a Threat-Hazard Analysis. This document should consider the hazards to which the community is exposed, the likelihood of the occurrence of each different scenario, and the potential effects of each scenario based on the magnitude of the disaster, i.e., a category 1 hurricane versus a category 4 hurricane. Typically, these documents consider loss of life, number of injuries, damages to homes and businesses, etc. However, most of these assessments stop there. I have never seen a Threat-Hazard Analysis which also quantified a range of potential financial losses, nor the amount of money that would be needed for even a minimal level of recovery.

Such analysis should involve the agency's senior financial officials, the emergency manager, the risk manager, and other senior administration officials. This should begin the process of recognition of the disaster potential for a community of any size, as well as how best to allocate scarce resources to reduce the levels of risk which are present in almost every community.

One of the most pervasive of all the "self-inflicted wounds" a local agency may suffer is failing to have a staff member with any knowledge or recent experience with FEMA's Public Assistance program. Because of the nearly constant program and policy changes, experience from years ago may not provide sufficient working knowledge of the current process. However, someone with any level of previous FEMA Public Assistance experience is much better than no experience at all.

While FEMA's Public Assistance process continues to change, and always will, there are certain fundamentals which have changed little or not at all in the past 45 years, including proper record-keeping, the basic principles of eligibility, making a thorough damage inventory, etc.

When an agency has a knowledgeable staff person, that person should have their fingers in every departmental pie, if only to advise leadership of possible consequences of proposed actions, even actions which at the local level we see as inconsequential in the larger scope of the disaster recovery.

When dealing with the Public Assistance program, most department personnel are wandering blindly through the maze of regulations, and the leadership does not know what they do not know. They may decide arbitrarily to make changes in the "scope of work," or method of work, because that is what they normally do as senior staff. However, they seldom realize that when FEMA approves a Project Worksheet, FEMA treats this document as a legally binding contract, and FEMA must approve ANY changes. Project Worksheets are not suggestions or guides about how to do the work; Project Worksheets are specific and detailed instructions from which we cannot vary without some level of risk. How much we vary may change the level of risk from a minor wound to a financially fatal injury. Stepping outside the closely defined boundaries written into each Project Worksheet is a temptation akin to opening Pandora's Box.

If a local agency is in a part of the country where disasters are relatively uncommon, this is a risk that may be accepted. However, if the local agency is in a part of the country where disasters are literally an annual occurrence (at least in some part of the region or state), then this is indeed a very high-risk situation, and the risk potential repeats all over again every year.

I have recommended to clients that they consider having access to an Executive Emergency Management Consultant. This person would not actually be involved in the day-to-day work of disaster cost recovery, but would instead be brought in immediately after the disaster to address the local elected officials and senior department heads to inform their level of expectations vis-a-vis both FEMA and Other Federal Agency assistance, and to help manage both staff and community expectations in a time of crisis.

Developing Local Recovery Priorities

Immediately following a disaster, everyone affected wants their own lives returned to normal as quickly as possible. In the early days of the Covid-19 pandemic, almost everyone wanted N-95 masks and hand sanitizer on tap. Simply not available. All other post-disasters are no different. Therefore, local agencies must prioritize their recovery goals. There is almost never enough money to fix everything that was damaged or destroyed, and most certainly not everything simultaneously. This is especially important because FEMA also needs to know what our priorities for recovery are, particularly as our priorities will affect our needs for Project Worksheet development. If we as the local agency cannot define our priorities, then FEMA cannot and will not do so.

The development of the local agency's disaster recovery priorities should prompt a realization of how stressfully different local government operations will be than during normal pre-disaster operations. George Doorley, then the Auditor-Controller for Santa Clara County, California, told me that he informed his staff that in an Emergency Operations Center environment he expected they would take necessary actions that on any other day of the year would be cause for discipline, because of the urgent need for saving lives and property. By extension, at the local level, while maintaining as unalterable certain things such as proper recordkeeping, 2 CFR, Part 200-compliant purchasing, and compliance with environmental and historic preservation issues, we still must look for innovative ways to respond to the needs of the community as the disaster recovery continues. What this picture of creative and innovative government looks like will vary from one community to another and from one disaster to the next. Local government going about its business of disaster recovery in the same way it approached problems before the disaster will almost certainly fail miserably.

Cost Recovery Planning and The Willingness to Risk All Without Preparation

I have medical insurance; I have fire insurance for my home; I have automobile insurance. I cannot imagine having some level of insurance for the classic rainy day. Many if not most local government agencies also have liability, property casualty, and worker's compensation insurance. The risks of not having these insurance coverages are too great to be without it. However, many local agencies have never given a thought to having disaster insurance. Not insurance in the purest form of the word, but insurance in having a basic working knowledge of FEMA's Public Assistance program, insurance in necessary plans in place, the insurance in having well trained staff. And regarding well trained staff, I am not only talking about fire, police, and emergency medical personnel, but for having all staff with an appropriate level of knowledge and training for what could be the most challenging assignment of their entire working career.

Certainly, many local agencies have some form of disaster preparedness and response plans. But very few have anything that resembles a working disaster cost recovery plan, which is infinitely more complex than the disaster response plan, if only because the response may last a few days or a couple of weeks but the recovery will go on for years to come. I have reviewed many alleged "disaster cost recovery" plans over the years. There is only one city – Houston, Texas – that has something close to a good working plan. Most of the so-called plans I have reviewed largely consist of the FEMA forms for tracking labor, equipment, and materials, and sometimes little else. There may be some agencies with excellent plans; however, I have not seen them.

In the late summer of 2023, we witnessed the near total destruction by fire of the town of Lahaina, Hawaii. In a mere 12 hours, the town was destroyed, and one hundred or so lives were lost. The rest was basically clean-up and the search for survivors and fatalities. However, the recovery will most likely go on for years to come.

Maui Fire of 2023 – Business as Usual

It is ironic to read in September of 2023 the Report on Wildfire Prevention and Cost Recovery on Maui published in July of 2021, two years after unprecedented "devastating" fires plagued Maui in 2019. First, the "cost" the report discusses is the cost of providing everyday fire protection for the island of Maui. So, the title is a bit of a misnomer, insofar as disaster cost recovery is simply not mentioned in the report, except as a passing thought. "According to a damage assessment from the Pacific Disaster Center (PDC) and FEMA, Maui County experienced $5.52 billion in 'capital exposure,' which is the estimated cost to rebuild following damage by the Lahaina

Fire."[2] According to the report, at the current level of fire services funding and unadjusted for inflation, it would take until nearly the year 2200 to spend the money lost in the Lahaina fire, at the current costs.

Clearly, with an estimated $5.52 billion dollars of damage done by this one fire, this would be a singular example of how to monetize the disaster risk and begin taking steps to be much better prepared for the drawn-out cost recovery process.

Bullets and Bandages

Some of the following paragraphs are marked with either a bullet (bad) or a bandage (solution), which local agencies should be aware of and take advantage of to the greatest extent possible to improve their capabilities for disaster cost recovery with a collateral reduction in the likelihood of deobligations.

Pre-Disaster Damage Assessment Plan

An important element of a usable disaster cost recovery plan is the local agency's Damage Assessment plan. As discussed in Chapter 20: The Local Damage Assessment Process, the local agency cannot request financial assistance from FEMA if it does not know what was damaged. City Hall is in a heap, that's obvious damage. The public library burned to the ground, that's obvious damage, and so on. But what about a backup emergency water pump that on average kicks in once a year? What about a county road that has been under floodwaters for the past 4 months? How does the local agency know, in total, what was damaged? On another level, does the local damage assessment account for the loss in revenue for a community with a significant seasonal tourism business, where 12 months' worth of revenue is realized in a 4-month window each year? Although lost revenue is not FEMA-reimbursable, it is money that is not available for making necessary repairs. This case from Texas may be a classic example of not having a damage assessment plan or process.

"During the incident period, February 11–21, 2021, Texas experienced severe winter storms and a major disaster, FEMA-4586-DR-TX, was declared for all Texas counties. The Applicant requested Public Assistance funding. A Recovery Scoping Meeting (RSM) was held on August 3, 2021. In a February 17, 2022 letter, the Applicant requested FEMA approve a late Damage Inventory (DI) request, due to extenuating circumstances, citing staff turnover and issues due to COVID-19. The request was made four months after the deadline and requested an additional 60 days to submit damages. FEMA denied the request on April 15, 2022. The Applicant submitted a first appeal in a letter dated July 1, 2022, arguing that extenuating circumstances prevented them from meeting the damage submission deadline. The Texas Department of Emergency Management (Recipient) forwarded the appeal, with its support. FEMA denied the Applicant's appeal, finding that that Applicant did not demonstrate extenuating circumstances beyond its control that would justify an extension to the deadline. The Applicant filed a second appeal, reiterating first appeal arguments."[3]

"FEMA finds that neither the Applicant nor the Recipient has demonstrated extenuating circumstances beyond either party's control to justify the untimely identification and reporting of damages."[4]

As a result of the missed deadline, the city lost all opportunity to receive any Federal funding for this disaster. What those losses might have been is not easy to determine since the Consolidated Annual Financial Report (CAFR) for the 2021 fiscal year is not published on the city's webpage, unlike the reports for other recent years. Since I was on the city's web page, I also looked at their purchasing policy. In my opinion, it is inadequate vis-à-vis Federally funded procurements and rife with typographic errors. Based upon a reading of the very limited purchasing policy, had the city submitted its damage inventory in a timely manner, it would have still fumbled the football when it came to procurements. In this case, the apple has not fallen far from the tree.

Debris Management and Debris Monitoring Plans

Another critical set of plans which will affect the local agency's ability to financially recover from a disaster are the debris management and debris monitoring plans. Absent these plans, it will be difficult if not impossible to recover the costs for cleaning up the community after the disaster.

"From 2004–2005, Hurricanes Frances, Jeanne, and Wilma caused damage in Florida. FEMA prepared various Project Worksheets (PW) for damages incurred by the City of Lake Worth (Applicant), 23 of which are at issue here. In 2011, FEMA deobligated $3,119,435.94 across 3 of these PWs due to insufficient documentation to support debris removal costs. In 2012, the Office of the Inspector General (OIG) audited Public Assistance funding awarded to the Applicant, recommending that FEMA recover $8,152,776.00. FEMA concurred with the OIG and deobligated the funding. In 2012–2013, the Applicant submitted several first appeals. On December 28, 2021, the FEMA Region IV RA partially granted the Applicant's first appeal. FEMA determined that Section 705(c) of the Stafford Act precluded the deobligation of $16,105.00 from PW 602; however, it was not precluded from deobligating costs from the remaining projects because the Applicant had not demonstrated the eligibility of the questioned costs. On February 25, 2022, the Applicant submitted a second appeal, asserting that it substantiated the eligibility of all costs and that Section 705(c) of the Stafford Act prevents FEMA from deobligating the costs."[5] At issue here is a total of $4,239,861.93, which FEMA is proposing to "clawback" years after the hurricanes.

"It is the applicant's responsibility to show that the damage is disaster-related. It is critical that the applicant establish and maintain accurate records of events and expenditures related to disaster recovery work. All of the documentation pertaining to a project should be filed with the corresponding PW and maintained by the applicant as the permanent record of the project. These records become the basis for verification of the accuracy of project cost estimates during validation of small projects, reconciliation of costs for large projects, and audits."[6]

"In 2011, FEMA performed a project closeout review, finding that the supporting documentation only substantiated eligible costs of $224,740.19, which resulted in an underrun of $1,927,591.61. FEMA explained that the variance was due to the lack of load tickets necessary to validate completed work, as well as accurate truck certifications. FEMA conducted numerous meetings with the Applicant to overcome the lack of documentation, but the Applicant was unable to provide documentation to verify the remaining costs. The Applicant submitted a first appeal, stating that it was unable to locate some load tickets, and other load tickets did not document where the debris originated, but the Applicant asserts that it originated in public/utility rights of way and properties."[7]

A well-crafted debris management plan would have specific forms and procedures included to fully document the work done and show effective record management.

No Routine Maintenance Plan, No Inspection Reports

One of FEMA's go-to tactics following a disaster is to request from the local agency both the agency's written maintenance inspection program, and the multitude of maintenance inspection reports that should be generated by a formal regular inspection and maintenance program. The shortfall for many, many agencies is that they have neither. In some appeals cases, representatives from local agencies are quoted in the appeals case as stating, "We don't have a formal maintenance program, or we only fix stuff when it gets broken," or words to that effect. These kinds of comments are a suicide note to FEMA.

Without documented proof that the damage was caused by the disaster, and only by the disaster, FEMA has no documentation to affirmatively establish the cause of the damage. This is particularly true for roads, bridges, culverts, and roofs, although it will also apply to any claimed damage. How this is managed and enforced may vary from FEMA Region to FEMA Region, but it generally holds true across the country.

Of course, the problem is that smaller, arguably less sophisticated, by-the-seat-of-the-pants local government operations have little knowledge of these requirements. Because of limited resources and staffing, many local agencies fail to keep proper records even for their own purposes. This lack of a well-documented maintenance program, however, often extends itself to large jurisdictions as well.

This business of having a formal maintenance program and regular annual inspections is no small task. In researching available resources on the internet, there is a plethora of "inspection" forms which might be used by a local agency. But many of these forms are merely "safety" inspection forms and have little content that would provide the type of information FEMA is seeking. A more appropriate search for "home inspection" forms yields some interesting material, but it is focused on a pre-purchase home inspection. These forms ask questions about chimneys, garages, bathrooms, and kitchens, which have limited applicability for local government facilities. Much of the material contained in this kind of home inspection form is clearly unsuitable for FEMA's required purposes.

Prioritize Maintenance and Documentation for High-Risk Properties and Infrastructure

- Regarding disaster-caused damage, this strategy occurred to me as I was working on this book. It could apply to those local agencies facing relatively frequent flooding events. Topography being what it is, the low spots in communities which flood repeatedly, repeatedly flood. The high spots never or very seldom flood. Therefore, there are two practices which could make FEMA reimbursement easier to get. First, frequently inspect, photographically document, and maintain buildings, roads, bridges, and culverts which are known flood risks, i.e., they often flood. Put another way, don't waste money on roads that never flood, if your community frequently floods.

Second, always before a flooding event is imminent, visit the most at-risk locations and take photos prior to the storm to prove that the facility, building, or road, etc., was in very good condition before the storm, and any damage which may have occurred was due to the storm and only due to the storm. In short, prioritize the risks the community faces, and take care of them in the order of their risk-based priority.

FEMA won't penalize you for not maintaining all your roads; they are only concerned with those claimed to be disaster-damaged. However, if this strategy is adopted, absolutely ensure that the low-lying (and likely to be damaged) roads are very well maintained AND that there is an abundance of documentation (written and photographic) to make this case.

FEMA probably will, however, look at all your roads and extrapolate that if some of the roads are poorly maintained, then all the roads must be poorly maintained. The responsibility for proving otherwise falls completely on the local agency.

The Pre-Disaster Maintenance Inspection Toolbox

In the Appendix, Form 55, there is a sample 8-page FACILITY inspection form. This is not a FEMA form, and its use is not required. However, absent the agency having its own form, this may be a working substitute.

Of course, this is just the inspection form. There should also be an accompanying written inspection plan which details how inspections should be performed, and the schedule for making the inspections, which may be tied to an agency's annual threat hazards, such as hurricane season, severe winter weather, etc. Ideally, there would also be a training syllabus for the employees making the inspections.

In the Appendix, Form 56, there is a sample 4-page ROOF inspection form which I found online from the Canadian Northwest Territories Provincial government. Clearly this is not a FEMA form and not required. However, based upon the many appeals cases I have researched, this form, properly and regularly used, would have saved the bacon of many agencies which suffered catastrophic roof damage, particularly in hurricane country and Tornado Alley.

For roadway, bridge, and culvert inspection forms, most states have inspection forms which may be easily adapted, if not used outright, to regularly document the condition of these facilities. Similarly, for those agencies which have utility departments, there are forms available from their regional or national associations. The important thing is to get a form, develop a program, and regularly make inspections to protect the local agency's ability to document disaster damage.

The same level of effort should also be made by those agencies with special facilities, such as dams, airports, harbors, water treatment plants, etc. Each of these different facilities will have differing documentation requirements that need to be addressed to constitute a proper inspection.

If the local agency cannot provide the required level of documentation, don't even bother to file a claim for damages with FEMA. Generally, if a facility is in bad condition prior to the disaster for any reason, FEMA will often sniff it out and deny funding.

Lack of Needed Pre-Disaster Policies

Following many disasters, several local agencies file claims for expenses which could be eligible if, and only if, the agency had a pre-disaster policy or agreement in place to cover those specific costs. These policies include:

- Disaster pay policies (for either/or both hourly and salaried employees);
- Disaster feeding policies for employees;
- Disaster lodging policies (in some cases);
- Mutual Aid
- Private Non-Profit agency (PNP) assistance to the local government
- Private Property Debris Removal (PPDR)
- Donation Acceptance
- Volunteers
- File Retention
- Disaster Purchasing Policy

When the local agency has these policies and agreements in place as described in Chapters, 2 and 3 and policies are consistently followed, the skids will be greased to get FEMA funding for these costs. The FEMA Appeals Database is strewn with the broken bodies of those who applied for funding these costs without a proper policy.

The critical piece here, except for the file retention policy and PNP assistance, is that these policies must be in place BEFORE the disaster strikes. Once again, there are many instances in the Appeals Database where local agencies have post-disaster adopted policies, which FEMA routinely ignores because they were not in effect at the time of the disaster. Every unadopted policy represents a financial loss of some degree to the local agency.

Lack of Disaster Cost Recovery Training

In a manner like the table at the beginning of Chapter 15 on Debris Monitoring and Debris Management, I can make a case that virtually every department in a local government agency may be involved in the disaster cost recovery process. This of course will depend on the nature, extent, and severity of a given disaster. But in accepting the premise of an "all-hands-on-deck" effort to financially recover from a disaster, the entire staff should have some level of training in preparation for a worst-case or lesser event.

In particular, non-public safety employees need this kind of training. Normally fire, police, and EMS personnel receive continual training for their jobs, which do not change all that much in a disaster, except for the severity and total call volume. Non-public safety employees, however, seldom receive the kind of training they need so they can make a maximum contribution to the disaster cost recovery process. Effective training helps avoid the quandary of "Making the maximum effort to produce the minimum result."

Non-public safety employees all should have some baseline training in how to correctly account for their own hours worked and for any equipment and materials which they may use in doing their work. At that point, the training needs go in different directions. Engineers and project managers need to be trained in how to avoid changes in the scope of work and how to properly process vendor invoices. Procurement staff need special training in compliance with Title 2 of the Code of Federal Regulations, Part 200. Disaster Cost Recovery staff need training on a variety of administrative protocols for the Public Assistance process.

FEMA's Independent Study Program for Public Assistance

To address this great need for knowledge regarding the Public Assistance program, FEMA offers an extensive set of independent study programs which are available FREE online. These courses cannot substitute for years of experience but are definitely a great start down the road.

Course #	Course Title[8]
IS-1000	Public Assistance Program and Eligibility
IS-1001	The Public Assistance Delivery Model Orientation
IS-1002	FEMA Grants Portal – Transparency at Every Step
IS-1006	Documenting Disaster Damage and Developing Project Files
IS-1007	Detailed Damage Description and Dimensions
IS-1008	Scope of Work Development (Scoping and Costing)
IS-1009	Conditions of the Public Assistance Grant
IS-1011	Roads and Culverts
IS-1012	Direct Administrative Costs
IS-1014	Integrating 406 Mitigation Considerations into Your Public Assistance Grant
IS-1015	Insurance Considerations, Compliance, and Requirements

IS-1016   Environmental and Historic Preservation (EHP) Considerations/Compliance for Public Assistance Grants
IS-1017   Scope Change Requests, Time Extensions, Improved/Alternate Project Requests
IS-1018   Determination Memorandums and Appeals
IS-1019   Codes and Standards
IS-1020   Public Assistance Donated Resources
IS-1021   Bridge Damage Considerations
IS-1022   Substantiating Disaster-Related Damages to Buildings, Contents, Vehicles, and Equipment
IS-1023   Electrical Systems Considerations
IS-1025   Grant Administration Decisions for Tribal Governments
IS-1026   Eligibility of Private Nonprofit Organizations

Effective and Long-Term Records Management

Previously in this chapter we addressed the need for a regular inspection program for the local agency's various facilities and infrastructure. Following hard on the heels of making regular inspections is the need to have all the files properly indexed and immediately available when FEMA requests them. Even if this is a basic method, such as creating a file structure in DropBox, Sugar Sync, Google Docs, etc., and then scanning the written reports into their appropriate file folder, it will be better than bankers boxes full of documents which now, when time is at a premium, have to be sorted into some logical order.

An ideal arrangement would be to have an electronic document management system. However, these may be too costly for many jurisdictions. But an ad hoc system will be better than no system at all.

Taking and Organizing Pre-Disaster Photographs

Similarly to organizing and filing various maintenance reports, every inspection report should include mandatory photographs. The photos should show both the good condition of the facilities inspected and the deficiencies which may be noted in the inspection reports. These photographs must also be organized in a coherent manner, usually by the facility name (or address or GPS coordinates) and date, with photos clearly identified as to the location where the photo was taken, and the deficiency noted as appropriate. When digital cameras are used, the metadata is embedded in each photo taken. The metadata shows the date, the time, the f: stop, the compass direction, and other important data related to each different photo. The important thing is to have pre-disaster photos showing no damage to the facilities in question.

As the reader may surmise, many agencies do not do a very good job of documentation. They don't have the forms necessary, or if they have the forms, they are not in the habit of using them. The result is the same: great difficulty in proving the damage was disaster-caused. Each department will have different ways of working on a day-to-day basis. However, those standard operating procedures may not, and in many cases absolutely do not, meet FEMA's rather stringent documentation requirements. Therefore, each agency should have some consistent practices (and training) for proper documentation which will meet FEMA's requirements.

It is very important that employees responding to a disaster know how to adequately document their time. Previously, we have seen instances where an employee documents their time with notations such as storm work, disaster clean-up, etc., without any specifics. Employees need to be trained to use full descriptions, such as "Boarded-up the Community Center at 151 Broad Street, covered 16 each of 4' by 4' broken windows with ½" plywood." Their report should also include any equipment which may have been used for the work and the other materials used.

I have one ICS-214 form, written by a police lieutenant, where the Emergency Operations Center tasks he included read: "Research, compile and analyze data" or "Attended leadership meeting," etc. Descriptions such as these are completely useless. They could be identical to work done on any other day of the year and provide absolutely no proof that the tasks were in any way disaster-related. FEMA routinely disallows so-called disaster work when it is described in this manner. In this case, the lieutenant could have more properly written: "Research, compile, and analyze data regarding Covid-19 infection spread rates," or "Attended a leadership meeting regarding the establishment of a Covid-19 inoculation center in the city."

No Properly Adopted and Enforced Codes and Standards

As we saw in Chapter 34, the lack of properly adopted and enforced codes and standards can be a major expense for the local agency, when they may be required by regulation to perform work to a newly revised code or standard but be ineligible to receive FEMA funding for that same work because they did not properly adopt the code or standard in question. This applies to buildings, roads, bridges, dams, bridges, culverts – in short, everything!

Liberal 'Storybook' Reading of Contracts and Agreements

Another major failing of local agencies is to misunderstand how existing documents can work against the agency. Some local agencies are often their own worst enemy because they interpret rules, regulations, contracts, and agreements in the most permissive manner possible. "Ah, the rule says thus, and therefore we can do this; it's only a slight stretch of the language."

FEMA, on the other hand, will read the very same document in the most restrictive manner possible and say: "This document does not explicitly require this action," or "this document does not allow this action."

There is a great case from Alabama that beautifully illustrates this principle. This is a complex case, and I have extracted the key information and rewritten the essence of the appeal.

University of Alabama Mutual Aid Case – Conflicting Plans and Agreements

We previously reviewed this case in Chapter 19, and here we take a second look at this important case. "In April 2011, a multi-vortex tornado hit Tuscaloosa County, Alabama, and destroyed the County EOC."[9] The County requested the University of Alabama to open their EOC in support of the disaster. The University of Alabama provided law enforcement personnel to do search and rescue, provide security, and road control throughout the County, including areas outside of the campus property.

The University of Alabama was operating under the terms of a 1994 Mutual Aid agreement which stated that no party shall reimburse another for assistance rendered under this agreement. The University of Alabama is one of 5 parties signing the agreement, including the City of Tuscaloosa, the County of Tuscaloosa, The City of Newport, and the Tuscaloosa County Sheriff.

At issue here is $516,000 for Mutual Aid law enforcement activity. The Project Worksheet was denied funding because of the "no pay" clause.

The University of Alabama filed its first appeal in March of 2012. (Now one year into the problem.)

The University of Alabama cited a 2004 Emergency Operations Plan as the governing document for the Mutual Aid rendered. However, the 2004 Emergency Operations Plan made reference to the 1994 Mutual Aid plan as a separate document, as though it were still in force.

Separately, in April of 2011 the cities of Tuscaloosa and Newport signed a post-dated (to April 27th) disaster Mutual Aid agreement under which those agencies were reimbursed for Mutual Aid expenses. The University of Alabama claimed that FEMA should pay University of Alabama under a theory of "equity and fairness" to avoid inconsistent treatment of the sub-grantees.

The FEMA Regional Administrator denied the first appeal because the University of Alabama derived its authority from the 1994 Mutual Aid agreement, not the 2004 Emergency Operations Plan.

The University of Alabama filed a second appeal in October of 2012 (now 17 months into the problem)

The applicant reiterated the issue of "equity and fairness," because the cities of Tuscaloosa and Newport had been reimbursed for their disaster response work under the terms of their postdated Mutual Aid agreement.

FEMA requested further information from the University of Alabama to support its position that the 1994 Mutual Aid agreement was not in force. However, the University of Alabama had not signed any document that stated that the 1994 Mutual Aid agreement was no longer in force or that it was withdrawing from the agreement. In fact, the University of Alabama had not signed the 2004 Emergency Operations Plan and therefore was not a party to the new agreement. And the 2004 Emergency Operations Plan did not assign any roles or responsibilities specifically to the University of Alabama.

Furthermore, the two documents are different types of agreements; one is an Emergency Operations Plan and the other is a Mutual Aid Agreement. The Emergency Operations Plan cited previous other Emergency Operations Plans, but not other Mutual Aid Plans. It includes Mutual Aid Plans in the glossary to substantiate further that they are different plans. The Emergency Operations Plan language provides for harmonizing of previous and future Mutual Aid plans as an indication that these are separate plans and not similar documents.

FEMA, as a Federal agency, is bound to follow its laws and regulations and cannot provide relief on the basis of theories of equity and fairness.

FEMA requested further information from the University of Alabama regarding where its officers provided Mutual Aid assistance. The University of Alabama responded with a map showing the locations where its officers provided law enforcement services. The map showed that University of Alabama officers provided service outside of the campus jurisdictional areas. The University of Alabama also cited sections of the Alabama state codes, giving it law enforcement authority. FEMA replied that the language of the codes did not broadly apply to actions off the university property.

FEMA requested that the University of Alabama submit a request for a legal opinion from the Alabama State Attorney General. In July 2014 (now 39 months into the issue), the Alabama AG provided a supporting opinion that the University of Alabama did have the authority to conduct law enforcement operations off-campus. The University of Alabama won the second appeal.

The University of Alabama could have saved 39 months of staff time and costs and received a timely reimbursement had they ensured that their emergency plans and Mutual Aid agreements were current, actually in force, and were harmonized and contained clear and unambiguous language which would not have given FEMA cause to make such adverse interpretations.

Absent the favorable ruling from the state's attorney general, the school would have lost half a million dollars on this lack of proper attention to details.

Relying on Verbal or Tacit Approval for Work Done

A sub-theme which appears frequently in appeals cases is that of the "verbal or tacit authorization." "Our (unnamed) FEMA representative told us to go ahead with the project and we would sort out the details at close-out time." Or "our FEMA representative was at the work site three different times, and never said that we couldn't do that." This is a death wish come true. FEMA will never, never, never honor an alleged verbal authorization. Not even once. If an approval isn't in writing, it simply doesn't exist.

The very same thing goes for a "tacit" approval. "They knew we were doing this and said nothing, so it must be OK." This logic is right up there with believing in Santa Claus, the Easter Bunny, and my dog ate my homework. It's a nice fantasy, but it never comes true.

Failure to Properly File Appeals, Request SOW Changes, Etc.

Many appeals cases are D.O.A.: Dead on Arrival, because they are filed after the statutory date for filing the appeal has passed. There is no automated external defibrillator manufactured that can bring this one back to life. No matter what the issue is, and how much documentation the agency may have to prove its point, a late filing is fatal to the cause. This mandatory compliance with deadlines applies to the local agency for all aspects of Public Assistance. The Damage Inventory must be complete within 60 days (generally) of the Recovery Scoping Meeting; Requests for Information must be responded to within the timeframe given, etc.

Another aspect of filing a "Dead-on-Arrival" appeals case is that in filing an appeal, particularly a second appeal, sufficient consideration is not given to exactly how much time will have to be spent on preparing the first appeal, and if that appeal is not successful (a 50% chance of success), how much time will go into the second appeal (a 33% chance of success). Also, with a second appeal, the appeal is elevated from the Regional level to the Headquarters level, and an arguably a more experienced and knowledgeable FEMA staffer will review the case. Sometimes during this review, this more experienced FEMA staffer will recognize that the appeal is a moot issue because of some other fundamentally fatal flaw in the project.

This is a case on this point, from Missouri: "From April 29-July 6, 2019, the state of Missouri experienced severe storms, tornadoes, and flooding. On July 9, 2019, the President issued a major disaster declaration (DR-4451) for the areas affected. The Missouri Department of Transportation (Applicant) requested $943,386.88 in Public Assistance (PA) funds for emergency work to clear vegetative, silt, and construction debris from five road sites in three counties that it claimed resulted from this disaster. The Applicant estimated the initial total quantity of debris across all project sites but later reduced the quantity via several contract change orders to reflect the actual debris removed and bid each of the project site's damaged items as a separate contract, choosing the lowest bidders for each item. FEMA wrote Grants Manager Project (GMP) 132669/Project Worksheet (PW) 1274 to capture completed debris removal work. FEMA issued a Determination Memorandum (DM), determining that the mobilization charges and *reducing the requested costs, including mobilization and erosion control, by $322,969.08* in direct proportion with the actual quantity of debris work performed. FEMA then obligated $620,417.80 in funding for the debris removal for GMP 132669/PW 1274."[10]

The case continues: "The FEMA Region VII Regional Administrator denied the appeal. FEMA found all of the debris removal work and costs were ineligible for PA funding because: 1) the Applicant's invoices were not supported by debris monitoring reports demonstrating that the debris was eligible for removal or generated by the disaster; 2) the Applicant did not provide adequate load tickets to show debris pick-up locations, type of debris removed, quantity, and eligibility; 3) the Applicant acknowledged in the second RFI response that some of the damage captured in GMP 132669/PW1274 may have been the result of DR-4435; (a previous disaster) and 4) without adequate and proper documentation showing that the Applicant adequately monitored the work, FEMA could not verify that the claimed costs were reasonable, were associated with eligible work, or that the debris removed posed an immediate threat to life, health, safety, or economic recovery. *FEMA also deobligated $620,417.80* in previously awarded funds after it determined that section 705(c) of The Robert T. Stafford Disaster Relief and Emergency Assistance (Stafford) Act did not prohibit recovery of those payments as two prongs of section 705(c) were not met."

So in this case, after being denied $322,969.08 in ineligible costs, the agency filed a second appeal, wherein FEMA deobligated the balance of $620,417.80. This is worse than a total loss when all the staff time is added in.

The other side of this coin is promptly notifying FEMA in writing, <u>and then waiting for FEMA's written approval</u>, any time there is a change in the scope of work. Beginning work prior to receiving a <u>written</u> approval for that work is futile and likely to cost the agency whatever amount of money might have been available had FEMA approved the change. I am cynical enough to think that some FEMA staff may give a verbal approval or say something like "It looks good to go," knowing that some unsophisticated local staff member may take the comment as an authorization, only later to find out it wasn't. It is particularly important that the local agency's engineers and project managers understand this issue. Stopping a project in midstream to wait, possibly weeks, for FEMA approval will cost money. But that loss must be measured against the cost i.e., the loss of funding which will occur if the work is done without FEMA approval.

Failure to complete an approved project within the designated time is another reason why local agencies' projects are deobligated. The Period of Performance or POP must be complied with, or a time extension request be timely filed to extend the POP.

This case from Mississippi is a good if extreme example insofar as the project was delayed for years past the original period of performance for permanent work, which is normally 18 months.

"In August 2005, ocean surge, high winds, and flooding resulting from Hurricane Katrina (FEMA-DR-1604-MS) caused damage throughout the City of Waveland (Applicant), including to the Applicant's 50,000-gallon water tank located on Davis Street. FEMA prepared Project Worksheet (PW) 6364 to the capture costs of restoring the water tank, which totaled an estimate of $60,618.00. At the time of PW 6364's formulation, the Applicant intended to not restore the tank but, instead, apply the funds toward constructing a new, larger tank in a different location as an improved project."[11]

"In 2007, the Applicant sent a letter to the Mississippi Emergency Management Agency (Grantee) requesting a time extension on multiple PWs, including PW 6364, beyond an August 28, 2007 project deadline. The Grantee granted the request in a letter dated October 4, 2007, allowing an extension to August 28, 2009."[12]

"The Applicant requested a further extension in a letter dated June 29, 2009. The Applicant requested an extension until January 1, 2011, citing the need to resolve an insurance dispute related to the project. In a letter dated January 29, 2010, the FEMA Region IV Regional Administrator granted a time extension on 42 projects under FEMA-1604-DR-MS, including PW 6364, that encountered delays relating to insurance recoveries. The Regional Administrator granted an extension on PW 6364 to January 1, 2011. Prior to granting that extension, FEMA had reduced eligible costs under PW 6364 to account for anticipated insurance proceeds that FEMA determined the Applicant failed to pursue. The October 2009 reduction brought the eligible amount under PW 6364 to $29,569.50."[13]

"The Applicant again requested an additional extension in a letter dated December 20, 2010, seeking a new project deadline of February 1, 2012, and explaining that the insurance dispute had been resolved. The Regional Administrator granted an extension on numerous Applicant PWs, including PW 6364 to July 1, 2011. Prior to granting that extension, the Mississippi State Rating Bureau issued a letter to the Applicant dated January 21, 2011, stating that the Applicant should timely repair or replace the water tank and that failure to maintain storage capacity could hurt the Applicant's fire rating."[14]

"The Applicant submitted a letter dated April 14, 2011 to the Grantee, indicating its decision to repair the water tank to bring it into compliance with Rating Bureau requirements and avoid an adverse effect on its fire rating. The Applicant provided a repair cost estimate totaling $234,740.00. In July 2011, the Grantee developed an analysis and response to the new estimate, determining that $168,977.12 of the estimate is eligible for reimbursement and recommending to FEMA that PW 6364 be revised to reflect that cost estimate."[15]

"Through a letter dated July 12, 2011, the Applicant requested an additional extension until January 1, 2012, explaining its decision to repair the water tank – rather than demolish it as originally planned – in order to maintain its fire rating, and stating that it planned to begin the bid process by August 2011. The Regional Administrator granted the request in a letter dated August 12, 2011."[16]

"On September 19, 2011, FEMA issued an eligibility determination reaffirming that eligible costs under PW 6343 amounted to $29,596.50 – the amount of the original, 2005 estimate, less anticipated insurance proceeds. FEMA rejected the Applicant's proposed new cost estimate, explaining that the increased costs and associated expanded scope of work of the project resulted from the Applicant's initial decision not to repair the tank but to demolish it and, therefore, the increased costs were not a direct result of the disaster."[17]

"Under Public Assistance Program project performance regulations, a PA permanent work project (such as the Applicant's water tank project) must be completed within 18 months of the applicable major disaster or emergency declaration. A Grantee may extend this deadline for an additional 30 months if warranted by extenuating circumstances or unusual project requirements beyond the control of the subgrantee. Any time extension requests beyond that point must be submitted to the Regional Administrator and include (1) the dates and provisions of all previous time extensions on the project, and (2) a detailed justification for the delay and a projected completion date."[18]

"In this case, the Applicant requested a total of five time extensions for PW 6364, four of which were granted. In each of the three extensions granted by FEMA, the Grantee was asked to remind the Applicant that, under PA Program regulations, no federal funding would be provided if the Applicant's project was not completed. Despite these explicit reminders, the Applicant failed to begin work on its water tank project, let alone complete the work, at the time it submitted its final time extension request at the end of 2011 – more than six years after the disaster event. In its second-to-last request, the Applicant revealed that, after years of pursuing a plan to demolish the water tank and build a replacement, it had decided to restore it. The Applicant stated that the bid process on the project would begin by August 2011 and asked for an extension until January 2012. In its final time extension request submitted just a few months later, the Applicant stated that the bid process would then begin in February 2012. In light of the lack of progress on the project, the numerous time extensions awarded, and the length of time that had elapsed since the disaster event, the Regional Administrator properly exercised his discretion in denying the Applicant's final time extension request and withdrawing funding. The Regional Administrator's decision is consistent with prior agency decisions regarding repeated time extension requests involving long-delayed projects."[19]

This case points out some important issues, which will bear repeating. 1) Clearly the local agency did not have its priorities in place relative to this project. To risk damaging its fire insurance rating is a serious issue for the entire community. 2) If a local agency does not consider a project to be important, neither will the state nor FEMA. 3) FEMA has thousands of projects in hundreds of jurisdictions who will put the available funding to good use when the local agency drags its heels and delays, almost indefinitely. In this instance, 6 years later, had the state not pressed the city on the matter of its fire insurance rating, the project might still be pending.

Another potential loss for local agencies derives from failing to timely file a "Net Small Project Overrun," or NSPO, which will be addressed in Chapter 42, Close-Outs. When the agency has many small projects, and when all the small projects are completed in aggregate, at more than the originally obligated costs, FEMA can provide additional funding so long as all the projects complied with the scope of work. However, this must be done within 60 days of completion of the last small project.

In another case from Louisiana, the parish lost more than $20,000 because of a late filing for an NSPO. "This is in response to a letter from the Louisiana Governor's Office of Homeland Security and Emergency Preparedness (Recipient) office dated May 4, 2023, which transmitted the referenced second appeal on behalf of St. Mary Parish Consolidated Gravity Drainage District #1 (Applicant). The Applicant is appealing the U.S. Department of Homeland Security's Federal Emergency Management Agency's (FEMA) denial of $20,831.26 in costs pertaining to a Net Small Project Overrun. <u>Pursuant to Title 44 of the Code of Federal Regulations (44 C.F.R.) § 206.204(e)(2) (2018), when an applicant discovers a significant overrun related to the total final cost for all small projects, it may submit an appeal for additional funding, in accordance with 44 C.F.R. § 206.206, within 60 days following the completion of all its small projects.</u> According to the Administrative Record, the Applicant completed work on small project PW 369 by February 28, 2021. The Applicant's other small project, PW 394, is a management cost project, so the Applicant was able to claim management costs for up to 180 days after completion of its last project, or up to August 27, 2021. However, the Applicant submitted its appeal on October 26, 2022, which was after the 60 calendar-day timeframe required by FEMA's regulations, making the first appeal untimely. Therefore, this appeal is denied."[20]

On the other hand, if all the small projects come in with a combined net under the obligated amounts, the agency may retain the funds when it files a timely NSPO request. The local agency loses money either way unless the overage or underage is an insignificant amount of money.

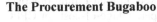

Similarly, if the local agency is participating in the Public Assistance Alternative Procedures process and the project(s) come in under budget, the agency can file a request to use the available excess funds for other qualified disaster-related uses, provided they file the request and the plan for using the funds in a timely manner.

The Procurement Bugaboo

In the world of Public Assistance program, there is no sin greater than the failure to fully comply with Title 2 of the Code of Federal Regulations, Part 200 (2 CFR, Part 200). And this is a sin which no priest or minister can forgive. FEMA believes that its best chance of controlling costs is to strictly enforce 2 CFR, Part 200. FEMA does not and will not evaluate our disaster contracts for compliance. We are on our own. When requested, FEMA will provide training on 2 CFR, Part 200. But unless the local agency takes the training to heart and revises its own procurement policies, there will be no salvation.

- Previously in this chapter we discussed pre-disaster policies that should be in place. A compliant purchasing policy is critical among these necessary policies. Also highly recommended is a "disaster purchasing policy" which, when properly drawn up and approved, may provide some flexibility of action for the local agency during the heat of battle, i.e., the crisis phase of a disaster. However, absent such a policy the local agency must follow its own regular procedures, so long as they are compliant with 2 CFR, Part 200, and between the two sets of requirements, always conform to the stricter requirements of both policies.

As a reprise to Chapter 9, one of the most common failings of local agencies when purchasing for any aspect of a disaster is the failure to realize that once Federal money, even one dollar, is used, every dollar the local agency spends must comply with 2 CFR, Part 200.

Piggybacking is almost always a very bad idea. There have been a few very limited exceptions to this rule, primarily when public health is endangered. The following case from Oklahoma is a good example of this problem: "An ice storm from December 8, 2007, through January 3, 2008, deposited large quantities of vegetative debris in the Applicant's maintained and owned properties. FEMA prepared PW 690 for the debris monitoring service. The state of Oklahoma Department Emergency Management (DOEM) (sic) audit suggested that FEMA increase the eligible funding amount to $75,000. However, the additional funding was denied because of what appeared to be a 'piggyback' contract. The amount of the claim exceeded the maximum amount stated in the contract; and the monitors did not meet contract requirements in the field writing load tickets at loading sites. In addition, FEMA file memos and photos, demonstrate that the contractor loads were 'fluffed' to exaggerate actual volume; ineligible debris was removed from private property and undeveloped areas; and monitors did not write load tickets at point of origins thereby allowing ineligible debris to be invoiced. The Applicant submitted its second appeal dated May 29, 2009. The Applicant provided a copy of a February 6, 2008, addendum to the monitoring contract, increasing the cost ceiling from $42,364 to $75,000. FEMA 322 Public Assistance Guide and FEMA 325 Public Assistance Debris Management Guide, both clearly state that if FEMA receives a request for reimbursement of costs derived from a piggyback contract, FEMA will review eligible work performed and determine reasonable costs on a case-by-case basis. In this instance the Applicant failed to provide documentation that the increased monitoring cost are reasonable for the eligible volume of debris."[21]

As we have previously seen, the use of buy groups is similar to walking a tightrope without a net. Local agencies are prohibited from using out-of-state buy groups, and if using an in-state buy group, the local agency must provide full documentation that the procurement was made in compliance with 2 CFR, Part 200. I have on file a buy group contract made for the use of a statewide college system, where the final agreement, while doing an excellent job of compliance with 2 CFR, Part 200, tumbles and falls down because the contractor tacked on their billing practices which include a 21% mark-up, rendering the contract a cost-plus-a-percentage-of-costs or CPPC contract. Any of the participants in that buy group will be in for a very nasty surprise upon use of the contract.

Many local agencies fail to have pre-disaster contracts in place for those services and commodities they are likely to need following a disaster. Water, fuel, emergency meals, port-a-potties, and disaster cost recovery consultant fees are just a few of the items which may be needed. If another local agency does have a pre-disaster contract in place for these items, then FEMA may use that price as the "reasonable" going rate and pay no more than that amount, regardless of what another agency had to pay.

Tacitly included in the previous bullet (no pun intended) are pre-disaster contracts for debris management and debris monitoring. These two contracts may be the most important pre-disaster contracts an agency can have in place. Without these pre-disaster contracts, the local agency is most likely going to pay much more for the clean-up; the clean-up will be slower to get started, the clean-up will take longer to finish, and the chances of unanticipated and costly problems will be greater.

Insurance Losers

Many local agencies do not have designated risk managers, nor do they have a formal risk management program. Insurance issues are sometimes handled on a piecemeal basis, i.e., Human Resources handles Worker's Compensation; facilities or possibly the city/county clerk handles property insurance; the agency attorney handles liability claims, etc. This lack of a formal coordinated risk management program invites serious problems when a disaster strikes.

Blanket insurance policies may be a great tool for everyday coverage, but they are an invitation to trouble because FEMA will evaluate the percentage of eligible losses to the ineligible losses and withhold that percentage of funds from the reimbursement, unless the blanket policy somehow allocates, in writing, how much of the policy may be for business interruption versus the amounts for property damage.

Agencies will, and often for sound business reasons, accept less than the full or face value of their insurance claim. However, the difference between the policy face value and the settlement received from the insurer is not a FEMA-eligible expense. Only if the local agency pursues a full settlement could FEMA be moved to pay. Usually this involves filing a lawsuit and once the court settles the question of coverage, FEMA will consider reimbursement.

Flood insurance, or more properly the lack thereof, can result in a major hit when flooding is the disaster. If a facility is in a mapped flood zone, it must be covered by a FEMA flood insurance policy. No other flood insurance policy from a private insurer is acceptable to FEMA. If the facility is FEMA-flood insured but for a lower amount than is required for the facility, then FEMA will deduct that insurance shortfall from the otherwise eligible work.

There are professional firms, i.e., public adjusters, which will go into battle with insurers to obtain much higher settlements for their clients. If the agency's property damage losses are significant, it may be well worthwhile to consult with an experienced public adjusting firm.

Obtain & Maintain (O&M): Once a facility has received FEMA funding for disaster damages, there is attached a "forever" requirement that the local agency "obtain and maintain" insurance coverage in the amount of the FEMA funds received for as long as the agency owns the facility, including equipment. The O&M requirement does not apply to Category B emergency work, only to permanent work. If a local agency does not obtain and maintain insurance to cover the type of disaster that caused the loss to the level of FEMA funding received, then that facility will not be eligible for FEMA funding in a future disaster.

This case from Louisiana is straight on point regarding the O&M requirement: "In 2005, Hurricane Katrina (DR-1603), caused extensive damage to properties owned by Plaquemines Parish (Applicant) and FEMA prepared numerous Project Worksheets (PWs) to address the damage. These PWs required that the Applicant obtain and maintain (O&M) insurance coverage for the damaged sites as a condition of receiving future Public Assistance (PA) funding. In 2012, Hurricane Isaac damaged several of the Applicant's sites including the same sites as Hurricane Katrina. FEMA prepared PW 1527 to address the damage and subsequently obligated $650,022.68, which was the value of eligible costs, less reductions and duplications. In total, this included O&M reductions in the amount of $797,809.92 for the four sites on appeal. FEMA applied the reductions to several sites because it determined that the Applicant had not met the necessary O&M requirement for them and as a result, the Applicant was not eligible to receive PA funding for those sites. The Applicant appealed claiming that FEMA: 1) improperly identified insurance coverage for multiple sites; 2) did not consider the State Insurance Commissioner (SIC) certificates obtained by the Applicant; and, 3) at the time of the disaster, did not require the Applicant to satisfy O&M requirements as a condition for subsequent assistance. The FEMA Region VI Regional Administrator denied the appeal, finding that the Applicant failed to satisfy the O&M requirements because it did not obtain insurance or had too little insurance for the sites on appeal. **Therefore, all claimed funding, was deemed ineligible.** On second appeal the Applicant maintains its previously asserted claims. The Applicant also claims that FEMA did not provide notice that it might deny the appeal due to an issue with its compliance with the SIC's certificate. The Applicant was required to obtain and maintain insurance coverage as a result of PWs written after Hurricane Katrina. When Hurricane Isaac struck, the Applicant either did not have any insurance coverage or had insufficient insurance coverage for the sites on appeal. Therefore, the Facilities in question are ineligible for PA funding, and the appeal is denied."[22]

Perhaps one of the most dangerous yet completely avoidable problems stems from the gratuitous statements local agency employees sometimes make to FEMA. In this case from Florida, an agency employee adds to the troubles by speaking out of turn: "For the NW 190th Road and NE 48th Avenue sites, FEMA found that the administrative record lacked sufficient documentation to demonstrate that the culverts were damaged by the event and required replacement. Further, the SIRs (*Site Inspector's Report*) noted that the Applicant had stated that it planned on replacing the culverts as a maintenance issue."[23] (Emphasis Added)

In the same way most local agencies restrict their employees from speaking with the media, unless they are the Public Information Officer, Mayor, City/County Manager, or similarly authorized spokesperson, all employees should be trained to direct ALL inquiries from either the state or FEMA to the authorized disaster cost recovery spokesperson. In any case, all employees should be cautioned against making gratuitous statements to anyone, especially FEMA. Naturally, someone in authority needs to be officially designated as the state/FEMA point-of-contact and all employees notified of this designation. This designated point-of-contact will not necessarily know all the answers, but their job is to be an active conduit for communication between the agency's employees and FEMA.

Perhaps the single greatest reason, absent procurement problems, that projects are either partially or completely deobligated once they have been FEMA-approved and funded, arise when the local agency arbitrarily makes changes to the scope of work. I don't know why this is so, but there are hundreds of appeals cases where the scope of work is an issue. In reading these cases, it is as though the engineers or project managers have a pathological need to make changes and make those changes without first notifying FEMA and awaiting FEMA's approval or denial. On average, when the local agency arbitrarily changes the scope of work, the very best which they can hope for is to receive the amount of funding originally approved, and not a penny more. In the most egregious cases, FEMA will deobligate the entire project. If the local agency doesn't want to do the project the way that FEMA specifies, it needs to be prepared to front the extra costs, and in some cases, pay for the entire project. Public Assistance projects are funded with Federal tax dollars, and therefore they need to be done as FEMA has specified or risk the lot.

Often commingled with changes in the scope of work are improved or alternate projects. My general advice to my training clients is to avoid improved and/or alternate projects as you would the bubonic plague.

First, improved projects. FEMA's initial position is "like for like" replacement. That is (relatively) the simplest and economically safest way to repair disaster damage. However, the temptation seems to be irresistible for many agencies to insist on doing improved projects their way, as opposed to the FEMA approved way. FEMA only funds the work to the level necessary to restore the facility to its pre-disaster condition. If something goes wrong during the repair and reconstruction, it is difficult to clearly separate out costs which relate to the "like for like" work versus the improvements. Most local agencies do not do a very good job of tracking job costs in a manner which will satisfy FEMA.

When the local agency opts for an improved project, and a change in the footprint of the facility is made, the agency may find itself in a lengthy delay while FEMA attends to all of the "special considerations," i.e., the environmental and historic consultations and requirements therefrom. The Joplin (Missouri) School District environmental report came out 11 months after the tornado devastated the town. In the meantime, the district could not begin construction. In that case, there was no option available because some of the school buildings had been totally destroyed. But that is not always the case.

For Alternate Projects, the case is not any better; if anything, alternate projects are riskier. First, the funding for a standard alternate project, as opposed to an Alternative Procedures project, is capped at 90% of the funding which FEMA would have provided for a "like for like" project. The same triggers exist for the environmental and historic concerns that FEMA must address. Alternate projects may be a good solution in some cases, but they are always a high-risk roll of the dice as opposed to "like for like" replacement.

The National Environmental Policy Act (or NEPA) can, and in appeals cases often does, result in a total deobligation of funding. This is because the local agency <u>BEGINS</u> repair or construction work <u>BEFORE</u> FEMA has completed its required reviews. The NEPA review will almost always result in a delayed project, but that is part of the cost to the local agency in exchange for receiving Federal tax dollars.

This next case is from Pennsylvania. "In September 2011, rains from Tropical Storm Lee caused severe flooding in Plymouth Township (Applicant), located in Luzerne County, Pennsylvania, resulting in severe erosion of Tilbury Terrace Road. Due to a slope failure, a portion of the road and shoulder collapsed. In February 2012, FEMA approved funding under Project Worksheet (PW) 394 for permanent repairs to the flood damaged portion of Tilbury Terrace Road. In April 2012, the Applicant submitted to the Pennsylvania Emergency Management Agency (Grantee) a request to change the scope of work (SOW) and a request to build a temporary access road for use while Tilbury Terrace Road was closed for repair. The Applicant stated Tilbury Terrace Road would be closed for a minimum of 90-120 days and as the damaged road was the only means of access for the community, consisting of 65 homes, a temporary road would be needed. The Applicant proposed building the temporary road on property it owned to the rear of the community and attached an estimate from its engineering firm that outlined the construction of a 20 foot wide paved surface with two foot wide shoulders on each side, a concrete slab slope, and rip-rap lined swales."[24]

"FEMA sent the Grantee a letter dated August 21, 2012, denying the Applicant's SOW change request. Specifically, FEMA found the 20 foot wide paved surface with two foot wide shoulders on each side, and a full roadway drainage system with concrete headwalls and rip-rap lined swales, went beyond what was required for a temporary road and such work would be more properly classified as a permanent road. However, FEMA agreed temporary access was needed while Tilbury Terrace Road was closed, and approved a temporary access road of the same length and width, with an aggregate surface six inches thick and drainage pipes at two locations. FEMA calculated a total cost estimate of $235,000.00 to complete the project and noted: (1) that a separate PW would be prepared for the temporary road; and (2) that if the Applicant still desired to construct its proposed access road as a permanent road, it could request FEMA classify it as an improved project. However, funding for an improved project, such as a permanent road, would be limited to the $235,000.00 cost estimate."[25]

In this case, the local agency built the temporary road to the standards of permanent work and FEMA disallowed any additional costs beyond what had been originally approved as an unpaved temporary access road. In this case, in the second appeal, FEMA headquarters determined that none of the work was eligible and deobligated the entire $235,000 in previously awarded costs.

An area of great wastes of time and money occurs when local agencies confuse eligible disaster-related costs with "increased operating expenses." FEMA simply does not pay for everything. This case from New York illustrates the issue of confusing disaster caused expenses with increased operation expenses: "From October 27 to November 8, 2012, Hurricane Sandy caused severe damage to the City of Long Beach's (Applicant) water and sewer system. FEMA wrote Project Worksheet (PW) 3956 for $253,412.39 for work to repair the sewer system that included 92 'cut and caps' performed between November 9, 2012 and July 17, 2013. A 'cut and cap' terminates a residential sewer or water line that is no longer required (i.e., the resident has demolished the property). FEMA also wrote PW 4201 for $1,524,159.78 to repair the water distribution system, which included 406 'cut and caps' that took place between around October 28, 2012 and July 30, 2014. On April 14 and 20, 2016, the New York State Division of Homeland Security and Emergency Services (Grantee) requested a scope of work change to include 306 (PW 3956) and 193 (PW 4201) additional 'cut and caps' for disaster damaged homes. FEMA denied the requests after determining that the additional 'cut ad caps' were not performed to repair damage caused by the disaster, and that the Applicant charged homeowners a $500.00 fee for the service. FEMA determined the requested 'cut and caps' were an ineligible increased operating expense. FEMA denied the Applicant's first appeal for similar reasons and explained that the original 'cut and caps' were only eligible because they were short-term increased operating expenses directly related to specific emergency tasks. The Applicant submitted a second appeal stating that FEMA arbitrarily defined 'short-term' as it relates to the policy for increased operating expenses. The Applicant states that the City had to perform this work to prevent an immediate threat to health and safety. The requested 'cut and cap' services were performed at the request of individual homeowners and are not tied to any repair or restoration work eligible for PA funding."[26] (Emphasis Added)

As the local agency, we always want to obtain the maximum reimbursement for our disaster-related costs. However, in some cases, requesting reimbursement for these "normal" increased operation expenses if denied is usually not worth the time and effort to file an appeal. At least in the interest of saving a lot of time, go to the Appeals Database[27] at FEMA.gov and see if there are any appeals cases which are similar to the one being contemplated. A few minutes of searching the database may save hours and days of work on a fruitless appeal.

Direct Administrative Costs (or DAC) may be a huge waste of time for many agencies. In my opinion, DAC is often a game of "three-card-monte" or the equally classic "pea-in-a-walnut-shell" game. Attempting to track the Direct Administrative Costs enforces an administrative burden on staff who, except for attorneys and certified public accountants, seldom have to track their time minute by minute and constantly consult a list to see if the work which they are doing is on the list of eligible tasks. The issue is that the local agency is eligible for DAC up to 5% of the total obligated cost of a Project Worksheet. Meanwhile, as the employees are attempting to track their DAC, other eligibility killers are hard at work. Tracking the direct administrative costs takes a lot of time and judging by the number of appeals cases is not very financially rewarding. Depending on the search terms used, "direct administrative costs" or "DAC," there are nearly 500 cases on this issue, or nearly 20% of all appeals cases. Furthermore, in the Appeals Database, one agency, utilizing a professional disaster cost recovery consulting firm, lost over a million claimed dollars for its alleged DAC expenses. For some agencies, DAC is nothing more than a diversionary trick. However, if the staff of the local agency is well trained in disaster cost recovery and attentive to details, the added (maximum) 5% is certainly a plus.

As explained in the previous chapter, FEMA's 50% rule on "repair versus replace" is a potential maelstrom for those uninitiated into the world of disaster cost recovery. Getting a new replacement facility may be a very attractive possibility, but it is critical to independently verify the accuracy of the calculations prior to accepting this option. It is equally important to strictly adhere to the defined scope of work. The issue with a replacement facility is that there is a great deal of money involved, often millions of dollars, and FEMA will be assiduously monitoring all aspects of the project to ensure that everything is done properly to minimize the Federal government's out-of-pocket expense.

The greatest point on the risk scale for a repair versus replace project comes at the project close-out. The work is done, and now FEMA examines all the project records to ensure that all complies with Federal regulations. Any substantive misstep can be a reason for deobligation.

A very frequent failing, but a failing often not understood or realized until it's too late, is the lack of financial and training support for local agency staff regarding the Public Assistance process. This is not an issue easily dealt with because of the general lack of revenue available to local government agencies, as opposed to the multitude of demands placed upon them every day. If a local agency had twice its current revenue, elected officials would have no trouble in spending the extra revenue.

But allocating some level of funding for disaster cost recovery is akin to saving for retirement, except no one knows what day a disaster may strike, as opposed to an eventual retirement which may be many years down the road. A disaster may be likened to buying a home with a balloon payment due in the future. The problem with a disaster is that this balloon payment may be called for any day of the year with virtually no notice. Thus, the prudent course is to provide some steady level of funding and training for a day which no one hopes will ever come.

All one must do is watch the Weather Channel to observe that disasters seem to be increasing in both frequency and cost, particularly in certain parts of the United States. While some states have relatively little experience in dealing with disasters, other states have an annual exposure to devastating events, such as hurricanes, tornadoes, wildfires, and severe flooding. Therefore, each local agency should, depending on its geography, need to spend more, or less, on disaster financial preparedness.

Yet another common failure of local government agencies is not understanding that there is a multitude of other Federal agencies which may, but not always, play a role in disaster recovery and disaster cost recovery. As described in Chapter 22, Other Federal Agencies, there are many different Federal agencies which may, depending on various factors, provide financial assistance for roads, bridges, transportation networks, water-related infrastructure, etc.

The local agency should not waste valuable time and energy on applying to FEMA for projects which FEMA cannot, under current legislation, provide funding. Furthermore, each of the programs of the different Federal agencies has different deadlines for filing, work completion, etc. Each of the Federal agencies also may have different regulations than FEMA does, which makes mastery of the disaster cost recovery process that much more difficult.

Across the Federal government, no one actually knows how much the U.S. spends each year on disaster recovery because there are so many different Federal agencies providing financial and in-kind disaster assistance, not only to local government, but also to eligible private non-profit organizations, homeowners, individuals, etc. Additionally, many states help financially support their local jurisdictions, which adds another layer of dense fog to our inability to know a single dollar amount for the total national cost of disasters. Even ChatGPT © cannot determine the total number for disaster spending.

Another very significant failure devolves from the individual state's collective failures to properly support their cities, counties, and special districts, etc. in learning about and properly managing their disaster cost recovery efforts. Some years ago, I looked at every audit issued by the Department of Homeland Security, Office of the Inspector General. In fully one-half of the audits issued, in addition to the findings of the specific local agency, a dozen states were taken out to the woodshed for their failures to properly support their own local agencies' disaster cost recovery efforts.

Some years ago, I took the disaster cost recovery training from one state's office of emergency services. The title of the training was a slight misnomer because they also discussed the "Individuals and Households Assistance" program, which is out there in another universe. Additionally, much of the training centered on how to make the process easier for the state, rather than how to maximize how much money the local agencies might get from FEMA.

Much like local agencies, the states have limited resources, and no one wants to spend money on preparing for a disaster that everyone hopes will never happen. But disasters do happen, and happen often enough, at least in certain states, that preparations do need to be made.

The same may be said for counties which fail to help their cities and special districts be better prepared for disasters. The point here is that, for example, every jurisdiction in the state of Florida should have 1) a debris management plan, 2) a debris monitoring plan, 3) a debris management pre-disaster contract, and 4) a debris monitoring pre-disaster contract. Florida has approximately 67 counties and 411 cities, towns, and villages. Why is there not a single statewide master debris

management plan and companion debris monitoring plan? Why should every unit of local government have to do this work on their own? The intent here is not particularly to pick on Florida, but
because of the state's annual hurricane exposure this is a fair question to ask. And the very same
set of questions can be asked for the majority of the 50 states, if not all of them.

Rental agreements and leases for both buildings and equipment can be a relatively minor scrape
or an issue which results in a financial quadruple bypass. To be eligible for FEMA Public Assistance, the interested party must be a local government agency or an eligible private non-profit
agency. When the local agency leases a facility (building), the lease should specifically address
the issue of which party is responsible for repairing disaster-caused damage. FEMA doesn't care,
but we do.

If a leased building is disaster-damaged and the lease is silent on the responsibility for repairing
disaster damage, then the owner of the building is almost always responsible. The local agency
may be able to claim damages related to equipment, furnishings, and supplies in the building,
but the building repairs themselves are not usually an eligible expense. If, however, the lease or
rental agreement specifically assigns (under the <u>written</u> terms of the contract) the responsibility
for repairs to the tenant (the local agency) for disaster-caused damage, then the repair work will be
eligible for FEMA funding. If the local agency owns the building and leases it to another a) government agency, b) an eligible private non-profit, or c) a private for-profit organization, the same consideration must be given to the assigned responsibility for the repair of disaster-caused damages.

The same thought must be given to the lease of equipment. For example, if a local agency
leases all of its photocopier/laser printers from XYZ Business Solutions, and those machines are
all ruined because of flooding, who has the responsibility for cleaning/repairing or replacing those
machines? The lease must specify responsibility for there to be eligibility. Under the terms of the
lease, the local agency may be responsible for any damage which occurs while in the possession of
the agency. But without very specific language addressing disaster-caused damage, the costs will
not be eligible for reimbursement. Very rarely when drawing up lease agreements is any consideration given to this issue.

And finally, the last bullet in the chamber. Local agencies of all stripes, cities, counties, special
districts, etc., are often unknowing and careless in the language they use in conversations with
FEMA, and in the documentation which they provide to FEMA during the disaster cost recovery
process. This unknowing and careless use of certain words are tip-offs to FEMA personnel that the
locals do not know what's going on. While the use of the term "stand-by time" may be acceptable
and an eligible expense under certain circumstances, it is not always so. Therefore, the use of that
term should be avoided whenever possible. If emergency response workers are assigned to a "staging area," then "Assigned to Staging" is the proper terminology, not "stand-by." The word "levee"
is another red-flag word that should not be used carelessly. If the facility is a "water retention basin
berm," the use of the word "levee" is an invitation to more intense scrutiny from FEMA. The
proper use of language plays a key role in the Public Assistance process.

In closing, FEMA's Public Assistance program is a complex and easily misunderstood process
which will continue for years after a disaster. In many states, second-, third-, fourth-, and sometimes more generation disasters are layered upon certain disaster-prone states.

Some years ago, I was invited to present my disaster cost recovery training program to a major
metropolitan city in the southern U.S. I was concerned. I knew this city and state were frequently
the victims of disasters of all sizes. I did not know what I could possibly tell this audience about
disaster cost recovery. Based upon their recent experiences, I thought they must know the process inside-out. Not so. We got along famously. They previously had little training; the staff with

disaster experience was often promoted into other jobs with the agency, retired, or left government. Those attending the class were very appreciative of the training, and since then I have presented the training on at least six other occasions in that general area for multiple other agencies.

This chapter is a litany of the most common failings of local agencies in their dealings with FEMA and the Public Assistance program. There is a universe of things to botch during the Public Assistance process, but in avoiding these most common errors, any agency will be so much better prepared and recover a great deal more Federal funding than would be otherwise possible.

Perhaps one of the most pervasive of all the "self-inflicted wounds" a local agency may suffer is failing to have a staff member with any knowledge or recent experience with FEMA's Public Assistance program.

While FEMA's Public Assistance process continues to change and always will, there are certain fundamentals which have changed little or not at all in the past 45 years, including proper record-keeping, the basic tenets of eligibility, making a thorough damage inventory, etc.

Notes

1 Kelly, W. 1972. *Pogo: We Have Met the Enemy and He Is Us*. Simon and Schuster, New York.
2 https://ksltv.com/577852/combined-residential-reconstruction-value-after-maui-fires-estimated-at-1–3-billion/#:~:text=According%20to%20a%20damage%20assessment,damage%20by%20the%20Lahaina%20Fire.
3 https://www.fema.gov/appeal/application-procedures-2
4 Ibid.
5 https://www.fema.gov/appeal/debris-disposal-and-monitoring-force-account-labor-equipment-costs-duplication-benefits-work
6 Ibid.
7 Ibid.
8 https://training.fema.gov/is/searchis.aspx?search=public%20assistance&all=true
9 https://www.fema.gov/appeal/legal-responsibility-6
10 https://www.fema.gov/appeal/debris-disposal-and-monitoring-0
11 https://www.fema.gov/appeal/time-extension-2
12 Ibid.
13 Ibid.
14 Ibid.
15 Ibid.
16 Ibid.
17 Ibid.
18 Ibid.
19 Ibid.
20 https://www.fema.gov/appeal/net-small-project-overrun-22
21 https://www.fema.gov/appeal/debris-removal-61
22 https://www.fema.gov/appeal/insurance-14
23 https://www.fema.gov/appeal/result-declared-incident-11
24 https://www.fema.gov/appeal/scope-work-environmental-compliance-705c
25 Ibid.
26 https://www.fema.gov/appeal/direct-result-disaster-11
27 Search for the Appeals Database using quotation marks as shown to quickly find the Appeals Database.

37 Private Non-Profit Agencies

At this point, the reader may have formed the opinion that the Public Assistance process is complex and challenging. That may be the case; however, for Private Non-Profit organizations the Public Assistance program is even more complex and challenging than for local government agencies, tribal nations, and the U.S. Territories.

For perspective, I researched the FEMA Appeals Database for cases originating from private non-profit organizations of all types. Depending upon the search term used, there may be as many as 450 appeals cases, or approximately 19% of all appeals filed and published. Therefore, this is an important chapter for all those in the private non-profit world. The eligibility of private non-profit organizations is a highly technical matter and may often hinge on minute facts. The first part of this chapter will rely a great deal on information from the Public Assistance Program and Policy Guide (2020 edition) and the Disaster Operations Legal Reference (2020 edition).

Let us first discuss ineligible Private Non-Profit organizations. Not all private non-profit organizations are eligible for Federal disaster assistance from FEMA. Community centers as a class of private non-profits are generally not eligible as delineated here:

"Ineligible Community Center Services *(As opposed to eligible community center services beginning on page 6.)*

* Training individuals to pursue the same activities as full-time paying careers (for example, vocational, academic, or professional training)
* Meetings or activities for only a brief period, or at irregular intervals
* Other education or training including:
  * Athletic, vocational, academic training, or similar activities
  * Political education

Other Community Services

* Advocacy or lobbying groups not directly providing health services
* Cemeteries
* Conferences
* Day care services not included in following table of eligible services
* Flood control (e.g., levees, berms, dunes)
* Land reclamation facilities
* Irrigation solely for agricultural purposes
* Job counseling

DOI: 10.4324/9781003487869-42

- Property owner associations with facilities such as roads, bridges, and recreational facilities (except utilities or emergency facilities)
- Public housing, other than low-income housing
- Recreation
- Parking not in direct support of eligible facility"[1]

"PNP recreational facilities are not eligible for permanent repair/replacement work."[2] However, under very limited circumstances they may be eligible for emergency work, such as debris clearance.

If the private non-profit organization is one of those listed here, there's little chance that it will be eligible for FEMA funding.

It is important to understand that for those other potentially eligible private non-profit organizations, there remains a steep road ahead to climb in the effort to obtain FEMA funding. "FEMA must determine whether the PNP (*Private non-profit*) owns or operates a facility that provides an eligible service in order to determine whether the Applicant is eligible."[3]

"An eligible PNP facility is one that provides educational, utility, emergency, medical, or custodial care, including for senior citizens or individuals with disabilities, and other essential social-type services to the general public."[4]

"If a PNP operates multiple facilities, or a single facility composed of more than one building, FEMA must evaluate each building independently, even if all are located on the same grounds. Buildings that are part of a complex that includes outdoor facilities (e.g., swimming pools, athletic fields, or tennis courts) are not evaluated separately from the rest of the complex when determining eligibility of the building. For example, an outdoor pool usually has a building for bathrooms and controlling entry. In such cases, FEMA does not evaluate the building for eligibility separately because it is an intrinsic part of the pool complex."[5]

"Therefore, FEMA requires additional documentation and information with PNP (private non-profit) RPAs (Requests For Public Assistance) to evaluate eligibility. PNP Applicants must also submit its facility-specific information in Grants Portal with all applicable documentation."[6]

Private Non-Profit Critical versus Non-Critical Facilities

"PNP Applicants should also separate critical service facilities into separate projects from non-critical service facilities so that projects with critical service facilities are not delayed pending the Small Business Administration (SBA) determination."[7] (The SBA loan process is described later in this chapter.)

Only Certain Private Non-Profits Are Eligible Applicants

"To be an eligible PNP Applicant, the PNP must show that it has:

- A ruling letter from the U.S. Internal Revenue Service that was in effect as of the declaration date and granted tax exemption under sections 501(c), (d), or (e) of the Internal Revenue Code; or
- Documentation from the State substantiating it is a non-revenue producing, nonprofit entity organized or doing business under State law."[8]

"If the organization is not required to obtain 501(c)(3) status or tax-exempt status under applicable State law, the organization must provide articles of association, bylaws, or other documents indicating that it is an organized entity, and a certification that it is compliant with Internal Revenue Code section 501(c)(3) and State law requirements."[9]

"Additionally, prior to determining whether the PNP is eligible, FEMA must first determine whether the PNP owns or operates an eligible facility. For PNPs, an eligible facility is one that provides one of the services listed below (the declared incident must have damaged the facility):

- A facility that provides a critical service, which is defined as education, utility, emergency, or medical; or
- A facility that provides a noncritical, but essential social service AND provides those services to the general public. PNP facilities generally meet the requirement of serving the general public if ALL of the following conditions are met.

  - Facility use is not limited to any of the following:

    - A certain number of individuals;
    - A defined group of individuals who have a financial interest in the facility, such as a condominium association;
    - Certain classes of individuals; or
    - An unreasonably restrictive geographical area, such as a neighborhood within a community;

  - Facility access is not limited to a specific population (such as those with gates or other security systems intended to restrict public access); and
  - Any membership fees meet all of the following criteria:

    - Are nominal;
    - Are waived when an individual can show inability to pay the fee;
    - Are not of such magnitude to preclude use by a significant portion of the community; and
    - Do not exceed what is appropriate based on other facilities used for similar services.

  - Certain types of facilities, such as senior centers, that restrict access in a manner clearly related to the nature of the facility, are still considered to provide essential social services to the general public."[10]

"In cases where the facility provides multiple services, such as a community center, FEMA reviews additional items to determine the primary service that facility provides. Facilities established or primarily used for political, athletic, recreational, vocational, or academic training, conferences, or similar activities are ineligible."[11]

Private non-profit organization services are further divided into "eligible critical services" and "eligible non-critical essential social services." Eligible critical services include education, utilities, emergency medical services, and emergency services. For each of these different eligible critical services, there are certain requirements which must be met.

Education

- "Primary or secondary education as determined under State law and provided in a day or residential school, including parochial schools; OR
- Higher-education institutions that meet ALL of the following criteria:

  - Admit students or persons having a high school diploma or equivalent;
  - Are legally authorized to provide education beyond a secondary level;

- Award a bachelor's degree or 2-year degree that is acceptable as full credit toward a bachelor's degree or provides at least a 1-year training program to prepare students for gainful employment in a recognized occupation; and
  - Are accredited by a nationally recognized agency or association (as determined by the Secretary of Education).
- Educational facilities that meet the above criteria are eligible without regard to religious character or use for religious instruction."[12]

Utility

- "Communications transmission and switching, and distribution of telecommunications traffic
- Electric power generation, transmission, and distribution.
- Irrigation to provide water for drinking water supply, fire suppression, or electricity generation
- Sewer and wastewater collection, transmission, and treatment
- Water treatment, transmission, and distribution by a water company supplying municipal water."[13]

Emergency Medical

- "Emergency medical care (diagnosis or treatment of mental or physical injury or disease) provided in:
- Clinics
- Dialysis facilities
- Facilities that provide in-patient care for convalescent or chronic disease patients
- Hospices and nursing homes
- Hospitals and related facilities, including:

  - Central service facilities operated in connection with hospitals
  - Extended-care facilities
  - Facilities related to programs for home-health services
  - Laboratories
  - Self-care units
  - Storage, administration, and record areas

- Long-term care facilities
- Outpatient facilities
- Rehabilitation centers."[14]

Emergency Services

- "Ambulance
- Fire protection
- Rescue
- Public broadcasting that monitor, receive, and distribute communication from the Emergency Alert System to the public.

Administrative and support facilities essential to the provision of the PNP critical service are eligible facilities."[15]

These eligible facilities are separate and distinct from the following eligible non-critical essential social services.

PNP Eligible Non-critical, Essential Social Services

"Community centers established and primarily used for the following services (or similar) to the general public:

- Art services authorized by a SLTT government, including, but not limited to:
- Arts administration
- Art classes
- Management of public arts festivals
- Performing arts classes
- Community center activities that serve the public
- Educational enrichment activities that are not vocational, academic, or professional training. Examples include hobby or at-home pursuits, such as:

  - Car care
  - Ceramics
  - Gardening
  - Personal financial and tax planning
  - Sewing
  - Stamp and coin collecting

- Multi-purpose arts programming
- Senior citizen projects, rehabilitation programs, community clean-up projects, blood drives, local government meetings, and similar activities
- Services and activities intended to serve a specific group of individuals (e.g., women, African Americans, or teenagers) provided the facility is otherwise available to the public on a non-discriminatory basis
- Social activities to pursue items of mutual interest or concern, such as:

  - Community board meetings
  - Neighborhood barbecues
  - Various social functions of community groups
  - Youth and senior citizen group meetings

- Performing arts centers with a primary purpose of producing, facilitating, or presenting live performances, including:

  - Construction of production materials
  - Creation of artistic works or productions
  - Design
  - Professional training
  - Public education
  - Rehearsals"[16]

"Facilities that do not provide medical care, but provide:

- Alcohol and drug treatment and other rehabilitation services
- Assisted living

- Custodial care, even if the service is not provided to the general public (including essential administration and support facilities)
- Childcare
- Center-based childcare, even if not provided to the public
- Day care for individuals with disabilities or access and functional needs (for example, those with Alzheimer's disease, autism, muscular dystrophy)
- Food assistance programs, including Food Banks and storage of food for Food Banks
- Health and safety services, including animal control services
- Homeless shelters
- Houses of worship
- Libraries
- Low-income housing (as defined by Federal or SLTT law or regulation)
- Museums:
- Constructed, manufactured, or converted with a primary purpose of preserving and exhibiting a documented collection of artistic, historic, scientific, or other objects
- Buildings, associated facilities, fixed facilities, and equipment primarily used for the preservation or exhibition of the collection, including:

  - Permanent infrastructure, such as walkways and driveways of outdoor museum-type exhibition areas
  - Historic buildings, such as barns and other outbuildings, intended for the preservation and exhibition of historical artifacts within a defined area
  - Permanent facilities and equipment that are part of arboretums and botanical gardens
  - Infrastructure, such as utilities, and administrative facilities necessary for support

- The grounds at museums and historic sites are ineligible.
- Open natural areas/features or entities that promote the preservation/conservation of such areas are ineligible.

  - Residential and other services for families of domestic abuse
  - Residential services for individuals with disabilities
  - Senior citizen centers
  - Shelter workshops that create products using the skills of individuals with disabilities
  - Zoos"[17]

In this quotation taken from the Public Assistance Program and Policy Guide, it is not immediately clear what the differences may be between "childcare" and "center-based childcare." The Disaster Operations Legal Reference (DOLR) is likewise silent on the matter, although the DOLR does mention childcare within the context of Individual Assistance (IA) and ONA (Other Needs Assistance), both of which are outside the scope of this book.

"With exception of custodial care facilities and museums, administrative and support facilities essential to the provision of PNP noncritical service are ineligible facilities."[18]

PNP Facility Eligibility

"Facilities owned or operated by homeowners' associations can present challenges. Such associations are generally formed as non-profit corporations to provide services, including managing, maintaining, and governing the use of property within a housing subdivision. Membership is restricted to property owners, and access to facilities may be restricted to members and their guests. Eligibility of facilities owned or operated by a homeowners' association depends on the type of facility and whether it is required to be open to the general public."[19]

Private non-profit homeowner's associations (HOAs) and their first cousins, Community Development Districts, are generally ineligible applicants. This case is from Florida, where Community Development Districts are quite common and often Public Assistance program appellants. "Between September 4 and October 18, 2017, wind, rain, and storm surge from Hurricane Irma caused damage throughout Florida, including where Sumter Landing Community Development District (Applicant) is located. The Applicant is a special community development district (CDD). The Applicant owns and maintains golf courses, pools, and recreation centers (Facilities); which are open to residents and their registered guests. FEMA prepared two Grants Manager Projects (GMPs) (26222 for $68,736.83) and (26244 for $27,004.16) in the amount of $95,740.99 for damage sustained to the Facilities, as well as for debris removal from the roads and rights of way in the district. On December 11, 2018, FEMA issued a Determination Memorandum denying the Applicant's request for funding, in part, because the Facilities were not open to the public and therefore did not meet the eligibility criteria for a CDD."[20]

In February of 2019, the Applicant appealed FEMA's eligibility determination.

"On June 14, 2019, FEMA issued a request for information (RFI), requesting documentation demonstrating that: (1) the Applicant has legal responsibility for operation and maintenance for the roads within that district; and (2) the Facilities serve the general public without exclusion to membership, and facility access is not prohibited by gates or other security features. The Applicant timely responded to FEMA's RFI stating that: (1) it does not own, operate or maintain any roads in the district; and (2) it disagreed with the assertion that its Facilities must be open to the general public to be eligible for reimbursement. On September 25, 2019, the Region IV Regional Administrator (RA) denied the appeal. FEMA found that: (1) the Applicant is not legally responsible for costs associated with debris removal because it does not own the roads in the district; and, (2) its facilities are not open to and do not serve the general public."

"On November 25, 2019, the Applicant filed a second appeal, claiming that: (1) the costs claimed for debris removal are eligible costs for the individual numbered districts that own the roads and rights of ways and FEMA should apportion these costs; (2) its water resource management system (Maxicom) and the adjoining road each provide a critical service to the general public by ensuring that flooding from the impoundments does not impair adjacent public road and thus endanger life and public health; and, therefore any related costs are eligible. . ."[21]

"FEMA issued an RFI on June 10, 2020, requesting additional documentation to substantiate that the work associated with Maxicom repairs constitutes eligible emergency protective measures. Specifically, FEMA asked the Applicant to: (1) describe what Maxicom is; (2) explain what services or systems Maxicom provides and who or what properties does Maxicom provide services/systems to; (3) provide timesheets and specific details of all work listed on the contractor's invoices; and (4) explain how the contracted work meets criteria for emergency protective measures."[22]

"In response, the Applicant stated that Maxicom system provides a critical service to the general public by ensuring that flooding from the Sumter Landing Community Development District (SLCDD) storm water impoundments does not impair adjacent public roads and thus endanger life, safety, public health, and/or improved property. It submitted a brochure on the Maxicom system and stated that Maxicom is a central control system for the irrigation conducted at the Applicant's Facilities. The Applicant asserted that its system controls levels in its storm water basins by monitoring their levels and adjusting irrigation amounts accordingly."[23]

What is interesting is that an internet search for a Maxicom water management system returns information on what appears to be a sophisticated sprinkler system, according to the website.

Provided that the private non-profit passes through the preceding gauntlet, the process is just getting started. Now the PNP must prove that it is legally responsible for making repairs to the disaster-damaged facility.

PNP Facility Legal Responsibility

"An eligible PNP applicant must be legally responsible for disaster-related repairs whether it owns a facility or leases it. An eligible PNP applicant that leases an asset of an ineligible applicant and uses it for eligible services may be eligible for PA funding. The lease must pre-date the disaster and must clearly specify that the eligible applicant is responsible for losses and major damage to the facility, not just maintenance or minor repairs. Lease agreements are often poorly drafted and not always clear as to whether the lessor or lessee is legally responsible for losses and major damage to the facility.

Legal review in such circumstances will be necessary. In some instances, the answer as to who has legal responsibility may turn on which party in the lease is required to carry insurance, such as an all-perils or commercial property policy to protect the facility."[24] (Emphasis Added)

Proving Legal Ownership and Responsibility

Many private non-profit organizations are often small and informally run organizations. These organizations rely on public contributions, the occasional grant, and sometimes service fee income from local government agencies that pay the non-profits for providing community services, such as substance abuse prevention programs and shelters for battered spouses. Hence, these organizations seldom have excess financial resources to pour into administrative procedures they may see as unnecessary. However, when the time comes to apply for FEMA disaster assistance, they may be woefully unprepared for the onslaught of documentation which FEMA typically requires.

Sometimes the non-profit may undergo minute, but very important, changes in their administrative structures over time. The following case illustrates one facet of this issue: "Severe storms, straight-line winds, and tornadoes impacted various areas of Tennessee during the incident period of December 10–11, 2021. The Dresden Cumberland Presbyterian Church (Applicant) submitted a Request for Public Assistance (RPA) as a Private Nonprofit (PNP), seeking Public Assistance (PA) funding for repair of its church (Facility), which was damaged during the disaster. FEMA found conflicting information regarding the address of the Facility, along with information that indicated the Facility was owned by the Cumberland Presbyterian Church (CPC), rather than the Applicant."[25]

"FEMA sent the Applicant a Request for Information (RFI) asking for: (1) the name, location, and primary purpose of the Facility; (2) a copy of articles of incorporation or bylaws; and (3) proof of ownership/operation of the Facility. The Applicant responded to FEMA's RFI and clarified the address of the Facility and provided its articles of incorporation and bylaws. However, FEMA found that neither of the addresses listed in these documents matched the address of the Facility as provided by the Applicant in its RFI response."[26] (Emphasis Added)

"On August 3, 2022, FEMA issued a Determination Memorandum denying the Applicant's RPA. FEMA acknowledged that worship services were conducted at the Facility and determined the Applicant demonstrated it is a PNP based on its tax-exempt status, but stated that the Applicant had not demonstrated that it owned or operated the Facility and provided no documentation (i.e., lease, deed, etc.) to indicate that it was legally responsible to repair the Facility. In addition, the Applicant had not applied for a Small Business Administration (SBA) loan."[27]

First Appeal

"In a letter dated September 27, 2022, the Applicant appealed FEMA's denial of its RPA and provided documentation that included: (1) A copy of its SBA loan approval letter; (2) a Certificate of Survey that recorded the Applicant as the owner of the Facility; and, (3) a letter from CPC, which stated that the Applicant had operated the Facility since its inception in 1889 and was responsible for all expenses and repairs. The Tennessee Emergency Management Agency (Recipient) supported the appeal in its October 4, 2022 transmittal to FEMA."[28]

"On March 28, 2023, the Applicant submitted its second appeal, providing additional documentation, including: (1) a letter from CPC stating that the Applicant is a connectional church, and as such, is legally responsible for all expenses related to the repair and upkeep of the Facility; (2) a letter from an insurance carrier stating the Applicant has had property coverage for the Facility since 2012; (3) the property insurance declarations page for the Facility, in the Applicant's name, with a policy period of May 20, 2021, to May 20, 2024; and, (4) the Applicant's 2021 financial statement showing income from offerings, and operational expenditures, such as pulpit supplies, personnel costs for a church pianist, church utilities, church repairs and maintenance, and church insurance premiums. The Applicant states that it has been operating as a PNP religious institution under the connectional legal authority of CPC since 1889, and claims that the letter from CPC authenticates the legal operation of the church, as well as the Applicant's responsibility for repair of the Facility."[29]

In the second appeal decision, FEMA writes: "Here, the Applicant is a PNP, and the Facility is an eligible PNP facility that provides eligible noncritical, but essential social services. The Applicant's documentation submitted on second appeal demonstrates ownership of and legal responsibility for the Facility. The Certificate of Survey outlines the property boundaries of the lot where the Facility is located, as shown on the tax map in the County Property Accessor's Office. The survey includes the specific deed book and page number located in the County Register's Office and states the lot is the property of the Applicant. CPC confirms that the Applicant has been operating the Facility since its inception in 1889 and is legally responsible for all expenses and repairs. The Applicant's 2021 financial statement shows income and expenditures associated with operating the Facility, including repairs and maintenance. The Applicant carries property insurance for the Facility, which was in effect at the time of the disaster. <u>The statements from CPC, supported by the insurance documents, deed, and financial statement, demonstrate that the Applicant owns and operates the eligible PNP Facility. Accordingly, the Applicant is legally responsible for the repairs.</u>"

Certainly in this case, a lengthy (but successful) appeals process could have been entirely avoided had the non-profit initially provided the correct information and, where there may have been some confusion in the documentation provided, attached a letter of explanation to clarify any apparent discrepancies.

More Pre-Disaster Administrative Burden to Prove Eligibility

This is a Covid-19 case out of Kentucky. Although we have little discussed Covid-related issues, the facts in this case make it applicable to a wide range of disasters. "The coronavirus (COVID-19) pandemic caused a major disaster to be declared for the state of Kentucky on March 28, 2020, with an incident period of January 20, 2020, to May 11, 2023. The Divine Providence Inc. (Applicant) is a Private Nonprofit (PNP) organization that operates a 134-bed facility that provides congregate shelter, meals, and basic living services in the community. The Applicant requested Public Assistance (PA) funding totaling $129,750.24 for costs associated with operating its facility in a COVID-19 environment and providing non-congregate sheltering (NCS) services. The Applicant's request included materials costs (including thermometers, cleaning supplies, paper products, food distribution supplies, hand soap, a refrigerator for medication, and electrical supplies), and $121,370.02 in contract costs (for meal delivery, facility sanitization, security, trash collection, utilities, and building repairs). The Applicant explained that the number of individuals with severe medical conditions (high-risk individuals) seeking shelter increased as a result of COVID-19, and that in order to facilitate Centers for Disease Control social distancing recommendations, it placed individuals in NCS at Cliffview Center, a retreat/conference center the Applicant began leasing in November 2019.[1] The Applicant received approval from state building and fire officials to make necessary alterations (e.g., measures to comply with fire safety and the Americans with Disabilities Act requirements), required to operate the Cliffview Center as an NCS. The Applicant completed the work from February 25 to August 2, 2020."[30]

"FEMA prepared Grants Manager Project 158914 to document the claimed costs. FEMA then issued a Request for Information seeking documentation to demonstrate the Applicant was legally responsible for NCS. The Applicant responded providing a letter from its county health department in support of the Applicant's sheltering operations and referenced a state guide listing the Applicant as a shelter. FEMA issued a Determination Memorandum (DM) on January 6, 2023, denying the requested costs, finding that the Applicant acted independently of a legally responsible government entity, and the Applicant did not possess the legal responsibility to provide NCS as an emergency protective measure. Accordingly, FEMA denied $129,750.24 in requested PA funding."[31]

"To be eligible for PA funding, an item of work must be the legal responsibility of an eligible applicant. Measures to protect life, public health, and safety are generally the responsibility of the state, local, tribal and territorial (SLTT) governments. Therefore, PNPs are generally not legally responsible for those services and FEMA does not provide PA funding to PNPs for the costs associated with providing those services. When a PNP provides emergency services at the request of, and certified by, the legally responsible government entity, FEMA provides PA funding through that government entity as the eligible applicant. In limited circumstances, FEMA may reimburse costs related to NCS. Under the COVID-19 declarations, FEMA will consider requests for reimbursement of NCS for health and medical-related needs, such as isolation and quarantine resulting from the public health emergency. The NCS must be at the direction of and documented through an official order signed by an SLTT public health official and approved by the appropriate FEMA Regional Administrator. For PNPs, operating costs are generally not eligible even if the services are emergency services, unless the PNP performs an emergency service at the request of and certified by the legally responsible government entity."[32]

"The Applicant is a PNP that, as part of its ongoing mission, provides shelter to individuals in need. Here, the Applicant states that it saw an increase in the number of homeless residents coming to its shelter as a result of the pandemic and that, based on warnings that congregate sheltering was dangerous for high-risk individuals, it provided NCS at the Cliffview Center. It provides a letter from the Lexington-Fayette County Commissioner of Health supporting its application for PA. However, the Applicant did demonstrate that it provided NCS at the request of and certified by the government entity legally responsible for measures to protect life, public health, and safety, nor did it establish that NCS was done at the direction of and documented through an official order signed by an SLTT public health official. Even if the Applicant had provided NCS at the request of and certified by the legally responsible government entity and NCS was done at direction of an SLTT public health official, the Applicant, as a PNP, is not eligible for direct reimbursement of the claimed NCS costs. Therefore, based on the above, costs associated with NCS (e.g., repairs to retrofit the facility for NCS requirements), are not eligible for PA funding."

The object lesson to be learned here is that the Private Non-profit could have, should have worked through a local government agency that did have the legal responsibility for providing these various services. The fact that the Lexington-Fayette Health Officer wrote a letter in support of the application indicates the county government was unaware of these issues.

PNP Facility Alternate Use

"If, at the time of the disaster, an applicant is using a facility for purposes other than the use for which it was originally designed, FEMA limits the eligible cost of work to restore the facility to the lesser of (1) the cost of restoring the facility to its original design and capacity, or (2) the cost of restoring the facility to the immediate pre-disaster alternate use. Another consideration is whether the facility is eligible based on pre-disaster use. PA funding is for the purpose of repairing, restoring, and replacing facilities that serve a public purpose. In the case of a PNP, the primary purpose of the facility is relevant to an eligibility determination. For example, a recreation center might be used as a homeless shelter, while its primary purpose remained a recreation center. It would be ineligible based on the primary or majority use. Facilities with mixed activities (eligible and non-eligible) may be eligible if the facility has over 50 percent of its space dedicated to eligible uses."[33]

Community Center or Church? Church or Community Center?

PNPs should be forewarned that FEMA will look deeply into the origins of a facility. In more than one case, FEMA has looked closely at the articles of incorporation and other key documents to determine eligibility. Facilities originally established for one purpose and then converted (even on an informal basis) to a substantively different use may find that any chance for eligibility has vanished based upon the original founding principles.

PNP Mixed-Use Facilities

"PNP organizations offer so many types of services that eligibility issues can be multi-tiered and complex. Funding will depend on whether the facility is an eligible type and whether the PNP has legal responsibility for the facility's repair. PNPs may share facilities with for-profit or other entities that are not eligible for PA, and a facility may be partially used for eligible services and partially used for ineligible services. Overall facility eligibility is based on the primary use of that facility. A facility must have over 50 percent of its space dedicated to eligible uses for the facility to be eligible as a whole. Common spaces are not included in the calculation. When a space is used for purposes both eligible and ineligible for PA funding, the primary use of that space is determined by looking at the time used for each activity. FEMA considers damage to the entire facility, however, and assistance is provided in proportion to the space dedicated to eligible services."[34]

Mixed-use facilities often involve complexities and require substantial knowledge and experience to get the application for a Project Worksheet approved. For further detailed information, refer to the current editions of both the Public Assistance Program and Policy Guide and the Disaster Operations Legal Reference.

Houses of Worship (HOWs)

"HOWs are treated like any eligible, non-critical PNP facility and may be eligible applicants for financial assistance (1) if their facilities suffered damage from an emergency or a major disaster declared on or after August 23, 2017, or (2) if they had applications pending with FEMA for damage suffered in an emergency or major disaster declared prior to August 23, 2017, that as of January 1, 2018, had not been resolved. HOWs are also eligible for assistance without regard to their secular or religious nature.

The Bipartisan Budget Act also included a provision that prohibits for all eligible PNP facilities, including educational facilities, the exclusion of buildings and items used primarily for religious purposes or instruction, and makes clear that such facilities are eligible regardless of their religious character or use for religious instruction."[35]

Small Business Administration Loan Requirements

For some private non-profit organizations, this requirement can be a killer requirement.

"Following a Major Disaster Declaration, the U.S. Small Business Administration (SBA) can provide loans to individuals and businesses for facility restoration. For PNPs with facilities that provide noncritical, essential social services, FEMA only provides PA funding for eligible Permanent Work costs that an SBA loan will not cover for those facilities. Therefore, noncritical PNPs must also apply for a disaster loan from the SBA and receive a determination for Permanent Work on facilities that:

- Provide noncritical services; or
- Are mixed-use facilities and the eligible portion of the facility is used to provide services that are entirely noncritical.

If the PNP misses the SBA application deadline, including any SBA approved extension, the Permanent Work is ineligible for FEMA PA funding. If the PNP declines an SBA loan, PA funding is limited to the costs that the loan would not have otherwise covered. This applies even when the PNP cannot accept the terms of the loan, and SBA therefore denies the loan, which may occur when the entity does not meet a collateral requirement.

PNPs do not need to apply for a disaster loan from the SBA for facilities that:

- Provide critical services; or
- Are mixed-use and the eligible portion is either entirely or partially used to provide critical services."[36] (Emphasis Added)

This case from Alabama demonstrates what happens when the private non-profit, in this case a church, fails to apply or perfect an SBA loan. "From September 14–16, 2020, Hurricane Sally impacted southern Alabama, with severe winds, rain and flooding. St. Bartholomew Parish, Elberta (Applicant), a Private Nonprofit (PNP) House of Worship, requested Public Assistance (PA) funding for the permanent repair of claimed damage to its church, hall, and kitchen/BBQ building.

FEMA advised the Applicant that it was first required to apply for a loan from the Small Business Administration (SBA) prior to seeking PA funding. The SBA denied the Applicant's loan application on March 21, 2021, because the Applicant, due to its own rules, could not offer the requested collateral. In a Determination Memorandum issued June 21, 2021, FEMA denied all costs. FEMA stated that the Applicant did not properly apply for the SBA loan as required and that the Applicant had not provided documentation validating its claims of damage or demonstrating that claimed damage was a result of the declared disaster."[37] (Emphasis Added)

However, there is also a dark side to the matter of obtaining an SBA loan. In a second look at a previous case, but a different aspect of that same case is evidenced by this appeal from Mississippi following Hurricane Katrina. "High winds and heavy rainfall from Hurricane Katrina in

August 2005 caused extensive damage on the St. Thomas the Apostle Catholic Church campus. FEMA determined that the Family Life Center was an eligible private nonprofit (PNP) community center. The Small Business Administration (SBA) estimated $2,355,160 in damages at the Family Life Center comprising 41 percent of the total of $5,536,033 estimated by the SBA for damages to the five campus buildings and their contents. SBA approved $1,500,000, the legislative limit, to reconstruct disaster-damaged facilities. FEMA prepared PW 10679 for $2,890,016 for FEMA's estimated replacement cost of the eligible facility. <u>FEMA determined that the approved SBA loan covered eligible and ineligible damages. Based on the ratio of eligible SBA estimated damages to ineligible SBA estimated damages, FEMA reduced eligible assistance by $614,653.</u>"[38] (Emphasis Added)

The case continues: "In a letter dated April 10, 2008, the Applicant submitted its second appeal. The Applicant reiterates its position that it was not the intent and purpose of the SBA requirement to hinder the recovery of ineligible facilities by depriving them of the full use of the SBA funds for which they qualified. The Applicant re-asserts that if it were to apply to the SBA for additional funds to be used toward the Parish Life Center it would receive $0 and would result in $0 offset to the Parish Life Center. Finally, the Applicant requests that if FEMA decides to apportion SBA loan proceeds that it includes building contents that were not included in the SBA estimate. The Applicant provided an inventory of destroyed building contents in the amount of $841,400."[39]

"I have determined that FEMA properly apportioned the SBA loan proceeds for the facility and its contents. When an SBA disaster loan covers damages for both eligible and ineligible facilities <u>without specifying the apportionment of the loan proceeds</u> against respective damaged facilities, FEMA deducts the proportionate amount of loan proceeds from available permanent work assistance based on a ratio of eligible damages to ineligible damages, consistent with FEMA's practice apportioning insurance proceeds."[40] (Emphasis Added)

The apparent message here is that the private non-profit should if at all possible request that the loan be made for specific purposes which arguably might reduce any FEMA deobligation of benefits.

Private Non-Profit Request for Public Assistance Documentation and Information Requirements

So far, we see that private non-profits must carry a heavier burden of documentation to establish eligibility for 1) the agency itself, and 2) the specific facility which was disaster-damaged. The following are additional documentation requirements which will vary depending on the type of private non-profit agency or institution making the request for Public Assistance and specific Project Worksheets.

"All PNP Applicants

- A ruling letter from the Internal Revenue Service that was in effect on the declaration date and granted tax exemption under sections 501(c), (d), or (e) of the Internal Revenue Code; OR documentation from the State substantiating it is a non-revenue producing, nonprofit entity organized or doing business under State law. If exempt from both the requirement to apply for 501(c)(3) status and tax-exempt status under State law, the organization must provide articles of association, bylaws, or other documents indicating that it is an organized entity and a certification that it is compliant with Internal Revenue Code section 501(c)(3) and State law requirements. **(Required)**
- If the Applicant owns the damaged facility, proof of ownership **(Required)**

- If the Applicant leases the damaged facility, provide lease or other proof of legal responsibility to repair the incident-related damage **(Required)**
- List of services provided in the damaged facility, when, and to whom **(Required)**

Membership Organization

- Who is allowed membership **(Required)**
- What fees are charged **(Required)**
- Policy regarding waiving memberships **(Required)**

Childcare Facility

- Proof that the State Department of Children and Family Services, Department of Human Services, or similar agency, recognizes it as a licensed childcare facility **(Required)**

Education

- Proof that the school is accredited or recognized by the State Department of Education **(Required)**. State regulations for private schools vary and some states do not require accreditation. A PNP school must demonstrate that it is recognized by the state as providing elementary or secondary education. Depending on state requirements, documentation may include, but is not limited to, the following (must have been in existence at the time of the incident):
  - Accreditation documents
  - Certification from the State Department of Education that the Applicant operated the facility as a PNP school at the time of the incident
  - Documentation demonstrating compliance with the State's compulsory attendance laws
  - School-year calendar
  - School budget
  - Complete list of students and teachers
  - Educational instruction property and equipment owned by the PNP
  - Tax records for the school
  - Documents reflecting school curriculum, transcripts, health and safety, disciplinary, or other records kept for students
  - Tuition receipts
  - Financial statements
  - Commencement documents
  - Inclusion in the U.S. Department of Education's National Center for Education Statistics Private School Universe Survey data
  - State Department of Education electronic and paper homeschool declaration or registration forms

Mixed-Use Facility

- Proof of the established purpose of the facility with documentation **(Required)**, such as:
  - U.S. Internal Revenue Service documentation;
  - Pre-incident charter, bylaws, and amendments; or
  - Evidence of longstanding, routine (day-to-day) use (e.g., a calendar of activities)."[41] (Emphasis Added)

For all private non-profit organizations this will be more time-consuming, particularly for educational private non-profits. And of course, these requirements are layered upon all the other documentation requirements for local government agencies and tribal nations.

Federal Procurement Rules Apply, Too!

As discussed in Chapter 9, Procurement, Title 2 of the Code of Federal Regulations, Part 200 applies equally to private non-profit organizations. In this case from Massachusetts, a major religious organization lost money on a series of 17 deobligations, in part due to defective procurement practices. These cases are moderately complicated, so we shall focus on the procurement aspects. "On June 1, 2011, severe storms and tornadoes caused damage to the Roman Catholic Bishop of Springfield's (Applicant) Cathedral High School and St. Michael's Academy (Facilities). FEMA prepared Project Worksheets (PWs) 251, 252, 253, 254, 255, 256, 257, 258, 264, 268, 271, 272, 276, and 277 to document emergency and permanent work for the Applicant's Facilities. Those PWs also included direct administrative costs (DAC) for contractor labor and travel expenses associated with grant administration services the Applicant received from Witt O'Brien's LLC (Witt), which the Applicant procured by executing a purchase order through the Houston-Galveston Area Council of Governments' (HGAC) cooperative purchasing program."[42]

"On June 16, 2014, FEMA notified the Applicant that it had not provided all documentation necessary to demonstrate its procurement of Witt's services complied with Federal procurement standards, and requested additional information regarding the Applicant's procurement process used to obtain those services through HGAC's cooperative purchasing program. FEMA specifically requested HGAC's: (1) solicitation for the Planning and Consulting Services contract awarded to Witt; (2) method used to advertise the solicitation; (3) evaluation of Witt's solicitation response; and (4) assessment of Witt's ability to perform successfully under the contract's terms and conditions. FEMA also requested documentation showing the Applicant: (1) prepared a rationale, cost analysis, and scope of work prior to executing the purchase order for Witt's services; (2) competed the Witt contract or could provide an explanation of why such competition was impractical; (3) made positive efforts to utilize small businesses, minority owned firms, and women's business enterprises as required under Title 2 of the Code of Federal Regulations (C.F.R.) § 215.44(b); and (4) executed a purchase order for Witt's services with all contract provisions required under 2 C.F.R. § 215.48 and 2 C.F.R Part 215, Appendix A."[43] (These are the pre-2014 code citations regarding procurement.)

"The Applicant responded on July 15, 2014, to provide additional information regarding the process used to procure Witt's services. The Applicant stated that it established a scope of work, researched firms, reviewed the list of vendors on HGAC's website, interviewed prospective vendors, and checked references prior to executing the purchase order for Witt's services. Based on that process, the Applicant concluded Witt was the only vendor that could offer: (1) competitive pricing, (2) solid recommendations from former clients and other Roman Catholic Dioceses, (3) a reputation as a national leader in providing the services required, and (4) the staff needed to complete the required scope of work."[44]

"The Applicant also contended that HGAC's sealed bidding process met all procurement requirements, and asserted that the Department of Homeland Security (DHS) Office of Inspector General (OIG) has previously confirmed HGAC's compliance with Federal procurement standards in OIG Audit Report DD-11–05 for FEMA-1791-DR-TX, Chambers County. Accordingly, it argued that it was not required to perform its own cost analysis or make positive efforts to utilize small businesses, minority-owned firms, and women's business enterprises pursuant to 2 C.F.R. § 215.44(b) because HGAC already fulfilled those requirements. The Applicant noted that it performed an additional cost analysis by comparing Witt's pricing with other

HGAC vendors. It also explained that it could have selected a historically underutilized business from HGAC's vendor list, but chose not to after considering 'such matters as contractor integrity, record of past performance, financial and technical resources and accessibility to other necessary resources.'"[45]

"As a condition of receiving PA funding, an applicant must comply with Federal procurement standards when securing contracts for its eligible work. Here, the Applicant did not provide full and open competition to the maximum extent practical as required by 2 C.F.R. § 215.43 because it selected Witt on a sole source basis from HGAC's nationwide list of pre-qualified contractors without a competitive procurement process."[46]

"When an applicant does not comply with Federal procurement standards, FEMA has the authority to fully or partially deobligate funding, and may also award reasonable costs it determines based on information such as: (1) historical documentation for similar work; (2) average costs for similar work in the area; (3) published unit costs from national cost estimating databases; and (4) FEMA cost codes, equipment rates, and engineering and design services curves."[47] (Emphasis Added)

There are four different appeals from this private non-profit in the Appeals Database, and in reviewing them, there is an interesting pattern in 3 of the 4 cases. Following the denial of the first appeals, the organization then raised the claimed amount of disaster damages 310%, 30%, and 187%, respectively, for an average of 175% over the three different appeals. The fourth appeal was denied forthwith, as it was filed after the appeal deadline expired, so it is quite difficult to know how much money in fact was in play: $3,583,103 based upon the first appeal amounts, or $6,800,061 based on the second appeal amounts. All the appeals dealt with the same essential issues of procurement, Direct Administrative Costs (DAC), and a lack of comprehensive documentation in support of the claimed damage. Another factor involved the large campus of 35 acres, in which some of the facilities were eligible and other facilities were not eligible.

Inactive or Partially Inactive Facilities

As is the case for local government facilities, a private non-profit organization's facilities must be fully in use to merit full eligibility under the Public Assistance program. "To be eligible, a facility must have been in active use at the start of the incident period. Inactive facilities are ineligible, unless one of the following conditions is met:

- The facility was only temporarily inactive for repairs or remodeling (provided a contractor is not responsible for repair of disaster-related damage);
- The Applicant firmly established future active use in an approved budget; or
- The Applicant can clearly demonstrate its intent to begin use within a reasonable amount of time.

The above criteria also apply to facilities that are partially inactive at the start of the incident period. Inactive portions are ineligible unless one of the exceptions noted above applies.

When eligible repairs benefit an area that was not in active use, FEMA prorates funding based on the percentage of the facility that was in active use. For example, if the roof of a partially used building is destroyed, FEMA limits the eligible cost to a prorated amount of the total cost to replace the roof based on the percentage of the building that was in active use.

For PNP mixed-use facilities to be eligible, more than 50 percent of the facility had to be in active use for an eligible purpose at the time of the incident.

A Facility Scheduled for Repair or Replacement

Facilities that are not yet under contract but are scheduled for repair or replacement using non-Federal funds are eligible provided that the claimed damage did not exist prior to the incident (FEMA may review procurement and contract documents to validate). If damage existed prior to the incident, only the repair of damage caused by the incident is eligible.

A facility scheduled for replacement within 12 months of the start of the incident period using Federal funds is ineligible. In such a case, the Applicant should coordinate with the agency funding the project to expedite replacement, if possible."[48]

This next case is a revisit of a case from Texas we looked at in Chapter 8 on Photo Documentation. This is a private non-profit organization which is a frequent flyer within the appeals process, having had 11 different appeals cases filed and published since Hurricane Harvey in 2017. "Hurricane Harvey caused high winds, severe storms, and flooding in Texas from August 23 through September 15, 2017. The Ethician Foundation (Applicant), a Private Nonprofit (PNP) entity, sought FEMA assistance to repair damage caused by Harvey to the chimney at its Baird House, also known as the 1844 George Washington Rogers House (Facility).

FEMA inspected the Facility on May 23 and June 6, 2018. The Facility is a two story, roughly 4,000 square foot wood-framed structure with wood floors, wood siding and a metal standing seam roof originally constructed in approximately 1845. The Facility has a 30-foot-tall brick chimney, constructed (or reconstructed) in the 1980s. According to FEMA's Site Inspection Reports (SIRs), the chimney was leaning away from the Facility at an angle of approximately 5 to 7 degrees. This lean began when the slope destabilized in 2005, following Hurricane Rita, and worsened following Hurricanes Ike (2008) and Harvey."[49]

"FEMA found the Facility to be ineligible for Public Assistance (PA) funding in an October 11, 2018 Determination Memorandum (DM). FEMA determined that both of its SIRs showed that the Facility was neither in active use nor undergoing temporary repairs during Hurricane Harvey. FEMA also noted that the Applicant had failed to establish that the Facility had been or would be in use within a reasonable time. Further, FEMA found, and the Applicant acknowledged, that the chimney began leaning away from the Facility before the disaster. FEMA therefore determined that the claimed damage was not the direct result of the disaster."[50]

The case continues: "Relevant here, a museum is a type of non-critical facility 'that preserves and exhibits a documented collection of artistic, historic, scientific, or other objects.' Regardless of whether an eligible facility is publicly owned or owned by a PNP, 'a facility must have been in active use at the start of the incident period.' An inactive facility may only qualify for PA funding if an applicant demonstrates that the facility meets at least one of three possible exceptions. To render an inactive facility eligible, an applicant must: 1) show that the facility was only temporarily inactive for repairs or remodeling (provided a contractor is not responsible for repair of disaster-related damage); 2) firmly establish active future use via an approved operating budget; or 3) clearly demonstrate its intent to begin use of the facility within a reasonable amount of time."[51]

"Here, the Applicant, a PNP entity, asserts that the Facility currently functions as a museum. If it could establish this assertion, the Facility would be a qualifying non-critical, essential social service. Although the Applicant states that the Facility is open to the general public by appointment, the Applicant never provided FEMA with documented evidence regarding the number or frequency of museum tours. The Applicant did not provide FEMA with evidence of an approved budget for the Facility's operation and/or repair, nor did the Applicant establish any scheduled end date for its historical restoration work on the Facility. The photographs in the record from FEMA's site visit show that the Facility posed numerous safety hazards to any visitors, such as foundation leveling problems, missing and broken windows, and missing exterior siding. Therefore, the

Applicant has not shown, with supporting documentation, that the Facility was in active use at the time of the disaster, or that it met one of the exceptions for an inactive facility to receive PA funding."[52]

The following section applies to museums, and to other institutions which may have collections of rare artifacts.

Irreplaceable Collections and Individual Objects

"Collections and individual objects are artifacts, specimens, artworks, archives, public records, and other items that are often considered irreplaceable because of their artistic, educational, historic, legal, scientific, or social significance. They are nonliving and, therefore, do not include animals or plant material, and are usually one-of-a-kind. Eligible collections and individual objects may be in storage or on display in a public or PNP facility and may include items located outdoors, such as sculptures and public art installations."[53]

In this case, one strategy would be to insure the collections and individual objects, rather than the facility in which they are housed. Unless, of course, the facility is 1) located in a mapped flood zone and required to have FEMA flood insurance, or 2) the facility was previously damaged in a disaster, the agency received funding from FEMA for that prior disaster damage, and the O&M (obtain and maintain) requirement is in force.

A second strategy that may be considered regards post-disaster donations. Should the agency be offered a post-disaster "legacy" donation of hundreds of thousands or millions of dollars, the agency should only accept the donation for "the full restoration or replacement of the damaged works of art or rare collections" which are not FEMA-eligible. By specifying the precise limitations of the donation for "otherwise FEMA non-eligible damages" this should, if properly written and implemented, reduce the likelihood of FEMA making a deduction to avoid a duplication of benefits. In the world of the Internal Revenue Service, this would be smart tax planning.

The following Office of the Inspector General audit comes out of Hurricane Katrina. A substantial part of this audit dealt with procurement; however, there was a multi-million-dollar bite taken by FEMA for donations made for rebuilding this high school in New Orleans. Arguably, proper handling of this donation could have greatly reduced or completely eliminated the finding of a duplication of benefits. Had the donations been designated to repair the chapel (not an eligible facility at that time) or to restore the campus landscaping (not FEMA-eligible), the school might have been able to retain the entire $4.6 million AND receive full funding for the FEMA-eligible repair work.

Private Non-Profit Codes and Standards

"FEMA does not recognize codes or standards adopted by a PNP specifically for its facilities when determining whether compliance with codes or standards is eligible."[54]

In this case, the private non-profit must rely on the building codes and standards adopted and enforced by the local government agency within the jurisdiction they fall.

Stafford Act Section 705

Yet another challenge for private non-profit organizations is that they are not covered by Section 705 of the Stafford Act (Robert T. Stafford Disaster Relief and Emergency Assistance Act, PL 100–707, as amended).

"Stafford Act Section 705 imposes a 3-year limit on FEMA's authority to recover payments made to SLTT (*state, local, tribal, and territorial*) government Recipients and Subrecipients unless there is evidence of fraud. Section 705 does not apply to PNPs."[55]

This means that FEMA may come back forever to "clawback" disaster relief funds when it discovers that all the conditions covering a Public Assistance grant were not met.

Disposition of Purchased Equipment

"In accordance with Federal regulations, State and Territorial government Applicants dispose of equipment in accordance with State and Territorial laws and procedures. When equipment purchased with PA funding are no longer needed for response to or recovery from the incident, Tribal and local governments and PNP Applicants may use the items for other federally funded programs or projects. When an individual item of equipment is no long (*sic*) needed for federally funded programs or projects, Tribal and local governments and PNP Applicants must calculate the current fair market value of the individual item of equipment. The Applicant must provide the current fair market for items that have a current fair market value of $5,000 or more. FEMA reduces eligible funding by this amount. If the individual item of equipment has a current fair market value less than $5,000, FEMA does not reduce the eligible funding. Tribal and local governments and PNP Applicants must comply with all disposition requirements described in 2 C.F.R. 200.313(e), Disposition."[56]

Temporary Relocation of Essential Services

"If the Applicant provides essential community services at a facility that is unsafe, inaccessible, or destroyed as a result of the incident, temporarily relocation of these services to another facility is eligible. Essential community services are those services of a governmental nature that are necessary to save lives, protect property and the public, and preserve the proper function and health of the community at large. These services differ from the list of eligible PNP essential social services. FEMA evaluates the criticality of the service and safety of the facility to determine the need for temporary relocation. FEMA does not incorporate funds from temporary facilities into fixed cost projects."[57]

Eligible for Temporary Relocation

"Essential community services provided by an eligible Applicant are eligible to be relocated. The following services are considered essential community services (these differ from the list of PNP essential social services):

- Education;
- Election and polling;
- Emergency, including police, fire, and rescue;
- Homeless and domestic violence shelters;
- Emergency medical care;
- Prison;
- Utility; and
- Other facilities that provide public health and safety services of a governmental nature."[58]

While some of these services, i.e., elections and polling and prisons are seldom, if ever, operated by a private non-profit, the other services are often provided by eligible private non-profits.

"Services provided in administrative and support facilities essential to the provision of the essential community service are also eligible for relocation. These include administration buildings, student housing, hospital and prison laundry and cooking facilities, parking, and storage if items are needed on-site. Athletic fields and student unions are not considered essential administrative or support services and are ineligible. If the Applicant provides the service at a leased, private facility prior to the incident, the service is still eligible to be relocated."[59]

Ineligible for Temporary Relocation

"Facilities that do not provide essential community services are ineligible for temporary relocation. These include facilities and services such as museums, zoos, community centers, shelter workshops, performing arts centers, recreation and parking, athletic stadiums, houses of worship, housing and residential services, custodial care, assisted living, senior citizen centers, alcohol and drug rehabilitation, childcare, libraries, research and warehouse facilities, burial, vocational, academic, athletic, political training, and student union buildings."[60]

While these listed facilities may be important, especially to those who participate in these activities and services, the regulations are specific and do not provide relocation assistance.

For additional and specific information regarding how to determine the eligibility for temporary relocations, and whether to lease, purchase, or construct such temporary facilities, please refer to the Public Assistance Program and Policy Guide, Version 4, June 1, 2020, or current edition.

PNP Medical/Custodial Facility Evacuations

"PNPs that own or operate a medical or custodial care facility are eligible for direct reimbursement of costs related to patient evacuation."[61]

However, the eligible costs are limited to the actual evacuation costs. Once the patients have been relocated, FEMA does not provide any additional funding for their care and feeding as it considers these to be "increased operating costs." There are many useless appeals cases filed by agencies requesting full funding for the entire duration of the relocation, sometimes including the cost of feeding employees. With very rare exceptions, these added costs are simply ineligible. Therefore, the key here is to maintain a strict accounting of the actual evacuation and relocation costs, exclusive of "increased operating costs."

This case on point comes from South Carolina: "From September 8, through October 8, 2018, Hurricane Florence caused damage to Berkeley County, South Carolina. Berkeley Citizens Inc. (Applicant), in response to the Governor's executive order evacuated its residents, who required specialized care, to another facility from September 11 to September 16, 2018. The Applicant requested costs for evacuation as well as force account labor overtime, meals, and supplies for evacuees once they were at the shelter in the amount of $151,959.30. FEMA denied $133,178.68 in Public Assistance (PA) funding finding the costs post-evacuation were increased operating costs. The Applicant appealed the determination stating that FEMA classified it as a Private Nonprofit (PNP) when it should be treated as a special purpose district (quasi-state agency). In addition, the Applicant stated that given the specialized care required for the evacuated patients, the costs claimed were necessary due to the emergency. FEMA Region IV denied the Applicant's first appeal, noting both publicly available documentation and the Applicant's own Request for Public Assistance classifies it as a PNP. Furthermore, FEMA found the costs incurred for operating the temporary facility are ineligible increased operating expenses. The Applicant filed a second appeal reiterating prior arguments."[62]

Conclusion

"The Applicant's costs incurred at a temporary facility are increased operating costs and are not eligible for PA. Therefore, this appeal is denied."[63]

Another related issue, particularly for colleges and universities, is student evacuations. While student safety is very important to any school at any level, the evacuation of students before a disaster is usually not a legal requirement of the school, but rather a legal responsibility of the local government agency.

This case is one of three appeals from this university dealing with student evacuations: "From August 31 to September 6, 2019, Hurricane Dorian caused damage throughout South Carolina. On September 2, 2019, South Carolina's Governor issued an executive order (effective until its September 6, 2019 rescission) closing state government offices, colleges, and universities in all six coastal counties, including Horry County where the Coastal Carolina University (Applicant) is located. That same day, the Applicant's football team, volleyball team, men's and women's track teams, women's and men's golf teams, and women's and men's soccer teams departed from the campus to various hotels."[64]

"At the time of the disaster, the Applicant's emergency procedures required all students residing on-campus to complete Personal Evacuation Plans (PEPs) prior to the start of a semester. Rather than activating PEPs and self-evacuating like the general student population, student-athletes for seven of the Applicant's athletic teams traveled to various hotels together prior to athletic competitions that were pre-scheduled, rescheduled, or cancelled. The Applicant requested $195,403.76 in Public Assistance (PA) for evacuation, sheltering at non-congregated shelters/hotels, transportation, and meals."[65]

"FEMA issued a Determination Memorandum (DM) on July 13, 2020, denying reimbursement for these costs. FEMA concluded that the costs for providing transportation, sheltering, and meals were not the legal responsibility of the Applicant, but rather of the local government, and consequently, those expenses were ineligible for PA funding."[66]

"The Applicant contended that its efforts to comply with FEMA's requirement to obtain prior approval for non-congregate sheltering were unsuccessful due in part to the conflicting information received from FEMA and the South Carolina Emergency Management Division (Grantee) as to which entity was the appropriate one to submit the required documentation for pre-approval. Due to time constraints the Applicant proceeded with the evacuation process without obtaining prior approval."[67]

"The FEMA Region IV Regional Administrator denied the appeal on June 3, 2021, stating that the Applicant did not have legal responsibility to provide evacuation and sheltering for its student-athletes and the actions undertaken did not constitute eligible emergency protective measures, because the student-athletes' departure from the campus appeared to be an effort to maintain the teams' competition schedule, not to provide shelter from the storm."[68]

"FEMA finds that the Applicant had authority to evacuate and shelter its students and legal responsibility to ensure the safety and well-being of its student population, while under its care and jurisdiction. However, the Applicant did not incur the claimed costs to evacuate and shelter those students unable to self-evacuate according to their PEP, but instead incurred expenses to transport and lodge its athletic teams between sporting events at multiple venues. Although the Applicant amended its request to exclude costs beyond $15.00 per night, per person, for lodging, it has not justified the difference between how the student-athletes were evacuated and sheltered, compared to the general student population."[69]

Given the outsized role that student athletics plays at most colleges and universities, it is easy to see how the school might have tried to bend the rules to maintain its schedule of competitions. However, nothing in the Stafford Act or FEMA regulations provides for this.

An Institute of Higher Education, or Not?

Because an organization or facility is closely allied with a bona fide institute of higher education and may even be integral to that institution, it does make it an eligible institute of higher education, as this case, also connected to the previously cited university, demonstrates: "During Hurricane Matthew, the State of South Carolina experienced strong winds, driving rain, and flying debris from October 4 through October 24, 2016. Because of the hurricane, an access road, a cottage and monitoring equipment located on the Waties Island/Anne Tilghman Boyce Coastal Reserve (Facility) incurred damage from debris. Coastal Carolina University (CCU) utilizes the Facility for its marine science program, and the monitoring equipment feeds data into National Weather Service models. The Coastal Educational Foundation, Inc. (Applicant) owns the Facility, including the improvements thereon, and at the time of the disaster, had legal responsibility for its repair and maintenance. The Applicant is a registered 501(c)(3) organization in good standing with the state of South Carolina."[70]

"On October 21, 2016, the Applicant submitted a Request for Public Assistance (RPA), requesting funding as a Private Non-Profit (PNP). In a Determination Memorandum attached to a letter dated January 12, 2017, FEMA denied the Applicant's RPA, finding that the Applicant was not an eligible PNP, as it does not 1) own or operate an eligible facility; 2) meet the definition of an educational institution; or 3) provide a non-critical, but essential governmental-type service that is open to the general public. Accordingly, FEMA concluded that the requested debris removal from the road and the rest of the Facility was not an eligible project, since it did not support an eligible critical service."[71]

"FEMA Region IV issued its first appeal determination on April 30, 2018, denying the Applicant's appeal. In support of this determination, FEMA noted that PNP educational facilities are eligible for Public Assistance (PA) funding as critical services, and that FEMA defines 'educational facilities' to include classrooms and the 'supplies, equipment, machinery and utilities of an educational institution.' Thus, although FEMA found that the Facility supports educational purposes, it found that the Applicant itself was not an institute of higher education. That is, because the Applicant was not the entity actually providing the educational services, FEMA found that the Applicant did not own or operate an eligible facility."[72]

"However, although the Facility appears to be an integral part of CCU's marine science program, the Applicant is not the entity which directly provides the educational services supported by the Facility. The Applicant does not meet any of the four criteria to qualify as an institute of higher education laid out in the PAPPG. The Applicant does not admit students having a high school diploma or equivalent; lacks legal authorization to provide education beyond the secondary level; does not award a bachelor's degree, 2-year degree, or provide 1-year training programs for employment purposes; nor is it accredited by a nationally recognized agency. Simply hosting programs administered by other organizations does not qualify a PNP as an eligible educational institution."[73]

These requirements also apply to "foundations," which are fundraising arms of most colleges and universities. The mere association, even integral connection, with a college, university, or any other private non-profit in and of itself does not create eligibility under the Public Assistance program. Even if classes were held in rooms provided in a "foundation" building, that in and of itself does not make the facility eligible.

Private Non-Profits Providing Emergency Services

"For PNPs, operating costs are generally ineligible even if the services are emergency services, unless the PNP performs an emergency service at the request of and certified by the legally responsible government entity. In such case, FEMA provides PA funding through that government entity as the eligible Applicant."[74]

In this case, the most important requirement is having a written agreement between the local government agency and the private non-profit organization which formalizes the understanding of what goods and/or services the private non-profit organization will provide at the behest of the appropriate level of government. Assuming that the services are true emergency services, the local government agency, with a signed agreement in hand, may then request funding from FEMA for the provision of those services. Currently, FEMA has allowed such agreements to be postdated. However, the safest plan is to have the appropriate agreements in place prior to the disaster in the event that FEMA should change this practice.

Under the terms of the agreement, the private non-profit organization provides the specified disaster services, then invoices the government agency for those costs. The local agency then reimburses the private non-profit organization and may then apply to FEMA as the eligible applicant for reimbursement.

However, as always, documentation and proper record keeping are critical to ensuring reimbursement. This case from California, following Hurricane Katrina, demonstrates the pitfalls resulting from a lack of documentation, and in this case closely following the approved scope of work. "After Hurricane Katrina, the State of California agreed to accept evacuees from the impacted areas in Louisiana. As part of that effort, the Applicant provided assistance, resources and short-term interim sheltering to the evacuees. On February 26, 2007, FEMA approved Project Worksheet (PW) 7 for actual costs of $27,692 for the provision of affordable housing location services, employment services, and transportation for Hurricane Katrina evacuees. The PW was written as a small project at 40% complete and noted that the Applicant's contract with the Volunteer Center of Silicon Valley had a not-to-exceed amount of $87,228."[75]

"On July 19, 2010, the California Emergency Management Agency (Cal EMA) forwarded the Applicant's Final Inspection Report (FIR) to FEMA with a recommendation to limit funding for the project at $27,692 because the Applicant did not request a Net Small Project Overrun within sixty days of completion of the project. In a letter dated August 17, 2010, FEMA identified final eligible funding of $27,692 and noted that it considered the project closed."[76]

First Appeal

"On October 22, 2010, the Applicant submitted its first appeal to Cal EMA and requested additional funding in the amount of $410,629 for costs associated with debit cards, furniture purchases and delivery, and housing rentals. In its appeal, the Applicant asserted that it was not informed that PW 7 had been approved as a small project. In its transmittal letter to the Regional Administrator, Cal EMA stated that the Applicant had requested funding in the amount of $438,422, with supporting documentation, in a letter dated May 21, 2007. However, Cal EMA further stated that this documentation was not forwarded to FEMA. In response to the first appeal, the Regional Administrator approved PW 7 as a large project and approved additional funding in the amount of $167,154. The Regional Administrator determined that the remaining $243,475 was not eligible due to the lack of supporting documentation, duplication of payments to vendors, and work being performed after the established deadline of March 1, 2006, for Section 403 interim sheltering costs for Hurricane Katrina evacuees."[77]

"The Applicant asserted that FEMA did not request additional supporting documentation until December 30, 2010, and that records from several contractors were no longer available. The Applicant also claimed that it was not adequately notified of the deadline for work to be performed related to sheltering of evacuees."[78]

"On December 29, 2010, FEMA requested invoices to substantiate the claimed costs and eliminate any duplicate claims. The Applicant responded in a letter dated April 7, 2011, stating that records and invoices from several of its contractors were no longer available and therefore, it could not provide the requested information. In accordance with 44 CFR §13.36(i)(11) (*the old pre-2014 citations*), Procurement, Contract provisions, Applicants must include a provision in their contractual agreements requiring contractors to retain all required records for three years after grantees or subgrantees make final payments."[79]

So, in this case, good people, doing good work, for a good cause, failed due to procurement violations, lack of proper documentation, and performance of work outside of the period of performance, or POP. To quote the Bard, "The quality of mercy is not strained."[80] However, nowhere in the Stafford Act does the word "mercy" appear. It is a simple matter of "comply or die." In fact, the only saving grace in this particular case is that this was not millions of dollars, but a mere $244,000.

If a local non-profit organization should provide disaster services at its own instigation without an agreement with the local government agency, then, even if the local government agency should reimburse the non-profit, those costs are not eligible. The work must be performed under the auspices and at the written direction of the local government.

Alternatively, the non-profit organization may provide eligible disaster related services and "donate" the value of those services to the local government, which in turn may, when properly documented, use the value of those services as an offset against the local government's cost share of disaster expenses. Once again, there needs to be a written document in place.

However, as with all things FEMA, there is an exception.

PNP Medical Care

"EMAC (the Emergency Management Assistance Compact) can be used to provide emergency medical care, and these costs may be eligible for reimbursement as well. Reimbursement claims made by Mutual Aid providers must comply with applicable FEMA policy. Public or PNP medical service providers working within their jurisdiction, however, do not qualify as Mutual Aid providers."[81]

Therefore, in a hypothetical case in Florida, private non-profit medical organizations located in and working in Dade County, even with an agreement in place, cannot provide Mutual Aid and be reimbursed for it. However, if a private non-profit organization from Dade County provides assistance in any county in Florida *other* than Dade County, properly documented Mutual Aid would be reimbursable.

PNP Fire Departments and FMAGs

Although FMAGs (Fire Management Assistance Grants) are not technically a part of the Public Assistance program, there is an important aspect which should be noted here: "After an FMAG declaration, FEMA and the recipient enter into a FEMA-State (or Tribal) Agreement that states the understandings, commitments, and conditions under which FEMA provides federal assistance. As in the regular PA program, eligible applicants are state, tribal and local governments; and these entities may apply for assistance through the recipient. Unlike the regular PA program, PNPs are not eligible applicants. Entities such as PNP fire departments may receive reimbursement but only through a contract, compact, or similar agreement with an eligible applicant."[82] (Emphasis Added)

However, "if a PNP volunteer fire department operates based on established agreements with a SLTT (state, local, tribal, or territorial) government that designates the volunteer fire department as an official recognized entity legally authorized to provide emergency services in areas of coverage specifically designated by the SLTT government, FEMA may reimburse the volunteer fire department directly as an eligible Applicant."[83]

Emergency Protective Measures Conducted by Private Non-Profit Organizations

"For PNPs, eligible emergency protective measures are generally limited to activities associated with preventing damage to an eligible facility and its contents."[84]

"Emergency services are usually the responsibility of SLTT governments. Therefore, PNPs are generally not legally responsible for those services and FEMA does not provide PA funding to PNPs for the costs associated with providing those services. When a PNP provides emergency services at the request of, and certified by, the legally responsible government entity, FEMA provides PA funding through that government entity as the eligible Applicant. These services include:

- Fire and rescue activities;
- Animal control;
- Emergency ambulance service for evacuation;
- 211 call services, if tracked and related to eligible work; and
- Other similarly urgent governmental services."[85]

Private Non-Profit Eligible Emergency Work

"For PNP Applicants, eligible Emergency Work is generally limited to that associated with an eligible PNP facility as follows:

- Debris removal from the facility property; and
- Emergency protective measures to prevent damage to the facility and its contents.

In limited circumstances, PNPs may be eligible for other types of Emergency Work when essential components of a facility are urgently needed to save lives or protect health and safety."[86]

PNP Debris Removal

"Debris removal from roadways owned by an association may be eligible for emergency access purposes if performed under the auspices of an eligible state or local government; however, permanent repair of private roads owned or operated by an association would not be eligible because roads are not eligible PNP facilities."[87]

Facility Located in a Special Flood Hazard Area (SFHA)

"SFHAs are areas that are subject to inundation during a 100-year flood (a flood having a 1 percent chance of occurrence in a given year)."[88]

The National Flood Insurance Program

"For an NFIP-insurable facility located in an SFHA, FEMA must reduce PA funding when the facility is:

- Located in an area that FEMA has identified as an SFHA for more than 1 year;
- Damaged by flooding; and
- Uninsured for flood loss."[89]

"If the Applicant believes that its property is incorrectly identified on a Flood Insurance Rate Map (FIRM) as being located within the SFHA, it may request a Letter of Map Amendment or Letter of Map Revision from FEMA within 6 months of the declaration. If the Applicant's request is approved and FEMA determines that the property is not located in an SFHA, FEMA may reinstate PA funding. Costs incurred in pursuit of a Letter of Map Amendment or Letter of Map Revision are ineligible for PA funding."[90]

"If the Applicant does not have flood insurance for the facility or carries inadequate flood insurance for the insurable facility, FEMA reduces eligible project costs by the lesser of:

- The maximum amount of insurance proceeds that could have been obtained from an NFIP standard flood insurance policy for the building and its contents; or
- The value of the building and its contents at the time of the incident."[91]

"FEMA does not apply this reduction to PNP facilities in communities that do not participate in the NFIP. However, for FEMA to provide PA funding for the PNP facility, the community must agree to participate in the NFIP within 6 months of the declaration and the PNP must purchase the required flood insurance; or the PNP must obtain and maintain flood insurance from another source."[92]

Notes

1 Public Assistance Program and Policy Guide, Version 4, June 1, 2020, FFP 104–009–2, p. 47.
2 Disaster Operations Legal Reference, Version 4.0, September 25, 2020, pp. 5–84.
3 Ibid, p. 38.
4 Ibid, p. 56.
5 Ibid.
6 Ibid, p. 37.
7 Ibid, p. 63.
8 Public Assistance Program and Policy Guide, Version 4, June 1, 2020, FFP 104–009–2, p. 43.
9 Ibid.
10 Ibid, pp. 43–44.
11 Ibid, p. 44.
12 Ibid, p. 45.
13 Ibid.
14 Ibid.
15 Ibid.
16 Ibid, p. 46.
17 Ibid.
18 Ibid.
19 Disaster Operations Legal Reference, Version 4.0, September 25, 2020, pp. 5–14.
20 https://www.fema.gov/appeal/legal-responsibility-immediate-threat-public-interest
21 Ibid.
22 Ibid.
23 Ibid.
24 Ibid, pp. 5–24–5–25.
25 https://www.fema.gov/appeal/request-public-assistance-private-nonprofit
26 Ibid.
27 Ibid.
28 Ibid.
29 Ibid.
30 https://www.fema.gov/appeal/legal-responsibility-immediate-threat
31 Ibid.
32 Ibid.
33 Ibid, pp. 5–21.
34 Disaster Operations Legal Reference, Version 4.0, September 25, 2020, pp. 5–15–5–16.

35 Ibid, pp. 5–12.
36 Public Assistance Program and Policy Guide, Version 4, June 1, 2020, FFP 104–009–2, pp. 57–58.
37 https://www.fema.gov/appeal/private-nonprofit-11
38 https://www.fema.gov/appeal/small-business-administration-loan
39 Ibid.
40 Ibid.
41 Public Assistance Program and Policy Guide, Version 4, June 1, 2020, FFP 104–009–2, pp. 47–48.
42 https://www.fema.gov/appeal/appeal-timeliness-16
43 Ibid.
44 Ibid.
45 Ibid.
46 Ibid.
47 Ibid.
48 Public Assistance Program and Policy Guide, Version 4, June 1, 2020, FFP 104–009–2, pp. 58–59.
49 https://www.fema.gov/appeal/inactive-or-alternative-use-facility
50 Ibid.
51 Ibid.
52 Ibid.
53 Public Assistance Program and Policy Guide, Version 4, June 1, 2020, FFP 104–009–2, p. 175.
54 Ibid, p. 147.
55 Ibid, p. 203.
56 Ibid, pp. 75–76.
57 Ibid, p. 130.
58 Ibid.
59 Ibid.
60 Ibid, p. 130.
61 Disaster Operations Legal Reference, Version 4.0, September 25, 2020, pp. 5–15.
62 https://www.fema.gov/appeal/ineligible-costs
63 Ibid.
64 https://www.fema.gov/appeal/legal-responsibility-evacuation-medical-care-and-sheltering
65 Ibid.
66 Ibid.
67 Ibid.
68 Ibid.
69 Ibid.
70 https://www.fema.gov/appeal/request-public-assistance-pnp-applicant-eligibility-facility-eligibility
71 Ibid.
72 Ibid.
73 Ibid.
74 Public Assistance Program and Policy Guide, Version 4, June 1, 2020, FFP 104–009–2, p. 114.
75 https://www.fema.gov/appeal/interim-sheltering-costs-hurricane-katrina-evacuees
76 Ibid.
77 Ibid.
78 Ibid.
79 Ibid.
80 Shakespeare, William, *The Merchant of Venice* (Act 4, Scene 1)
81 Disaster Operations Legal Reference, Version 4.0, September 25, 2020, pp. 5–41.
82 Ibid, pp. 5–120.
83 Public Assistance Program and Policy Guide, Version 4, June 1, 2020, FFP 104–009–2, p. 113.
84 Ibid, p. 112.
85 Ibid, pp. 112–113.
86 Ibid, pp. 97–98.
87 Disaster Operations Legal Reference, Version 4.0, September 25, 2020, pp. 5–14.
88 Public Assistance Program and Policy Guide, Version 4, June 1, 2020, FFP 104–009–2, p. 162.
89 Ibid.
90 Ibid.
91 Ibid.
92 Ibid, p. 163.

38 U.S. Small Business Administration Loans for Private Non-Profits

"Blessed are the young, for they shall inherit the national debt."

Herbert Hoover

As mentioned in the previous chapter, certain eligible private non-profit organizations must apply to the U.S. Small Business Administration (SBA) for a loan prior to applying to FEMA for Public Assistance for permanent work, i.e., Categories C through G. Emergency work Categories A and B are usually otherwise eligible. However, regarding debris clearance, this needs to be coordinated with the appropriate level of local government if and when FEMA approves private property debris removal (PPDR).

Those private non-profit organizations that DO NOT have to apply to the Small Business Administration are the non-profits that provide the following services: "power, water (including water provided by an irrigation organization or facility), sewer services, wastewater treatment, communications, education, and emergency medical care."[1] All other private non-profits must apply to the SBA as a precondition to potentially receiving Public Assistance.

The SBA does not have a special program just for private non-profits, since the SBA also provides loans to qualified small businesses, homeowners, and renters.

Disaster Loan Assistance

"The SBA offers disaster assistance in the form of low interest loans to businesses, nonprofit organizations, homeowners, and renters located in regions affected by declared disasters. SBA also provides eligible small businesses and nonprofit organizations with working capital to help overcome the economic injury of a declared disaster."[2] (Emphasis Added)

Federal Disaster Loans for Businesses, Private Non-Profits, Homeowners, and Renters

Business Physical Disaster Loans

"If you are in a declared disaster area and have experienced damage to your business, you may be eligible for financial assistance from the SBA. Businesses of any size and most private non-profit organizations may apply to the SBA for a loan to recover after a disaster."[3] (Emphasis Added)

DOI: 10.4324/9781003487869-43

Loan Amounts and Use

"SBA makes physical disaster loans of up to $2 million to qualified businesses or most private nonprofit organizations. These loan proceeds may be used for the repair or replacement of the following:

- Real property
- Machinery
- Equipment
- Fixtures
- Inventory
- Leasehold improvements"

"The SBA Business Physical Disaster Loan covers disaster losses not fully covered by insurance. If you are required to apply insurance proceeds to an outstanding mortgage on the damaged property, you can include that amount in your disaster loan application. If you make improvements that help reduce the risk of future property damage caused by a similar disaster, you may be eligible for up to a 20 percent loan amount increase above the real estate damage, as verified by the SBA."[4]

"You may not use the disaster loan to upgrade or expand a business, except as required by building codes."[5] (Emphasis Added)

Eligibility and Terms

A business of any size or most private non-profit organizations that are in a declared disaster area and have incurred damage during the disaster may apply for a loan to help replace damaged property or restore its pre-disaster condition.

The interest rate will not exceed 4% if you cannot obtain credit elsewhere. For businesses and non-profit organizations with credit available elsewhere, the interest rate will not exceed 8%. SBA determines whether the applicant has credit available elsewhere. Repayment terms can be up to 30 years, depending on your ability to repay the loan.

How to Apply

You can apply online for an SBA disaster assistance loan. SBA will send an inspector to estimate the cost of your damage once you have completed and returned your loan application. You must submit the completed loan application and a signed and dated IRS Form 4506-C giving permission for the IRS to provide SBA with your tax return information.

For additional information, please contact the SBA disaster assistance customer service center at 1–800–659–2955 (if you are deaf, hard of hearing, or have a speech disability, please dial 7-1-1 to access telecommunications relay services) or e-mail disastercustomerservice@sba.gov.

Small Business Administration Loan Requirements

"Following a Major Disaster Declaration, the U.S. Small Business Administration (SBA) can provide loans to individuals and businesses for facility restoration. For PNPs with facilities that provide noncritical essential social services, FEMA only provides PA funding for eligible Permanent Work costs that an SBA loan will not cover for those facilities. Therefore, noncritical PNPs must also apply for a disaster loan from the SBA and receive a determination for Permanent Work on facilities that:

- Provide noncritical services; or
- Are mixed-use facilities and the eligible portion of the facility is used to provide services that are entirely noncritical.

If the PNP misses the SBA application deadline, including any SBA approved extension, the Permanent Work is ineligible for FEMA PA funding. If the PNP declines an SBA loan, PA funding is limited to the costs that the loan would not have otherwise covered. This applies even when the PNP cannot accept the terms of the loan, and SBA therefore denies the loan, which may occur when the entity does not meet a collateral requirement.

PNPs do not need to apply for a disaster loan from the SBA for facilities that:

- Provide critical services; or
- Are mixed-use and the eligible portion is either entirely or partially used to provide critical services."[6]

If the private non-profit applies for an SBA loan and receives full funding to cover the costs associated with the disaster-caused damage, then they do not need to apply for Public Assistance.

However, if the SBA denies the loan, then the private non-profit should apply to FEMA for Public Assistance. In a third possible case, the SBA provides some but not all of the needed funding, then the private non-profit may apply to FEMA for the remaining unfunded balance.

The private non-profit should file a "Request for Public Assistance" (or RPA) at the same time it files a loan application with the SBA. Without proof of filing a loan application with SBA and getting eventual approval of a loan, FEMA will not consider the private non-profit eligible for Public Assistance.

National Flood Insurance Program (NFIP) Coverage Requirement

"An applicant who had a prior NFIRA (National Flood Insurance Reform Act of 1994) requirement for federal disaster assistance such as IHP *(Individual and Households Program)* or an <u>SBA loan</u> is ineligible for future federal assistance for flood-damaged real and personal property if he or she did not obtain and maintain flood insurance . . . SBA flood insurance coverage requirements are for the life of the loan."[7]

Following are appeal cases dealing with private non-profits and the requirement for applying for an SBA loan.

"In September 2021, Hurricane Ida caused extensive damage throughout New York State. The Kingsway Jewish Center (Applicant), a Private Nonprofit organization (PNP), owns and operates the Kingsway Jewish Center (Facility), a house of worship (HOW) that provides a noncritical essential social service. The Applicant requested $30,760.29 in Public Assistance (PA) funding to repair damage to the Facility and for hazard mitigation (HM). However, FEMA issued a Determination Memorandum on August 12, 2022, finding that the Applicant failed to demonstrate that it had timely applied for a Small Business Administration (SBA) disaster loan, a prerequisite to its eligibility for PA funding for permanent work. Therefore, FEMA found the permanent work was ineligible for PA and because HM was tied to and dependent upon eligible permanent work, the requested HM funding was similarly ineligible."[8]

First Appeal

"The Applicant appealed for $30,760.29 on October 14, 2022, stating it was not aware of the SBA requirement for FEMA assistance. The Applicant provided a signed SBA application dated October 13, 2022."[9]

"The FEMA Region 2 Regional Administrator denied the appeal on February 28, 2023. FEMA noted the SBA Fact Sheet for the disaster established that the deadline to apply for SBA loans was January 4, 2022, and that the Applicant did not apply until October 13, 2022. FEMA determined the Applicant did not apply for the SBA loan in a timely manner and was therefore not eligible for PA funding for permanent work."[10]

"The Applicant did not apply for an SBA disaster loan until October 13, 2022, approximately nine months after the January 4, 2022 deadline. The SBA did not extend the deadline. Therefore, the SBA loan application requirement was not satisfied. Notably, the Applicant does not dispute this. Rather, the Applicant relies on lack of knowledge concerning this requirement to support its request for PA. However, lack of knowledge and understanding of PA requirements does not justify submitting the SBA loan application after the required deadline."[11]

In the next case, the result was favorable for the private non-profit agency.

"EDU is a private nonprofit (PNP) organization that was founded to aid and assist Total Community Action, Inc. (TCA), in planning, designing, programming, funding, and operating projects for the purpose of permitting economic growth in the community, and providing social services and facilities for the residents of the community. As a result of Katrina, EDU is requesting reimbursement of approximately $326,000 for repairing flood damage, removing debris, and remediating mold at its Jefferson Davis Parkway and Thalia Street facility that was not covered by insurance. FEMA did not accept EDU's RPA because it was submitted nine months after the March 1, 2006, deadline. The Regional Administrator denied the first appeal on September 27, 2007, because EDU did not demonstrate extenuating circumstances that were sufficient to warrant the petition. In addition, the Regional Administrator determined that EDU did not provide the type of services that would make it eligible for Public Assistance."[12]

"In its second appeal, EDU states that it contacted FEMA in February 2006 and was directed to submit a loan application to the Small Business Administration (SBA) before applying to FEMA for assistance. In a letter dated July 17, 2006, SBA denied EDU's loan application and stated that it would forward EDU's application to FEMA. After several attempts to locate its application, EDU contacted the State of Louisiana Governor's Office of Homeland Security and Emergency Preparedness and was advised to apply for a Public Assistance Grant."[13]

"EDU's second appeal also argues that its Articles of Incorporation state that EDU exists to develop and expand the social service delivery systems of TCA. It leases its facility to TCA and is legally responsible for repairing the facility. Therefore, it claims that EDU is eligible for assistance from FEMA. Section 7.C.3 of Response and Recovery Policy 9521.1, Community ety [sic] of services to the people of New Orleans. These services include early childhood development, job counseling and guidance, transportation for the elderly and disabled, commodity distribution, individual and family development accounts, homelessness prevention, free tax preparation assistance for low-income individuals, Family Matters (a program for unwed parents), youth work experience and energy assistance, weatherization. These activities are eligible PNP community center functions. Section 7.C.1 of Response and Recovery Policy 9521.1, Community Center Eligibility, states that if 51 percent of the facility qualifies as eligible, the facility is eligible. However, assistance is based on the percent of eligible use. EDU provided evidence that TCA's activities occupy approximately 90 percent of its facility. TCA's activities are open to the general public, and the established and primary use of the facility as a gathering place for a variety of social, educational enrichment, and community service activities is consistent with Response and Recovery Policy 9521.1, Community Center Eligibility."[14]

"Based on a review of all information submitted with the appeal, I have determined that EDU presented a compelling justification for submitting its RPA to FEMA after the established deadline. In addition, EDU's facility is an eligible community center. Accordingly, I am granting the second appeal."[15]

In this second case, the private non-profit prevailed upon appeal. However, we cannot assume that this same finding would result in other appeals in other regions of the country.

In a third and final case regarding SBA loans, ill winds blew across the Gulf of Mexico and resulted in a denial of eligibility. This is another multi-issue case, so we shall focus on the SBA loan element of the case.

"FEMA may provide PA funding to an eligible PNP only if it has applied for a disaster loan from the SBA, and demonstrates either that the PNP is ineligible for such a loan, or that the PNP has obtained such a loan in the maximum amount for which the SBA determines the facility is eligible and that amount does not cover fully the eligible damage under the PA program. Here, the SBA loan denial letter that the Applicant provided was for an individual home loan in the name of its president. It provided other SBA loan application documents in the organization's name, but did not provide a determination letter from the SBA. FEMA inquired with the SBA, and learned that the Applicant initiated, but had not completed an SBA loan application for this disaster. As the RA (Regional Administrator) correctly found, without an SBA disaster loan determination, FEMA may not provide PA funding to the Applicant."[16] (Emphasis Added)

As we have previously seen, attention to the details is critical in dealings with FEMA, and private non-profit agencies are not exempt.

Notes

1 Disaster Operations Legal Reference, Version 4.0, September 25, 2020, pp. 5–15.
2 https://disasterloanassistance.sba.gov/ela/s/
3 Ibid.
4 Ibid.
5 Ibid.
6 Public Assistance Program and Policy Guide, Version 4, June 1, 2020, FFP 104–009–2, pp. 57–58.
7 Disaster Operations Legal Reference, Version 4.0, September 25, 2020, pp. 6–45.
8 https://www.fema.gov/appeal/private-nonprofit-13
9 Ibid.
10 Ibid.
11 Ibid.
12 https://www.fema.gov/appeal/request-public-assistance
13 Ibid.
14 Ibid.
15 Ibid.
16 https://www.fema.gov/appeal/private-nonprofit-legal-responsibility-direct-result-disaster-support-documentation

Part 5

Wrapping Up

39 Fraud

Figure 39.1 Chat GPT depiction of a local government official caught with their hand in the cookie jar.

"We are not doing anything that fraudulent."
– Email from consultant to ICS members relating to payment of individuals for project management and
Direct Administrative Costs[1]

One might ask, why is there a chapter on fraud in a book about FEMA?

Because fraud committed against the Federal government is big business, and it deeply affects what FEMA does and why it makes the process so difficult for those of us who are merely seeking to restore their communities and their lives to some sense of normalcy.

In researching this chapter, the internet gods smiled down upon me many times. I recently ran across an article which proves my point, even though this particular case does not involve FEMA.

DOI: 10.4324/9781003487869-45

The headline reads "A Houston Power Couple Has Been Sentenced To A Combined 35 Years In Federal Prison After Being Convicted of Fraud."[2] (Emphasis Added) The case involved fraud related to Worker's Compensation and a healthcare program for veterans, which is all Federal money.

According to the article, the accused siphoned off nearly $126,000,000 dollars from the Federal government and the Department of Labor.

Former Mayor Pleads Guilty to FEMA Fraud

During another foray into the wilds of the internet, I found this FEMA-connected fraud: "GULF-PORT, Miss. – The former Mayor of Gulfport, Mississippi, Gregory Brent Warr entered a plea of guilty and was sentenced today for felony Katrina fraud, announced Stan Harris, United States Attorney for the Southern District of Mississippi, and Richard Skinner, Inspector General for the United States Department of Homeland Security."[3]

"Gregory Brent Warr entered a guilty plea before Senior United States District Judge Walter J. Gex, III, to one felony count of stealing U.S. Government funds from the Federal Emergency Management Agency (FEMA). Following his plea of guilty, Warr was sentenced to three years of supervised probation, 100 hours of community service, and restitution to FEMA of $9,558.00. In addition, a judgment of forfeiture was entered against Warr in the amount of $9,558.00. All of the remaining counts against Warr, and his wife Laura Warr, were dismissed in consideration for his plea of guilty."[4]

"As part of his guilty plea, Warr admitted in federal court to the accuracy of the factual basis set forth by the Government regarding his criminal conduct. Warr admitted that on September 14, 2005, co-defendant Laura Warr registered with the Federal Emergency Management Agency for Katrina Disaster Assistance claiming that she, her husband and their two children were living at 1814 Beach Drive, Gulfport, Mississippi when the proof would show that they did not."[5]

"On November 26, 2005, the defendant, Gregory Brent Warr, met with a FEMA inspector at 1814 Beach Drive and represented that, at the time of Hurricane Katrina, the house was occupied by the Warr family. As a result of these fraudulent actions, the Warrs received three payments from FEMA: 1) $2,000.00 on September 15, 2005; 2) $2,358.00 on October 18, 2005; and, 3) $5,200.00 on November 29, 2005; for a total of $9,558.00 to which they were not entitled."[6] While this case relates to FEMA's Individual Assistance program (IA), it is nonetheless Federal funding.

Next in line: **"Manhattan U.S. Attorney Announces $5.3 Million Proposed Settlement Of Lawsuit Against New York City For Fraudulently Obtaining FEMA Funds Following Superstorm Sandy."**[7]

"Geoffrey S. Berman, the United States Attorney for the Southern District of New York, Mark Tasky, Special Agent in Charge of the New York Regional Office of the Department of Homeland Security Office of Inspector General (DHS-OIG), and Margaret Garnett, Commissioner, New York City Department of Investigation (DOI), announced today that the United States filed a civil fraud lawsuit today against the City Of New York (the 'City') alleging that the New York City Department Of Transportation (NYCDOT) fraudulently obtained millions of dollars from the Federal Emergency Management Agency (FEMA) by falsely claiming that numerous NYCDOT vehicles were damaged during Superstorm Sandy (Sandy). The United States also submitted a proposed settlement of the lawsuit to the U.S. District Court for review and approval. Under the proposed settlement, the City agreed to pay and revert to the United States a total of $5,303,624 and admitted to conduct alleged in the Government's complaint, including seeking reimbursement from FEMA for vehicles that were not damaged by Sandy."[8]

"Following Sandy, the NYCDOT created a list of vehicles within the agency's fleet that had been damaged by the storm and submitted it to FEMA for indemnification pursuant to the Public Assistance program. The NYCDOT personnel responsible for generating the list of damaged vehicles, to whom the City provided no training on the Public Assistance program, made no effort to inspect the vehicles or otherwise determine whether any reported damage was attributable to Sandy. In fact, a number of the vehicles included on this list were inoperable long before Sandy."[9] (Emphasis Added)

"In 2014, based on this faulty list, the City submitted a request for indemnification to FEMA seeking to recover the full cost of replacing 132 NYCDOT vehicles. The City submitted a certification to FEMA as part of the program and a request for indemnification that falsely attested that all costs were incurred as a direct result of Sandy. Many of the vehicles for which the City sought full replacement costs had been nonoperational or not in use prior to the storm. As a result of these false certifications, FEMA paid the City millions of dollars to which it was not entitled."[10]

"As part of the proposed settlement, the City will pay the United States a total of $5,303,624. Specifically, the City will make a cash payment of $4,126,227.34 and relinquish rights to an additional $1,177,396.66 that FEMA had previously approved for disbursement. During this Office's investigation, the City withdrew another $3,196,376 in indemnity requests, acknowledging that the costs were ineligible for reimbursement."[11] (Emphasis Added)

Yet another case: "**Two Maryland Men Facing Federal Indictment for Their Roles in a Scheme that Allegedly Stole Government Benefits, Including More Than $8 Million in Federal Emergency Assistance.**"[12]

"Greenbelt, Maryland – A federal grand jury returned an indictment charging John Irogho, age 38, of Upper Marlboro, Maryland, for conspiracy to commit wire fraud, and charging Irogho and Odinaka Ekeocha, age 33, of Laurel, Maryland, for conspiracy to commit money laundering, in connection with a scheme to fraudulently obtain federal benefits. The indictment was returned on July 31, 2019, and unsealed today upon the arrests of the defendants."[13]

"The indictment was announced by United States Attorney for the District of Maryland Robert K. Hur; Special Agent in Charge Mark I. Tasky of the Department of Homeland Security (DHS) – Office of Inspector General; Special Agent in Charge Michael McGill of the Social Security Administration (SSA) Office of Inspector General; Special Agent in Charge Matthew S. Miller of the U.S. Secret Service – Washington Field Office; and J. Russell George, Treasury Inspector General for Tax Administration (TIGTA)."[14]

"'While many come forward in the wake of disasters to help selflessly, some use disasters to enrich themselves through theft and fraud,' said U.S. Attorney Robert K. Hur. 'The U.S. Attorney's Office will pursue criminals who steal funds intended to help actual disaster victims.'"[15]

"According to the two-count indictment, from 2016 through 2018 Irogho and several co-conspirators purchased hundreds of Green Dot debit cards, which co-conspirators then registered with Green Dot using the stolen personal information of identity theft victims from around the country. In 2017, amidst Hurricanes Harvey, Irma, and Maria, and the California wildfires, co-conspirators allegedly applied online with FEMA for CNA (*Critical Needs Assistance*) using the stolen personal information of additional victims of identity theft. According to the indictment, FEMA paid at least $8 million in amounts of $500 per claim to the Green Dot debit cards purchased by Irogho and his co-conspirators."[16]

Lynn Haven Mayor and City Attorney Indicted for Corruption and Fraud Charges Stemming from Hurricane Michael Clean-up Activities

"PANAMA CITY, FLORIDA – Lynn Haven City's Mayor and Attorney are the subjects of a 64-count indictment returned yesterday by a federal grand jury in Panama City, Florida. Lynn

Haven Mayor Margo Anderson, 65, of Jacksonville, Florida, and Lynn Haven City Attorney Joseph Adam Albritton, 33, of Lynn Haven, Florida, have been indicted for conspiring to commit wire fraud and honest services fraud, substantive counts of wire fraud, honest services fraud, and theft concerning federal programs. Anderson is also charged with making false statements to FBI agents. Albritton is charged with submitting a false invoice to an insurance company for hurricane debris removal from his residence."[17]

"Anderson was arrested by FBI agents this morning at her Jacksonville, Florida, residence. Her initial appearance is scheduled for 2:30 p.m. EST today at the United States Courthouse in Jacksonville. Albritton was arrested by deputies of the Bay County Sherriff's Office this morning in Lynn Haven, Florida. His initial appearance is scheduled for 4:00 p.m. EST today at the United States Courthouse in Tallahassee."[18]

"Following Hurricane Michael, on October 16, 2018, the City of Lynn Haven adopted a local state of emergency for post-disaster relief and planning. The City also approved a resolution waiving the procedures that are normally required under Florida law so that timely action could be taken to ensure the safety, welfare, and health of the citizens of Lynn Haven. The resolution delegated emergency powers to Mayor Anderson or her designee, meaning they could independently enter into contracts and spend public funds. Although the emergency declaration was ended by Lynn Haven two weeks later, the city entered into an emergency agreement with David White, owner of Erosion Control Specialists (ECS) to perform hurricane clean-up services."[19]

"The indictment returned yesterday alleges ECS was paid for services that were not authorized under the emergency contract. According to the indictment, unauthorized work valued at over $48,000 was performed at the private residences of Anderson, her mother, and a neighbor, and an additional $25,000 worth of unauthorized work was performed at the private residences of Albritton and his girlfriend. The indictment alleges that ECS invoices falsely claimed this work was provided to Lynn Haven public areas. After the unauthorized work was performed, Albritton went on to file a fraudulent claim with St. John's Insurance Company that his residence had been damaged by Hurricane Michael, according to the indictment. Albritton is charged with providing the insurance company with a false invoice from ECS indicating he had paid for tree removal, debris removal, and installation of a tarp to his residence totaling $9,600."[20]

"Anderson and Albritton are also charged with devising a scheme to defraud Lynn Haven and its citizens of their right to honest services of Anderson, as Mayor, and Albritton, as City Attorney. The indictment alleges that both Anderson and Albritton solicited and received bribes or kickbacks from City projects that they approved."[21]

"After the initial emergency declaration by Lynn Haven expired, the indictment alleges Albritton conspired with then-City Manager Michael White to award a trash pick-up project to ECS. Although Lynn Haven waste trucks had the ability to perform the same work at no additional cost to the city, ECS was paid $300 per hour, per crew for this task. The indictment charges Albritton with demanding, and receiving, $10,000 in cash for each weeks of trash services billed to Lynn Haven by ECS from mid-October 2018 through January 2019. The city of Lynn Haven was ultimately billed $1.8 million for unnecessary trash pick-up according to the indictment."[22]

"The indictment alleges that Anderson halted progress on plans to permit a city-owned site for disposal of vegetative debris, even though using the city-owned site would have saved Lynn Haven millions of dollars in disposal fees. Instead, the indictment alleges Anderson told the City Manager to use a privately owned company (Company B) for vegetative debris disposal. According to the indictment, the city of Lynn Haven paid disposal fees in excess of $2 million to Company B. Additionally, the indictment charges that between 2015 and the present date, Anderson helped Company B win multiple other multi-million dollar contracts with the city of Lynn Haven. In return, the indictment charges Anderson with accepting things of value from the owner of Company B, including travel in a private airplane, lodging aboard a private yacht, meals and entertainment. According to the indictment, Anderson and her husband also received a $106,000 motorhome from Company B in February 2018."[23]

Is Lynn Haven a Hotbed for FEMA Fraud?

Here is still another case of Lynn Haven, Florida officials taking pleas and doing time for FEMA related fraud.

"LYNN HAVEN, Fla. (WMBB) – The men and women responsible for a massive fraud that federal prosecutors once tagged as more than $5 million were – in most other respects – responsible members of society, a judge suggested at their sentencing Monday. 'I suspect these are fine people that if they found your wallet they would give it back,' said Federal Judge Robert Hinkle. However, he noted that many people who are often honest in other walks of life, 'take the opportunity to steal money from the government.'"[24]

"This phase of the case involved work done after Hurricane Michael and massive overbilling of the city, FEMA, and ultimately, the taxpayers. David White, the owner of a construction company, Mike White, the former city manager, Josh Anderson, the owner of a lawn service, Shannon Rodriguez, one of David White's employees and his sister, and David Horton, Lynn Haven's former leisure services director, all plead guilty between February and July 2020."[25]

"Hinkle also said he wished he could impose a 10-year sentence on the group as a warning to others in public office. 'Our institutions are important,' Hinkle said. Adding, 'Our institutions are very much under stress.'"[26]

Prosecutors Push Forward in Lynn Haven Case

"Mike White and David White were both sentenced to 42 months in prison. They will report on July 7. Anderson and Horton were sentenced to 9 months of house arrest as part of their one year of probation. Rodriguez was sentenced to one year of probation with no house arrest."[27]

"Mike White wept while his wife Amy told Hinkle that the situation had changed her husband's heart and humbled him."[28]

This litany of fraud and abuse against FEMA and local agencies could go on indefinitely. But the point is made: that fraud is the dark-side companion of FEMA and other Federal agencies providing disaster assistance in its many forms.

There is also a lesser evil which stops short of prosecutable fraud, and that is the nickel-and-dime dishonest billing in whatever a vendor or contractor believes they can get away with. As a result, while providing much needed disaster assistance to both local government agencies and individuals and households, FEMA is constantly on guard to detect fraudulent behavior. Local agencies making applications for repairs to facilities which have seldom had any maintenance, or facilities which should have been repaired or replaced years or even decades ago has created an environment where the local agencies must prove everything regarding their allegations of disaster damage.

In short, FEMA accepts little at face value without substantial documentation.

Not Fraud, But Still Fraud-Related

However, disaster fraud is generally in the domain of the Federal government, although the states might also play a role. In this next example, again from Florida, we have this case. "Following Hurricane Opal, the Florida Department of Business and Professional Regulation (DBPR), the subgrantee, formed two task forces to provide public assistance to residents of the declared disaster areas of Bay and Walton Counties. According to the subgrantee, these task forces were deployed to protect disaster victims from contractor and consumer fraud in the aftermath of the hurricane by conducting public seminars and meetings with local building officials; appearing on or producing material for the broadcast media; distributing brochures and pamphlets; handling and investigating questions and reports regarding this threat; posting warning information on transportation routes; and conducting a public information and assistance campaign."[29]

"On February 2, 1996, damage survey report (DSR) 62077 was written for $64,762 to reimburse the subgrantee for expenses incurred during this public assistance campaign. Expenses included in the DSR are labor, equipment, material, communications, and travel costs. Upon review of DSR 62077, it was determined that the activities were ineligible for funding on the basis that the work performed was not eliminating immediate threats to life and property as provided for under Section 403 of the Stafford Act."[30]

"Relevant emergency measures in a situation such as this may include structural analysis to determine the integrity of buildings so as to avert immediate threats to life and property. Conversely, warning that work may be performed which would result in unsound structural integrity, or directly confronting unlicensed contractors, such as in this situation, would not be eligible. The immediate threat to personal and property safety would be an unsound structure, not an unlicensed contractor. An example of disseminated information eligible for funding may be literature concerning unsafe drinking water. If drinking water were tainted such that use would present an immediate threat to the health of a community, public assistance campaigns and documents would be valid examples of emergency measures provided for under Section 403."[31]

Therefore, there may a be a legitimate role for either state or local governments to be alert for fraud and make timely notice to the public, but this is done at either local or state expense, and with the exceptions noted in the previous paragraph, it's not FEMA-eligible.

Watch Those Consultants Closely, Too

Headline: "████████ (The Consultant) to Pay $11.8 Million to Resolve False Claims Act Allegations in Connection with Hurricane Disaster Relief"[32]

"████████, (the consultant) an architecture and engineering firm based in Dallas has agreed to pay $11.8 million to resolve allegations that it violated the False Claims Act (FCA) by knowingly submitting false claims to the Federal Emergency Management Agency (FEMA) for the replacement of certain educational facilities located in Louisiana that were damaged by Hurricane Katrina."[33]

"Under the Robert T. Stafford Disaster Relief and Emergency Assistance Act and corresponding rules, FEMA provided institutional applicants, such as schools and universities, with public assistance (PA) funds for the repair or replacement of facilities damaged by Hurricane Katrina. Funding was limited to the cost of repairing a damaged facility, unless that cost exceeded 50% of the facility's replacement cost, in which case full-replacement funding was available."[34]

"Between 2006 and 2010, ████████ (the consultant) served as a technical assistance contractor in support of FEMA disaster recovery efforts following Hurricane Katrina. In this role, ████████ (the consultant) prepared requests for PA funds on behalf of applicants that included, among other things, damage descriptions, estimates of the cost to repair damage and estimates of the cost to replace structures."[35]

"The settlement resolves allegations that an ████████ (consultant's) project officer deployed to Louisiana for the Hurricane Katrina recovery effort submitted to FEMA fraudulent requests for disaster assistance funds for several educational facilities in New Orleans, which resulted in certain applicants receiving PA funds in excess of what FEMA rules permitted, including in some cases because the facility was entitled only to repair rather than replacement costs. These facilities included the gymnasium, student center and electrical grid at Xavier University of Louisiana and a cafeteria building at the Roman Catholic Archdiocese of New Orleans' St. Raphael the Archangel School. According to the allegations in the government's complaint, ███████ (the consultant's) supervisors reviewed and did not correct disaster assistance applications that included materially false design, damage and replacement eligibility descriptions."[36]

"The settlement with ██████ (the consultant) resolves claims brought in a lawsuit filed under the qui tam or whistleblower provisions of the False Claims Act, which permit private parties to file suit on behalf of the United States for false claims and share in a portion of the government's recovery. The United States may intervene in the action, as it did in part in this case. The lawsuit is captioned United States ex rel. Robert Romero v. ███████, Inc (the consultant)., et al., No. 16-cv-15092 (E.D. La.). As part of the settlement with ██████ (the consultant), the whistleblower, Robert Romero, will receive more than $2.4 million."[37]

"The United States has now recovered nearly $25 million in connection with the disaster assistance applications prepared by ██████ (the consultant). The United States previously settled with Xavier University of Louisiana and the Roman Catholic Archdiocese of New Orleans with respect to their alleged role in the submission of the false certifications for FEMA funding prepared by ████████ (the consultant)."[38]

Closing Thought on Fraud

Disasters cause millions upon millions of dollars in damages. But disasters also make untold millions of Federal tax dollars available to the affected cities, counties, special districts, and private non-profits for their recovery.

But all this money, apparently flowing freely from Washinton, D.C., brings with it temptations which only the honest can resist. The fraudsters and grifters will either arrive on the next bus into town or they already live in town, and they see the disaster as a chance to make a once-in-a-lifetime score. Some will seek to re-victimize the survivors and take what money the survivors may have. Others will seek to defraud the local governments and, by extension, the Federal government.

Beware: along with so many wonderful people and organizations arriving to help, there will also be those seeking to unjustly and cruelly benefit from so much suffering.

Notes

1 https://www.wvsao.gov/SpecialInvestigation/Default
2 https://atlantablackstar.com/2023/10/17/houston-power-couple-sentenced-to-a-combined-35-years-in-federal-workmans-comp-fraud-scheme/
3 https://www.oig.dhs.gov/sites/default/files/assets/pr/OIGpr_092509.pdf
4 Ibid.
5 Ibid.
6 Ibid.
7 https://www.justice.gov/usao-sdny/pr/manhattan-us-attorney-announces-53-million-proposed-settlement-lawsuit-against-new-york
8 https://www.oig.dhs.gov/news/press-releases/2019/02202019/manhattan-us-attorney-announces-53-million-proposed-settlement-lawsuit-against-new-york-city-fraudulently-obtaining
9 Ibid.
10 Ibid.
11 Ibid.
12 https://www.oig.dhs.gov/news/press-releases/2019/08022019/two-maryland-men-facing-federal-indictment-their-roles-scheme-allegedly-stole-government-benefits-including-more

13 Ibid.
14 Ibid.
15 Ibid.
16 Ibid.
17 https://www.justice.gov/usao-ndfl/pr/lynn-haven-mayor-and-city-attorney-indicted-corruption-and-fraud-charges-stemming
18 Ibid.
19 Ibid.
20 Ibid.
21 Ibid.
22 Ibid.
23 Ibid.
24 https://www.mypanhandle.com/news/lynn-haven-corruption-case/two-sentenced-to-prison-in-lynn-haven-corruption-case/
25 Ibid.
26 Ibid.
27 Ibid.
28 Ibid.
29 https://www.fema.gov/appeal/emergency-response
30 Ibid.
31 Ibid.
32 https://www.justice.gov/opa/pr/aecom-pay-118-million-resolve-false-claims-act-allegations-connection-hurricane-disaster
33 Ibid.
34 Ibid.
35 Ibid.
36 Ibid.
37 Ibid.
38 Ibid.

40 Audits

"We basically had a real-time audit by Arthur Andersen ongoing, all the time."
Kenneth Lay, former Chairman and CEO of Enron[1]

Like few other words in the English language, the word "audit" can instill fear and loathing in the stoutest and kindest of hearts. For those readers who are not financial mavens, an "audit" can take on many different forms, and the audit may come from a variety of sources.

First, there is the Federally required "single audit." "The Single Audit Act requires an annual audit of non-Federal entities, including Tribes, which expend $750,000 or more of Federal Financial Assistance in a fiscal year. The Single Audit must be performed by an independent auditor and the reporting package (which includes the audit report) must be submitted to the Federal Audit Clearinghouse within 30 days after your organization receives the audit report or 9 months from your organization's fiscal year end."[2]

"The Single Audit is a tool to help program and Tribal management monitor Federal program activities. A Single Audit includes an audit of both your organization's financial statements and compliance with Federal award requirements for those programs identified as "major programs" (based on application of the risk-based approach and criteria outlined in 2 CFR § 200.518 and 200.519) for the audit. Through the audit process the auditors determine whether your organization's financial statements fairly present the financial position of the organization and whether they are presented in accordance with Generally Accepted Accounting Principles (GAAP) or another comprehensive basis of accounting. Both the financial statement audit and the compliance audit provide information on the internal controls design appropriateness and operating effectiveness, which enables management to identify systematic weaknesses in a timely manner."[3]

The "single audit," however, is routine for many local agencies, and is not the one truly feared by recipients of FEMA's Public Assistance program; that is, an audit conducted by the Department of Homeland Security, Office of the Inspector General. But before we go on to those audits, we should detour first to the informal but continual "auditing process" that is the heart and soul of the Public Assistance program.

From the moment that the President signs a Federal major disaster declaration, FEMA is in an informal but very real and <u>active audit state</u>. Virtually nothing about the disaster and the claims of disaster damage are taken at face value by FEMA, nor should they be. Even the legal existence of a local agency is not taken for granted. For example, part of the submitted documentation should include the articles of incorporation of a local government agency, or its charter by the state. Private non-profit organizations also must prove their very existence as part of the qualification process for being eligible to receive Public Assistance funds for response, repairs, and recovery.

DOI: 10.4324/9781003487869-46

Audits in general are looking for different things. Some audits are <u>financial</u> and look at the appropriate use of funds; some audits are <u>performance-based</u> and look at how the local agency completed the projects for which it was funded; and some audits are <u>compliance-related</u>, i.e., did the local agency meet the requirements of 2 CFR, Part 200 or other Federal requirements? Some audits may look at one, two, or all three of these issues in the same audit.

State financial authorities may also conduct audits when there are indications that things may not be as they seem, or merely for routine checking.

What Is FEMA Looking for on a Routine (Non-Formal-Audit) Basis?

The Application Process

Has the local agency or private non-profit filed the necessary documents to notify FEMA that they will apply for Public Assistance?

Verification of Eligibility

Has the local agency filed the necessary documents that prove that it is a legal local government or private non-profit entity?

Eligibility Determination

Are the facilities and the work which have been requested otherwise eligible?

Documentation Requirements

Has the agency provided all the necessary documentation regarding the cause and existence of the damage or emergency response work done?

Documentation Review

With all the information provided by the local agency, is everything in order?

Verification of Information

Are all the documents which require signatures properly signed and dated?

Compliance with Regulations

Has the local agency fully complied with Title 2 of the Code of Federal Regulations, and completely addressed all issues regarding environmental and historical compliance?

Fraud Detection

Does all the information provided present a complete picture of the facts, and are there any "loose ends" which might indicate otherwise?

On-site Inspections

During any on-site inspections, did the inspection confirm or contradict the documentation provided by the local agency?

Record-Keeping

Has the local agency retained all the Project Worksheet files, including all procurement-related documentation?

Consequences of Failed Audits

The consequences of audits can be chilling . . . or worse. FEMA and or the DHS-OIG auditors can recommend deobligation of all or part of the funds approved for a Project Worksheet. In extreme cases, the penalties may include deobligation of an entire series of Project Worksheets, as we have seen for DAC or Direct Administrative Costs, and failures to comply with 2 CFR, Part 200.

In the most extreme cases, the DHS-OIG auditors may refer individual cases to the Department of Justice for Federal prosecution for fraud. And as we saw in the previous chapter, that is not an idle threat.

Some Quasi-Good News

First, when the DHS-OIG auditors prepare an audit with adverse findings, this is the auditor's recommendation of a particular course of action, generally to deobligate some or all the Federal funding audited. FEMA does not have to accept the auditor's finding and enforce a particular finding. FEMA has the discretion to enforce or not or take other appropriate action as FEMA determines is warranted. The following case illustrates this.

"The Imperial Irrigation District is a countywide 'special district' established in 1911 under California's Irrigation District Act. Although the District is a local government, a board of directors manages operations as a 'public agency,' relying primarily on non-tax revenue such as user charges. The District provides water for agricultural and municipal use and is a source of energy for residential, commercial, and industrial use. With facilities such as the All- American Canal, the District provides water and energy to an area of approximately 1,658 square miles, including approximately 521,800 acres of farmland. On April 4, 2010, a magnitude 7.2 earthquake, centered 29 miles southwest of Mexicali, Mexico, causing widespread damage throughout Imperial County, California, and to the District's facilities at All-American Canal. Specifically, the earthquake damaged the canal's embankments; concrete linings and structures; drain embankments; and gates, pipes, and roads."[4]

Results of Audit

"The District did not always account for and expend FEMA grant funds according to Federal regulations and FEMA guidelines. The District awarded contracts totaling $3.6 million without taking the required affirmative steps to ensure the use of small and minority firms, women's business enterprises, and labor surplus area firms when possible. As a result, FEMA has no assurance that these types of firms had opportunities to bid on Federal work as Congress intended. The District's claim also included $45,408 of ineligible contract costs and $1,473 of unsupported equipment costs. Therefore . . . FEMA should disallow \$3.6 million of ineligible and unsupported costs. FEMA should also deobligate \$2.5 million from four large projects and put those funds to better use because the District completed those projects and no longer needs those funds."[5]

For those not familiar with Imperial County, CA, it is the southeasternmost county in the state and borders Arizona to the East and Mexico to the South. The population is approximately 80% Hispanic or Latino. Therefore, many of the businesses located in the county are by definition minority businesses. In repairing the damage the earthquake caused to the water and wastewater systems, the agency predominantly contracted with minority-owned businesses. However, the agency did not have a written and adopted policy stating that it would comply with 2 CFR, Part 200, particularly Section 200.321, Contracting with small and minority businesses, women's business enterprises, and labor surplus area firms.

My colleague at Imperial Irrigation District told me that only two of the contractors hired by the district were from outside the county, and they had special engineering expertise not available in-county.

Following the audit, FEMA determined that the district had in fact complied with 2 CFR, §200.321 and FEMA waived that issue because of substantial compliance, even without the written policy in place. However, the district could have saved itself from this adverse audit finding and the resulting staff work to dig out from under this mess if they had previously adopted such a policy.

So, in some cases, an adverse audit finding is not necessarily a fatal wound, but it is certainly professionally embarrassing and a serious drag on staff time to refute the finding. However, in many other cases, FEMA will concur with the audit findings, and deobligate, in whole or in part, the Project Worksheet(s) funds.

Yet More Audit Semi-Good News

Neither every applicant nor every Project Worksheet is audited by the DHS-OIG auditors. In fact, the last audit of a local government agency posted on the Office of the Inspector General's website was in September of 2020. Since then, the OIG has focused its efforts on auditing various aspects of FEMA and how it operates. The DHS-OIG is also charged with auditing all the agencies falling under the Department of Homeland Security, i.e., CBP, ICE, TSA, USCG, etc. This of course could all turn on a dime, particularly when there is another catastrophic disaster on the scale of Hurricane Katrina or a similar-sized event. The very real threat of an audit is always, as Tom Clancy once said, a "clear and present danger."

The Answers to the Test

For several years, the DHS-OIG auditors released an annual "Capping Report," which was a summary of the previous Federal fiscal year's audits of local agencies. However, it has been some years since these reports have been posted on the DHS-OIG website. The good news is that despite the fact that these reports seem to have vanished, those still available on the DHS-OIG webpage are still generally good. These reports are still tantamount to the answer sheet for a multimillion-dollar test. If the local agency avoids these findings, they may consider themselves well on the way to a successful disaster cost recovery effort.

Where Do Audits Come From?

In almost every class that I teach, this question comes up: "Who decides whom to audit?"

This is a great question, and it has many different answers. A disgruntled employee or a contractor who didn't get a job they bid on may drop a dime on the Audit Hotline at DHS. In one extreme case, the local agency auditor/controller called and requested that their own agency be audited because the director of public works insisted on doing things (incorrectly) their way, and they needed to get that individual's attention.

Also, the famous Depression-era bank robber Willie Sutton phrased it nicely: "I rob banks because that's where the money is." This is sometimes the impetus for a Federal audit: when a local agency, especially one that may not be terribly sophisticated in high finance, receives a very large amount of FEMA funding, the auditors will swoop in to examine the books.

So, there is no knowing from whence an audit may spring, and therefore the best audit defense is to be prepared with excellent documentation. It is in the auditor's job description to find our mistakes. We just want them to be of a minor and technical nature, not of the catastrophic variety.

Notes

1 Enron was one of the largest corporate frauds ever inflicted on the U.S.
2 https://oig.hhs.gov/reports-and-publications/featured-topics/ihs/training/understanding-single-audits/content/#/
3 Ibid.
4 DHS-OIG Audit 15–35-D: FEMA Should Recover $6.2 Million of Ineligible and Unused Grant Funds Awarded to the Imperial Irrigation District, California, February 13, 2015, pp. 1–2.
5 Ibid, p. 2.

41 Appeals

Figure 41.1 Depiction of money down the drain from mis-guided appeals.

How Badly Can an Appeal Go?

"The University of Texas Medical Branch (Applicant) owns and maintains a healthcare, research, and educational campus consisting of over 100 inter-related facilities in Galveston, Texas. On August 1, 2007, before the declared event, the Applicant entered into a non-exclusive disaster restoration and recovery services contract (Contract) with a third party vendor. The contracted services included project management, water damage recovery, moisture control, heating, ventilating and air conditioning decontamination and cleaning, document and equipment recovery, and other remediation services."[1]

"On September 12 and 13, 2008, storm surge and flooding from Hurricane Ike inundated the basements and first levels of many buildings across the Applicant's campus. In response, the

DOI: 10.4324/9781003487869-47

Applicant activated the Contract and extensive emergency protective measures were performed. [2] FEMA prepared Project Worksheet (PW) 435 to provide Public Assistance (PA) funding for the cost of this work. The Applicant completed the emergency protective measures on December 31, 2009,[3] and FEMA obligated funding for $102,890,992.00 in eligible costs."[2]

"In July 2011, the Texas Department of Public Safety, Division of Emergency Management (Grantee) audited PW 435 reimbursement requests and identified a cost overrun in the amount of $5,403,295.70. FEMA awarded funding for this additional amount, increasing total eligible PA costs to $108,294,287.70. This left a difference of $14,835,080.30 between the $123,129,368.00 actual costs incurred by the Applicant and the amount awarded. The Applicant's subsequent cost analysis found the deficiency to be $12,220,830.92, comprised of $3,408,379.16 for contracted work and $8,812,451.76 for force account labor compensatory time.[4] The contract work was for rented generator and related equipment expenses, and for fuel and water delivery costs."[3]

First Appeal

"The Applicant submitted its first appeal in a letter to the Grantee on January 18, 2012, appealing the denial of costs totaling $12,220,830.92."[4]

"On June 18, 2014, the RA issued a first appeal decision and determined that the Applicant acted prudently during the initial procurement and rental of the generators. However, after an initial period, the Applicant had ample opportunity to rent the generators at a lower monthly rate rather than more costly daily ones and did not do so. The RA determined that the Applicant's failure to pursue the lower rates was not prudent. Consequently, the RA performed a cost reasonableness analysis ***and further reduced eligible funding by $1,351,167.00*** to account for the monthly versus daily rate differential."[5]

This was bad, and then it got even worse.

"During adjudication of the Applicant's second appeal, FEMA identified new issues related to procurement that were not identified by the region on first appeal. For purposes of fundamental fairness and to facilitate an Applicant's ability to appeal a determination, potentially new issues identified on second appeal are remanded to the region to ensure applicants receive two levels of appeal.[24] Accordingly, this appeal is remanded to Region VI to consider the procurement issues below."[6]

This is not a one-time occurrence. In reviewing hundreds of cases for the book, I found several appeals with a similar situation. The local agency files a first appeal and is denied. The local agency then files a second appeal, and this time in addition to losing the issues first appealed, the second appeal results in even further reductions of funding. And sometimes these further reductions in funding are not just for the appeals case at hand, but for many or even all of the local agency's previously approved Project Worksheets.

Appeals in General

Appealing a partial deobligation or outright denial of funding is a risky proposition at best. First appeals are only successful 50% of the time, and second appeals are only successful in one out of three cases.

The dice are further loaded with the risk that perhaps more or even all of the Project Worksheet funding may be denied upon further review at FEMA, if the denial is not total to begin with.

For filing two appeals, the statistical chances of success are 1 in 6. Therefore, filing an appeal should not be a preordained course of action.

I attribute much of this very low success rate to the fact that applicants simply do not understand the Public Assistance process and its many nuances to begin with.

A great many of the second appeals cases which I have read are dead-bang losers from the very beginning, and yet time after time, agencies file appeals with great hope but little chance of success.

Once the decision is made to file the appeal, agency staff often approach the process with the same lack of process knowledge and lack of thorough preparation that got them denied in the first place.

In my training programs, the students do an exercise to create a memo to their elected officials explaining a denial of FEMA funding. As a starting point, they work from a list of over 30 different reasons which I have culled from audits and appeals which ostensibly explain the denial. However, not one of these statements in defense of the applicant holds any water. Even when the local agency has been misinformed by the respective state emergency management agency staff and/or FEMA staff, as is frequently alleged in appeals rebuttals, it is ultimately the sole responsibility of the applicant's staff to know the regulations and to properly file the appeal.

Another deadly failing of an applicant's staff is failure to timely and thoroughly respond to FEMA's Requests for Information (RFI). In reading appeals case after appeals case, applicants fail to submit the requested information. I can surmise that in many cases, information is not provided simply because the documentation does not exist, or it only partially exists, and what does exist is insufficient to prove the applicant's case.

FEMA, by regulation, has 90 days to respond to appeals. However, this regulation is honored much more often in the breach than in the observance. In part, I attribute this slow response time to the fact that FEMA must respond to all appeals, even when the appeal is a complete waste of the applicant's time and money, because the applicant doesn't really understand what is happening.

An important consideration should pop up anytime the applicant is considering filing an appeal with FEMA. The appeal case must be worth the effort involved, or it's like hauling snow up the mountain in the dead of winter. One appeal I read began at $1,008 and was subsequently reduced by the applicant to $924. This amount of money, even if fully recovered, might not begin to cover the staff time, and certainly would not begin to cover the legal fees, if any, involved in pursuing the appeal.

A couple of years ago, a colleague called me to discuss the possibility of filing an appeal. My first question was: "How much money are we talking about?" My colleague replied that the amount was $5,000. I recommended that the agency simply walk away. The staff time and legal fees would be more than the amount in question, even with a 100% chance of success. But with the current combined denial rates for first and second appeals hovering around 83%, what I call (perhaps inaccurately) the real net present value of the appeal was closer to $850. It later turned out that the appeal would have most likely been denied on a finding of duplicate funding because this was a local road which at the city's prior request (some years previously) had been mapped as a Federal Aid Road and therefore was ineligible.

Stafford Act: Like for Like

It has never been the Stafford Act's nor FEMA's intention to improve a community to something better than what it was prior to the disaster. And in fact, as has been pointed out, there are some disaster-related costs that are simply ineligible for FEMA financial assistance, or in some cases, depending on the case specifics, a cost may or may not be eligible.

This said, care and caution must be applied when researching cases in the Appeals Database. Here are two different appeals cases, one of which was a winner, and the other a loser.

BIMA and Art Scroll Library Appeals Case

"The Cedar Fire started on October 25, 2003, and swept through San Diego County, California, destroying the Chabad Hebrew Academy (Academy). The Academy is an eligible private non profit accredited educational facility, which serves 320 students from preschool through 8th grade. The Academy is appealing the ineligible determination for the replacement of a Bima (platform) and an Art Scroll library in the amount of $69,000. FEMA originally denied funding for PW 836 based on the function of the building the items were housed in as a Temple. The Academy submitted its first appeal for $550,000. The State supported funding $18,172 for damages to the non-religious contents of the Temple, and provided a table showing the multipurpose uses of the Temple by hours per day, demonstrating that the Temple was used for non-religious purposes over 90 percent of the time. FEMA determined that the Temple was used for primarily educational purposes, in accordance with Recovery Policy 9521.3, Private Nonprofit Facility (PNP) Eligibility, and approved $12,943.59 ($14,076 less $1,132.41 in anticipated insurance proceeds), for non-religious educational equipment. The Academy submitted a second appeal requesting reconsideration of the Bima and Art Scroll library in the amount of $69,000. Additional information provided by the Academy explained that Bima was used primarily for non-religious purposes similar to the overall uses of the Temple building and that the Art Scroll library was a collection of books, while Jewish in theme, were educational in nature and consistent with a library reference collection."[7] In this case, FEMA found that these artifacts were indeed educational materials and therefore eligible.

Tanya Books Appeals Case

"The Cedar Fire started on October 25, 2003, and swept through San Diego County, California, destroying the Chabad Hebrew Academy (Academy). The Academy is an eligible private non profit, accredited educational facility, which serves 320 students from preschool through 8th grade. FEMA initially denied $2,550,000 in funding for 30,000 Tanya books (120 sets with each set containing 250 books) because of their use as a religious teaching tool. The Academy's first appeal asserted that the books were not used for primarily religious purposes, but rather for 'non-religious, educational, literary, and cultural purposes.' FEMA denied the Academy's first appeal on October 28, 2004, stating that 'the large number of copies indicated that the books were for religious education, not research and education by the public.' The Academy submitted a second appeal in which the Academy stated that the Tanya books were stored by the main library, rather than kept in the main library collection itself and not directly accessed by the students. Instead they were distributed to external individuals and institutions."[8]

The case continues: "The Tanya books were stored at the school and distributed as part of the mission of the Friends of Chabad Lubavitch, San Diego, California, and not for the education of the students at the school. While the Academy may be a subsidiary of the Friends of Chabad Lubavitch, San Diego, California, Public Assistance Program funding is intended for restoring the function of the Academy, not the Friends of Chabad umbrella organization. Items that are unrelated to the education of the students at the Academy are not eligible for reimbursement."[9]

So we have two appeals cases out of the same event, the Cedar Fire, from the same institution, and yet the results based upon the differing facts in each case resulted in eligibility for one case but not the other.

It is also very important to note that there is a separate Appeals Database for Hazard Mitigation Issues.

Mitigation Appeals Case Study

"The Missouri State Emergency Management Agency (SEMA) submitted an application on behalf of Drury University for the construction of a community safe room. The terms of the HMGP grant approval noted that use of the funds were permitted for design activities and that construction activities were not permitted until FEMA had approved the detailed design. Construction was initiated prior to design approval, and the Grantee was not provided by FEMA the notice to proceed. FEMA Region VII sent a Termination notice and determined that construction costs were ineligible."[10]

Reason for Denial

"Region VII based the denial of the 1st appeal on the fact that the construction had been initiated prior to design approval by FEMA per terms of the grant and that the construction costs were not eligible."[11]

Editorial: The Bottom Line on Appeals

After reading and annotating over 500 appeals cases for this book, it is my considered opinion that most appeals are a waste of time and money for the local agency. In some cases where the denial or deobligation is substantial, say over $50,000 to $250,000, then depending on the size and budget of the local agency, it may be worthwhile to pursue an appeal. But in many cases, filing an appeal may be more of an emotional and political decision than a well-reasoned and financially viable one.

I mention to clients that filing an appeal may be like moving from your first t-ball game to the World Series playoff game in a single heartbeat. I further suggest that if the appeal is truly worthwhile, the agency retain the services of a reputable and well-established consultant to assist them in the pursuit of the appeal. And the cost of hiring outside experienced help adds another variable to the equation for determining the true cost and true value of filing the appeal. In my somewhat-limited experience, it appears that many consultants will not (if not previously on contract) take on an appeals case for much less than $100,000. Therefore, to throw $100,000 in consultant fees for an appeal which only has a total value of $100,000 is an exercise in futility. And there's always the risk that FEMA will, upon second reading, find other faults in the Project Worksheet, or as is often the case, procurement errors which may void out not only the current appeal, but also other Project Worksheets.

In filing an appeal, the agency will likely have to do much more work to prosecute the appeal than they would have done if the proper documentation was presented on the initial Project Worksheet application.

It is also important to understand that if a local agency requests their disaster cost recovery consultant to file an appeal, it will be done, even, in many cases where there is little or no chance of prevailing on the appeal. The only sure winner in this scenario is the consultant who will be paid whether or not the appeal is ultimately successful.

Appeals Questions

The following is a list of questions which should be appropriately asked and answered before making the decision to file an appeal.

1) Is the denial of eligibility worth the time and expense of filing an appeal?
2) If so, which other projects and issues will lie fallow due to the pursuit of this appeal?

3) Do we have the in-house experienced resources for filing and pursuing the appeal?

4) If we do not have the in-house expertise necessary, is the success of the appeal worth the money it will cost us for outside expert help?

5) Are our records complete enough to substantiate our appeal position?

6) Have we done preliminary appeal research in FEMA's Appeals Database to understand the real issues?

7) If so, what have the relevant appeals in the Appeals Database shown regarding our case, and other similar cases?

8) For filing the appeal, do we like the statistical odds of 1 chance in 6 of success?

Let Hard-Nosed Financial Logic Prevail

Filing an appeal is sometimes an angry, emotional, gut-wrenching response from a local agency that has been truly hammered by a disaster and any resulting complications with FEMA. Certainly, in some of the appeals cases I have read, this would seem to be the case. This is a reprise of a case we saw earlier in the book, but one which supports my point.

"During the adjudication process, the Regional Administrator (RA) sent a Final Request for Information (RFI) to the Applicant. The Final RFI advised the Applicant that the Administrative Record did not validate reimbursement for incurred costs. The Final RFI made detailed requests for multiple, specific pieces of information, including but not limited to:

- Payroll information for all the Applicant's employees involved in the disaster work.
- Individual name, job title, and function to include the day the work was performed.
- Equipment logs and usage records, hourly pay rates and equipment rates, cost of materials purchased.
- Documentation of the City of Sweetwater's procurement process for this project.
- The request for proposal outlining the scope of work for each site.
- Any Mutual Aid agreements to which the Applicant may have been a party.

The Applicant responded to the Final RFI by sending FEMA a USB flash drive containing over 12,000 separate files.
On January 13, 2016, the RA issued a decision denying the Applicant's appeal. The RA determined that the Applicant did not adequately document costs incurred for the projects. The Applicant's Final RFI response, provided on electronic media, did not contain a cover letter or any indication as to how the files document the eligible work performed or costs incurred for multiple projects. In upholding the deobligation, the RA found that the information provided did not assist FEMA in analyzing the 29 appealed PWs."[12] (Emphasis Added)

Once again, the local agency poked the bear with a sharp stick. Or, to quote Tommy Lee Jones in the original "Men in Black": "No, ma'am. We at the FBI (*The Federal Government*) do not have a sense of humor we're aware of."

More Appeal Pitfalls

Another frankly rare issue occurs often enough to mention here. This is when the local agency timely files its appeal with the state emergency management agency, and there it sits indefinitely; if and when it is filed with FEMA, it is rejected as a late filing. This is an issue over which the local agency has little control, except to be a thorn in the side of the state office of emergency management to ensure that the appeal is forwarded to FEMA on time.

"This is in response to a letter from your office dated May 17, 2021, which transmitted the referenced second appeal on behalf of Martin County Drainage Authority (Applicant). The Applicant is appealing the U.S. Department of Homeland Security's Federal Emergency Management Agency's (FEMA) denial of $686,600.00 in costs pertaining to additional repairs and proposed mitigation to repair the Judicial County Ditch."[13]

"Section 423(a) of the Stafford Act provides that any decision regarding eligibility for assistance may be appealed within 60 days after the date on which the applicant is notified of the award or denial of assistance. Implementing this provision, Title 44 of the Code of Federal Regulations, Section 206.206(c), requires that applicants must file appeals within 60 days after receipt of a notice of the action that is being appealed. Grantees must then review and forward appeals within 60 days after receipt of the appeal from the applicant."[14]

"According to the Administrative Record, the Applicant filed its first appeal on July 30, 2020. However, the Minnesota Division of Homeland Security and Emergency Management did not transmit the appeal until September 30, 2020. This was after the 60-day timeframe required by FEMA's regulations, making the first appeal untimely. Therefore, this appeal is denied."[15]

Deadlines Really Are Dead Lines

"This is in response to a letter from your office dated November 12, 2019, which transmitted the referenced second appeal on behalf of the City of Houston (Applicant). The Applicant is appealing the Department of Homeland Security's Federal Emergency Management Agency's (FEMA) decision to uphold the deobligation of $70,082.31, based on an untimely first appeal."[16]

"Section 423(a) of the Stafford Act provides that any decision regarding eligibility for assistance may be appealed within 60 days after the date on which the applicant is notified of the award or denial of assistance. Implementing this provision, Title 44 of the Code of Federal Regulations, section 206.206(c), requires that applicants must file appeals within 60 days after receipt of a notice of the action that is being appealed."[17]

"According to the administrative record, the Applicant received notice of FEMA's lump sum deobligation by October 30, 2018. However, it did not submit its first appeal until it transmitted a letter dated January 31, 2019. *(More than 2 years later.)* In its second appeal, the Applicant states it could not respond timely because it needed additional information from the Texas Division of Emergency Management (Grantee) before it could prepare an appeal response. Notwithstanding this assertion, since the Applicant submitted its first appeal after the 60-day timeframe required by FEMA's regulations, it is untimely. Consequently, because the Applicant's appeal rights lapsed, the protections of Stafford Act section 705(c) do not apply. For these reasons, this appeal is denied."[18] (Emphasis Added)

It would appear that in this case, the city should have filed an appeal within the 60-day window and fully anticipated that FEMA would issue a Request for Information (RFI). This would have preserved the appeal rights and gained some additional time, as FEMA seldom can or does act on appeals within the 90-day timeframe specified in regulations. This is somewhat akin to the practice in pre-computerized banking of "floating" checks, knowing that the bank needed several days to physically transport and process the check.

Appeals and Time Extensions

For cases under appeal, the POP or "Period of Performance" timeclock keeps running and requires time extensions as necessary. FEMA does not automatically extend the timelines for any project. For every approved Project Worksheet running behind schedule, the local agency must file timely requests through the state for time extensions. The nominal time for emergency work is 6 months, and the time for completion of permanent work projects is 18 months. Requesting a first-time extension is normally a routine matter, and a first-time extension may be granted by the state. Subsequent time extensions must be approved by FEMA. Time extension requests are not appeals.

Based upon my reading of these hundreds of appeals cases, filing an appeal for a missed deadline has an almost-100% chance of denial. Typically, in making a denial for a missed deadline, FEMA will not even address any of the substantive issues it might have considered had the appeal been timely filed.

The Civilian Board of Contract Appeals (CBCA)

Another option exists for limited cases where the appeals process is proving unsatisfactory for the local agency in the form of the Civilian Board of Contract Appeals.

Eligibility for Arbitration

"To be eligible for arbitration, a PA (Public Assistance) applicant's request must meet all three of the following conditions:

1. The dispute arises from a disaster declared after January 1, 2016; and
2. The disputed amount exceeds $500,000 (or $100,000 if the applicant is in a 'rural area,' defined as having a population of less than 200,000 living outside an urbanized area); and
3. The applicant filed a first-level appeal with FEMA within the timeframes established in 44 C.F.R. § 206.206 and FEMA denied the first appeal, or has not provided a first appeal decision within 180 calendar days of receiving the first appeal submission."[19]

Request for Arbitration (RFA) Deadlines

"If a PA applicant wishes to arbitrate a dispute, it must file a Request for Arbitration (RFA) within 60 calendar days from the date of the Regional Administrator's first appeal decision. Alternatively, if FEMA does not issue a first-level appeal decision within 180 calendar days of the first appeal's receipt, the applicant may withdraw the first-level appeal and file the RFA within 30 calendar days of withdrawal."[20]

The Arbitration Process

"The CBCA is the forum in which PA arbitrations are conducted. CBCA regulations at 48 C.F.R. §§ 6106.601–6106.613 detail the CBCA arbitration process. Applicants must follow these procedures, which include emailing the RFA simultaneously to:

- the CBCA at cbca.efile@cbca.gov;
- the Recipient; and
- the applicable FEMA Regional Administrator.

The request must include:

- a written statement specifying the amount in dispute;
- all documentation supporting the position of the applicant;

- the disaster number; and
- the name and address of the applicant's authorized representative or counsel."[21] (Emphasis Added)

Arbitration and Second Appeals

"If the applicant does request an appeal or arbitration within the regulatory timeframes, the applicant no longer has a right to appeal or arbitrate. If an Applicant submits a request for arbitration, it may not submit a second appeal for the same matter. Similarly, if an Applicant submits a second appeal, it may not withdraw the second appeal to request arbitration instead."[22]

Costs

"The CBCA arbitrates at no cost to the parties. Other expenses, including attorney's fees, representative fees, copying costs, costs associated with attending any hearing, or any other fees not listed in this paragraph will be paid by each party incurring such costs."[23]

Finality of Decision

"A majority decision from the CBCA panel serves as a final decision and is binding on all parties. Final decisions are not subject to further administrative review."[24]

When filing a case with the Civilian Board of Contract Appeals, it is highly recommended that the local agency hires experienced counsel to guide the agency through the process.

The Bottom Line on Appeals and Arbitration

The Public Assistance process will not always go in favor of the local government agency or private non-profit organization. For these adverse situations, the local agency has the right to make a first appeal to their respective FEMA region. If the first appeal fails, which happens statistically in one out of every two cases, then the local agency may file a second appeal, which is then forwarded to FEMA Headquarters for review. If the second appeal fails, that's it and there are no further appeals available.

However, in limited cases, the local agency may opt to file a request for arbitration with the Civilian Board of Contract Appeals, whose decision is final.

There may be more cases, but I have only found one single instance where the private non-profit following denial of their second appeal filed a motion with a Federal District Court on the issues.

"In 2008, severe storms hit Indiana. Columbus Hospital sustained significant damage. President Bush authorized FEMA assistance through disaster grants under the Stafford Act, 42 U.S.C. 5121–5206. The state agreed to be the grantee for all grant assistance, with the exception of assistance to individuals and households. FEMA reserved the right to recover assistance funds if they were spent inappropriately or distributed through error, misrepresentation, or fraud. Columbus apparently submitted its request directly to FEMA, instead of through the state. FEMA approved Columbus projects, totaling approximately $94 million. Funds were transmitted to Columbus through the state. In 2013, the DHS Inspector General issued an audit report finding that Columbus had committed procurement violations and recommended that FEMA recover $10.9 million. FEMA reduced that amount to $9,612,831.19 and denied Columbus's appeal. Columbus did not seek judicial review. FEMA recovered the disputed costs from Columbus in 2014."[25]

"In 2018, Columbus filed suit, alleging four counts of contract breach and illegal exaction. The Claims Court dismissed Columbus's illegal exaction claim, holding that Columbus did not have a property interest in the disputed funds and that FEMA's appeal process protected Columbus's rights to due process, and dismissed Columbus's contract-based claims, finding that Columbus had no rights against FEMA under that contract or otherwise. The Seventh Circuit affirmed the dismissal of the illegal exaction and express and implied contract claims. The court vacated the dismissal of the third-party beneficiary contract claim."[26]

Sometimes, enough is enough. Disasters are awful events, and sometimes there is little equity and fairness in them. Best to get on with life as best we can. That said, going forward, local agencies and private non-profits once bitten should then look internally to see what may be done prospectively to eliminate the risk of FEMA denials and take steps to improve their disaster cost recovery processes for future successes as may be needed.

Notes

1 https://www.fema.gov/appeal/reasonable-costs-procurement
2 Ibid.
3 Ibid.
4 Ibid.
5 Ibid.
6 Ibid.
7 https://www.fema.gov/appeal/bima-and-art-scroll-library
8 https://www.fema.gov/appeal/tanya-books
9 Ibid.
10 https://www.fema.gov/hmgp-appeals/1676/6-1st
11 Ibid.
12 https://www.fema.gov/appeal/appeal-timeliness-support-documentation-705c
13 https://www.fema.gov/appeal/appeals-13
14 Ibid.
15 Ibid.
16 https://www.fema.gov/appeal/appeal-timeliness-705c-6
17 Ibid.
18 Ibid.
19 https://www.fema.gov/sites/default/files/documents/fema-pa-arbitration-fact-sheet.pdf
20 Ibid.
21 Ibid.
22 Ibid.
23 Ibid.
24 Ibid.
25 https://law.justia.com/cases/federal/appellate-courts/cafc/20-1226/20-1226-2021-03-10.html
26 Ibid.

42 Close-outs

Figure 42.1 Depiction that the job is not done until the last of the paperwork is completed.

As we approach the final chapter of this book, I began additional research into the close-out process. Searching for the word "close-out" (also "close out" and "closeout") in the Appeals Database yields 501 cases, or nearly 21% of all appeals cases, which in one way or another present close-out issues. Small wonder. If the local agency or private non-profit cannot or does not know and follow the Federal regulations for the Public Assistance program, it should be no surprise that they also do not know how to properly close-out a Project Worksheet file.

It is important that the local agencies understand that disaster recovery, particularly disaster cost recovery, is a long-haul event. The Loma Prieta Earthquake in 1989 took 22 years to fully close. For many local agencies Hurricane Katrina remains open, as do hundreds of other disasters across the country.[1]

This will require very long-term and methodical recordkeeping to ensure that all the files required for Project Worksheet close-out are available when the close-out happens.

DOI: 10.4324/9781003487869-48

What's Involved with the Close-out Process?

The close-out process involves virtually everything that has been a part of the Public Assistance process from the very beginning. Specifically, the following areas and all the supporting documents are needed to finalize all aspects of the Project Worksheet:

- Check for documentation errors, and provide a comprehensive and precise record of all expenses for labor and materials used and all contracts, if any.
- Compliance and eligibility: the project must adhere to all FEMA guidelines and regulations.
- For cost reconciliation, the record must show a balance of actual costs with the estimated or approved costs.
- Audits and reviews may be conducted by FEMA to ensure that all costs and activities comply with their regulations.
- Are there any revisions or Project Worksheet versions which might have occurred after the initial submission of the worksheet?
- Communication and coordination are always important up to the last signature.
- Financial reconciliations must show a balance among the financial aspects, including reimbursements, expenditures, and any outstanding payments.
- Were there any regulatory or legal issues, particularly procurement, insurance, or environmental and historic considerations?

Close-out Information Is Critical to Maintaining Project Eligibility

This next case comes out of Texas. "During the incident period of September 7, 2008, through October 2, 2008, Hurricane Ike struck the State of Texas with high winds, severe storms, and flooding. Surfside Beach (Applicant) requested FEMA Public Assistance (PA) to repair its flood damaged roads and sewer system. FEMA prepared two Project Worksheets (PWs):

(1) PW 7032 to repair damaged roads with estimated costs of $112,870.88; and
(2) PW 12862 to repair the Applicant's sewer system with estimated costs of $107,582.57 and $1,312.00 in associated direct administrative costs."[2]

"In 2011, the Applicant submitted final cost information for both projects. From May through July 2022, the Texas Division of Emergency Management (Recipient) transmitted close-out documentation for both projects, submitting its certification of project completion and final accounting for each PW. The Recipient identified $4,199.47 in substantiated costs for PW 7032 and $11,122.44 for PW 12862, and requested close-out for both. FEMA reviewed the documentation and prepared amendments based on a finding for each PW that the Applicant had not provided documentation to support all the previously awarded costs. In August 2022, FEMA deobligated all previously awarded costs for PW 7032 $112,870.88, and $97,772.13 for PW 12862."[3] (Emphasis Added)

First Appeal

"On October 7, 2022, the Applicant submitted a first appeal of both projects, requesting reinstatement of $210,201.15, contending that FEMA did not conduct a review of all its documentation, and provided invoices, load tickets, and cancelled checks for consideration."[4]

"On May 4, 2023, the FEMA Region 6 Regional Administrator partially granted the appeal, finding that the Applicant provided documentation supporting $64,264.61 in costs for eligible work. FEMA also determined that the protections of Stafford Act section 705(c) did not apply because the Applicant did not provide adequate documentation to support its actual costs."[5]

Second Appeal

"The Applicant submitted a June 29, 2023 second appeal, requesting the reinstatement of $134,813.70 and restating its first appeal arguments."[6]

"Here, the Applicant seeks the reinstatement of the remaining deobligated project costs but does not provide additional information, explanation, or documentation that demonstrates the costs are either directly tied to the performance of eligible work, or the completion of an approved scope of work. The Applicant asserts that it has provided ample and adequate documentation, emphasizing statements from public officials attesting to the accuracy of its close-out cost claims while including previously submitted documentation. However, the Applicant does not show how the documents it submitted relate to the approved scopes of work, FEMA's cost estimates, or the Applicant's current claim. FEMA cannot rely on assertions that the costs are eligible; rather, supporting documentation is required, and the Applicant must explain how that documentation supports its claim."[7] (Emphasis Added)

"FEMA finds that the Applicant has not substantiated that the costs are directly tied to the performance of eligible work or that final costs are based on the actual documented cost of the completed approved scope of work. Consequently, FEMA properly corrected the project funding at close-out based on properly supported actual costs, which does not implicate a section 705(c) analysis. Therefore, this appeal is denied."[8]

Due to the lack of a full and complete set of project records, this agency lost nearly $135,000, and at this point, following a second appeal, there is no recourse to reworking the documentation.

Documentation Needed for Close-Out

This list may not be all-inclusive. Nonetheless, it shows how much and how varied the required documentation is. Some of the documents required are:

- "Summary of work performed.
- Summary of Expenditures
- Force account labor (time sheets, fringe benefits, etc.) Force account equipment (proof of ownership, hours used, operators' hours, etc.)
- Materials and supplies (invoices, inventory, proof of payment, disposition)
- Contract expenses
- Insurance documentation (full insurance policy and final Statement of Loss)
- Project-related correspondence (Alternate/Improved project approval, etc.)
- Contracting and Procurement documentation, if applicable (e.g., change orders, advertisements, bid tabulations, evaluation)
- *(Cost)* Under/Overrun Information
- Personnel pay policies, if applicable
- Applicable codes and standards
- Documentation required to demonstrate compliance with EHP conditions.
- Sampling results necessary to support claimed costs (e.g., invoices, time sheets, work orders, trip tickets, etc.)
- Mutual Aid agreements, if applicable
- Photos, if applicable"[9]

Record Retention and Close-outs

"From September 7 to October 2, 2008, Hurricane Ike struck Texas with high winds, heavy rains, and storm surge. FEMA prepared and obligated Project Worksheet (PW) 4321, awarding

$132,715.52 for force account labor (FAL) and force account equipment (FAE) associated with Category B emergency protective measures completed from September 13 to 26, 2008 to protect the Applicant's buildings from further damage. FEMA also included $1,312.00 in to-be-completed direct administrative costs (DAC) in the approved costs. FEMA noted in the PW that pursuant to Title 44 of the Code of Federal Regulations (C.F.R.) § 13.42, the Applicant must maintain work-related records for three years from closure and that all records relative to this PW were subject to examination and audit by FEMA and must reflect work related to disaster-specific costs."[10]

"The Applicant submitted a project completion and certification report (P4) on September 12, 2013, certifying all work and costs were eligible and all work was completed. On December 10, 2021, the Texas Division of Emergency Management (Recipient) submitted a Financial Compliance Review (FCR) for close-out to FEMA recommending FEMA deobligate all funding because the Applicant had not substantiated the costs. On January 11, 2022, the Recipient rescinded the FCR recommendations and instead recommended FEMA approve the FAL costs but deobligate the FAE (force account equipment) costs and the DAC (direct administrative costs). For the FAL (force account labor) costs, the Recipient stated that, although the Applicant was unable to provide a record of bank statements or copies of cancelled checks, the Applicant provided other documentation to support payment for the claimed FAL costs. Additionally, the Recipient stated the project was initially written at 99 percent completion and the final project amount is within the approved costs FEMA found to be reasonable at the time of project formulation. On April 7, 2022, FEMA issued a close-out letter deobligating all previously awarded project funding. FEMA stated that, in the absence of payroll support documentation, it could not determine whether the costs were reasonable or whether the Applicant had accomplished the purpose of the grant."[11]

"The Applicant also noted that the Recipient's delay in performing the FCR resulted in specific Applicant-banking records no longer being available. The Applicant stated that cancelled checks and bank records from 2008 were no longer available due to a change in bank ownership and a 2019 flood that destroyed the Applicant's copies of those documents. The Applicant stated it provided sufficient alternative documentation in the form of timesheets and payroll registers which included payroll names, employee numbers, pay periods, banking numbers, check numbers, check dates, and net payment amounts for each employee, along with Wage and Tax Statement (W-2) forms to substantiate the hourly labor amounts claimed. The Applicant provided a document retention policy, records of data shredding in 2019 and 2020 with notes on records destroyed by the 2019 flood, and electronic correspondence from the banking institution stating the records were no longer available."[12]

"In a September 26, 2022 decision, the FEMA Region 6 Regional Administrator denied the appeal, finding that the Applicant neither provided adequate documentation to support the claimed costs, nor demonstrated the work associated with the claimed FAL and FAE costs eliminated or lessened threats to lives, public health, and safety, or threats of additional damage to improved property. FEMA stated that standards for financial management pertain to all grant-related accounting records and source documentation, including FAL costs. FEMA also noted that applicants are required to retain project records for three years from the day the Recipient submits its final expenditure report. <u>FEMA stated that applicants are required to provide</u> physical evidence <u>to verify work was completed, therefore, the Applicant must support its accounting records through source documentation.</u>"[13] (Emphasis Added)

"<u>The Applicant acknowledged it did not have all the documentation requested due to a flood and change in bank ownership,</u> but nevertheless asserted the previously provided documentation supported its appeal. However, the Applicant has not explained how the documentation provided supports the costs in dispute. Here, the Applicant provided timesheets and payroll registers which included payroll names, employee numbers, pay periods, banking numbers, check numbers, check dates, and net payment amounts for each employee, along with W-2 forms to substantiate the hourly labor amounts claimed. However, the documentation the Applicant provided does not establish the date of work with activities performed and the equipment used for each activity with associated costs. The timesheets, payroll registers, and equipment logs contain generic descriptors of the work such as transporting and patrolling but contain no details on what type of work each employee performed. For instance, the entries do not describe the 'who, what, when, where, and why, and how much' for each item of disaster recovery work nor do they demonstrate how the actions eliminated or lessened threats to lives, public health and safety, or threats of additional damage to improved property. In addition, the Applicant's documentation shows that more than 90 percent of the Applicant's claimed FAL costs are for ineligible straight-time labor costs, rather than for overtime costs. Finally, similar to the FAL and FAE costs discussed above, due to missing documentation for the claimed DAC, the Applicant did not provide documentation that establishes those costs are tied to the performance of eligible work."[14] (Emphasis Added)

Thus, this appears to be another "the dog ate my homework" story. Although the local agency cannot prevent a change in bank ownership, at the completion of the work, it should have obtained copies of the required records and then maintained them in a locked, fireproof, flood-proof vault. Absent the required records, one cannot expect FEMA to do any different than what it did: deobligate the funding. The money lost on this one case, $132,715.52, would have bought a very nice vault, or paid for long-term record storage with a professional records storage firm.

So, in both cases, because of the lack of proper documentation, these two agencies lost more than a combined $260,000, despite all the good work that may have been done to return these two organizations to their pre-disaster conditions.

Hindsight is always 20/20, and in these cases we can clearly see the need for VERY strong records retention policies and procedures. This is important, because often once projects are completed the local agency is often in no hurry to get them properly closed out and begin the minimum three-year records retention period.

Small Projects Versus Large Projects at Close-out

Small projects, currently set at less than $1,037,000 per project (in Federal Fiscal Year 2023–24), are funded upon obligation by FEMA. Large Projects, on the other hand, are funded on a reimbursement basis predicated on the amount of work done in the previous billing cycle. As the local agency works on its approved small projects, there is no checking how well the agency is managing all aspects of the project, including all recordkeeping activities and procurement matters. Thus, it all comes to a head at close-out. Not only is one specific project endangered, but those issues that cut a wide swath in the process, i.e., procurement, may endanger every Project Worksheet. But of course no one knows this until the final paperwork is submitted and reviewed.

It is also a sad fact of life that the local agencies in many states cannot fully rely on their respective state offices of emergency management/services (OEM/OES) to give them accurate and complete guidance. This is proven repeatedly when the various state OEM/OES offices, acting in their role of Grantee (wherein the states administer the Public Assistance on behalf of FEMA) recommend an approval of certain Project Worksheets, only to have FEMA deny those recommendations.

In reviewing hundreds of appeals cases, it sometimes appears that the state, acting as the Grantee, will approve certain actions, if only to avoid angering the local agencies. In such cases, the state may come out smelling like a rose, while FEMA is then cast in the role of the bad guy.

Therefore, particularly with Small Projects, the local agency may be doing many things improperly, or not at all, and be blissfully unaware of the danger lurking in the dark. In the meantime, the local agency is moving forward, but the forward motion is an illusion, because they are floating on the Niagara River and Niagara Falls is just around the next bend in the river.

During close-out, there are many different and dangerous monsters under the bed, and they are quite real. One of those monsters is the specter of a unilateral change in the scope of work. In this case from Missouri, the local agency lost more than $275,000.

"From December 23, 2015, through January 9, 2016, severe storms, winds, and tornadoes caused widespread flooding throughout St. Louis County, Missouri. Metropolitan St. Louis Sewer District (Applicant) experienced a slope failure, which caused a channel collapse at the Dellridge Storm Channel (Facility). FEMA prepared Project Worksheet (PW) 573 to record the Applicant's request for costs to repair the Facility, including excavation and replacement of the concrete sides, chain link fence, and sod. The PW also included a Hazard Mitigation Proposal (HMP) for geotechnical shoring/soil stabilization behind the reconstructed Facility for $125,000.00. The PW noted that any changes to the approved scope of work (SOW) would require additional review for Environmental and Historic Preservation (EHP) compliance. FEMA obligated PW 573 for a total cost of $485,037.00 including the $125,000 in hazard mitigation."[15]

"On October 10, 2019, in a letter to the Missouri State Emergency Management Agency (Grantee), the Applicant requested a time extension on the project, advising that it had installed a drain behind the Facility which failed resulting in a failure of the slope. The Applicant explained that its engineering staff concluded that placement of a secant pile wall[16] was necessary to stabilize the sliding affecting the Facility. The Applicant provided a work schedule, justification for the proposed work, and a cost estimate of $1,698,479.83."[17]

"On December 16, 2020, the Grantee requested a large project close-out of $206,465.29 representing actual costs of repairs, and recommended removal of all the Applicant's hazard mitigation costs because the Applicant had exceeded the HMP SOW without prior FEMA approval and EHP review."[18]

"FEMA deobligated $275,321.71, including $125,000.00 in hazard mitigation because the Applicant changed the SOW and increased the HMP costs without previously notifying FEMA."[19]

"On July 27, 2021, the FEMA Region VII Regional Administrator denied the appeal, finding that the Applicant exceeded the approved HMP SOW without prior FEMA approval, which did not afford FEMA the opportunity to review the project to determine if the Applicant met all EHP requirements."[20]

"<u>Applicant acknowledges that it performed additional work but states that FEMA and the Grantee knew about it because the Applicant had informed them in its time extension request.</u>"[21] (Emphasis Added)

In this instance, the local agency made a fatal error in what may have been an attempt to save time by filing two notices/requests in the same document. A time extension request should always be a single filing, with no other purpose. Similarly, a request for a change in the scope of work should be a single filing, combined with no other document. The FEMA staff member approving a routine time extension request will not necessarily be the same person reviewing the request for a change in the scope of work.

Closing Out Projects When the Local Agency Is Ready, and Not Before

For the local agency, disasters are hopefully a one-off event, not something to be repeated many times. (However, there are certain parts of the country where the threat of disasters, particularly hurricanes, do potentially threaten on an annual basis.)

This one-off disaster experience for the local agencies starkly contrasts with both state and FEMA experiences, particularly for FEMA where disasters are an everyday occurrence. FEMA treats the business of disasters as, well, a business. FEMA employees are encouraged (or pushed) to close-out disasters as quickly as possible. Things roll downhill, and so the states as FEMA's program administrators are also "strongly encouraged" to close-out projects as quickly as possible.

To this end, there is constant pressure to close, close, and close some more. However, the locals should resist this push to close projects before they are truly finished. That is not to say that sometimes the local agencies don't need a boot to "encourage" them to finish projects in a timely manner. Following a disaster, the local jurisdictions are generally overwhelmed physically, mentally, and administratively. There are never enough staff members to properly do all that is required by Federal regulations to qualify for Public Assistance. But it is important that the local agencies realize that there are other pressures on both the states and FEMA to move the recovery along as quickly as possible, and when this does not happen, there may be consequences.

FEMA, under the terms of the FEMA-State Letter of Agreement signed for every Presidentially disaster declared, pays the states to administer the program a flat percentage, but only for a term of eight years. Therefore, after eight years, the states are continuing to manage the Public Assistance program without additional Federal funding. Naturally, the states will want to close-out as many projects as possible before the Federal funding vanishes.

The Net Small Project Overrun (NSPO)

Unlike large projects, small projects generally do not have versions written when there are changes to the approved scope of work. Prior to actually making the change in the scope of work, FEMA must be notified and must approve, in writing, any changes requested.

The Net Small Project Overrun is best illustrated by example. In a hypothetical situation an agency has 10 different projects at $100,000 each for a total of $1,000,000. If for all 10 small projects, the actual project costs were $1,050,000, then the agency is in arrears by $50,000. If the NSPO is timely filed and all is in order, FEMA will pay an additional $50,000 to the local agency.

On the other hand, if for these same 10 projects, the actual costs came in at $950,000, then there is a surplus of $50,000. Again, If the NSPO is timely filed and all is in order, the local agency may retain the $50,000. However, the agency must file the request for the NSPO within 60 days of the close-out of its last small project.

"Title 44 of the Code of Federal Regulations, section 206.204(e)(2), requires that applicants appeal for additional funds related to a NSPO, in accordance with 44 C.F.R. 206.206, within 60 days after the competition *(completion of construction, not completion of the paperwork)* of its last small project."[22]

If the local agency is pursuing a net small project overrun and the actual costs are below the approved costs, there may be some limitations on how the excess funds may be used, generally for future disaster preparedness projects.

In either case, the local agency must retain all the necessary information for each Project Worksheet until all is finalized, and then for not less than 3 years from the specified date of closure.

For large projects, there is no equivalent to a NSPO, as large projects have versions issued as changes may be approved, and the entire large project is paid against the actual documented costs.

This case is from Pennsylvania and illustrates an important nuance in the NSPO process. "This is in response to a letter from the Pennsylvania Emergency Management Agency (Recipient) dated July 10, 2023, which transmitted the referenced second appeal on behalf of the Pennsylvania Department of Conservation and Natural Resources (Applicant). The Applicant is appealing the U.S. Department of Homeland Security's Federal Emergency Management Agency's (FEMA) denial of $133,060.04 in costs pertaining to a Net Small Project Overrun (NSPO) request/first appeal."[23]

"Pursuant to Title 44 of the Code of Federal Regulations (44 C.F.R.) § 206.204(e)(2) (2018), when an applicant discovers a significant overrun related to the total final cost for all small projects, it may submit an appeal for additional funding, in accordance with 44 C.F.R. § 206.206, within 60 days <u>following the completion of all its small projects</u>."[24] (Emphasis Added)

"The Administrative Record does not contain documentation verifying the exact date that the Applicant completed the work on its last small project. <u>However, the Recipient acknowledged in its first appeal letter that the Applicant completed work on its last small project sometime prior to the February 27, 2023 period of performance deadline.</u> On second appeal, the Recipient concedes that the Applicant untimely submitted its NSPO request on May 7, 2023, and additionally, the Applicant does not dispute FEMA's untimeliness determination. <u>However, the Applicant asserts that it was not possible to meet the regulatory deadline because it received the last project's invoice on April 20, 2023. Notwithstanding that this was before the 60-day deadline, FEMA has previously determined that the 60 calendar-day timeframe to submit an NSPO request/first appeal starts when an applicant</u> completes work <u>on its last small project, and not at the time of invoice payments.</u> As a result, FEMA finds that the Applicant submitted its appeal after the 60 calendar-day timeframe required by FEMA's regulations, making the first appeal untimely. Therefore, this appeal is denied."[25] (Emphasis Added)

Therefore, for an agency that wants to file an NSPO, it is hypercritical that it tracks each and every project as it is completed to be able to determine that all projects are complete and the 60-day clock has started running to file the NSPO. FEMA will look at the timecards of the force account labor or contract documents which stipulate the date of project completion. This is a serious challenge when the local agency has perhaps dozens of small projects that may be divided up among many different departments. If no one is designated the project completion date monitor, then the chances of successfully filing an NSPO are grim. Furthermore, an NSPO is considered an appeal, so all matters which should be included in an appeal must be a part of the NSPO filing.

As we saw in the previous chapter on appeals, there is a small element of risk in filing an NSPO. In a California case, this was the net result. "The Applicant provided sufficient documentation to demonstrate that additional work in the amount of $6,740.77 was necessary to restore damaged components of the Facility. Specifically, work associated with Woeste invoices CCO#3–7049, CCO#3–6489, CCO#3–6490, CCO#3–6491, CCO #2–7046, CCO #2–7044, and CCO #2–7045 is eligible for PA funding. <u>The Applicant has not demonstrated that the work documented in the Wallace Group and CES invoices was required as a result of the disaster and is therefore ineligible. FEMA Region IX must deobligate $9,026.80 from PW 1156 so that the same work is not reimbursed twice. The net deobligation is $2,286.03.</u>[26] (Emphasis Added)

Final Thoughts on Close-outs and Net Small Project Overruns

The burden of full and complete documentation continues long after the projects have been completed, all the way until the final project, large or small, has been finished. Once the administrative record is finalized, then and only then does the three-year record retention period start to run, if there are no remaining issues on any of the projects which would require record retention for a longer period of time.

While Net Small Project Overruns may be useful, and a great opportunity to either capture additional funds when project costs exceeded the estimates, or to retain any excess funds when construction costs were less than the estimates, the NSPO process must be carefully monitored, particularly for knowing when the last small project is complete. Further, as an appeal, the NSPO may unearth problems which have been thus far undiscovered by FEMA.

Notes

1 https://www.fema.gov/about/openfema/Datasets-disaster-declaration-summaries
2 https://www.fema.gov/appeal/financial-accounting-reconciliation-section-705
3 Ibid.
4 Ibid.
5 Ibid.
6 Ibid.
7 Ibid.
8 Ibid.
9 https://www.fema.gov/sites/default/files/documents/fema_pa-validate-as-you-go-factsheet_0.pdf
10 https://www.fema.gov/appeal/force-account-labor-equipment-costsfinancial-accounting-reconciliation-section-705
11 Ibid.
12 Ibid.
13 Ibid.
14 Ibid.
15 https://www.fema.gov/appeal/change-scope-work-environmental-and-historic-preservation-compliance-0
16 Ibid. (A secant pile wall is a series of interlocking vertical concrete columns used to shore up basements and waterwalls.)
17 Ibid.
18 Ibid.
19 Ibid.
20 Ibid.
21 Ibid.
22 https://www.fema.gov/appeal/appeals-net-small-project-overrun
23 https://www.fema.gov/appeal/net-small-project-overrun-23
24 Ibid.
25 Ibid.
26 https://www.fema.gov/appeal/net-small-project-overrun-18

43 Summary and General Rules

General Rules and Guidelines

1) <u>**Document, Document, Document:**</u> Every visit to an incident or worksite must be documented with the appropriate paperwork, every day.

2) <u>**Contemporaneous Records Beat All:**</u> Activities for every shift of every disaster working day must be documented immediately. Failure to daily document disaster activities and expenses will result in lost financial recovery.

3) <u>**Verbal or 'Handshake' Agreements Are Deadly:**</u> In disasters, with the critical press of time, the temptation to rely on a verbal or handshake agreement may be the worst thing a government official can do. Unwritten agreements or contracts are tantamount to financial suicide. FEMA will NEVER honor this type of agreement or contract.

I personally know of one case from Texas where the debris contractor lost $900,000 on a verbal agreement with a local school district. Worse, such an agreement may give the local agency the impression that things are getting done, and we'll get the money from FEMA. Wrong, Wrong, Wrong, every time.

4) <u>**Never Leave a Box Blank:**</u> Completely fill out all FEMA, state, and local forms for tallying damage and tracking response and repair costs. This especially applies to form fields requiring a signature or a date. Where information is not known or does not apply, enter "DNA" (does not apply), "unk" (unknown), "Φ," or a similar notation to indicate that the box was not merely overlooked.

5) <u>**Take Pictures of Everything:**</u> Take still photographs of the damage done before beginning the cleanup or repair work. Take still photographs of the work in progress, and take still more photographs once the work is complete. Ideally, the local agency will have a full set of photographs of facilities and infrastructure taken prior to the damage to provide matching sets of "before" and "after" photos of the damage done by the disaster.

6) <u>**More on Photos:**</u> Even if individuals and work crews do not continuously document their activities, if they continuously but intermittently take photos of where they are and what they are doing, at the end of each shift they will be able to reconstruct their daily activities with a high degree of certainty. One way to constantly remind crews to take documentation photos is to have staff set their smartphone alarm to go off every 30 minutes as an alert to pause work to take a photo.

7) <u>**Lease or Rent, Rather Than Purchase:**</u> When obtaining additional equipment for the disaster response or repairs, it is almost always better to lease or rent rather than outright purchase equipment. With purchased equipment, typically FEMA will only reimburse for the actual

DOI: 10.4324/9781003487869-49

hours used for the disaster-related work done based upon the FEMA Equipment Rate Sheet. Equipment purchased for disaster use is often reimbursed for pennies on the dollar.

8) **Estimations of Time Worked and Costs Incurred Are Not Allowed:** FEMA does not allow the apportionment of time or costs incurred on a percentage basis, i.e., 50% of an employee's time was for disaster-related work. All times and costs must be documented using numbers and fractions/decimals or dollars and cents.

9) **There's Always an Exception, and There's Always Change:** This book makes every effort to explain the written regulations FEMA generally follows. However, there are exceptions to the rules, and the different FEMA regions may choose to follow or not follow some of these regulations on a case-by-case basis. Similarly, different FEMA employees may focus on compliance with certain rules and downplay compliance with other regulations. Furthermore, some FEMA regulations may appear to be self-conflicting with other FEMA regulations. Finally, there are so many different regulations that many FEMA staffers, particularly the newer employees, simply cannot know all the rules and which rules take precedence over another rule.

10) **Proper Procurement:** Compliance with Title 2 of the Code of Federal Regulations is absolutely required when spending Federal grant funds. Without compliance, FEMA may deobligate all or part of otherwise eligible costs.

11) **Changing the Scope of Work:** NEVER make unilateral changes to a "scope of work." Always notify FEMA when a change in the scope of work is required, and ALWAYS wait for FEMA's written approval before BEGINNING the work, or you may risk the deobligation of project funds.

12) **Special Considerations:** Never ignore the importance of the "Special Considerations" issues, particularly the environmental and historical issues. Failures in this area can lead to a total deobligation of project funds.

13) **After Action Reports:** Following the tactical response to a disaster, it is a common practice to conduct and write up an After-Action Report, or AAR, which will normally discuss those operations that went well, those tasks that need improvement, and those issues that were a significant problem and need to be immediately addressed. I have never seen a similar report prepared by a local agency. This is likely for several reasons: 1) Staff turnover: All those who participated have long since left the agency; 2) No one wants to remember the pain and hard work, much less address it; 3) The financial disaster doesn't stop suddenly but drags on for years in many cases, so when does an agency reach that point where self-reflection becomes possible?

14) **Use Correct Procedures Everyday:** To the extent possible, and there's always room for improvement, the local agency should seek to institutionalize policies and procedures to meet on a day-to-day basis the documentation requirements of the Public Assistance program. Every small step taken today or tomorrow will provide a huge return on the investment of the time and money it takes to have more rigorous documentation procedures in place when the next disaster hits.

15) **Adopt Codes and Standards:** If the local agency has not already done so, it should ensure that prior to the disaster, it has adopted all the codes and standards which may come into play for the repair and reconstruction after the disaster.

16) **Establish a Disaster Cost Recovery Team:** Formally establish a disaster cost recovery team and program to begin the process of being better prepared for the next disaster.

17) **Designate a Point of Contact for Cost Recovery:** Formally designate one or more employees (with a hierarchy) as the liaison with FEMA and the state OES/OEM.

18) **<u>Develop Pre-Disaster Contracts:</u>** Begin to develop pre-disaster contracts for the goods and services needed for the disaster response and recovery, including a disaster cost recovery consultant if the need arises.

19) **<u>Support Cost Recovery Mutual Aid:</u>** If at all possible, send staff to assist other local agencies in their Emergency Operations Center activations of their Finance and Administration Section when requested. If a neighboring agency is hard hit, do not expect that they will have the presence of mind to request assistance. Call and offer them assistance.

In Closing

I wrote this book to assist local government agencies of all types that are charged with the awesome responsibility of recovering their communities following a disaster.

This is a monumental task, but it is accomplished in much the same way as we do all tasks, in small, incremental, and prioritized steps.

I hope that this book will provide a new and expanded awareness of the depth and breadth of the Public Assistance program and all that it can offer to disaster-afflicted communities.

This book intentionally does not mention, except in passing, one of FEMA's important Public Assistance offerings: Hazard Mitigation. For almost every agency, there is more than enough work suggested in this book to occupy the most diligent staff for many months and years. If the local agency can understand and maneuver through the Public Assistance program as described in this book, Hazard Mitigation will be relatively easy to incorporate into Project Worksheets. Typically, both FEMA and their state counterparts are programmed to suggest and recommend specific Hazard Mitigation measures on a project-by-project basis.

Appendix

All forms listed below can be accessed in the Support Material at www.routledge.com/9781032770338

Form #	Title	Chapter	# Pages	File Type	Source
1	Public Assistance Initial Damage Assessments	20	4	PDF	FEMA
2	PDA Narative Report	21	1	PDF	FEMA
3	Disaster Overtime Burn Rate Estimator	12	1	Excel	MEM
4	Force Account Labor Summary	5	1	PDF	FEMA
5	Force Account Equipment Summary	5	1	PDF	FEMA
6	Materials Summary Record	5	1	PDF	FEMA
7	Rented Equipment Summary	5	1	PDF	FEMA
8	Contract Work Summary Record	5	1	PDF	FEMA
9	Applicant's Benefit Calculation Worksheet	5	1	PDF	FEMA
10	Disaster Field Unit Incident Work Report	5	2	PDF	MEM
11	City/County/District Annual Building Inspection Report	6	6	PDF	FEMA
12	Disaster Cost Recovery File Checklist	6	1	PDF	FEMA
13	EOC Finance & Administration Talking Points	3	1	PDF	MEM
14	Mutual Aid For Hire or Mutual Assistance Cost Reimbursement Agreement	19	2	PDF	MEM
15	Building Inspector Mutual Aid Daily Expense Report	19	1	PDF	MEM
16	Mutual Aid Expense Reconcilliation Form	19	1	Excel	MEM
17	Building Inspector Mutual Aid Log For Expense Tracking	19	2	Excel	MEM
18	Emergency Management Mutual Aid Information Request Letter Sample	19	1	PDF	FEMA
19	Staging Area Check In Sheet for Cost Recovery	19	2	PDF	MEM
20	Memorandum of Understanding for Building Inspector Mutual Aid	19	3	PDF	Cal-OES
21	Disaster Operations Meal Sign-In Sheet	3	1	PDF	MEM
22	Memorandum of Understanding between Agency and Private Non-Profit	3	33	Word	MEM
23	Disaster Response and Relief Donations Form	3	2	PDF	MEM
24	Pre-Season Disaster Financial Preparation Checklist	28	4	PDF	MEM

Form #	Title	Chapter	# Pages	File Type	Source
25	LEM-5 L, E, & M Cost Tracking Spreadsheet	5	11	Excel	MEM
26	Facility Initial Damage Report Form	20	2	PDF	MEM
27 A	Master Facilities List	20	1	Excel	FEMA
27 B	Facilities Damage Reporting Status	20	1	Excel	FEMA
27 C	Disaster Loss Estimation Form	20	1	Excel	FEMA
28	Office Furnishings and Equipment Damage Report	22	1		
29 A	Office Relocation Expense Report	20	2	Excel	MEM
29 B	Office Relocation Expense Report	20	2	Excel	MEM
30	Disaster Damage Documentation Checklist	20	1	PDF	MEM
31	Post Disaster Vehicle Damage Report	20	4	PDF	MEM
32	Initial Damage Estimate fpr the City of …	20	2	PDF	MEM
33	Damage and Needs Assessment Summary	20	12	Excel	MEM
34	Disaster Impact Financial Summary	20	2	PDF	MEM
35 A	Property Damage Report - Owner Occupied Homes	20	1	Excel	MEM
35 B	Property Damage Report - Rental Housing	20	1	Excel	MEM
35 C	Property Damage Report - Business and Commeercial	20	1	Excel	MEM
35 D	Property Damage Report - Public & Private Non-Profits	20	1	Excel	MEM
36 A	Private Non-Profit Request For Public Assistance Documentation Checklist	20	1	PDF	FEMA
36 B	Applicant Documentation for the Kickoff Meeting (Recovery Scoping)	20	1	PDF	FEMA
36 C	Documentation to Support Damage Claim	20	1	PDF	FEMA
36 D	Information to Develop Scope of Work	20	2	PDF	FEMA
36 E	Information to Support Change in Scope of Work	20	1	PDF	FEMA
36 F	Documentation to Support Costs Claimed	20	2	PDF	FEMA
36 G	Information to Support Time Extension	20	1	PDF	FEMA
37	Disaster Cost Recovery Documentation Filing Assignment Check list	20	2	PDF	MEM
38	30 Up Labels for Filing (Bates Stamping)	20	1	PDF	MEM
39 A	Category A EEI Questionnaire (Essential Elements of Information)	20	2	PDF	FEMA
39 B	Category B EEI Questionnaire (Essential Elements of Information)	20	1	PDF	FEMA
39 C	Category C EEI Questionnaire (Essential Elements of Information)	20	2	PDF	FEMA
39 D	Category D EEI Questionnaire (Essential Elements of Information)	20	2	PDF	FEMA
39 E	Category E EEI Questionnaire (Essential Elements of Information)	20	2	PDF	FEMA
39 F	Category F EEI Questionnaire (Essential Elements of Information)	20	2	PDF	FEMA

Form #	Title	Chapter	# Pages	File Type	Source
39G	Category G EEI Questionnaire (Essential Elements of Information)	20	2	PDF	FEMA
40	Purchasing Department Bid Worksheet	9	1	PDF	MEM
41	Procurement Documentation Checklist	9	1	PDF	MEM
42	Sole Source Purchase Justification	9	4	PDF	MEM
43	Materials Average Costing Worksheet	9	1	Excel	MEM
44	Office Relocation Expense Report	9	2	Excel	MEM
45	Price/Cost Analysis Worksheet	9	3	PDF	MEM
46	Cost Analysis Spreadsheet	9	1	Excel	MEM
47	Load Ticket (Debris Management)	15	1	PDF	FEMA
48	Truck Certification (Debris Management)	15	2	PDF	FEMA
49	Tower Monitor Log (Debris Management)	15	1	PDF	FEMA
50	Roving Monitor Report (Debris Management)	15	1	PDF	FEMA
51	Daily Issue Log (Debris Management)	15	1	PDF	FEMA
52	Disaster Debris Survey Form	15	1	Excel	MEM
53	Right of Entry & Insurance Information Form	15	12	PDF	Other
54	Calculating Repair vs. Replacement	23	2	Excel	MEM
55	Annual Facility Inspection Checklist	36	8	PDF	MEM
56	Roof Inspection Checklist	36	4	PDF	Other
57	Project Worksheet Direct Administrative Costs Tracker	32	5	PDF	MEM
58	9901-Direct Administrative Costs	32	2	PDF	FEMA
59	Special Disaster Operations Report	3	1	PDF	MEM
60	Daily Shelter Report for Cost Recovery	3	6	PDF	MEM
61	Request For Public Assistance	28	1	PDF	FEMA
62	Special Considerations Questions	30	1	PDF	FEMA
63	Project Worksheet	28	5	PDF	FEMA
64	PNP Facility Questionnaire	28	1	PDF	FEMA
65	Time Extension Request	28	1	PDF	FEMA
66	Materials Summary Record (Improperly Filled Out)	9	6	PDF	Other
			220		

Index

Note: Page numbers in *italics* indicate figures. Page numbers in **bold** indicate tables in the text, and references following "n" refer to notes.